Which
Destination

Which? Holiday Destination

An A–Z guide to where to go on holiday

CONSUMERS' ASSOCIATION

Which? Books are commissioned and researched by
Consumers' Association and published by
Which? Ltd, 2 Marylebone Road, London NW1 4DF
Email address: books@which.net

Distributed by The Penguin Group:
Penguin Books Ltd, 27 Wrights Lane, London W8 5TZ

Acknowledgements Morag Aitken, Jane Anderson, Eric Bailey, Ros Belford, Diccon Bewes,
Eileen Brennan, Philip Briggs, Reg Butler, Sophie Carr, Johnathan Cox, Alexander Craig,
Mick Diffley, Jan Dodd, Frank Dunne, Caroline Ellerby, David Else, Simon Evans, Anna
Fielder, Rebecca Ford, Simon Gaul, Christina Gibbons, Patricia Goldstraw, Emma Gregg,
Jason Harris, Anne Harvey, Emily Hatchwell, Huw Hennessy, Audrey Herbert, Sasha
Heseltine, Paula Hodgson, Lucy Hooker, Lindsay Hunt, Roger Lakin, Julie Lennard, Alison
Lindley, Nicola and Charles Liu, Linda Lobendahn, James Luckhurst, James Lyon, Shereen
Makarem, Fred Mawer, Conor McCutcheon, Robin McKelvie, Ella Milroy, Johnathan
Mitcham, Steven Murray, Rob Nash, Graham Norton, Helen Oldfield, Christine Osborne,
Mike Pedley, Perrott Cartographics, Polly Phillimore, Tony Pinchuck, Paul Pontone, David
Prest, Gordon Robison, David Rodwell, Tony Rooney, Seychelles Tourist Board, Lucy
Smith, Ann and Frank Spowart Taylor, Hugh Taylor, Neil Taylor, Bob Tolliday, Richard
Trillo, Julia Tweed, Neil Walkling, Gill Williams, Kim Winter, Pat Yale, Patricia Yates,
Nancy Yuill

First edition January 1997
Revised edition January 1998
This edition March 2001
Copyright © 1997, 1998, 2001 Which? Ltd

British Library Cataloguing in Publication Data
A catalogue record for this book is available from the British Library

ISBN 0 85202 851 2

For a full list of Which? books, please write to Which? Books, Castlemead,
Gascoyne Way, Hertford X, SG14 1LH, or access our web site at www.which.net

Holiday Which? regularly inspects holiday destinations both in Britain and abroad, as well
as reporting on airfares, hotel safety and other issues of interest to holiday-makers. To
keep up to date with the best information, take out a subscription. For details of a free
trial, write to *Holiday Which?*, Consumers' Association, PO Box 44, Hertford SG14
1SH, tel (01992) 822804.

Typographic design by Sarah Watson
Cover photograph by BRITSTOCK-IFA/ICS/Darrell Jones

Typeset by CentraServe Ltd, Saffron Walden, Essex
Printed and bound by Clays Ltd, Bungay, Suffolk

CONTENTS

CONTENTS

INTRODUCTION

THE WORLD is getting smaller. As many of us now take more than one holiday a year, we are seeking out more unusual destinations – African game reserves; the snowscapes and forests of Finland; remote tropical islands; and the newly accessible countries of the former Soviet Union. The choice of destinations has never been greater. So where do you start? *Which? Holiday Destination* will help you when you are planning your holiday, trying to cut through the brochure hype and deciding where to go. It provides, in a nutshell, all the key facts about a wide range of holiday spots around the world. Since its first edition, it has been expanded to include a further 30 destinations, reflecting the growing popularity of unusual destinations available to those on package holidays as well as independent travellers.

Our concise overviews of each place highlight what each country or region has to offer the holidaymaker. Each will give you a pretty good idea of whether it is the sort of place that is right for you and the type of holiday you envisage.

The key features of each destination are listed under the following headings, so you can see at a glance whether your own interests are represented:

Beaches Good ones are those with golden sand, preferably gently shelving, with plenty of room for everyone, taking into account the size of the resort or island*

Culture Includes museums, galleries, theatre, music and architecture

Family holidays Bases for those with young children

Flora Flowers, shrubs and trees, whether cultivated or in the wild

Food/wine Resorts which offer a wide selection of restaurants serving good-value food, not just expensive gourmet haunts. This category also covers beer as well as wine and fortified wine like port or sherry, including areas where it is produced

History Denotes historically significant sites, e.g. American Civil War battlefields, Hiroshima, the Inca ruins at Machu Picchu

Local colour Places where local traditions and customs still live on – and not just as nightly 'folklore' shows put on for the benefit of tourists

Nightlife If you want to spend your holiday enjoying the local bars, nightclubs and restaurants, this is the resort or city for you

Outdoor activities Specialising in one or more sports, such as golf, water sports, walking or trekking, cycling, sailing or diving

Romantic escapism For getting away from it all, avoiding crowds

Scenic landscape Memorable mountains and lakes, desert wilderness, stunning seascapes, good for touring or walking

Shopping For those who need more than a couple of souvenir stalls and postcard stands

Wildlife Including birds, whales and big game

Cost of living ££ is equivalent to the cost of living in the UK.

For each country we list tour operators offering holidays there, including smaller specialist operators whose brochures you may not see in a high-street travel agency but which rate higher satisfaction levels than the big names in the *Holiday Which?* biennial survey of tour operators. All are bonded, so your money is safe if the company goes bust. The tour operators' telephone numbers are listed on pages 606–11.

Travel is one of the most popular topics researched on the Internet: even if people are not confident enough to book online, they often check out individual hotel web sites, or garner other travellers' opinions in chat rooms or news groups. In this book we include web site addresses for tourist boards and other useful organisations. You may also find it helpful to visit the ANTOR UK (Association of National Tourist Offices in the United Kingdom) web site, which represents 90 national and regional tourist offices. For each country you can access useful information, tour operator listings and details of web sites of further interest. The ANTOR UK web site can be found at *www.tourist-offices.org.uk*

We also give advice on getting around independently, whether you need a visa, and whether there are any specific health or safety concerns. Hints on applying for a visa are on page 17. For advice on health and safety, see pages 10–12. A checklist on what to do before you go away is given opposite, and information on how to complain if something goes wrong with your holiday is provided on pages 13–16.

---

* Our assessments do not take into account the quality of the bathing water, as this changes from year to year. The European Union awards Blue Flags to beaches in member countries that meet mandatory minimum standards for bacteria and viruses and publishes the results of its surveys every year.

HOLIDAY CHECKLIST

Health Seek advice about immunisations two months before travel to exotic locations. Take your vaccination certificate with you. Supplement malaria tablets on holiday with use of mosquito nets, repellent and other anti-bite measures, and be sure to complete the course of tablets on your return. Form E111 (available from the post office) entitles you to receive urgent medical treatment on the same basis as a national of the country concerned (free or at reduced cost) while visiting a European Union (EU) member state, Norway or Iceland. The Department of Health produces booklet T5 *Health Advice for Travellers* (updated regularly), available from post offices with Form E111 or via the Health Literature Line, tel (0800) 555777. Details are also on *www.doh.gov.uk/traveladvice/index.htm*

House Do your best to make your house look occupied. You could get a house-sitter – a friend or a specialist company such as Homesitters Ltd, tel (01296) 630730 or Housewatch Ltd, tel (01279) 777412 (both operate nationwide). Failing that, set your lights and radio on timers and arrange for somebody to check the house.

Insurance Take out insurance as soon as you have booked your holiday (almost one-third of claims are for cancellation). Remember to pack the policy document and your insurer's emergency number.

Money For uncommon currencies give your bank or exchange bureau at least 72 hours' notice: choose US$ travellers cheques for the USA, Eastern Europe, Latin America and the Caribbean. Local currency cheques are best in France and Germany. Euro travellers cheques could be useful if you're visiting several European countries on one trip.

Motoring If taking your own car abroad, extend your car insurance cover. Take the vehicle registration document. Check your spare tyre. Adjust your headlamps for driving on the right, with an adhesive or clip-on converter. Some countries require you to carry a warning triangle and/or first aid kit, spare bulb and fire extinguisher.

Passports and visas The UK Passport Agency aims to process all correct applications for passports within 10 working days. Alternatively, you can hand in your application to main post offices and branches of World Choice travel agents, who, for a small handling charge, will check that your application is correctly completed and deliver it to the Passport Agency for processing; your passport should be returned within four days. See *www.ukpa.gov.uk/index.htm*

HOLIDAY HAZARDS

YOU DO not have to go on holiday to get ill or be mugged. But unfamiliar surroundings, language problems, strange food and drink, and too much sun can increase the risks. Here are some tips to help ensure you have a healthy and safe holiday.

Altitude sickness Altitude sickness, or mountain sickness, can be fatal but is largely avoidable. The best way to prevent it is to ascend gradually. If you are travelling by road, air or rail to high altitudes, you should allow a couple of days for your body to acclimatise. Rest as much as you need, drink plenty of liquids and avoid alcohol.

Animal and insect bites Do not approach any animal if there is a risk of rabies; cover arms and legs (especially at dawn or dusk, when mosquitoes bite). Use insect repellent, spray rooms with insecticides and sleep under nets. Check whether you need to take anti-malaria pills.

Ear infections They can be caused by polluted or warm tropical water – shower in fresh water after swimming and dry the ear canal by shaking the head.

Heat exhaustion and sunburn Stay in the shade or cover up between 11am and 3pm. Wear a broad-brimmed hat and sunglasses. Spread sun cream evenly and thickly and re-apply every two hours.

Lost credit/charge cards Advise the card issuer and inform the police as soon as the theft comes to light to limit your liability for any unauthorised purchases made with your card. Keep the issuer's 'lost card' telephone number to hand and note your card number and expiry date in order to help speed up its cancellation (keep separately from the card). Some card issuers can make cash advances to help tide you over – check that yours offers the facility before departure.

Plane travel Flying can be a health hazard, particularly to long-haul destinations. Side-effects include tiredness, swollen ankles, headache, sore throat, dry or watery eyes and dehydration. There is also some concern that cramped seating in economy class can lead to blood clots that could be fatal. Get up and move around regularly during the flight. People with heart, respiratory or neurological problems may suffer from hypoxia (lack of oxygen) owing to atmospheric pressure; symptoms resemble mild drunkenness. Jet lag, which occurs because the body's natural rhythms take time to adjust to a new time zone, can cause tiredness, poor concentration, inability to sleep at night, loss of appetite, bowel problems and headaches (the effects may be worse on eastward flights). For a more comfortable journey, choose a daytime flight to minimise sleep loss and tiredness. Walk frequently around the cabin or exercise in your seat; on long flights, get off at refuelling points for some fresh air and a walk. Avoid alcohol to combat dehydration and maximise your exposure to bright light to help the body clock readjust. If you get air sickness, sit over the wings, where the plane moves least. To avoid painful pressure in the ears, yawn or suck a sweet.

Pregnant travellers Before travelling, check with your GP or a travel clinic. Most airlines will not accept you for travel after 32 weeks of pregnancy – check before booking. You may also need to arrange additional insurance cover. Steer clear of places with a high malaria risk such as East and West Africa and Thailand. Beware of horse-riding, mountain climbing and other activities that may cause a fall. Observe the same food precautions as you would at home; in addition, drink only bottled water. For the *Travelling in Pregnancy* brochure from the Royal College of Obstetricians and Gynaecologists, which costs £1.50, call 020-7772 6275.

Road accidents Check a hired vehicle fully before driving off, especially tyres; make sure you have a spare wheel, test all the lights (especially brake lights) and seat belts. Wear a helmet and protective clothing if riding a motorbike or moped (check first if your holiday insurance covers you). Learn the rules of the road and local speed limits.

Travel Advice Unit

The Foreign and Commonwealth Office (FCO) has set up a Travel Advice Unit offering information on the risks to tourists in different countries. The information comes from British embassies and consulates and security agencies and is updated as necessary. The FCO also has close links with the travel trade – if it advises against visiting a country, ABTA tour operators will generally pull out and give refunds to people who have already booked. Individual travellers, however, cannot be prevented from visiting a country against its recommendations. The FCO Travel Advice Unit can be contacted on 020-7238 4503/4504. Travel advice is also available on BBC2 Ceefax, page 564 onwards, on travel agents' computer systems, and can be accessed on the Internet at:
www.fco.gov.uk/travel/

Sports injuries Check the condition of any equipment you hire or use. Check whether your insurance covers 'hazardous activities'.

Stomach upsets Beware of food left on display uncovered at room temperature. Drink boiled or bottled water or use purifying tablets if you are unsure of the water. Beware of salads, shellfish, ice-cream, and ice-cubes in drinks. The best treatment is rehydration.

Theft If you must take valuables with you, leave them in a safety-deposit box in your hotel. Lock the doors and windows of your hotel room or apartment securely. Keep the safety chain on in your room, and never open the door unless you know who is there. Get local advice on no-go areas and wear a money belt under your clothes. Hide valuables from view even if you are in the car and do not leave anything in the car overnight. Put personal safety first and if you are threatened, hand over your possessions.

Water sports Do not swim after eating a heavy meal or drinking alcohol. Take note of warning signs or flags on beaches. Check the condition of equipment you are using and insist on a full briefing on unfamiliar equipment and procedures. Always check the depth of the hotel pool before you dive in.

MAKING A CLAIM

Check that you have adequate insurance cover for your possessions. If you are robbed, report the theft to the local police and fill out a report form, keeping a copy to show the insurance company; if something is stolen from your hotel room or apartment, most insurers also require you to notify the hotel manager and tour operator's rep; if the theft occurs during a flight, report it to the airline straight away and fill out a Property Irregularity Report – some policies will not pay out unless thefts are reported within 24 hours.

IF THINGS GO WRONG

TRAVEL AGENCIES

When you ask a travel agent to book a holiday for you the agent is legally obliged to pass on your holiday booking and to make all other travel arrangements you requested. If the agent fails in this duty, and you suffer loss as a direct result of negligence, you can claim compensation from the agent. If you have special requirements – for example, llocation of a ground-floor room – make them a condition of your booking. This means that if the tour operator fails to take notice of your requirements, it is in breach of contract. Put your requirements to the travel agent in writing, and ask for written confirmation that the tour operator has been made aware of your special needs.

If things go wrong
● Write to the agent as soon as possible, referring to both your letter of instruction and the agent's letter confirming your instructions have been acted on. Ask for a reply with settlement proposals within 14 days.
● The ABTA code of conduct obliges agents to acknowledge complaints within 14 days and to send a detailed response within 28 days. If the agent does not comply, or the response is unsatisfactory, you can complain to ABTA (see page 16).
● If all else fails, consider going to the small claims court or to arbitration (see page 16).

BROCHURES

The brochure description plus the associated photographs and any maps are part of the contract between you and the tour operator. If the company fails to deliver what it has promised, you can claim compensation. The Package Travel Regulations 1992 state that 'descriptive matter concerning a package must not contain any misleading information'. In addition, the Trade Descriptions Act 1968 makes it a criminal offence for a tour operator to publish a brochure which it knows (or should know) contains false or misleading information.

If things go wrong
● Your local Trading Standards Department can prosecute alleged offenders.
● The Advertising Standards Authority (ASA), 2 Torrington Place, London WC1E 7HW, tel 020-7580 5555, is able to investigate complaints that brochures or other advertising material are dishonest or misleading.

● Always take a copy of the brochure with you on holiday so that you can see what you were promised.

FLIGHTS

If a tour operator tells you that your flight times have been changed, you should check that the booking conditions allow this. In most cases, when we went to press 'minor' changes could be made without any entitlement to compensation; minor in this case usually means up to 12 hours. Clause 2.2 (i) of the ABTA tour operators' code of conduct outlaws major changes within 14 days of your departure date. Where late alterations are made in defiance of the ABTA code you are entitled to compensation and to a full refund if you decide to cancel.

If things go wrong
● Write to the tour operator immediately, setting out your claim for compensation.
● If the change of flight time leaves you out-of-pocket – for instance, you need to take a taxi to the airport to catch an early-morning flight – your letter to the operator should accept the change under protest and reserve your rights to claim additional compensation beyond that set out in the brochure.

RESORT AND ACCOMMODATION

The first rule of complaining is to do it straight away, and give the hotel or tour operator a chance to sort out your problem. If you do not, the operator – and the court in any subsequent action – may decide that you have 'failed to mitigate your loss' and are entitled to reduced compensation, if any.

If things go wrong
● Ask the management to sort out any problems you encounter.
● Tell your holiday rep of your complaint at the first opportunity. Be polite, but firm. If you feel that the brochure seriously misrepresents the facilities available, show it to the rep and ask to be moved to a hotel or apartment in line with the brochure description. Most reps have the authority to do this on the spot.
● Complete a claims form, and retain a copy for future reference.
● Keep a diary detailing requests to the hotel and rep to put things right and their responses. Note down all meetings, telephone calls and any expenses that you incur.
● Take photographs to back up your case. These are particularly useful if your complaint relates to substandard accommodation and misleading brochure descriptions. Swap contact details with other guests.

● Write down the names and addresses of any witnesses who can confirm your complaints.

● Think carefully before accepting any offer of on-the-spot compensation. Some companies pay compensation in the resort but require a disclaimer stating that the holidaymaker accepts this in full and final settlement of any claims. It may be easy to undervalue your claim in the heat of the moment.

● Curtail your holiday and return home only as a last resort. If your accommodation is unacceptable, and the rep is unable or unwilling to move you, you should try to arrange a suitable alternative, at a cost and with facilities similar to those originally booked – remember the duty to mitigate your loss. Keep receipts to substantiate your claim to the tour operator when you return.

● List your grievances on any 'welcome home' questionnaire you may be given or sent.

LETTERS OF COMPLAINT

Write to the tour operator as soon as you get home, or at any rate within 28 days of your return, detailing your complaint. Aim to be concise, logical, honest and thorough. Show determination but do not whinge. Your letter should:

● be headed with your name, holiday dates, accommodation booked, and booking reference

● deal with your story chronologically, and give dates, times and names of parties involved

● explain any breach of contract by detailing discrepancies between the brochure description and the actual situation encountered, referring to any special requirements notified and not met

● indicate that photographs and witnesses are available, if this is appropriate

● indicate the amount of compensation claimed, based on the factors below.

The amount of compensation you are likely to recover depends on the impact the deficiencies had on your enjoyment of your holiday. Your claim is made up of three elements:

Loss of value – the difference between the holiday you got and the one you paid for, e.g. if you are moved to inferior accommodation due to overbooking this figure will be the difference in the value of the accommodation. Or, if the holiday was a 'complete disaster', this figure will amount to the cost of the holiday.

Loss of enjoyment – compensation for distress, disappointment and inconvenience. This is a difficult figure to assess, but courts often allow very reasonable amounts of compensation for this part of a claim.

Out-of-pocket expenses – the refund of any reasonable extra costs incurred.

Keep a copy of the letter with all subsequent correspondence. As stated earlier, the ABTA code of conduct requires tour operators to acknowledge your letter within 14 days, and to reply within 28 days.

COURT OR ARBITRATION?

If your letter fails to win you acceptable compensation you must decide how to proceed with your claim. In this situation you have two options:

The small claims court

This is a cheap, informal procedure designed to let people argue their cases in person, without any need for lawyers, and without the risk of being liable for the tour operator's legal costs if they lose. The maximum sum you can claim in England and Wales is £5,000. The court fee is between £27 and £115, depending on the sum claimed. In Scotland, the upper limit for small claims in the sheriff court is £1,500, and the fee is up to £36. In Northern Ireland the limit is £1,000 and the fee is up to £55.

Arbitration

The Chartered Institute of Arbitrators runs an independent, legally binding arbitration scheme on behalf of ABTA. This is a documents-only scheme. However, because there is no hearing, the impact of your personal testimony – often a potent consideration in small claims – will be lost. You may, however, submit video evidence of your holiday problem. The maximum award is £1,500 per person or, in the case of large parties, £7,500 per booking form. Holidaymakers who use the scheme pay a registration fee of between £65 and £112. Decisions made by the arbitrators are binding on both sides – so you cannot go to the small claims court if you lose. You do have a right of appeal to the courts but this is likely to leave you out of pocket.

The ABTA codes of conduct

Many travel agents and tour operators are members of the Association of British Travel Agents (ABTA). Its members agree to comply with a code of conduct which forms part of your contract with the member concerned.

ABTA
68–71 Newman Street
London W1P 3LA
tel 020-7637 2444
web site: *www.abtanet.com*

APPLYING FOR A VISA

THIS INFORMATION is for holders of British Citizen passports only. Check with the relevant embassy about regulations and always apply well in advance of departure. If booking a late bargain, check with the travel agent that there is enough time to get a visa before you leave. Remember, a visa doesn't guarantee you entry. Any immigration official can refuse to admit you. For more detailed information about individual countries, see the appropriate chapters.

In person The cheapest option, but requires access to an embassy and time to queue. Check payment methods: some embassies prefer cash or postal orders. Also check opening times. The country may have consulates you could visit in UK cities other than London.

By post Apply well in advance: it can take up to six weeks to issue some visas. Phone the consulate to obtain application forms, then send everything by registered mail, enclosing a registered sae. Make sure application forms are completed correctly and check what form of payment is required – credit cards are rarely accepted.

Visa agencies
These add a service charge on top of the basic visa fee. Prices vary enormously and sometimes 'difficult' visas can cost more to procure. Agencies can give discounts for groups and work fairly quickly. The downside is the expense.

Tour operators
Few offer any comprehensive kind of visa procurement service. Most point out clearly in their brochures that it is your responsibility to sort out visas before travelling. Escorted tours are often covered by a group visa: confirm this when you book.

Travel agents
Most do not offer a visa service. Their advice can be at best sketchy, at worst plain wrong and it is wise not to commit yourself until you actually book a holiday and have a contract with the agent or tour operator.

Countries included in this edition which require a visa

Australia, China, Cuba, Dominican Republic (Caribbean), Egypt, India, Jordan, Kenya, Nepal, Oman, Russia, Tanzania (Zanzibar), Turkey, Vietnam

---

AUSTRALIA

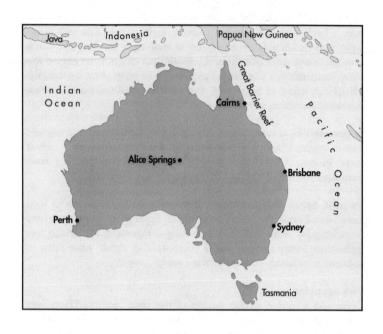

HIGHLIGHTS

Beaches
New South Wales, Queensland

Culture
New South Wales, Outback

Flora
New South Wales, Queensland, Western Australia

Food/wine
Melbourne, Perth, Sydney

Nightlife
Cairns, Sydney

Outdoor activities
New South Wales, Outback, Queensland,
Western Australia

Scenic landscape
New South Wales, Queensland, Victoria, Western Australia

Shopping
Sydney, Victoria

Wildlife
New South Wales, Outback, Queensland, Western Australia

NEW SOUTH WALES
Good for beaches, culture, flora, food/wine, nightlife, outdoor activities, scenic landscape and wildlife

OVER A third of Australia's population lives in New South Wales, but it's hardly crowded; the coastline north and south of Sydney is a chain of often empty beaches pounded by Pacific surf; superb World Heritage national parks run the length of the Great Dividing Range. The spectacular valleys and escarpments of the Blue Mountains are in Sydney's backyard, while the Hunter Valley to the north is a must for wine-lovers.

SYDNEY AND AROUND

VIBRANT, COLOURFUL and cosmopolitan Sydney is a beach city *par excellence*, boasting at least a dozen world-famous beaches, such as Bondi and Manly, as well as many interesting but less well-known spots stretching from Palm Beach to Cronulla. The eclectic mix of cultural influences provides a huge choice of restaurants, galleries, museums, pubs and clubs.

BEST SIGHTS

Port Jackson (the harbour area's proper name) has one of the world's great natural settings, giving Sydney its unique and immediately recognisable face. Visit the iconic Sydney Opera House, the Harbour Bridge, the Botanical Gardens and the Rocks, where Sydney put down its roots.

The concrete jungle of Darling Harbour has some excellent museums, including the Maritime Museum and the Powerhouse Museum, as well as the stunning Aquarium, where you can walk beneath stingrays and sharks in long, clear plastic tunnels. For great views, climb the Harbour Bridge, visit Sydney Tower, or take a ferry trip to Manly.

BEST RESORTS

The key to picking the right beach resort for your needs is to decide what nightlife (it varies from wild to non-existent) you prefer.

Byron Bay
● Brilliant beaches and surfing, and laid-back atmosphere.
● Off-beat residents contribute to the distinctive mix of art and crafts shops, veggie and wholefood restaurants.

Coffs Harbour
● Major resort with a wide selection of accommodation suitable for families, and a string of good beaches.

Port Macquarie
● Large, family-oriented resort with various theme parks and river-front area as well as beaches.
● Koalas have quite a presence here, in both the Koala Hospital and Billabong Koala Park.

BEST SCENIC LANDSCAPE

Barrington Tops
Great walking through a UNESCO World Heritage Site of rainforest. Bush bungalows are set among beautiful scenery and rivers.

Blue Mountains
The region's vertiginous cliffs, rugged gorges and eucalyptus forest (whose oily haze gives the mountains their name) were impenetrable to early settlers. Today, Sydney residents come for adventure activities. Accommodation to suit all budgets abounds in the main centres of Katoomba, Leura and Wentworth Falls. Jenolan Caves, Australia's best-known limestone caverns with wonderfully surreal rock formations, are worth a visit.

Dorrigo
Just inland from Coffs Harbour, Dorrigo is worth a detour for the drive alone, quite apart from the bushwalking opportunities and the rainforest canopy walks among the orchids of Dorrigo National Park.

Snowy Mountains and Mount Kosciusko National Park
It is possible to ski here from July to September, and in other seasons there is white-water rafting, hiking and beautiful alpine flowers.

BEST EXCURSION

Hunter Valley
Australia's most famous wine region boasts about 50 wineries, many of which welcome visitors for tastings.

QUEENSLAND
Good for beaches, flora, outdoor activities, scenic landscape and wildlife

BEST CITIES

Brisbane
Brisbane has little of Sydney's jet-set image and cosmopolitan nightlife. Colonial architecture is overshadowed by gleaming high-rise towers of concrete and glass, while broad walkways line the river's edge, and several impressive bridges span its muddy reaches. George Street has the best central colonial buildings, while the excellent art gallery and Queensland Museum are a good way to spend a morning. For great views over the city and Gold Coast head out to Mount Coot-tha park.

Cairns
The main tourist base for exploring the highlights of the rainforest in north Queensland. Downtown are cafés, bakeries, T-shirt shops and cheap hostels and motels, with smarter high-rises along the Esplanade. There is no beach; Palm Cove is the nicest resort north of Cairns.

BEST SCENIC LANDSCAPE

Atherton Tablelands
West of Cairns is a volcanic landscape of crater lakes, splendid water-falls, rich farmlands and quaint little towns such as Yungaburra, where you can spot platypuses in the nearby river. Kuranda's markets are reached via a spectacular railway and cable car, and wildlife cruises on Lake Barrine can often provide sightings of cassowary (a large flightless bird), eels, pelicans and pythons. The Curtain Fig and the Cathedral Fig are fine examples of strangler figs, while Millaa Millaa is the centre of a series of waterfalls.

Daintree and Cape Tribulation
Plenty of day-tips from Cairns and Port Douglas take in the unique eco-system of rainforest and reef around Cape Tribulation; for a memorable experience stay in an eco-lodge. Try Mossman Gorge for swimming, rapids or rainforest walks, while Daintree village, on the banks of the eponymous river, is a good base for wildlife cruises.

Further north are superb beaches at Cow Bay, Thornton Beach and Cape Tribulation itself; beyond this point you need a four-wheel-drive vehicle.

BEST RESORTS

Noosa

● A surfers' mecca since the 1960s, this trendy resort has old beach houses, bougainvillea and acacia trees in a gorgeous setting.
● Town centre at Noosa Heads has the vibrant Hastings Street.
● The cape at the northern tip is Noosa National Park, a stunning mix of eucalyptus, rocky coves and sandy bays.

Surfers Paradise and Broadbeach

● Looming skyscraper hotel blocks.
● Tacky shopping malls and pink stretch limousines exude an air of brash wealth.
● Unbeatable for a lively time.

ISLANDS OF THE BARRIER REEF

THE GREAT Barrier Reef has over 600 islands interspersed between the reef formations. Most are uninhabited, but around 20 have resort and hotel facilities.

Dunk Island

Arguably the most attractive of the islands, thanks to dense rainforest, large numbers of birds and butterflies and views from Mount Kootaloo.

Fraser Island

The world's largest sand island – complete with rainforest – located south of the Great Barrier Reef. Stunning, though popular with the tour crowds.

Great Keppel Island

This large island off the coast at Yeppoon is heavily promoted for its activities and superb beaches.

Green Island

Green Island's Coral Bay is a popular destination for day-trips from Cairns. The island offers Melanesian art and artefacts as well as an underwater observatory.

Heron Island

The huge array of marine life makes it a diver's paradise, while reef herons and other feathered friends are of interest to birdwatchers.

Hinchinbrook Island

A national park with extensive walks. There are also some fine stretches of beach and you can also see fantastic rainforest and wildlife, including crocodiles.

Lady Elliot Island

Shipwrecks and access to reefs direct from the beach make this a hit with divers. A simple, no-frills place, the island has a lighthouse and airstrip.

Lady Musgrave Island

An emerald isle set in a perfect turquoise lagoon. Day-trips or campers only.

Lizard Island

Remote, secluded, and pricey, but for your money you get pristine coral and superb diving as well as fantastic fishing.

The Whitsundays

A group of 70-odd islands, several of which have been developed into resorts. Boats from Shute Harbour serve the islands, although the beaches are uninspiring.

WESTERN AUSTRALIA

Good for flora, food/wine, outdoor activities, scenic landscape and wildlife

MUCH OF this vast region (ten times the size of the UK) is desert; most of the population lives in the south-west. The area is rich in gold and Aboriginal culture, but resorts are scarce – most lie south of Perth.

PERTH AND AROUND

THE WORLD'S most isolated city (1,242 miles from its neighbour Adelaide) offers good beaches and cheap accommodation. The port district of Fremantle is worth a visit for its market and café society. Northbridge has many good restaurants and clubs and Cottesloe boasts a stunning beach. The weekend markets at Subiaco are worth a visit.

Only 11 miles from Perth, Rottnest Island is home to quokkas – small marsupials – and has good snorkelling. Further afield you can also visit the limestone pillars of the Pinnacles Desert, swim with dolphins at Monkey Mia, see wild flowers in the Darling Ranges, try an

Australian white burgundy at the Swan Valley vineyards or make the 200-mile drive to Wave Rock.

BEST SIGHTS

Albany
A pleasant old whaling settlement surrounded by dramatic scenery, Albany is well placed for visiting the Valley of the Giants tree-top walk.

Broome
Once a pearling centre, Broome has a laid-back yet cosmopolitan charm, with a small Chinatown and a Japanese cemetery testifying to the dangers of pearl fishing. The superb Cable Beach lies nearby.

Esperance
Esperance has a pink lake, day-trips to see the seals and penguins in the wildlife sanctuary of Woody Island, and organised four-wheel-drive trips to Cape Le Grand National Park.

Kalgoorlie
The gold-mining town that brought prosperity to Western Australia is surrounded by endless barren outback. The rough and ready frontier atmosphere makes it well worth visiting.

Margaret River
The home of Western Australia's surfers and cosmopolitan *bon vivants* is a good place to relax, visit a cave, drink excellent local wine and surf the 'big one'. Margaret River is often fully booked during the school holidays.

Pemberton
Pemberton has the famous Gloucester Tree, reputedly the highest fire lookout tree in the world, but few manage the vertiginous 120 feet to the top. Like the rest of the south-west, the area has become a centre for crafts, especially wood-turning.

BEST SCENIC LANDSCAPES

Bungle Bungles (Purnululu)
These are extraordinary beehive formations, comprised of sandstone covered in alternating layers of silica and lichen. They are so fragile that climbing is forbidden. Accessible only by helicopter from Kununarra or Turkey Creek or by four-wheel drive from the latter, the Bungle Bungles are worth the journey for the intrepid.

Nearby is the Argyle Diamond Mine, which accounts for about a third of the world's diamonds.

Ningaloo Reef
Less famous than its eastern counterpart, the Great Barrier Reef, Ningaloo offers a chance to see humpback whales, turtles and manta rays. Whales and whale sharks are a seasonal attraction.

Reef tours leave from Exmouth, also the starting-point for the area's major diving site, the Peak Islands.

Pilbara and the Kimberleys
Red earth is common to these two vast, hot and underpopulated areas of Western Australia, but green waterways, orange beaches, gorges and boab trees are the main attractions of the Kimberleys.

BEST FLORA

Tall Trees
A tree-top walk along a suspended metal walkway, which meanders through the canopy of tall and extremely rare tingle trees.

OUTBACK AUSTRALIA
Good for culture, outdoor activities, scenic landscape and wildlife

THESE TIMELESS red landscapes of searing bone-dry wilderness hold the key to understanding Australia's soul and the ancient culture of the Aborigines.

BEST SIGHTS

Alice Springs
'The Alice' is a modern town built on a grid layout and is a good base from which to explore the Red Centre, with a range of shops, restaurants, and Aboriginal art and crafts.

Ayers Rock (Uluru) and the Olgas (Kata Tjuta)
The village of Yulara makes a visit to the Uluru National Park an easy prospect. The immense rock is a site of deep religious and cultural significance for the region's Aboriginal tribes. Climbing the Rock is dangerous and against the wishes of the Aborigines. The Olgas, or Kata Tjuta ('many heads') are a fragmented version of Ayers Rock and just as impressive in their own way.

Coober Pedy
The name means 'white fellow's hole in the ground'. This is a unique

25

redneck town of opal miners living in underground dug-outs in a post-apocalyptic landscape. Rough, ready and ugly, yet oddly compelling. Try your luck at 'fossicking' for opals.

Kakadu National Park

One of Australia's most famous parks, situated in the Northern Territory bordering Aboriginal Arnhem Land. The location for *Crocodile Dundee*, this vast, varied terrain of wide plains is punctuated with giant rock formations, waterfalls, billabongs (waterholes) and mangrove swamps and is inhabited by snakes and crocodiles.

Rich in Aboriginal rock art, the park boasts Nourlangie, and Ubirr Rock which has about 7,000 paintings dating back 20,000 years. Don't be disappointed if you discover images repainted in the 1960s – it's an Aboriginal tradition to touch up rock art. Boat trips and guided tours highlight the best of the park's wildlife – especially the myriad birdlife – and Aboriginal art.

Katherine Gorge (Nitmiluk National Park)

A chain of red, majestic gorges, linked by a series of rapids. Boat trips and canoeing excursions explore the fiery canyon with its steep-sided escarpments. The rapids are not difficult to negotiate – when the waters are low you may have to carry your canoe over slippery rocks, but the spectacular scenery merits the challenge.

VICTORIA
Good for food/wine, scenic landscape and shopping

THIS IS fast becoming a very fashionable state and has long left behind the rather conservative, agrarian image it had in the past. In recent times the Grand Prix, the Comedy Festival and the Melbourne Cup have brought the state on to the international stage. Fiercely competitive with New South Wales in everything from Australian Rules Football to having the tag of the country's finest city, the 'Garden State' is keen to capture more of the tourist market. Cooler than most Australian states, Victoria is home to some of the most spectacular but overlooked scenery on the continent, particularly along the Murray River.

MELBOURNE AND AROUND

THE STATE'S cultural and demographic heart. Established in the early nineteenth century, the city is located on the immense Port Phillip Bay and has some of the finest restaurants and nightlife in Australia. What it perhaps lacks in terms of sunshine, it more than makes up for in terms of ambience, diversity and charm.

Brunswick Street and St Kilda are two of the most popular thoroughfares in which to linger over a *caffè latte* and watch the world pass by. The latter has an attractive marina and pier. Several popular markets are located around the city as are some excellent galleries, the National Gallery of Victoria being foremost among them. For shopping, head for the centre of town around Elizabeth Street and the South Gate Centre on the Yarra river opposite Flinders Street station. Sports fans will probably wish to savour the legendary environs of the MCG (Melbourne Cricket Ground), and the Botanical and Zoological Gardens located centrally are also worth a visit. However, the city's charm lies in its eateries and the good-natured and unhurried *viveurs* who frequent them.

BEST SIGHTS AND EXCURSIONS

Lakes Entrance
This boating destination is popular with Victorians.

Murray river
The tranquil meanderings of this vast river lie inland, along with the haunting expanse of the Mallee, for those who want to escape the surf.

Twelve Apostles
These towering stacks of limestone, located south-west of Melbourne, rise up from the Great Southern Ocean. They can be accessed from the Great Ocean Road, which takes you along a magnificent tract of coast – one of the world's great ocean drives.

Wilson's Promontory
A stunning national park three hours' drive south-east of Melbourne, this is just about close enough for a day visit and perfect for camping.

WHEN TO GO

THE CLIMATE in Australia varies from north to south throughout the year, so you should find somewhere to suit you at any time. If travelling the length of the east coast, go in spring or late autumn (Australian seasons).

Festivals are important in the Sydney calendar. The January arts festival features open-air music in the parks. Chinese New Year celebrations occur in January or February, followed by the Gay and

Lesbian Mardi Gras in February or March. The Royal Show at Easter has a cattle and rodeo theme, and the rest of the year is liberally sprinkled with many film and arts events, as well as the Sydney-to-Hobart yacht race on Boxing Day.

	Average daily maximum temperature °C											
London	6	7	10	13	17	20	22	21	19	14	10	7
Sydney	26	26	24	22	19	16	16	17	19	22	23	25
	JAN	FEB	MAR	APR	MAY	JUN	JUL	AUG	SEP	OCT	NOV	DEC
Sydney	14	13	14	14	13	12	12	11	12	12	12	13
London	15	13	11	12	12	11	12	11	13	13	15	15
	Average number of rainy days per month											

	Average daily maximum temperature °C											
London	6	7	10	13	17	20	22	21	19	14	10	7
Perth	29	29	27	24	21	18	17	18	19	21	24	27
	JAN	FEB	MAR	APR	MAY	JUN	JUL	AUG	SEP	OCT	NOV	DEC
Perth	3	3	5	8	15	17	19	19	15	12	7	5
London	15	13	11	12	12	11	12	11	13	13	15	15
	Average number of rainy days per month											

	Average daily maximum temperature °C											
London	6	7	10	13	17	20	22	21	19	14	10	7
Cairns	32	32	31	29	27	26	26	27	28	30	31	32
	JAN	FEB	MAR	APR	MAY	JUN	JUL	AUG	SEP	OCT	NOV	DEC
Cairns	16	16	19	15	12	10	8	8	7	7	10	12
London	15	13	11	12	12	11	12	11	13	13	15	15
	Average number of rainy days per month											

PACKAGE TRAVEL

ALL THE specialist tour operators offer a great deal of flexibility. The airfare will be a substantial part of the total cost, though some internal flights may be included with your flight to Australia.

As long-distance travel is likely it is wise to organise at least part of your holiday before you arrive. Travel and accommodation passes, car and camper-van hire, coach tours, short stop-over tours, self-drive itineraries, scenic train tours, day trips and adventure tours are all on offer. You can take part in activities such as walking, birdwatching, camping safaris, canoeing and diving on the Great Barrier Reef.

Tour operators

Coach tours: AAT Kings, Australian Pacific Tours, Contiki **Flora**: Cox & Kings **General and specialist**: Airtours, All-Ways Pacific, Austravel, Bridge the World, British Airways Holidays, Cadogan, Flightbookers, Jetset, Kuoni, Qantas Holidays, Quest Travel, Trade-winds, Trailfinders, Travelbag, Travel Bug, Travelmood, Travel-pack **Walking/adventure**: Explore Worldwide, Imaginative Traveller, Ramblers Holidays, Walks Worldwide, World Dreams, World Expeditions **Wildlife/birdwatching**: Abercrombie & Kent, Limosa, Naturetrek, Ornitholidays, Sunbird, Wildlife Worldwide **Wine**: Arblaster & Clarke, Winetrails **Other activities**: Dive Worldwide (scuba), Equitour (horse-riding), Ffestiniog Travel (rail tours)

INDEPENDENT TRAVEL

MANY CHEAP flight deals exist. November to February is the most expensive time; April and May are the cheapest months. If you have lots of spare time, a round-the-world ticket can be an excellent option.

It is easiest to use internal airlines for national travel. Qantas and Ansett Australia are the two main carriers. Advance booking is strongly advised and can save you money, as can airpasses. Some have to be bought in advance before you reach Australia – check with the airlines.

Driving is the best way to appreciate the scale of Australia provided you have enough time and stamina for long stints at the wheel (it is 1,600 miles from Cairns to Sydney). Driving is on the left; a British driving licence with passport is acceptable. In the outback, plan your route carefully and keep to main roads – it's easy to get lost in the bush. Carry plenty of water, and stay with your vehicle if you break down.

The coach network is highly developed and the cheapest means of travelling, though the vast distances mean long hours. Greyhound-Pioneer offers a variety of Aussie passes allowing hop-on, hop-off travel over pre-set routes for up to 12 months.

Railways link the main south and east coastal cities and some of the inland towns. Trains are comfortable, but often pricier than coaches. Passes are available to overseas travellers and can be bought before you arrive.

Accommodation is in American-style comfortable hotel and motel chains. Budget backpacking hostels offer a wide accommodation network; standards vary. B&Bs and guesthouses are on offer, mostly in the south and east. In the outback, bush camping may be the only option.

RED TAPE, HEALTH AND SAFETY

BRITISH TOURISTS need a visa, which is free for visits of less than three months and can be issued instantly and electronically. Your travel agent should be able to arrange this for you, but may charge an admin fee. Alternatively, apply to the Australian High Commission in London (open 9am to midday, Monday to Friday).

No vaccinations are necessary, but take care in the sun (Australian rays are far stronger than those in northern Europe, and the country has one of the world's highest incidences of skin cancer). Flies and mosquitoes can be constant irritants during the summer: cover up arms and legs, especially at dusk and dawn, and take plenty of repellent. A sting from the poisonous box jellyfish can be fatal – steer clear of the beach when it is around (generally November to March, north of the Tropic of Capricorn).

MORE INFORMATION Australian Tourism Commission, First Floor, Gemini House, 10–18 Putney Hill, Putney, London SW15 6AA, tel (09068) 633235 (60p per minute), web site: *www.australia.com*

Australian High Commission, Australia House, Strand, London WC2B 4LA, tel 020-7379 4334, visa information (09065) 508900 (premium rate number), web site: *www.australia.org.uk*

COST OF LIVING £–££

AUSTRIA

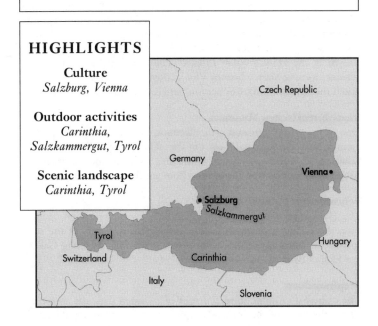

HIGHLIGHTS

Culture
Salzburg, Vienna

Outdoor activities
*Carinthia,
Salzkammergut, Tyrol*

Scenic landscape
Carinthia, Tyrol

Czech Republic

Germany

Vienna

Salzburg
Salzkammergut

Tyrol

Switzerland

Italy

Carinthia

Hungary

Slovenia

VIENNA
Good for culture

STATELY AVENUES, squares, palaces and museums make Vienna an
excellent city for sightseeing. Many of Vienna's great cultural attractions – and traditional coffee houses – line the Ringstrasse (or Ring),
a grand boulevard that follows the line of the former medieval city
walls.

BEST SIGHTS

As well as the traditional 'sights' there are events such as the opera, and
performances by the Vienna Boys' Choir and the Spanish Riding
School. Getting tickets can be complicated, however: contact the
tourist office for advice.

Belvedere
Baroque summer palace housing three museums: works by *Jugendstil*
(Viennese art nouveau) artists such as Klimt, Schiele and Kokoschka in
the Upper Belvedere; the Austrian Baroque Museum in the Lower
Belvedere; and a good collection of medieval art in the Orangery.

Hofburg

The state rooms of this huge imperial palace recall Franz Josef's reign (1848–1916) – among them, his wife Elisabeth's 'gymnasium' appears incongruous. The Albertina has superb graphic art by Dürer, Klimt, Schiele and Rubens, while the *Schatzkammer*, or Treasury, displays the Crown of the Holy Roman Empire. The chapel is best seen during Sunday morning Mass, when the Vienna Boys' Choir sings. Alternatively, watch the Spanish Riding School in the Hofburg on Sunday morning.

Kunsthistorisches Museum

One of the world's greatest art collections, housed in one of a pair of monumental domed buildings on the Ring. The galleries contain paintings by Rubens, Cranach, Dürer and Holbein, and a particularly good Italian section. On the ground floor are the Egyptian antiquities.

Schönbrunn Palace

The Habsburgs' summer palace, 20 minutes by underground or tram from the centre of Vienna, has beautiful gardens. Tours of the state apartments cover 40 of the 1,500 rooms, including the Long Gallery and Hall of Mirrors.

Stephansdom

The cathedral's Gothic spire and roof of coloured tiles soar above the city at the heart of the Ring. The towers give great views; the north one allows a close-up look at the roof tiles. Magnificent Gothic and baroque altars, fine tombs of emperors Rudolf IV and Friederich III and of the famous warrior Prinz Eugen.

SALZBURG
Good for culture

A BEAUTIFUL baroque city in a dramatic mountain setting, Salzburg is the product of 700 years of ecclesiastical rule, and its attractions are mainly architectural and cultural. It is also a paradise for music-lovers, as Mozart's birthplace and the home of the renowned Salzburg Festival.

BEST SIGHTS

Cathedral and Dommuseum

The stern stone exterior of the first Italianate baroque church north of the Alps belies the marble and stucco fripperies of the vast interior. Art-lovers should visit the Dommuseum, which has rare treasures ranging from an eighth-century Northumbrian cross to Gothic altarpieces.

Hellbrunn

About 15 minutes from the centre, Hellbrunn's main claim to fame is the water-spraying trickery of the fountains in its baroque garden. Aquatic gags abound as the tour guides pull levers and press buttons to unleash the superb intricacies of the seventeenth-century plumbing.

Mönchsberg and the Hohensalzburg Fortress
One of the most pleasant ways of spending the day, in fine weather, is to take the funicular up the Mönchsberg cliff and visit the fortress, and then walk along the top where there is a path to the lift.

Mozart's birthplace
In a third-floor apartment on Getreidegasse, Mozart's birthplace is more a place of pilgrimage than a museum, with its stone stairway, a simple cold kitchen and barren floorboards. Family portraits and a few exhibits, including the violin he played as a child, are on display.

Residenz
The remains of the art collection of the Prince-Bishops contains paintings of the seventeenth- and eighteenth-century European schools hung in a classical setting of grand rooms. Guided tours of the state rooms are monotonous unless you have a good grasp of German.

SALZKAMMERGUT
Good for outdoor activities

THE SALZKAMMERGUT area, 12 miles east of Salzburg, is a region of gentle mountains and glistening lakes. It is easy to visit on day-trips from Salzburg – there are plenty of excursions, and public transport to the area is efficient.

BEST RESORTS
Hallstat
● Neatly tiered houses crowd the hillside and a sliver of flat land by a lake ringed by mountains.
● The town is a good base for exploring the Dachstein massif.

St Gilgen
● Pretty old town with painted stucco buildings and haphazard layout.
● Horses and traps whose drivers wear traditional dress are a feature.

BEST SIGHTS AND EXCURSIONS
Churches
The church at Mondsee, nicknamed 'Salzkammergut's Cathedral', merits a visit for its 13 superbly ornate altars, while that at St Wolfgang has an exquisitely carved winged altar by Gothic master Michael Pacher.

Dachstein Caves
Reached by cable-car, the caves are full of wonderful formations of stratified ice, including a complete ice chapel. Take a sweater.

BEST MOUNTAIN TRIPS

Dachsteinbahn
The cable-car to the glaciers rises in a single, unsupported loop to the top station on the rocky pinnacle of the Hunerkogel mountain.

Schafberg
The cog railway to the top of the Schafberg gives superb views over the lakes; the lovely walk back down takes about three hours.

TYROL
Good for outdoor activities and scenic landscape

MANY RESORTS are in the less beautiful eastern Tyrol, among bland towns such as Soll and Kirchberg. West of Innsbruck are higher and more spectacular mountains, emptier roads and undeveloped villages.

BEST RESORTS

Alpbach
● Peaceful, notably pretty resort bursting with flowers.
● Located in a rural valley near the rugged Kitzbüheler Alps.

Kitzbühel
● A large, busy town with solid, well-established hotels, picturesque churches and a skiing museum that is a shrine to local heroes.
● A chairlift and cable-car network provides easy access to the uplands.

Mayrhofen
● Big resort with large hotels, glossy shops and breathtaking scenery.

Obergurgl
● Quirky mix of traditional Tyrolean charm and hi-tech sophistication in the shape of gleaming hotels and futuristic cable-car stations.

BEST SIGHTS

Innsbruck
Stroll around the old centre, and watch for the shimmering Gothic 'Golden Roof' of copper tiles and the extravagantly rococo Helbling-haus. The Hofkirche houses 28 larger-than-life bronze royal statues. They include a statue of England's King Arthur. The Tyrolean Folk Museum recreates old pine-panelled rooms and tiled stoves.

Rattenberg
Top of the tourist itinerary for its glassworks and the Höfemuseum, showing the different styles of building in the Tyrolean regions.

Schwaz
You can tour the remains of the silver mines – an entertaining two-hour trip on an electric train into the mountain through a tiny tunnel.

BEST MOUNTAIN TRIPS

Nordketterbahn
At the top you can look down to the man-tamed landscape of the Inn valley or north across the uninhabited Karwendelgebirge massif.

Pitztaler Gletscherbahn
You can reach the top of the Hinterer Brunnenkogel via cable-car and funicular for views of the Wildspitze, the highest mountain in the Tyrol.

Zugspitze
Staggering views down into Germany, where the Eibsee is a glistening mass of constantly changing colour.

CARINTHIA
Good for outdoor activities and scenic landscape

AUSTRIA'S SOUTHERNMOST province is an oval basin, its central lakes rimmed by mountains. Visit Romanesque churches, hill fortresses and Roman remains, or try Carinthia's ample outdoor sports facilities.

BEST RESORTS

Bad Kleinkirchheim
● High-altitude spa/ski resort, which provides a refreshing change from lakeside resorts and boasts indoor and outdoor thermal pools.

Millstatt
● Resort on the northern shore of Millstättersee, geographically divided in two by its small and intimate abbey.
● Quiet, yet very close to the motorway – a good base for touring.

Pörtschach
● On the largest lake of Wörthersee, Pörtschach is on a promontory.
● An attractive lakeside promenade is lined with hotels and restaurants.

St Veit an der Glan
● Peaceful fortress city with a medieval street plan and old town wall.
● The ornate town hall inhabits the main square.

BEST SIGHTS AND EXCURSIONS

Friesach and Gurk
The slopes around the town of Friesach contain many ruined churches and castles; Gurk's onion-domed cathedral is one of Austria's best-known Romanesque buildings.

Grossglockner Hochalpenstrasse
One of the first commercial Alpine roads to be built, this gives magnificent views of glacial scenery on a fine day.

Hochosterwitz
This imposing hilltop fortress with 14 towered gates contains displays of weapons and armour – be prepared for a stiff climb up to it.

Magdalensburg
At this excavated Roman settlement you can see remains of public baths, temples and a centrally heated villa. There is also a museum.

Maria Wörth
This small promontory, with two pretty churches on its tip, is popular as a photographic subject. Just south is the peak of Pyramidenkogel.

Spittal an der Drau
In the centre stands the Italianate Schloss Porcia, whose inner courtyard contains three tiers of superb Renaissance arcades.

WHEN TO GO

MAY, JUNE and September are good months to visit Vienna. In July and August you will miss the Spanish Riding School, the Vienna Boys' Choir and the opera. In winter it is easier to get tickets for the opera and other attractions, but be prepared for very cold weather.

Book accommodation early for the Salzburg Festival (late July–August) and for the similar, smaller-scale Easter and Whitsun Festivals.

	Average daily maximum temperature °C											
London	6	7	10	13	17	20	22	21	19	14	10	7
Vienna	1	3	8	15	19	23	25	24	20	14	7	3
	JAN	FEB	MAR	APR	MAY	JUN	JUL	AUG	SEP	OCT	NOV	DEC
Vienna	15	14	13	13	13	14	13	13	10	13	14	15
London	15	13	11	12	12	11	12	11	13	13	15	15
	Average number of rainy days per month											

In the high Alps, many hotels and facilities close after the skiing season (which lasts from December to early April), open in late May and close again in early October.

PACKAGE TRAVEL

THERE IS a wide choice of packages to resorts in the Tyrol, Carinthia and Salzkammergut. Single or two-centre holidays in mountain villages and towns let visitors make the most of facilities in the local area or use good public-transport links to explore further afield. Resorts offer a range of sporting activities, including organised walks, so unless you want a specialist holiday you will not necessarily need to book an activity package. Fly-drive packages and car hire can be arranged.

Tour operators

Birdwatching: Limosa, Ornitholidays, Sunbird **Camping**: Canvas, Eurocamp, Eurosites, Keycamp **City breaks**: British Airways Holidays, Cresta, Crystal, DER, Hungarian Air Tours, Inghams, Made to Measure, Moswin, Osprey, Sovereign, Thomson, Time Off, Travelscene **Coach tours**: Bowens, Excelsior, Shearings, Travelsphere, Wallace Arnold **General and specialist**: Airtours, Austria Travel, Cosmos, Crystal, First Choice, Lakes & Mountains, Headwater, Inghams, Thomas Cook, Thomson **Walking**: Exodus, HF Holidays, Inntravel, Ramblers Holidays, Sherpa, Waymark **Other activities**: Ace Study Tours, Anglo Dutch (cycling), Erna Low (spa), Great Rail Journeys (rail tours), Inter-Church Travel (religious tours), Martin Randall (cultural), Solo's Holidays (singles), Travel for the Arts (opera), Winetrails (wine)

Tour operators may use Munich airport as well as Innsbruck for holidays in the Tyrol. Accommodation is in hotels, guesthouses and self-catering farmhouses.

Most city-break tour operators go to Vienna and Salzburg; a few also feature Innsbruck and Graz in their brochures. Vienna can also be combined with other central European cities such as Budapest and Prague. Activity holidays focus on cycling, walking, music and birdwatching.

INDEPENDENT TRAVEL

IT IS easy to organise your own holiday. Scheduled flights go to Vienna and Salzburg, but western Austria is also easily reached via Munich in Germany, which has a bigger (and cheaper) choice of flights.

Taking your own car is quite feasible – the crossings to Belgium or Holland are the most convenient. Main roads are reliable, but tolls exist on many tunnels and on some scenic mountain roads. Many mountain passes are narrow and twisting, and may be barred to cars towing caravans. If taking your car over in spring, check its tyres, as some roads may still be snowy and icy. Use of seat-belts is compulsory, and drivers must carry a first-aid kit and warning triangle. All petrol is unleaded. If you are hiring a car, an international driving licence is recommended.

Electrified rail lines connect the main cities, and branch lines (some narrow-gauge and privately owned) run up side valleys. Trains are clean, comfortable and punctual, though fast expresses are few. Fares are high, but several value-for-money train passes are available – some give unlimited travel for a set number of days, others allow a set number of kilometres (useful if you intend to do only a few day-trips).

Even small villages usually have a yellow postbus service, to access the remotest corners, although long delays over short distances are common.

Standards of accommodation are high (though cheap city hotels can be basic). Hotels are graded from one to five stars, less formal gues-thouses (*Gasthäuser*) from one to three stars. In country areas many hotels are built in an informal chalet style, but will often have up-to-date facilities such as swimming-pools and saunas. Pensions are graded separately from hotels, at one to three stars. They do not usually serve meals. Best value of all are rooms in private houses and farmhouses (look for *Zimmer frei* signs, or book through tourist offices).

Self-catering consists mainly of apartments in chalet-style buildings. Local tourist offices have lists. Campsites are usually well organised, with good facilities, though those near popular resorts can get very crowded.

RED TAPE, HEALTH AND SAFETY

BRITISH PASSPORT-HOLDERS do not need a visa.

Austria has no particular health or crime problems: just take the usual precautions (see pages 10–12).

MORE INFORMATION Austrian National Tourist Office, 14 Cork Street, London W1X 1PF, tel 020-7629 0461, web site: *www.austria-info.at/*

Vienna tourist board tel 0043-1211 114222

COST OF LIVING £££

BELGIUM

HIGHLIGHTS

Culture
Antwerp, Bruges, Brussels

Family holidays
Ardennes, Flanders Coast

Food/wine
Brussels

History
Ieper

Local colour
Bruges, Ghent, Tournai

Nightlife
Antwerp, Flanders Coast

Outdoor activities/ scenic landscape
Ardennes, Flanders Coast

North Sea

Netherlands

Ostend • •Bruges •Antwerp
•Ghent
•Ieper •Brussels
•Tournai

France

Ardennes

BRUSSELS
Good for culture and food/wine

DESPITE BRUSSELS' reputation as a dull centre of commerce and bureaucracy, the city contains some interesting museums, a beautifully preserved medieval centre and some of Europe's best restaurants.

BEST SIGHTS

Cathedral
This fine Gothic church was begun in 1220 and has been restored many times. The wonderful stained glass in the transepts is sixteenth-century.

Grand Place
The indisputable centre of Brussels, this magnificent square was once a market-place. The elaborate façades of guildhouses and the Gothic

Hôtel de Ville make a great backdrop for a drink in one of the overpriced cafés.

Musées Royaux des Beaux Arts
Belgium's best fine-art collection occupies two linked museums: the Musée d'Art Ancien has works by Bruegel, Rubens and Cranach; the Musée d'Art Moderne has Belgian Surrealists Delvaux and Magritte.

Musée Victor Horta
This house, designed by Belgium's most famous architect, Victor Horta, is a marvellously fluid, sensuous example of art nouveau.

BRUGES
Good for culture and local colour

EVEN THOUGH Bruges heaves with tourists during the summer, its gloriously preserved medieval buildings, cobbled streets and winding canals make it an unmissable destination.

BEST SIGHTS

Groeninge Museum
An outstanding collection of Flemish paintings. The early works, plus several paintings by Jan van Eyck, who lived and worked in Bruges, are the best of the collection.

Hans Memling Museum
The fifteenth-century artist's works are in the church of St Jan's Hospital.

Markt and Burg squares
These adjacent squares are the old town's focus. The Markt is lined with gabled buildings and the thirteenth-century Belfry; in the smaller Burg the Heilig Bloed Basiliek contains a phial reputed to contain Holy Blood.

Onze Lieve Vrouwekerk
Huge church with a marble Madonna and Child by Michelangelo.

GHENT
Good for local colour

ALTHOUGH NOT as compact or well-preserved as nearby Bruges, Ghent has character, some fine medieval buildings and far fewer tourists than its neighbour.

BEST SIGHTS

St Baaf's Cathedral
Mostly Gothic church with a priceless early fifteenth-century altarpiece.

's Gravensteen
The imposing twelfth-century 'Castle of the Counts' is complete with battlements, arrow slits, narrow winding corridors and a dungeon.

ANTWERP
Good for culture and nightlife

ONCE ONE of the busiest ports in Europe, Antwerp is a gritty, lively city that has several excellent museums and an outstanding cathedral.

BEST SIGHTS AND EXCURSIONS

Museum voor Schone Kunsten
Eclectic collection housed in huge neo-classical building. Among the most important works are paintings by Rubens, Van Eyck and Matsys.

Onze Lieve Vrouwe Cathedral
One of Belgium's finest Gothic churches dates mainly from the fifteenth century and has a beautiful nave. Four works by Rubens hang here.

Rubenshuis
Impressively restored house of painter Peter Paul Rubens (1577–1640).

TOURNAI
Good for local colour

A RELAXED, low-key town dominated by its superb cathedral.

BEST SIGHT

Cathédrale Notre Dame
A wonderful, five-towered twelfth-century church, probably Belgium's finest example of Romanesque-Gothic architecture. It features exquisite transepts, some glorious paintings and an interesting treasury.

IEPER
Good for history

IEPER (YPRES), a once-prosperous medieval town, was ruined in the First World War. Some important old buildings have since been rebuilt.

BEST SIGHTS AND EXCURSIONS

First World War battlefields
The 43-mile '14-'18 Route takes in museums and many battle sites. However, beautifully kept cemeteries (like Tyne Cot near Zonnebeke) provide the most moving testament to the scale of the slaughter.

THE ARDENNES
Good for family holidays, outdoor activities and scenic landscape

A WORLD away from the flat industrial north and west, the Ardennes is a sparsely populated region of wooded hills and peaks, stunning river valleys and wild beauty. The Hohes Venn is the highest part, but the most popular, attractive areas and famous cave systems lie further west.

BEST SIGHTS

Dinant
This town is a centre for boat trips along the Meuse and for canoeing on the wilder Lesse. Its much fought-over citadel now contains a historical museum. The nearby Parc National de Furfooz is worth visiting.

Namur
The 'gateway to the Ardennes' is a pleasant town with several museums and the region's liveliest nightlife. A citadel stands where the Meuse and Sambre rivers meet. Its three main sections are the Terra Nova bastion, the imposing Donjon, and the Mediane works – part of a citadel to the east, including the stronghold of the Counts of Namur.

BEST RESORTS

Bouillon
- Resort attractively sited in a loop of the River Semois.
- Stunning castle, modified by Louis XIV's military engineer, Vauban.

Han-sur-Lesse
- Site of the most spectacular cave system in the Ardennes.
- Plenty of accommodation and restaurants but overrun in summer.
- In one of the region's most beautiful areas, offering great walking.
- Near a wild animal reserve with bison, bears and boar, the Belgian space and satellite station at Lessive and a château at Lavaux Ste-Anne.

La Roche-en-Ardenne
- A picturesque summer resort hidden away in the hills. It can be overcrowded with tourists in season.
- Topped with a ruined castle and at the centre of dramatic scenery.

Rochefort
● Less touristy than Han, with its own caves and access to country-side.

St-Hubert
● Popular resort in the most densely forested region of the Ardennes.
● Good base for gentle hiking and for a wild animal reserve (Parc à Gibier), an open-air museum of rural life and the Euro Space Centre.
● Fine sixteenth-century Gothic basilica.

Stavelot
● Small, pretty town in the eastern Ardennes, dominated by its abbey, and site of a lively annual carnival (third weekend before Easter).
● Close to famous (though not very interesting) health resort of Spa.

FLANDERS COAST
Good for family holidays, outdoor activities and nightlife

EASILY REACHED by one-hour drive from Calais, the Belgian Coast features 43 miles of safe, golden beaches mostly backed by sand dunes and nature reserves. Each of the dozen resorts has its individual character and atmosphere. The entire coast is served by an efficient scheduled tram service. Access to Bruges is easy from here.

Blankenberghe
● The wide promenade, overlooked by eight-storey hotels and apart-ments, is pedestrianised, giving maximum room for kids' bicycles and go-carts.
● Sea Life Centre includes a rescue centre for wounded or orphan seals.

De Haan
● A low-profile resort, ideal for families, with well-marked routes for cycling, walking and horse-riding.
● The charm and variety of the architecture is worth exploring.

Knokke-Heist
● An elegant upmarket resort based on five beaches that stretch for seven miles. Many wealthy Belgians own villas or apartments for holidays and weekends, making the resort extra lively. Luxury shops and 70 art galleries are open all day on Sundays.
● Look into Knokke Casino's magnificent entrance hall, fitted with a seven-ton Venetian chandelier and murals by Magritte.

Ostend

● The liveliest resort of the coast, with numerous bars, fish restaurants, the Wellington Racetrack and a Casino.

● Excellent shopping at reasonable prices.

● Visit the yacht harbour, and the Belgian training ship the three-master *Mercator*.

WHEN TO GO

CITY BREAKS are popular at any time of year. The Ardennes is crowded in July and August, when you should book accommodation in advance.

	Average daily maximum temperature °C											
London	6	7	10	13	17	20	22	21	19	14	10	7
Brussels	4	7	10	14	18	22	23	22	20	15	9	6
	JAN	FEB	MAR	APR	MAY	JUN	JUL	AUG	SEP	OCT	NOV	DEC
Brussels	21	17	17	18	16	15	17	18	13	17	20	19
London	15	13	11	12	12	11	12	11	13	13	15	15
	Average number of rainy days per month											

PACKAGE TRAVEL

MOST TOUR operators to Belgium offer city breaks to Bruges and Brussels for any number of nights by air, ferry, coach or rail (including Eurostar). Other choices outside the cities include self-catering holidays in a holiday park, B&B in the Ardennes, coach tours and accommodation in hotels and guesthouses throughout the country. Activity holidays include art and music tours, battlefield tours and wine tours.

Tour operators

City breaks: Bridge Travel Service, British Airways Holidays, City Holidays, Cresta, Crystal, Eurostar Holidays Direct, Inghams, Inntravel, Kirker, Made to Measure, Magic Cities, Osprey, Premier Holidays, Simply Travel, Time Off, Travelscene, VFB **Coach tours**: Crusader, Excelsior, Kirker, Leger, Shearings, Wallace Arnold **Special interest**: Anglo-Dutch Sports (cycling), Arblaster & Clarke (wine), Ffestiniog Travel (rail tours), Holts' Tours (battlefields), Martin Randall (art), Midas (battlefields) **Specialists**: Belgian Travel Service

---

INDEPENDENT TRAVEL

FREQUENT FLIGHTS run to Brussels from the UK, but it is easy (and cheap) to go via the Channel Tunnel on Eurostar. There are also ferry connections via Ostend.

The best way to explore Belgium is by train. The country's small size and the efficient and relatively cheap rail network mean that few places are more than a couple of hours from Brussels. Bruges, for example, is only one hour away. If you intend to travel extensively by train, a range of rail passes is available. In contrast, buses are mainly useful for travel within the towns and in some remoter parts of the Ardennes.

Travellers without a car will have most difficulty getting around in the Ardennes. Rail links are few, and sporadic bus services are often the only option. Cycling is a possibility. If you do not take your own cycle you can participate in a scheme run by Belgian railways that allows you to hire a bike from one railway station and return it to any other of your own choosing.

Car hire can be expensive. A British driving licence is accepted by car hire companies. Signposts can cause confusion, as all towns are referred to in Flemish in the north of the country and in French in the south.

In addition to hotels, cheaper private accommodation is also some-times available, and an extensive network of official and unofficial youth hostels operates, many with private and family rooms. Camping is a popular alternative: there are many well-equipped campsites in Belgium. These are graded from one to four stars. Another option is working holidays on farms. Tourist offices can supply leaflets on all these options and will book accommodation for you, usually without charge.

RED TAPE, HEALTH AND SAFETY

UK CITIZENS do not need a visa to travel to Belgium. Your passport must be valid for three months beyond your date of departure from Belgium.

Belgium has no particular health or crime problems: just take the usual precautions (see pages 10–12).

MORE INFORMATION Belgian Tourist Office, 29 Princes Street, London W1R 7RG, tel 020-7629 1988, brochure line (09001) 887799 (premium rate number), web site: *www.belgiantourism.net*

Another useful web site is: *www.tourist-offices.org.uk/Belgium/index.html*

COST OF LIVING £££

BOLIVIA

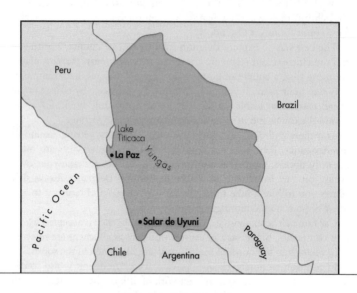

HIGHLIGHTS

Culture	Romantic	Local colour	Scenic
Potosi, Sucre	**escapism**	*La Paz*	**landscape**
	Lake Titicaca,		*Lake Titicaca,*
History	*Salar de Uyuni,*	**Shopping**	*Salar de Uyuni,*
Tiahuanaco	*The Yungas*	*La Paz*	*The Yungas*

LA PAZ
Good for local colour and shopping

THE FIRST impression of La Paz is unforgettable, with the snow-capped Andean peaks in the distance and the pastel-coloured houses climbing up the edge of the steep canyon in which the city nestles. It provides a wonderful introduction to this diverse country, and is also a good place in which to spend a few days acclimatising to the altitude – simply wander around and absorb the bustling atmosphere. Stroll down the lively main street, The Prado, to one of the excellent coffee shops here.

BEST LOCAL COLOUR

The markets are fine spots in which to observe local life. Traditionally dressed Indian women in bowler hats sell everything imaginable from exotic freeze-dried potatoes to llama foetuses and herbal potions to coca leaves. The best place for handicrafts and in particular alpaca jumpers is Calle Sagamaga. The best place to sit in the sun and people-watch is Plaza Murillo.

BEST SIGHT

Museo Nacional de Arte

Housed in a beautiful baroque palace, the museum boasts works of contemporary local artists as well as an impressive collection of colonial paintings. The city contains many other museums, two of which exhibit some of the best statues from the ancient site of Tiahuanaco.

TIAHUANACO
Good for history

TIAHUANACO IS thought to have been an Aymara ceremonial complex which existed at the heart of a large empire around the ninth century AD. The specialities of the inhabitants were raised fields for cultivation and skull deformation.

THE YUNGAS
Good for romantic escapism and scenic landscape

FOR THOSE adventurous enough to brave the terrifying roads leading to Coroico, this lush mountainous region, verging on the edge of the Amazon basin, is a tranquil haven. It is a place to relax, admire the wonderful views and enjoy the semi-tropical climate. Many pleasant walks can be taken through the orange and banana groves that cover the mountainside.

LAKE TITICACA
Good for romantic escapism and scenic landscape

THIS CALM, beautiful inland sea, at a height of nearly 13,000 feet, is the highest navigable water in the world. From the pleasant town of Copacabana, boats take visitors out to the unspoilt Islas del Sol and de la Luna where you can spend the night. The tranquillity and the vistas across the still blue waters which reflect the distant mountains are magical.

SUCRE
Good for culture

NAMED IN 1825 after the first president of the new Republic, Sucre is the official capital of Bolivia. It is a pretty city where all the buildings in the centre are traditionally painted white.

BEST SIGHTS

Casa de la Libertad
Elegant buildings surround the central square, where Bolivia's Declaration of Independence was signed in 1825.

Ecclesiastical buildings
Sucre's cathedral and the monasteries of La Recoleta and San Felipe Neri are worth a visit.

Tarabuco
This village, about 40 miles from Sucre, is worth a visit. Its Sunday market is thronged with villagers wearing traditional costume.

POTOSI
Good for culture

THIS PICTURESQUE city has narrow, winding streets, much colonial architecture and Baroque churches. You can visit the Mint to which all the locally mined silver was brought. It is an enthralling place.

BEST SIGHTS

Potosi mines
The mines have been worked since the sixteenth century, yielding silver, copper, lead and now mostly tin. Meet the miners and witness the harsh conditions endured by many of Potosi's inhabitants – it is a fascinating, if rather disheartening and claustrophobic experience. On the streets leading to the mines stall-holders sell dynamite and fuses plus copious amounts of coca leaves the miners chew before starting work each day.

Geothermal lake at Tarapaya
This is a good place to sit and relax for free. In the village itself are several thermal baths popular at weekends.

SALAR DE UYUNI
Good for romantic escapism and scenic landscape

EMERGING FROM this vast and surreal dried-up salt lake, or *salar*, are curious 'islands', for example the Isla de Pescado with a marked circular walk, covered in giant cacti. A Salt Hotel has been built on the *salar* where the walls, tables, chairs and beds are carved out of salt. However, there would appear to be a lack of plumbing if you want to stay.

BEST EXCURSIONS

Tour companies in Uyuni offer two-, three- and four-day trips. Prices vary considerably. You get what you pay for but the better companies charge about $90 for a four-day tour. Even so, the accommodation will be very basic with a number of people sharing bunk-bedded rooms and primitive toilet facilities. It is an extraordinary journey from Uyuni by jeep past the *salar*, onward through phenomenal scenery to the Chilean border and back. The trip across the desert takes in salt flats, geysers, volcanoes and the startling jade-coloured Laguna Verde and Laguna Colorado, dotted with hundreds of pink flamingoes. Conditions are harsh: go well-prepared with plenty of food, water, warm clothes and good company.

WHEN TO GO

THE BEST time to visit Bolivia is from May to November during the dry season. June and August are the coldest months. Warm clothing is essential at all times of year, and you should always be prepared for the drastic changes in temperature, which can plummet as low as − 25°C.

	Average daily maximum temperature °C											
London	6	7	10	13	17	20	22	21	19	14	10	7
La Paz	17	17	18	18	18	17	17	17	18	19	19	18
	JAN	FEB	MAR	APR	MAY	JUN	JUL	AUG	SEP	OCT	NOV	DEC
La Paz	21	18	16	9	5	2	2	4	9	9	11	18
London	15	13	11	12	12	11	12	11	13	13	15	15
	Average number of rainy days per month											

PACKAGE TRAVEL

ONLY A few specialist tour operators offer a variety of holidays in Bolivia. Most feature the country as part of a two-week tour in combination with Peru and/or Chile, allocating around four or five days for exploring the north of the country including La Paz, the Inca ruins by Lake Titicaca, the Islas del Sol and Copacabana.

Specialists offer tailor-made tours with suggested itineraries that include Sucre, Potosi and the Yungas region. Spectacular rail journeys from Santa Cruz to the Brazilian border and four-wheel-drive exploration of the salt flats around Uyuni can also be arranged as inclusive tours.

Accommodation ranges from de luxe city hotels and comfortable town hotels to very basic accommodation with primitive facilities and camping on more adventurous trips. Special-interest holidays include mountain biking, trekking, wildlife and adventure camping trips.

Tour operators

Adventure: Dragoman, Encounter Overland, Kumuka Expeditions **General**: Cox & Kings, Hayes & Jarvis, Kuoni **Mountain biking**: KE Adventure **Specialists**: Austral Tours, Journey Latin America, Magic of Bolivia, Nomadic Thoughts, Passage to South America, South American Experience, Veloso Tours **Walking**: Exodus, Explore Worldwide, Guerba

---

INDEPENDENT TRAVEL

BOLIVIANS ARE not the friendliest or most helpful of South Americans and as a tourist you will often encounter an aloof, disinterested manner in the people you come across. However alienating this may be, it can come as a welcome change to the constant attention one tends to attract in most other countries on the continent. An even greater advantage is the distinct sense of safety their indifference generates. Bolivia not only *feels* safe but *is* one of the safest countries in South America.

Bolivia is extremely popular with travellers since it is cheap and relatively easy to get around. Many buses ply between the main tourist destinations, and although the roads are poor (especially during the rainy season), the scenery is breathtaking and the distances endurable. There are railway lines connecting Bolivia with neighbouring Brazil, Argentina and Chile. However, it is uncertain whether there are trains on some of these routes at present. Check well in advance. Flights are cheap, but since much of Bolivia's appeal lies in the dramatically changing landscape, overland travel is really the only way to appreciate the country.

Simple accommodation is easy to find in most places, but more upmarket hotels should be booked in advance.

Those who wish to trek should head for Sorata, a small town on the edge of the Cordillera Real, a five-hour bus journey from La Paz. It is possible to walk from there on your own, to arrange fully supported treks, or to hire single guides and mules. Demanding treks include a 7-8 day circuit of Illampu and Ancohuma and to Mapiri in the Yungas.

RED TAPE, HEALTH AND SAFETY

BRITISH PASSPORT-HOLDERS do not require a visa and will be granted three months on entry into Bolivia.

The main health complaint suffered by travellers is caused by the altitude and it is vital on arrival in the Andes to take time to acclimatise and not over-exert yourself – see page 10 for hints on combatting the symptoms. To avert stomach problems be sure to avoid tap water, ice and salads at all times. Bottle water is readily available.

Inoculations against typhoid and hepatitis are recommended, as are malaria tablets if you are visiting the lowlands. Yellow fever inoculations are also required if you arrive from an 'infected' country (not if you go direct from the UK).

MORE INFORMATION Tourist Department, Bolivian Embassy, 106 Eaton Square, London SW1W 9AD, tel 020-7235 4248/2257, fax 020-7235 1286, web site: *www.bolivia.com*

COST OF LIVING £

BRAZIL

HIGHLIGHTS

Beaches	**Scenic landscape**	**Culture**	**Flora/ wildlife**
North-east Brazil, Rio de Janeiro	*Iguaçu Falls, Rio de Janeiro*	*Olinda, Ouro Prêto, Rio de Janeiro, São Paulo, Salvador*	*The Amazon, the Pantanal*
Local colour	**Nightlife**		**Romantic escapism**
North-east Brazil	*Rio de Janeiro, São Paulo*	**Food/wine** *North-east Brazil, São Paulo*	*Ouro Prêto, Praia do Forte*

RIO DE JANEIRO
Good for beaches, culture, nightlife and scenic landscape

THE BUZZING atmosphere on the streets is one of Rio's biggest attractions – never more so than during the February carnival. As the archetypal city of extremes, however, Rio de Janeiro is not for the faint-hearted.

BEST SIGHTS AND EXCURSIONS

Folklore Museum
A small but excellent museum devoted to folk art from all over Brazil.

Santa Teresa
This hilltop residential district contains lovely colonial architecture, and is blissfully quiet by Rio standards. The tram ride through cobbled streets to get there from the city centre is part of the fun.

Viewpoints
Sugar Loaf Mountain, or Pão de Açúcar, and the Corcovado peak (crowned with the much-photographed statue of Christ) are the two places that every tourist visits, for their superb views over the city. Expect crowds unless you go early or late in the day.

BEST BEACHES

Copacabana
The beach at Copacabana is not so much the focal point as the setting: this is a place to people-watch as much as swim or sunbathe – as long as you can cope with the hawkers. At night, Rio's most outrageous nightclubs come into their own.

Costa Verde
If you want to escape the hubbub of Rio, there are lovely beaches and tropical islands along the Costa Verde, several hours' drive to the west: in particular, Augra des Reis, Ilha Grande and Paraty.

Ipanema and Leblon
These adjacent beaches are more chic but not as lively as Copacabana. The sand is cleaner and the atmosphere more relaxed.

THE SOUTHERN INTERIOR
Good for culture, flora, food/wine, nightlife, romantic escapism, scenic landscape and wildlife

BEST SIGHTS

Brasilia
Brazil's space-age capital is a curiosity rather than a must-see destination. Located miles from anywhere, it might appeal to those interested in 1950s architecture but is otherwise best left alone.

Ouro Prêto
The best of a remarkable group of colonial towns set in the lush hills

of Minas Gerais state, Ouro Prêto is chock-a-block with beautifully preserved mansions and churches and was once a gold and diamond mining centre. While dangerously close to being a living museum, with its lovely hotels and restaurants Ouro Prêto is a relaxing place to stay and a good base for exploring the nearby towns.

São Paulo

Brazil's largest city is certainly not its most beautiful, but it hums with energy and cosmopolitan bustle. Here are the country's best and greatest concentration of museums and art galleries (including MASP – the Museu de Arte de São Paulo – the largest and most impressive art collection in Latin America). The city also has the greatest variety of restaurants in Brazil, and in Liberdade district, the largest population of Japanese immigrants outside Japan. São Paulo's nightlife is also superb, with everything from mega rock concerts to intimate Latin jazz clubs.

BEST SCENIC LANDSCAPE

Iguaçu Falls

These magnificent waterfalls spanning the Brazilian–Argentinian border are higher than Niagara and broader than the Victoria Falls. The best overall view is on the Brazilian side, but for a close-up view of the Falls and surrounding jungle you should nip over to Argentina. The Falls are at their most dramatic in summer.

BEST WILDLIFE

The Pantanal

This vast swamp has more wildlife than anywhere else in Brazil, and with its open grasslands and waterways it is pleasantly easy to observe. The birdlife is particularly rich, with everything from macaws to emus. Safaris are by truck, foot, canoe or horseback, and sleeping arrangements range from very basic to luxurious packages in upmarket *fazendas*, or ranches.

NORTH-EAST BRAZIL

Good for beaches, culture, food/wine, local colour and romantic escapism

BEST SIGHTS AND EXCURSIONS

Cachoeira

A couple of hours by road from Salvador, Cachoeira is one of Brazil's most atmospheric colonial towns – thanks partly to its state of picturesque decay. Ideal for a peaceful overnight excursion.

Olinda

This delightful place, overlooking the ocean near Recife, boasts some of the nation's best-preserved colonial architecture. Would-be guides pester tourists, but they do not ruin the place. Its carnival is known as one of the best in Brazil – full of local colour and atmosphere.

Salvador

The African flavour is strong in Salvador, visible in the city's music and dance, religion and wonderful food. Tourists pour in to explore its cobbled streets and admire its colonial architecture, but this city is as chaotic as it is entrancing, and some people find it unnerving.

BEST BEACHES

Fine sandy beaches line much of the north-east coast, but many have not been developed for tourism. Salvador and Fortaleza offer about the liveliest beach scene in the north-east, but if you are more interested in the quality of the sand and peace and quiet, head out of the cities.

Costa do Sauipe

North of Salvador, this purpose-built mega-resort, due to open at the end of 2000, is being heralded as Brazil's answer to Mexico's Cancún. Beachside accommodation will offer everything from intimate *pousadas* (guesthouses) to all-inclusive international resort hotels.

Ilha de Tinharé

South of Salvador, this island's magnificent beaches are among the best in Brazil. The growing crowd of trendy Brazilians and foreign tourists mostly gather around the once-quiet fishing village of Morro de São Paulo.

Porto Seguro and Arraial da Ajuda

Mid-way between Salvador and Vitoria to the south, the historical old town of Porto Seguro has been developed into a major resort, with excellent beaches, luxury hotels and watersports. Nearby Arraial da Ajuda has magnificent beaches too, some of which attract a younger crowd wanting to escape the masses.

Praia do Forte

North of Salvador, Praia do Forte has miles of glorious beaches and is perfect for a week away from it all – particularly with the improved facilities of the developing resort.

BEST CARNIVAL

Rio's carnival is best-known, but experts assert that carnival is better in Salvador, Recife and Olinda – thanks to the African influence.

THE AMAZON
Good for flora and wildlife

YOU SHOULD not go to the Amazon just for the varied scenery or for guaranteed sightings of exotic wildlife or indigenous people. Go expecting an adventure and a taste of the mystery of Amazonia and you should not be disappointed.

BEST BASES

Belém
The departure point for boat services up the Amazon River, Belém is the Amazon's most attractive city and explorable in a day.

Manaus
The only reason to go to Manaus, a shabby, million-strong city in the heart of the Amazon, is to organise a trip into the rainforest (though many Brazilians come for the duty-free shops). You need at least four days to make a jungle trip worthwhile. Manaus's outstanding – and bizarre – architectural attraction is the Opera House, built during the city's nineteenth-century spectacular rubber boom, with marble from Italy and French chandeliers.

WHEN TO GO

THE Amazon is hot and wet for most of the year, but it is the high humidity which causes most discomfort. The seasons are much more defined in the southern states, where summers are hot and winters cool. It can rain at any time, but the wettest months are between October and April (during the Brazilian summer). The incessant rains and extreme heat make the Pantanal off-limits during the peak of the wet season. Generally, though, Brazil is a year-round destination.

Many Brazilians are on holiday from December to February, when seats on planes and buses get booked up.

Anyone thinking of visiting in February but who is not interested in carnival should consider changing their plans: during the carnival chaos reigns, hotels are full and flights are heavily oversubscribed.

	Average daily maximum temperature °C											
London	6	7	10	13	17	20	22	21	19	14	10	7
Rio de Janeiro	29	29	28	27	25	24	24	24	24	25	26	28
	JAN	FEB	MAR	APR	MAY	JUN	JUL	AUG	SEP	OCT	NOV	DEC
Rio de Janeiro	13	11	12	10	10	7	7	7	11	13	13	14
London	15	13	11	12	12	11	12	11	13	13	15	15
	Average number of rainy days per month											

PACKAGE TRAVEL

GENERAL TOUR operators offer holidays in Rio de Janeiro with excursions to the Iguaçu Falls, or two-week tours of Brazil's highlights also taking in Manaus and maybe Brasilia, Salvador or the Pantanal close to the western border of Brazil. Specialists offer more flexibility and more options such as two or three days in jungle lodges around Manaus observing wildlife, the colonial mining town of Ouro Prêto, exploring offshore islands around Paraty, or breaks to Natal beach.

Accommodation varies considerably according to budget, from luxurious, colourful *pousadas* (guesthouses) to simple or basic accommodation in jungle lodges. Activity holidays include walking, cruising expeditions on the Amazon, birdwatching and wildlife holidays in the Pantanal swamplands or Amazon jungle.

Tour operators

Adventure: Explore Worldwide, Guerba, KE Adventure **Birdwatching**: Limosa, Sunbird **Cruising**: Abercrombie & Kent **General**: Airtours, Bales Tours, British Airways Holidays, Cox & Kings, Hayes & Jarvis, Kuoni, Unijet **Inclusive**: Club Med **Specialists**: Austral Tours, Journey Latin America, Nomadic Thoughts, Passage to South America, South American Experience **Wildlife**: Naturetrek, Wildlife Worldwide

---

INDEPENDENT TRAVEL

THERE ARE direct flights to Rio from the UK, but you can save money by taking an indirect route – by changing, for example, in Madrid or a US city. Flights direct to Recife are worth considering if you are interested only in the north-east.

Brazil covers an area larger than Europe so flying is the only sensible way to get around if you are not planning a one-centre holiday. Air passes cut the price of internal flights, but these must be purchased outside Brazil. Shop around if you are buying individual fares, and you will get a better deal if you buy ahead. Brazil has a couple of scenic train rides, but otherwise rail services are minimal. The buses are excellent. Services between cities are frequent and often non-stop, and there are sleeper (*leito*) services too, which are worth considering for long journeys. Think carefully before hiring a car. In the big cities, traffic and theft are real problems. The main roads are generally in reasonable shape, particularly along the coast and in the south.

There are scheduled boat services along the Amazon between Belém, Sautarém and Manaus. To really explore the Amazon go on an organised trip. In Manaus umpteen agencies and guides compete for tourists' custom, so it is a good idea to get a recommendation. Organised trips are the best option in the Pantanal too.

The words 'hotel' and '*pousada*' (guesthouse), the most common forms of lodgings in Brazil, are used to describe anything from a smart resort hotel to a fleapit. In cities with beaches, the hotels in the beach areas tend to be more expensive but are closer to bars and restaurants. Some surprisingly comfortable lodges are on offer in the Amazon, but normally you will have to sleep in a hammock or in a simple shelter.

RED TAPE, HEALTH AND SAFETY

UK CITIZENS do not require a visa but must show on arrival: a passport valid for six months, a return or outward ticket, and proof of means of subsistence.

The chief health risks are malaria (which affects inland areas including the Amazon, the Pantanal and the Iguaçu Falls), dengue fever and yellow fever. See your GP or a travel clinic before departure and ensure that you are inoculated against hepatitis A, polio and typhoid. In the coastal cities, the main threat to your health is from the tap water – especially in the north-east – so drink bottled water. Also in the north-east, watch out for *bichos de pé*, which are small parasites that live in the sand and burrow into people's feet.

Petty theft plagues all the large cities – especially Rio, Salvador and Manaus. Be watchful on city buses and on the beach. Follow the precautions on page 12 and take particular care during carnival time.

MORE INFORMATION Tourist Information Department, Brazilian Embassy, 32 Green Street, London W1Y 4AT, tel 020-7499 0877 ext. 218, web site: *www.embratur.gov.br*

COST OF LIVING £

CANADA

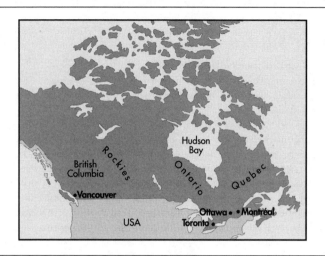

HIGHLIGHTS

Beaches
Atlantic provinces, British Columbia

Flora/ wildlife
British Columbia

Culture
Atlantic provinces, British Columbia Ontario, Quebec

Outdoor activities
Alberta, British Columbia

Nightlife
Ontario, Quebec

Family holidays
British Columbia, Ontario, Quebec

Food/wine
British Columbia, Quebec

Scenic landscape
Atlantic provinces, British Columbia

BRITISH COLUMBIA
Good for beaches, family holidays, flora, outdoor activities, scenic landscape and wildlife

---

BRITISH COLUMBIA (BC) advertises its attractions as 'Super Natural British Columbia'. With over 16,000 miles of coastline and countless inland lakes and rivers, boating, canoeing, fishing, cruising, and just plain sightseeing are easy and affordable practically anywhere.

You can also experience the peace of the great forest on the plentiful hiking trails. Just driving up the main highway east to Alberta, on the first stretch of the 4,970-mile Trans-Canada Highway through the Fraser River Canyon, will give you an idea of the majestic landscape.

BEST SIGHTS

Banff and Jasper National Parks

The former is Canada's oldest national park. It is as large as Lincolnshire, while the even bigger Jasper, at 4,000 square miles, is less crowded and developed. The main attractions here are scenic: majestic mountains, lakes and valleys. Wildlife-spotting is good too, with bighorn sheep frequently on the road and mountain goats on the peaks. Deer, elk, bear, moose and eagles are among the fauna you can, and must, admire from a distance. The Columbia Icefields straddle both parks, and you can travel on these huge glaciers by snowcoach.

The rest of Alberta east of the Rockies is Canada's Wild West. Its major cities, Edmonton and Calgary, are nearby and worth visiting for the former's Klondike Days and the latter's famous Stampede.

Vancouver

Canada's third-largest city – its most booming by far – enjoys a dramatically scenic location between the imposing Rockies and the outlet of the Fraser river into the Pacific Ocean. A bus or trolley tour will show you the main attractions, such as the photogenic inlet of Kettle Creek, the expanding Chinatown, the tourist village of Gastown, and the sandy beaches of Spanish Banks. Granville Island is a lively market area, great for souvenir shopping. At the scenic campus of the University of British Columbia on Point Grey Cliffs, the Museum of Anthropology is the finest research collection of aboriginal artefacts in North America, including a captivating assembly of heavily carved totem poles and ceremonial masks.

Only five minutes from downtown lies Stanley Park, one of North America's most stunning natural parks with lots of amusements for children. Both adults and children will enjoy a drive over Lions Gate Bridge or a trip on the SeaBus to North Vancouver, and then a ride on the tram up to the top of Grouse Mountain.

Victoria

The car ferry from Vancouver to the provincial capital on Vancouver Island is an excellent trip in its own right, meandering between the beautiful Gulf Islands. Once in Victoria, see the Parliament Buildings, the Empress Hotel, and the Royal British Columbia Museum. Then tour the beautiful Butchart Gardens and the gardens of Government House, open year-round because of the mild climate.

ONTARIO
Good for culture, family holidays and nightlife

ALTHOUGH THE province is four times the size of Britain, the north is a virtually untouched vastness, and most inhabitants live in the south, a varied area of rich farmland and prosperous small towns, with all sorts of reconstructed settlements, restored villages, recreational trails and museums. Algonquin Provincial Park, near Ottawa, is even larger than Banff National Park, and offers many wild lakes and forests, rivers, cliffs and beaches: you can reach large parts only on foot or by canoe. Ontario also borders four of the five Great Lakes.

BEST SIGHTS

Niagara Falls
More film is used here than at any other location in the world – from the roadside or from cruise boats, such as the famous *Maid of the Mist*. Only a 20-minute drive away, at Niagara-on-the-Lake, the Shaw Festival has presented world–class international theatre every summer since 1962. The even older Stratford Festival is only two hours away by car.

Ottawa
The nation's capital, well-cared for by federal funds, is a graceful, elegant city. Most of the architecture is traditional, as you will see if you walk around the compact downtown area. The House of Commons and the Senate are contained in the Gothic Revival buildings overlooking the Ottawa River. The Château Laurier and the National Arts Centre are perched on the Rideau Canal (which becomes the world's longest skating-rink in winter).

Two excellent, very modern, museums are the Art Gallery of Canada and the Museum of Civilisation.

Toronto
The Harbourfront Centre, a complex of theatres, galleries and shops, is a leading cultural attraction, along with the Art Gallery of Ontario and the Royal Ontario Museum. You can stroll around the huge yet charming campus of the University of Toronto, right beside Queens Park, where the large, impressive, provincial Parliament stands. City Hall in Philips Square is also interesting. The CN Tower is worth going up, either for the revolving restaurant, or just to look down over Toronto and across Lake Ontario to Niagara Falls and Buffalo, New York.

You can tour the harbour on a yacht, or take the ferry that goes every half-hour to the Toronto Islands with their amusement park, lagoon with waterfowl, and bikes, quadracycles and canoes to rent. Children will also enjoy the zoo and the Ontario Science Centre uptown, and lakeside Ontario Place, an imaginative park with a panorama of attractions and activities.

QUEBEC
Good for culture, food/wine, nightlife, scenic landscapes, wildlife

BEST SIGHTS

Montréal
The world's second-largest French-speaking city is popular with American tourists because it is old, exotic and safe. The old port, recently refurbished, consists mostly of seventeenth- to nineteenth-century buildings and offers many summer festivities and activities. Most of the interest for visitors lies in the old town: handsome cobbled streets, inviting cafés and restaurants. The Museum of Archaeology at Pointe à Callière offers an insight into the city's past. The Musée des Beaux Arts is worth a visit in the downtown area.

Built for the 1976 Olympics, the stadium and its huge leaning tower are not as interesting as the nearby Botanical Gardens or the Biodôme: the latter re-creates four ecosystems, from polar to tropical, presenting 1,000 types of fish, amphibians, reptiles, birds and mammals in their natural habitats.

Quebec City
The only walled city in America north of Mexico looms on the cliffs above the St Lawrence river, where Wolfe beat Montcalm in 1759 to ensure that Canada remained British rather than French. Walk around its historic buildings and museums, and see them again from the river as you cruise to the Ile d'Orléans. Don't miss the top-class Museum of Civilisation's exhibition of Quebecois Indian and Inuit lifestyles. The city has excellent facilities for all winter sports and a huge winter carnival. Good restaurants abound.

Quebec Province
The Charlevoix region (the scenic north bank of the vast St Lawrence river) is designated a UNESCO Biosphere reserve. Visit the artists' town of Baie St Paul and the basilica at Ste Anne de Beaupré, or Tadoussac for whale-watching trips around the mouth of the Saguenay Fjord.

The Gaspé Peninsula offers rugged scenery and historic sights on the south bank of the St Lawrence. Percé makes the best base, a relaxed seaside resort famed for the huge offshore rock pierced by an archway. Visit historic waterfront warehouses at Paspébiac; the Museum of Acadian History at Bonaventure; and Pointe-à-la-Croix where the timbers and artefacts salvaged from the warship *Machault* are displayed.

ATLANTIC PROVINCES
Good for beaches, culture and scenic landscape

NEWFOUNDLAND, MAINLAND Nova Scotia and New Brunswick each have lots to offer – an almost endless variety of bays, coves, beaches, scenic drives and vistas, charming villages and fresh seafood. Halifax, Nova Scotia, is the regional capital. An important and historic port, it makes an ideal base.

BEST SIGHTS

New Brunswick
● There are an awful lot of trees in New Brunswick. Most sights of interest to visitors are in the south along the Bay of Fundy.
● Fredericton is the province's genteel capital. Visit the York-Sunbury Museum and the art gallery. Nearby the Kings Landing living museum recreates the lifestyle of a pioneer community.
● Saint John is the largest city – push beyond the industry and stinking paper mills on the outskirts to the rewarding heart of Victorian red-brick streets.
● In the Fundy National Park you'll find walking trails along wild coastline with the world's biggest tides. Cape Enrage and Hopewell Rocks are highlights.

Newfoundland
● This huge island has a rich history of settlers from the Vikings to the present day; it feels like a separate country.
● St John's is the buzzing capital. Marconi received the first transatlantic wireless message on Signal Hill. St John's inhabitants have a taste for serious partying after dark – head for the pubs on George Street.
● The Avalon Peninsula in the south is popular for whale-watching trips and boat trips to offshore puffin colonies; Cape St Mary's is home to a colony of gannets; Ferryland has the archaeological site of the English Colony of Avalon, established in 1621.
● The Bonavista Peninsula has the time-warp historic town of Trinity, all gabled wooden houses and neat picket fences; in Boyd's Cove, the Beothuk centre tells the story of a native Newfoundland people who became extinct after European colonisation; boat trips leave from Twillingate island for a close-up view of icebergs.

● The Great Northern Peninsula is a long drive from St John's, but holds Atlantic Canada's top scenic feasts in Gros Morne National Park. At the extreme tip lies the amazing Viking settlement at L'Anse aux Meadows.

Nova Scotia
● The capital Halifax has an outstanding Maritime Museum with displays on the *Titanic* and the 'great explosion' that levelled the city in 1917. Lively nightlife and restaurant scene centres on the restored warehouses of the waterfront Historic Properties.
● Lunenburg is an excellent historic fishing and shipbuilding port, with the superb Fisheries Museum of the Atlantic.
● At Annapolis Royal, Samuel de Champlain set up the first permanent European settlement in Canada at Fort Royal.
● Cape Breton Island boasts a thoroughly Scottish heritage; Cape Breton Highlands National Park offers stunning scenery and endless hiking trails.
● Baddeck on the shore of Lake Bras d'Or makes a good base, and there's a good museum dedicated to the inventor Alexander Graham Bell.
● Don't miss Louisborg fortress, a reconstructed French military town.

Prince Edward Island
● Gentle bucolic scenery immortalised in Lucy Maud Montgomery's *Anne of Green Gables* – an inescapable presence on PEI, as it's known by all.
● Anne fans have to visit Cavendish – but be prepared for an awful lot of company.
● Charlottetown is the 'big city' on PEI, an agreeably relaxed and elegant town; the nation of Canada was born in the splendour of Province House.
● PEI National Park on the north coast offers beaches, dunes, cliffs and pleasant seaside resorts between Cavendish and Rustico.

WHEN TO GO

MUCH OF Canada has year-round tourism, but most activities for visitors run from June to August. The autumn foliage season, mid-September to mid-October, is worthwhile too. You can ski in Quebec and the Rockies from November to May, but the best period is December to March.

Average daily maximum temperature °C

	JAN	FEB	MAR	APR	MAY	JUN	JUL	AUG	SEP	OCT	NOV	DEC
London	6	7	10	13	17	20	22	21	19	14	10	7
Montréal	-6	-4	2	11	18	23	26	25	20	14	5	-3
	JAN	FEB	MAR	APR	MAY	JUN	JUL	AUG	SEP	OCT	NOV	DEC
Montréal	17	15	15	14	13	12	13	10	13	12	15	17
London	15	13	11	12	12	11	12	11	13	13	15	15

Average number of rainy days per month

Average daily maximum temperature °C

	JAN	FEB	MAR	APR	MAY	JUN	JUL	AUG	SEP	OCT	NOV	DEC
London	6	7	10	13	17	20	22	21	19	14	10	7
Vancouver	6	7	10	14	17	20	23	22	19	14	9	7
	JAN	FEB	MAR	APR	MAY	JUN	JUL	AUG	SEP	OCT	NOV	DEC
Vancouver	20	16	17	13	10	10	7	7	10	15	18	21
London	15	13	11	12	12	11	12	11	13	13	15	15

Average number of rainy days per month

PACKAGE TRAVEL

Tour operators

Birdwatching: Limosa, Naturetrek, Ornitholidays, Sunbird **Camping/adventure**: AmeriCan Adventures, Trek America **City breaks**: British Airways Holidays, Cresta, Crystal, Inghams, North America Travel Service, Sovereign, Time Off, Travelscene **Coach and rail tours**: APT International, Archers Direct, Bales Tours, Cosmos, Explorers Tours, Page & Moy, Saga, Titan HiTours, Travelsphere, Wallace Arnold **Specialists**: All Canada Travel, British Airways Holidays, Canadian Affair, Canadian Connections, Hamilton Travel, Jetsave, Jetset, Just America, Kuoni, Travelpack, Vacation Canada **Walking**: Explore Worldwide, Ramblers Holidays, Waymark **Wildlife**: Discover the World, Wildlife Worldwide **Other activities**: American Adventures, American Round-Up (ranch riding), Anglers World (fishing), Arctic Experience (Arctic wilderness), Cox & Kings (flora), Solo's Holidays (singles)

TOUR OPERATORS offer a choice of eastern or western seaboard holidays and tours, with a few whistlestop trans-Canadian tours by rail, coach or air for those who want to sample all the highlights of Canada.

Fly-drive packages or self-drive tours by car, motor home or even motorbike give you the flexibility to set your own pace. You can also travel by rail through the Rockies or cruise along the Inside Passage. Inland, you can stay in lodges or hotels in the mountains and tour by car. City breaks are offered to Montréal and Toronto.

Canada also offers a wide variety of activity holidays. They include grizzly bear tours, polar bear adventures, whale watching, cycling, ranching, river-rafting, canoeing, wagon trekking and trail riding.

INDEPENDENT TRAVEL

IT IS best to choose one of three options – British Columbia and the Rockies, Ontario and Quebec, or the maritime provinces.

Hiring a car is by far the best way of getting around. Both cars and petrol are comparatively cheap. The Canadian Automobile Association (the CAA) works very closely with its US counterpart, the AAA, and has reciprocal agreements with both the AA and the RAC in the UK. The CAA, which also acts as a travel agency, can provide information on accommodation, restaurants and attractions, and offers maps and trip kits (excellent custom-made detailed road-maps). Get other useful information from local libraries and chambers of commerce as well as the ubiquitous tourist information centres.

You can no longer cross the country on a single train, but VIA Rail offers 50 per cent discounts, seven days a week, as well as a runabout ticket. Children can sometimes travel free.

You can rent bikes, tents and even motor homes. (Ask the rental agency which hotels in major cities are best for parking them.)

Like other Canadian cities, Montréal offers museum passes (for 19 museums in Montréal). There are also passes that are valid for 1–3 days on the buses or speedy metro, for individuals or families.

Comfortable accommodation of all kinds abounds. Prices, like those of most goods and services, are very reasonable by British standards. For accommodation in Ontario, phone toll-free 1–800-ONTARIO; in Quebec, use toll-free Hospitality 1–800–665–1528. Budget travellers should check out university and college accommodation, particularly during vacation periods.

RED TAPE, HEALTH AND SAFETY

BRITISH VISITORS do not need a visa to visit Canada. Check US visa requirements if you are thinking of dropping into the US, the border of which is often very close.

There are no particular health or crime problems: just take the usual precautions (see pages 10–12).

MORE INFORMATION Tourism Department, Canadian High Commission, Macdonald House, Grosvenor Square, London WC2N 5DN, tel (09068) 715000 (premium rate number), web site: *www.canada.org.uk*

Travel and holiday information is also available at *www.tourworld.com*

COST OF LIVING £

THE CARIBBEAN

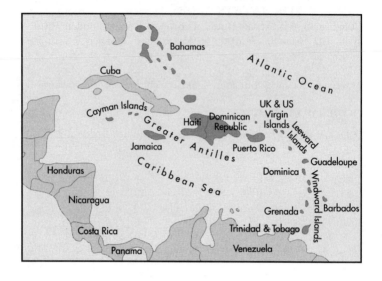

HIGHLIGHTS

Beaches
*Bahamas,
Barbados,
Caymans,
Dominican
Republic,
French
Antilles,
Jamaica,
Leewards,
Tobago,
British and US
Virgin Islands*

Local colour
*Trinidad and
Tobago*

Food/wine
French Antilles

**Romantic
escapism**
*Bahamas,
French
Antilles,
Leewards,
Tobago, British
Virgin Islands*

Nightlife
*Barbados,
French
Antilles,
US Virgin
Islands*

**Outdoor
activities**
*Bahamas,
Barbados,
Caymans,
Dominican
Republic,
French
Antilles,
Jamaica,
Trinidad and
Tobago,
Windwards,
British and US
Virgin Islands*

**Scenic
landscape**
*Dominican
Republic,
Jamaica,
St Lucia,
US Virgin
Islands*

**Flora/
wildlife**
*Caymans,
Dominican
Republic,
Trinidad and
Tobago,
Windwards,
US Virgin
Islands*

BAHAMAS
Good for beaches, outdoor activities and romantic escapism

BEST ISLANDS

Abaco Islands
The best beach is on Great Guana Cay; the islands offer many peaceful sandy stretches while calm waters provide fine sailing. You can hire boats in Hopetoun, Marsh Harbour and Treasure Cay.

Andros
Find sheltered beaches in the east, or dive at resorts near Andros Town.

Berry Islands
Popular with anglers, the islands provide fantastic diving facilities at the underwater cliffs around Tongue of the Ocean.

Bimini Islands
Ernest Hemingway's favourite islands have the best deep-sea fishing areas in the world. Trips are arranged from Alice Town.

Eleuthra
This is a long, thin island with sandy beaches along the sheltered west coast. On the windward side the waves are big enough for surfing. Tiny Harbour Island is famous for Pink Beach on the east coast.

Exuma Cays
The area is mostly uninhabited. Some stunning beaches are located at Elizabeth Harbour and Stocking Island, a short sail away.

Grand Bahama
Freeport/Lucaya boasts hotels, beaches, casinos, marinas and shops. The best beaches outside Freeport include William's Town to the south, remote Barbary Beach, and Gold Rock Beach on the south coast. Trails in the Lucayan National Park lead to limestone sinkholes.

New Providence
Nassau, the Bahamian capital, is the centre of the island's nightlife, with lots of American-style bars, clubs and restaurants. The main tourist enclaves are Cable Beach and Paradise Island, the latter a thin sandy strip noteworthy for its wonderful beaches. Many beaches are private; exceptions include Lighthouse, Adelaide and South beaches.

Rum Cay
Rum Cay numbers a tiny village, a few bars, palms and endless beaches.

BARBADOS
Good for beaches, outdoor activities and nightlife

BEST BEACHES AND WATER SPORTS

A continuous strip of beach winds along the protected west coast, north of Bridgetown. Try Paradise Beach, Treasure Beach and Mullins Bay. The south coast as far as South Point has small, sandy, rock-protected bays, ideal for children. On the south-east coast Crane Bay, spectacular views and surfing – also at attractive Bottom Bay. True surfing pros go to Soup Bowl bay, at Bathesheba on the Atlantic coast, where rough seas make swimming dangerous. Picnic here among the cliffs from Conset Bay to Gay's Cove – it's a bit like Cornwall.

Windsurfing is good at Silver Sands beach, South Point, popular with locals. From some points around the island glass-bottomed boats and a submarine take you out to the reefs, and snorkelling and line and rod fishing are available. The Folkestone Marine Reserve and Museum (on the west coast near Holetown) is a good place to start.

BEST SIGHTS

St Nicholas Abbey and Sunbury Plantation House recall Barbados's sugar-plantation past. The Garrison Savannah – a vast grassed former British army parade ground – has fine Georgian buildings, one containing the excellent national museum. Learn about and taste rum at the Mount Gay Visitor's Centre. Andromeda Gardens overflows with orchids, hibiscus and flowering trees. See green monkeys, imported exotic animals, at the Wildlife Reserve at Farley Hill, with the huge ruined plantation house and tree park.

BEST NIGHTLIFE

Head for Oistins or St Lawrence Gap for rum shops, wine bars, restaurants and clubs to suit all tastes.

CAYMAN ISLANDS
Good for beaches, flora, outdoor activities and wildlife

BEST ISLANDS

Cayman Brac and Little Cayman
Seven miles apart, smaller and less developed than Grand Cayman, these islands suit serious divers. The main underwater attraction is Bloody Bay, north of Little Cayman. Little Cayman also has Booby Pond, home to red-footed booby birds as well as whistling ducks and snowy egrets.

Grand Cayman
The largest and most developed island also has the best stretch of sand, Seven Mile Beach. Behind this are most hotels and condominiums. Queen Elizabeth II Botanic Park is an excellent woodland trail where you might spot parrots or agouti among the air plants and trees. Suitable diving sites are too numerous to list; the most famous is Stingray City, where the eponymous fish eat squid from divers' hands.

DOMINICAN REPUBLIC
Good for beaches, flora, outdoor activities, scenic landscape and wildlife

BEST BEACHES

The north (Atlantic) coast tourist centre, Puerto Plata, has splendid beaches at Playa Dorado and Long Beach: hundreds of others lie to the east. Luperon is good for watersports. International windsurfing tournaments are held at Cabarete, near Sosúa. Sosúa is noisy and bustling with an overcrowded beach. The beach at Cabo Frances Viejo is not crowded but more exposed and the waves are big with a strong undertow. Some of the country's best beaches can be found at Las Terrenas, on the interesting peninsula of Samana in the north-east. Once remote, development is now under way.

In the south, Boca Chica is the nearest beach to the capital, Santa Domingo. It gets very crowded and unpleasant at weekends. Go further east – to La Romana, to the beaches of Catalina island. Casa de Campo, the country's chief tourist centre, is close by. Remote Bayahibe beach and fishing village are 16 miles away.

BEST SIGHTS

The Atlantic coast in the north is the most interesting, and the foothills of the Dominican Alps are worth exploring. Take the Carratera Turistica road to Santiago for a picturesque drive. Puerta Mata and Santiago both have ornate late-nineteenth-century houses built by sugar-cane merchants.

Santa Domingo was the first colonial city of the New World. The reputed remains of Christopher Columbus lie in the gigantic, modern, British-designed Columbus Lighthouse, having been transferred from the venerable (1514) cathedral. The old town has a quiet old quarter of Spanish-style houses with grilled windows and tall shuttered windows, ruined churches and shady cloistered mansions. Some of them have been ruined by past earthquakes. It is eerily atmospheric.

At the end of the Samana peninsula, humpbacked whales occupy the Bahia de Samana in winter. Boat trips to see them are pricey.

BEST SCENIC LANDSCAPE

The interior landscape ranges from plantations to mountains. Four national parks can be visited with a guide – Isla Cabrito, Armando Bermúdez, Los Haitises and the National Park of the East. Permission to visit comes from the Department of Ecotourism in Santo Domingo. Take food and water, as the parks have few facilities.

FRENCH ANTILLES
Good for beaches, food/wine, nightlife, outdoor activities and romantic escapism

BEST ISLANDS

Guadeloupe

Of the island's two 'wings', the easterly Grande-Terre has the sandiest beaches: Caravelle Beach is crowded, but beyond St-François, the Plage des Salines is often deserted. Strong currents prohibit swimming on the east coast. The Basse-Terre half island lies to the west – granulated golden sand beaches in the north. Windsurfing boards can be hired on the south coast of Grande-Terre, yachts from Pointe Pitre and Deshaies. Jacques Cousteau's marine reserve on Ilet de Pigéon is a must for divers. Deep-sea fishing trips are arranged in St-Anne and St-François. In Basse-Terre's national park, trails meander through rainforest, and there are walks to La Soufrière (an active volcano), its lava flows and nearby waterfalls. Grande-Terre resounds nightly to the sounds of *zouk* music, with hundreds of clubs and bars along the south coast. Of the three islands off-shore, Marie Galante produces sugar and has attractive, uncommercialised beaches; Les Saintes is particularly scenic but now suffers from day-trippers; La Désirade is dry and not much visited.

Martinique

The best beaches are on the Ste-Anne peninsula; Grande Anse des Salines is packed at weekends, as is Point de Marin, while Diamant and the remote Baie des Anglais are tranquil. Cap Chevalier is good for windsurfing and L'Anse d'Arlets is ideal for snorkelling.

The island's main sight is the former capital, St-Pierre, totally destroyed in the eruption of Mount Pelée in 1902. A Caribbean Pompeii – except that life has returned, with houses, bars and cafés among the ruins. The bay and volcano are beautiful. The superb eighteenth-century Plantation Leyritz, near Basse-Pointe, has an excellent restaurant, old buildings and beautiful grounds. There are over 300 restaurants, some on the beach – you can see the fish being landed – serving anything from spicy Creole cuisine to the best of French cooking.

St-Barthélemy
This island is the amazingly expensive playground of France's elite. Beaches are busiest on the south coast and quieter to the north. Gentle seas at Anse de Flamands and Lorient are ideal for children. Gustavia and St-Jean, the main towns, support clusters of tax-free French boutiques around their marinas. St-Barthélemy's nightlife is low-key.

St-Martin
Baie Orientale is one of the best beaches on the Atlantic coast – but beware of the undertow. Several resorts are being developed along the coast. On the sheltered Caribbean side, Long Bay has a magnificent beach. Ilet Pinel and Ile Tintamarre are secluded and can be reached via the fishing village of Cul-de-Sac.

JAMAICA
Good for beaches, outdoor activities and scenic landscape

BEST RESORTS AND BEACHES

Most resorts are on the north coast.

Montego Bay
● Close to the airport, with family hotels and water-sports facilities.
● Admission charged to two beaches: Cornwall and Doctor's Cove. Cornwall has music and action.
● Burwood Beach is quieter, and a favourite with windsurfers.

Ocho Rios
● To escape the crowds and jet skiers, head west for Mammee Bay.
● At nearby Port Maria beaches are sheltered and uncrowded.

Port Antonio
● Air of faded grandeur and an incomparable setting between two bays.
● Renowned for deep-sea fishing.
● For beaches take the ferry to Navy Island, or search out Dragon Bay and the deserted beaches beyond Long Bay.

Other beaches
● Kingston's Port Henderson beach, which gets crowded with locals, is the ultimate Jamaican experience and has live music most weekends.
● On the western tip of Jamaica, Negril stretches along miles of sandy beaches and cliffs. Just south lie Bloody Bay and pretty Miskito Cove.

BEST SIGHTS AND EXCURSIONS

Jamaica is scattered with plantation houses; Devon House is in the suburbs of Kingston, Harmony Hall near Ocho Rios, Rose Hall and

Greenwood close to Montego Bay. Noel Coward's house, Firefly, perches high above Port Maria. Reggae fans seek the Bob Marley Museum in Kingston and his birthplace in Nine Mile. Be aware that the city has a high crime rate.

Trails cross the Blue and John Crow Mountains. Climb the 7,400-foot Blue Mountain Peak (take a guide and go before dawn). Bamboo Avenue leads to Black River – take a boat to Great Morass swamp.

Dunn's River Falls, south of Ocho Rios, tumble 600 feet. Visit Rockland Bird Sanctuary at feeding time in the afternoon. Tropical gardens are at Hope, on the outskirts of Kingston, and Castleton in the Wag Valley. The Enchanted Gardens and Coyaba are south of Ocho Rios.

LEEWARD ISLANDS
Good for beaches and romantic escapism

BEST ISLANDS

Anguilla
Anguilla's beaches are arguably the finest in the world. Shoal Bay in the north is the busiest, while to the west Mead's Bay and Shoal Bay West are quieter. Misanthropes head north-east, to a series of tiny coves and Captain's Bay. Uninhabited cays (small, low islands made of sand and coral fragments) can be visited by arrangement with local fishermen. You can enjoy snorkelling at Little Bay on the west coast.

Antigua
Beaches get busy north of St John's; those at Half Moon Bay and Darkwood Beach are more remote. Try visiting sandy inlets like Galleon Bay by water-taxi. Windsurfers can head for Dickenson Bay on the north-west coast, and sailors will be able to hire yachts in English Harbour and Parham Harbour. Nelson's Dockyard at English Harbour was a Georgian British naval base. Now restored, it is packed with nostalgia – and yachties every spring.

Barbuda
Near-deserted beaches and few hotels characterise Barbuda; petrol is still hand-pumped. Thousands of frigate birds nest in Codrington Lagoon.

Nevis
Nevis has a slow, stately charm: little major development occurs outside private resorts. The best beach is Pinney's, on the west coast, while Oualie Beach to the north has golden sands and views across the Narrows to St Kitts. Many plantation houses in the hills have now been converted to splendid, pricey hotels.

St Kitts

St Kitts is busier than Nevis, possessing more hotels and water-sports facilities. Friar's Bay is an exceptional sandy beach on the south coast. You can hire water-sports equipment at neighbouring Frigate Bay; catamaran and deep-sea fishing charters are also booked here. Take a walking trip up 4,000-foot Mount Liamuiga, or tour old plantation houses (some of the island's best hotels are in renovated plantation houses). Take a guide if venturing up into the hills.

TRINIDAD AND TOBAGO
Good for beaches, flora, local colour, outdoor activities, romantic escapism and wildlife

BEST BEACHES

Sleepy Tobago is home to splendid sandy beaches, sheltered by palms and ringed with reefs (with clear blue sea, in contrast to Trinidad's silt-clouded waters). Pigeon Point is one of the best. Englishman's Bay is more secluded.

Trinidad has comparatively few quality beaches, although the sand along the east coast is soft. The remote coves at Balandria and Salibia bays look out towards Tobago. The capital, Port of Spain, is quite far from the sea; most trippers go to Maracas Beach on the north coast. Inland, try river bathing at the Maracas Falls, north of St Joseph.

BEST LOCAL COLOUR

On Trinidad, Port of Spain's 500,000 inhabitants have Indian, Chinese, South American, Asian, African and European origins. The resulting cultural pandemonium of music, architecture, religion and style has produced a vibrant city bursting with calypso, reggae and steel-pan and soca music, notably during the carnival before the beginning of Lent. Pubs and clubs buzz all year round – but take care after dark. On Tobago, the 'Sunday School' in Buccoo starts at 9.30pm with a steel band down by the beach before moving to nearby bars.

BEST NATURAL HISTORY

Although quite heavily industrialised, Trinidad boasts the Caribbean's best flora and fauna. Aficionados should seek out the Royal Botanical Gardens in Port of Spain's Savannah Park and the Asa Wright Nature Centre above Arima. There is a bird sanctuary at Caroni Swamp (scarlet ibis and snow-white egrets), and the Pointe-à-Pierre Wildfowl Trust. North of the Oropouche river, turtles creep up the beach at Matura Bay. An amazing natural sight is Pitch Lake, which has produced bitumen for roads all over the world.

BEST FOR ROMANTIC ESCAPISM

For escapism, seek Castara and Englishman's Bay on the north coast of Tobago, and stay in a traditional hideaway. For more action, Pigeon Point and Store Bay have beach bars, and are popular with the locals.

BEST WATER SPORTS

Tobago is a water-sports haven. Hire gear and boats from Pigeon Point. Buccoo Reef is popular with snorkellers and scuba divers, but is damaged; try beautiful less-visited reefs off the eastern coast. Water-sports facilities on Trinidad are not top-notch, but you can hire boats, boards and fishing lines around Bayshore in Port of Spain and from larger hotels.

WINDWARD ISLANDS
Good for flora, outdoor activities and wildlife

BEST ISLANDS

Dominica
The poorest of the group, Dominica has craggy, cloud-topped slopes. As the beaches are mostly volcanic black sand, river bathing on the Rosalie river and at Trafalgar Falls is popular. Much of the interior is national park, with walking trails through the rainforest, which is home to 150 species of bird including three species of parrot. Between May and October, whale-watching is a popular tourist activity.

Grenada
The capital, St George's, is the prettiest town in the Caribbean. Most hotels are located around Grand Anse with its stunning beach. Water-sports equipment can be hired here. For privacy, try Dr Groom or Magazine Beach to the west. Sailors could potter around the inlets of the south coast or cruise up to the Grenadines. Bareboat charters are available in L'Anse aux Epines. Organised walks explore rainforest in the National Park. Join a trek to the volcanic lake of Grand Etang, or try an easier hike to Concord Falls.

St Lucia
The most developed of the Windwards, St Lucia boasts white sandy beaches on its leeward coast and a tradition of delicious Creole food, thanks to the French. The most popular beach is Reduit. The best windsurfing is off the south of the island. Divers' choice is Anse Chastanet, on the west coast. The scenery is dramatically beautiful, especially in the south near the volcanic Pitons.

St Vincent and the Grenadines

Like several other islands among this incredibly unspoilt group, Mustique is an exclusive retreat of the rich and famous. On St Vincent, walkers can attempt the three-hour climb up the Soufrière (take a guide) or follow the gentler Vermont Nature Trails. The islands are a sailing paradise, with clear seas, a backdrop of volcanic peaks on the horizon, and playful dolphins. Divers and snorkellers should head for Bequia, which is surrounded by reefs, or the Tobago Cays, five deserted islands encircling a protected reef.

BRITISH VIRGIN ISLANDS

Good for beaches, outdoor activities and romantic escapism

BEST ISLANDS

Anegada

Lying less than 35 feet above sea-level, Anegada has miles of sandy beaches. There is a big scuba and snorkelling centre on the reef, with over 300 wrecks to explore. You can hire equipment from the Anegada Reef Hotel.

Jost van Dyck

A great place for escapists, the island has strips of idyllic beach and few hotels. The best beaches are at Great Harbour and White Bay, or try Sandy Spit (off Green Cay) with its palm trees and white sands.

Tortola

Tortola's sandiest beaches are on the north coast; try Cane Garden Bay or Smuggler's Cove, the best on the island. Scuba divers should head for the wreck of the *Rhone* off Salt Island, while snorkellers should try the coral reefs. The Sage Mountain National Park has trails through rainforest. You can charter bareboats in Roadtown, Nanny Cay and West End.

Virgin Gorda

The most popular beaches are in the south-west. From Mad Dog Bar, footpaths lead to the Baths, with deep sand and clear water. To the north, Spring and Trunk bays are popular with the yachting crowd, and Long Bay has views to Tortola. You can charter crewless boats (known as bareboat charters) at North Sound and the main yacht harbour. Hire water-sports gear from sailing clubs and hotels. It is expensive to dive here.

US VIRGIN ISLANDS
Good for beaches, flora, nightlife, outdoor activities and wildlife

BEST ISLANDS

St Croix
Less developed than St Thomas and a laid-back holiday location, St Croix features beaches in isolated coves. In the north-east Isaac's Bay, off the road, is good for snorkelling. In the south-west, head for Sandy Point between May and July to see leatherback turtles laying eggs. On the northern coast, the shallow waters of sandy Chenay Beach are ideal for children. Water-sports equipment can be hired.

St John
With tranquil white beaches lining the north-west coast from Trunk Bay to Francis Bay, St John is another snorkellers' mecca. Two-thirds of the island is national park and paths criss-cross the rainforest. Guides lead tours which include picnic and snorkelling stops (5,600 acres of the park cover offshore reefs).

St Thomas
Hotels and private resorts fringe St Thomas's coastline. The tax-free shopping attracts cruise ships to the island's port and capital Charlotte Amalie, which was once a Danish colony. Forts and elegant buildings remain. At night, Charlotte Amalie and Frenchtown buzz; tastes are eclectic, with sushi bars ranged alongside piano bars and nightclubs. Muggings are becoming more common. The most popular beach is Magen's Bay on the north coast; you can hire water-sports equipment here. For total seclusion, sail south to Buck Island. Now a national park, it is guarded by a vast reef and snorkelling here is superb.

WHEN TO GO

THE OFFICIAL hurricane season in the Caribbean runs from 1 June to 30 September, though recent hurricanes have struck between the end of August and the end of September extending occasionally into early November.

Carnival is the main celebration in the Caribbean; although this is traditionally a pre-Lenten festival, some of the smaller islands alter the dates of festivities to avoid competing for performers and visitors. Thus, for example, Trinidad, Dominica, St Lucia and most of the French islands celebrate in February or March; Barbados and St Vincent in July; Anguilla and Grenada in August; Montserrat and St Kitts in December.

	Average daily maximum temperature °C											
London	6	7	10	13	17	20	22	21	19	14	10	7
Bridgetown	28	28	29	30	31	31	30	31	31	30	29	28
	JAN	FEB	MAR	APR	MAY	JUN	JUL	AUG	SEP	OCT	NOV	DEC
(Barbados)	13	8	8	7	9	14	18	16	15	15	16	14
London	15	13	11	12	12	11	12	11	13	13	15	15
	Average number of rainy days per month											

	Average daily maximum temperature °C											
London	6	7	10	13	17	20	22	21	19	14	10	7
Kingston	30	30	30	31	31	32	32	32	32	31	31	31
	JAN	FEB	MAR	APR	MAY	JUN	JUL	AUG	SEP	OCT	NOV	DEC
(Jamaica)	3	3	2	3	4	5	4	7	6	9	5	4
London	15	13	11	12	12	11	12	11	13	13	15	15
	Average number of rainy days per month											

PACKAGE TRAVEL

MOST TOUR operators feature packages to hotel complexes with the emphasis on relaxation and water sports. The Caribbean is notable for the number of all-inclusive holidays on offer. These vary slightly in what is covered, but generally all meals, entertainment and sporting activities are included in the price. In some packages drinks are also thrown in. Some hotels are for couples only, others have more of a family appeal. All-inclusive holidays save money, but encourage guests to stay in the hotel rather than exploring the island they are staying on.

Self-catering on the popular islands is in apartments and also in purpose-built villas. Several operators offer private villas. These tend to be at the upper end of the market, with private pools and maid service (sometimes even fully staffed). Two-centre and island-hopping holidays are also available; the latter will be more expensive than a standard package.

Activities on offer include sailing, scuba diving and deep-sea fishing. You can charter bareboat (crewless) or crewed sailing boats and pick your own route or join a sailing trip as part of your holiday. Cruising can be on a four-masted sailing ship or on a full-size cruise ship. Birdwatching holidays are on offer in Trinidad and Tobago, and walking in Jamaica.

Tour operators

Birdwatching: Abercrombie & Kent, Limosa, Ornitholidays, Sunbird, Wildlife Worldwide **General**: Abercrombie & Kent, Airtours, British Airways Holidays, Caribbean Connection, Caribtours, Club Med, Cosmos, CV Travel, Elegant Resorts, First Choice, Harlequin, Hayes & Jarvis, Jetsave, Kuoni, Made to Measure, Meon, Sunset Faraway Holidays, Thomas Cook, Thomson, Tradewinds, Tropical Places, Unijet, Virgin Holidays

INDEPENDENT TRAVEL

LONDON AND Paris are the main European gateways for flights to the Caribbean; otherwise you can transit through the United States. If you have lots of time to spare, a 'banana boat' cargo ship might appeal.

LIAT is the main airline providing connections between the islands, and offers a range of discounts and passes. Smaller airlines, like Winair or Air Guadeloupe, cover more limited areas or island groups.

Ferries, catamarans and cargo boats are options, or you can charter bareboat or crewed yachts. It is easiest to sail north to south, with the prevailing winds; some yacht charter companies allow you one-way hire.

Buses are a cheap mode of transport on individual islands. The word 'bus' also covers vehicles such as minivans or pick-up trucks. Taxis are cheap and offer more comfort. If you plan to hire a car, you may have to buy a temporary local driving permit. Driving is on the left on former British islands, and on the right on French and Dutch islands.

RED TAPE, HEALTH AND SAFETY

EACH OF the islands has its own entry rules and regulations – check with the appropriate tourist office or your tour operator, and with your GP or travel clinic for health advice.

Most visitors to the Caribbean enjoy trouble-free holidays (but note months affected by the hurricane season under 'When to go'). The Foreign Office Travel Advice Unit issues notices about various islands, particularly Jamaica and Trinidad and Tobago. Leave valuables and large amounts of cash in your hotel, do not resist if threatened with a weapon, and take local advice on areas to avoid, especially at night. For further advice see page 12.

MORE INFORMATION Caribbean Tourism Organisation, 42 Artillery Row, London SW1P 1RR, tel 020-7222 4335, web site: *www.caribtourism.com*

Individual offices

Anguilla Tourist Office
7 Westwood Road,
London SW13 0LA
tel 020-8876 9025

Antigua & Barbuda Tourist Office
15 Thayer Street,
London W1M 5LD
tel 020-7486 7073

Bahamas Tourist Office,
3 The Billings, Walnut Tree Close
Guildford, Surrey GU1 4UL
tel (01483) 448900
Grenada Board of Tourism
Address: as Dominica Tourist
Office
tel 020-7370 5164

Jamaica Tourist Board
1–2 Prince Consort Road
London SW7 2BZ
tel 020-7224 0505

St Kitts & Nevis Tourism Office
10 Kensington Court
London W8 5DL
tel 020-7376 0881

St Lucia Tourist Board
421A Finchley Road
London NW3 6HJ
tel 020-7431 3675

Barbados Tourism Authority
263 Tottenham Court Road
London W1P 9AA
tel 020-7636 9448

Cayman Islands Department of
Tourism, 6 Arlington Street
London SW1A 1RB
tel 020-7491 7771

Dominica Tourist Office
1 Collingham Gardens
London SW5 0HW
tel 020-7835 1937
St Vincent & the Grenadines
Tourist Office
10 Kensington Court
London W8 5DL
tel 020-7937 6570

Trinidad & Tobago Tourist Office
66 Abbey Road, Enfield,
Middlesex EN1 2RQ
tel 020-8350 1015

US Virgin Islands Tourist Office
Molasses House, Clove Hitch Quay
Plantation Wharf, London SW11 3TN
tel 020-7978 5262

COST OF LIVING ££–£££

CHINA

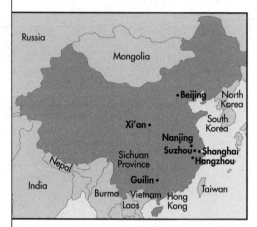

BEIJING
Good for culture

BEIJING (PEKING), the power base of modern China and its ancient northern capital, lies at the heart of the Middle Kingdom and is not to be missed. A visit to this extraordinary city also offers a chance to sample typical northern food (try the Mongolian hotpot and steamed dumplings, or *jiaozi*).

BEST SIGHTS

Forbidden City
The massive, sealed quarters of the emperors of China, just off Tiananmen Square, date back to the fifteenth century and provide a perfect example of classical Chinese architecture (Bernardo Bertolucci's lush and lavish 1987 film *The Last Emperor* was shot here). Allow a day for the City and neighbouring sights around the square.

Great Wall and the Ming Tombs

Construction of the Great Wall began in 221 BC. You can escape the many visitors by walking far enough along from its Badaling access point to be afforded spectacular mountain views. Then visit the nearby Ming Tombs, especially for the ancient spirit walkway.

Summer palaces

The summer palace (Yiheyuan) in Haidian district is set in an exotic lakeside royal garden, with temples, pavilions and bridges. It can be crowded, hot and tiring in the summer, but in midwinter when the lake freezes it is pleasant to watch the skaters. Or try the old summer palace (Yuanmingyuan) nearby. Looted by Europeans in 1860, the melancholy ruins and tranquil gardens provide a haven from modern China.

Tiantan Park

Home to the Temple of Heaven, this is a favourite spot for local city-dwellers, with lots of greenery and trees. The temple, with its blue-tiled roof and white marble terrace, the 'altar of heaven', is the central attraction. Nearby is an excellent silk shop.

XI'AN
Good for culture

XI'AN WAS the imperial capital (Changan) during the Tang dynasty (AD 618–907). It has the best-preserved city walls in China and many interesting historical sites. See in particular the Shaanxi History Museum on Xiaozhai Road; the nearby Big Wild Goose Pagoda (seventh century); the Banpo neolithic village in the eastern suburbs; and the Great Mosque in the old Muslim quarter. And fit in a visit to the forest of stone steles (tall, thin gravestones), housed in a former Confucian temple at the Shaanxi Provincial museum. Nearby is the Bell Tower and a market selling local food.

BEST SIGHTS

Huashan Mountain

One of China's sacred mountains, this lies 75 miles east of Xi'an at Huayin. Allow half a day to climb its extremely steep slopes. Daoist temples abound. It is not suitable for sufferers of vertigo or inexperienced walkers, but provides an excellent antidote to city blues. (And it could inspire you to seek out China's other sacred mountains: Hengshan, south of Datong; Songshan, home to the Shaolin Temple in Henan province; Taishan, north of Qufu in Shandong province, birthplace of Confucius; Emeishan, in Sichuan; and Huangshan – perhaps the most beautiful mountain in China – in Anhui province.)

Qin terracotta army

Twenty-five miles north-east of Xi'an in Lintong county lies one of China's most famous sights. An army – over 2,000 years old – of 8,000 life-sized terracotta warriors form an eternal imperial guard for the Emperor Qin Shi Huang. The exhibit lives up to all the hype – it is an extraordinary glimpse of China's past. Inevitably, it's crowded. Nearby, the thermal complex of Huaqing hot springs dates back to the Tang dynasty.

SICHUAN PROVINCE
Good for culture, food/wine and scenic landscape

CHENGDU IS the capital of Sichuan, whose people have a reputation for a fierce intelligence; many of China's ancient heroes come from this enclosed land. The food is superb – but be warned, it is spicily hot.

BEST SIGHTS

Chengdu

The ancient city of Chengdu is famous for its bamboo tea-houses and Du Fu, one of China's great Tang poets and a son of Sichuan (you can visit the shrine where his house used to stand).

Chengdu is also a good base for excursions – maybe to the Dujian-gyan Dam (31 miles north-west), an irrigation project engineered in 306 BC but still in operation today; the sacred mountain of Emeishan (100 miles south); or the Wolong panda reserve.

Chongqing

Chongqing was the wartime capital of the Nationalist (Guomindang) government in the 1940s; today it is the main base for trips down the Yangtze river. It is a fascinating place of mists, steep streets and houses that cling to the hills, but scorching summer temperatures make it one of the 'fiery ovens' of China. Sit by the docks and sample the air, attempt a cable-car crossing of the Yangtze, or rest at Pipashan Park (in the south-west) and the northern hot springs (in the north-west).

Yangtze

From Chongqing you can travel down the Yangtze ('Changjiang') and its gorges by boat. Do it now, while it is still there. The gorges will be submerged under a 370-mile reservoir, part of an ambitious – and contentious – dam project under way. Take a book and some food to supplement what's on offer and enjoy a two- to six-day cruise through beautiful surroundings. After the spectacular Qutang Gorge you carry on through Wu and Xiling gorges, as far as Yueyang, Wuhan or Shanghai. But if you like the rapids and can afford the pricey fare, leave the boat at Wushan and try the small gorges of the Daning River.

GUILIN
Good for scenic landscape

A LANDSCAPE fit for poets, artists and the gods, consisting of limestone hills, networks of caves and clear waterways, all to be explored by boat or raft. Especially worth visiting are the Reed Flute Cave, Fuboshan Mountain and Elephant Trunk Hill (Xiangbishan).

Take a boat trip 37 miles down the Li river to Yangshuo, to absorb the scenes that inspired Chinese poets and painters of old. You can travel back by bus to get a feel for the countryside. Guilin is filled with the scent of cassia trees in the autumn (but it is stifling in summer). The area is, sadly, in danger of becoming overdeveloped.

HANGZHOU
Good for scenic landscape

HANGZHOU'S WEST Lake is a 'pearl in the city', a place of bridges, pavilions, causeways and islands, again at risk of being overwhelmed by tourism. The carved laughing Buddha at Feilai Feng (the 'peak that flew from afar') is one of 380 sculptures dating from the tenth to the fourteenth centuries. Combine this with a visit to Lingyin Si (the Temple of Spiritual Retreat). Or step on a pleasure boat or gondola and sail away into a Chinese scroll painting. Hangzhou is also famous for its silk and its Dragon Well tea; the silk factories are good value.

Further afield, the village of Meijiawu (20 minutes by car heading south) and the mountain Moganshan (37 miles to the north) offer a chance to escape the crowds. Boat trips down the Grand Canal to Suzhou offer the experience of 'a slow boat in China'.

SUZHOU
Good for scenic landscape

'IN HEAVEN there is Paradise, on earth there is Suzhou', according to a Chinese saying. Suzhou is given over to gardens and canals. Chinese gardens encapsulate harmony, poetry and water, tree and stone: they attempt to create the universe in a small space. See especially the Xi Yuan Garden (with a temple filled with 500 Buddhist Luohan statues at its heart), the Liu Yuan Garden (200 designs of window) and the Zhuozheng Yuan Garden (where water reigns). In summer the Wangshi Yuan Garden remains open in the evening and traditional Chinese music is played.

SHANGHAI
Good for culture, nightlife and shopping

SHANGHAI – THE Paris of the Orient – is one of the great cities of the world: huge, phenomenally crowded and with a past that speaks of glamour, danger and excitement. But it is not the best place to take young children (too busy, too tiring). Nor should it be your first taste of the country – visit it after northern or central China.

Much of Shanghai's waterfront architecture (along the Bund) is rooted in European tradition: China's history of colonisation is there for all to see. Shanghai was, and is, a capitalist's dream (and a communist's nightmare), with a sophisticated identity of its own (as the Shanghainese love to remind other Chinese). And the shopping is all-consuming.

NANJING
Good for culture

ONCE THE south's ancient capital, Nanjing is a civilised city of maples, chrysanthemums and mausoleums – or rather, one mausoleum. The tomb of the 'father of modern China' and its first President, Sun Yatsen, is worth a visit. Also interesting are the Linggu Temple, the Confucius Temple and Chaotian Palace. Enjoy views from the cable-car as it ascends the purple-and-gold mountains, and visit the lake at Xuanwu Park. Another of China's 'fiery ovens', Nanjing is very hot in summer.

WHEN TO GO

IF YOU are planning to visit both northern and southern China, spring or autumn are the best times to avoid extremes of temperature. Spring Festival, or Chinese New Year, is a three-day celebration in January or February, depending on the lunar calendar, and is best avoided, as transport is even more crowded than usual.

	Average daily maximum temperature °C											
London	6	7	10	13	17	20	22	21	19	14	10	7
Guangzhou	17	17	21	25	30	31	33	33	32	28	25	21
	JAN	FEB	MAR	APR	MAY	JUN	JUL	AUG	SEP	OCT	NOV	DEC
Guangzhou	5	8	11	12	15	17	16	13	10	4	3	5
London	15	13	11	12	12	11	12	11	13	13	15	15
	Average number of rainy days per month											

	Average daily maximum temperature °C											
London	6	7	10	13	17	20	22	21	19	14	10	7
Shanghai	8	8	13	19	25	28	32	32	28	23	17	12
	JAN	FEB	MAR	APR	MAY	JUN	JUL	AUG	SEP	OCT	NOV	DEC
Shanghai	6	9	9	9	9	11	9	9	11	4	6	6
London	15	13	11	12	12	11	12	11	13	13	15	15
	Average number of rainy days per month											

	Average daily maximum temperature °C											
London	6	7	10	13	17	20	22	21	19	14	10	7
Tientsin	1	4	11	20	27	32	32	31	26	20	9	2
	JAN	FEB	MAR	APR	MAY	JUN	JUL	AUG	SEP	OCT	NOV	DEC
Tientsin	1	<1	2	2	4	6	10	9	4	1	2	1
London	15	13	11	12	12	11	12	11	13	13	15	15
	Average number of rainy days per month											

PACKAGE TRAVEL

MOST PACKAGES featured in brochures are two- or three-week escorted tours starting from Beijing and including internal coach, rail and air travel. A 10- or 12-day tour may include Beijing, Chengdu, Xi'an, Guilin, Suzhou and Shanghai. Longer tours could also include Nanjing and Hangzhou or you could follow the old Silk Route. A three-week tour may also include a five-day cruise on the Yangtze river from Chongqing to Wuhan. Alternatively, go for a two-centre stay based in Beijing – with day-trips to sights such as the Great Wall – and Shanghai, or combine China with destinations such as Hong Kong, Bali or Penang.

Tour operators

Activities: Exodus (cycling, trekking), Explore Worldwide (trekking), KE Adventure (trekking), Ramblers Holidays (walking), Prospect (culture), Solo's Holidays (singles), Sunbird (birdwatching)
General: Abercrombie & Kent, Bales Tours, British Airways Holidays, Distant Dreams, Dream Journeys, Far East Gateways, Hayes & Jarvis, Kuoni, Peregrine Adventures, Premier Holidays, Saga, Tradewinds, Travelsphere, Voyages Jules Verne, World Dreams
Specialists: China Travel Service

Specialists such as China Travel Service also include the Trans-Siberian Express travelling from Moscow to Beijing independently or travelling into Tibet from Chengdu. Activity tour operators offer adventure and trekking tours, birdwatching, battlefield tours and rail tours.

INDEPENDENT TRAVEL

DIRECT FLIGHTS run from London to Beijing; other destinations involve stopovers. Many people enter China via Hong Kong, by train or boat; the truly adventurous can take the Trans-Siberian Express, the Karakoram Highway from Pakistan, or cross the border from Vietnam.

If you decide to go it alone – without guide, coach and trappings – then do research first, and at all times take it easy. Independent travel in China brings an exhaustion quite different from package holiday 'hotel fatigue'. But the sense of achievement along the way is wonderful. The chances of having an unforgettable holiday shoot up if you go it alone.

Language is unlikely to be a problem, provided you speak English and have a bilingual phrase-book of even the most basic kind. A smattering of Chinese (far easier to pick up than it sounds) will open unexpected doors. When you are trying to communicate, politeness and patience win every time. Smile frequently and learn some courtesy phrases. The new entrepreneurial spirit sweeping China means that there should be no shortage of people willing to help you. However, beware of overcharging.

Train and aeroplane ticket prices are still higher for visitors than for most Chinese. Train tickets can be harder to come by, but be persistent, because a train journey is an excellent way to get a feel for the real China. Ask for *ying wo* (second-class with a berth) and bring your own mug.

You can also get around China by bus and boat. Try, for example, the boat from Shanghai up to Qingdao in Shandong (and from there to Qufu, to see the grave of Confucius, or to Taishan to climb the sacred mountain). Study your maps and guide books before you go: varying journeys can reveal different glimpses of China. A little courage, a little luck . . . and, if Buddha smiles on you, China will show her best face.

RED TAPE, HEALTH AND SAFETY

ALL BRITISH passport-holders, including transit passengers, require a visa to enter China. Tour groups will probably travel on a group visa; individual travellers should contact the Chinese Embassy, which will supply an application form; this is also obtainable on *www.chinese-embassy.org.uk* To obtain a visa you must submit a completed form, a valid passport and one passport photograph, plus evidence of booked accommodation in China, details of your itinerary, and a return ticket. Apply in person between 9am and 12pm Monday to Friday or courier your application to the Visa Section at the Chinese Embassy enclosing a strong sae. A single-entry tourist visa is valid for three months and costs £30 (cash or postal order) to personal applicants while postal applicants must add £20 extra towards handling charges; a double-entry tourist visa costs £45. You must enter China within three months of issue.

The Chinese swear by garlic to fend off stomach upsets brought on by food or water contaminated with bacteria – or simply by a diet your digestive system is not used to. Don't let this put you off sampling local restaurants. It is unlikely that you will catch anything serious, as long as you are as careful as you would be in your own country. Hotel food does not have the same cachet, and is far more expensive. The fastidious among the urban Chinese use *gao meng suan jia* (potassium permanganate) to wash fresh fruit before they eat it; you can buy it at any pharmacy.

It is worth noting that hard toilet paper is the norm in China (apart from in the major hotels), so if you regard soft paper as a must, you can buy a roll in any shop. (Sanitary towels and tampons are widely available.)

A final word of warning: China can be dangerous for independent travellers. Be on your guard, as anywhere, and keep your money, passport and other valuables out of sight. For the latest advice, contact the Foreign Office Travel Advice Unit (see page 11).

MORE INFORMATION China National Tourist Office, 4 Glentworth Street, London NW1 5PG, tel 020-7935 9787, also information on (09001) 600188 (premium rate number)

No tourist office web site exists, but you can access information about China at: *www.tourist-offices.org.uk/China/index.html*

Chinese Embassy, 31 Portland Place, London W1N 3AG, tel 020-7631 1430, visa information (0891) 880808 (premium rate number), web site: *www.chinese-embassy.org.uk*

COST OF LIVING £

COSTA RICA

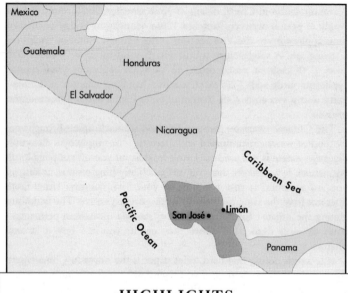

HIGHLIGHTS

Beaches
*Manuel
Antonio
National Park,
Nicoya
Peninsula*

Flora
*Braulio
Carillo*

*National Park,
Santa Rosa
National Park,
Volcán Poás
National Park*

**Outdoor
activities**
*Braulio
Carillo National
Park,*

*Pacuare river,
Tortuguero
National Park*

**Romantic
escapism**
*Nicoya
Peninsula,
Tortuguero
National Park*

Wildlife
*Monteverde
Cloud Forest
Reserve,
Tortuguero
National Park*

THE NATIONAL PARKS
**Good for beaches, flora, outdoor activities, romantic escapism
and wildlife**

THE NATURAL world is the big attraction in Costa Rica, almost 30
per cent of which is protected. Much of the countryside is stunningly
beautiful and home to an amazing abundance of wildlife, and there are

great beaches too. This is not a place for culture vultures, although the capital, San José, has a couple of excellent museums.

BEST WILDLIFE

Corcovado National Park
This park on the Osa Peninsula, comprising empty Pacific beaches, tropical forest interior, and swampy lagoon, is very remote but is home to an astounding array of wildlife.

Monteverde Cloud Forest Reserve
Costa Rica offers the best chance to see the elusive, resplendent quetzal, found only in Central America, and this reserve has the highest-known density of this beautiful bird.

Santa Rosa National Park
Santa Rosa, in the north-west, has glorious beaches and abundant wildlife which is easy to spot, particularly in the dry season when the animals gather around the exposed water holes.

Tortuguero National Park
Few people would venture over to the Caribbean coast if it weren't for Tortuguero. It is inaccessible by road, and the boat ride through jungle-lined canals from Limón is part of the attraction. The park is named after the sea turtles which come ashore to lay eggs on the beach every year between June and August.

BEST VOLCANOES

Poás and Irazú volcanoes in the Central Valley are both easily accessible by road from San José and offer good views inside their craters and of the landscape below. The most dramatic of Costa Rica's volcanoes, the Arenal, is best seen from a distance: its constant emissions of white-hot ash and lava light up the sky at night.

Volcán Poás National Park
This live – and currently lively – volcano looms to the north of San José. You can look down into its huge crater from a lookout point, or take a nature trail to another nearby, lake-filled crater, through lush vegetation of ferns, bromeliads and colourful flora.

BEST RESORTS AND BEACHES

Cahuita National Park
● A small resort to the north with a Caribbean atmosphere.
● The town is off the main tourist route.

● There are gorgeous palm-fringed beaches and a coral reef within swimming distance of the shore.

Manuel Antonio National Park
● Contains some of the most accessible rainforest and cutest monkeys in Costa Rica but many people – locals and tourists – come just for the blue Pacific beaches.
● The area possesses the largest concentration of smart resorts in Costa Rica, so you will not be alone.

Nicoya Peninsula
● Not the most scenic part of the country, but boasts some of Costa Rica's best beaches.
● Tamarindo is developed but not spoiled.
● Montezuma is popular with backpackers and the nearby Cabo Blanco Nature Reserve is home to various marine birds and some exotic mammals.
● Nosara, Samara and Carrillo are other good resorts.

BEST OUTDOOR ACTIVITIES

You don't have to walk anywhere to enjoy the scenery, but hiking will enable you to see the most pristine areas, where you will have minimal human company. The national parks and other areas of natural beauty offer a range of nature safari and sporting opportunities, including mountain biking, kayaking, windsurfing, surfing, diving and snorkelling.

Braulio Carrillo National Park
The park contains Costa Rica's most rugged countryside, with densely forested mountains cut through by countless rivers.

Cerro Chirripó National Park
A mix of tropical forests and peaks, including the nation's highest mountain, Cerro Chirripó (12,500 feet).

Reventazón and Pacuare rivers
Rafting is the most popular adventure sport in Costa Rica. The River Reventazón is ideal for beginners, while the River Pacuare is more challenging.

Rincón de la Vieja National Park
Trails run deep into the forest, where there are springs, waterfalls and a volcano to climb.

Tortuguero National Park
Costa Rica is well known for its blue-water fishing: sporting anglers

flock to the Pacific coast, and some say the waters between Puerto Limón and Tortuguero National Park provide the best tarpon fishing in the world – the large, silvery fish are common in tropical waters.

WHEN TO GO

THE INLAND valleys and Pacific coast have two distinct seasons: dry, from December to April; rainy, from May to November. Costa Rica is at its most lush and beautiful during the wet season, and the short downpours every afternoon are predictable enough to be tolerable – at least outside the wettest months of September and October. You will be lucky to avoid rain along the Caribbean coast, where the two short dry seasons are barely discernible. The climate in the mountains is often pleasantly cool – and chilly at night – with temperatures rising significantly along the coast.

Average daily maximum temperature °C											
London	6	7	10	13	17	20	22	21	19	14	10	7
San José	24	24	26	26	27	26	25	26	26	25	25	24
	JAN	FEB	MAR	APR	MAY	JUN	JUL	AUG	SEP	OCT	NOV	DEC
San José	3	1	2	7	19	22	23	24	24	25	14	6
London	15	13	11	12	12	11	12	11	13	13	15	15
Average number of rainy days per month											

PACKAGE TRAVEL

A GOOD range of tours making the most of the remarkable diversity of the country are available through tour operators, visiting the many national parks and reserves that constitute around 20 per cent of Costa Rica. A typical escorted tour would start from San José, visiting the Poás volcano, the Monteverde reserve and the Tortuguero National Park with perhaps a couple of days on the Caribbean or Pacific coast exploring the parks, cruising the offshore islands or staying in a beach hotel. Specialists offer tailor-made itineraries and escorted tours.

Accommodation varies from top-of-the-range to basic. At the reserves accommodation is usually in comfortable lodges and the beach hotels on offer are of a good standard.

The diversity of birdlife makes Costa Rica a popular destination for specialist birdwatching and wildlife tour operators. Other activities include trekking, white-water rafting, camping and mountain biking.

> **Tour operators**
>
> **Adventure**: Exodus, Explore Worldwide, Guerba, Journey Latin America, KE Adventure (mountain biking) **Birdwatching**: Abercrombie & Kent, Limosa, Naturetrek, Ornitholidays, Sunbird, Wildlife Worldwide **General**: Bales Tours, British Airways Holidays, Cox & Kings, Cricketer, Hayes & Jarvis, Kuoni, Sunvil, Voyages Jules Verne **Specialists**: Journey Latin America, South American Experience, Trips Worldwide **Walking**: Exodus, Explore Worldwide, Guerba, Journey Latin America, Reef and Rainforest, Veloso Tours

INDEPENDENT TRAVEL

NO DIRECT scheduled flights are available from the UK. The best connections are via Miami, Amsterdam or Madrid.

Costa Rica is small – just twice the size of Scotland – but getting around can be time-consuming owing to the topography. Specialist tour operators in the UK can arrange Central American air passes, fly-drive and hotel voucher schemes for travellers in advance.

Internal flights are worth considering if you have a tight schedule. Bus services are efficient along the Pan-American Highway and other main routes and within the Central Valley, but are otherwise patchy. If you are dependent on local transport you will have a hard time getting to and from most national parks. Many visitors opt to take a tour, and the many agencies in San José offer a wide choice. You can hire a car for a moderate cost; some agencies hire out camping gear too. The topography can make for some dramatic journeys, but keep your eye on the road: Costa Rica has the highest road accident rate in Central America.

As wealthy North Americans love to escape to Costa Rica, there are plenty of good-quality hotels and longer-stay apartments and villas. You will find conventional luxury hotels in San José, but outside the city – mainly along the Pacific coast – the good hotels are usually small, tasteful, wood-built affairs set in lovely grounds. You can expect more basic facilities in remoter areas where American package tourists do not go. While the most visited national parks have comfortable lodges, most others have either simple refuges or camp sites.

RED TAPE, HEALTH AND SAFETY

BRITISH PASSPORT-HOLDERS do not need a visa and can stay in Costa Rica for three months.

The tap water is safe to drink in the main towns, and the healthcare is the best in the region. There is a risk of dengue fever in Puntarenas, the Pacific coast, Guanacaste and Limón. Ensure that your hepatitis A, polio and typhoid inoculations are up to date and consult your GP or a travel clinic for further health advice.

Take strict precautions against the 'aedes aegypti' mosquito and use lots of repellent. It is unlikely you will encounter one of Costa Rica's poisonous snakes, of which there are several varieties, but because so much of the countryside is accessible they are a potential danger.

Costa Rica likes to promote itself as a peaceful, 'civilised' place, but the country has its fair share of crime. You should take the same care in San José and the port of Limón as you would in any big city (see page 12), and do not presume that your belongings are safe in the beautiful surroundings of a national park.

MORE INFORMATION Tourist Information, Costa Rican Embassy, 14 Lancaster Gate, London W2 3LH, tel 020-7706 8844 (*please send an A4 sae with four first-class stamps*).
Web site: *www.embcrlon.demon.co.uk*

COST OF LIVING £

CUBA

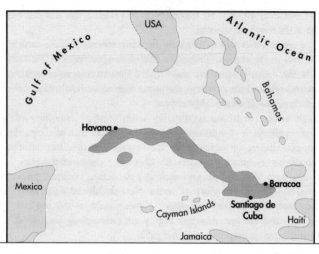

HIGHLIGHTS

Beaches
*Cayo Largo,
Varadero,
Cayo Coco,
Cayo Guillermo,
Playa Santa
Lucía,
Guardalavaca,
Baracoa*

**Scenic
landscape**
Viñales Valley,

*Baracoa,
Sierra Maestra*

Culture
*Havana,
Trinidad,
Santiago de
Cuba*

Nightlife
*Havana,
Santiago de
Cuba*

**Outdoor
activities**
*Cayo Largo,
Isla de la
Juventud,
Varadero,
Cayo Coco,
Cayo Guillermo,
Playa Santa
Lucía,
Guardalavaca*

Local colour
*Havana,
western, central
and eastern
Cuba*

**Romantic
escapism**
*Viñales Valley,
Remedios,
Baracoa*

HAVANA
Good for culture, local colour and nightlife

CUBA'S CAPITAL was once Spain's most important colonial port and from the 1930s to 1950s was a Mafia-run prostitution and gambling den. Now it is a cocktail of decrepit seediness and architectural splendour, at times overpoweringly romantic, at times frustrating and exhausting.

OLD HAVANA

The colonial city is as rewarding for its grand palaces and dusty backstreets as for any individual sights. Much of it is undergoing radical, and much-needed, restoration. The showpiece squares of Plaza de la Catedral and Plaza de Armas, and several of the surrounding streets, have dazzling mansions. Work continues apace on Plaza Vieja, while the backstreets are still very dilapidated. The finest thoroughfare is the Prado, lined with gaily painted mansions.

Morro and Cabaña castles

These imposing fortresses commanding Havana's harbour deliver magnificent views over the city.

Museo de la Revolución

Everything you wanted to know about the history of Castro's revolution (and a lot more besides).

Palacio de los Capitanes Generales

Havana's grandest palace, the former residence of Cuba's colonial governors, is now the city museum. The sumptuously furnished galleries remember Cuba's nineteenth-century independence heroes.

NEW HAVANA

Cementerio de Colón

An enormous, dreamy marble city of the dead, with giant mausoleums and poignant tombs.

Museo Hemingway

This country house at the edge of Havana's suburbs is furnished much as it was when the American writer Ernest Hemingway lived here on and off between 1939 and 1960; sadly, you can only peer through the windows.

Partagás cigar factory

The country's biggest cigar factory; tours look at the whole process of cigar-making, from sorting and rolling the tobacco leaves to bundling and banding the cigars.

Plaza de la Revolución

Cuba's governmental hub is a vast square surrounded by ugly ministry buildings and a towering obelisk which is 460 feet high – a lift goes to the top. At its base is an exhibition to José Martí, Cuba's most important independence hero.

BEST NIGHTLIFE

Cuba's most famous bar/restaurants are the plush El Floridita, noted for its daiquiris, and the graffiti-scrawled El Bodeguita del Medio. The Tropicana lays on showily kitsch open-air cabaret extravaganzas. For a less touristy experience, catch top contemporary Cuban salsa bands at the Casa de la Música.

BEST HOTELS

Some of Havana's hotels are sights in their own right. They include the ostentatious Nacional, emblematic of the Mafia era, and half-a-dozen historic places in Old Havana such as the opulent Santa Isabel, the Sevilla (with Graham Greene associations), Conde de Villanueva, a fine colonial house, and the Inglaterra, the island's oldest hotel.

WESTERN CUBA
Good for beaches, local colour, outdoor activities, romantic escapism and scenic landscape

BEST RESORTS

Cayo Largo
● This small island, devoted exclusively to tourism, has six mediocre hotels and Playa Sirena, one of Cuba's best beaches. Boredom may soon set in, however.

Isla de la Juventud
● Backwoods island with little to offer except the best diving in Cuba (from the Hotel Colony).

Varadero
● Far and away Cuba's largest resort, comprising a ribbon of massive hotel complexes along a 12-mile-long beach.
● Drawbacks are the continuing construction work, the lack of a real centre, limited entertainment outside hotels, and sulphurous wafts from nearby oil wells at its western end.
● Pluses are a dazzling, white-sand beach, comfortable accommodation, good water sports and excursions to almost everywhere in Cuba.

BEST SIGHTS AND EXCURSIONS

Playa Girón
The failed US Bay of Pigs invasion landed here on the coast of the vast Zapata swamp in 1961; a small museum tells the story.

Viñales Valley

Tobacco fields ploughed by oxen, and giant limestone outcrops covered in thick vegetation (called *mogotes*) define this romantic, peaceful idyll; it has two memorably sited hotels.

CENTRAL CUBA
Good for beaches, culture, local colour, outdoor activities and romantic escapism

BEST RESORTS

Cayo Coco and Cayo Guillermo
● Isolated islands, linked to the mainland by a causeway, being rapidly developed for tourism with outsize, luxury hotel complexes.
● Fantastic beaches and excellent water sports, but nothing else to do.

Playa Santa Lucía
● Five moderate hotels strung out along a fine beach providing super diving. Three miles away is the memorable beach of Playa Los Cocos.

BEST SIGHTS AND EXCURSIONS

Camagüey
Aside from its clutch of crumbling baroque churches, Cuba's third largest city has more sombre architecture than Havana or Santiago. However, it is also far less touristy and an ideal place in which to immerse yourself in day-to-day Cuban life.

Remedios
This often overlooked colonial backwater has a stunning main square and church.

Santa Clara
A mecca for Che Guevara fans. On the outskirts of the city, beneath a towering statue of Che, lies a mausoleum housing the revolutionary hero's bones, and the reverential Museo Comandante Ernesto Che Guevara.

Trinidad
Cuba's most touristy but also most complete small colonial town, designated a UNESCO World Heritage Site, has beautifully restored mansions (now museums) and sleepy, cobbled backstreets.

EASTERN CUBA
Good for beaches, culture, local colour, nightlife, outdoor
activities, romantic escapism and scenic landscape

BEST RESORTS

Guardalavaca
● Cuba's prettiest resort, surrounded by verdant countryside, has half-a
dozen hotels along a scenic, shady beach. Further hotels sit next to
smaller, but equally lovely, Playa Esmeralda, a few miles west.

BEST SIGHTS AND EXCURSIONS

Around Guardalavaca
Close to the resort lie: Chorro de Maíta, a well-presented excavated
Indian burial ground; Gibara, a little port with tumbledown colonial
buildings; and a moving memorial at Bahía de Bariay, where Columbus
landed in 1492 while seeking a new trade route from Europe to Asia.

Baracoa
Remote and magical, this little-altered, languorous colonial port sits
ensconced in cocoa and coconut groves. There are a couple of
memorable, simple hotels, and magnificent beaches nearby such as
Maguana.

Santiago de Cuba
Cuba's laid-back, number-two city has bewitching, lazy backstreets. It
also offers some superb music: try the Casa de la Trova, where bands
play all day. The top historic sights are: Casa de Velázquez, said to be
the oldest house in the Americas; the Moncada Barracks, against which
Castro launched an unsuccessful attack in 1953; and Cementerio Santa
Ifigenia, where many Cuban heroes are buried.

Sierra Maestra
Cuba's largest mountain range is wild and very impressive. The new
coastal road skirting the mountains from Marea del Portillo to Santiago
de Cuba is the country's most stunning drive.

WHEN TO GO

THE BEST time to travel is from November to April, when the
temperature is normally pleasantly warm and there is little rain. In
summer, it is too hot and humid for energetic sightseeing, tropical

thunderstorms are frequent, and hurricanes a distinct possibility. Santiago hosts Cuba's most famous carnival around 26 July.

	Average daily maximum temperature °C											
London	6	7	10	13	17	20	22	21	19	14	10	7
Havana	26	26	27	29	30	31	32	32	31	29	27	26
	JAN	FEB	MAR	APR	MAY	JUN	JUL	AUG	SEP	OCT	NOV	DEC
Havana	6	4	4	4	7	10	9	10	11	11	7	6
London	15	13	11	12	12	11	12	11	13	13	15	15
	Average number of rainy days per month											

PACKAGE TRAVEL

THE MOST popular packages to Cuba involve a stay-put beach holiday, often on an all-inclusive basis. Caribbean sun-and-sand holidays are available in sanitised but comfortable resorts with superb beaches. Varadero is the most popular choice.

Specialists offer a wider choice of options and generally stay away from the more commercialised beach resorts. Fortnight-long coach tours (sometimes also involving internal flights) visit places such as Havana, Santiago de Cuba, Trinidad, Cienfuegos and the Viñales Valley. Many companies combine a week on the beach with a week-long cultural tour.

A number of themed specialist packages are also on offer, from cigar tours and Hemingway tours to politically oriented holidays that visit hospitals and schools. Fly-drive holidays also feature, as do activity holidays including scuba diving, steam train tours, cycling and multi-activity breaks.

Tour operators

General and specialist: Airtours, Archers Direct, British Airways Holidays, Captivating Cuba, Carefree World, Cosmos, Cox & Kings, Cresta, Cricketer, Explore Worldwide, First Choice, Golden-joy, Hayes & Jarvis, JMC Holidays, Journey Latin America, Kuoni, Regent Holidays, Saga, Sun Modilex, Thomson, Tradewinds, Travel-sphere, Voyages Jules Verne **Tailor-made specialists**: Interchange, South American Experience, Trips Worldwide **Other activities**: Club Med (multi-activity), Exodus (cycling), Railtours (rail tours), Sunbird (birdwatching)

INDEPENDENT TRAVEL

CHEAPEST SCHEDULED flights are normally with Cubana, from Gatwick to Havana. However, travellers should note that the airline has an appalling safety record, with several fatal crashes in recent years, and that it also comes rock bottom for comfort and service in airline surveys. Alternatives include non-stop flights with British Airways, and indirect services with Air France and Iberia.

There have been reports of theft from luggage on flights out of Havana; to reduce this risk, consider using shrink-wrap facilities.

The tourist industry in Cuba is geared towards package holiday-makers, but no restrictions are imposed on independent travellers. That said, dealing with Cuba's often infuriating bureaucracy and the limitations of its decrepit transport system can be very trying. However, you'll only learn what Cuba is really like if you leave the confines of package hotels and explore without a tour guide. Outside the resorts, conditions are generally far more primitive, but compensations include superb Spanish colonial buildings, a rich musical heritage and a fascinating culture little changed since the late 1950s when Fidel Castro imposed communism on the island. For example, classic American Cadillacs and horse-and-carriages are typical forms of transport. Some Spanish is a great advantage: away from hotels, English is spoken only sporadically.

The best way to get around is to take internal flights and hire a car. Though car hire is relatively expensive and vehicles are often in dubious condition, roads are blissfully empty and you'll meet hordes of Cubans if you give lifts – hitching is ubiquitous. Hire cars are very conspicuous: never leave any possessions on display. The only decent train service runs from Havana to Santiago (about 14 hours). Buses can be horrifically overcrowded and infrequent. However, seats for dollar-wielding tourists have become significantly easier to secure in recent years. Though it is illegal, many Cubans drive tourists around for the day in their old Cadillacs.

Most resort accommodation is prohibitively expensive for independent travellers. However, there are affordable, atmospheric hotels in Havana and Santiago, and cheap hotels in all the other cities. The cheapest accommodation is renting a room in a private house. To avoid immigration hassles on arrival at the airport, it is best to pre-book accommodation for your first few nights.

Independent travellers can also experience *paladares* – mini family-run restaurants where you eat very inexpensively in someone's living room. Service, atmosphere and food are usually far better than in state-run restaurants.

RED TAPE, HEALTH AND SAFETY

BRITISH HOLIDAYMAKERS need a visa to enter Cuba; these are available from tour operators, specialist travel agencies and the Cuban Embassy. The visa is valid for 30 days and must be used within six months of issue. It costs £15 and is extendable once in Cuba. To acquire a visa you will need your passport (or a photocopy if applying by post) and flight and accommodation details. Enclose an s.a.e. with posted applications.

Vaccinations are recommended against typhoid, tetanus, polio and hepatitis A. Dengue fever is reported in Santiago and southern Cuba – use mosquito repellent and cover your arms and legs between dusk and dawn. Take all medicines and bathroom essentials with you from home, as they are expensive and/or hard to come by locally.

Tourists use US dollars in Cuba. Go with as much cash as possible, plus some dollar travellers cheques and a credit card: neither can be American Express because of the US embargo against Cuba.

Though crime is on the increase, Cuba is still a very safe destination compared with many developing countries. While crime against the person is virtually unheard of, bag-snatching and pickpocketing have become problems in parts of Old Havana (particularly south of Calle Obispo), in the district called Centro, and at festivals. Bigger problems include being harrassed by locals for money, gifts and the purchase of black-market cigars, and above all being pestered by prostitutes, who are especially prolific in Havana.

For the latest travel advice contact the Foreign Office Travel Advice Unit (see page 11).

MORE INFORMATION Cuba Tourist Board, 154 Shaftesbury Avenue, London WC2H 8JT, tel 020-7240 6655, web site: *www.caribtourism.com/*

Cuban Embassy, 167 High Holborn, London WC1V 6PA, tel 020-7240 2488

Also helpful are specialist tour operators such as: Regent Holidays, tel (01983) 864212; and South American Experience, tel 020-7976 5511

COST OF LIVING £-££

CYPRUS

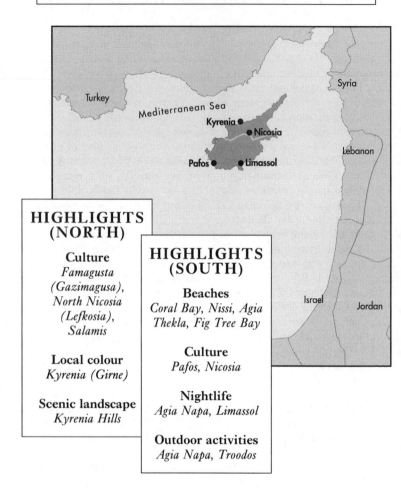

HIGHLIGHTS (NORTH)

Culture
Famagusta (Gazimagusa), North Nicosia (Lefkosia), Salamis

Local colour
Kyrenia (Girne)

Scenic landscape
Kyrenia Hills

HIGHLIGHTS (SOUTH)

Beaches
Coral Bay, Nissi, Agia Thekla, Fig Tree Bay

Culture
Pafos, Nicosia

Nightlife
Agia Napa, Limassol

Outdoor activities
Agia Napa, Troodos

SINCE THE 1970s a buffer zone (the 'Green Line') patrolled by the UN has split Cyprus between the Greek south and the Turkish north. The Greeks control the island south of this line and the Turks the north. Northern Cyprus is not recognised by any country except Turkey, which makes it less accessible than the south.

Hostility runs deep, and free movement across the Line is forbidden. If you visit Northern Cyprus, ask the officials to stamp your entry visa on a separate sheet of paper, as you may otherwise be forbidden entry to southern Cyprus and possibly mainland Greece.

SOUTHERN CYPRUS

BEST RESORTS

Pafos

● Interesting local market and historic sights, but good beaches are lacking (the nearest decent stretch is Coral Bay, 5 miles away).

● Waterside cafés along the harbour do a roaring trade, while huge package hotels stretch eastwards along the rocky coastline.

● Over 20 third-century mosaics were discovered here in 1962.

● Excavations also continue on the Tombs of the Kings, a vast necropolis hollowed out beneath the rocky landscape.

Protaras

● Excellent beach along Fig Tree Bay with good hotels and restaurants, but not too developed.

● Some nightlife and activities but plenty more in Agia Napa, a few miles away and easy by bus or cab.

● Hiring a car lets you explore the panoramic Cape Gkreko peninsula and nearby beaches of Nissi and Agia Thekla.

BEST SIGHTS AND EXCURSIONS

Folk Art Museum

Housed in an eighteenth-century stone house in Geroskipou is a variety of Cypriot implements and crafts.

Kourion

On a high promontory lie the extensive Greek and Roman remains of the town of Kourion, notable for its theatre and mosaics. The nearby Sanctuary of Apollo, destroyed by an earthquake in AD 76–7, has been partly rebuilt. A museum in Episkopi shows items retrieved from the votive pit.

Kykkos

The most famous monastery on the island feels more like a showpiece than a religious centre. The tomb of Archbishop Makarios III, who fought against British rule, is nearby.

Lefkara

Two pretty mountain villages (Pano and Kato Lefkara), the centre of lacemaking and silverwork, offer scenic shopping options.

Limassol

Good for shopping and strolling along the seafront, Limassol also has a small archaeological museum, and a twelfth-century castle housing Venetian stone engravings and medieval buckles. Alternatively, you can take a guided tour of the local brewery.

Nicosia (Lefkosia)
Nicosia is a divided city, the Green Line runs through the middle. The city is encircled by vast sixteenth-century walls stamped with the Venetian lion. The Cyprus Archaeological Museum gives pride of place to the eighth-century BC contents of the Salamis royal tombs, including a throne decorated with gold; rulers were buried with their chariots and horses in Greek epic tradition. There is a small museum at Salamis itself. In the Byzantine Museum, 144 icons from churches throughout Cyprus have been gathered for safe keeping. The Leventis Museum charts Nicosia's history, while the National Struggle Museum records the struggle for independence from Britain in the 1950s.

Panagia Angeloktistos, Kition
The main focus of attention in this light stone, domed church is the miraculously preserved Byzantine mosaic of the Virgin and Child.

Panagia Chrysorrogiatissa
Founded in 1152 by a monk, Ignatius, the monastery commands lovely views over the hills. You can buy wines from the vineyards.

Troodos Mountains
A cool day in the mountains comes as a relief after the baking coastal heat. A leisurely stroll around villages like Omodhos, Phini and Kato Platres reveals a way of life unchanged for centuries. The best walking base in the mountains is Troodos, at the foot of Mount Olympus. Nature-trails are signposted through forests of black pine and cypress.

NORTHERN CYPRUS

BEST RESORT
Kyrenia
● The main base for visitors to Northern Cyprus, Kyrenia has a picturesque fishing harbour ringed with outdoor cafés.
● A Venetian castle overlooks the harbour.
● The Shipwreck Museum has the oldest wreck ever to be recovered.

BEST SIGHTS AND EXCURSIONS
Famagusta
The city's impressive Lusignan-Venetian walls failed to keep out the

Ottomans, but inside them is a thriving centre with business conducted in and around the narrow streets that separate the ruins. The attractive Lala Mustafa Pasa Camii (St Nicholas Cathedral) was where Lusignans were crowned honorary kings of Jerusalem.

Outside the walls, in Famagusta new town, the beach hotels of Varosha have been deserted since 1974. View this crumbling embryonic Benidorm from the Palm Beach Hotel.

Kyrenia Hills
The ruined abbeys and Crusader castles in the Kyrenia Hills are best explored by car. St Hilarion is the best-preserved; Buffavento is the hardest to reach and has the most extensive views; Kantara is more accessible, with fine views over the Karpas peninsula. Bellapais, a hill village dominated by a ruined Gothic abbey, was the home of writer Lawrence Durrell in the 1950s, immortalised in his novel *Bitter Lemons*.

North Nicosia
Despite the blight cast by the wall dividing it from South Nicosia, sleepy North Nicosia is worth visiting for its medieval churches (now mosques) and small museums. The best sights are Selimiye Camii (Church of Aya Sofya), the lovely French-Gothic cathedral where Lusignan kings were crowned kings of Cyprus, and the Ethnography Museum (the actual collection is of limited interest but is housed in a seventeenth-century lodge where dervishes whirled until 1954). Finally, the Turkish bath of Buyuk Hamam is worth frequenting if you are not visiting mainland Turkey.

Salamis
These extensive Roman ruins lie within a taxi-ride of Famagusta. At the nearby Royal Tombs horses were sacrificed, as described by Homer.

WHEN TO GO

	Average daily maximum temperature °C											
London	6	7	10	13	17	20	22	21	19	14	10	7
Nicosia	15	16	19	24	29	34	37	37	33	28	22	17
	JAN	FEB	MAR	APR	MAY	J UN	JUL	AUG	SEP	OCT	NOV	DEC
Nicosia	14	10	8	4	3	1	<1	<1	1	4	6	11
London	15	13	11	12	12	11	12	11	13	13	15	1
	Average number of rainy days per month											

IN JULY and August Cyprus is extremely hot; June and September are better months in which to visit. North Cyprus is not as crowded as the rest of the Med, but temperatures at these times are more comfortable.

PACKAGE TRAVEL

Southern Cyprus

All the major tour operators to southern Cyprus offer one- or two-week packages to the main coastal resorts of Limassol, Pafos, Protaras, Larnaka and Agia Napa in either hotels or apartments. Some combine a week on the coast with a week in a resort-style hotel in the Troodos mountains, or with a week staying in simple village houses. Purpose-built villas with pools in the hill villages are available only through a handful of tour operators. Car hire is sometimes included in the package price. If not, budget for it, as public transport is limited.

If you want to explore, several companies offer self-drive tours where you stay in pre-arranged hotels, or if you want more freedom you can take a fly-drive package and make your own way around the island. Mini-cruises to Israel and Egypt lasting from two to seven nights are on offer from many tour operators, and a couple combine a holiday in Cyprus with a trip to Jordan.

Specialist activity holidays to Cyprus feature birdwatching (the best time is in the spring), walking, cycling, scuba diving, golf, botany and cultural tours.

Tour operators: Southern Cyprus

Birdwatching: Limosa, Naturetrek, Ornitholidays **Diving**: Airglobe, Sunvil **Flora**: David Sayers Travel, Naturetrek **General and specialist**: Airglobe, Airtours, Amathus, Anemone, Argo, Aspro, Aztec, Best of Greece, Cadogan, Cosmos, Cyplon, Cyprair, Delta, First Choice, Greece & Cyprus Travel Centre, Golden Sun, InterSky, JMC, Libra Holidays, Magnum, Manos, PriceRight, Sovereign, Sunvil, Thomas Cook, Thomson, Travel Club of Upminster **Walking**: Alternative Travel Group, Exodus, Explore Worldwide, Waymark **Other activities**: Headwater (walking), Inter-Church Travel (religious tours), Wildlife Worldwide (wildlife), Winetrails (Wine)

Northern Cyprus

Few tour operators include Northern Cyprus in their brochures, and lack of competition rules out rock-bottom prices. Most packages are based in Kyrenia.

Tour operators: Northern Cyprus

Alternative Travel Group, Andante, Celebrity, Cox & Kings (flora), Cricketer (flora), Paradise Found, Prospect, Ramblers Holidays, Regent Holidays

---

INDEPENDENT TRAVEL

Southern Cyprus

In southern Cyprus you are unlikely to save money by going independently, and accommodation can be difficult to find, as it will invariably be fully booked by tour operators.

Large towns are linked by regular bus services and shared taxis, but to explore extensively you will need to hire a car. Stick to the main roads, as minor ones can be lethal, and do not be afraid to use the horn (except at night). Driving is on the left-hand side of the road.

You will find well-equipped, self-contained hotel complexes, and plenty of villas and apartments. Some smaller tour operators offer 'agro-tourism' programmes on the Akamas peninsula and in the Troodos mountains, where·you can stay in traditional village houses, mixing with local people and experiencing their way of life.

Northern Cyprus

In Northern Cyprus, provided you do not want to stay in the few resort-class hotels, it can be cheaper to make your own arrangements. The international boycott means that flights to Nicosia's Ercan airport have to transit Turkey; if you have time to spare the cheapest way to reach North Cyprus is to fly to Istanbul and then take a 'domestic' flight to Ercan or a bus south to Alanya, Tasucu or Mersin and the Kyrenia ferries. Kyrenia, Nicosia and Famagusta are linked by cheap, shared taxis called *combos*. For reaching outlying sites, ordinary taxis are a godsend.

The international car rental companies do not operate in Northern Cyprus. Not all hire cars are well maintained; look them over carefully before accepting one.

Hotels are not officially graded and standards are generally lower than in the south. Kyrenia has plenty of clean and well-run pensions. Elsewhere, they may double as homes-from-home for Turkish soldiers.

RED TAPE, HEALTH AND SAFETY

UK PASSPORT-HOLDERS do not require a visa to visit southern Cyprus, but your passport must be valid for three months after your date of departure. Visitors to Northern Cyprus have their passports stamped with an entry visa when they arrive: ask for it to be stamped on a separate piece of paper, if you want to visit southern Cyprus or mainland Greece on a future occasion.

Sensitivity about the Green Line runs deep, and trouble occasionally flares up. It is advisable to pay attention to signs forbidding access, photography, etc. For the latest advice contact the Foreign Office Travel Advice Unit (see page 11).

No vaccinations are required. Tap water is safe to drink, but the water in the south-eastern part of the island has a slightly funny taste, and even the locals drink bottled water here.

MORE INFORMATION

Southern Cyprus
Cyprus Tourism Organisation, 213 Regent Street, London W1R 8DA, tel 020-7734 9822, web site: *www.cyprustourism.org/cyprus.html*

Northern Cyprus
North Cyprus Tourist Office, 29 Bedford Square, London WC1B 3EG, tel 020-7631 1930, web site: *www.trnclondon.demon.co.uk*

COST OF LIVING £

CZECH REPUBLIC

HIGHLIGHTS

Culture
Prague, Tabor, Telč

Local colour
Moravia

Scenic landscape
Bohemia, Giant Mountains and Český Ráj, Moravský Kras, Šumava National Park

---

PRAGUE
Good for culture

THE HEART of historic Bohemia, Prague is one of the world's most beautiful cities. An incredible mix of Gothic, Romanesque, baroque and art nouveau architecture forms the backdrop to an unbeatable literary and musical calendar. The centre is overrun by tourists in summer, but there are still many parts of the city that remain relatively quiet.

BEST SIGHTS

Hradčany (castle district)
The largest ancient castle in the world is Prague's biggest crowd-puller – go early or late to avoid crowds. It dates from the ninth century and incorporates a series of courtyards with fascinating chapels, halls, gateways and gardens. Do not miss St Vitus Cathedral with its spectacular stained-glass windows, and the historic Old Royal Palace.

Beyond the castle walls, Hradčany teems with palaces. The main trio are the Sternberg, Schwarzenberg and Archbishop's. In Loretánské Náměstí, visit the impressive Loreta and Chapel of Our Lady of Sorrows with its treasury. Malá Strana is a picturesque area for a stroll.

Tourists, hawkers and buskers (and pickpockets) pack the Charles Bridge (Karlův Most) for the best views of the city from the river.

Staré Město (old town)
Staroměstské Náměstí, the Old Town Square, is significant in Czech history and a focal point today. Look out for the Astronomical Clock, with its hourly show, the baroque façade of St Nicholas Church, and the towers of the Gothic Týn Church. The old Jewish quarter of Josefov is very atmospheric and has an important museum and a unique multi-level cemetery.

BOHEMIA
Good for culture and scenic landscape

BEST TOWNS AND VILLAGES

Český Krumlov
Blessed with an outlandish castle, cobbled streets and a lazy river, this is one of the most picturesque small towns in Europe. Despite the summer bus parties, walking through the streets of UNESCO World Heritage Listed Ceský Krumlov is still a fairytale experience.

Kutná Hora
Once a wealthy town with grand palaces and churches, due to its now defunct silver mines, Kutná Hora resembles Prague on a friendlier, more accessible scale. The gothic ossuary in nearby Sedlec is the unmissable attraction – built with the skulls and skeletons of over 40,000 people.

Loket nad Ohří
This medieval walled village in a splendidly romantic setting was one of Goethe's favourite spots for courting. The castle, altered over the centuries but still magnificent, gives great views over the countryside.

Tabor
Tabor's gorgeous winding streets, the former stronghold of the revolutionary anti-Catholic Hussites, are fronted by Gothic and Renaissance houses. Tour the underground passages linking their cellars.

BEST SCENIC LANDSCAPES

Giant Mountains (Krkonoše)
The highest peak on the border with Poland in Eastern Bohemia is Sněžka, at over 4,800 feet. Skiing (in winter) and walking are good, although the forests have suffered from acid rain. Accommodation is not of a very high quality in the resort centres. In the foothills lies Český Ráj, or 'Czech paradise', a surreal sandstone landscape with a web of walking trails, and the interesting 'rock villages' of Prachovské

Skaly and Hrubá Skala. Their sandstone labyrinths of caves, towers and passageways are unmissable. Bring your own camping gear on longer hikes.

Šumava National Park
Attractions of this thickly forested, mountainous area are walking and cross-country skiing in pristine forest, untouched by pollution. Boubin Forest, designated a UNESCO protected landscape, is particularly prized.

BEST SPA TOWNS

The Czech Republic's famous trio of spas, Karlovy Vary (Karlsbad), Mariánské Lázně (Marienbad) and Františkovy Lázné (Franzenbad), were, in their heyday, the playgrounds of Goethe, Kafka, Wagner, Schiller, Beethoven and Gogol. Nowadays tourists flock there for the cure, and even if you are not there to ingest noxious fumes and sulphurous waters, great pleasure can be found in the spas' sedate and dignified ambience. Of the three, Karlovy Vary is the most magnificent – and the most overrun with tour groups.

BEST BEERS
České Budéjobicé
At the heart of this town is a gorgeous arcaded square with baroque, Gothic and Renaissance façades. The Budvar, or Budweiser, brewery is outside the centre and runs tours for six or more people.

Plzeň
This industrial town with some Renaissance houses is home to Pilsner, and has enough historical interest for a day-trip. The Prazdroj (Urquell) Brewery and beer museum explain the brewer's ancient and noble art.

BEST CASTLES
Karlštejn
An unashamed tourist Mecca, overrun by the tour groups, that still has an appealing Disney-esque charm. Admire from the outside and avoid the queues and extortionate guided tours.

Krivoklat
Worth a visit for the train trip along the forested Berounka valley and mostly free of tour groups, Krivoklat's Gothic features are more evocative than Karlštejn's remodelled face.

Rožmberk

A romantic fusion of Gothic and Renaissance styles, Rožmberk's interior is stuffed with fascinating furniture, porcelain and sculpture.

MORAVIA
Good for local colour and scenic landscape

BEST SIGHTS

Brno

Moravia's capital is the second largest city in the Czech Republic. Often ignored by tourists it has an easy-going charm and a more lived-in feel than Prague, as well as an impressive castle and many good local bars and restaurants.

Moravské Slovácko

This region of south-east Moravia is a suitable place to sample local folk traditions including colourful costumes, singing and dancing, and painted houses. The best-known festivals are held at Strážnice, Blatnice and Vlčnov. The local wine is also the best in the Republic.

Rožnov pod Radhoštěm

This resort town is home to one of the country's best open-air museums, including a reconstructed Wallachian shepherds' village and pub.

Telč

Founded in the thirteenth century, Telč's pastel gingerbread façades, centred on a square which has remained unchanged for centuries, qualify it to be a UNESCO World Heritage Site.

BEST SCENIC LANDSCAPE

Moravský Kras

The Moravian karst lies to the north of Brno. It is a hilly area slashed by canyons and porous with hundreds of caves, the most spectacular of which are Punkevni and the Macocha Abyss. A boat tour on the underground river is an eerie and popular way to see these caves. The karst formations are hewn by acidic rainwater passing through limestone, resulting in wonderfully coloured stalactites and stalagmites.

WHEN TO GO

IF YOU intend to focus on Prague, any time of year is suitable. The crucial factor will be your tolerance of crowds, which are worst from May to August, at Easter and over the Christmas/New Year period, when Austrians, Germans and Italians take over Prague and the mountains. November to April is distinctly chilly, with snow on the ground in higher regions, though you will avoid crowds and rip-off prices.

Prague's major cultural event is the Spring International Music Festival in May through to June, when concerts are held in the city's historic churches and palaces. Easter and Christmas have shed most of their religious significance thanks to the Communist era, but are still major holidays. Prague is particularly romantic with a sheen of winter snow.

Average daily maximum temperature °C												
London	6	7	10	13	17	20	22	21	19	14	10	7
Prague	0	1	7	12	18	21	23	22	18	12	5	1
	JAN	FEB	MAR	APR	MAY	JUN	JUL	AUG	SEP	OCT	NOV	DEC
Prague	13	11	10	11	13	12	13	12	10	13	12	13
London	15	13	11	12	12	11	12	11	13	13	15	15
Average number of rainy days per month												

PACKAGE TRAVEL

MANY TOUR operators offer city breaks to Prague (some in combination with other central European cities such as Budapest and Vienna) in a choice of accommodation ranging from five-star hotels to one-star pensions, apartments or rooms in private homes.

Specialists such as Cedok offer the widest choice of holidays outside Prague, including visits to the spa towns of Bohemia such as Karlovy Vary or Mariánské Lázně, Brno in Moravia and the mountain and lake resorts north of Prague. Self-catering houses in the countryside, self-drive tours and coach tours are also on offer. Coach tours from the UK offer holidays based in a hotel (usually within striking distance of Prague) and include daily excursions.

Activity holidays include battlefield tours, birdwatching, cultural, music and study tours, walking, horse-riding and golf.

Tour operators

City breaks: Bridge Travel Service, British Airways Holidays, Cresta, Crystal, Inghams, Kirker, Osprey, Sovereign, Thomson, Time Off, Travelscene **Coach tours**: Crusader, Shearings, Wallace Arnold **Cultural/music/study tours**: Ace Study Tours, Martin Randall, Travel for the Arts **Specialists:** Bridgewater, Cedok, Danube Travel, Hungarian Air Tours, Lanzotic Travel, Peltours, Regent Holidays, Travellers Czech **Walking**: Exodus, Explore Worldwide, HF Holidays, Ramblers Holidays, Sherpa **Other activities**: Alternative Travel Group, Andante (archaeology), Cedok (horse-riding, golf), Midas (battlefields), David Sayers (flora), Solo's Holidays (singles), Sunbird (birdwatching)

INDEPENDENT TRAVEL

PRAGUE IS well served by scheduled and charter flights, and has regular internal connections to Brno and Ostrava. You can go from London to Prague by rail in about 36 hours, or with a quicker, and more expensive route using Eurostar from London to Paris and then the night train to Prague.

There are car rental agencies in the Czech Republic, but it is cheaper to book before you arrive. A UK or European licence plus passport are all you need. Seat-belts are compulsory. On-the-spot fines are levied for speeding and other minor offences. If you want to use toll roads you must pay in advance for a sticker, valid for one year, that you must display on your windscreen. You can buy stickers at petrol stations, border crossings and various retail outlets. Unleaded petrol is widely available. Be warned if you plan to take your own car: a thriving market in stolen Western cars with foreign numberplates operates, especially in Prague.

The Czech Railways network is extensive, covering most of the country. Fares are cheap by Western standards. You can also buy a regional or network ticket valid for a week, a month, or a year, for the whole network or for Bohemia or Moravia and Silesia. To buy a pass you need your passport and a photo. You can also buy passes before you arrive.

Book accommodation well ahead at all times and especially for the spring music festival, when Prague is overflowing. B&B in private homes is the best budget option, as Prague hotels tend to be expensive. Accommodation agencies can find you flats or rooms in central Prague. Most will have photos of the room and show you the address on a map. In recent years an increasing number of temporary youth hostels, of greatly varying quality, have been opening for the summer months.

RED TAPE, HEALTH AND SAFETY

BRITISH PASSPORT-HOLDERS do not need a visa to visit the Czech Republic for visits of up to 90 days.

Petty theft is common, especially in Prague: watch out for pickpockets around Charles Bridge, the castle area, Wenceslas Square, Old Town Square and the Jewish Cemetery. Thieves also operate on trains and trams and around the main railway station. Leave valuables in a hotel safe and carry a photocopy of your passport for identification purposes. Beware of cowboy taxi drivers who charge exorbitant fares and can get violent. For the latest information contact the Foreign Office Travel Advice Unit (see page 11).

MORE INFORMATION Czech Tourist Authority, Czech Centre, 95 Great Portland Street, London W1N 5RA, tel 020-7291 9925, web site: *www.visitczech.cz*

COST OF LIVING £

DENMARK

HIGHLIGHTS

Culture
Copenhagen,
Jutland, Zealand

Beaches
Funen, Zealand

Family holidays
Copenhagen, Jutland

Nightlife
Copenhagen,
Jutland

Outdoor activities
Jutland

Scenic landscape
Jutland

COPENHAGEN
Good for culture, family holidays and nightlife

DENMARK'S CAPITAL is a charming and likeable city. Its compact centre is pedestrian-friendly, its people are welcoming and it has excellent museums, churches and streetlife and offers the best value for money of any of the Scandinavian capitals. New districts are currently being rediscovered and gentrified, notably Vesterbro, Norrebro and Osterbro, which are becoming popular for their clubs and restaurants.

BEST SIGHTS

National Museum
Fascinating displays include the newly re-opened Viking exhibition, Egyptian mummies and a priceless collection of Danish bronze horns.

Ny Carlsberg Glyptotek
The city's best gallery contains Egyptian, Greek and Roman sculptures and antiquities, as well as works by Gauguin, Degas and Rodin.

Rosenborg Castle
The Danish Crown Jewels, which are kept in the basement treasury, are what most people come to see, but the seventeenth-century buildings with their green polygonal spires are a joy in themselves.

Tivoli Gardens
Copenhagen's famous amusement park has been the place to see and be seen since 1843. It has fairground rides, stage shows and fireworks and is great for a family night out.

ZEALAND
Good for beaches and culture

BEST SIGHTS

Helsingør
The best-known sight in this prosperous port is the sixteenth-century castle, which was the model for Elsinore in Shakespeare's *Hamlet*, where the tortured prince wandered the battlements.

Hillerød
Most visitors to this busy town come to admire the many towers, spires and Gothic arches of Frederiksborg Castle, largely the work of Christian IV's extensive rebuilding in the early seventeenth century. The interior is a museum devoted to Danish history while the newly renovated gardens and recreated cascade are not to be missed.

Humlebaek
A delightful old fishing village which is home to the famous Louisiana gallery. American works are particularly well represented.

Roskilde
Just half an hour west of Copenhagen, this town was once the Danish capital. The Domkirke, which dominates the city's skyline, is a must-see, with its ornate chapels, crypts and the tombs of 37 Danish monarchs.

Rungsted
Opposite the busy yachting harbour sits an inspiring museum which is dedicated to Karen Blixen, author of *Out of Africa*.

BEST BEACHES AND ISLANDS

Bornholm
A delightfully unspoilt holiday island, which was briefly occupied by Germany during the Second World War, with everything from medieval forts to spectacular gatherings of birdlife. Also famed for its yachting, smoked herrings, sea cliffs and unique round churches. A six-hour ferry trip or short flight from Copenhagen.

Møn
The most interesting of the islands off the south coast of Zealand has white chalk cliffs and neolithic burial sites.

Northern Zealand
A series of fine beaches and sleepy villages – such as Hornbaek and Gilleleje – stretch along the peninsula west of Helsingør and are ideal for a couple of days' relaxation.

FUNEN
Good for beaches

BEST SIGHT

Odense
Denmark's third largest city is the only sizeable settlement on the island of Funen. The cobbled streets and half-timbered houses give this university town a certain charm. Children's author Hans Christian Andersen was born here and there is now a museum in his honour.

BEST BEACHES AND RESORTS

Aerø
● The most interesting island off Funen's south coast.
● Excellent beaches and ancient burial places as well as a fine medieval town, Aerøskøbing.

Southern Funen
● Known for its many inviting, sandy beaches (which can become uncomfortably crowded in summer).
● Best bases are Svendborg and Fåborg. The latter is generally quieter and contains the excellent Museum of Funen Painting.

JUTLAND
Good for culture, family holidays, nightlife, outdoor activities and scenic landscape

BEST SIGHTS

Aalborg
A lively city and the gateway to the wild far north of the peninsula. The North Jutland Art Museum is a stunning modern art collection featuring works by Warhol and Oldenburg, and on the outskirts of the city lies the haunting Lindholm Hoje, Denmark's largest Viking burial ground.

Århus
Denmark's second city is best seen on foot. It has some superb buildings, including the fifteenth-century Domkirke with its long nave and glorious frescos. The Århus Art Museum is worth a visit as well as the botanical gardens at Botanisk Have. Den Gamle By is a charming museum village within the city where all of the 70 mainly seventeenth-century buildings have been transported here from around the region. To the south of the city there is also a fine museum housing one of the world's largest collections of fire engines.

Ribe
Remarkably well-preserved medieval trading centre, which is often claimed to be the oldest town in Scandinavia.

Silkeborg
Walkers use this respectable and airy town as a base for treks in the surrounding lakes and woodland. It is also the home of Tollund Man, the 2,000-year-old peat bog body discovered nearby and now preserved at the town's Cultural Museum.

Skagen
The popular 'artists' colony' holiday town of bright houses perched on top of the windswept peninsula. Its museum has work by the 'Skagen Artists'.

Vejle
A delightful fjord town which many visitors stop at on their way to Legoland at the village of Billund. This extraordinary theme park is dedicated to the phenomenon of the plastic toy brick that was devised by Ole Kirk Christiansen in the 1930s. Over 45 million bricks were used to build Legoland itself, and it has been welcoming visitors since 1968.

Viborg

At the centre of Denmark's region of rolling hills, wind-ravaged heaths and wooded valleys, Viborg makes a convenient base for walking. The town itself has a vibrant old quarter reflecting its aristocratic past. It was also the place where a succession of early Danish kings were crowned.

WHEN TO GO

COPENHAGEN IS best visited during the Tivoli season, which lasts from May to September. Summer is the best time for the rest of the country too; temperatures are similar to those of southern England, but Denmark is noticeably sunnier – and slightly wetter.

Copenhagen's carnival, with flowers and processions, is held in early June.

	Average daily maximum temperature °C											
London	6	7	10	13	17	20	22	21	19	14	10	7
Copenhagen	2	2	5	10	16	19	22	21	18	12	7	4
	JAN	FEB	MAR	APR	MAY	JUN	JUL	AUG	SEP	OCT	NOV	DEC
Copenhagen	17	13	12	13	11	13	14	14	15	16	16	17
London	15	13	11	12	12	11	12	11	13	13	15	15
	Average number of rainy days per month											

PACKAGE TRAVEL

Tour operators

City breaks: British Airways Holidays, Cresta, Crystal, Inghams, Osprey, Premier Holidays, Time Off, Thomson, Travelscene
Specialists: DFDS Seaways, Scandinavian Travel Service, Scan-Meridian, Scantours, Specialised Tours **Other activities**: Ace Study Tours, Anglers World (fishing), Eurocamp (camping), Holts' Tours (battlefields), Martin Randall (cultural), Solo's Holidays (singles)

TOUR OPERATORS offering Denmark tend to concentrate on city breaks in Copenhagen or visits to Legoland. Self-drive tours are popular and themed tours based around golf, birdwatching, Hans Christian Andersen or fishing are also on offer.

INDEPENDENT TRAVEL

SEVERAL FLIGHTS run every day between Britain and Denmark, some with low-cost airlines. There are also ferry crossings from Harwich and Newcastle to Esbjerg. The newly opened Kulturbro, or 'Bridge of Culture', now links Copenhagen with Malmö in Sweden, offering a wide range of possibilities for combining visits to the two countries. Trains and buses within Denmark are frequent, efficient and cheap, and because the country is small, travelling times are short. Cycling is very popular and, with about 6,000 miles of signed cycle routes, often the best way to appreciate the mainly flat countryside. Bikes can be hired at most tourist offices, youth hostels and bike shops. The Copenhagen Card, available from tourist offices, provides free transport and entrance to all the city's museums.

Accommodation in Denmark is cheaper than in the rest of Scandinavia but still a major expense. It is worth looking around for pensions and country inns, which often offer similar facilities to hotels but are cheaper. Rooms in private houses are a good-value alternative. Camping is cheap, and some campsites have the option of cabins, which are excellent value for several people sharing.

RED TAPE, HEALTH AND SAFETY

BRITISH PASSPORT-HOLDERS do not need a visa to visit Denmark.

There are no particular health or crime problems in Denmark. Just take the usual precautions (see pages 10–12).

MORE INFORMATION Danish Tourist Board, 55 Sloane Street, London SW1X 9SY, tel 020-7201 3976, web site: *www.dtb.dt.dk*

COST OF LIVING £££

ECUADOR

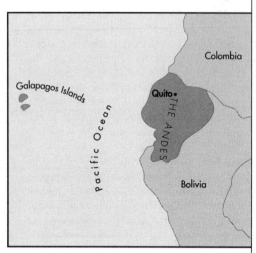

THE ANDES
Good for culture, local colour and scenic landscape

BEST CITIES

Cuenca
This is Ecuador's prettiest colonial city and a well-sited base for exploring the surrounding area, which includes the Inca ruins of Ingapirca (small but the best in Ecuador), traditional villages and national parks.

Quito
Much of the capital of Ecuador is congested with human as well as motor traffic, but it has a gorgeous setting and the cobbled streets of Old Quito boast lovely colonial architecture. Its impressive range of art and history museums are a good introduction to the rest of the country. Just outside the city is the Mitael del Mundo – Equatorial Line Monument – where you can straddle the northern and southern hemispheres.

BEST LOCAL COLOUR

Otavalo

Tourists pour into the home of Ecuador's most famous market, to admire the villagers from all over the island dressed in their colourful traditional clothes. Although the market was until recently devoted mainly to the sale of livestock, this has now been overwhelmed by craft stalls catering for the tourist trade with a massive array of products from around Ecuador and other South American countries.

Saquisilí

The Thursday market in Saquisilí, south of Quito, is rated by many to be the country's best – both commercially for the locals and for its tourist colour and interest. It does not attract as many people as Otavalo's market but, so far, it has retained an authentically indigenous atmosphere.

BEST SCENIC LANDSCAPE

The magnificent scenery of the Andes, above all the so-called Avenue of the Volcanoes south of Quito, can be enjoyed from the road or as a backdrop to the towns of the Sierra.

You need to be a serious climber to tackle the highest peaks, including Cotopaxi (19,500 feet) and Chimborazo (20,700 feet). The easiest volcano to climb is Tungurahua (16,500 feet), which is accessible from Baños.

THE ORIENTE
Good for flora, outdoor activities and wildlife

ECUADOR'S MAGNIFICENT and varied landscapes, abundant wildlife and rich indigenous culture have made it one of the top destinations in South America. Two-thirds of Ecuador, the so-called Oriente, forms part of the Amazon basin.

BEST WILDLIFE

The Amazon

There is little virgin jungle within easy reach, but you can see an abundance of tropical flora and fauna and have the opportunity to stay with indigenous communities and families.

Podocarpus National Park

In the far south of Ecuador, this national park's varied habitats provide some of the best chances to see native mammals and a huge abundance of birds.

GALAPAGOS ISLANDS
Good for wildlife

LOCATED 600 miles off the South American coast, these volcanic islands are prized for their unique wildlife, which seems to show no fear of humans. The cost of the trip doesn't deter visitors, the number of whom is limited by the government to 40,000 a year.

WHEN TO GO

THE COASTAL, mountain and jungle regions of Ecuador each have a very different climate. The Amazon is hot and wet all year round, and roads may close after heavy rain. In the Andes, on the other hand, temperatures can fluctuate enormously during a single day, and the sudden changes in weather conditions are a potential hazard for climbers. Quito is pleasantly fresh all year round and is cool at night. The weather should cause minimal disruption whatever time you go. The period from June to October is the driest in many areas.

	Average daily maximum temperature °C											
London	6	7	10	13	17	20	22	21	19	14	10	7
Quito	22	22	22	21	21	22	22	23	23	22	22	22
	JAN	FEB	MAR	APR	MAY	JUN	JUL	AUG	SEP	OCT	NOV	DEC
Quito	16	17	20	22	21	12	7	9	14	18	14	16
London	15	13	11	12	12	11	12	11	13	13	15	15
	Average number of rainy days per month											

PACKAGE TRAVEL

AN IMPRESSIVE variety of package holidays is available. You can journey from Ecuador's tropical coastline high up into the Andes and back down into the jungle, staying in all manner of accommodation from upmarket city hotels to jungle lodges. Travel choices range from public transport to coach, boat or raft.

Specialists offer flexibility with tailor-made tours and suggested itineraries. A tour starting from Quito might include a visit to the market at Otavalo, the Cotopaxi National Park, the spectacular 'Devil's

Nose' highland train journey from Huigra to Riobamba, and a cruise to the Galapagos Islands.

Nearly all the tour operators offer cruises to the Galapagos Islands, either as part of a tour or on their own. Specialist cruises suiting a range of budgets from economy to luxury and catering for groups of 15 to 90 people visit a selection of islands; most vessels have naturalists and guides on board.

Activity holidays include wildlife and birdwatching, adventure, trekking and white-water rafting.

Tour operators

Adventure: Adrift, Dragoman, Encounter Overland, Exodus, Guerba **Birdwatching/wildlife**: Abercrombie & Kent, Cox & Kings, Kuoni, Limosa, Sunbird **Cruising the Galapagos Islands**: Explore Worldwide, Journey Latin America, Naturetrek, Noble Caledonian, Reef and Rainforest, Regal Holidays, South American Experience, Wildlife Worldwide, Worldwide Journeys **Cultural**: British Museum Traveller **General**: Hayes & Jarvis, Sunvil, Titan HiTours, Voyages Jules Verne **Specialists**: Journey Latin America, Passage to South America, South American Experience, Veloso Tours **Tailor-made specialists**: Nomadic Thoughts, Scott Dunn World **Trekking**: KE Adventure

---

INDEPENDENT TRAVEL

THERE ARE no direct flights to Ecuador from the UK, but there are numerous routes via European and US cities. Demand is high, however, so if you plan to travel in the high season (June to August and December to January), book your flight at least three months in advance.

Ecuador's comparatively small size makes the country easy to explore. Internal flights are reasonably frequent, but almost always originate either in Quito or Guayaquil. Trains are a fine way to travel if you want a long, slow look at the scenery – the ride from Riobamba to Huigra is one of the most dramatic in the world. Buses are faster and serve most towns, while glorified trucks operate along minor routes. Hiring a car is expensive compared with most things in Ecuador, and can be more of a worry than an asset in such a poor country. Many national parks are difficult to reach by public transport, but you can normally arrange trips in the nearest town or in Quito.

Most people go on organised trips to the Galapagos Islands, but it is possible to plan a tour once in Ecuador. It is important to book your flight to the islands in good time: i.e. before you leave home.

Accommodation tends to be simple, although the rise in tourism means that guesthouses are more comfortable than previously. If you have your heart set on a particular place, book ahead, but otherwise rooms are easily found on the spot – although they will be in short supply the day before and after market days, or big festivals.

RED TAPE, HEALTH AND SAFETY

BRITISH PASSPORT-HOLDERS do not need a visa and can stay for three months in Ecuador. When entering the country, you must show a passport valid for six months and a return ticket.

Parts of Ecuador, including the northern Oriente, have a reputation for a particularly virulent form of malaria, and the whole country lies within a yellow fever zone. Altitude sickness can affect people in the Sierra, and you should take time to acclimatise before attempting any big mountain climbs.

Crime is a big problem in Quito, and you must guard against bag snatchers and pickpockets in the old city; evenings here are best spent in the new city. Do not venture down any dark streets at night and try to avoid walking alone – a rule which applies to all Ecuadorean cities. The Ecuador/Peru border is open but sensitive: stay on well-marked paths, as there are still land-mines in the area. For up-to-date information, contact the Foreign Office Travel Advice Unit (see page 11).

MORE INFORMATION Tourist Information, Embassy of Ecuador, 3 Hans Crescent, London SW1X 0LS, tel 020-7584 1367 (*please send an sae with two first-class stamps*)
Web site: *www.ecuaworld.com*

COST OF LIVING £

EGYPT

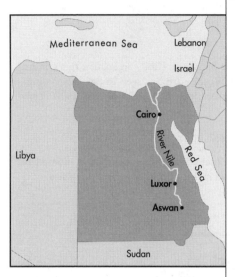

HIGHLIGHTS

Beaches
*Red Sea,
western Mediterranean
coast*

Culture
*Alexandria, Cairo,
Luxor*

Local colour
*Alexandria, Aswan,
Cairo, Luxor, Minya,
Rosetta, Siwa*

Outdoor activities
Red Sea, Sinai, Siwa

CAIRO
Good for culture, history and local colour

AFRICA'S LARGEST city, Cairo is a teeming metropolis of some 15 million people and countless taxis, all honking their horns. The noise and pollution make it hard to love, but the old quarter is a fascinating microcosm of Islamic history with thousands of mosques and tombs. Khan el-Khalili bazaar is packed with crafts and traditional coffee shops. The Coptic Christian area with ancient churches, the Nilometer on Roda Island and the gardens of the Agricultural Museum are pockets of calm in the maelstrom. For stunning Nile views, frequent the 'Windows on the World' restaurant-bar in the Ramses Hilton.

BEST SIGHTS

The Citadel
Muhammad Ali's great mosque and a panorama of old Cairo.

Museum of Egyptian Antiquities
Housing treasures from the Pharaonic era, this collection is a must-see, but queues are long and the entrance fee is steep at LE60 (about £12). All museums charge extra if you have a camera.

Pharoanic Village

Take a boat trip along a waterway lined with papyrus grass. Exhibitions include excellent models of the building of the pyramids, mummy embalming and Christian Egypt, plus the history of Islamic culture. Ideal for families.

Pyramids

The three pyramids and the Sphinx at Giza – in ancient times among the Seven Wonders of the World – are best seen in the early morning from the desert side. Diversions include camel rides and *son et lumière* presentations.

BEST EXCURSIONS

Saqqara is the site of King Zoser's Step Pyramid and other monuments from 27 BC. The Suez Canal makes a good day-trip from Cairo.

LUXOR
Good for history and local colour

THE WEST bank of the Nile in Luxor is the site of ancient Thebes, Egypt's capital for 15 dynasties. Hotels are located on the east bank whose lingering colonial air is spoilt by hassle from locals selling goods and services.

BEST SIGHTS

Queen Hatshepsut's Temple

An amphitheatre of bare cliffs provides a dramatic backdrop for this mighty temple to Egypt's only female Pharoah. It is reached by ferry, followed by a long walk or donkey ride.

Temple of Karnak

With its avenue of sphinxes and awesome Hypostyle Hall of 134 colossal stone columns covered in hieroglyphics, the temple is truly imposing. For the best light, visit at midday.

Tombs of the Nobles

The murals here give a fascinating insight into ancient funerary practices. Long queues are inevitable.

ASWAN
Good for local colour

ASWAN ENJOYS the most salubrious climate in Egypt, and is a handy spot for taking a traditional *felucca* to some of the nearby river islands. Kitchener's Island has a fine botanic garden, while Philae Island with its Temple of Isis and *son et lumière* shows is worth seeing.

BEST EXCURSION

Abu Simbel and the High Dam
A 30-minute flight south of Aswan, Abu Simbel is a stunning site. Four giant seated statues of Ramses II look across Lake Nasser, formed by the great High Dam. A smaller temple is dedicated to Nefertari – the only Egyptian temple built for a Pharoah's wife.

MINYA
Good for local colour

TWO HOURS' train ride south of Cairo, the old-world town of Minya has a sizeable Christian population. It has been off-limits since 1992, and tourist police are much in evidence, but the area is now considered safe and small tourist groups are filtering back. Sightseeing is by horse-carriage (good for excursions along the Nile) or taxi.

BEST SIGHTS

Deir al Adhra
Fourth-century Coptic church perched on a mountain, with an icon of the Virgin Mary which is said to weep oil. Fantastic views of Nileside farms.

Zawiyet el-Mayiteen
A Muslim necropolis with thousands of mausolea.

ALEXANDRIA
Good for local colour and culture

THE SHABBY but dignified old Mediterranean city is a two-hour train journey from Cairo. The most cosmopolitan city in Egypt, its old bars and tea rooms – such as Pastroudis – evoke lingering literary images from Lawrence Durrell's *Alexandria Quartet*. The Greco-Roman Museum holds Egypt's premier collection of images from the classical era, with masterly sculptures of Marcus Aurelius, Aphrodite and other legendary personae.

BEST EXCURSIONS

Rosetta
An hour by minibus from Alexandria, the town is notable for traditional architecture including *mishrabiya* wooden screens. The Rosetta stone, which made possible the translation of hieroglyphics, was discovered nearby in 1799.

Siwa Oasis
Fascinating landscape and a strong local culture, with the mud-built town of Shali a highlight.

RED SEA
Good for outdoor activities

THE RED SEA coast offers excellent scuba diving on the coral reefs. Other activities include snorkelling, fishing, sailing and desert safaris.

BEST RESORTS

Hurghada
● Egypt's premier resort on the Red Sea coast, aimed at package tours.

Sharm el Sheikh
● On the tip of the Sinai peninsula, it attracts divers, pilgrims and backpackers.
● Most hotels are basic but new luxury establishments have upped the stakes.
● A good base for visiting the Greek Orthodox Monastery of St Catherine.

WHEN TO GO

SPRING SANDSTORMS and summer heat restrict the best visiting months to October to March. From April onwards, temperatures soar and sightseeing is pushed to the very beginning or end of the day. Life slows down during Ramadan when many shops open only after evening prayers. People tend to live by night during the fast, when everything stays open late and streetlife is even noiser.

	Average daily maximum temperature °C											
London	6	7	10	13	17	20	22	21	19	14	10	7
Aswan	24	26	30	35	40	42	42	42	40	37	31	26
	JAN	FEB	MAR	APR	MAY	JUN	JUL	AUG	SEP	OCT	NOV	DEC
Aswan	<1	<1	<1	<1	<1	0	0	<1	<1	<1	<1	<1
London	15	13	11	12	12	11	12	11	13	13	15	15

Average number of rainy days per month

	Average daily maximum temperature °C											
London	6	7	10	13	17	20	22	21	19	14	10	7
Cairo	19	21	24	28	32	35	35	35	33	30	26	21
	JAN	FEB	MAR	APR	MAY	JUN	JUL	AUG	SEP	OCT	NOV	DEC
Cairo	3	2	1	1	1	0	0	0	<1	1	1	2
London	15	13	11	12	12	11	12	11	13	13	15	15

Average number of rainy days per month

PACKAGE TRAVEL

MOST PEOPLE take packages to Egypt: a tour leader eases your way through the bureaucracy by a well-judged distribution of small amounts of money (small-scale bribery is part of Egyptian life); it can be exhausting and time-consuming to make your own arrangements, and Egypt is a country where first-time travellers may feel less confident. Most package holidays also provide Egyptian guides, whose standards vary. The more scholarly tours provide specialist lecturers as well.

A Nile cruise is a unique and very relaxing part of most Egyptian holidays, and it is the easiest way to see the temples at Esna, Edfu and Kom Ombo, between Luxor and Aswan. However, all the other major sights can be seen from comfortable land bases at Cairo, Luxor and Aswan. Hotel rooms are usually larger than the often cramped cruise boat cabins, and the food is often safer.

Most tour operators offer Nile cruises or the resorts of the Red Sea as part of a package to Egypt. Typically, cruises last from four to seven days. Cruise boats are often luxurious and air-conditioned, though travel by *felucca* (small sail boat) is also available on a package. Luxor and Aswan are the main starting points for cruises and some operators offer cruises on Lake Nasser.

You can extend your holiday on the banks of the Nile or add on a trip to Cairo or the Red Sea resorts of Hurghada, Sharm el Sheikh and Dahab. When comparing brochure prices look out for 'optional excursions', which can add a lot to the basic cost of a package. Activity holidays include desert safaris in the Sinai, birdwatching and adventure tours. Many specialists offer diving packages in the Red Sea, based in hotels or on live-aboard vessels, or camping safaris along the coast.

Tour operators

General and specialist: Abercrombie & Kent, Airtours, Bales Tours, British Airways Holidays, Cosmos, Cox & Kings, Explore Worldwide, Goldenjoy, Goodwood Travel, Guerba, Hayes & Jarvis, Kuoni, Longwood, Peltours, Saga, Seafarer, Soliman Travel, Somak, Sunvil, Thomas Cook, Thomson, Tradewinds, Voyages Jules Verne **Scuba diving**: Acacia, Explorers Tours, Oonas Divers, Regal Holidays **Other activities**: British Museum Traveller (archaeology), Exodus (walking), Dragoman (adventure), Explore Worldwide (adventure, walking), Holts' Tours (battlefields), Jasmin Tours (desert experience), Peregrine Adventures (horse-riding), Martin Randall (cultural), Solo's Holidays (singles), Sunbird (birdwatching)

INDEPENDENT TRAVEL

TRAVELLING INDEPENDENTLY can be stressful due to hassle in the popular tourist spots. Otherwise people are very welcoming although a knowledge of Arabic is useful for directions and bargaining. Major carriers to Egypt are British Airways, Egypt Air, KLM and Air France. Charter flights go to Luxor and Sinai. Egypt Air maintains a domestic service to major centres. Flights are frequently overbooked so double-check your reservations on both domestic and international routes before travelling.

Rapid trains operate between Cairo and Alexandria, and south to Aswan via Minya, Assiut and Luxor. First class is air-conditioned with reclining seats and refreshments. Fares are very cheap. Except during rush-hour, the Cairo metro is ideal for city sightseeing – the first two carriages are for women only. Shared service-taxis are good value on common routes. Minibuses are very cheap but you can waste time waiting for a full complement of 14 passengers. For longer distances choose an air-conditioned coach. Egyptian roads are chaotically dangerous (drivers make up their own rules) and self-drive is strongly discouraged, although the roads are less congested in the Sinai Peninsula. River travel is possible by *felucca*; the fare will depend on your bargaining skill. Some sleep 6–8 people – take a sleeping bag.

International hotels such as the Hilton, Sheraton, Marriott, Meridien and Oberoi chains are well represented but pleasant mid-range accommodation tends to be lacking. Traffic noise and the call from 15,000 minarets makes sleep impossible in downtown Cairo. Hotels in Heliopolis or Giza tend to be quieter, but the journey into town can take more than an hour in the traffic.

RED TAPE, HEALTH AND SAFETY

BRITISH PASSPORT-HOLDERS require a visa to enter Egypt. You can obtain this at the Egyptian Consulate in London for £15 (one passport photo is required), or it is available for £10 (no photo) at Cairo International Airport. Make sure your passport is valid for six months after your date of travel.

Women travellers should dress modestly. Bikinis will attract unwanted attention on a public beach. Men should not wear shorts for sightseeing in Cairo. A jacket is essential for cold nights and chilly air conditioning.

Upset stomachs are common – avoid tap water, ice, salads and in most cases hotel buffets. Tetanus is the only essential injection but if concerned, consult your GP.

The Islamic fundamentalists behind the killings in Egypt during the 1990s have been greatly weakened by a government crackdown. Tourist police maintain a high profile at places frequented by tourists and while the situation is vastly improved, an armed escort is provided for your safety in Middle and Upper Egypt at the time of writing. For up to date information, contact the Foreign Office Travel Advice Unit (see page 11).

MORE INFORMATION Egyptian Tourist Board, Egyptian House, 170 Piccadilly, London W1V 9DD, tel 020-7493 5282, web site: *www.touregypt.net/*

Egyptian Consulate, Lowndes Street, Knightsbridge, London SW1X 9ET, tel 020-7235 9777, visa information (0891) 887777 (premium rate number)

COST OF LIVING £

ESTONIA

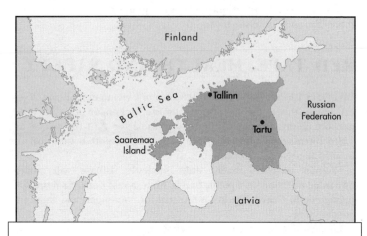

HIGHLIGHTS

Food/wine *Tallinn*	**Nightlife** *Tallinn*	**Outdoor activities** *Saaremaa Island*
Family holidays *Lahemaa National Park*	**Culture** *Tallinn, Tartu*	**Scenic landscapes** *Lahemaa, Saaremaa Island*

TALLINN
Good for culture and nightlife

CUT OFF from the outside world for 40 years when part of the Soviet Union, Estonia has caught up rapidly since 1991 when its independence was restored. The capital, Tallinn, is a fully westernised city. The medieval Old Town has kept its cobbled streets, its impenetrable city walls and its massive church spires, but local people now use mobile phones, eat at Thai, French, Italian and Greek restaurants and frequent nightclubs.

BEST SIGHTS

Adamson-Eric Museum
Estonia's most famous artist operated in every possible medium – he painted, he wove, he engraved and then moved on to ceramics,

sculpture and theatre design. When a stroke paralysed his right hand, he simply learnt to paint with his left one. See 1,000 items of his work from the twentieth century here.

Alexander Nevsky Cathedral
The one Czarist legacy that has been allowed to remain, this church was built in the 1890s at the top of the Old Town to symbolise Russian power. The mosaics, icons and 15-ton bell all came from St Petersburg.

Rocca al Mare Open-air Museum
Seventy houses, farmsteads, churches and workshops from all over Estonia have been reassembled to demonstrate country life in the early twentieth century. Festivities are at their best around midsummer (23 June) or just before Christmas, and centre on bonfires.

Town Hall Square
With a choice of 15 restaurants (and beer at £1 a pint), many tourists spend their entire holiday here. Yet it is worth returning to the fourteenth century with a tour of the Town Hall, lavishly furnished by generations of Baltic Germans who built up Tallinn as a major port in the Hanseatic League.

TARTU
Good for culture

ESTONIA'S OXBRIDGE, this university town has nurtured all the country's famous politicians, scientists and writers. The main university building, the Town Hall square and the neighbouring narrow streets all date from the late eighteenth century. The contemporary world is hidden discreetly behind shop windows.

BEST SIGHT

St Peter and St Paul Cathedral
The remains of one of the largest Gothic churches in the Baltics, a stiff walk up the hill behind the university.

LAHEMAA NATIONAL PARK
Good for family holidays

A CONVENIENT hour's drive from Tallinn, Estonia's largest National Park has been protected since its founding in 1971. Walk or cycle through the woods and visit manor houses and fishing villages. Do not expect any nightlife in this remote and rural region, even along the coast.

BEST SIGHTS

Kasmu Maritime Museum
Estonia's turbulent maritime history – smuggling, piracy, bootlegging and Soviet border controls – is all explained here, together with a £1 note from 1918, when sterling was the only safe currency.

Palmse Manor
Estonia's best-known country house was built around 1800, probably from English designs. Generations of a benevolent Baltic German family lived in it for 200 years. You can play their music boxes, pianos and harpsichords and visit greenhouses and orchards. Boulders are scattered erratically through the surrounding woods.

SAAREMAA ISLAND
Good for outdoor activities and scenic landscape

LIFE HAS stood still here since 1945 when the Soviet army invaded and prevented even Estonians from visiting. As a result, pollution and high-rise buildings do not exist; instead you will find wooden cottages, medieval churches, lighthouses and isolated alcoves for swimming in the sea. An hourly ferry takes buses and cars from the mainland.

Kuressaare
A massive castle overlooks the capital of the island; the museum here details the 700 years of invasions the island has endured since it was first conquered in the thirteenth century.

WHEN TO GO

THE GULF Stream protects Estonia from the worst of the Russian winter so temperatures do not fall much below freezing point. However, the short hours of daylight from November to February are hardly inviting. Spring through to autumn is the best time to visit. Be ready for rain at any time, although showers do not last long.

Average daily maximum temperature °C											
London	6	7	10	13	17	20	22	21	19	14	10	7
Tallinn	-4	-4	0	7	14	19	20	19	15	10	3	-1
	JAN	FEB	MAR	APR	MAY	JUN	JUL	AUG	SEP	OCT	NOV	DEC
Tallinn	19	16	13	11	12	10	13	15	16	17	18	19
London	15	13	11	12	12	11	12	11	13	13	15	15
Average number of rainy days per month											

PACKAGE TRAVEL

GROUP TOURS usually link Estonia with Latvia and Lithuania to create week-long escorted tours of the Baltic States. Year-round city breaks in Tallinn offer a range of three- to five-star hotels and can be combined as a two-centre break with Helsinki, Riga or Vilnius. Little in the way of sightseeing excursions are on offer in Tallinn, but day trips to Parnu, Tartu and Haapsalu are all possible using local buses. Guides can be hired locally. Activity packages include cultural tours and walking tours taking in Lahemaa National Park.

Tour operators

City breaks: Norvista, ScanMeridian, Yes Travel **Cultural**: Ace Study Tours, Martin Randall **Cycling**: Exodus, Regent Holidays **Specialists**: Intourist, Norvista, Regent Holidays, Specialised Tours **Walking**: Explore Worldwide, Ramblers Holidays

---

INDEPENDENT TRAVEL

TALLINN IS now easily reached from all over Britain. Estonian Air has a daily flight from Gatwick, and SAS Scandinavian Airlines has several connections every day via Copenhagen and Stockholm from the London airports, Birmingham, Manchester, Glasgow and Edinburgh. An attractive route in the summer is to fly to Helsinki and then continue by ferry or hydrofoil to Tallinn. Discount air fares are available from travel agents that specialise in the Baltic States. Such companies also offer reduced hotel rates compared to the normally high prices in Tallinn (prices outside the capital are much lower).

Car hire firms use modern Western cars; prices are quite high and you may prefer to limit car use to difficult-to-reach areas. An extensive bus network with very low fares covers the country, and buses also link

Estonia with Russia, Latvia and Lithuania. Passenger train services hardly exist.

RED TAPE, HEALTH AND SAFETY

BRITISH PASSPORT-HOLDERS do not require a visa for Estonia.

Medical care in local hospitals is of a high standard. With Estonia in the first wave of new EU members, hygiene and safety standards are strictly imposed in restaurants and cafés. English is widely spoken by young people in hotels, shops and restaurants. Many signs are now in English as well.

Tourists are much less affected by crime than in other European countries. Problems can arise late at night outside nightclubs, when rich tourists are a vulnerable target for thieves. Be sure to take the usual precautions (see page 12). Car theft is common and vehicles should be left overnight in a guarded car park. Pavements may be poorly maintained; watch out for loose cobblestones and uncovered manholes. Museums often close for two days a week (usually Monday and Tuesday) and have erratic opening hours.

MORE INFORMATION Estonian Embassy, 16 Hyde Park Gate, London SW7 5DG, tel 020-7589 3428. Check out the Tourist Board web site at: *www.tourism.ee*

COST OF LIVING £

FIJI

HIGHLIGHTS

Beaches
Yasawa Islands

Culture
Suva

Outdoor activities
*Coral Coast, Kadavu,
Mamanuca Islands,
Ovalau*

Scenic landscape
*Vanua Levu, Viti Levu,
Ovalau*

I N MAY 2000 there was a coup d'état in Fiji. Some violent incidents have severely damaged inter-racial relations (45 per cent of the Fijian population is Indian). At the time of writing the military is continuing its direct role in the maintenance of law and order.

The implications of this unrest for travellers are uncertain. According to the Fiji Visitors Bureau, the situation has returned to normal and there are no safety concerns for tourists. However, those wishing to travel to Fiji are advised to check with the Foreign Office Travel Advice Unit (see page 11) for up-to-date information and advice on the current political situation.

A popular destination with Antipodean tourists and transpacific fliers, Fiji has seen most development focused on the southern coast of the main island, Viti Levu, and on the smaller islands just off its western seaboard. For anyone willing to travel further afield, the scattered islands which make up this welcoming nation offer some of the most dramatic and enticing scenery in the Pacific.

VITI LEVU
Good for culture, outdoor activities and scenic landscape

THIS IS the more developed of the two main islands, the other being Vanua Levu to the north. Lautoka on the western seaboard is the departure point for several popular island chains such as the Mamanuca and Yasawa groups. Nadi is a bustling town awash with touts and vendors who will compete vigorously for your attention. Most people enter and depart Fiji from the airport at Nadi and cruises around the popular island chains pick up passengers from hotels here.

BEST SIGHTS

Coral coast
Travelling south from Nadi, the Queen's Road winds its way east through Sigatoka and along Viti Levu's stunning southern coastline, the Coral Coast. The region offers a concentration of both beauty and resorts which should cater for most preferences and pockets.

Nananu-i-Ra
Nananu-i-Ra is a beautiful, compact little island fringed by coral reef on the King's Road, north of Lautoka. Access is by boat from Rakiraki.

Suva
Suva, the capital, is in the south-east of the island. It is both the cultural centre of Fiji and the main port for other islands, such as Kadavu. The excellent museum includes among its artefacts many items of cutlery, such as brain forks, used in the ritualised cannibalism which was widely practised until the end of the nineteenth century, but which quickly disappeared with the coming of Christianity and the end of tribal warfare.

VANUA LEVU
Good for scenic landscape

THIS IS the second largest island after Viti Levu and is much less developed. Tourism has secured a foothold here but is localised to certain areas and is still a long way from the developed resorts of its southern neighbour.

BEST BASE

Savusavu
Savusavu, on the south of the island, is the largest town on Vanua Levu

and the main point of entry. It is a colourful, though small town, and is really a base for diving and exploring the rest of the island.

OTHER ISLANDS
Good for beaches and outdoor activities

DIVING AND snorkelling are excellent throughout the various island groups, and water sports abound. These activities can be arranged through specialist diving shops and most local hotels.

Kadavu
Fast becoming one of the premier diving spots in Fiji, owing to the spectacular Astrolabe reef, this island is located to the south of Viti Levu and accessed primarily either by air from Nadi or by boat from Suva. Check the timetable if you intend to arrive by sea.

Mamanuca Islands
Several boat trips arrive here from Lautoka, taking advantage of the islands' perfect setting for laid-back cruising and water sports. The Mamanucas are more expensive than other island groups.

Ovalau
Ovalau is part of the Lomaiviti Islands. Its main town, Levuka, is the old capital of Fiji. It boasts one of the oldest and most charismatic hotels in the South Pacific, the Royal Hotel. Here complimentary Kava (a mildly intoxicating brew made from a ground root) is served daily.

The Lovoni Valley is one of the island's most scenic locations. From Ovalau, you can venture further on to other more isolated islands, such as Caqelai, where the snorkelling and beaches are superb.

Yasawa Islands
This group of islands, which runs roughly north to south to the west of Viti Levu, forms an ideal South Pacific paradise. Unspoilt stretches of pristine sand and translucent water are punctuated by lush headlands; each island has its own character and unhurried charm. It was just off the northern extreme of the Yasawas that Captain Bligh, adrift after the mutiny on the *Bounty*, was almost captured and eaten by irate locals before escaping through a gap in the reef.

Cruise ships regularly stop off at the islands. For most independent travellers, however, arriving by boat from Lautoka is the favoured approach. Be prepared for rudimentary facilities on board.

WHEN TO GO

THE IDEAL time to visit is during the drier and cooler months, which run from May through to November. Outside this period the humidity, temperatures and rainfall can all be uncomfortably high, especially at the beginning of the year.

	Average daily maximum temperature °C											
London	6	7	10	13	17	20	22	21	19	14	10	7
Suva	29	29	29	29	28	27	26	26	27	27	28	29
	JAN	FEB	MAR	APR	MAY	JUN	JUL	AUG	SEP	OCT	NOV	DEC
Suva	18	18	21	19	16	13	14	15	16	15	15	18
London	15	13	11	12	12	11	12	11	13	13	15	15
	Average number of rainy days per month											

PACKAGE TRAVEL

FOR THE UK holidaymaker, Fiji is generally featured as a popular stopover destination on round-the-world flights to or from Australasia rather than as the place for a two-week holiday. Consequently, there are few specialist brochures. As Fiji is marketed as somewhere to escape the rigours of intercontinental travel, all arrangements can be tailor-made to suit your requirements.

Most tour operators offer a choice of hotels on Viti Levu – either close to the airport at Nadi or on the Coral Coast, about an hour and a half away. Resorts like Castaway, Treasure and Breakaway Islands are easily accessible from the airport by plane, helicopter or boat, and transfer times are often quicker than to the Coral Coast. Study the resort details carefully to ensure you choose the right island for your requirements. Two-, three- or six-night cruises throughout the islands are also available. Specialist options include tall ship cruising and scuba diving.

Tour operators

Cruising: Noble Caledonian **General**: Austravel, Cadogan, Classic Connection, Eastravel, Elegant Resorts, Kuoni, Qantas Holidays, Sunset Faraway, Tradewinds, Trailfinders, Travel 2, Travelpack, World Dreams **Sailing**: Explore Worldwide **Specialists**: Anderson's Pacific Way, All-Ways Pacific, Destination Pacific

---

Accommodation is usually upmarket and of decent quality, with lots of facilities laid on – particularly water sports. Entertainment is low-key and generally hotel-based.

INDEPENDENT TRAVEL

THERE IS a wide range of accommodation on Fiji, ranging from dormitory beds for backpackers to very upmarket hotels. The tourist desk at the airport in Nadi is a useful source of information.

Roads through the lush interior of Viti Levu are limited and if you are driving you should exert extreme caution as the highways, especially the northern loop, are notoriously chaotic. Buses run between Nadi, Suva, Raki Raki and Lautoka, making it possible to travel round Viti Levu by public transport.

An inexpensive and interesting way to travel to Levuka on the island of Ovalau is by bus from Suva to Natovi, from where a car ferry takes you to Buresala on Ovalau. You then catch another bus around the island to Levuka.

RED TAPE, HEALTH AND SAFETY

VISAS CAN be obtained on entry and extended while in Fiji.

Tropical diseases present in Fiji include hepatitis A, dengue fever, polio and typhoid. If you are arriving from a country where yellow fever is present, immunisation against the disease is essential. Tourists should consult their doctor or a travel centre before travelling to Fiji.

Shark attacks, bites from venomous sea snakes and stings from cone shells are relatively rare. Seek local advice when you are snorkelling or diving if unsure of currents, rips and other considerations.

Fiji is generally no more or less dangerous than elsewhere in the South Pacific, although petty theft is not uncommon. The main urbanised areas, such as Suva, are where you are most likely to encounter crime.

At the time of writing, travel into the jungles on the north-eastern side of Viti Levu is not advised. Check with the Fiji High Commission or Fiji Visitors Bureau in Suva (see below) for up-to-date information.

MORE INFORMATION Fiji High Commission, 34 Hyde Park Gate, London SW7 5DN, tel 0120-7584 3661, Fiji Visitors Bureau web site: *www.fijifvb.gov.fj*

COST OF LIVING £

145

FINLAND

HIGHLIGHTS

Culture
Helsinki, Savonlinna, Turku

Outdoor activities
Lapland, National Forest, Lakeland

Winter adventures
Levi, Rovaniemi, Ylläs

Family holidays
Lakeland, Lapland

F INLAND MAY be tucked away in the north-eastern corner of Europe, but it's a year-round favourite with visitors who value the unspoilt and undisturbed peace of a country landscape that's still just as Mother Nature intended. It's a relatively young country, having gained its independence from more than a hundred years of Russian rule as recently as 1917. Prior to 1809 it was part of Sweden. Consequently it draws on eastern and western cultural influences more than any other European country.

By and large, the Finns do not conform to the typical Scandinavian image of blond hair and blue eyes – and the simple explanation for this is that they do not share common ancestors with their Swedish and Norwegian neighbours. Though no one knows for sure, it's thought the earliest settlers moved into Finland from beyond the Ural Mountains, on a circuitous route via the Baltic and Estonia.

HELSINKI
Good for culture, history and nightlife

THE CAPITAL is best explored on foot, and will bring rewards for the visitor keen to sniff out art, music and culture, as well as quality glassware and bargains from the many markets. Like the rest of Finland, Helsinki changes with the seasons. Wearing its heart on its sleeve for the brief but spectacular summer, the city withdraws quietly as the nights close in and the first winter snows send city dwellers hurrying for refuge in one of the cosy bars or sophisticated cafés.

BEST SIGHTS

Cathedrals
For dramatic effect, the Lutheran and Orthodox cathedrals are best viewed from the sea. The former, white and multi-domed, dominates the central Senate Square, designed by J.L. Engel between 1822 and 1852. Its austerity is offset by the eastern mystery of the Orthodox Uspensky Cathedral, Scandinavia's largest Orthodox church, just five minutes' walk away.

Church in the Rock
Entering this architectural masterpiece dating from 1967 feels like stepping into a great cave. A single strand of copper wire circles the church's ceiling, adding to its fabulous acoustic.

Olympic Stadium
Helsinki originally expected to host the Olympic Games of 1940, but the Second World War prevented the event, and it was not until 1952 that they took place here. The view of the city from the top of the Olympic Stadium is stunning.

Senate Square
As well as the Lutheran Cathedral, the Square is home to the Council of State and the main University building, both creations of Engel. A statue of the Russian Czar Alexander II, dating from 1863, stands in the centre of the Square.

Suomenlinna
The old island fortress lies just a 15-minute boat ride away from the city centre. Fortified by the Swedes in the eighteenth century, it is now on the UNESCO World Heritage list.

TURKU
Good for history and local colour

TURKU WAS for 500 years the capital of Finland. It was only in 1812 that Czar Alexander I decided Turku was too close to Sweden to be the Finnish capital, so Helsinki took over.

BEST SIGHTS

Castle
Dating from 1280, the castle was further fortified in the sixteenth century at the time the Swedish King Gustav Vasa appointed his son John as Finland's first duke. The 'Little Knights' castle tour is designed specially for children.

Cathedral
An amazing mix of architectural styles from early medieval through to late Romantic.

Forum Marinum Maritime Centre
A must for anyone interested in sea travel and maritime history. New interactive technology even brings a Baltic storm to life.

Moomin World
Twenty minutes' drive from Turku, the home of the author Tove Jansson's lovable creatures can be found in the town of Naantali.

THE SAIMAA LAKELAND
Good for culture, outdoor activities and scenic landscape

EUROPE'S MOST extensive lake district is a world away from the busy life of Helsinki. Culture is never far away, and visitors flock to enjoy the magic of grand opera performed on the stage of Savonlinna's medieval castle and the breath-taking pulse of Kuopio's annual dance festival.

Away from the cities there are quite literally thousands of lakes and rivers that make the region a paradise for sailing, rowing, canoeing and fishing and provide a home for a rare breed of freshwater seal.

BEST SIGHTS

Kuopio
This small eighteenth-century city boasts a bustling market, an Ortho-dox Church Museum and a spectacular annual dance festival. Pano-

ramic views over the city and its surrounds can be enjoyed from the top of the nearby Puijo Tower, where a well-timed visit could coincide with the thrills of the nearby 90-m ski jump.

Punkaharju
The four-mile-long Punkaharju Ridge provides an awesome but narrow drive between the lakes Pihlajvesi and Puruvesi.

Retretti
Situated along the Punkaharju Ridge is the extraordinary Retretti art gallery, made up of a network of caves.

Savonlinna
The town grew up on a number of islands and is dominated by the fifteenth-century Olavinlinna Castle – Finland's largest – where an opera festival is held in July each year.

BEST RESORTS

North Karelia
Strong Eastern influences on architecture, religion and lifestyle prevail in the region. Particularly notable is Heinävesi, Scandinavia's only Orthodox monastery; the Bomba House, an authentic Karelian mansion; and the town of Ilomantsi, at the time of writing the easternmost point of the European Union.

LAPLAND
Good for family holidays and outdoor activities

THIS WINTER wonderland has also made a seasonal name for itself as the home of Santa Claus. Lapland's mainstream resorts offer downhill and cross-country skiing, snowmobile safaris, dog-sledging and ice-fishing. In the smaller villages cosy cabins provide a warm welcome from the Arctic chill.

BEST RESORTS

Levi
● Finland's premier downhill ski resort, with slopes to suit all standards.
● Excellent nightlife centred around the hotels of Sirkka, on the northern side of the hill.

Rovaniemi
● Home of Santa Claus, with attractive wooden Santa Village and Santa Park theme park situated in a cave.

● Plenty of accommodation, with winter sports opportunities close to hand.

Saariselkä
● Spectacular National Park location more than 125 miles north of the Arctic Circle.
● Cosy log cabins with sauna and fireplace, and top-class winter sports.

Ylläs
● 34 Alpine pistes with 155 miles of floodlit cross-country ski trails.
● Up-to-date resort facilities, yet retaining its old Lappish charm.

WHEN TO GO

FINLAND'S NORTHERLY location ensures four very distinct seasons. Summers are sunny and settled, with long hours of daylight in the south and temperatures regularly soaring above 25°C. The north of Finland enjoys the midnight sun during the months of June and July, though the flip side of this is a two-month period of little or no daylight during the winter. The mercury can plunge in the winter months, though daytime temperatures of around −10°C are more usual.

Helsinki and Turku city breaks are popular all year round, though the cities tend to empty in July when most Finns take their annual holidays. The Lakeland is at its best in June and July, whilst there is usually snow in Lapland from late November through until the end of April.

Average daily maximum temperature °C											
London	6	7	10	13	17	20	22	21	19	14	10	7
Helsinki	-3	-4	0	6	13	19	22	20	15	8	3	0
	JAN	FEB	MAR	APR	MAY	JUN	JUL	AUG	SEP	OCT	NOV	DEC
Helsinki	20	18	14	13	12	13	14	15	15	18	19	20
London	15	13	11	12	12	11	12	11	13	13	15	15
Average number of rainy days per month											

PACKAGE TRAVEL

TOUR OPERATORS to Finland offer city breaks to Helsinki and Turku, sometimes in tandem with other Scandinavian and Baltic cities such as Stockholm and Tallinn. Other options include self-catering in traditional log cabins and cottages in the Lakeland and Lapland. Ski operators include some of the resorts of Lapland in their brochures, while a number of tour operators offer short breaks to visit Santa Claus. Flights operate on several weekends before Christmas from many regional airports.

Tour operators

Birdwatching: Abercrombie & Kent, Birding, Limosa, Ornitholidays, Sunbird **City breaks**: Bridge Travel Service, Cresta, Crystal, Sovereign, Thomson, Travelscene, Yes Travel **Specialists**: Norvista, Scandinavian Travel Service, Scantours, ScanMeridian, Specialised Tours **Wildlife**: Naturetrek, Wildlife Worldwide **Other activities**: Ace Study Tours, Inntravel (walking/biking), Inter-Church Travel (religious tours), Martin Randall (cultural), Thermalia (spa)

INDEPENDENT TRAVEL

GETTING TO Finland by air is simple. There are several daily flights with Finnair and British Airways from London Heathrow, while Finnair operates from Gatwick and Manchester as well. Buzz flies twice daily from Stansted to Helsinki. Driving to Finland takes a little more planning and time; the most efficient route is via the north German port of Rostock for the Baltic crossing to Helsinki.

Getting around Finland is best done in a hired car, though this is generally expensive. The train system is reliable and very reasonably priced. Long-distance coaches connect the major cities, while much travel – especially in the Lakeland and western archipelagos – relies on ferries.

Hotel accommodation in Helsinki ranges from standard to de luxe. Regional city hotels cater by and large for business travellers; in rural locations you can find luxurious spa resorts. Farmhouse bed and breakfast is a popular option for many travellers, although to find the true wilderness of Finland it is considered essential to sleep under canvas, or make use of the free forest shelters found in National Parks.

RED TAPE, HEALTH AND SAFETY

BRITISH PASSPORT-HOLDERS do not need a visa to visit Finland.

Health care is of a high standard and crime levels are low. However, take the usual precautions to safeguard your personal safety and possessions (see pages 10–12).

MORE INFORMATION Finnish Tourist Board, 30 Pall Mall, London SW1Y 5LP, tel 020–7839 4048, web site: *www.finland-tourism.com*

COST OF LIVING ££

FRANCE

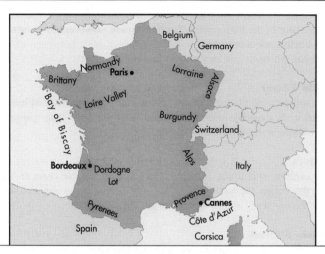

HIGHLIGHTS

Beaches
*Brittany,
Corsica,
South of
France*

**Family
holidays**
*Atlantic coast,
Brittany,
Ile-de-France*

History
Normandy

Food/wine
*Alsace,
Atlantic coast,
Brittany,
Burgundy,
Dordogne,
Loire valley,
Normandy,
Paris,
South of
France*

**Nightlife/
shopping**
Paris

Culture
*Burgundy,
Ile-de-France,
Loire valley,
Paris,
South of
France*

Local colour
Alsace

**Outdoor
activities**
*Alps, Alsace,
Brittany,*

*Corsica,
Dordogne,
Normandy,
Pyrenees,
South of
France*

**Scenic
landscape**
*Corsica,
Dordogne,
Pyrenees,
South of
France*

PARIS
Good for culture, food/wine, nightlife and shopping

SAUNTERING IS the best way to sample the city, whether strolling the riverside embankments or simply 'licking the panes' (*lèche-vitrines*), as the French call window-shopping.

BEST SIGHTS

If you have been to Paris before, you will have your own ideas about exploring – perhaps the mansions and antique shops of the Marais, or even a tour of the Paris sewers. For first-timers, however, the attractions listed below are unmissable.

Some museums and local shops close on Mondays.

Eiffel Tower
The top viewing platform of this '300-metre flagpole', as Eiffel himself called it, is accessible only by lift, and there are hour-long queues in the middle of the day – visit early or late.

Louvre
Star exhibits include the *Mona Lisa* (La Joconde) and the *Venus de Milo*. Use the leaflets explaining the layout of the museum to pinpoint what you want to see – or you will never get out.

Musée d'Orsay
This turn-of-the-century station picks up French art from 1848, where the Louvre stops. As well as the Impressionists, it displays sculpture by Rodin, art nouveau glass and furniture.

Notre Dame
This beautiful Gothic cathedral is mirrored in the water of the Seine and lit by the searchlights of passing boats. If you are feeling strong, you can tackle the 402 steps to the top of the towers.

Pompidou Centre
The main interest inside the centre is the Modern Art Museum, where canvases by Picasso, Bonnard, Léger and Matisse dominate the huge galleries.

ILE-DE-FRANCE
Good for culture and family holidays

MANY ATTRACTIONS, including Disneyland Paris, can be visited on day-trips from the capital via public transport, while Chantilly and Fontainebleau are excellent bases for drivers.

BEST SIGHTS

Chantilly
The château contains an excellent art collection, while the stables now house a Horse and Pony Museum.

Chartres
The cathedral is a masterpiece of Romanesque and Gothic carving and sumptuous stained-glass. Use binoculars to appreciate details close-up and climb the New Tower for unrivalled views.

Fontainebleau
Lively town with royal château used as a base by French kings hunting in surrounding forest. Highlights include the Farewell Court, where Napoleon said goodbye to his soldiers before exile in Elba.

St-Denis
The world's first Gothic cathedral contains the tombs of all but three of the kings of France.

St-Germain-en-Laye
The château where Louis XIV was born houses the excellent National Museum of Antiquities.

Vaux-le-Vicomte
Finely restored château and gardens built by Louis XIV's ambitious Minister of Finance, Nicolas Fouquet.

Versailles
Most visitors tour the grandiose state apartments and the Hall of Mirrors – but do not neglect the gardens, which are particularly stunning when the fountains are switched on (summer Sunday afternoons).

BEST THEME PARKS

Disneyland Paris
Smaller and more manageable than its American counterparts, Disneyland recreates the familiar concept of five themed 'lands'. Most of the queues – and several good attractions – are sensibly under cover. There are plenty of attractions for younger children.

Parc Astérix
Themed park and Disney alternative based on the popular comic strip set in ancient Gaul. Most of the rides are gentle.

LOIRE VALLEY
Good for culture and food/wine

THE REGION'S undisputed magnets are the châteaux. These fanciful Renaissance palaces, severe medieval fortresses and sumptuous classical mansions saw the high life and scurrilous deeds of France's aristocracy.

BEST CHATEAUX

Chambord
The château is covered with carved salamanders – the insignia of François I – and is remarkable for its astonishing skyline.

Chenonceau
The most romantic château, reflected in the Cher.

Langeais
This comprehensive collection of late medieval furnishings is intensely atmospheric.

Plessis-Bourré
The bawdily decorated guard room is one of the highlights of this lesser-known château.

Villandry
A subdued house surrounded by magnificent gardens, renowned for their topiary.

BEST BASES

Chinon
This is a riverside town of narrow streets where oriel and bay windows overhang the cobbled paths below the ruins of a medieval château.

Loches
Cafés and gift shops occupy houses on cobbled lanes winding up towards the walls of an intact medieval city. A rampart walk connects the château at the northern end with the eleventh-century keep.

Vendôme
The old town is enclosed within a bend in the Loir, and channels from the river run between the streets of small stone and half-timbered houses.

BURGUNDY
Good for culture and food/wine

TO APPRECIATE the beauty of the wine villages, take the side road designated the Route du Vin running parallel to the N74. Here the signposts read like an exclusive wine list. There are around 750 miles of navigable waterway in Burgundy, so it is a good place for a boating holiday. The most scenic routes are the Canal du Nivernais, which cuts through the Yonne valley from Auxerre to Decize, and the Canal de Bourgogne, from Migennes to the Sâone plain.

BEST SIGHTS

Ancy-le-Franc
This sober, classical Renaissance château has a superb interior by Italian artists Primaticcio and Niccolo dell'Abate.

Beaune
Capital of the wine trade, and a perfect base for touring the famous wine villages. Sample some wine at the Marché aux Vins. The Hôtel-Dieu contains Van der Weyden's *Last Judgement* polyptych.

Dijon
The Dukes of Burgundy ruled from this capital for 500 years. John the Fearless and Philip the Bold's tombs occupy the Musée des Beaux-Arts, surrounded by Renaissance courtyards and half-timbered houses.

Fontenay Abbey
The finest surviving example of a Cistercian monastery.

Tanlay
Château notable for its exterior, more interesting architecturally than that of its neighbour at Ancy-le-Franc.

Vézelay
The outstanding Romanesque basilica at Vézelay has a lofty interior striped with Moorish bands. The pillar capitals depict gruesome allegories.

THE ALPS
Good for outdoor activities

THE MONT Blanc area is a summer playground for climbers, walkers and cable-car riders. More peaceful are the Queyras region and the Vercors; to escape further, try the national parks of Vanoise or Ecrins.

BEST LAKESIDE RESORTS

Annecy
● A fashionable town with good shops and ancient Savoyard houses.

Meillerie
● A small fishing village off the tourist track in a prime site on Lac Léman (the French shore of Lake Geneva).

Talloires
● Village with superb views, well placed for watching sunsets.
● Prestigious hotels line the waterfront.

BEST EXCURSIONS

Chambéry
Chambéry consists of a network of tunnels and lanes, with a castle at its heart. The cathedral displays extraordinary *trompe l'oeil*.

Manigod
This tiny village in the most alluring of the valleys makes a good excursion from Lac d'Annecy. From the Col de la Croix-Fry the peaks of Chaîne des Aravis can be seen.

BEST MOUNTAIN BASES

Chamonix
Crowded, sunny, fashionable Chamonix – a mountain activity base – has a nineteenth-century core of pastiche alpine village style.

Pralognan
This steeply enclosed climbers' and hikers' village just on the edge of the Vanoise National Park offers guided excursions.

St-Gervais
Despite a traffic-ridden main street, St-Gervais is surrounded by unspoilt countryside.

St-Véran
One of the highest villages in Europe (6,600 feet), St-Véran is a delightful combination of resort and rustic village in the Queyras Regional Park. Excellent walks and views to Italy.

Valloire
Traditional alpine village and all-year resort in the Ecrins.

Villard-de-Lans
Sprawling resort in the pre-alpine massif of the Vercors that caters for recreational tastes both leisurely and energetic.

BEST MOUNTAIN TRIPS

Aiguille du Midi
This spectacular cable-car trip from Chamonix provides stunning views of the peaks. A further cable-car takes you over the wastes of snow behind Mont Blanc to Helbronner on the Italian frontier.

Mer de Glace
A rack railway from Chamonix leads you to a cave in the glacier, where sculptures include a bathroom complete with ice lavatory.

Mont Blanc tramway
An old rack railway ascends a spur of Mont Blanc from St-Gervais to reach the Nid d'Aigle (eagle's nest) peak on the edge of the snow line.

Vercors massif
A limestone plateau ringed by fearsome vertical cliffs on all sides. The Gorges de la Bourne, the Grands Goulets and the Combe Laval all involve driving alongside hair-raising chasms.

BRITTANY
Good for beaches, family holidays, food/wine and outdoor activities

ITS 1,000-PLUS miles of sandy coastline make Brittany a good choice for quiet family and beach holidays, especially for campers and self-caterers. By French standards, sightseeing could be limited, and the cuisine, notable for seafood and crêpes (pancakes), uncomplicated.

BEST RESORTS

Beg-Meil peninsula
● Excellent camping area. Sandy stretches and charming coves surround the Cap-Coz promontory, Beg-Meil and Pointe de Mousterlin.

Bénodet
● The south-west's popular yachting centre, ranged picturesquely around the mouth of the Odet estuary.
● Good beaches and plenty of boat trips.

Carantec
● A sleepy peninsular resort with reasonable beaches.
● There is a large nautical club.

Dinard
● Sophisticated town that is host to an annual film festival.
● It also offers a big beach, water sports and boat trips.

Pink Granite Coast
● Weird shoreline rock formations from Perros-Guirec to Ploumanach.

BEST SIGHTS AND EXCURSIONS

Medieval inland towns
Dinan boasts fine half-timbered houses, Vitré and Josselin have conical-towered castles, while Fougères has an awesome medieval fortress.

Medieval ports
St-Malo's ramparts enclose the old town, destroyed in the Second World War and now sensitively rebuilt; at low tide, walk across the sands to islets. The huge fishing port of Concarneau has a fortified old quarter.

Parish closes
North-western Brittany has a concentration of unique sixteenth- and seventeenth-century ecclesiastical architecture. Do not miss the parish closes at Lampaul-Guimiliau, Guimiliau and St-Thégonnec.

Prehistoric sites
Southern Brittany is awash with monuments dating from around 5000–2000 BC: amazing rows of menhirs (long stones) and a prehistory museum at Carnac, and a fine dolmen (tomb) on Gavrinis Island.

NORMANDY
Good for food/wine, history and outdoor activities

THE MOST varied of France's northern coastal regions is also of great architectural and historical interest. In the countryside, cider and calvados complement the rich, dairy-based cuisine. The region has a history of invasions, from the Norsemen to D-Day.

BEST BASES

Les Andelys
Town comprising Petit and Grand Andelys; the former is one of the prettiest spots on the Seine above Rouen and packed at weekends.

Barneville-Carteret
This small fishing port on the west coast of the Cotentin peninsula lies within reach of deserted sand dunes and spectacular beaches.

Clécy
Rarely overcrowded village in the heart of lovely Suisse Normande. Canoeing and walking are the main activities.

Etretat
Popular French family resort with spectacular cliff scenery. It is lively in season, and has a fair range of facilities.

Honfleur
Boudin and Monet both worked here and are commemorated in the Boudin Museum. Artists still thrive and several galleries exist.

BEST SIGHTS AND EXCURSIONS

Bayeux
Bayeux is most famous for its striking tapestry (actually embroidery) commemorating the Norman invasion of England in 1066.

Coutances
The big draw here is the cathedral, widely held to be a masterpiece of Norman Gothic architecture, with soaring lines and clusters of turrets.

Deauville
Deauville has turn-of-the-century neo-rustic villas and the smartest hotels, shops, nightlife and people.

Dieppe
Attractive port with a bustling fishmarket. Shops line the Grand Rue, while the castle museum contains an exquisite ivory collection.

Giverny
See the famous bridge at Monet's house, now housing Japanese prints.

Jumièges Abbey
The ruins of the Romanesque abbey church loom over the peaceful green lawns where the monks once had formal gardens.

Mont St-Michel
Abbey, fortress and natural curiosity atop a granite mound in the marshy mouth of the Couesnon river. Invariably crowded.

Rouen
Half-timbered houses, energetic street life and magnificent churches, including the cathedral. Best museums are the Musée des Beaux-Arts; Musée le Seq-des-Tournelles (a collection of wrought ironwork); and the Musée Flaubert (the novelist's house, now a medical museum).

BEST D-DAY MUSEUMS AND MEMORIALS

On 6 June 1944 all five designated Normandy beaches – Sword, Juno, Gold, Omaha and Utah – were taken by the Allies. From this base they went on to liberate the rest of Europe.

American Normandy Cemetery
The largest of the war cemeteries. Many buried here were killed during the assault on 'bloody Omaha', the most difficult of the landings.

Arromanches
See the remains of the Mulberry Harbour, built in Britain for troop embarkation in the Normandy landings. The museum shows an explanatory film.

Normandy Memorial at Caen
This huge modern complex traces the history of the last war, with films of the D-Day landings and hopes for future peace. Unmissable.

Pegasus Bridge and Café Gondrée
The first building in France liberated by the Allies. Small museum.

Pointe du Hoc
With its battery in a bunker surrounded by shell craters, this was the scene of an extraordinary D-Day assault by American Rangers.

ALSACE AND LORRAINE
Good for food/wine, local colour and outdoor activities

ALSACE HAS singular traditions and character. The streets and houses gleam with Teutonic spruceness, and hearty local dishes delight in Germanic names such as *bäckeoffe* (meat and potato hotpot) and *ziwelküeche* (onion tart). France's prettiest wine route stretches for about 113 miles from Marlenheim in the north to Thann in the south.

The neighbouring *département* of Lorraine is much less attractive to tourists, but Nancy and Verdun are well worth visiting.

BEST BASES
Strasbourg
The seat of the Council of Europe is excellent for weekend breaks. The River Ill surrounds the old centre with its magnificent cathedral. Château Rohan contains three museums, the best of which is the Museum of Applied Arts. The Alsace Museum explains local traditions.

Wine Road (Route du Vin)
Practically any of the prosperous medieval villages on the Wine Road would be a suitable base for exploring. Ribeauvillé offers enticing shops; Riquewihr is one of the most attractive walled towns; tiny Eguisheim is surrounded by ramparts.

Wissembourg
Right on the German border, Wissembourg has a charming centre with bridges over branches of the River Lauter, and a Gothic church.

BEST SIGHTS AND EXCURSIONS
Château du Haut-Koenigsburg
Rebuilt by Kaiser Wilhelm at the turn of the century to his idea of a medieval castle, the château contains neo-Gothic panelling and frescos.

Colmar
Main administrative focus of Alsace's wine trade with unspoilt centre. The Unterlinden Museum has work by Schongauer and Grünewald.

Ecomusée d'Alsace
Half-timbered houses from all over Alsace have been reconstructed to form a working village at this open-air museum.

Nancy
Capital of Lorraine, noted for baroque buildings, fountains and iron-work. Art-nouveau buffs should visit the Musée de l'Ecole de Nancy.

Route des Crêtes
Road along the ridge of the Vosges. Superb views of glacial lakes, rolling pastures and gulleys from the Grand Ballon and the Hohneck.

Verdun
Over half a million soldiers died in the Battle of Verdun (1916). Visit a memorial museum, defensive forts and the Ossuary.

DORDOGNE AND LOT
Good for food/wine, outdoor activities and scenic landscape

SUNNY, RURAL France at its best, this popular region is small enough for most sights to be seen in a day's drive. Farmhouse-style *gîtes* for self-catering are widely available. Properties here get booked up quickly.

BEST BASES

Brantôme
Hugging the Dronne, the 'Venice of Périgord' has narrow streets with open spaces filled by riverside cafés and bars, and a lovely abbey.

Carjac
This large village is well organised for tourism but manages to feel relaxed and friendly. It is a good base for exploring the Lot valley.

Domme
Well positioned for exploring the chief sights of the Dordogne valley, this beautiful fortified town looks best in quiet mornings and evenings.

Martel
This medieval town surrounded by attractive countryside features magnificent houses, and is an ideal spot from which to explore the Upper Dordogne.

Montignac
Characterful small town, a good base from which to visit nearby prehistoric sights. Self-caterers favour the pretty countryside to the east.

Puy l'Evêque
The town is medieval and full of character; it is also well placed for exploring the Cahors vineyards and hidden countryside to the north.

Ribérac
This town on the Dronne is renowned for its market. The gentle countryside to the north-west is a popular self-catering area.

BEST SIGHTS AND EXCURSIONS

Caves
The prehistoric paintings in the brilliant reproduction cavern of Lascaux II and the genuine Font-de-Gaume are unmissable. Pech-Merle is also fascinating. Rise early to get one of the (limited) tickets.

Châteaux
Most French châteaux are best seen from the outside; Dordogne exceptions include Hautefort, Montal, Castelnaud and Castelnau-Bretenoux. Particularly scenic examples are at Belcastel, Beynac and Montfort.

Churches and abbeys
The abbey church of St-Amand-de-Coly has fortress-like walls. Beaulieu and Carennac have two of the best examples of the region's Last Judgements and Christs in Glory carved above the doorway.

Towns and villages
Visitors throng the charming domestic areas, particularly the honeypot villages of La Roque-Gageac and Domme on the Dordogne and St-Cirq-Lapopie on the Lot. Pretty Autoire and Limeuil are less crowded. The towns of Périgueux and Brantôme north of the Dordogne are worth exploring. Sarlat is touristy, but its architecture is worth a visit.

ATLANTIC COAST
Good for family holidays and food/wine

ENDLESS SANDY beaches on which Atlantic rollers break form the backdrop for family beach and camping holidays. Most resorts are straightforward and unsophisticated; sightseeing trips often involve a considerable drive inland. Bordeaux and its surrounding châteaux provide an alternative focus for wine buffs.

BEST RESORTS

Arcachon
- Large, lively and smart with a promenade and a casino.
- The beaches are muddy.

Biarritz
- Big and ritzy, Biarritz attracts surfers, families and the smart set.
- Splendid beaches, promenades and gardens.

Maubisson
- Good sports activities at this lively, well-maintained little resort.
- Sited in a corner of the huge Etang d'Hourtin-Carcans.

La Rochelle
- Handsome port, now a popular yachting centre.
- Medieval towers guard the harbour; the old quarter is lively.

Les Sables d'Olonne
- A modern family resort with a sandy beach.
- Apartment blocks, hotels and older villas line the wide promenade.

St-Jean-de-Luz
- Popular, stylish fishing port with traditional Basque houses.
- Good swimming in the sheltered bay.

St-Martin-de-Ré
- A lively little port surrounded by seventeenth-century ramparts.

BEST SIGHTS AND EXCURSIONS

Bayonne
- Appealing port on the Nive; the old town lies below the cathedral.
- The Musée Léon Bonnat has an excellent art collection.

Bordeaux
Central Bordeaux has grand eighteenth-century architecture, seen best around the Place de la Bourse. The old town has elegant shopping areas. The Musée des Beaux-Arts contains a fine collection, while the Maison du Vin offers tastings and information on vineyard visits.

Poitiers
Though not conspicuously charming, Poitiers has some fascinating churches including the Baptistery, Notre-Dame-la-Grande and St-Hilaire-le-Grand. Futuroscope is the jazzy theme park of the cinema.

Saintes
An architectural foretaste of the coastal style, Saintes offers a river cruise on the Charente and a well-preserved Roman amphitheatre.

Vineyards
To get a feel for the region and its history it is best to join one of the vineyard tours organised by the tourist office. Commentary in both French and English explains wine-tasting and wine-making. Book at least a day in advance, either directly with the châteaux or through the tourist office. The prettiest wine town is St-Emilion.

SOUTH OF FRANCE
Good for culture, beaches, food/wine, outdoor activities and scenic landscape

TRAFFIC JAMS, crowds and high prices are the hazards of a holiday on the glamorous Côte d'Azur – to the west, the purpose-built resorts of Languedoc are aimed more at the family self-catering and camping market. Inland, the most visited area is round the Lubéron and Mont Ventoux. If you really want to get away from it all, head for the Alpes-Maritimes, for stupendous valley views and bracing alpine air.

BEST RESORTS

For a seaside holiday, choose a resort west of Cannes. Most beaches here are public, with good sand; some are on splendid bays.

Argelès-Plage
● Central beach with smart collection of hotels and apartments bordering boulevard of palms, pines and gardens.
● Greater number of campsites than at any other resort in France.

Canet-Plage
● One of the best of Languedoc's purpose-built resorts, with plenty of bars and a degree of sophistication.
● Three museums and a tropical aquarium.

Cannes
● Manicured sandy beach, mostly divided up into pay beaches.
● Classy promenade, La Croisette, with hotels and restaurants.
● Attractive shopping streets, covered antique market and Le Suquet, a sleepy old town.

Cassis
● Most picturesque little resort west of St-Tropez.
● Boat trips explore the fjord-like inlets known as *calanques*.

Collioure
● The port is overlooked by the Château Royal, the beaches by the pink-domed church.
● Steep alleys house artists' studios and shops. It is extremely picturesque.

St-Raphael
● Lacks some Riviera style, but has a casino and lively nightlife.
● Broad sandy beaches, some of the best on the coast.

St-Tropez
● In season, the port cafés and boutiques are crammed with people; the historic back streets are full of trend-setting shops and galleries.
● Attractive hill villages on wooded Maures massif such as Ramatuelle, Gassin and Grimaud.
● Unspoilt beaches on the Ramatuelle peninsula are spacious, shady and sandy, but some distance from the main road and charge hefty entrance fees. Best to get there on two wheels or town shuttle bus.

Ste-Maxime
● More relaxed and less ostentatious than its famous neighbour.
● Resort beach is mostly public, with fine clean sand; there is another long public beach to the west.
● Palmy promenade with simple, colourful houses and pedestrianised streets behind.

NICE AND AROUND

THOUGH NO longer the super-fashionable resort of the British *beau monde*, Nice is still prosperous. It combines the charm of an old Italian port town with parks and flowers and candy-floss architecture from the Riviera's *belle époque*, despite traffic and high-season crowds.

BEST SIGHTS

Splitting the city into four distinct areas can be helpful when you are planning your sightseeing. Diverting museums, such as the Modern and Contemporary Art Museum, and galleries abound in the modernist 'new town'. In contrast, the dense old town has baroque chapels, small squares, colourful market stalls and pavement cafés. The outstanding Matisse and Marc Chagall Museums are in the smart Cimiez suburb, once the Roman settlement of Cemenelum. Back in town, Nice's most famous landmark, the Promenade des Anglais, edges the Bay of Angels.

BEST COASTAL EXCURSIONS

Abbaye de Fontfroide
Restored Cistercian abbey, a good place to escape the tourist bustle.

Antibes
The Grimaldi château houses one of the finest collections of Picasso's works. The old town is full of life and has a very colourful market.

Cathar hillforts
The Cathars, an unorthodox Christian sect, were condemned as heretics by the Pope. Among fortresses the Cathars built as refuges, Carcassonne was reconstructed in the nineteenth century, while the most spectacular are Peyrepertuse and Quéribus.

Corniche roads
Of the three coast roads, the Corniche Inférieure runs its length, serving all the resorts, inadequately. The exciting, precipitous Grande Corniche is the far-from-straight Roman road from Nice to Genoa. The Moyenne Corniche gives the best sea views and access to Eze, an astonishing perched village with a castle and exotic cactus garden.

Menton
Attractively Italianate old town; the new town resembles a spa town. The Cocteau Museum and his design of the town's register office are outstanding artistic features.

Monaco
This tiny principality occupies less than a square mile of ground and makes an excellent day out. Touristy old Monaco boasts a miniature palace and a stunning Oceanography Museum. Monte Carlo, the principality's playground, has a casino, luxury hotels and exclusive shops.

St-Paul-de-Vence
This artists' village is a tasteful tourist trap, full of smart little galleries. The Maeght Foundation is an excellent collection of modern art.

Vence
A less crowded walled town with shops and galleries and the Rosaire Chapel, conceived in its entirety by Matisse.

BEST SIGHTS

Abbeys
Three Cistercian abbeys are the splendidly isolated Abbaye de Sénanque, the Abbaye de Silvacane above the River Durance and the Abbaye du Thoronet, offering insights into monks' lives.

Aix-en-Provence
The fascinating old town has a colourful flower market. Artists can seek out Cézanne's studio and the Vasarély Foundation.

Arles
The site of Van Gogh's last years, Arles has a Roman arena, an older ruined theatre and the beautiful church of St-Trophime.

Avignon
An exciting and cosmopolitan city, especially during the summer arts and music festival, Avignon is renowned for its Popes' Palace.

Les Baux
The 'dead' village is an atmospheric ruin providing a glorious panorama; the 'living' village's narrow streets are lined with expensive and very tourist-orientated shops.

Nîmes
Chic and stylish, Nîmes' centre is pedestrianised. The Maison Carrée is a perfect Roman temple and there is also an amphitheatre. The Pont du Gard, a spectacular Roman aqueduct, straddles the Gard 14 miles away.

Orange
Orange's unique theatre is the best-preserved of all Roman theatres.

Vaison-la-Romaine
Extensive Roman remains include a theatre, houses and an elegant portico. A small museum houses excellent mosaics.

Verdon
At the Grand Canyon, cliffs up to 2,300 feet high plunge down to the river. Here you can canoe, walk or raft; by car, the best views are from the Belvedere Trascaire, Balcons de la Mescla and the Pont de l'Artuby.

BEST TOURING

Alpes-Maritimes
For real escapists, a remote and adventurous landscape of imposing gorges and plunging valleys. Barcelonnette is a lively town, while St-Martin-Vésubie is a good base for walkers, riders and canoeists.

The Camargue
A harsh, uncompromisingly beautiful triangle of reedy marsh, the Camargue is ideal to explore in one or two days. To really experience the Camargue take a guided tour on a horse to see the herds of black bulls, wild white horses and pink pelicans. The main resort is Stes-Maries-de-la-Mer – a lively, and somewhat tacky, outpost with an attractive square.

Lubéron and Vaucluse plateau
The Petit Lubéron's gentle hills cradle fetching villages such as Bonnieux, Lacoste and Ménerbes. The wooded Vaucluse plateau hides a network of underground caves and passages, notably the Fontaine-de-Vaucluse. Attractive villages are Gordes, Roussillon and Rustrel.

Tarn gorges
The forested gorges of the Tarn, Jonte and Dourbie are popular with walkers, canoeists and climbers. Base yourself in Meyrueis or Ste-Enimie, or, for more seclusion, in the Cévennes. Aven Armand is an enormous cavern filled with a forest of stalagmites, while Montpellier-le-Vieux is a fantastic jumble of limestone outcrops sitting above the Dourbie.

Var
This forested area gives way to vineyards and olive groves. Attractive villages are Moissac Bellevue, Fox-Amphoux, Cotignac and Tourtour.

Mont Ventoux
Highest mountain between the Alps and the Pyrenees.

PYRENEES
Good for outdoor activities and scenic landscape

THE CENTRAL Pyrenees have the highest and most spectacular scenery, while the east and west are best for attractive touring.

BEST BASES

Lescun
Pleasantly sleepy village in the mountains, a good base for walking.

Bagnères-de-Luchon
Fashionable, lively Pyrenean spa in a wide flat bowl surrounded by mountains. Its waters are the most radioactive in France.

Luz-St-Saveur
Combined spa resort and old village in a beautiful mountain valley.

Pau
This cosmopolitan and relaxed regional capital has an imposing château and famous views of the mountains.

St-Jean-Pied-de-Port
St-Jean-Pied-de-Port, a popular stopping-place for pilgrims *en route* to Santiago since medieval times, has a pretty, if rather touristy, old town.

BEST SIGHTS

Caves
Niaux's cave paintings rival those at Lascaux in the Dordogne, but numbers are strictly limited and you will need to reserve a place in advance (call 00 33 561 05 8837). See vast groups of stalagmites and stalactites at Lombrives and Labouiche (the latter involves a magnificent underground boat trip).

Romanesque churches
The fine abbeys of St-Michel-de-Cuxa and St-Martin-de-Canigou, both near Vernet-les-Bains, date from the ninth and tenth centuries. St-Martin is remarkably sited on top of a rocky crag.

BEST TOURING

Cirque de Troumouse
Vast amphitheatre of snow-patched rocky peaks, more coming into view as you ascend numerous hairpin bends.

Col d'Aubisque
Lovely col curving along a long, smooth ridge with views across the peaks. Spectacular Cirque de Litor and pretty Col de Soulor.

Col d'Erroymendi
Winding up through forest from Larrau, you reach open slopes and a plateau with splendid views.

Col de Tantes
You can look down on Spain from the top of this col. Climb the grassy knoll of Pic des Tantes for wide views of the cirque and valley.

Col de Tourmalet
Vast grassy slopes with rocky outcrops. The col seems rather Scottish in character.

Gorges de Galamus
Spectacularly steep and narrow chasm, with rock overhanging the road in parts. Steps down the rockface lead to the hermitage of St-Antoine.

Haute Vallée de l'Aude
From Quillan to Mont-Louis the road passes between sheer rock walls, then through wild wooded scenery with several lakes.

Route du Pic du Midi de Bigorre
Narrow road climbing above the snowline by steep hairline bends. Stupendous views of a forest of jagged peaks, and the plain of Gascony.

CORSICA
Good for beaches, outdoor activities and scenic landscape

THE MOST mountainous Mediterranean island combines dramatic landscapes and good beaches. Nationalist protests about over-development have prevented most of the building-site eyesores. There have been stories about (rare) attacks on holidaymakers by Corsican nationalists.

BEST RESORTS

Bonifacio
● Attractive, bustling port with a dramatic harbour set in a fjord.
● Boat trips are available. You need transport to get to a beach.

Calvi
● Good for a stay-put holiday, with a long beach and interesting shops.
● Excursions are available on land and sea. The citadel is impressive.

Porticcio
● Porticcio, with its excellent beach, is rapidly developing.
● Vegetation shrouds slopes rising gently to the peak of Monte Rosso.

Porto-Vecchio
● Peaceful town near superb beaches at Palombaggia and Santa-Giulia.
● Olive groves divide old town from modern harbour.

BEST SIGHTS AND EXCURSIONS

Ajaccio
The old town, with its waterfront cafés, feels more French than anywhere else on the island. Napoleon's birth house disappoints, but Cardinal Fesch's museum contains an excellent art collection.

Les Calanche and Gorges of Spelunca
From Piana the road to Porto snakes through Les Calanche: misshapen towers and stacks of pink granite. From Porto to Evisa the road hugs the Gorges of Spelunca. Ample stopping places to view the precipices.

Col de Bavella
The D638 from Porto-Vecchio to Zonza passes cork groves and pine forests. From the Col de Bavella the dramatic Aiguilles de Bavella seem to glow in the sunshine.

Corte
The former capital of Corsica is on a gigantic outcrop, encircled by peaks that provide challenging terrain and picturesque backdrops for walkers. Narrow stairways lead up to the belvedere, a dramatic look-out point.

Filitosa
A row of five 4,000-year-old statue-menhirs has faces, swords and belts eroded but still visible. They are the first Western European representations of human portraiture in stone.

Gorges of Asco

The road narrows and climbs along the cleft forged by the Asco beneath the sheer crags on either side. After Asco it widens as it runs up to Haut-Asco, the starting point for some tough mountain walks.

WHEN TO GO

FRANCE HAS something to offer most times of the year. If you are looking for out-of-season sunshine, the south coast has the mildest climate, and the Riviera resorts are lively from March to October. The time to avoid is the French peak holiday period of late July and early August. The same advice applies to Paris, which looks its best in spring and autumn (though September sees a lot of trade fairs); in July and August many restaurants and museums are closed.

Average daily maximum temperature °C											
London 6	7	10	13	17	20	22	21	19	14	10	7
Paris 6	7	12	16	20	23	25	24	21	16	10	7
JAN	FEB	MAR	APR	MAY	JUN	JUL	AUG	SEP	OCT	NOV	DEC
Paris 17	14	12	13	12	12	12	13	13	13	15	16
London 15	13	11	12	12	11	12	11	13	13	15	15
Average number of rainy days per month											

Average daily maximum temperature °C											
London 6	7	10	13	17	20	22	21	19	14	10	7
Nice 13	13	15	17	20	24	27	27	25	21	17	13
JAN	FEB	MAR	APR	MAY	JUN	JUL	AUG	SEP	OCT	NOV	DEC
Nice 9	7	8	9	8	5	2	4	7	9	9	9
London 15	13	11	12	12	11	12	11	13	13	15	15
Average number of rainy days per month											

PACKAGE TRAVEL

WELL OVER 150 tour operators feature France in their brochures – far too many to list here. The very useful *Reference Guide for Travellers in France*, published by the French Government Tourist Office, has a comprehensive list of tour operators with a region-by-region break-down of types of holiday featured. A selection of tour operators is listed to get you started. The variety of holidays and activities in France is enormous, ranging from cookery courses and gastronomy tours, wildlife and golfing holidays to multi-activity sporting holidays in the Alps.

Tour operators

Activity holidays: Action Vacances (multi-activity), Andante (archaeology), Belle France (cycling), Blakes, Andrew Brock Travel, French Country Cruises (boating), French Golf Holidays (golf), Hoseasons (boating), Susi Madron's (cycling), VFB (multi-activity) **Battlefields**: Midas, Holt's Travel **Camping**: Canvas Holidays, Carisma, Club Cantabrica, Eurocamp, Eurosites, Keycamp, Select France, Sunsites **City breaks**: Airtours, British Airways Holidays, Cresta, Crystal, Inghams, Kirker, Made to Measure, Osprey, Thomson, Time Off, Travelscene **Cultural**: Andante, British Museum Traveller, Cox & Kings, Martin Randall, Prospect, Travel for the Arts **Self-catering gîtes, villas and apartments**: Air France, Allez France, Bowhills, Bridgewater, Brittany Direct, Club Cantabrica, Collineige, Corsican Affair, Corsican Places, Cresta, Crystal, Destination Provence, Dominiques Villas, Driveline Europe, Eurovillages, Fourseasons, French Life, Headwater, Inghams, Inntravel, Interhome, Just France, Lagrange, Lakes & Mountains, Meon, Motours, Normandie Vacances, Palmer & Parker, Simply Corsica, Something Special, Sovereign, Sunselect, Travelscene, Vacances en Campagne, VFB, Vintage Travel, Voyages Ilena **Walking**: Alternative Travel Group, Exodus, Explore Worldwide, Headwater, HF Holidays, Inntravel, Naturetrek, Ramblers Holidays, Sherpa, Waymark **Wildlife/birdwatching**: Limosa, Ornitholidays, Sunbird, Wildlife Worldwide **Wine**: Arblaster & Clarke, Winetrails

---

INDEPENDENT TRAVEL

THERE ARE direct flights from Britain to many French airports, and ferry/catamaran/hovercraft services from Dover to Calais; Ramsgate to Dunkirk; Folkestone to Boulogne; Newhaven to Dieppe; Portsmouth to Le Havre, Caen, Cherbourg and St Malo; Southampton to Cherbourg; Poole to St Malo; and Plymouth to Roscoff. Ferry fares are grouped into bands that depend on the time of day, time of year, and day of the week you intend to travel. To find the best possible deal you need to travel outside July and August, but if you are tied to school holidays it is wise to avoid Friday and Saturday departures and Saturday and Sunday returns.

Le Shuttle transports cars from Folkestone to Calais; foot passengers can take Eurostar from London Waterloo or Ashford to Paris Gare du Nord.

France is quite well served by its motorway system, though tolls make motorways expensive. N-roads (similar to British A-roads) link the main towns and cities but can become clogged by lorries using them as toll-free options. In contrast, D-roads are usually empty, fast and often arrow-straight. Official *Bison Futé* motoring maps, indicating major bottlenecks and alternative routes, are available from the French Government Tourist Office or from service stations in France. Seat-belts are compulsory in France, and you must carry a warning triangle unless your car has hazard warning lights. You are also obliged to carry your vehicle registration document, full driving licence and current insurance certificate. The minimum driving age is 18. Unleaded petrol is widely available; petrol stations on motorways are usually more expensive.

Rail travel is an efficient and fast alternative to taking your own car. Eurodomino Rover Tickets offer unlimited travel on any three, five or ten days in one month. There are few long-distance buses; local services are run by SNCF and link with trains.

Hotels are officially graded from one up to four stars, with a four-star luxury category. Probably the best-known guide to hotels and restaurants is the *Michelin Red Guide*, but a good source of information on cheap, family-run hotels is the *Logis de France* guide, available from the French Government Tourist Office, which also publishes a guide to *Café Couettes* (B&B accommodation).

Self-catering accommodation ranges from simple country cottages to modern purpose-built blocks.

Camping and caravan sites are graded from one to four star. Those in the main seaside areas are often large and organised, with lots of facilities. Sites in rural areas are usually smaller and simpler.

RED TAPE, HEALTH AND SAFETY

BRITISH PASSPORT-HOLDERS do not need a visa to visit France. Mainland France does not have any particular health or safety problems – just take the usual precautions.

Bomb attacks, mainly on public buildings, continue throughout Corsica. Take care in town centres and near public buildings, and look out for suspicious packages. There have been some attacks on British-registered yachts. For the latest advice contact the Foreign Office Travel Advice Unit (see page 11).

MORE INFORMATION French Government Tourist Office, 178 Piccadilly, London W1V 9AL, tel (09068) 244123 (premium rate number), web site: *www.franceguide.com/gb/france.html*

COST OF LIVING £££

GAMBIA

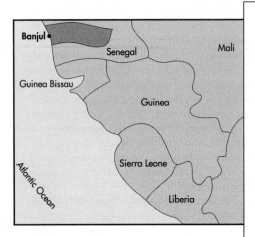

F OR THOSE looking for a taste of Africa with minimal hassle, the
Gambia has the advantages of being English-speaking, accessible
(direct flight time from London is under six hours, with no time
zone change), and affordable. Tourist development has progressed at
the laid-back pace that characterises the Gambian way of life. Even the
most visited areas are relatively unspoilt but facilities can be basic.

BEST RESORTS

● Most tourists stay at beach hotels in **Bakau**, **Fajara**, **Kololi** or **Kotu**,
on the palm-fringed Atlantic coast south of the Gambia river.
● The hotels in Bakau and Fajara are within walking distance of Bakau
village which has a market and a few shops; Kotu and Kololi are
remoter and more exclusive. Hotels are small-scale, with buildings set
in lush gardens with birds and tropical flowers.
● Beaches outside resort areas stretch for 25 miles, wild and deserted.
● The run-down capital, **Banjul**, is a relic of colonial days with a busy
market but otherwise little to offer tourists.
● Many hotel tour programmes include a cruise up the Gambia river
by motor-powered *pirogue* (dug-out canoe). The river banks are almost
completely undeveloped and home to a vast bird population.

BEST SIGHTS AND EXCURSIONS

Abuko Nature Reserve
This is a small but rewarding forest reserve to explore on foot. Families

of monkeys, including patas, green monkeys and red colobus, are easy to spot in the trees, and with a little patience you should also see many migrant and resident birds, including parrots, kingfishers and sunbirds.

Boat trips

Record-breaking catches of barracuda, shark and marlin have been made off Cape Point, east of Banjul, and several charter companies will provide anglers with a fully-equipped ocean-going boat with skipper and crew for full-day or half-day sport fishing trips.

For those who prefer calmer waters, the maze of mangrove creeks at the mouth of the Gambia river is a paradise for birdwatchers, and the fishing here is so plentiful that even a novice stands an excellent chance of hauling in a ladyfish, butterfish or grouper. Fishing boats and tackle can be hired through hotel representatives or direct from the private operators at Oyster Creek, off the highway outside Banjul.

Juffure

Many hotels offer unashamedly touristy *Roots* tours to this, the supposed birthplace of Kunta Kinte, the Mandinka ancestor of the African-American writer Alex Haley. Juffure is a simple village of thatched, mud-brick huts off the north bank of the Gambia river. Present-day members of the Kinte family allow visitors to take photos, for a fee.

Markets

The market at Serekunda, the Gambia's largest town, is a maze of rickety stalls and makeshift pitches selling everything from palm oil by the cupful to chickens by the crateful. Colourful but chaotic and definitely not for the faint-hearted, this is an excellent hunting-ground for batik cloth, beads and locally made jewellery. Banjul's Albert Market is smaller and tamer, good for cheap tapes of West African music. For woodcarvings, musical instruments and antique masks, the market at Brikama, a small town south of Serekunda, is worth a visit.

Wrestling

Late in the afternoon on Saturdays and Sundays, lively inter-tribal wrestling matches take place in open-air arenas in Serekunda. Cheering on contestants as they strut around the arena accompanied by teams of whistlers and drummers is all part of the ritual.

WHEN TO GO

THE GAMBIA'S main tourist season runs from October to April, with almost guaranteed sunshine by day, and cool nights. Although the Gambia is a predominantly Muslim country, enthusiastic Christmas celebrations, with music and processions, take place in Banjul and on the coast. The rainy season is from June to September, bringing oppressively humid weather broken by sudden downpours. The brilliant displays of fresh green growth are more than adequate compensation, and most of the rain falls at night. Late September and October are hot and dry, like a Mediterranean summer.

Average daily maximum temperature °C												
London	6	7	10	13	17	20	22	21	19	14	10	7
Banjul	30	31	32	30	30	31	31	30	31	32	32	30
	JAN	FEB	MAR	APR	MAY	JUN	JUL	AUG	SEP	OCT	NOV	DEC
Banjul	<1	1	0	1	1	7	17	22	18	9	1	1
London	15	13	11	12	12	11	12	11	13	13	15	15
Average number of rainy days per month												

PACKAGE TRAVEL

FOR RESORT-BASED beach holidays, the best deals are packages from the UK. The main options in the brochures are a beach holiday or a birdwatching holiday, both in the winter months (October to April).

Tour operators

Beach packages: Airtours, Cosmos, First Choice, Gambia Experience, Thomson **Birdwatching**: Limosa, Ornitholidays

INDEPENDENT TRAVEL

IF YOU prefer to rough it in simpler accommodation, or to tour independently, you can choose between a scheduled flight or a flight-only charter deal from Gatwick or Manchester.

Many visitors come here purely to soak up the winter sun (and enjoy the riotous sunsets), barely venturing outside their hotel, but the more adventurous can head inland to explore the Gambia's open bush country and sample something of traditional village life.

The Gambia has a few car-hire firms in the Banjul and coastal areas; rates are high. If you plan to venture up-country in the rainy season a four-wheel-drive vehicle is essential. Private taxis can be hired by the half-day or day. The main hotels have their own taxi ranks and discourage guests from using 'unauthorised' taxis for security reasons.

Local transport by bus or bush taxi (shared cars, minibuses or vans which travel along fixed routes) can be uncomfortable but is very cheap. The transport hub for inland destinations is Serekunda. The bush taxi stands are near the market; touts round up travellers and collect fares for their vehicles, which leave when full.

The atmosphere and quality of accommodation at package resort hotels vary a great deal, with some catering predominantly for young singles and couples (offering water sports and nightlife), some geared to families (though none has much in the way of facilities for very young children), and some more sedate in style. All the larger hotels stage regular evenings of traditional music (*balafon*, *kora* and drumming) and tribal dancing. There is no official hotel grading system, and standards are generally more modest than in Europe – only the top hotels have air-conditioning, fridges, telephones or televisions.

Although you will not find them in the package tour brochures, the Gambia also has a good choice of small, simple guesthouses, catering for independent travellers, expatriate volunteers and locals.

RED TAPE, HEALTH AND SAFETY

NO VISA is required by British nationals staying for less than three months. Airport tax of £10 is levied on travellers leaving by air.

Visitors are strongly advised to take anti-malaria tablets – see your GP or a specialist travel clinic for advice on what tablets to take as well as other recommended vaccinations. Anti-malaria tablets do not, however, provide total protection against infection, and it is best to avoid being bitten by using insect repellents, electric vaporisers and mosquito nets. Cover up arms and legs, especially at dawn and dusk.

One of the Gambia's greatest assets is the genuine warmth and hospitality of its people. Newcomers should, however, bear in mind that outside wealthier residential and hotel areas the gulf between tourists and local people can be acutely felt. Hustlers – young locals who make a living by badgering tourists to buy souvenirs or drugs, change money, or employ them as a guide – can be a nuisance. It is 7unwise to walk along empty stretches of beach alone, and inadvisable to venture far outside your hotel compound after dark without a trusted driver or guide. Women travelling alone may feel particularly vulnerable. For the latest Foreign Office advice see page 11.

MORE INFORMATION Gambian National Tourist Office, 57 Kensington Court, London W8 5DQ, tel 020-7376 0093, web site: *www.thegambia-touristoff.co.uk*

COST OF LIVING £

GERMANY

HIGHLIGHTS

Culture
*Bavaria, Berlin,
eastern Germany,
Munich*

Nightlife
Berlin

Local colour
*Bavaria,
northern Germany*

Outdoor activities
*Bavaria,
Black Forest*

Scenic landscape
*Bavaria, Black Forest,
Rhineland*

BERLIN
Good for culture and nightlife

THE INFAMOUS Berlin Wall is down, the German parliament is back from Bonn and the city is once again at the helm of a united Germany. Today Berlin is a city on the move with the biggest construction project in Europe since the Second World War.

BEST SIGHTS

Brandenburg Gate
When the Wall existed, the area round the Brandenburg Gate was part of no-man's-land, and sealed off. Today this imposing edifice is the centre of a trade in alleged bits of Wall and military memorabilia.

Checkpoint Charlie Museum
This vivid, if partisan, history of the Wall includes accounts of escape schemes. The best section of the old wall by the Muhlenstrasse was covered in celebratory paintings back in 1989, but these, like the wall itself, are fading into a memory.

Dahlem

Berlin's best-known museums are housed in an enormous complex south-west of the city. Highlights include the Museums of Oriental Art, Ethnology and Islamic Art, and the Picture Gallery.

Museum Island

Formerly in East Berlin, the Pergamon is a superb collection of Greek, Roman and Mesopotamian antiquities. Other collections include the Egyptian Museum and the Early Christian and Byzantine exhibits.

Reichstag

Since it reopened in 1999 the Reichstag, the German parliament, has become one of the city's most popular tourist attractions. Sir Norman Foster's innovative glass dome is open to the public, offering sweeping views of the city.

MUNICH
Good for culture

MUNICH IS a great cultural centre for film, art, theatre and music. Its *Oktoberfest*, a two-week beer festival in late September, is the world's biggest homage to beer with over six million litres consumed.

BEST SIGHTS

Alte and Neue Pinakothek

The 'old' collection has fine Dutch and Flemish works, Bruegel's *Land of Cockayne*, and Dürer's Christ-like self-portrait. The 'younger' collection includes sculpture by Rodin and some of Goya's Black Paintings.

Dachau

The former concentration camp in this market town ten miles from Munich is overwhelmingly flat and grey: 28 of the 30 barrack blocks have been flattened and all that remains are numbered beds of gravel.

Haufbrahaus

Munich more than any other German city flows with beer. Outside the Oktoberfest the Haupbrauhaus offers a slice of Bavarian beer culture as well as hearty local food in atmospheric surrounds.

Nymphenburg Palace

Rococo palace in a formal park that includes botanical gardens. In the grounds is the blue-and-white hunting lodge of Amalienburg.

St John Nepomuk Church
A superb Bavarian baroque church which resembles an opera house.

BAVARIA
Good for culture, local colour, outdoor activities and scenic landscape

FLYING THE blue-and-white regional flag, Bavaria retains a strong independent identity, flaunting the national dress of *Lederhosen und Dirndl* and celebrating with legendary drinking sessions.

BEST SIGHTS AND EXCURSIONS

Augsburg
Grand Renaissance mansions line Augsburg's main street, symbolic of the city's former wealth. To the east is the Fuggerei, the world's first social housing project for the poor.

Bamberg
This gem of a city on the River Regnitz has an eighteenth-century town hall at its base. An imposing Gothic cathedral stands high above the town. This 1,000-year-old city is arguably the most beautiful in Germany. UNESCO declared it a World Heritage City in 1993.

Bayreuth
Wagner's house is now a museum. The spartan *Festspielhaus*, acoustically perfect, is packed each August during the Bayreuth Festival.

Oberammergau
Famous for its Passion Play, staged every ten years, the village is attractive, but the shops selling woodcarvings make the biggest impression.

Ottobeuren Abbey
This extravagant baroque church is a profusion of sugar almond, pink and yellow, with arches decorated with gold and white stucco.

Passau
This cathedral city sits on a narrow neck of land where the Rivers Inn and Ilz meet the Danube. The old town is a cheerful jumble of stone houses and towers; boats on the quay take trippers on pleasure cruises.

Regensburg
The knobbly twin towers of Regensburg's cathedral dominate huddled

medieval stone houses. Ludwig I set up Walhalla, an unnerving shrine of 118 marble busts just outside the city, to honour German heroes.

Rothenburg ob der Tauber
So perfect it is almost a parody: the medieval town centre, surrounded by ramparts, has remained completely untouched. Charming, less-famous Dinkelsbühl and Nördlingen are similarly pristine.

Royal castles
Between 1864 and 1886 Bavaria's mad King Ludwig II spent vast amounts of state funds to build three fantastic castles. Neuschwanstein, bristling with white turrets and never finished, was designed by a stage painter; its interior is painted with heroic scenes. Linderhof, a smaller, completed rococo castle, has lovely grounds containing a Moorish pavilion with cascades of water. Uncompleted Herrenchiemsee was to have been the grandest, a replica of Versailles, but money ran out. Opposite Neuschwanstein is Hohenschwangau, where Ludwig grew up.

Würzburg
The official start of the famed 'Romantic Road'. The baroque *Residenz*, once home to the prince-bishops, has a fine chapel, a magnificent two-tier staircase and also a huge ceiling fresco by Tiepolo. Würzburg is also the centre of Franconian wine production.

BEST RESORTS

Berchtesgaden
● Facing the peaks of the Watzmann, Berchtesgaden is in the most beautiful region of the German Alps.
● Go boating on the ice-green waters of nearby Königssee.
● Take a bus trip up the spectacular road to Kehlstein, or Eagle's Nest, built for Hitler on his fiftieth birthday.

Garmisch-Partenkirchen
● A busy town with smart shops and hotels, lying below the Zugspitze.
● On offer are mountain rides and easy walks.

Lindau
● Small island in the Bodensee with a relaxing harbourside promenade.
● Steamers carry day-trippers to Switzerland.

RHINELAND
Good for scenic landscape

ONE OF the great transport arteries of Europe, the Rhine valley can be disappointing, industrialised and traffic-ridden. But the tributaries, such as the Mosel and the Nahe, have some attractive scenery.

BEST SIGHTS

Cologne (Köln)
See the city best from the river, where the twin spires of the stunning Gothic cathedral dominate the skyline. Next door is the Roman-Germanic Museum, built around a Dionysos mosaic. The Wallraf-Richartz Museum has modern sculpture and pop art as well as Cologne masters.

Heidelberg
Heidelberg's romantic Neckar valley setting, its part-ruined castle and informal student bars attract many tourists. The courtyard and gardens are the best parts of the castle. Take the Philosopher's Path for fine views.

Mainz
The Gutenberg Museum houses the famous bible, also the hand press used to print it. Mainz also has a reconstructed Romanesque cathedral.

Trier
Birthplace of Karl Marx, Trier has some unmissable Roman remains: the Porta Nigra, an arcaded gate, and the Kaiserthermen, a heated bathing complex.

Worms
The cathedral's western chancel is a celebration of Rhineland Romanesque style, while the Luther Monument commemorates the city's association with the great Protestant reformer.

BEST CASTLES

Many of the Rhine's castles are best regarded as part of the scenery, and in most cases do not merit the uphill trek which their closer investigation usually requires.

Eltz
A nest of sharply pointed turrets rising from an outcrop in the Eltz valley. In the treasure chamber is a glittering array of gold and silver drinking vessels.

Marksburg
The only medieval castle on the Rhine never to be blown up or stormed stands above Braubach, on a narrow cone of rock.

Rheinfels
This desolate rambling ruin is a good spot for watching the barges manoeuvring around the Lorelei rock.

Stolzenfels
Rebuilt in the 1830s by Friedrich Wilhelm IV, the castle attempts an interesting, if self-conscious, recreation of the spirit of the Middle Ages.

BEST TOURING

Ahr valley
A smaller Rhine valley, with vineyards and castles. The prettiest scenery is at Altenahr, the most dramatic between the Ahr valley and the Mosel.

Lahn valley
The least crowded of the Rhine's tributaries enjoys tranquil countryside. Bad Ems, a sedate riverside spa, was Kaiser Wilhelm's favourite resort. Limburg is a medieval town, now encircled by modern development.

Mosel valley
Between Trier and Koblenz the Mosel river curves through a valley of terraced vineyards. The landscape is broken by wine villages and the occasional ruined castle. Bernkastel is a handsome old town, packed with wine cellars.

Rhine gorge
A V-shaped furrow in the schist massif, the Rhine gorge is the most beautiful and most crowded area. To escape take the Rheingoldstrasse, a scenic route linking Boppard, St Goar, Oberwesel and Bacharach.

BLACK FOREST
Good for outdoor activities and scenic landscape

FOR A civilised break combining spa baths and gentle woodland walks, a holiday in the Black Forest is hard to beat.

BEST BASES

Baden-Baden
The resort centres on a park and an avenue of plane trees. Visit ornate nineteenth-century buildings, an art nouveau *Trinkhalle* where you can taste saline waters, and a sumptuous neoclassical *Kurhaus* and casino.

Freiburg

A 370-ft cathedral spire dominates this city, spiritually ruled by its university. Near the cathedral are medieval and eighteenth-century houses and terrace cafés. The Augustiner Museum houses religious art.

BEST SIGHTS AND EXCURSIONS

Furtwangen

The Black Forest, not Switzerland, is the home of the cuckoo clock – a fact celebrated in this collection of over 1,000 timepieces.

Gutach

The Schwarzwald Freilicht Museum, a collection of reconstructed sixteenth-century buildings, forms Germany's most impressive open-air museum.

Triberg

The Heimatsmuseum is a collection of pianolas and organs. It displays mannikins which burst into life when you put a coin in the slot.

NORTHERN GERMANY

Good for local colour

FEW OF the bigger cities in this area have much charm. The real gems are the small historic towns, not visited by many foreign tourists.

BEST SIGHTS

Bremen

The focus of the city is the market square: a large, irregular, cobbled area bordered by ornate medieval town-houses and the massive, twin-towered Romanesque cathedral.

Goslar

The medieval old town is finely preserved, with fan-shaped carvings, oriels and crooked arcades adorning streets of half-timbered houses.

Lübeck

This medieval town of gateways, red-brick houses with stepped gables, intimate courtyards and fine churches makes for enjoyable exploring; the soaring Gothic Marienkirche is a particular highlight.

EASTERN GERMANY
Good for culture

BEST SIGHTS

Potsdam
About 12 miles south-west of Berlin, the summer retreat of the Prussian kings contains many houses and villas. Best are Frederick the Great's Sans Souci Palace, with fine marquetry, and the grotto of the Neue Palace.

Weimar
Weimar is a picturesque town with museums commemorating the German cultural giants – from Goethe and Schiller onwards – who graced its heyday.

WHEN TO GO

ROSENMONTAG, THE day before Shrove Tuesday, is celebrated with huge carnivals in the Rhineland area around Cologne and Mainz. In August and early September, wine festivals abound throughout the same region. Munich is perhaps best known for its *Oktoberfest*, which usually takes place in the second half of September. In December, nearly every large town holds festive Christmas fairs, with decorated stalls and carol-singing. The most impressive Christmas fair is held in Munich's Marienplatz.

Average daily maximum temperature °C											
London 6	7	10	13	17	20	22	21	19	14	10	7
Berlin 2	3	8	13	19	22	24	23	20	13	7	3
JAN	FEB	MAR	APR	MAY	JUN	JUL	AUG	SEP	OCT	NOV	DEC
Berlin 17	15	12	13	12	13	14	14	12	14	16	15
London 15	13	11	12	12	11	12	11	13	13	15	15
Average number of rainy days per month											

Average daily maximum temperature °C											
London 6	7	10	13	17	20	22	21	19	14	10	7
Munich 1	3	9	14	18	21	23	23	20	13	7	2
JAN	FEB	MAR	APR	MAY	JUN	JUL	AUG	SEP	OCT	NOV	DEC
Munich 16	16	13	15	15	17	16	16	13	13	15	15
London 15	13	11	12	12	11	12	11	13	13	15	15
Average number of rainy days per month											

PACKAGE TRAVEL

PACKAGES ARE by air, rail or ferry. Many of the UK tour operators to Germany are coach tour operators offering stay-put holidays with daily excursions or coach tours of the Rhine and Mosel valleys, the Black Forest or Bavaria.

Other ways to get about include booking rail passes, arranging accommodation in advance, or following one of the self-drive itineraries – for instance the Romantic Road, which runs south from Würzburg in the north of Bavaria to Schwangau in the Alps along the Austrian border, or alternatively exploring the wine regions of the Mosel and the Rhine.

Accommodation includes holiday parks, self-catering apartments, staying with a family, farm-stays, guesthouses and hotels.

Activities include cruises on the Rhine and Danube, walking, sailing, cycling, canoeing, cultural and music tours, and wine and beer festivals.

Most city breaks offer Berlin and Munich for one or more nights, but a few operators also go to Cologne, Dresden, Frankfurt and Hamburg.

Tour operators

Battlefields: Holts' Tours, Midas **City breaks**: British Airways Holidays, Bridge Travel, Cresta, Crystal, Inghams, Made to Measure, Osprey, DFDS Seaways, Sovereign, Stena Line, Time Off, Travelscene **Coach tours**: Excelsior, Leger, Shearings, Wallace Arnold **Specialists**: DER, Moswin, Taber **Walking**: Bents, Ramblers Holidays, Sherpa, Waymark **Other activities**: Ace Study Tours, Anglo Dutch (cycling), Bents (cycling), Eurocamp, Select Sites (camping), Ffestiniog Travel (rail tours), Interhome, Peter Delmann (river cruising), Martin Randall (opera), Prospect (cultural), Solo's (singles), Swan Hellenic (river cruising), Travel for the Arts (cultural)

INDEPENDENT TRAVEL

THE COUNTRY is easy to reach from any of the eastern Channel ports, and reduced short-break ferry fares are good value. The major German airports are Berlin, Frankfurt and Munich. The advent of the budget airlines has also had a cost-cutting impact with Buzz flying to Berlin, Dusseldorf, Frankfurt and Hamburg. The extensive internal air network is expensive.

With the recent expansion of European high-speed trains, getting to Germany via Eurostar is an increasingly viable option.

Walkers and cyclists can use the wide-ranging and efficient rail network – various rover tickets are available. There are few long-distance bus services; most buses run between towns and villages not linked by rail. The exceptions are some scenic routes, such as the Romantic Road.

The Germans are wedded to their cars, and the network of motorways (*Autobahnen*) and other roads is good, except for some secondary roads in eastern Germany. No tolls are levied at the moment, though the idea is being discussed. Unleaded petrol is available everywhere. The speed limit of 80mph on *Autobahnen* is only a recommendation: that speck in your mirror is, within seconds, a Porsche three feet from your bumper. Overtake with extreme care, and be well insured. Seatbelts must be worn in the front and back, and children under 12 must sit in a special seat in the back. On-the-spot fines can be imposed for speeding.

Larger hotels tend to be characterless and unfriendly. The best-value accommodation is in smaller pensions and B&Bs, which offer spotless rooms and hearty breakfasts. Look out for signs saying *Zimmer frei*.

Germany also boasts a very well-developed system of clean and efficient youth hostels. Information on these is available on the web site: *www.hostellinginternational.com*

RED TAPE, HEALTH AND SAFETY

BRITISH PASSPORT-HOLDERS do not require a visa to visit Germany. The country has no particular health or safety problems: just take the usual precautions (see pages 10–12).

MORE INFORMATION German National Tourist Office, PO Box 2695, London W1A 3TN, tel 020-7317 0908, brochure line (09001) 600100 (premium rate number), web site: *www.germany-tourism.de*

Proceeds from the premium-rate number go towards postage and packing; people writing in are asked for £1.50.

COST OF LIVING £££

GREECE

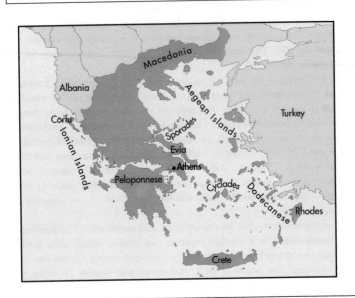

HIGHLIGHTS

Beaches
*North-east
Aegean,
Crete,
Cyclades,
Dodecanese,
Ionians,
Macedonia,
Sporades*

Culture
*North-east
Aegean,
Athens,
Attica,
Crete,
Cyclades,
central Greece,*

*Macedonia,
Peloponnese*

**Family
holidays**
*Crete,
Cyclades,
Dodecanese,
Ionians,
Macedonia,
Sporades*

Local colour
*Crete,
Cyclades,
Dodecanese,
central Greece,
Peloponnese,
Sporades*

Nightlife
*Crete,
Cyclades,
Ionians,
Macedonia,
Sporades*

**Outdoor
activities**
*North-east
Aegean,
Crete,
Cyclades,
central Greece,
Ionians,
Peloponnese,
Sporades*

**Romantic
escapism**
*North-east
Aegean,
Dodecanese,
Central Greece,
Sporades*

**Scenic
landscape**
*North-east
Aegean,
Crete,
Cyclades,
Dodecanese,
Evia,
central Greece,
Ionians,
Peloponnese*

ATHENS
Good for culture

IT IS polluted and noisy, the traffic is impossible and the view from the Acropolis is of shabby blocks and TV aerials. Yet Athens' ancient sites and museums are vital viewing for classical civilisation buffs.

Greece's main port, Piraeus, is connected to Athens by metro or by bus 040 from Filellinon off Syntagma Square. All ferries and the hydrofoil to Aegina leave from the main harbour; other hydrofoils leave from the smaller Zea harbour on the east of the peninsula.

BEST SIGHTS AND EXCURSIONS

The Acropolis
Highlights of this complex, on a rocky outcrop at Athens' heart, include the Erectheion, with replica caryatids, and the Parthenon, main temple to Athena. The original decorative sculpture is in the Acropolis Museum, at the south-east corner of the Acropolis.

Benaki Museum
Fabulous collection, from Mycenaean jewellery to regional costumes.

Byzantine Museum
The only European museum to cover solely Byzantine art.

Greek Agora
Just the foundations of Athens' ancient market-place remain, but acquire a plan and visit the museum first, and the site will come to life.

Museum of Cycladic and Ancient Art
A collection of Cycladic sculptures from 3000 BC – abstract figurines that influenced Picasso, Modigliani and Henry Moore.

National Archaeological Museum
Greece's best museum of antiquities. Highlights include Cycladic and Mycenaean pieces, a fifth-century BC Poseidon and frescos (1500 BC).

Roman Agora
Relics of the Roman market include a public lavatory as well as Tower of the Winds, a first-century BC octagonal tower that held a water clock.

Theatre of Dionysos
A fourth-century theatre carved into the Acropolis hill, where the tragedies of Aeschylus, Sophocles and Euripides were first performed.

ATTICA
Good for culture

ATTICA IS unappealing, and none of the resorts along the Apollo Coast is recommendable. There are, however, some sights worth a look.

BEST SIGHTS AND EXCURSIONS

Daphni
Eleventh-century monastery with mid-Byzantine mosaics.

Eleusis
Pilgrims were initiated in the Eleusinian Mysteries at this shrine.

Sounion
One of Greece's celebrated sights: a temple to Poseidon, 200 feet above the sea, on the jagged tip of the Attic peninsula. Best seen at sunset.

THE PELOPONNESE
Good for culture, local colour, outdoor activities and scenic landscape

THE FOUR-CLAWED Peloponnese peninsula is not only peppered with ancient sites, but has some of the loveliest landscapes in Greece.

BEST SIGHTS AND EXCURSIONS

Ancient Corinth
Riotous in ancient times, Corinth today consists of a ruined hilltop acropolis and a Roman town below, with an excellent museum.

Epidavros
This fascinating sanctuary dedicated to Asklepios, god of healing, boasts a famous theatre. A list of miracle cures performed stretches credulity.

Mistra
Byzantine outpost set on a lovely hill crowned by a Frankish fortress.

Mycenae

The evocative ruins of the 3,000-year-old royal palace from which Helen ran off with Paris and provoked the ten-year-long siege of Troy.

Nestor's Palace

To get the most out of these ruins, reputedly visited by Telemachus in *The Odyssey*, stop off at the museum in the nearby village of Hora first.

Olympia

Site of the original Olympic Games. Visit the gymnasium, the palaestra with baths and massage parlour, the stadium and an excellent museum.

Tiryns

A well-preserved and rarely visited Mycenaean fortress.

BEST RESORTS

Methoni

● Small coastal market town, with Venetian houses and fortress-walls.
● The beach, used as a road by some traffic, is popular with windsurfers. Good beaches north beyond Pylos at Gialova and Petrochori.

Stoupa

● A recently developed resort of low-rise, whitewashed apartments, with three golden sandy beaches.
● Well-placed for touring the Mani peninsula.

Tolon

● Good for family holidays, with lots of water sports too.
● Largest resort in the region, with a sheltered beach between two promontories. The sands are soft to the south, but skimpy to the north.
● Lots of seasonal cafés, tavernas, cocktail bars and discos.

BEST BASES

Areopolis

The Mani peninsula's major resort. Stay in converted tower houses.

Kardamili

With its charming, flower-scented village of fine old houses, Kardamili makes a good low-season base (in summer it gets very crowded). The beach is pebbly, but there is excellent swimming.

Monemvasia

A rock connected to the mainland by a causeway. The walled, medieval town, deserted after the nineteenth-century War of Independence against the Turks, was recently renovated. Transport is by donkey. The nearest suitable beach is on the mainland at Epidavros Limera.

Nafplion

This delightful Venetian coastal town is well placed for ancient sites. From May to September, hydrofoils run to the Peloponnese islands and Piraeus. Try Karathona's good beach, with picnic and parking areas.

Pylos

This stylish, attractive town has great views over Navarino Bay. Fine beaches are to be found to the north, at Gialova and Petrochori.

BEST ISLANDS

Aegina, Hydra, Spetses and Poros are all connected by hydrofoil with Athens and Nafplion and tend to get overrun with day-trippers in high season.

Hydra

The main village, Hydra, is pretty but very crowded in summer. Though no beaches exist, swimming off the rocks is enjoyable. To avoid crowds stay at Kamini, a half-hour's walk west of the port.

Kithira

The island is difficult to reach, and visited mostly by Australian *emigrés*. Villages are mostly inland; the prettiest is blue-and-white Kithira town. The modern port of Kapsali boasts a good, gently shelving beach. Market days – Saturday at Kalamos, Sunday at Potamos – are lively.

Spetses

The main port in Spetses town is crowded, but you will find pleasant villas in the upmarket area by the old harbour, Paleo Limani. Most beaches are shingle. The best out-of-town beach is Agia Anargyri, where some accommodation is available.

CENTRAL GREECE
Good for culture, local colour, outdoor activities, romantic escapism and scenic landscape

CENTRAL GREECE is a vast area with some magnificent sights and remarkable landscapes, though they are widely scattered.

BEST SIGHTS

Delphi
Ruined shrine of the most famous oracle of the ancient world, set on pine-clad slopes. It overlooks a huge sweep of olive groves.

Dodona
Not quite as perfect as Epidavros, the theatre of Dodona stands in a remote mountain valley and is rarely visited by tourists.

Ioannina
This undistinguished lakeside town boasts a superb archaeological museum and a folk art collection in a former mosque. In 1822, the monastery on the lake-island of Nissa was the scene of the assassination of tyrant Ali Pasha.

Meteora monasteries
Dating from the fourteenth century, these are fused to the summits of rock pillars on the Trikkala plain. You can visit Great Meteoron (the first established) and Varlaam; go early to avoid crowds, then try quieter Agios Nikolaos and Roussanou. Stay overnight in Kalambaka village.

Necromanteion of Ephyra
Ancient pilgrims hoping to consult the spirits of the dead here were duped: excavations found traces of lupin seeds and Egyptian jonquil (to induce hallucinations and giddiness), and a windlass for raising 'ghosts'.

Ossios Loukos
Tenth-century monastery with magnificent mosaics. Visit early.

Perama Caves
Caves discovered during the Second World War by locals sheltering from bombs. Impressive stalactite and stalagmite formations.

BEST BASES

Metsovo
On the slopes of a ravine, Metsovo is Epirus' most attractive town. People wear traditional costumes; some hotels exist in village houses.

Pilion peninsula
A lush, hilly peninsula with good beaches and picturesque villages; many traditional houses are now hotels. Best inland bases are Visitsa and Makrinitsa. For a seaside base, try Milopotamos or Chorefto.

Zagorahoria
Beautiful villages in mountain scenery. The Vikos Gorge is popular for hiking locally. Stay in converted traditional houses at Megalo Papingo.

BEST RESORT

Parga
● Red-roofed village on a castle-crowned hill with a harbour.
● Lower part of village is extremely commercialised and gets very busy in high season; upper village is virtually untouched by tourism.
● Beaches of Valtos and Lichnos are better than main beach. To escape the crowds in summer, take a land- or water-taxi to Loutsa.

MACEDONIA AND THRACE
Good for beaches, culture, family holidays and nightlife

THIS IS not a notably scenic area. Most people come to see the region's ancient Macedonian sites, or visit the Halkidiki peninsula on package holidays.

BEST SIGHTS

Halkidiki
A three-pronged peninsula offering different experiences: Kassandra, the westernmost prong, is most developed. Package hotels are often miniature resort complexes, charmless but with ample facilities. Sithonia, the central prong, is the prettiest. Vouvourou has a lovely sandy beach and good rooms to rent. For nightlife head for Nea Marmaras, with a crowded beach and ample rented accommodation. The third prong, Mount Athos, is a self-governing monastic state. Women are banned; men with a genuine interest in monastic life can apply for a visitor's permit from the British Consul in Athens.

Pella

Alexander the Great grew up in Pella. The town's white columns and mosaic floors recall its former elegance. The best mosaics are displayed in the museum.

Thessaloniki

You can see unmissable treasures from the Macedonian tombs at Vergina (where they are housed in the Archaeological Museum) and visit fine Byzantine churches here.

THE CYCLADES

Good for beaches, culture, family holidays, local colour, nightlife, outdoor activities and scenic landscape

THE LARGEST group of islands at over 30, the archipelago is great for island-hoppers (Naxos and Paros have excellent ferry connections).

BEST ISLANDS

Amorgos

The island of Amorgos is popular with hippies, hikers and intellectuals. Though its beaches are poor, both the villages and the landscape are extremely lovely. The best places to stay are the lively port of Katapola, or picturesque Hora.

Andros

A wealthy island with a pleasant resort, Batsi, and a fashionable yacht club. Andros town has a superb archaeological museum.

Ios

Hordes of backpackers are attracted to this rocky island, with only one village, because it has a couple of great beaches. Ios suffers high rates of theft and vandalism.

Mykonos and Delos

These islands are predominantly young, noisy, trendy, narcissistic and gay. The picturesque main town has good shops and pricey food. Visit some brilliant beaches (Paradise and Super Paradise), or make an excursion to Delos, birthplace of Apollo (take a picnic).

Naxos

The best place to stay is in the old part of Naxos town. Though the town beach is poor, good beaches lie a bus-ride away to the south. Many of the island's attractive villages are unaffected by tourism.

199

Paros

Parikia, the island's main town and port, is popular with backpackers and has lots of young, lively discos and bars. The second port of Naoussa does not have a beach, but you can find excellent ones nearby. The overdeveloped islet of Antiparos is not particularly interesting.

Santorini/Thira

Red-and-black beaches feature on this volcanic island, whose resorts are mostly sub-standard. The main town of Thira is spectacularly sited on the lip of a crater; most of the town was reconstructed after the earthquake of 1956. The town of Ia also has a clifftop site, with much accommodation in restored houses. Fine remains are visible at Akrotiri, buried by volcanic ash in 1500 BC.

Serifos

An island popular with backpackers in high season: come in spring or autumn, and hire a jeep to explore remote beaches along unmade tracks. The best beaches are Psilli Ammos, just over a mile along a rough track from the port, and Agios Iannis, just beyond.

Sifnos

Wealthy Europeans holiday on Sifnos. Visit the inland village of Apollonia, more pleasant and stylish than the port/resort of Kamares. The island is reputed to produce the best cooks in Greece – Apostoli restaurant, on Stylianou Prokou in Apollonia, is truly outstanding.

Tinos

Around 25 March and 15 August the island is overrun with pilgrims. Tinos town is very commercialised. Stay at Kolimbithra, with two sandy beaches, or Panormos, a fishing village with a small beach.

Remote islands

Avoid the islands of **Kouffonissi** and **Folegandros** in high season, as they become overcrowded. **Shinoussa** is not especially attractive, and is becoming commercialised. True islophiles should try heading for **Iraklia** and **Dhonnoussa.**

IONIAN ISLANDS
Good for beaches, family holidays, nightlife, outdoor activities and scenic landscape

TOURISM ON the Ionian islands is overwhelmingly British, and package holidays predominate – though it is possible to escape the crowds, even on the most 'packaged' islands of Corfu and Zante. The islands are not ideal for island-hopping: most ferry connections are to the mainland, although summer links between Lefkas, Ithaca, Zante and Cephalonia now exist.

BEST ISLANDS

Cephalonia
A large island with attractive scenery but few picturesque villages. The best area for touring is the beautiful northern peninsula. Assos and Fiskardo are lovely villages, but offer little to do. There are beaches within walking distance of Fiskardo, and you can use a boat to reach quality beaches a little further afield.

Corfu
Only 25 miles of Corfu's 125-mile coastline have been irreversibly ruined (the area around Corfu town). Avoid this region if you hate clubbing or drinking all night. Corfu town has a lovely Venetian centre and some interesting museums. The most spectacular scenery is in the centre of the west coast: Paramona is a quiet resort here. To the south-west lie mile upon mile of empty sands.

Ithaka
Mostly modern buildings occupy Ithaka, which has a few good beaches, accessible by boat. The nicest place to stay is peaceful Kioni, which retains some character. It is developing as a villa and flotilla resort.

Lefkas
Connected to the mainland by a causeway, Lefkas is convenient for Preveza airport. Day-trips to Ithaka and Cephalonia are possible by ferry. Vassiliki (a windsurfers' mecca) and Agios Nikitas are pleasant resorts. There are some excellent out-of-town beaches.

Paxos
Most accommodation is in villas, booked through small UK tour operators, with the option of renting a dinghy. Day-trippers from Parga and Corfu crowd the villages of Gaios and Lakka. The beaches on Paxos are mostly pebbly; you will find some good ones on the satellite island of Antipaxos.

Zante (Zakinthos)
The main package resort is Laganas, which boasts a long, sandy beach. Quieter options are Cape Gerakas, with sandy beaches and some

201

accommodation, and Agios Nikolaos, with a hotel and sandy beach. Boat trips take in the justly named Blue Grotto (good for snorkelling).

EVIA AND THE SPORADES
Good for beaches, family holidays, local colour, nightlife, outdoor activities, romantic escapism and scenic landscape

EVIA'S BEACHES and resorts are not notably attractive, excluding the spa town of Loutra Edipsos, but the landscape is gorgeous: mountains, farmland, lush valleys and tracts of uncharted coast. More part of the mainland than an island, Evia – linked to Athens by bridge and motorway – is more popular with Greeks than foreigners. The Sporades are fertile, close-knit islands with fine beaches, ideal for flotilla holidays.

BEST ISLANDS

Alonnisos
Quietest of the Sporades, Alonnisos has a small, scruffy modern port, Patitiri, sited in a lovely bay. It also boasts a pleasant part-ruined village, Palaia Alonnisos, and a dreary holiday development at Votsi. The best-quality hotels in Patitiri are on the clifftops. An arty crowd have started to restore ruined houses in Palaia Alonnisos. Most beaches are small and stony, but peaceful and rather pretty. The west coast is good for snorkelling, but watch out for dangerous currents.

Evia
Loutra Edipsos sits on a sweeping bay, with a long beach. The town is quiet and sedate, with few non-Greek visitors. Captivating landscapes are to be found in the lush river valley between Prokopi and Mantoudi. There are two good, secluded beaches near the port of Marmari.

Skiathos
Skiathos is the smallest, the most charming and the busiest of the Sporades, largely for its abundance of good beaches. Koukounaries is the most popular, a long arc of fine, yellow sand backed by pine trees and a lagoon. Other good beaches are Kanapitsa, Asselinos, Mandraki (Elias), Koutsouri and Krassas – also known as Banana Beach and now mainstream despite a reputation as the island's nudist spot. Busy Skiathos town sees much noisy international beer-swilling. It is, however, a pleasant place to stay in low season.

Skopelos
Skopelos town is outstandingly beautiful. Package tourism is a fairly

recent arrival, and of an exceptionally high standard. The atmosphere in town is restrained and civilised. The island's most popular beach is Stafilos, two and a half miles from Skopelos. For more space go to Velanio, or Limnonari and Milia (via tracks). Water sports are in evidence on many beaches.

Skyros
Tourism here is muted (most accommodation is in rooms), but Skyros is one of the Aegean's most trendy, offbeat destinations and, in keeping with the New Age ethos, the island is equipped with two holistic centres. Below the picturesque main hill-town is a fine long sandy beach. There is a beach with dunes at Agios Petros, and a pebble beach at Agios Fokas (within walking distance of the holistic centre at Atsitsa). Local crafts include sandal-making and ceramics.

CRETE
Good for beaches, culture, family holidays, local colour, nightlife, outdoor activities and scenic landscape

CRETE, GREECE'S largest island, has a mountainous backbone. In the north, gentle slopes cradle large towns; in the south the mountains drop sharply into the sea. Much of the north coast is built-up, but the south coast is less spoilt, and the far east and west are virtually wild.

BEST RESORTS

Agia Galini
- The pick of Crete's British package-holiday resorts.
- Pretty harbour, compact village-style layout, good tavernas and discos.
- Poor beach.

Chania
- A beautiful old port, the second largest town in Crete.
- Can be rough, with large numbers of soldiers and backpackers.
- To the west is a new town, Neo Hora, with beaches and restaurants.

Elounda
- A collection of hotels in grounds outside Elounda village.
- Small sandy beach and swimming from ladders fixed to the rocks.
- Lively village square opening on to the harbour in Elounda itself.
- Small hotels and rooms to rent, but no adequate local beaches.

Paleohora
- Not eyecatching, but far from the major resorts, Paleohora lacks large hotels, and has a good coarse sand beach with lively windsurfing.
- Popular with Greek families and foreign backpackers.

Rethymnon
- Interesting town with a mosque and minaret, Venetian fortress, fine old houses, sleepy waterside and, sadly, a scruffy, slum-like new annexe.
- Most visitors stay on the coastal strip: a long beach lined with hotels.

Sitia
- Peaceful, terraced town and a lively harbourfront with French and Italian tourists, tavernas and a quay where ships collect local sultanas.
- Coarse sand beach, mid- to lower-range hotels.
- Vai beach nearby, with a famous palm grove, is superb but crowded.

BEST SIGHTS AND EXCURSIONS

Gorge of Samaria
In summer, thousands tramp through the spectacular gorge daily. The hike is tough-going – so wear stout shoes and carry plenty of water.

Gortyn
This appealing Graeco-Roman site stands on the fertile Messara plain. Most of the ruins are enclosed, but others are scattered nearby.

Gournia
Interesting remains of a Minoan town with narrow cobbled streets.

Heraklion
The Archaeological Museum of this noisy city contains Minoan finds.

Knossos
Most famous Minoan palace and mythical home of the Minotaur, excavated and partly rebuilt by Sir Arthur Evans in the early 1900s.

Melidoni Cave
Against a backdrop of stalactites and stalagmites, altars commemorate 300 local people massacred here by Turks during the wars of the 1820s.

Phaistos
A Minoan palace atop a low hill. There has been no reconstruction,

and although the ruins are complex, they are more rewarding than Knossos.

Valsamonero Monastery
A medieval monastery with early fifteenth-century frescos.

THE DODECANESE
Good for beaches, family holidays, local colour, romantic escapism and scenic landscape

TUCKED UP along the Turkish coast are the Dodecanese. Some islands, like Rhodes and Kos, are hugely commercialised; others, like Astypalia, Nisyros and Tilos, are still unspoilt. Ferry links are fairly regular, and cheap charter flights leave frequently for Kos and Rhodes, making the Dodecanese an ideal choice for a varied island-hopping holiday.

BEST ISLANDS
Astypalia
A remote island shaped like a butterfly with an indented coast. The dazzling white village of Hora has a disco, a bouzouki club and great fish tavernas. Most tourists are Athenians who have holiday homes on the island. The best beach is at Livadia, where lush trees fringe the shingle and tavernas offer rooms to rent. Water sports are available. A wider range of beaches is accessible by boat.

Chalki
Tiny Chalki is a barren, rocky island with no fresh water. The harbour and only settlement is idyllic Emborio, with windmills, fishing boats and a few tavernas. The main beach, Pondamos, is ten minutes' walk away. Fishermen can take you to other beaches. In August many Chalkiots return to the island, and it can be difficult to find accommodation.

Karpathos
Dramatically beautiful, with crags looming over pine-forested slopes, Karpathos has a mountainous northern spine. The best places to stay at are Amopi, a growing resort, with beaches on serrated coastline; Finiki, a fishing village with a pretty harbour, a few tavernas and rooms to rent; and Lefkos, three bays of white sand reached via a rough road. Olympos was cut off from the rest of the island until recently, when a road was built. Village people still speak an ancient

form of Greek, and adopt traditional dress and customs. There are a few rooms to rent.

Kos

Kos has a fascinating town of minarets, ancient sites, mountains and fine beaches – and has embraced mass tourism. Best beaches are along the eastern side of Kefalos Bay, and east of Mastichari on the north coast.

Rhodes

Splendid medieval Rhodes town and large coastal areas are touristy, but unspoilt villages and beaches (on the west coast) exist. Archeangelos is the largest village; with its golden beach and rooms to let, it is a good base for family holidays. Haraki, a developing fishing village, has tavernas, self-catering accommodation and views down its shingle beach to Lindos. Vliha Bay has a sandy beach, tavernas and water sports. Steps of Lindos and Lindos Mare Hotels have family facilities. At Lindos houses like sugar cubes tumble down a hill, but the village is grossly over-commercialised and packed in high season. Lardos is a smart village. The bay below has mile upon mile of shingle and dunes.

Symi

The layers of neo-classical houses make Symi's harbour, Gialos, one of the most beautiful of any Greek island. An influx of day-trippers (between 10am and 3pm in high season) shatters the calm, but otherwise the island is very laid back. Labyrinthine Chorio, the ancient capital, is linked to Gialos by a vast staircase. Caiques run between the pebble and shingle beaches at Marathorinta, Nanon and Georgios. The shingly sand at Nimborio is also accessible via a coastal path from the harbour.

Minor islands

Craggy, remote **Kasos** has few beaches or tourists but good walking. Try accommodation at Phry, a charming port with a few tavernas. **Kastellorizo** (setting of the film *Mediterraneo*) is near Turkey. Yachts visit its magnificent natural harbour. No real beaches exist; you swim from hotel steps or rocks. The main village, Mandraki, has some pensions. Lovely, prosperous **Nisyros** has cube houses, fruit groves and a volcanic crater which draws a regular stream of day-trippers. Beaches are black volcanic sand, or pebble, and often empty even in summer. **Patmos** was home to St John, and is where his Revelation occurred. Except for the busy monastery of St John, a quiet island (beaches are poor). Rugged **Tilos** has quiet beaches. Stay in the main town, pretty Livadia, inland at the island capital, Megalo Chorio, or at Eristos.

NORTH-EAST AEGEAN ISLANDS
Good for beaches, culture, outdoor activities, romantic escapism and scenic landscape

BEST ISLANDS

Chios
This beautiful island sees relatively few tourists, perhaps because it has no quality beaches. The main town, Chios, is large, ugly and modern but very lively. Inland are fascinating fortified villages built for mastic-growers. Accommodation is available in Pirgi, the prettiest (and busiest) of them.

Ikaria
A wonderful place for Grecophiles who have enough Greek to appreciate the eccentricity of the island. Ikaria is a stronghold of the Left; you may meet Stalinists in village *kafeneions* and, on asking the price of a room, be asked what you can afford. A brilliant sand beach is to be found at Armenistis, and a small, mostly modern whitewashed village with rooms and tavernas is nearby. Lots of mountain villages can be explored.

Lesbos
A large island, peaceful even in summer. The main resort, Molivos, is a perfectly restored fortified village of timbered mansions. Nearby is a pebbly local beach, while sand and pebble beaches are further afield. Eressos, birthplace of Sappho, is a cheerful resort on a vast sandy beach. It is popular with lesbians and families of all nationalities. Sigri, a fishing harbour with a sandy crescent and tavernas, is a Greek resort used by some UK specialist operators. Many good local beaches exist here.

Limnos
The main town, Myrina, bustles above a fortified acropolis. Accommodation here is of a high standard. There are good beaches on the edge of Myrina, and better ones a little further afield at Platy, Thanos and Evgatis. Outside Myrina, most of Limnos is dominated by the army. Specialist archaeological sites are to be found at Hefestia, Kavirio and Poliochni.

Samos
Samos has few established resorts, yet is the most commercialised of all the islands. Most tourism involves package accommodation. The port/

resort of Samos town is known for its fine archaeological museum. Pythagorion, the main resort, is focused on the harbour. Kokkari is the island's best resort. To the west, the coast and hills are enchanting. Tzamadou is a popular pebble beach. Stay at Ormos Marathokampos or find accommodation along the miles of beach to the west. The hills offer fine touring and walking.

Thassos
Traditionally popular with Greeks, Thassos is also well used by UK tour operators. Accessible from mainland Kavala, it is not linked with other islands. A beautiful place of pine-covered mountains, its coastline fills up with campers and beach holidaymakers. Beware the vicious local mosquitoes. The main resort of Thassos town has a good beach, lively atmosphere and ruins of ancient Thassos dotted around town. Skala Potamios and Chrissi Amoudia are laid-back little resorts at each end of a mile-long crescent of fine white sand. Theologos is the most charming inland village.

Samothraki
Accessible only by ferry from Alexandroupolis on the mainland, this is an island of woods, waterfalls and towering mountains. Long, sandy Ammos is the only beach. The ruins of the Sanctuary of the Great Gods are impressive. Find accommodation at the port, Kamariotissa (lively but not pretty) or at the spa town of Therma, which attracts a mix of elderly Greeks and young hippies. Lots of remote places allow for free camping.

WHEN TO GO

APRIL, MAY and October are good months to visit the islands in peace and quiet, but even in July and August one can find empty or near-empty beaches on the remoter islands. Between November and March ferry schedules are skeletal. In August the Aegean islands are swept by the *meltemi* wind, which can affect hydrofoil services.

Athens is a better autumn/winter destination, as the air quality gets appalling when the heat rises. The climate is hottest in Halkidiki and Athens, next hottest are the Ionian and east Aegean islands.

The best pre-Lenten carnival celebrations take place on Skyros, Cephalonia and in the port of Patras. There are scores of local saint's-day festivals (all of which are celebrated the previous evening). St George's festival (23 April) is noted on Skyros and in the village of Arahova near Delphi.

Average daily maximum temperature °C												
London	6	7	10	13	17	20	22	21	19	14	10	7
Athens	13	14	16	20	25	30	33	33	29	24	19	15
	JAN	FEB	MAR	APR	MAY	JUN	JUL	AUG	SEP	OCT	NOV	DEC
Athens	16	11	11	9	8	4	2	3	4	8	12	15
London	15	13	11	12	12	11	12	11	13	13	15	15
Average number of rainy days per month												

Average daily maximum temperature °C												
London	6	7	10	13	17	20	22	21	19	14	10	7
Heraklion	16	16	17	20	23	27	29	29	27	24	21	18
	JAN	FEB	MAR	APR	MAY	JUN	JUL	AUG	SEP	OCT	NOV	DEC
Heraklion	14	9	10	6	4	1	<1	<1	2	6	11	14
London	15	13	11	12	12	11	12	11	13	13	15	15
Average number of rainy days per month												

PACKAGE TRAVEL

ALL THE mass-market tour operators go to Greece, often with a large programme in a dedicated brochure. Hotels, self-catering and simple rooms are on offer in mainland resorts and on the islands. Greek specialists are listed below.

Charter and scheduled flights to Thessaloniki are used for packages

Tour operators

Birdwatching: Limosa, Ornitholidays, Sunbird, Wildlife Worldwide **Pilgimage**: Highway, Inter-Church Travel, McCabe **Specialists**: Airtours, Amathus, Argo, Best of Greece, Catherine Secker (Crete), Club Cantabrica, Cosmos, Cricketer, CV Travel, Filoxenia, First Choice, Golden Sun, Greece & Cyprus Travel Centre, Greek Islands Club, Greek Sun, Ilios Travel, Inghams, Kosmar, Laskarina, Pure Crete, Simply Simon, Simply Travel, Skiathos Travel, Skopelos Villas, Sunvil, Thomas Cook, Thomson, Travel à la Carte, Travelux, Unijet, Voyages Ilena **Walking**: Explore Worldwide, Ramblers Holidays, Sherpa, Waymark **Other activities**: Ace Study Tours, British Museum Traveller, Cox & Kings (flora), Martin Randall (cultural), Midas (battlefields), Prospect (cultural), Solo's Holidays (singles), Swan Hellenic (cultural cruises) to northern Greece and Halkidiki. Athens is the charter and scheduled flight airport for the Peloponnese and the islands. The larger islands of Corfu, Crete and Rhodes and the smaller islands which have direct flights from the UK tend to be the busier island destinations.

Packages range from a one- or two-week stay-put hotel or self-catering holiday, to a two- or three-centre or a more active island-hopping holiday. Special-interest holidays include archaeological tours, island cruises, birdwatching, walking, cultural tours and sailing.

INDEPENDENT TRAVEL

DIRECT CHARTER flights (usually from May to October) go to many islands, including Corfu, Crete, Karpathos, Kos, Lesbos, Limnos, Mykonos, Rhodes, Samos, Santorini, Skiathos and Zante, as well as Athens, Kalamata, Kavala, Preveza and Thessaloniki on the mainland. All scheduled flights involve changing planes at Athens or Thessaloniki.

For island-hoppers, the best choices are well-connected islands such as the Cyclades or Dodecanese. The Sporades and Peloponnese islands also have regular hydrofoil and ferry services. It is best to 'hop' in May, June or September: in high season accommodation is scarce. Ferry timetables are unreliable (though improving), so keep a flexible itinerary. Internal Olympic Airways flights cover 30 island and mainland airports.

Car hire is expensive – rates do not include insurance and local tax, and the final bill may be double what you expect. What is more, even the international companies rent out cars in poor condition. Collision damage waiver (CDW) is usually included in pre-booked cars, but you may have to cover costs up to a certain amount. Car undersides are not insurable because of poor road surfaces, and the CDW will often also exclude windscreen and tyre damage. Many local firms do not offer CDW.

Fly-drive deals can often be cheaper than flying and adding on the cost of car hire. That said, rates charged by local rental firms are negotiable, especially in low season, so haggle.

All but the remotest islands have moped/motorbike operators. No one bothers with a helmet, and no questions are asked as long as you pay in advance, leave your passport as a deposit, and show you can ride a few yards. The accident rate is huge, and even if you are confident on a bike in the UK, you may come a cropper on Greece's rutted, pot-holed roads.

Taxis are cheap. You can negotiate a fixed rate with a driver for a day or half-day out – which can work out reasonably for a group. Also, the best taxi drivers make great guides, and if you hit it off they may even take you to a favourite remote beach, or to see their country relatives.

The railway network is limited, and trains are very slow. Long-distance buses are faster, and usually air-conditioned. The bus network is vast; and even remote villages are regularly served. On islands and in rural areas buses also deliver the post and supplies. On local buses, pay the driver. For long-distance buses it is wise to buy your ticket in advance in high season and on popular routes. Seats are numbered.

Haggling is still the norm – so in low season, or on islands experiencing a lull in tourism, you can get good deals on accommodation in rooms. Try bargaining even in summer, although on oversubscribed islands such as Paros, Mykonos and Ios discounts are unlikely.

Greek hotels are officially graded from E-category up to A and L (luxury). Rooms fall into three classes: A, B and C. Rooms in D- and E-class hotels can be as cheap as room-only accommodation; conversely, facilities in rooms can be as good as in an A- or B-class hotel. Fascinating ethnic village houses, restored to hotels or holiday homes by the National Tourist Board of Greece, can be found at Papingo (Epirus), Monemvasia, Vathia, Areopolis (Peloponnese), Makrynitsa, Vizitsa (Pilion), Mestá (Chios), Psara (Chios) and Ia (Santorini).

Hundreds of campsites exist, from basic pitches to those with bungalows, huts, restaurants, beach bars and sports facilities. Camping outside official campsites is illegal, and local police are now vigilant about moving people on, especially if there are vacant rooms or hotels. However, on the really remote islands (perhaps with no accommodation anyway), the locals will usually accept you, if you live cleanly and modestly. Even in summer you will probably need a sleeping bag if sleeping under the stars on a beach, as nights can be quite cold.

RED TAPE, HEALTH AND SAFETY

BRITISH PASSPORT-HOLDERS do not need a visa to visit Greece.

In the late 1990s, there were problems with boat thieves in Corfu. British citizens visiting Corfu by boat should stay overnight in harbours where the boat can be guarded. The Foreign Office has advised holidaymakers to avoid marinas between midnight and 6am; for the latest advice see page 11.

MORE INFORMATION Hellenic Tourism Organisation, 4 Conduit Street, London W1R 0DJ, tel 020-7734 5997, web site: *www.gnto.gr*

COST OF LIVING £-££

GUATEMALA

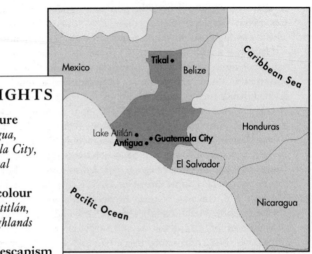

Mexico — Tikal ● — Belize — *Caribbean Sea* — Honduras — Lake Atitlán ● — **Antigua** ● — ● **Guatemala City** — El Salvador — *Pacific Ocean* — Nicaragua

MUCH OF the interest of Guatemala lies in the rich culture of its people, 50 per cent of whom are indigenous – descendants of the ancient Maya civilisation. But it is also an astonishingly beautiful country.

GUATEMALAN CITIES
Good for culture and romantic escapism

Antigua
This peaceful colonial gem is firmly on the *gringo* trail (young travellers come here to learn Spanish) but is still a delight. There are good places

to sleep, drink and eat, making Antigua an excellent base (although random attacks on visitors have tainted its image and tourist police now maintain a reassuring presence).

Guatemala City

The vast Guatemalan capital is an unsavoury place, but it is worth staying at least a day to visit the fine museums. The excellent Museo Popol Vuh has a superb Maya collection, while the indigenous weavings and costumes at the Museo Ixchel merit a browse.

Tikal

The greatest Maya city, where towering pyramids poke up above the tree canopy, attracts hordes of tourists to the remote Petén jungle region. However, it is easy to lose the crowds in the jungle, where you are more likely to have parakeets and howler monkeys for company.

SOUTHERN AND EASTERN GUATEMALA

Good for local colour, romantic escapism and scenic landscape

BEST SCENIC LANDSCAPE

Lake Atitlán

Surrounded by perfect cone volcanoes, Lake Atitlán is the most beautiful spot in Guatemala. The resort of Panajachel is totally dominated by tourism but is a relaxed enough base for exploring the indigenous villages around the lake – the main attraction after the scenery.

Río Dulce

Boat trips up the Río Dulce from Livingston on the Caribbean coast to Lake Izabal take you through lush jungle scenery and away from the normal tourist route. Rich local wildlife includes birds, alligators and the shy, placid manatee (sea cow).

THE HIGHLANDS

Good for local colour, romantic escapism, scenic landscape and shopping

BEST LOCAL COLOUR

The highland villages are fascinating places to observe the rich culture of the local people with their colourful clothes, religion and festivals.

Chichicastenango

'Chichi' is too much on the tourist trail for some people's tastes, but Guatemala's most famous market attracts traders from all over the highlands. There is also bizarre pagan-style worship amalgamating different cultural traditions in the local Catholic church.

Todos Santos Cuchumatán

The inhabitants of this remote village in the western highlands wear particularly distinctive traditional clothes (the men's costume is said to have been inspired by that of Spanish noblemen), which you can see and buy at the weekly market.

Zunil

People in this small, friendly town follow the curious cult of Maximón, a mischievous, dualistic saint whose favourite gifts are cigarettes and alcohol. A visit to his shrine is an unforgettable experience, although you should be respectful of local etiquette, and only take photographs if specifically approved.

WHEN TO GO

GUATEMALA HAS a rainy season (May to October) and a dry season (November to April). The latter is a good time to be in the highlands, when temperatures are warm and the skies clear. The nights are usually fairly cool all year round. In the Petén, it can rain solidly all day (even out of the peak of the wet season), making the paths around Tikal very slippery. Visitor numbers increase during the usual peak winter and summer periods, but generally booking flights and hotels is not a problem – except during big festivals such as Holy Week.

Every town and village has its own special festival, but some are particularly famous. At Easter, Antigua hosts Guatemala's most celebrated Holy Week processions; in mid-August Joyabaj holds a festival of traditional dances rarely seen elsewhere; on All Saints Day

	Average daily maximum temperature °C											
London	6	7	10	13	17	20	22	21	19	14	10	7
Guatemala City	23	25	27	28	29	27	26	26	26	24	23	22
	JAN	FEB	MAR	APR	MAY	JUN	JUL	AUG	SEP	OCT	NOV	DEC
Guatemala City	4	2	3	5	15	23	21	21	22	18	7	4
London	15	13	11	12	12	11	12	11	13	13	15	15
	Average number of rainy days per month											

(1 November) a chaotic horse race occurs in Todos Santos; on the Day of the Dead (1 November) giant kites are flown at Santiago Sacatepequez; and in mid-December a festival of dancing, worship and processions takes place in Chichicastenango.

PACKAGE TRAVEL

ONLY A handful of tour operators offer holidays in Guatemala on its own. The country is mostly offered as part of a two-week tour visiting the Maya sights of central America which combines Mexico and/or Belize with around five days in Guatemala. Tours usually take in Guatemala City, Lake Atitlán, Chichicastenango, Antigua and Tikal. Accommodation is generally in hotels of reasonable quality.

Special interest holidays include adventure tours such as camping, walking, wildlife safaris, caving, potholing, river rafting, minibus or truck travel, and public transport tours.

Tour operators

Adventure: Dragoman, Encounter Overland, Exodus, Explore Worldwide, Guerba, Imaginative Traveller **General**: Bales Tours, Cox & Kings, Kuoni, Sunvil **Specialists**: Cathy Matos, Journey Latin America, Passage to South America, Scott Dunn World, South American Experience, Trips Worldwide, Veloso Tours **Study tours**: Ace Study Tours

---

INDEPENDENT TRAVEL

IN THE absence of direct flights from the UK, the best links to Guatemala City are via Amsterdam or Madrid, although you can also get good deals via Miami; Mexico City and Cancún are also possible changeover places. Once in Guatemala, there is only one internal air route, from Guatemala City to Tikal, which is how virtually everyone travels to the Petén. Rail services are limited, so most people rely on the buses. Public buses can be poorly maintained and dangerous. The services along or close to the Pan-American Highway are reasonably good, so you can reach most main towns easily; you can also flag down buses from the side of the road but you will probably have to stand once on board. First-class buses (which are faster and more comfortable) are available along some routes. Car hire is not particularly expensive and is worth considering if you want to be free of timetables. The main

215

roads are generally good, but surfaces deteriorate rapidly as you head into remoter areas. Security will be a worry wherever you are.

There are international-standard hotels in the capital, Chichicastenango, Antigua, Panajachel and around Tikal, and reasonable hotels or guesthouses in towns used to putting up tourists – but you should always ask to see the room before committing yourself. In remoter villages, guesthouses will be very basic. The price for accommodation, as for most things in Guatemala, is exceptionally low.

RED TAPE, HEALTH AND SAFETY

NO VISA is required by British passport-holders. On arrival, you must show a passport valid for six months which will be stamped allowing you to stay for 90 days in Guatemala.

Have yourself immunised against yellow fever, hepatitis A, polio and typhoid. Take anti-malaria pills if you plan to travel to jungle regions such as the Petén. The main problem most visitors face is a bout of diarrhoea: the best protection is to follow the advice on preventing stomach upsets on page 12.

Pickpocketing and bag-snatching are common on the streets of Guatemala City, particularly in the downtown district known as Zone 1. Petty thieves also operate in popular tourist centres such as Chichicastenango, Lake Atitlán, Antigua and even Tikal (cling on to your belongings carefully in markets).

Guatemala has a long history of civil war, and while peace accords have been signed between the government and Indian guerrillas, the situation has not been resolved. You are strongly advised not to go off hiking in remote highland areas, where bandits have occasionally attacked travellers. There is little public transport on the road after 7pm – an unofficial curfew that has not ceased with the end of the war. Violent and armed crime is common throughout Guatemala. Visitors are advised to register with the British Embassy on arrival (tel (502) 3675425) for an update on the latest situation. Specific, current information is available from the Foreign Office Travel Advice Unit (see page 11), and specialist travel agencies should also know the latest situation.

MORE INFORMATION Tourist Information, Guatemalan Embassy, 13 Fawcett Street, London SW10 9HN, tel 020-7351 3042, web site: *www.travel-guatemala.org.gt*

COST OF LIVING £

HONG KONG

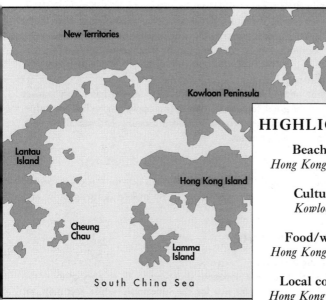

New Territories

Kowloon Peninsula

Lantau
Island

Hong Kong Island

Cheung
Chau

Lamma
Island

South China Sea

HIGHLIGHTS

Beaches
Hong Kong Island

Culture
Kowloon

Food/wine
Hong Kong Island

Local colour
*Hong Kong Island,
Kowloon, islands*

Shopping
*Hong Kong Island,
Kowloon*

A SPECIAL Administrative Region within China since 1997, Hong Kong's unique way of life has been preserved following the handover from British rule. East collides with west in a noisy, colourful mix of cultures. Compact enough to ensure that shopping and sights are always within reach, the city squeezes in towering skyscrapers and nearly 9,000 restaurants. Scattered around Hong Kong Island and the Kowloon Peninsula are 235 other islands, some rocky outcrops, others ideal day-trips.

HONG KONG ISLAND
Good for beaches, food/wine, local colour and shopping

ITS NORTHERN coast a narrow ribbon of high-rises, Hong Kong Island is the administrative and transport centre of the city.

BEST SIGHTS

The Peak
This sought-after residential district has superb vistas of Kowloon (from the Lion's Viewing Pavilion), plus luxuriant vegetation and multi-hued butterflies away from the crowds. The precipitous ride on the Peak Tram is stunning – sit on the right for the best views.

South Shore
The far side of the island is a little less hectic. Stanley has a daily market and a string of good restaurants. Aberdeen could not be less Scottish – high-rise blocks of flats crowd around a teeming harbour filled with junks and wooden sampans.

Western District
The British first landed and planted a Union flag on Possession Street. Wander the streets to see traditional coffin makers, ginseng shops and dried shrimps.

BEST SHOPPING

Markets and malls
Central Market shows Cantonese shopping in all its gory glory – the meat and fish sections are not for the squeamish, while you may not recognise half the fruit and veg.

At the more genteel Western Market you'll find cheap silk. Des Voeux Road West is the place for dried shellfish, fantastic fungi, glass jars of birds' nests and sharks' fins galore – many traders here still use Chinese scales and abacuses.

For antique and curio shops visit Hollywood Road, or browse the bric-a-brac stalls at Upper Lascar Row (known as Cat Street).

At Causeway Bay, Japanese giants dominate the shopping malls. Times Square is the biggest and best mall, while the street market in Jardine's Bazaar is fun and frantic.

BEST BEACHES

Repulse Bay
This wide sweep of golden sand is reached only by a flight of steps. Crossing the ornamental bridge to the gaudy temple apparently extends your life by three days.

South Bay
A good, secluded spot for swimming – on weekdays you will virtually have the beach to yourself.

KOWLOON
Good for culture, local colour and shopping

THE FRENETIC channel of the Victoria Harbour separates the Kowloon Peninsula from Hong Kong Island.

BEST SIGHTS

Museums
The excellent collection of the Natural History Museum focuses on the British colonial period; the Art Museum's ceramics section will help you sort a Ming from a Qing. In the Science Museum, try hands-on displays to test your reflexes.

Star Ferry
Not so much a sight as an experience – this scenic seven-minute ride across Victoria Harbour from Kowloon to Hong Kong Island (and back) costs only pennies, and provides a splendid view of the waterfront tower blocks and water-borne harbour life.

Temples
In the shady courtyard outside the colourful Tiu Hau Temple, old men bet micro-fortunes on cards or dominoes. At Wong Tai Sin, a huge complex near the MTR station, you can have your fortune told by shaking a bamboo cup containing 'fortune sticks'.

Tsim Sha Tsui
Hong Kong's brightest and brashest commercial district – the sky blazes with rainbow colours at night. Electronics shops on Nathan Road are two a penny – but make sure you know exactly what you're paying for.

BEST SHOPPING

Markets
Reclamation Street Market has cheap clothes and butchers' shops. The jade market in Kansu Street is good for browsing, while Temple Street Night Market starts at about 7pm and sells CDs and fake designer goods. The noisy Bird Garden on Yuen Po Street has an avian theme.

ISLANDS
Good for local colour

YOU CAN visit outlying islands by ferry.

Cheung Chau
A peaceful island small enough to explore in a couple of hours, with traditional Chinese shops.

Lamma
Walk through the hills and market gardens of this traffic-free island or eat at the waterfront restaurants of Sok Kwu Wan.

Lantau
Po Lin Monastery is home to a huge bronze Buddha. Tai O is a fishing village with houses on stilts.

WHEN TO GO

HONG KONG is an all-year-round destination, but due to the high levels of humidity in the summer months (June to August) it is more enjoyable to visit when the weather is cooler, from September onwards until the end of February.

A number of sporting events feature: dragon boat racing takes place in June/July and the Hong Kong Golf Championship in November/December. Horse-racing is popular between September and June (on Wednesdays in Happy Valley and Saturdays at Shatin).

	Average daily maximum temperature °C											
London	6	7	10	13	17	20	22	21	19	14	10	7
Hong Kong	18	17	19	24	28	29	31	31	29	27	23	20
	JAN	FEB	MAR	APR	MAY	JUN	JUL	AUG	SEP	OCT	NOV	DEC
Hong Kong	4	5	7	8	13	18	17	15	12	6	2	3
London	15	13	11	12	12	11	12	11	13	13	15	15
	Average number of rainy days per month											

PACKAGE TRAVEL

MANY TOUR operators offer city breaks in Hong Kong and it is a popular stopover destination on long-haul flights to the East and Australasia. Brochures generally offer a choice of three- to five-star hotels and excursions can be pre-purchased or organised locally. Day tours can include a trip to Macau and a full-day tour of Shekou and Guangzhou (ten hours), while shorter tours include Hong Kong Island. Three-day cruises visiting Vietnam, China and Hainan Island can be taken or you could combine Hong Kong with any number of tropical island resorts.

Tour operators

General: Bales Tours, British Airways Holidays, Distant Dreams, Far East Gateways, Gold Medal, Hayes & Jarvis, Japan Experience, Jetset, Kuoni, Magic of the Orient, Premier, Silverbird, Somak, Sunset Faraway, Travel 2, Travelbag, Travelsphere

---

INDEPENDENT TRAVEL

HONG KONG has an excellent transportation system. The efficient, high-speed airport railway to Kowloon and Hong Kong Island is well connected with the MTR (Mass Transit Railway) underground network. Buses go to all destinations from the airport's coach terminal, while double-decker street trams (packed in rush hour) are a local option.

If you're going to do quite a bit of travelling during your stay you would be wise to buy an Octopus Card. This permits travel on the MTR, KCR (Kowloon–Canton Railway), LRT (Light Rail Transport, in the New Territories), city buses and the airport express, and allows you to feel like a local. Cards can be purchased from ticket offices or customer service centres in the MTR and KCR and can be 'reloaded' from machines or the customer service offices located in every station. Smoking, eating and drinking are forbidden on the MTR and KCR and are subject to heavy fines. No bikes are allowed and there are no toilets on board.

Hong Kong taxis are licensed, air-conditioned and metered. Red taxis serve Hong Kong Island and Kowloon; green taxis serve the New Territories and blue taxis serve Lantau. Taxis charge extra for luggage and large amounts of shopping.

Many goods are cheaper than in the UK. Always make sure you know what you are buying before splashing out, and if possible get a worldwide guarantee with a full record of your purchase.

Most hotels are located in Central and Wan Chai (Hong Kong Island) and Tsim Sha Tsui. A growing number of resort-style hotels in the New Territories offer relaxing alternatives. No official star rating system exists, but competition generally ensures top-notch standards.

RED TAPE, HEALTH AND SAFETY

BRITISH PASSPORT-HOLDERS do not require a visa to visit Hong Kong. On arrival visitors must satisfy immigration officers that they possess an onward or return ticket and that they have adequate funds for their stay, if without a work visa (a confirmed hotel reservation and a valid international credit card generally suffice). It is advisable to carry at all times some form of ID (e.g. passport) as police carry out spot checks.

Medical facilities are excellent and most hotels have a medical clinic.

Hong Kong is one of the safest cities in the world, even at night. Nevertheless you should take the usual precautions against pickpockets – see page 12.

The water is safe to drink, although most people drink bottled water. Care is necessary in some rural and island areas where the water is drawn from wells. The official swimming season is from April to October when all public beaches have lifeguards and shark nets (as a precaution).

MORE INFORMATION Hong Kong Tourist Association, 6 Grafton Street, London W15 4EQ, web site: *www.hkta.org*

COST OF LIVING ££

HUNGARY

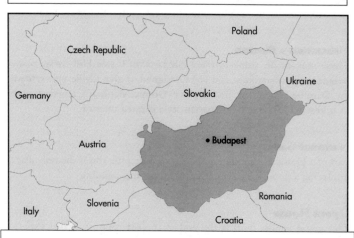

HIGHLIGHTS

Food/wine	**Family holidays**	**Nightlife**	**Culture**
Eastern and southern Hungary	*Western Hungary*	*Budapest*	*Budapest, Danube Bend, eastern and southern Hungary*
Flora/wildlife	**Outdoor activities**	**Scenic landscape**	
Great Plain	*Western Hungary*	*Eastern and southern Hungary*	

BUDAPEST
Good for culture and nightlife

YOU CAN visit the main tourist sights of both Buda and Pest in two days. But Hungary's lively capital repays closer attention. Trace the history of the region in its streets, from Ottoman thermal baths to bullet marks in the walls from the uprising in 1956. The capital boasts plenty of reasonably priced restaurants, bars, cafés and nightclubs. In many of these, gypsy musicians play.

BEST SIGHTS

Coffee houses
Three fine examples of the turn-of-the-century coffee-house culture

have survived: Becsi Kávéház, Café Gerbeaud, Müvész Kávéház, Lukacs, New York Kávéház and Szalai. Drink coffee, eat cream cakes, and make intellectual conversation in great central European tradition.

Fisherman's Bastion
These man-made, stone-turreted ramparts on Castle Hill attract many buskers and entertainers, and were designed to give idyllic views down the Danube. They surround the neo-Gothic Matthias Cathedral, with its unusual Turkish and Hungarian-style painted interior.

National Gallery
Part of a pleasant museum complex on Castle Hill, this is the only place displaying a good-sized collection of Hungarian painting.

Opera House
This grand venue, built at the end of the last century, is best experienced during a performance. Budapest has an impressive musical heritage: Liszt, Bartók and Kodály were all Hungarian.

Parliament building
You can take a guided tour around the excessively ornate parliament next to the Danube. Modelled on Westminster, it was built to mark Hungary's increased independence from Vienna 100 years ago. The red star that capped the spired dome was removed in 1990.

St Stephen's Basilica
Splendid nineteenth-century Catholic basilica in central Pest.

Thermal Baths
Budapest's many natural thermal baths vary greatly in atmosphere and clientele. The most picturesque are in Secessionist style: in the Gellért Hotel, and the Széchényi Fürdő outdoor pool in the City Park, where wide-girthed men soak and play chess.

DANUBE BEND
Good for culture

JUST NORTH of Budapest, where the Danube curves through a narrow valley, is a trio of historic towns and ruins that make a long but interesting day-trip out from the city.

BEST SIGHTS

Esztergom

Hungary's first capital is dominated by a huge domed Catholic cathedral.

Szentendre and Visegrád

Szentendre, the traditional home of Hungary's creative types, attracts thousands of tourists to its well-preserved nineteenth-century streets with folk arts and crafts sales. Visegrád boasts an impressive ruined castle atop a hill giving views of the Danube as it winds towards Budapest.

WESTERN HUNGARY
Good for family holidays and outdoor activities

BEST BASES

Lake Balaton

The southern shore is a tacky series of crowded, unremarkable resorts. Shallow water and no waves mean that children are safer than at the seaside and beginners can try sailing and windsurfing. Equipment hire is cheap. Concern is rising about the cleanliness of the water, though.

The vine-cultivating hills of the northern shore are more secluded and more upmarket. Tennis courts are generally plentiful and cheap.

BEST SIGHTS AND EXCURSIONS

Badacsony is a hilltop town with volcanic soil producing quality vines. It has a lively wine harvest. At Keszthely the baroque Festetics Palace, home to the eponymous Hungarian aristocratic family, was the country's first public forum for literary criticism. A medicinal spa is nearby at Hévíz. North of the lake, Herend makes famous delicate porcelain. The idyllic streets of the Tihány peninsula get overrun with tourists and folk craft sellers, but try to visit the abbey-church with its 900-year-old crypt, and maybe walk inland to see the lakes and geysers.

Sopron

A horseshoe-shaped town with a medieval layout, Roman walls and baroque architecture. Austrians come for dental treatment and cheap shopping. A music and dance festival is held in early summer.

EASTERN AND SOUTHERN HUNGARY
Good for culture, food/wine, outdoor activities and scenic landscape

BEST SIGHTS

Eger
The city's ecclesiastic and secular architecture is fascinating; the castle saw the Hungarians' last stand against the Turks in the sixteenth century. The nearby 'Valley of the Beautiful Women' is home to Bull's Blood red wine.

Pécs
With two mosques and a synagogue, Pécs reflects Hungary's multi-cultural past. A collection of work by the Hungarian illusionist artist Victor Vasarély and the Zsolnay porcelain exhibit are the best museums.

BEST SCENIC LANDSCAPES

Bükk Hills
These rolling, wooded hills with underground stalactite caves span Hungary's northern border with Slovakia.

Great Plain
This expanse of prairie and lakes is home to rare, aquatic birds and other wildlife, also to the original Hungarian cowboys.

Tokaj and Zemplèn
The unspoilt, wild, wooded hills of the Zemplèn region sit along-side the villages of the tamer Tokaj, where the world-famous dessert wine is made. Wine tastings are held in labyrinthine, mould-covered cellars.

WHEN TO GO

TEMPERATURES HIT extremes in January (-5°C) and August (35°C). Air-conditioning is still uncommon, so Budapest swelters in July and August. Budapest holds a film festival in February and a Spring Festival in March (with national and international contributions). Sopron's festival in early summer features ancient music and dance.

Average daily maximum temperature °C												
London	6	7	10	13	17	20	22	21	19	14	10	7
Budapest	1	4	10	17	22	26	28	27	23	16	8	4
	JAN	FEB	MAR	APR	MAY	JUN	JUL	AUG	SEP	OCT	NOV	DEC
Budapest	13	12	11	11	13	13	10	9	7	10	14	13
London	15	13	11	12	12	11	12	11	13	13	15	15
Average number of rainy days per month												

PACKAGE TRAVEL

CITY BREAKS to Budapest and holidays to Lake Balaton are the main package destinations. City breaks feature hotel or pension accommodation and self-catering apartments. Opera tickets and excursions can be booked in advance by specialist tour operators, as can Spring Festival packages. Two- or three-centre holidays featuring Budapest with Prague or Vienna are on offer, as are Danube cruises.

Outside Budapest your options are to take a fly-drive tour visiting towns such as Pécs or Sopron, or stay put on the shores of Lake Balaton.

Activity holidays include walking, riding, cycling and spa holidays.

Tour operators

Birdwatching: Birding, Limosa, Naturetrek, Ornitholidays, Sunbird **City breaks**: Bridgewater, British Airways Holidays, Cresta, Crystal, Inghams, Made to Measure, Moswin, Osprey, Sovereign, Sunvil, Time Off, Thomson, Travellers Czech, Travelscene **Music**: Travel for the Arts **Spa**: Hungarian Air Tours, Thermalia **Other activities**: Anglo Dutch (cycling), Arblaster & Clarke (wine), Martin Randall (cultural)

INDEPENDENT TRAVEL

BUDAPEST IS ideal for a weekend city break. Hungary is a budget destination (food, drink, travel and entry to tourist sights are all cheap) so travelling independently is inexpensive if you want to see all the country.

Travel agents such as IBUSZ, the state tourist agency, Budatours and Co-optourist can help with accommodation and travel. They also offer bus sightseeing trips, wine tastings and grape picking, horse-riding excursions, goulash parties with gypsy music, folk dancing evenings, and boat trips on the Danube. If you are short of time, the organised trips are a reasonably priced way to get a flavour of the country.

Direct flights go to Budapest, or you can fly to Vienna and take the hydrofoil down the Danube to Budapest for a more scenic route. Cheap packages transport you on a gruelling 30-hour bus journey. Budapest is a convenient starting-point for visiting Slovakia to the north and Transylvania, in Romania, to the south-east.

Within Hungary buses and trains provide an extensive and cheap, if not particularly fast, service. Car hire is expensive, but easy if you have a passport and credit card. If you are planning to take the hire car across the border to Slovakia or Austria, mention this in the hire office to get the requisite papers. Most offices are unhappy about you taking their cars into Romania and may charge extra. Hungary's motorway network is still primitive and some country roads are narrow and badly lit. Queues at the Austrian and Romanian borders are usual in summer.

Budapest and most major towns are crawling with taxis, which can be very cheap if you choose carefully and avoid the swanky Mercedes. The public transport system is also cheap and reliable. One recently renovated part of the underground is Europe's oldest after London and is a tourist sight in itself. Heavy traffic, difficult parking and one-way systems mean that it is not usually worth driving in Budapest yourself.

Hotels follow the star grading system and Budapest is well served with de luxe hotels as well as a good range of three- and four-star establishments. Of the top hotels, the art nouveau Gellért Hotel has the most character. Most are unattractive constructions from the 1960s in dire need of renovation.

Preferable are the privately run pensions – the equivalent of British B&Bs – which are found all over Hungary at various prices and standards. Find out about budget accommodation from IBUSZ, which has offices all over Hungary. Co-optourist, Budatours, Eravis and Vista Visitor's Centre handle bookings for private rooms and flats, rentable on a daily, weekly or monthly basis at reasonable rates. During the summer holidays the halls of residence belonging to Budapest's universities serve as cheap youth hostels, with four to a room and shared facilities. Students accost you at the major train stations with fliers to send you in the right direction.

Hungarian campsites are generally well-equipped with a complete range of facilities. Some, particularly around Lake Balaton, provide accommodation in wooden huts for those without a tent.

RED TAPE, HEALTH AND SAFETY

BRITISH PASSPORT-HOLDERS do not require a visa.

Everyone is supposed to carry identification with them at all times. However, pickpocketing is common and you must weigh up the risk of being stopped by the police when you may not have your passport against that of losing it to a pickpocket. If you decide to carry it with you at all times, keep it in a money belt worn *under* your clothes.

Signs and labels are hard to decipher, as Hungarian is un-related to other European languages apart from Finnish. But many young Hungarians speak English. The older generation speaks German.

MORE INFORMATION Hungarian National Tourist Office, 46 Eaton Place, London SW1X 8AL, tel 020-7823 1032 or (0891) 171200 web site: *www.hungarytourism.hu*

Danube Travel Ltd, 45 Great Cumberland Place, London W1H 7LH, tel 020-7724 7577

COST OF LIVING £-££

ICELAND

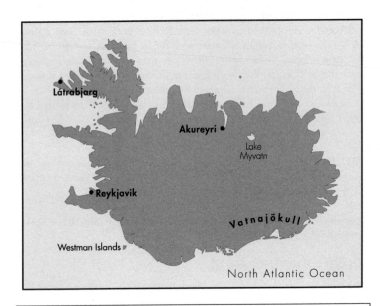

HIGHLIGHTS

Local colour	**Outdoor**	**Scenic**	**Wildlife**
West Fjords,	**activities**	**landscape**	*North coast,*
Westman Islands	*Blue Lagoon,*	*Golden Circle,*	*West Fjords*
	Glaciers,	*Glaciers, Lake*	
Nightlife	*north coast,*	*Myvatn area,*	
Reykjavik	*the interior*	*the interior*	

REYKJAVIK
Good for nightlife

ICELAND'S MINI metropolis is home to two-thirds of the country's
population but is pint-sized in comparison to Europe's other capital
cities. Surrounded by the sea on three sides, and with snow–capped
mountain ranges in the distance, Reykjavik enjoys a striking setting. Its
two main sights are the Hallgrímskirkja, a modern church seemingly
fronted by a giant set of organ pipes, with a lift up to a good viewpoint
in the steeple, and Perlan, a revolving restaurant on geothermally

heated water silos. Drinkers and diners inside can enjoy the 360° vista during a two-hour rotation.

Reykjavik's inhabitants exhibit a *joie de vivre* entirely at odds with Iceland's isolation and inhospitable climate, and after dark the proliferation of pubs and clubs becomes apparent. This abundant nightlife, plus a selection of interesting restaurants and various shopping opportunities (specialities include knitwear, glassware and ceramics) make Reykjavik a good base from which to explore the rest of the island on day trips. Alternatively, the island can be explored in more depth by touring – by car, bus or bicycle – along the ring road that follows the coastline – either independently, or as part of an escorted group tour.

BEST SIGHTS AND EXCURSIONS

Akureyri and Lake Myvatn

Day trips include return flights to Akureyri, the 'capital of the north,' and coach tours of the nearby Lake Myvatn geothermal area. Akureyri has some pretty art-deco houses, plus an idyllic setting at the head of a narrow fjord. The town museum is stuffed with folksy artefacts, while the botanical gardens come as a shock after exposure to Iceland's predominantly tree-free landscape. Lake Myvatn sits in a shallow basin surrounded by craters and geothermal phenomena such as lava columns, spitting mud-pots and black lava. Legend suggests the lake was formed from the Devil's urine. Watch out for midges. Europe's most powerful waterfall, Dettifoss, is two to three hours' drive north-east of Lake Myvatn, via one or other of two rough dirt roads either side of a deep gorge. The awesome falls are fed by meltwater from the Vatnajökull glacier.

Blue Lagoon

The bluish-white waters of this spa deep in the lava fields south of Reykjavik are the result of naturally high levels of silica, minerals and algae. The pool, which is dug into the rock, is distinguished by steel chimneys and plumes of steam and run off water from a geothermal power station. Experiencing the water is like sharing a vast outdoor bath where hot and cold currents swirl at ankle level.

Glaciers

A ninth of Iceland's surface is covered with permanent glaciers, the sooty tongues of which spill meltwater into rounded valleys. Snowmobiling on glaciers is popular: skidoos (motorcycles with twin skis and a tank-track instead of wheels) follow guides clued-up on the where-abouts of crevasses in the eerie, undulating blue-white landscape. Vatnajökull is Europe's largest glacier, covering an area almost the size of Corsica. At Skaftafell you can walk to one of its tongues (40 minutes) or explore trails to waterfalls on the slopes, and at Jökulsárlón you can take an amphibious bus on to an opalescent lake, drifting between milky blue icebergs.

Golden Circle

The name was coined to describe a round trip from Reykjavik, passing ploughed-up lava fields, black mountain peaks and metallic blue water. Along the way you can stop off to admire thundering waterfalls (Gullfoss); hot springs (the Great Geysir – originator of the generic name for hot springs – no longer spouts regularly, but its baby brother Strokkur erupts into a 66-ft column every five minutes or so); and the historic origins of Iceland's parliament at Þingvellir – the extraordinary landscape here is the meeting-place of two tectonic plates which interrupt a flat plain with an astonishing escarpment of fractured basalt. A natural amphitheatre here was the site for Iceland's first national assembly in AD 930.

The interior

Ice-caps and highland desert make much of the interior habitable only by sheep and stocky Icelandic horses. The dirt tracks across the interior are negotiable for just a few weeks in summer. For a taste of the interior accessible by saloon car (as opposed to four-wheel-drive) take the Kaldidalur Pass between Þingvellir and Husafell (allow at least two-and-a-half hours).

Snæfellsness

The Snæfellsjökull ice-cap conceals the route to earth's core according to Jules Verne's *Journey to the Centre of the Earth*. Exploration of the peninsula might centre on the lava fields and skerries of the north coast, the rugged stacks and black sand at Dritvík or the clifftop walk between Hellnar and Arnarstapi.

West Fjords

Virtually anywhere in Iceland, outside of Reykjavik, feels remote, though the feeling is further exaggerated in the isolated reaches of the West Fjords. The cliffs at Látrabjarg end in the most westerly point in Europe. The 9-mile sheer black cliffs are home to vast colonies of kittiwakes, cormorants and puffins. Isafjordur, the principal town in the region, has an interesting Maritime Museum, giving a sanitised flavour of the town's nautical history, with telescopes, trawl nets and model boats. For a more earthy experience, drop in on the Ósvör Maritime Museum on the road from Isafjordur to Bolungarvik – oddities at this small living museum include fish-skin footwear and drying lumpfish carcasses.

Westman Islands

In 1973 a volcano erupted on the principal outpost, Heimaey, engulfing the port in ash and increasing the land mass of the island by 20 per cent. Day-trips to the island include a tramp across the still-steaming earth, a film of the eruption, a boat ride to see local bird colonies and a bus ride to see the puffin colony.

Whale watching

Boats can be taken from several harbours on the west and north coasts, though Husavik, on the north-east coast, is the main centre for whale watching. Two companies run three-hour trips across the bay and claim virtually 100 per cent records for sightings – though that can mean just a distant glimpse of a minke whale's dorsal fin, and not necessarily the fully airborne humpback whales on the promotional posters.

WHEN TO GO

THE TOURIST season in Iceland is short – generally from May to September. Many visitors come to see the midnight sun in June, but touring throughout the long days of July and August is also popular. It can still get bitterly cold, however, even in summer, and the weather is very changeable: always have sweaters and waterproofs available, even if you set out for the day in T-shirt weather. Some tour operators offer Reykjavik as a winter city break; although prices are often cheaper then, bear in mind that having only a few hours of daylight each day will seriously cut down on sight-seeing time.

	Average daily maximum temperature °C											
London	6	7	10	13	17	20	22	21	19	14	10	7
Reykjavik	2	3	4	6	10	12	14	14	11	7	4	2
	JAN	FEB	MAR	APR	MAY	JUN	JUL	AUG	SEP	OCT	NOV	DEC
Reykjavik	20	17	18	18	16	15	15	16	19	21	18	20
London	15	13	11	12	12	11	12	11	13	13	15	15
	Average number of rainy days per month											

PACKAGE TRAVEL

MANY VISITORS check into a bland but comfortable hotel in Reykjavik for three or four nights and spend substantial amounts of money on daily excursions to glaciers, hot springs, waterfalls and whale-watching harbours. Alternatively, several UK tour operators offer escorted group tours lasting from a long weekend to 14 days.

The tourist office in Reykjavik is excellent for planning and booking excursions, though prices of pre-booked tours through UK operators are similar.

Tour operators

Birdwatching: Island Holidays, Limosa **City breaks**: Bridge Travel Service, Cresta, Crystal, Inghams, Osprey, Premier, Sovereign, Thomson, Time Off, Travelscene, Yes Travel **Cultural**: Prospect **General and specialist**: Bales, Cricketer, Donald MacKenzie, Icelandair, Regent Holidays, Scandinavian Travel Service, ScanMeridian, Scantours, Shearings, Titan Hitours, Travelsphere, Wallace Arnold **Other activities**: Arctic Experience, Discover the World, Naturetrek (wildlife), Explore Worldwide, David Oswin Expeditions, Northern Lights Tours (explanatory and special interest tours), Go Fishing

---

INDEPENDENT TRAVEL

PLAN AND book your itinerary in advance; accommodation is limited, usually fully booked in the summer, and can be a long way apart. Be generous when planning journey times.

If you have two or three weeks, you can set off round the coast by bike, bus or car, staying in basic hotels, farmhouses, guesthouses or campsites and refuelling at petrol stations that act as focal points for scattered rural communities (almost all garages sell food or have a restaurant – likely to be your only option in some areas). This way you can discover grass-roofed hamlets, clifftop bird colonies and moorland trails that are off-limits to most day-trippers.

Car hire is very expensive in Iceland, and if you intend to remain in Reykjavik you will not need a car as the city is compact and public transport is good. The 'Ring Road' encircling the island is comfortably negotiable by a mid-size, two-wheel-drive car, though progress can be slow on bumpier stretches. Local tour operators offer 'jeep safaris' to the interior to sample gravel deserts and bathe in hot springs, or you can hire your own four-wheel-drive if you are sufficiently experienced. Mountain roads and some parts of the national highway are surfaced with loose gravel, so motorists should take extra care. A leaflet entitled *Mountain Roads* is available from Tourist Information Centres. Off-road detours are forbidden and drivers must keep their headlights on at all times.

Air Iceland and Islandsflug are the two airlines which both offer domestic flights, and both have a variety of air passes available.

An extensive bus network covers most parts of the country, including the Highlands. A variety of passes are available (including The Full Circle passport allowing travel on buses around the Ring Road) from the main bus station in Reykjavik or specialist travel agencies in the UK and Iceland.

RED TAPE, HEALTH AND SAFETY

BRITISH PASSPORT-HOLDERS do not need a visa, but your passport does need to be valid for at least another three months after your return date. English is widely spoken in Iceland.

No vaccinations are required for tourists travelling to Iceland.

Only experienced drivers of four-wheel-drive vehicles should tackle the interior, and then only in July and August, with at least one other vehicle, after consulting the Public Roads Administration (tel 563 1500). Always take a detailed map.

Pack a swimsuit; outdoor bathing – whether in craters, rock-crevice pools or geothermally heated municipal baths – is part of Icelandic culture.

MORE INFORMATION The Icelandic Tourist Board has no office in the UK. Information is available from Icelandair Holidays, 172 Tottenham Court Road, London W1P 0LY, tel 020–7874 1000, web site: *www.icetourist.is*

COST OF LIVING £££

INDIA

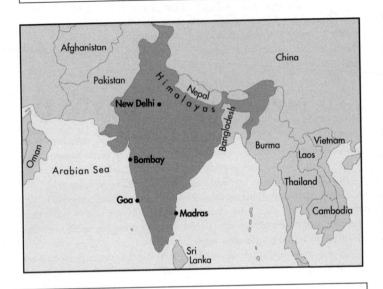

DELHI
Good for culture and local colour

DELHI IS really two cities – Old Delhi, the capital of Muslim India until the nineteenth century, and New Delhi, the administrative capital created by the British. Old Delhi is crowded, colourful and crazy; the shopping bazaar of Chandni Chowk is the focal point, and represents India at its most frenetic: full of people, rickshaws and cows. New Delhi has wide streets and government buildings.

BEST SIGHTS

Feroz Shah Kotla
A ruined fortress-palace incorporating a 43ft-high pillar inscribed with Ashoka's edicts dating from 1354, this site gives a glimpse of one of Delhi's earliest incarnations as a powerful city.

Gallery of Modern Art
A good collection of works by Indian and colonial artists.

Humayun's Tomb
A precursor to the Taj Mahal and interesting example of early Mughal architecture – domed roof, arched entrances and spacious excess.

India Gate
A 140ft-high stone arch commemorating the 85,000 Indians who died fighting for the British in the First World War.

Jama Masjid
The largest mosque in India, built by Shah Jahan (who also built the Red Fort and Agra's Taj Mahal) offers views over Delhi from the top of the 133-ft southern minaret.

National Museum
Good bronzes, terracotta and wood sculptures, miniatures, mural paintings and tribal costumes. Some exhibits are from the third century BC.

Raj Ghat
Not much to look at, but fascinating to the endless stream of pilgrims, this large field is where Mahatma Gandhi was cremated in 1948. Indira Gandhi and her son Rajiv were also cremated in the area, as were Sanjay Gandhi and Jawaharlal Nehru. You can see memorials to the leaders here.

Rashtrapati Bhavan
Immense palace-like official residence of the President, built in 1929; architecturally a mixture of Mughal and Western styles.

Red Fort
Built by Shah Jahan between 1638 and 1648, this was an impressive Mughal power base, with over a mile of ramparts up to 110 feet high. Inside are mosques, palaces, baths and a small archaeological museum.

Qutab Minar
A fine early Afghan work dating from 1193, when the last northern Hindu kingdom fell to the Muslims. A red sandstone-and-marble 243-ft tower is the centrepiece, along with a mosque and an iron pillar.

NORTHERN INDIA
Good for culture, local colour, romantic escapism and scenic landscape

BEST SIGHTS

Agra
The Taj Mahal is the romantic symbol of India, and rightly so. Between 1631 and 1653 experts from Iran, France and Italy laboured to build a monument in memory of Shah Jahan's dead wife. The result is magical – a floating white building with minarets and *pietra dura* (inlaid semi-precious stones).

The size of the nearby Red Fort bears testimony to Agra's position as capital of the Mughal empire. Set on the bank of the Yamuna river, it contains luxurious living quarters as well as warlike halls for public and private audiences. Fatehpur Sikri, a perfectly preserved example of a Mughal city, is a day-trip from Agra.

Amritsar
The Golden Temple, the holiest shrine for the Sikhs, has a dome said to be gilded with 220kg of gold, and is surrounded by an artificial lake set in a complex constructed almost entirely of white marble. Amritsar itself is not an attractive town.

Varanasi
This is the holiest city in India, and also one of the most chaotic, although unbearably hot in the summer. Pilgrims flock to bathe in the River Ganges, and it is every devout Hindu's dream to be cremated on the burning *ghats* here. The bathing *ghats* are the focal point of the city, bustling with every imaginable activity, from buffalo-washing to sitar concerts.

The Golden Temple, built in 1776, is hidden in the back streets, but the constant stream of pilgrims ringing the bells makes it easy to find. It is small, yet covered with three-quarters of a ton of gold plate. The Durga Temple, also called the Monkey Temple because of its resident simian population, has regular goat sacrifices to appease the goddess Durga.

Six miles outside Varanasi, Sarnath, a good day-trip, is the place where the Buddha first preached after being enlightened in Bodhgaya.

RAJASTHAN
Good for culture, local colour, romantic escapism and scenic landscape

BEST SIGHTS

Jaipur

The walled 'pink city' – pink signifies hospitality in traditional Rajput culture – has wide streets and is a heady brew of exotic shops, constant traffic and colourful Rajasthanis. The palace dates from 1727; it houses a good museum. Johari Bazaar is the centre of the gem trading industry and is a fascinating place. Hawa Mahal, or the Palace of the Winds, built in 1799, is little more than a façade, but it is a beautiful example of Rajput artistry, intricately fashioned in pink sandstone. Jantar Mantar, an enormous observatory, is the largest in India. The sundial has a 99-ft gnomon casting a shadow that moves up to 13 feet an hour.

About 7 miles out of Jaipur, Amber is a fortress–palace set high on a hill with fine views.

Jaisalmer

A magical walled city in the desert, Jaisalmer is essentially a fort, built in 1156 by Rawal Jaisal. Tourism is big business, but Jaisalmer retains an exotic feel, evocative of camel trains, riches and romance. The old city is filled with temples and *havelis* – sandstone mansions with intricate façades. Camel treks leave from here and you can buy locally made fabrics and wallhangings, embroidery and *appliqué*.

Jodhpur

A classic example of a noisy, dirty and polluted Indian city, Jodhpur nevertheless contains the most impressive of the Rajasthani forts. Enter through a series of gates, the first of which displays cannonball scars; the last, handprints of Maharaja Man Singh's 15 wives, who committed *sati* by throwing themselves on his funeral pyre in 1843. The palace museum is good, as are views from the ramparts over the city.

If you want to splash out, stay at the plush Umaid Bhawan Palace. Built shortly before Independence in 1947, it is one of India's most atmospheric hotels.

Pushkar

Hindu pilgrims visit this pretty town on the edge of the desert for its calm, its temples and lake with bathing *ghats* (steps down to the river). Pushkar has an extraordinary Camel Fair each autumn.

Udaipur

The old part of the city (the 'Venice of the East') is full of whimsical

239

palaces, temples, *havelis* and parks, but the centrepiece is beautiful Lake Pichola, with its magical Lake Palace Hotel. See also the City Palace that towers above the lake, and go to Jagmandir Island for the view of the lake and city. Udaipur is a centre for the performing arts, painting and crafts.

THE HIMALAYAS
Good for outdoor activities and scenic landscape

BEST SIGHTS

Darjeeling
A hill station, Darjeeling is best approached in the toy train. Set amid vast tea plantations, it boasts views of Kanchenjunga and the peaks. The town is full of colourful mountain folk, curio shops and pony-wallahs. It also has excellent walks, tea plantation tours and local Buddhist monasteries nearby.

Dharamsala
This wooded hill resort is the home-in-exile for the Dalai Lama, and as a result has become a captivating Tibetan village, complete with spinning prayer-wheels and strings of colourful flags. Lord Elgin, a Viceroy of India, was buried in 1863 in the Church of St John in the Wilderness.

Ladakh
On the other side of the Himalayas, Ladakh is still unspoilt. The people wear traditional dress, and practise an ancient form of Buddhism. Leh, the capital, has a palace like a small version of the Potala in Tibet. Try to visit the region in summer, when the monasteries hold their festivals – those at Hemis and Lamayuru are the most flamboyant, but others, especially at Shey and Tikse, are also fascinating.

Manali and the Kulu Valley
Since Kashmir became off-limits to tourists, Manali has boomed as a base for trekking, boat trips along the Beas river, and day-trips to some of the alluring nearby villages. Conditions of travel can be tough. It is possible to take a day-trip to the Rohtang Pass, a spectacular tour through the mountains along one of the highest driveable roads in the world.

Simla
The former 'summer capital' of the British Raj sits high on a ridge in

the foothills; cool even in the hot season, it makes a welcome escape from the sweltering plains. The Mall, or main street, is lined with stately mansions and churches. Indians were barred from it until the First World War. There are several magnificent walks locally. The Rashtrapati Niwas, a huge building with beautiful gardens, was the British Viceroy's home.

CENTRAL AND EASTERN INDIA
Good for culture and nightlife

BEST SIGHTS

Ajanta and Ellora
Spectacular, isolated examples of Buddhist, Hindu and Jain cave temples from 200 BC. Ajanta is noted for wall paintings, Ellora for sculptures.

Bombay (Mumbai)
The business capital of India is also the home of Bollywood, India's thriving film industry. A dynamic, cosmopolitan, but dirty and crowded city, Bombay has excellent shops and restaurants.

The most important landmark, the Gateway of India, was built to commemorate the visit of George V in 1924. The boat to Elephanta Island leaves from here to visit the impressive rock–cut temples carved 1,500 years ago. Chowpatty Beach is not for swimming but is a great place for carnival atmosphere and *bhelpuri* snack stands. The Prince of Wales Museum, built in Indo–Saracenic style, is interesting inside and out.

Calcutta
Best visited after getting acclimatised to India's extremes, Calcutta is the old Raj capital and a lively cultural centre, where film, poetry, art, music, drama and dance events take place every day. The Indian Museum is one of the biggest and best in all Asia. The Maidan is a vast expanse of parkland surrounding Fort William and the Victoria Memorial, and recalls the days of the Raj – with mounted police patrol, cricket fields, gardens and cows. The Memorial is a large marble museum full of relics of British India's heyday.

The Hooghly river runs near the hub of BBD Bagh (formerly Dalhousie Square and site of the 'Black Hole of Calcutta') and the main street, Chowringhee. It is spanned by the famous Howrah Bridge, the world's busiest. Across the river are the Botanical Gardens, birthplace of Darjeeling and Assam teas.

Khajuraho

These Indo-Aryan temples are a major site and well worth seeing. Sculpted 1,000 years ago, they depict vivid images of gods, warriors, animals and mythological creatures. They are most famous for their erotica.

SOUTHERN INDIA

Good for beaches, culture, local colour, nightlife, romantic escapism and scenic landscape

BEST RESORTS

Goa

● For beaches, Goa's the ticket, but do not anticipate crystal-clear water.

● Old Goa was the Portuguese capital. Unique colonial villas and churches line verdant streets. Fascinating markets at Mapusa and Anjuna.

● Best beaches are at Baga, Vagator and Cavelossim. For total peace (but basic facilities) head north to Arambol.

Kovalam

● Almost at India's southernmost tip, Kovalam is a tiny beach resort with huge crashing breakers, worthy of a longer stay.

Mahabalipuram

● About 37 miles south of central Madras, and well connected by bus, the small coastal town of Mahabalipuram (also known as Mamalla-puram) has impressive rock carvings and a shore temple dating from the seventh century.

● The road into the town is dotted with beach resorts, many of which are reasonably priced and which offer access to private, unspoilt beaches.

BEST SIGHTS AND EXCURSIONS

Hampi

The ruined capital of one of India's largest empires sprawls over 13 square miles. Hampi is relatively undeveloped but well worth an excursion. The city was founded in 1336, and by the mid-sixteenth century controlled the southern half of India. Today it is a magical place of temples and statues, hidden among rocks, and a bazaar. Beware the vicious mosquitoes.

Kanyakumari

Three bodies of water – the Bay of Bengal, the Indian Ocean and the Arabian Sea – converge at the 'Land's End' of India, Kanyakumari. A steady stream of pilgrims come here for their ritual bathing.

Kerala

This magical state of palm trees and sunlit rice paddies full of birds and monkeys is best appreciated by exploring the coastal lagoons. Cochin, a fishing port city of green islands set in lagoons and backwaters, has India's oldest church (the Portuguese explorer Vasco da Gama was initally buried here), a beautiful synagogue and Matancherry Palace, which can be visited by ferry.

Madras (Chennai)

Madras has lively street culture; famous for its vegetarian food, it is full of cheap, excellent restaurants. Try a *thali* – a complete meal with rice, sambhar (*dal*), curries and puddings arranged in little dishes on a big circular plate. Madras is the centre for Bharata Natyam, Tamil Nadu state's best-known classical dance, usually performed by women. Visit Fort St George for its British East India Company memorabilia, and the archaeological section of the Government Museum. Real temple country starts outside Madras; the best temple towns are Madurai, Kanchipuram and Mahabalipuram.

Mysore

An easy-going city with colourful markets, Mysore is a centre of incense manufacture, imparting sensuous pleasure at every turn. The walled Indo-Saracenic Mysore Palace – a confection of brash colours, solid silver doors, stained glass and vast mirrored halls – is hugely over the top, yet elegant and dignified. Chamundi Hill has views over the city and the surrounding villages as well as a seven-storey temple.

WHEN TO GO

OCTOBER TO April is the best time, although it starts getting hot by April. In the north it can be cold at night in January and February. The mountains are best visited after the monsoon in September and October, when the views are good. Ladakh is open for only a few weeks each year in July and August.

Average daily maximum temperature °C

	JAN	FEB	MAR	APR	MAY	JUN	JUL	AUG	SEP	OCT	NOV	DEC
London	6	7	10	13	17	20	22	21	19	14	10	7
Bombay	28	28	30	32	33	32	29	29	29	32	32	31
	JAN	FEB	MAR	APR	MAY	JUN	JUL	AUG	SEP	OCT	NOV	DEC
Bombay	0.5	0.6	0.7	1	2	7	11	10	9	9	4	0.8
London	15	13	11	12	12	11	12	11	13	13	15	15

Average number of rainy days per month

Average daily maximum temperature °C

	JAN	FEB	MAR	APR	MAY	JUN	JUL	AUG	SEP	OCT	NOV	DEC
London	6	7	10	13	17	20	22	21	19	14	10	7
Madras	29	31	33	35	38	38	36	35	34	32	29	29
	JAN	FEB	MAR	APR	MAY	JUN	JUL	AUG	SEP	OCT	NOV	DEC
Madras	0.1	0.1	0.2	2	7	25	27	25	15	10	5	1
London	15	13	11	12	12	11	12	11	13	13	15	15

Average number of rainy days per month

Average daily maximum temperature °C

	JAN	FEB	MAR	APR	MAY	JUN	JUL	AUG	SEP	OCT	NOV	DEC
London	6	7	10	13	17	20	22	21	19	14	10	7
New Delhi	21	24	31	36	41	39	36	34	34	34	29	23
	JAN	FEB	MAR	APR	MAY	JUN	JUL	AUG	SEP	OCT	NOV	DEC
New Delhi	2	2	1	1	2	4	8	8	4	1	<1	1
London	15	13	11	12	12	11	12	11	13	13	15	15

Average number of rainy days per month

PACKAGE TRAVEL

MASS-MARKET TOUR operators such as Thomson, First Choice, Manos, Somak and Inspirations have charter flights direct to Goa (some with extensions to Kerala) for one- or two-week beach holidays. Packages to Kovalam are available.

Several brochures feature tours of the north, typically starting from Delhi and visiting the palaces and fortresses of Rajasthan, Agra, Jaipur, Udaipur, Jodhpur, Varanasi and Khajuraho. Tours are by coach, train or car, and diversions such as visits to the Corbett National Park are on offer. Further north, Darjeeling and its tea plantations are featured on tours of the north-east starting from Calcutta, and walking and adventure holidays utilise the Himalayas. Extensions on offer are to Nepal or to the Andaman Islands in the Bay of Bengal. Southern tours from

Madras or Bombay include Bangalore, Mysore and Madras, Kanchipuram and Cochin. Visits to National Parks or a bird sanctuary may be included as well as trips to temples and forts.

Activity holidays include birdwatching, adventure tours, wildlife tours, rail tours and archaeological tours.

Tour operators

General and specialist: Abercrombie & Kent, Bales Tours, British Airways Holidays, Cosmos, Cox & Kings, Distant Dreams, Far East Gateways, First Choice, Hayes & Jarvis, Highlife Holidays, Inspirations East, Jasmin, Kuoni, Manos, Mysteries of India, Pettitts India, Somak, Thomson, Tradewinds, Trans Indus, Unijet, Voyages Jules Verne, World Dreams **Trekking/walking**: Classic Journeys, Exodus, Himalayan Kingdoms, Walks Worldwide **Other activities**: Holts' Tours (battlefields), Encounter Overland (adventure), Explore Worldwide (adventure), Peregrine Adventures, Sunbird (birdwatching), Swan Hellenic (cultural tours), Wildlife Worldwide (wildlife)

INDEPENDENT TRAVEL

INDEPENDENT TRAVEL in India can be uncomforatble, but worth it. The biggest problem is the bureaucracy and interminable queueing involved in booking transport. You will see India in the raw and you will get frustrated and hot, so if you are keen on getting about and seeing lots of sights in a short time, take a package. If you go it on your own, give yourself twice as much time as you think you will need, for everything. Take trains rather than buses, bargain with the rickshaw drivers, travel light, stay at the best hotels you can afford and keep your sense of humour.

India has an extensive domestic flight network. Book from home, but expect possible delays and overbookings. Indian Airlines, the main domestic carrier, has a 21-day flight pass, which must be bought in the UK when you buy your international flight ticket.

The train system, a phenomenon of efficiency in itself, is a great slice of Indian life. The network covers the subcontinent like a web; journeys are slow but give you the chance to feast your senses on what goes on both inside and outside the compartment. Travel in air-conditioned first class for overnight journeys, second class for shorter ones, keep an eagle eye on your luggage and befriend your travelling companions. Book trains in the UK through specialist travel agencies: rail passes from half a day to 90 days are available.

Buses tend to be hugely overcrowded. The air-conditioned ones operating in Rajasthan are OK. Buses are the only option in the mountains – sit near the front, but do not go if you have vertigo.

Self-drive is not an option, but it is possible to hire a taxi for a day or even longer. This way you get a rough-and-ready guide to the area as well. Do not be bullied by drivers who offer to go to places not on your itinerary – the chances are that it is a 'brother' with a gem shop. If the meter is not working, bargain and agree a rate before you start.

Accommodation comes in all standards, from super-luxury to total fleapit. Choose hotels recommended in guides. In some places you will have to rough it: carry your own secure lock, look for reasonable facilities and a mosquito net. One of the most unpredictable aspects of travel in India is accommodation, even for those on a package holiday. If you prefer international-standard hotels (and there are plenty) keep to the beaten track. The larger hotels are bookable from home. Do not think about camping.

RED TAPE, HEALTH AND SAFETY

VISAS ARE required. Application forms are obtainable from the High Commission. For a six-month visa, you need two passport-size photographs. The cost is £20; £21 by post. If you apply in person between 8.30am and midday Monday to Friday, the visa can be processed on the same day. Postal applications can take up to three weeks.

Check with your GP about vaccinations and malaria protection. The biggest health problem for visitors to India is usually 'Delhi belly'. See the tips on page 12 for how to avoid this.

We strongly advise travellers to read the Foreign Office Travel Advice web site India page (see page 11) for the latest advice on security and travel to and from Indian airports.

Do not travel to Jammu and Kashmir (except Ladakh).

MORE INFORMATION Indian Tourist Office, 7 Cork Street, London W1X 2LN, tel 020-7437 3677, brochure line (01233) 211999, web site: *www.indiatouristoffice.co.uk*

High Commission of India, India House, Aldwych, London WC2B 4NA, tel 020-7836 8484

COST OF LIVING £

INDONESIA

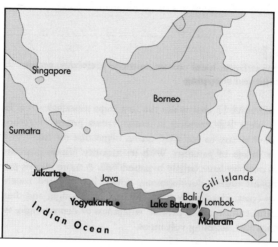

HIGHLIGHTS

Culture
Jakarta,
Ubud (Bali),
Yogyakarta
(Java)

Lake Batur
(Bali),
Lovina,
Mount Bromo
(Java)

Shopping
Ubud (Bali),
Yogyakarta
(Java)

Mount Bromo
(Java),
Ubud (Bali)

Local colour
Ubud (Bali),
Mataram
(Lombok),
Yogyakarta
(Java)

Scenic
landscape
Gili Islands
(Lombok),
Lake Batur
(Bali),

Outdoor
activities
Gili Islands
(Lombok),

Beaches
Gili Islands
(Lombok)

WOULD-BE VISITORS may have been put off visiting Indonesia after watching television images of the political and ethnic troubles there. However, the country is for the large part safe to visit, with volatile situations on only a handful of the 17,000 islands that make up the world's fourth most populous country. Travellers are strongly advised, though, to check with the Foreign Office Travel Advice Unit (see page 11) on the current situation before travelling to Indonesia.

The Indonesian archipelago is vast. Of the thousands of islands, a number of the larger ones – Sumatra, Kalimantan (Borneo), Sulawesi,

Maluku, Sumbawa and Flores – have been on the 'backpacker trail' for some years, and are increasingly accessible to travellers. In this chapter, however, we concentrate on those which are most developed and offer the best options to tourists – Bali, Lombok and Java.

BALI
Good for culture, local colour, outdoor activities, scenic landscape and shopping

LEGEND HAS IT that when the first ships stumbled across Bali their captains were left stranded as entire crews jumped overboard and deserted. It is easy to see why, on an island that for many visitors still fits their image of paradise. With its majority Hindu population, the political troubles have largely bypassed Bali. A more serious problem is the rampant tourist development, which has blighted much of the southern coast. Head away from the beaches, though, and there is still a bountiful culture and a pristine wilderness of dense jungle, sweeping mountains and rumbling volcanoes.

BEST TOWN

Ubud
An alternative to the tourist hell of the Kuta and Sanur beach resorts is the inland jungle town of Ubud. Over the last decade a number of upmarket hotels and traditional-style restaurants have brought modern facilities to a town that boasts plenty of authentic charm.

Ubud is the ideal place to stock up on traditional Balinese craftwork and fabrics such as batik, though owing to the unabated flow of tourists prices are not what they were. Shopkeepers vie for your attention and window-shopping here is a full-contact sport. Tarry for a second outside any of the market stalls and the owner will appear from nowhere in a flurry of quotes and offers. Don't take his or her first price too seriously, or feel flattered when offered the 'special morning price'. Find out from other travellers what the going rate is and work around that.

The Monkey Forest Sanctuary is a growing attraction at the bottom of Monkey Forest Road, though recently many tourists have reported losing bags and valuables to the increasingly spoilt and vicious monkeys.

BEST RESORTS

Candi Dasa
● Used to be a small fishing village; now a heavily touted, though mediocre, beach resort.

● The beach that attracted developers has now largely disappeared due to the damage caused by blasting the reef to provide concrete for the tourist hotels.

● Close by is Tenganan Village. Its people adhere most closely to the island's animistic past which predates its conversion to Hinduism.

Kuta

● At this brash resort located along a once-gorgeous beach, watch Antipodeans on holiday misbehave or party through to dawn. Not for the faint-hearted. You will either love it or loathe it.

● Kuta has now extended and blurred into Legian, its northerly neighbour on the coast.

● The *gangs* (alleyways) host a myriad of *losmen* (small and normally very competitively priced hotels), bars and restaurants.

● There is a stunning temple at Pura Tanah Lot, just north of Kuta.

● Over the last few years there has been a disturbing rise in tourist muggings and robberies.

● The constant hassling from persistent salesmen can ruin a day at the decent beach.

Lovina

● The main attraction of this quieter resort in the north of the island is the impressive black sand beaches.

● Snorkel, go dolphin-watching or visit the nearby waterfalls and hot springs.

● Less frenetic than Kuta, it has a reasonable selection of restaurants at which to try the local variation of *gado gado*.

Sanur

● An upmarket and more relaxed version of Kuta.

● Many Europeans choose it as part of a package; several expensive hotels cater for a well-heeled clientele.

● The beach, which is reasonable, is backed by an unending sequence of restaurants from where you can take in the view out towards Lombok.

BEST SIGHTS

Balinese temple dancers

By far the most dramatic spectacle is provided by the Balinese temple dancers. Bali is an island of festivals and many of these are celebrated in and around the temples of Ubud – check with the Indonesian Embassy in London or the tourist desk at Denpasar Airport for further details of events. Many upmarket hotels offer their own traditional dancing.

Goa Gajah and Yeh Pulu

These ancient sites, both close to Ubud, delight thousands of overseas visitors every year. Goa Gajah, which means Elephant Cave, is especially popular; Yeh Pulu has huge, stunning panels carved out of the rockface. The walk down to Yeh Pulu takes you through terraced rice paddy fields.

BEST SCENIC LANDSCAPE

Lake Batur

Towards the north of the island, the area combines the largest lake in Bali with some magnificent walks up the side of the adjacent and dormant volcano, Gunung Batur. The road up to Lake Batur from the south winds through some of the most arresting scenery on the island.

This is a popular spot from which to watch the dawn come up and most visitors set off for the rim of the volcano's caldera at around 4am to be at the top by sunrise. The walk starts quite gently through a lowland wood but soon inclines steeply so good walking shoes are essential. The guides who take you to the top are feverishly competitive so shop around, and agree the price with your guide before heading off. It is essential to check the level of volcanic activity, as Batur can throw ash and boulders out with little warning, but local guides still risk taking tourists up.

LOMBOK
Good for local colour

FOR YEARS savvy travellers have been escaping the tourist madness of southern Bali by fleeing east to its neighbour. Lombok boasts some magnificent scenery of lush paddy fields, coconut groves and towering volcanoes. Increasingly the island is opening up to tourism, despite some serious ethnic disturbances, and there is a wonderful sense of space if you have just arrived from Bali. Lombok can be reached by ferry from Padang Bai on Bali or from a number of places throughout Indonesia by air.

The road north of Mataram is especially dramatic as it winds its way up through mahogany forests before plunging down to the coast opposite the Gili Islands.

Lombok has a very different culture from Bali, being essentially Muslim, and rather than temples dotting the road, you will find mosques here.

BEST TOWN

Mataram

The main town on Lombok is essentially a conurbation of four separate towns – Mataram, Ampenan, Sweta and Cakranegara. Mataram is a thriving and relatively unreconstructed Asian town with all the aromas and bustling street life that you would expect, and is a good place to base yourself for exploring the rest of the island.

Worth visiting are the largest market on the island (next to the main bus terminal in Sweta), bursting with exotic fruits and spices, and a good museum in Ampenan. If the traffic gets too much then visit the relaxed environs of the Mayura Water Palace, located in the centre of town.

BEST RESORT

Senggigi
● A developed but still engaging coastal resort just to the north of Mataram, Senggigi is a long way from the excesses of Kuta on Bali.
● Wide range of bars and restaurants along the seafront.
● Enjoy nightlife here or in Mataram – there's not a great deal elsewhere on Lombok.

BEST SCENIC LANDSCAPE

Gunung Rinjani
This magnificent volcano rises up from the lush lowlands of central Lombok. Popular walking trails wind up to the crater rim, the most convenient leaving from the village of Senaru. From the summit you can look down on the stunning expanse of Segara Anak, the lake enclosed within the crater rim. Care is essential when choosing a guide, as this is a remote area.

BEST SIGHT

Narmada
This impressive palace and temple complex just to the east of Mataram was built in the early nineteenth century by the Raja of Mataram as a token of his enduring reverence when he became too infirm to climb the slopes of Gunung Rinjani to make his offerings to the gods.

BEST SHOPPING

Whereas on Bali no one leaves without buying a batik sarong or throw, the expertise on Lombok is demonstrated in beautiful handwoven cottons, bone whittling, boxes made from palm leaves, bamboo carving and pottery.

Selong
Selong is the bustling capital of East Lombok. Here you can purchase many crafts, though it is cheaper to buy them at source in the villages.

Village shopping

Some of the best villages to visit for craftwork include Kotaraja (pottery), Loyok (basket-weaving), Rungkang (pottery), Banyumulak (pottery) and Pringgasela (*endek* cloth).

GILI ISLANDS
Good for beaches, outdoor activities and scenic landscape

THESE SLENDER slips of sand are many people's idea of paradise. The days when the islands were a closely guarded backpacker secret are receding as tourist development takes hold. The three islands off the north-west coast of Lombok are circled by pristine stretches of silicone, beyond which lies some of the best coral around Lombok.

'Gili' simply means 'island', which gives these three a rather enigmatic ring in translation. Each island has its own character. Gili Meno is the quietest, Gili Trawangan the most lively and largest, with Gili Air somewhere in between. They all lie within easy reach of each other and can be accessed quickly by boat from Bangsal on Lombok. Many travellers report being badly ripped off when arranging these boat trips – the most popular scam is selling foreigners a whole boat and then reselling the seats to locals.

JAVA
Good for culture, local colour, outdoor activities, scenic landscape and shopping

THE COMMERCIAL and political hub of Indonesia, this predominantly Muslim island is one of the most populated parts of the world with over 160 million people living within its shores. It boasts a fantastic diversity of scenery, astonishing temples and a wonderfully vibrant people. Tension is still high in Java, as the legacy of President Suharto's regime hangs over the island.

BEST CITIES

Jakarta

Since Suharto's fall from power in May 1998 the situation in Jakarta has been as volatile as it has been unpredictable, with protests, riots and, in Autumn 2000, serious bomb attacks. This is the brash, urban heartland of Indonesia and the traffic and pollution are everything you might expect from a developing city. It takes a little time and patience to begin to appreciate its charms, and many tire of the place and leave before realising that it has much to offer. However, if you keep an open mind, Jakarta can provide a rewarding and diverse insight into Javanese life and culture.

Though Jakarta has none of the aesthetic appeal of Bangkok or the sophisticated *élan* of Hong Kong, it does have myriad superb restaurants and clubs. The old Dutch quarter (Kota) and Chinatown are both worth visiting and there are a few excellent museums, including the Indonesian National Museum, which is located on one side of the vast Merdeka Square. You may also choose to visit the Taman Ismail Marzuki (cultural centre), or the fascinating Textile Museum close to Tanah Abang railway station.

Yogyakarta

A far more relaxed alternative to the chaos of Jakarta, this compact and attractive town is famous for both its culture and its markets.

Much of the activity in the town radiates from Jalan (street) Marlioboro, near the railway station. There are many wonderful and historical buildings, such as the Kraton, and some excellent museums, such as the Museum Sono-Budoyo.

Yogyakarta is probably one of the best places in Indonesia (Solo is another) to buy batik. The two main areas for accommodation are in Sosro and Prawirotaman: Sosro has a unique charm and is favoured by most backpackers; Prawirotaman is more expensive.

BEST SIGHTS

Prambanan and Borobudur

These stunning UNESCO World Heritage Listed temple complexes are arguably Indonesia's greatest attractions. They are astonishing testimonies to the architectural acumen of the Javanese and constitute two of the most visually compelling religious sites in the region.

Prambanan is a series of Hindu temples – the eight largest and most comprehensively restored stand in the central area.

Borobudur, further from Yogyakarta, is a Buddhist temple that rises up impressively from the surrounding countryside. The complex construction of the main temple remains a mystery, and the site still retains an evocative ambience today. Nothing else exists on this scale in Indonesia and both complexes are definitely worth a visit.

BEST SCENIC LANDSCAPE

Mount Bromo

This is one of the most theatrical natural wonders on Java, located well to the east of the island. This is the most active of the popular volcanoes, with intermittent eruptions and lots of steam. Early morning trips to catch the sunrise are as popular as they are spectacularly rewarding.

WHEN TO GO

ROUGHLY SPEAKING, the best time to visit Indonesia is around April/May and October when you will probably avoid the humidity and torrential downpours of the wet season as well as the peak holiday weeks. However, strong regional fluctuations affect the start of the monsoon season, so you need to consider this before booking.

Seasonal smog is still a serious problem in many areas.

If you are interested in attending some of the larger festivals that occur throughout the year, check the dates with the Indonesian Tourist Office.

	Average daily maximum temperature °C											
London	6	7	10	13	17	20	22	21	19	14	10	7
Jakarta	29	29	30	31	31	31	31	31	31	31	30	29
	JAN	FEB	MAR	APR	MAY	JUN	JUL	AUG	SEP	OCT	NOV	DEC
Jakarta	18	17	15	11	9	7	5	4	5	8	12	14
London	15	13	11	12	12	11	12	11	13	13	15	15
	Average number of rainy days per month											

PACKAGE TRAVEL

TOUR OPERATORS allow you to choose your own itinerary by combining overland cultural tours of Java with beach holidays in Bali or Lombok and cruises of the Spice Islands (Maluku). Tours of Java may include internal flights to allow more time for sightseeing. A typical ten-day tour starting from Java will take in the sights at Borobudur and Yogyakarta on the south coast, visit the rim of the Mount Bromo volcano at sunrise and include a flight from Surabaya in Java to Bali for a few days' relaxation. Alternatively, choose a beach hotel on the smaller, less developed island of Lombok. Many operators also offer Spice Island cruises out of Bali – these involve three or four nights at sea, and drop in on the islands east of Bali including Lombok, Sabolan, Flores and Komodo. Other options include self-drive tours exploring the interior of Bali. Accommodation is generally in mid-range hotels on tours of Java, and in beach hotels ranging from simple to deluxe in Bali. Many operators cancelled trips to Indonesia in the late 1990s, with some even having to evacuate holidaymakers from Lombok, so tour programmes and brochure-advertised holidays are subject to change.

> **Tour operators**
>
> **Adventure**: Exodus, Explore Worldwide, Guerba, Travelbag
> **Birdwatching**: Naturetrek **Cultural**: Prospect **Cruising**: Noble
> Caledonian **General**: Abercrombie & Kent, Asean Explorer, Asian
> Journeys, Bales Tours, British Airways Holidays, Coromandel,
> Eastravel, Far East Gateways, Garuda Indonesia Holidays, Gold
> Medal, Hayes & Jarvis, Jetset, Kuoni, Magic of the Orient, Saga,
> Silverbird, Somak, Steppes East, Thomas Cook, Thomson, Trade-
> winds, Trailfinders, Tropical Places

INDEPENDENT TRAVEL

ACCOMMODATION IS plentiful, although less so at festival times,
and normally includes a complimentary breakfast of banana pancakes
and clove tea.

The three main internal airlines are Merpati, Sempati and Garuda's
domestic service. On Java the trains and air-conditioned coaches are
efficient and connect with the ferries. On Bali private minibuses run
the busy routes; *bemos* (the tiny public buses) are very cramped, and
only for the patient!

It is important to remember when visiting an Indonesian temple or
Pura that dress must be appropriate. Ceremonial sarongs are often
provided but it's useful to have one at hand in case they aren't.

Before setting out on independent travel in Indonesia travellers
should consider that they have less back-up than those on a package
tour if the political situation deteriorates.

RED TAPE, HEALTH AND SAFETY

AGAIN, ALL travellers should check the current political situation
before embarking on travel to Indonesia. During 2000 there were
dangerous disturbances in Jakarta, Ambon (Maluku), Poso (Sulawesi),
Aceh (Sumatra) and West Timor amongst others.

British passport-holders do not need a visa for trips of under 60 days,
unless on business. A 60-day tourist visa is issued upon entry if you
have an onward ticket out of Indonesia and at least six months still
remaining on your passport. This period is not extendable and you
must leave and re-enter if you wish to remain longer. It is worth
checking your flight routes as there is a risk of disruption over
Afghanistan owing to military activity.

Three major diseases you could be at risk of catching are malaria, typhoid and viral hepatitis. Polio is also a minor threat. Unless you have come from a country which is known to have yellow fever, you will not need to prove that you have been inoculated against the disease, but it is strongly recommended that you consult your GP or a travel clinic before leaving for the latest health advice.

Outbreaks of pickpocketing on Java have been reported over the years, especially in Yogyakarta – take the usual streetwise precautions (see page 12). Visitors are advised against mountain trekking without a professional guide.

MORE INFORMATION Indonesian Tourist Office, brochure line (09001) 600180 (premium rate number)

Embassy of the Republic of Indonesia, 38 Grosvenor Square, London W1X 9AD, tel 020-7355 3866, web site: *www.visit-indonesia.com*

COST OF LIVING £

REPUBLIC OF IRELAND

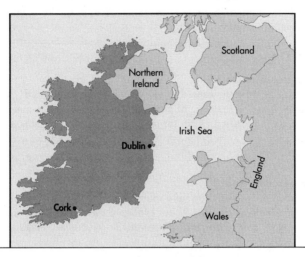

HIGHLIGHTS

Beaches *North-west, west coast*	**Culture** *Dublin, Kilkenny, Sligo, Wexford*	*Glendalough, Schull, River Shannon*	*south and south-west*
Local colour *Cobh, Kinsale, Youghal*	**History** *North-west*	**Romantic escapism** *South and south-west*	**Family holidays** *Cobh, Enniscrone, Mullaghmore*
Nightlife *Dublin, Galway, Westport*	**Outdoor activities** *Ben Bulben, the Burren,*	**Scenic landscape** *North-west,*	**Wildlife** *River Shannon, Saltee Islands*

DUBLIN
Good for culture and nightlife

DUBLIN HAS considerable charm; it is compact and easily explorable on foot, with fine Georgian squares and stately government buildings. The River Liffey bisects the city: most museums, churches and the

257

best choice of shops, restaurants and hotels are located on the south side of the river. There are a number of excellent walking tours to help the visitor get to grips with various aspects of the city's life and history. Many academic tours on historical or architectural themes leave from Trinity College. For more passion, join the 1916 Rebellion Tour. And be sure to find time to join the Fine Thespians who mount the excellent 'Literary Pub Crawl'.

BEST SIGHTS

Guinness Hopstore
Everything you ever wanted to know about 'the Black Stuff', with a comprehensive collection of the company's memorable and often innovative advertising. You can try your hand at designing a new Guinness poster, learn the secrets of the brewing process and complete your visit with a welcome pint.

Kilmainham Gaol
The place of incarceration (and sometimes execution) for generations of Irish Nationalists, this is an evocative and powerful sight. An excellent visitor centre boasts state-of-the-art display techniques to place Ireland's march to independence in its social and historical context.

National Gallery of Ireland
Good collection of British and Irish art, a sprinkling of Renaissance works and a comprehensive programme of visiting exhibitions.

National Museum of Ireland
Galleries cover Irish history from pre-Christian times to the twentieth-century struggle for independence. There are Celtic and Viking arte-facts and a glittering collection of Bronze Age gold.

Temple Bar
One of the city's oldest parts, rejuvenated as a trendy cultural centre. Cobbled streets are packed with interesting arts centres, theatres, cafés, pubs, live music, street theatre, ethnic restaurants and unusual shops. If you are interested in traditional music join the nightly 'Musical Pub Crawl'.

Trinity College
The peaceful gardens and cobbled squares of the oldest university in Ireland (founded 1592) are in the centre of the city. You can see the ninth-century *Book of Kells*, visit the magnificent old library and tune into 'The Dublin Experience' – an audio-visual introduction to the city.

St Patrick's and Christchurch Cathedrals

St Patrick's, the Church of Ireland's national cathedral, has important monuments to influential dignitaries, such as the eighteenth-century satirist and former dean, Jonathan Swift. Christchurch, at the other end of the street, is linked to a multimedia experience, 'Dublinia', an evocative account of the city's history.

SOUTH-EAST
Good for culture, outdoor activities and wildlife

IN THE 'Garden of Ireland' (County Wicklow) you can drive from green valleys to the bleak Sally Gap in the Wicklow Mountains within minutes. It is a good area in which to spend a week visiting the best sights, before spending a week by the beach on the west coast.

BEST BASES

Kilkenny
● Best example of an Irish medieval city, with intact cathedral and castle.
● Delightful setting on banks of the River Nore.
● Lots of craft and artists' workshops close to the city, and in addition an important arts festival in August.

Wexford
● Ancient, attractive harbour town, the south–east's commercial centre.
● International opera festival staged in October.

BEST SIGHTS AND EXCURSIONS

Glendalough
One of the most important early Christian sites in Ireland. Splendid setting with a high round tower above the glen and its two small lakes.

National Stud and Japanese Gardens
Formerly owned by Lord Wavertree, the 1,000-acre estate at Tully is now state-run. Visit the museum, then see thoroughbred horses in their paddocks. The superb gardens were created in the early 1900s.

Powerscourt Gardens and Waterfall
Stunningly set in the foothills of the Wicklow Mountains, these Italianate gardens were designed in the 1730s but took over 100 years to complete. Fire gutted the house in 1974. The waterfall, nearly three miles away, is worth visiting for its romantic setting.

Russsborough

A very pretty Palladian mansion, designed by Richard Castle (also architect of Powerscourt House) in the mid-eighteenth century. It has a notable art collection.

Saltee Islands

Great and Little Saltee Islands off the east coast are Ireland's largest bird sanctuary, with colonies of cormorants and guillemots.

SOUTH AND SOUTH-WEST
Good for family holidays, local colour, outdoor activities, romantic escapism and scenic landscape

THE GULF Stream hits the coast around Cork, and as you travel westwards towards Kerry the scenery turns almost tropical. Here you will find some good small family resorts, where high rocky shores alternate with long pale sandy beaches (strands). It is also a great area for touring, with lakes and mountains inland and a beautiful coastline enhanced by offshore islands, such as the Blasket Islands (good for beaches and seal-spotting).

BEST RESORTS

Cobh

● Attractive town with huge natural harbour which serves as international port for Cork. It was the *Titanic's* last port of call. Evocative visitor centre.
● Stony beach but good swimming and lots of facilities.
● International Sailing Centre offering all kinds of water-based sports, including a regatta weekend in August.
● Fota Wildlife Park and Arboretum a few miles north of Cobh.

Kinsale

● Narrow streets lined with painted houses and interesting shops.
● Charming harbour with a range of accommodation.
● Excellent restaurants – fish and seafood are specialities. Renowned countrywide for the quality of its food. Kinsale Gourmet Week is held here in October.

Schull

● Sheltered harbour, with sporting and sailing festivals in July.
● Mount Gabriel (1,339ft) is worth the climb for memorable views.

Youghal
- Ancient port at the mouth of the River Blackwater.
- Appealing architecture in and around Main Street.
- Lots of traditional music in local bars.

BEST SIGHTS AND EXCURSIONS

Blarney
The home of the infamous Blarney Stone, which is said to bestow the gift of eloquence on all who kiss it. Worth it for believers only.

Gallarus Oratory
This remarkable structure is thought to have been built in the eighth or ninth century. It is in the shape of an upturned boat and is the best example of dry-stone masonry in the country.

Garinish Island
Rocky island converted into an outstanding garden by John Allen Bryce just before the First World War.

Killarney National Park
Over 25,000 acres of lakes, mountains, peat bogs, gardens and woodland, most of which you can drive or walk around.

Ring of Kerry
This is the scenic circuit of the Iveragh peninsula – the standard route consists of a drive of about four hours. The views of Macgillycuddy's Reeks mountains, the valleys, lakes and sea are spectacular, but it is not worth going if it is raining or misty. The road also gets particularly busy in July and August, when crawling along the narrow roads behind gleaming tour buses can get frustrating. The town of Killarney is the best touring base for both the Ring of Kerry and Killarney National Park.

CORK

CORCONIANS CONSIDER their city more important than Dublin and the two compete both commercially and culturally. Cork has an international jazz festival in October, and lots of *craic*, pronounced 'crack' (loosely translated as 'fun'), all year round.

BEST SIGHTS

The Crawford Art Gallery and the Municipal School of Art offer a great variety of sculpture and paintings. St Anne's Shandon, a city

261

landmark with a huge tower of which two sides are red sandstone and the other two grey limestone, provides an excellent panorama of the city.

WEST
Good for beaches, culture, family holidays, nightlife, outdoor activities, romantic escapism and scenic landscape

THE WEST of Ireland is thought by many to be the 'real' Ireland, with some of the country's wildest and most beautiful landscapes. You are more likely to hear Irish spoken here than in any other part of Ireland. It is a good area for beach or walking holidays as well as touring.

BEST BASES

Galway
Galway's fine city walls have been painstakingly restored. Cultural events are frequent; the city boasts a July arts festival, in addition to year-round great music, theatre and exhibitions. A horse-racing festival is held in the last week of July. Try Clarinbridge Oyster Festival (7 miles south of Galway) in September – great 'crack' for the connoisseur.

Roundstone
Connemara's prettiest fishing harbour offers local accommodation – you will find B&Bs and hotels in the village. Two magnificent beaches, Dog's Bay and Gurteen Bay, are sited a mile or so to the north. Try the exceptional fish chowder in O'Dowd's pub.

Westport
This delightful town was designed in the eighteenth century by James Wyatt. It has an interesting variety of shops, and some of the best musical pubs in the west. Eighteenth-century Westport House, designed by Richard Castle and a mile from the centre, is open to visitors.

BEST SIGHTS AND EXCURSIONS

The Burren
This extraordinary multi-fissured limestone plateau in the north-west of County Clare covers more than 60 square miles and is a delight to potholers and botanists alike, with an intricate underground cave system and alpine and Mediterranean flowers growing side by side. There are a number of fine standing stones.

Ceide Fields
Stone Age farming settlement preserved beneath a peat bog and now revealed after some 5,000 years. Superb visitors' centre.

Cliffs of Moher
The five-mile stretch of cliffs reaches 660 feet in places. The birdlife is abundant and the views magnificent.

Croagh Patrick
The mountain from where St Patrick is said to have banished all snakes from Ireland is the west's holy symbol. The 2,500-ft climb takes about two hours; the views on a clear day are breathtaking.

Lough Corrib
The largest lake in the Republic is famous for its pike, trout and salmon fishing. Boat trips are available from many locations.

Twelve Pins and Maumturk Mountains
These spectacular mountain ranges dominate the Connemara landscape. Clifden makes a good base.

BEST ISLANDS

Aran Islands
Inishmore, Inishmaan and Inisheer: Irish is spoken everywhere. Good for craft, pre-historic monuments, natural history.

Clare Island
Good for ruins and Irish music.

Inishbofin
Historical interest, fascinating ruins and secluded sandy beaches are the main attractions of this island off County Galway.

NORTH-WEST
Good for beaches, culture, family holidays, history, outdoor activities and scenic landscape

---

THE POET William Butler Yeats and his brother Jack used the landscape of Sligo as the inspiration for their writing and painting. The county is also rich in archaeological remains. Donegal's rugged coastline is studded with fine sandy beaches. It has some of the oldest mountain ranges in the country and a strong Gaelic tradition.

BEST RESORTS

Enniscrone
● Long sandy beach on Killala Bay.
● Hot sea-water baths with seaweed and steam.

Mullaghmore
● Appealing harbour full of boats and a good sandy beach.
● Views across Donegal Bay to the Blue Stack Mountains.

BEST SIGHTS AND EXCURSIONS

Ben Bulben
The unforgettable, brooding profile of this mountain dominates all around it. Plateau-topped and solitary on the north Sligo plains, it is easy to climb. W.B. Yeats is buried, as he requested, 'Under bare Ben Bulben's head/In Drumcliff churchyard'.

Carrowmore
The largest Stone Age cemetery in Ireland, with over 60 passage graves.

Cliffs of Bunglass
The views of the south face of Slieve League dropping 1,980 feet into the sea are worth the climb.

Glenveagh National Park
Nearly 25,000 acres of lakes, woodlands and bog plus a romantic nineteenth-century granite castle and mature exotic gardens.

Knocknarea
See spectacular views from this 1,080-ft mountain. Queen Maeve's cairn, 540 feet round and containing a passage grave, lies on the summit.

Sligo
The County Museum and Art Gallery holds a memorial collection of W.B.Yeats' manuscripts and papers, and pictures by Jack B. Yeats.

MIDLANDS
Good for outdoor activities and wildlife

THIS LARGELY underrated region, spanning the great River Shannon, has small mountain ranges, ancient farmlands and peat bogs. Ireland's longest river is navigable from Carrick-on-Shannon in County Leitrim to Killaloe in County Clare. The restored Shannon–Erne

Waterway links the Republic to the North. You can hire cruisers from several locations. The Shannon frequently widens into loughs; the scenery is beautiful and the birdlife exceptional. River traffic is heavy in July and August when it is wise to moor early after a day's cruising.

BEST SIGHTS

Clonmacnois
The Republic's most famous monastic site. Founded in the sixth century, it is the burial place of the Kings of Connaught and Tara.

Lough Key Forest Park
An outstanding 350-hectare park near the Shannon. Climb the modern Moylurg Tower for spectacular views over Lough Key and nearby mountains. Boat trips on the lake, gardens and nature trails are on offer.

WHEN TO GO

IN SUMMER the weather is generally a bit wetter and cooler than it is in southern England. Late spring and early summer are often relatively dry.

	Average daily maximum temperature °C											
London	6	7	10	13	17	20	22	21	19	14	10	7
Dublin	8	8	10	13	15	18	20	19	17	14	10	8
	JAN	FEB	MAR	APR	MAY	JUN	JUL	AUG	SEP	OCT	NOV	DEC
Dublin	13	10	10	11	10	11	13	12	12	11	12	14
London	15	13	11	12	12	11	12	11	13	13	15	15
	Average number of rainy days per month											

PACKAGE TRAVEL

MOST TOUR operators offer inclusive holidays to Ireland by ferry and air. As car hire is relatively expensive in the Republic of Ireland you may do better to take your own car, or hire in Northern Ireland, where it is cheaper. Go-as-you-please options, including ferry crossings and pre-paid accommodation – from manor-house hotels to village inns and guesthouses – cater for varying budgets. You can also go on self-drive itineraries of the whole country or an area such as Cork and Kerry, staying in accommodation which you have to have booked in advance.

Self-catering accommodation featured in tour operators' brochures is often in purpose-built modern houses, arranged in small clusters; more individual and picturesque properties are thinner on the ground. Holiday parks are featured by various tour operators and include wet-weather facilities and activities.

City breaks to Dublin by air and ferry are based in a range of accommodation, from five-star hotels to guesthouses. With competitive airfares and budget accommodation or special offers in hotels you may find it cheaper to travel independently.

Specialists provide a wide range of activities, including touring by horse-drawn wagons, golfing, fishing, river cruising, walking and cycling.

Tour operators

City breaks: British Airways Holidays, Cresta, Crystal, Inghams, Osprey, Sovereign, Thomson, Time Off, Travelscene **Coach tours**: Excelsior, Leger, Shearings, Travelsphere, Wallace Arnold **Specialists**: Aer Lingus Holidays, CIE Tours, Drive Ireland, Irish Ferries, Kerry Holidays, PAB Travel, Ryan Holidays, Stena Line Holidays **Walking/cycling**: Bike Tours (cycling), Countrywide (walking), Exodus (walking), Headwater (cycling and walking), Ramblers Holidays (walking), Sherpa (walking), Waymark (walking) **Other activities**: Ace Study Tours, Anglers World (fishing), Blakes (river cruising), Cox & Kings (flora), Holts' Tours (battlefields), Limosa (birdwatching), Martin Randall (cultural), Prospect (Cultural), Solo's Holidays (singles), Travel for the Arts (music)

INDEPENDENT TRAVEL

AER LINGUS is the national carrier and flies from the UK to Dublin and regional airports all over the Republic. Ryanair, British Midland and Virgin Cityjet also fly from the UK to the Republic. There is not much difference between the SuperApex fares offered by these airlines, but it is worth ringing around for special offers.

All the major car-hire firms are represented at the airport in Dublin centre, the regional cities and some towns, but local firms are cheaper and generally reliable. A UK driving licence is acceptable. Petrol is significantly cheaper than in the UK.

Irish Ferries, Stena Sealink and Swansea Cork ferries run regular services to the UK. Stena operates the new HSS 90-minute ferry from Dun Laoghaire to Holyhead as well as the Sea Cat hydrofoil. Car ferry prices are extremely high, particularly in peak season; although all companies offer special rates, none is cheap. Even so, for a two-week touring holiday it is less expensive to bring your own car on the ferry than to fly and hire.

Getting to the Republic by bus and ferry is very cheap but time-consuming; train and ferry costs much less than flying. Once in the Republic the train system is run by CIE (Coras Iopair Eireann), which also operates the bus system. It is a bit archaic but good value and you will reach your destination, albeit by a circuitous route. Special travel cards offer the best value.

Accommodation, and plenty of it, is available to suit all pockets. Bookings are necessary in high season, and, if you are touring, the tourist offices offer an excellent booking service. Several organisations produce their own brochures, such as *Hidden Ireland*, featuring a collection of large, privately owned houses. *The Blue Book* is another popular collection, while Bord Faílte (the tourist board) has information on hotels, B&Bs, farmhouses and self-catering.

RED TAPE, HEALTH AND SAFETY

UK CITIZENS ARE not required to show passports, but entry formalities have been tightened to prevent illegal 'back-door' immigration, so take some form of identification.

Like many European cities, Dublin has a problem with street crime – take care of valuables and leave nothing on display in parked cars. Be particularly wary in O'Connell Street after dark. For other advice see page 12.

MORE INFORMATION Irish Tourist Board Information Line, 0800 0397000, web site: *www.ireland.travel.ie/home*

COST OF LIVING £££

ISRAEL

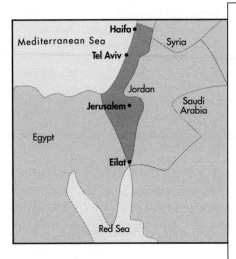

HIGHLIGHTS

Culture/history
The coast, Holy Land, Jerusalem

Beaches
The coast

Family holidays
The coast

Local colour
Jerusalem

Outdoor activities
The coast

Scenic landscape
Holy Land

JERUSALEM
Good for culture/history and local colour

PRESENT-DAY JERUSALEM continues to be driven by symbolism and dreams. The Old City is a labyrinth of alleyways that creep through the Arab, Christian, Jewish and Armenian quarters. The New City is vast and exhausting and much more European in outlook, apart from Me'a She'arim, the ultra-orthodox Jewish *shtetl*, which embraces the traditions of eighteenth-century Eastern Europe.

OLD CITY

Christian Quarter
The Way of the Cross traces Christ's route to crucifixion, ending at the Church of the Holy Sepulchre. Long queues form outside Christ's tomb here; many visit the alternative Garden Tomb in East Jerusalem.

Jewish Quarter
The Western (Wailing) Wall is the last remnant of Herod the Great's Second Temple and an important political and religious symbol. Underground, the Herodian mansions reveal life in Roman times.

Muslim Quarter
The Dome of the Rock is the city's most impressive sight, its huge golden dome dominating the skyline. At the centre is the rock from which, Muslims believe, Mohammed ascended to heaven.

Tower of David
This superb museum mixes archaeology, walks round ramparts and a trip into the city's history via dioramas, holograms, models and films.

NEW CITY

Israel Museum
Under the Shrine of the Book the frail leather of the Dead Sea Scrolls is displayed in a subtly lit, almost mystical setting. Allow half a day.

Vad Yashem
The memorial and research centre for the six million victims of the Nazi Holocaust explains the events in a simple and dignified way.

HOLY LAND
Good for culture/history and scenic landscape

FOR THOUSANDS, a trip to the Holy Land is the affirmation of a lifetime's faith: biblical place names that resonate deep in the consciousness.

BEST SIGHTS

Bethlehem
The humble manger has long since been engulfed by the cavernous Church of the Nativity, a fortress-like stone structure. The Grotto of the Nativity lies beneath. Christ's birthplace marked by a silver star.

Dead Sea
Most resort hotels are at En Bokek, which owes its spa status to therapeutic Dead Sea minerals. In AD 70, Jewish zealots took refuge in the spectacular rock fortress of Masada during a revolt against Rome: you can visit the remains. The celebrated Dead Sea Scrolls were found in the caves at Qumran: subsequent excavations unearthed several buildings of the Essene community. At the Ein Gedi Nature Reserve you can walk along an oasis-like ravine, past a gushing spring that flows into the Dead Sea.

Nazareth
The Roman Catholic Basilica of the Annunciation, boldly modern in

design, obliterates the spot where the Archangel Gabriel appeared to the Virgin Mary. Inside are the Grotto of the Annunciation and the remains of Byzantine and Crusader churches.

Sea of Galilee
Here are some of the Holy Land's loveliest areas, while the shore-side town of Tiberias has a lively, if tacky, resort buzz. At Tabgha, the Church of the Multiplication of the Loaves and Fishes marks the site of the feeding of the five thousand. The Church of Mensa Christi denotes the spot where Christ supposedly charged Peter with the keys of the kingdom; remains of what is said to be Peter's house are at Capernaum, complete with damaged fresco work.

THE COAST
Good for culture, beaches, family holidays and outdoor activities

BEAUTIFUL BEACHES stretch the length of the Mediterranean coast, while Eilat on the Red Sea has year-round water sports and beach safaris into the Negev Desert.

BEST RESORTS

Eilat
● Popular resort with every conceivable water sport on offer.
● Beaches indifferent but Eilat is a livelier place than Israel's Mediterranean resorts, and has year-round sun.
● Most evening entertainment based in and around hotels.
● Inconvenient for biblical sights: excursions involve an overnight stop.

Netanya
● Best Mediterranean resort: low-key, good for families and the elderly.
● Fine cliff-backed white sand beach, stretching for over five miles.
● Pedestrianised town centre with lively main square.
● Convenient for a visit to Petra in Jordan.

BEST SIGHTS AND EXCURSIONS

Akko
This Crusader city was once held by Richard the Lionheart. It is worth visiting the splendid eighteenth-century mosque of Ahmed Jezzar, and the now underground Crusader city in the heart of the Arab quarter.

Caesarea
This two-mile site includes a Roman amphitheatre and aqueduct, a

Byzantine street and a Crusader city. The restored amphitheatre where Christians and Jews were thrown to the lions is used for concerts.

Tel Aviv (Jaffa)
Laid back and arty, an ugly line of high-rise hotels along the seafront hides tree-lined streets of Bauhaus architecture divided by intimate shopping avenues. The Diaspora Museum has beautiful displays conveying the strong sense of nationhood felt by present-day Israelis. Jaffa's old port offers more local colour, while the cobbled alleyways of the reconstructed Crusader city house an artists' colony of craft shops.

WHEN TO GO

PILGRIMS MAY wish to spend Christmas in Bethlehem or Easter in Jerusalem. Spring is probably the best time for a coach tour, before it becomes too hot. Eilat excels for winter sun, with reliable temperatures. For summer sun, sea and sand, choose the Mediterranean coast.

	Average daily maximum temperature °C											
London	6	7	10	13	17	20	22	21	19	14	10	7
Jerusalem	13	13	18	23	27	29	31	31	29	27	21	15
	JAN	FEB	MAR	APR	MAY	JUN	JUL	AUG	SEP	OCT	NOV	DEC
Jerusalem	9	12	3	3	1	0	0	0	0	1	4	7
London	15	13	11	12	12	11	12	11	13	13	15	15
	Average number of rainy days per month											

PACKAGE TRAVEL

ALL THE major tour operators feature Israel; only specialists offer a wide variety of holidays. A week-long coach tour may feature the Dead Sea, Masada, Jericho, the Sea of Galilee, Lake Tiberias, Nazareth, Haifa, Caesarea, Bethlehem and Jerusalem, staying in hotels and guesthouses.

Fly-drive packages are available. Some specialists offer accommodation on kibbutzes, either in guesthouses or hotels. Kibbutz accommodation can also be booked directly with the Kibbutz or through the Israel Kibbutz Chain (tel: 03 5246161, fax 03 5278088, web site *www.kibbutz.co.il*)

On the Mediterranean, Netanya is an alternative to the Red Sea resort of Eilat. Peak season in Eilat is December. Accommodation is mostly in hotels, with some self-catering apartments.

Tour operators

Birdwatching: Ornitholidays, Sunbird **Diving**: Goldenjoy, Longwood, Superstar **General and specialist**: All Abroad (Dead Sea special), AMG, First Choice, Israel Travel Service, Pullmans Holidays, Peltours, Superstar, Thomson, Unijet, West End Travel **Pilgrimages**: Highway Journeys, Inter-Church Travel, McCabe Travel **Walking**: Explore Worldwide **Other activities**: Club Med (all-inclusive)

INDEPENDENT TRAVEL

SCHEDULED FLIGHTS go to Tel Aviv and charter flights to Eilat. Eilat has internal flights to Tel Aviv and Jerusalem, which can save you time if you want to combine a beach holiday with a bit of sightseeing.

Israel's internal transport system is well developed. Motorways link the main cities, and roads are of a high standard. For car hire, you need a valid UK licence and must be over 21. Road signs are in Hebrew, English and Arabic; driving is on the right. Public transport is efficient and cheap.

The national bus company, Egged, covers most of Israel. You can buy passes for up to a month. Trains are cheaper but less frequent and more limited. Public transport closes down on Friday afternoon and Saturday.

Within towns, taxis have meters; for taxis between towns or villages agree the fare in advance. *Sherut* (shared taxis) also link most places in Israel and, though more expensive than buses, are still reasonable.

Israel offers every kind of accommodation, from deluxe hotels and self-catering apartments to kibbutz guesthouses and campsites. Some Christian pilgrims stay at hospices run by various churches.

RED TAPE, HEALTH AND SAFETY

BRITISH PASSPORT-HOLDERS do not require a visa. The tentative nature of the Middle East peace process means that security is very tight, even before you arrive – extra baggage checks are required when you check in at the airport, so you should allow plenty of time. Passports may be required when crossing between Israel and the Occupied Territories and when entering Jerusalem.

If you are having a beach holiday on the Mediterranean coast or in Eilat you are unlikely to see any sign of the troubles. But if you plan to visit the West Bank cities you may find that unrest limits your travels. Bethlehem is the most likely of the biblical sights to be out of bounds. Organised tours may have to drop a destination from the itinerary.

In Jerusalem, the new city is relatively safe, but you are advised not to wander alone in the evenings around East Jerusalem and parts of the Old City. Personal documents, money and credit cards should not be kept in an outside pocket of a bag when walking through the crowded Old City of Jerusalem as they can be easily stolen. With the exception of the main road from Jerusalem to the Dead Sea, Jericho and the Jordan Valley, it is unwise to drive anywhere in the West Bank or Gaza Strip in a car with an Israeli number plate. Keep car doors locked when driving through the West Bank. Seek advice before you hire a car. If heading for East Jerusalem at night, you might be refused lifts from Israeli taxis. For the latest information on safety contact the Foreign Office Travel Advice Unit (see page 11).

MORE INFORMATION Israel Government Tourist Office, 180 Oxford Street, London W1N 9DJ, tel 020-7299 1111, web site: *www.infotour.co.il/*

COST OF LIVING ££££

ITALY

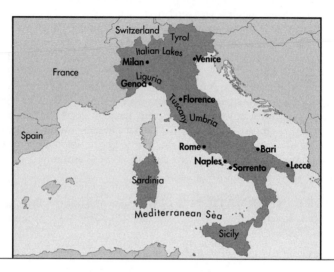

HIGHLIGHTS

Beaches
*Heel of Italy,
Liguria,
Sardinia*

**Family
holidays**
*Liguria,
Sicily*

History
*Florence, Rome,
Venice, Tuscany,
Sicily*

**Romantic
escapism**
*Neapolitan
Riviera*

Culture
*Florence,
Neapolitan
Riviera,
Northern cities,
Rome, Sicily,
Tuscany,
Umbria, Venice*

Food/wine
*Neapolitan
Riviera,
Northern cities,
Tuscany,
Umbria*

Local colour
Venice

Nightlife
Milan, Rome

**Outdoor
activities**
Lakes, Tyrol

**Scenic
landscape**
*Lakes,
Neapolitan
Riviera,
Sardinia, Sicily,
Tuscany, Tyrol,
Umbria*

NORTHERN CITIES
Good for culture and food/wine

DISCOVERING THE northern Italian cities is like a potted art history lesson, covering everything from the Romans to the Futurists.

BEST CITIES

Bergamo
The medieval alleys and brick herringbone streets of the upper part of this pretty hill town converge on a Venetian-style square. The lavish Colleoni chapel was built to house a fifteenth-century mercenary's tomb.

Bologna
An attractive university town, with miles of elegant porticoes, known for good food. The Basilica of San Petronio was originally intended to be larger than St Peter's in Rome. The Archiginnasio, the old university, houses a superb wood-panelled anatomical theatre.

Mantua
At the Palazzo Ducale, portraits by Mantegna of the Renaissance ruling family, the Gonzagas, decorate the Camera degli Sposi. At the other extreme, the Palazzo del Tè displays bawdy scenes by Giulio Romano.

Milan
Industrialised Milan has Italy's only High Gothic cathedral: visit the roof for distant views of the Alps. The Brera Gallery houses north Italian Renaissance paintings, while the Gallery of Modern Art has Italian modernists, French Impressionists and post-Impressionists.

Padua
Pilgrims make for the domed Basilica of Sant' Antonio, patron saint of lost property, to touch his sarcophagus. The other top attraction is Giotto's fresco cycle of the Redemption in the Scrovegni Chapel.

Parma
Parma was heavily bombed in the Second World War. At the Palazzo della Pilotta is the Teatro Farnese, based on Palladio's theatre in Vicenza. The cathedral dome displays a fresco of the Assumption by Correggio.

Ravenna
Exquisite Byzantine mosaics are dotted around town, sumptuous gold backgrounds setting off glowing robes and detailed flowers. To save money, buy a block ticket from the first church you visit.

Turin
A copy of the Holy Shroud, Christianity's most famous relic, can be seen in the cathedral (the original is so fragile it is rarely displayed). The

Egyptian Museum has a superb collection of antiquities, and a Museum of Cinema has opened in the distinctive old synagogue, the Mole Antonelliana.

Verona
The huge irregular Piazza Brà is the focus of Verona, with cafés on one side and a Roman arena at the northern end. Smaller but fringed by fine *palazzi* are Piazza delle Erbe and Piazza dei Signori. The loveliest of the many churches is San Zeno Maggiore, a striped Romanesque basilica.

Vicenza
Palladio's stately *palazzi* fill the town, also boasting his stucco and wood Teatro Olimpico and the symmetrical Villa Rotonda. Several Palladian-style villas surround Vicenza, not all designed by the architect himself.

VENICE
Good for culture, history and local colour

THE FRAGILE, melancholy, decaying beauty of Venice makes it incomparable. Despite the riches of its museums, churches and palaces, nothing compares with exploring the canals and back streets.

BEST SIGHTS
Accademia
Venice's foremost art gallery spans five centuries, starting with fine Byzantine-style altarpieces. The Renaissance collection includes work by the Bellini family, Carpaccio, Titian, Tintoretto and Veronese.

Basilica of St Mark
This exotic Byzantine basilica can be swamped by the number of visitors. Some of the most vibrant mosaics of the Old Testament stories are in the porch. Pay extra to see the stunning jewelled altarpiece, the Pala d'Oro (by the high altar).

Grand Canal
Venice's main thoroughfare flows past bubble-domed churches and extravagant palaces. The best and cheapest way to see the canal is from the No 1 waterbus: you can seldom walk along it, except around the Rialto Bridge. Try a night trip to see frescoed rooms lit by chandeliers.

Piazza San Marco
The city's most famous piazza, its series of repetitive arcades form a foil to the Gothic Doge's Palace and the basilicas, domes and mosaics.

FLORENCE
Good for culture and history

MOST OF the city's attractions are historical, and lie inside its galleries and museums; outside, life proceeds at twentieth-century pace.

BEST SIGHTS

Accademia
Queues form to see the original sculpture of David by Michelangelo, but do not overlook the sculptor's four unfinished Slaves.

Bargello
The best Italian collection of Renaissance sculpture has Donatello's David and Brunelleschi and Ghiberti's entries for the baptistery doors.

Cathedral and baptistery
Brunelleschi's masterpiece is built on a vast scale, but the interior is rather plain. The baptistery has stunning mosaics in the dome and copies of Ghiberti's beautiful bronze doors.

Museo dell'Opera del Duomo
The original panels from Ghiberti's baptistery doors are here, as well as two lovely musicians' galleries by Donatello and della Robbia.

Palazzo Pitti
Within the palace are several galleries. The Galleria Palatina includes works by Titian, Raphael and Veronese, while the Museo degli Argenti is a chaotic collection of marble, silver, ivory and porcelain.

Uffizi
The east wing gives a fine introduction to Florentine Renaissance art. Botticelli's *Birth of Venus* and *Primavera* are the main crowd-pullers.

TUSCANY
Good for culture, food/wine, history and scenic landscape

AN ENGAGING succession of medieval hill towns in a landscape of sunflowers and cool green cypresses sums up, for many, the essence of Italy. Chianti is the most popular area for renting a villa.

Arezzo

The church of San Francesco contains frescos of the True Cross by Piero della Francesca. Visit the house of Renaissance art historian Vasari, who designed the loggia along one side of the Piazza Grande.

Cortona

The massive city walls encircle a hilly mix of old *palazzi* embellished with architraves, scrolls and lions' heads.

Lucca

A handsome, walled, provincial capital with two superb Pisan Romanesque churches: San Martino's and San Michele in Foro. Pilgrims come to see the Holy Face in San Martino, a crucifix said to have been carved by Nicodemus.

Montepulciano

The main street, the Corso, has shops selling *vino nobile*, perfect for quaffing as you toil up to the cathedral on Piazza Grande. Beyond the walls, Antonio da Sangallo's church is a perfect Renaissance temple.

Pienza

The town's central tiny square is the model of a Renaissance city, built by Aeneas Sylvius Piccolomini on his election as Pope Pius II in 1458.

Pisa

The famous leaning tower adjoins a matching cathedral and baptistery, all aligned on the wonderfully traffic-free Campo dei Miracoli.

San Gimignano

Fourteen lofty towers remain out of 72. Climb the tallest, the Museo Civico's. The *collegiata* church has a veritable X-rated *Last Judgement*.

Sansepolcro

Piero della Francesca fans seek his mesmeric painting of a resurrected Christ. To the north-west, La Verna monastery, where St Francis received the stigmata, has fine enamelled terracotta by della Robbia.

Siena

A city of rosy pink alleys, free of traffic. At the central Campo piazza, climb the Museo Civico's tower for superb views. Inside is Simone Martini's famous Maestà. The cathedral has fine inlaid marble floors, sadly usually covered, and a library with frescos by Pintoricchio.

Volterra
Volterra's Roman theatre is well preserved. The Etruscan Museum has many alabaster sarcophagi; the stone is mined here for tourist souvenirs.

TYROL
Good for outdoor activities and scenic landscape

THIS REGION, melding two distinct ethnic traditions – Italian and Tyrolean – into one political entity, has experienced sporadic tensions. Visitors, however, will thrill to the majesty of the saw-toothed Dolomites. The walking season lasts from late June to late September.

BEST BASES

Bressanone
A baroque cathedral dominates the old quarter. The town hosts a festival every second August. Good base for Gardena and Pusteria valleys.

Merano
With its mild climate and spa status, Merano boomed in the nineteenth century. Visit arcaded shopping streets and the castle. Ideal base for the Venosta valley and Monte Giovo Pass.

Molveno
Pretty lakeside village with a pedestrianised centre, small gravel beach and good hotels. Handy for the Brenta Massif and the Rendena valley.

Ortisei
The Gardena valley's main resort with a museum on Ladin culture, derived from a local Roman garrison. Handy for Fassa and Ega valleys.

Solda
A quiet village in the Solda valley; visit a glacier by cable-car. Mountaineer Reinhold Messner has set up an Alpine climbing museum.

BEST SIGHTS AND EXCURSIONS

Bolzano
Stroll from cobbled Piazza Walther through the old town's arcaded streets. The Romanesque-Gothic cathedral has a lovely Gothic pulpit.

Trento
There is a Romanesque cathedral and treasury, a thirteenth-century castle and a lovely central square, with frescoed Renaissance buildings.

BEST SCENIC LANDSCAPES

Ega valley
The road hugs the base of a narrow ravine, opening out to reveal fir-covered hills and the dramatic distant Catinaccio mountains. From the pretty Lake Carezza the road climbs up over the Costalunga Pass.

Gardena valley
Guarded by the dramatic Gardena and Sasso Lungo passes, this crosses the Ladin people's land (street signs become trilingual) to reach the Sella Mountains. Great views of winding Pordoi Pass and Falzarego Pass.

Monte Giovo Pass
See snow-capped Austrian peaks from the top. The descent to the pretty tourist honeypot town of Vipiteno is spectacular.

Rendena and Genova valleys
The Rendena valley is fir-clad; Pinzolo, its most pristine village, is the starting-point for the more spectacular Genova valley, where a dead-end forest road follows the river to Bedole, a lovely picnic spot.

BEST MOUNTAIN TRIPS

Brenta Massif
The cable-car goes up 7,920 feet to the barren landscape of the Groste Pass. From here experienced walkers can hike east to Molveno.

Catinaccio
Multi-level walks bisect the splendour of the Catinaccio. The cable-car from Vigo di Fassa goes to the start. At sunset the rocks glow red.

Mount Paganella
Go by cable-car from Andalo to see the Brenta range and Lake Como.

LAKES
Good for outdoor activities and scenic landscape

GO TO the Italian lakes for a lazy, relaxing holiday. Take a boat trip, linger in cafés, stroll by the water and admire the scenery.

Lake Como

● At picturesque, unspoilt Bellagio, the grounds of Villa Serbelloni occupy a rocky outcrop between the two arms of the lake. Visit also the gardens of Villa Melzi.

● At Cadenabbia an avenue of plane trees leads to Tremezzo and Villa Carlotta, with attractive terraced gardens.

● Cernobbio is a relaxed resort near the splendid Villa d'Este, a grand hotel with famous gardens. Treat yourself to tea on the lakeside terrace.

● Como is a busy city with an interesting centre, the highlight of which is the cathedral with its fine Renaissance altar screen.

● Villa Monastero is now a conference centre but the gardens, shaded by an old magnolia tree, are lovely, with avenues of fruit trees.

Lake Garda

● Popular Gardone has a botanical garden and the fascinating Villa Vittoriale, home of the historian, fascist, womaniser and poet Gabriele D'Annunzio.

● Salo's splendid cathedral contains a gilt polyptych; Malcesine sits at the foot of Monte Baldo and is dominated by a castle once home to the Scaligers of Verona. Good views of the lake from Monte Baldo.

● Sirmione also has a Scaliger castle, and Roman poet Catullus' villa.

● Bardolino has an elegant Romanesque church, and famous wine.

Lake Lugano

● Subdued Morcote is below a steep hillside. Lots of fish restaurants.

● In busy Gandria, houses cling to the lakeside. Spectacular views.

● The Sighignola Belvedere, four miles east of Campione, is called the 'balcony of Italy' – on a clear day you can see Mont Blanc.

● There are also super views from Sacro Monte, which has a pilgrimage church dedicated to the Virgin, and from the Campo dei Fiori.

Lake Maggiore

● Stresa is the best base for island-visiting. A cable-car to Mottarone gives fine lake views.

● Boats ply among the Borromean Islands: Isola Bella is the prettiest. Count Charles Borromeo III's palace and gardens are here. Isola Madre has an elegant villa; unspoilt Isola Pescatori has many restaurants.

● Pallanza's quays are flower-decked. Nearby are Villa Taranto's gardens.

● Cannero is a pretty ferry stop where cafés on wooden platforms overhang the lake. A ruined castle stands on a tiny island to the north.

● Angera's castle has fine frescos depicting life in the Middle Ages.

Lake Orta
● Orta San Giulio is a small resort on a tiny promontory on the eastern side of the lake. An arched town hall dominates the cobbled square.
● San Giulio Island is a tiny, tranquil place, whose houses cluster tightly around a Benedictine monastery and the twelfth-century basilica.

LIGURIA
Good for beaches and family holidays

THE COASTLINE between Tuscany and France divides into up-market eastern resorts – stopovers on the eighteenth-century Grand Tour – and unpretentious, family-oriented beach resorts in the west.

BEST RESORTS

Alassio
● Lively resort with a variety of large modern hotels and some older, more characterful ones catering for affluent, largely Italian market.
● Best sandy beach in Liguria, almost entirely divided into concessions.
● Good restaurants and late-night shopping around a long, narrow street behind the beach, known to the English as 'the Drain'.

Finale Ligure
● Splendid setting below craggy cliffs and wooded mountains.
● Long sandy beach with more free areas than most neighbours.
● Most hotels, shops and restaurants are in area called Finale Marina.
● Old quarter of Finalborgo is a knot of alleyways around a Gothic church and Renaissance convent.

Laigueglia
● Circled by hills draped in olive groves.
● Peeling network of alleyways in old fishermen's quarter.
● Long, broad sandy beach, much of which is divided into concessions along the length of the resort.

Santa Margherita Ligure
● Well-established, fashionable resort in beautiful Gulf of Tigullio.
● Swanky hotels, shops and restaurants, a harbour full of luxury yachts.
● No beach, though you could take a boat trip to the tiny, photogenic and even pricier resort of Portofino in neighbouring bay.

BEST SIGHTS AND EXCURSIONS

Cinque Terre

Five unspoilt fishing villages, improbably wedged into fissures or overhanging rock faces. Accessible by boat and train; best seen by taking the scenic footpath connecting all five. **Monterosso** is largest and most touristy, with a pebble beach and hotels; **Vernazza** is prettiest – an arcaded lane leads to a seafront piazza with bars and restaurants; **Corniglia** has a stony beach and dull old town; **Manarola** is a delightful huddle of houses hugging the rock face; **Riomaggiore** is really just one charming street shoe-horned into a ravine.

Genoa

Christopher Columbus's birthplace is still Italy's premier seaport; Genoa has unsightly docks, but the back streets (*carrugi*) of the old quarter house some atmospheric *trattorie*. Take a day-trip to see Genoese and Venetian paintings in the Palazzo Rosso, Antonello da Messina's *Ecce Homo* at the Palazzo Spinola and the Pisan-Romanesque cathedral of San Lorenzo.

UMBRIA
Good for culture, food/wine and scenic landscape

AS IN neighbouring Tuscany, soul-satisfying landscape and medieval hilltop towns are Umbria's main attractions. The main sightseeing cities are in the centre and north, but the best countryside is in the south.

BEST SIGHTS AND EXCURSIONS

Assisi

The Basilica of San Francesco boasts Giotto's wonderful frescos of the saint's life, now restored after the 1997 earthquake. Few tourists actually reach the town itself. Just out of town, the Porziuncola, the chapel where St Francis founded the Franciscan monastic order, is dwarfed by the seventeenth-century Basilica of Santa Maria erected around it.

Gubbio

A grey, frontier-like town. The Museo Civico contains seven Eugubine Tablets, the only record of the Umbrian language. The city's bishop-saint Ubaldo lies in a pink brick basilica reached by funicular.

Orvieto

High on a volcanic outcrop, Orvieto has a magnificent cathedral, with gruesome frescos by Luca Signorelli. Visit also a 12-sided belltower in the Piazza della Repubblica, and a sixteenth-century well.

Perugia
The city has a cosmopolitan feel, thanks to the Foreigners' University. The pink-and-white cathedral overlooks the Fontana Maggiore, a fountain with mythical scenes. The National Gallery of Umbria has works by locals Perugino and Pinturicchio.

Spoleto
In the Piazza del Duomo is a Romanesque cathedral. Nearby, four-teenth-century Ponte delle Torri was built to replace a Roman aqueduct.

Todi
Piazza del Popolo is a stunning medieval square with a cathedral, the crenellated Palazzo del Popolo and the Gothic Palazzo del Capitano.

BEST SCENIC LANDSCAPE

Sibillini Mountains
Towering cliffs stretch to Visso, before a thrilling climb up to the Gualdo Pass, overlooked by the bleak Sibillini Mountains. Nearby, wild horses roam the huge basin of the Piano Grande. Call in at Norcia for excellent local ham, sausages and lentils.

NEAPOLITAN RIVIERA
Good for culture, food/wine, romantic escapism and scenic landscape

THIS PART of the Italian coastline has stunning scenery, charming cliffside towns and some of the finest archaeological sites to be found anywhere in the world.

BEST BASES

Amalfi
The terraced houses and lemon groves are best admired from the sea. The town's focal point is a small piazza at the foot of the stairway to the cathedral. For a quieter side of town, take one of the little alleyways off the main street to emerge above the belltower.

Positano
There is no real centre to this town of sugar-cube houses, except Santa Maria Church. A one-way street leads to the beach and promenade.

Ravello
The escapist's choice, Ravello sits 200 feet above Amalfi at the end of a series of hairpin bends. Villa Rufolo and Villa Cimbrone have public gardens with wonderful coastal views. The plain cathedral has some fine mosaic pulpits and bronze doors.

Sorrento
Good for public transport and hotels. The attractive old town is lit up in the evening, but beneath the touristy veneer, Italian traditions and lifestyle linger. To escape most of the crowds, visit San Francesco's cloisters or the Marina Grande, a fishing port with a few good restaurants.

BEST SIGHTS AND EXCURSIONS

Capri
Most visitors seek the Blue Grotto – a pricey tourist trap. More interesting is the stylish Villa San Michele in Anacapri, built by the Swedish doctor Axel Munthe. Try a coastal walk from the Tragara terrace for cliff views, or see the ruins of Villa Jovis, one of Emperor Tiberius's haunts.

Herculaneum
Herculaneum was a wealthy suburb destroyed by the eruption of Vesuvius in AD 79. Don't miss the baths, the House of the Deer, and the House of the Neptune Mosaic, with two lovely multicoloured mosaics.

Naples
Brave the chaos and traffic for the National Archaeological Museum. Highlights are mosaics and paintings and a 'secret cabinet' of erotic art from Pompeii.

Paestum
Three magnificent Doric temples on windswept marshy plains south of Amalfi. The museum displays pottery, friezes and tomb murals.

Pompeii
The layer of pumice stone and ash that buried the city when Vesuvius erupted in AD 79 kept Pompeii – and some of its inhabitants – in an amazing state of preservation. Highlights include the Forum, the Forum Baths, the House of the Vettii, the theatres and the Villa of the Mysteries.

Vesuvius
A zigzag path leads to the top (about half an hour). The crater is a sheer-walled funnel filled with scree, ash and boulders. From the belvedere at the end of the path you can see Pompeii, on a clear day.

ROME
Good for culture, history and nightlife

A CORNERSTONE of Western civilisation and still the focus of the Roman Catholic faith, the Eternal City offers incomparable sightseeing for those fascinated by archaeology, ancient history or Renaissance and baroque art and architecture. But opening hours are maddening – and many restaurants shut for August.

BEST SIGHTS

Colosseum
This vast cauldron of brick and stone arches is one of Rome's most recognisable sights. Scene of gladiatorial combat and other 'entertainments' from the year AD 80, it has 76 entrances and was designed to accommodate 50,000 people.

Forum
The east side of the Capitoline Hill overlooks the columns and temples of the Roman Forum. Important buildings include the Curia, where the Senate met; the Temple of Castor and Pollux; the Temple of Vesta, with the House of the Vestal Virgins; and the Temple of Saturn.

St Peter's
The awesomely scaled church is the work of several architects, including Michelangelo, Bramante and Bernini – who designed the sweeping colonnades symbolising the church's embracing arms. Impressive interior highlights are the baroque *baldacchino* (canopy) above St Peter's tomb, and Michelangelo's exquisite Pietà. Splendid views from the roof.

Vatican Museums and Sistine Chapel
The Vatican museums are so vast as to leave you glassy-eyed. Signposted routes lead to the Raphael Rooms and the Sistine Chapel, where you can develop a rubber neck and lockjaw gaping at the stunning frescos.

HEEL OF ITALY
Good for beaches

ITALY'S POOREST regions – Apulia, Calabria and Basilicata – have traditionally been beyond the tourist pale, but more adventurous travellers will find much of interest here. The landscapes vary from the flat and fertile plains of Apulia to the stark mountain scenery of Basilicata. Calabria combines scenic wildness with near-deserted beaches. Lovers of art and architecture will find touring Apulia most rewarding.

BEST RESORTS

Gargano Peninsula
● The spur on Italy's heel has superb coastal scenery and corniche drives.
● Best resorts are Peschici and Vieste, both lively with sandy beaches.
● Best excursion is Monte Sant'Angelo, a pilgrimage town.

Maratea
● Best resort south of Campania, despite a poor beach.
● A deserted medieval quarter overlooks the Gulf of Policast.

Scilla
● Fishing village with a sandy beach and charming residential quarter.
● The rock Scylla (named in Homer's *Odyssey*) dominates the scene.

Tropea
● A decent coarse sand beach helped Tropea to become a lively resort.
● The fishing port and old town are picturesque.

BEST SIGHTS AND EXCURSIONS

Lecce
A small town full of flamboyant baroque churches, carved from soft local limestone that enables exuberant carving. Santa Croce is stunning.

Matera
An extraordinary town. The handsome new town has a fine cathedral; below is a honeycomb of squalid cave dwellings where the population lived until forced out in the 1950s.

Reggio di Calabria
The town boasts the superb National Museum, housing items from the

cities of Magna Graecia. Drive to the Aspromonte Mountains for views.

Romanesque churches

'Apulian Romanesque' style is mostly Norman (also Byzantine and Saracenic). Characteristics are a rose window above an elaborate portal. Best seen in cathedrals at Bari (San Nicola), Bitonto, Altamura and Molfetta. Those at Canosa, Barletta, Bisceglie and Trani are also good.

Sila Massif

The plateau is 3,300ft above sea-level, with mountains, forests and lakes. Accommodation is chalet-style.

Trulli

Trulli are whitewashed conical huts, unique to Italy, found between Locorotondo and Martina Franca. See them *en masse* at Alberobello, the *trulli* capital. The caves at Castellana make a worthwhile excursion.

SICILY
Good for culture, history and scenic landscape

SUCCESSIVE WAVES of invaders have bequeathed a rich architectural legacy. Classical, Norman and baroque masterpieces litter the entire island. Best bases for a stay-put package holiday are Taormina and Cefalù but a car is essential for seeing the island.

BEST RESORTS

Cefalù

● Delightful fishing port successfully developed as a resort.
● Characterful old town – a grid of narrow streets sloping down from a magnificent Arabo-Norman cathedral – remains unspoilt.
● Golden, sandy beach stretches out west of the town.

Taormina

● Picturesque hill town with beguiling views of Mount Etna.
● Lively town of designer boutiques in medieval *palazzi* and *al fresco* bars and restaurants lining mini-piazzas.
● Home to a Greek theatre, remodelled by the Romans.
● A cable-car takes you to the pebble beach at Mazzaró, though the broad, sandy beach at Giardini-Naxos, half a mile west, is better.

BEST SIGHTS AND EXCURSIONS

Agrigento

The Valley of the Temples is Sicily's best classical site. Ruins of nine temples from the sixth and fifth centuries BC are visible; the Doric Temple of Concord is the largest and best-preserved. There are also significant remnants of the Temples of Hera and Olympian Zeus.

Casale

Ruined Roman villa with spectacular mosaics laid by African artists for Emperor Maximian in the third century AD. Highlight is the long corridor mosaic showing the capturing and shipping of wild animals for display in Rome.

Monreale

The small hill town above Palermo is dominated by the Norman cathedral. The exterior is dull, but the interior is covered by glittering mosaics and a dominating Christ the Pantocrator. Parking is a nightmare, so take a bus from Palermo instead.

Mount Etna

Europe's largest active volcano dominates Sicily's eastern end and is spectacular during its frequent eruptions. Organised tours take you up for great views.

Noto

Showpiece Sicilian baroque town, built after the 1693 earthquake. Ornate churches line Corso Vittorio Emanuele and finely carved balconies line Via Nicolari. To the south lie the baroque towns of Ragusa and Modica. Inland is a scenic drive to the prehistoric necropolis of Pantalica or the ceramics town of Caltagirone.

Palermo

In two days in this melting-pot of Islamic, Latin and Byzantine cultures you should be able to see the twelfth-century cathedral; the Matorana, an Arabo-Norman church; the National Archaeological Museum; the mosaics of Cappella Palatina, created by Byzantine and Arab craftsmen; the Capuchin catacombs; and the dilapidated but vibrant local neighbourhoods with colourful daily markets.

BEST ISLANDS

Most interesting of the islands around Sicily are the **Aeolian Islands**.

Aeolian Islands

The largest is **Lipari**, a popular resort with a pebble beach and an archaeological museum in the old quarter. Find good hotels and restaurants here. **Stromboli** is volcanic and less developed for tourism with a black sand beach. Boat trips to see the eruptions by night go from Lipari. On **Vulcano**, bathe in sulphurous mud or visit the Great Crater.

SARDINIA
Good for beaches, history and scenic landscape

SARDINIA'S ATTRACTIONS are simple but beguiling: magnificent beaches, glorious coastal scenery and intriguing archaeological sites.

BEST RESORTS
Alghero
- Biggest, cheapest and most satisfying resort, with bustle and charm.
- Old town is maze of vibrant streets opening on to large square.
- Main beach stretches for over three miles.

Baia Sardinia
- Most pleasant resort on expensive north-east coast, Costa Smeralda.
- Small but delightful curving bay of white sand.
- Smart shopping centre of boutiques and cafés, with lively buzz.

Villasimius
- Likeable, uncomplicated little town in the south east, a couple of miles from fine, white-sand beaches and beachside hotels.
- Hire a bike to get around.

BEST SIGHTS AND EXCURSIONS
Ancient Nuraghic sites
The best can be found at Su Nuraxi, Santa Vittoria, Serri, and the 'Giants' Tombs' at Coddu Vecchio and Li Lolghi.

Cágliari
The National Archaeological Museum is the city's greatest sight, its highlight being the large collection of bronze nuraghic figures dating from around 1400 to 300 BC.

Sássari
The island's second city also has an excellent archaeological museum,

including Punic-era toby jugs and spindly prehistoric bronze statuettes in its collection.

WHEN TO GO

Italians seem to holiday *en masse* in August, deserting the cities in droves to head for the hills, lakes or coast. Prices shoot up, rooms become scarce, and some hotels and restaurants in the cities may close. Short city-breaks are popular all year round, but for self-catering and touring holidays it is better to avoid peak season if you can.

	Average daily maximum temperature °C											
London	6	7	10	13	17	20	22	21	19	14	10	7
Rome	6	9	13	17	22	26	28	28	24	20	13	8
	JAN	FEB	MAR	APR	MAY	JUN	JUL	AUG	SEP	OCT	NOV	DEC
Rome	8	5	8	8	7	7	4	5	6	8	11	9
London	15	13	11	12	12	11	12	11	13	13	15	15

Average number of rainy days per month

	Average daily maximum temperature °C											
London	6	7	10	13	17	20	22	21	19	14	10	7
Palermo	16	16	17	20	24	27	30	30	28	25	21	18
	JAN	FEB	MAR	APR	MAY	JUN	JUL	AUG	SEP	OCT	NOV	DEC
Palermo	12	8	8	6	3	2	0	2	4	8	8	10
London	15	13	11	12	12	11	12	11	13	13	15	15

Average number of rainy days per month

PACKAGE TRAVEL

ALL THE mass-market tour operators offer holidays in Italy, particularly on the Neapolitan Riviera, the Venetian Riviera and the Italian Lakes. Coach tours of the highlights of Italy or of a particular region of Italy such as Sicily or the lakes are also widely available. City breaks are on offer in numerous cities, sometimes with an activity included, such as opera in Milan or Verona.

Specialists in self-catering offer a wide variety of accommodation; anything from a modern apartment on the Neapolitan Riviera to a lavish villa in the hills of Tuscany or Umbria.

Tour operators

Battlefields: Holts' Tours **Birdwatching**: Limosa, Naturetrek
Camping: Canvas, Eurocamp, Eurosites, Keycamp, Select Sites,
Sunsites **City breaks**: Airtours, British Airways Holidays, Cosmos,
Cresta, Crystal, Inghams, Kirker, Made to Measure, Osprey, Prem-
ier, Sovereign, Thomas Cook, Thomson, Time Off, Travelscene
Cultural: Andante, British Museum Traveller, Martin Randall,
Prospect **Specialists**: Abercrombie & Kent, Airtours, Belleair Holi-
days, Bridgewater Travel, Carefree Italy, Citalia, Costa Smeralda,
Crystal, CV Travel, Hello Italy, Ilios Travel, Italian Expressions,
Italiatour, Magic of Italy, Page & Moy, Siesta International, Simply
Tuscany & Umbria, SMS, Sunvil, Vacanze in Italia, Voyages Ilena
Walking: Alternative Travel Group, Exodus, Explore Worldwide,
Headwater, HF Holidays, Inntravel, Ramblers Holidays, Sherpa,
Waymark **Wine**: Arblaster & Clarke, Winetrails **Other activities**:
Ace Study Tours, Andante (archaeology), Bike Tours (cycling),
Club Med (all-inclusive), Cox & Kings (flora), Ffestiniog Travel
(rail tours), Inter-Church Travel (religious tours), Solo's Holidays
(singles), Tasting Places (cookery), Thermalia (spa)

INDEPENDENT TRAVEL

CHEAP FLIGHTS with budget airlines are becoming easier to find.
There are scheduled flights to most large Italian cities. Charter flights
go to Rome, Venice, Milan, Pisa, Naples, Florence, Treviso, Rimini
and Catania – also to Bergamo, Turin and Verona in winter. Milan is
usually the cheapest charter destination.

Touring independently is not ideal, as car hire and petrol are
expensive, and motorway tolls can add up. In addition, local drivers
make sure that you never relax at the wheel, particularly in the cities,
and parking is often a nightmare. Nevertheless, it is often the only way
to see some of the countryside, and it gives you extra flexibility. If you
pre-book your car from the UK (usually the cheapest option), check
what is included in the price – you often have to pay extra for theft
protection when you pick up the car. A British driving licence is
acceptable.

The extensive, reasonably reliable and relatively cheap rail network is a good alternative to touring by car, especially if you are
visiting the northern cities. You can buy passes that are valid for
unlimited rail travel for a certain number of days or a set number of
kilometres.

Buses are often quicker than trains, but are usually also more expensive. In cities they usually charge a flat rate, and you must buy tickets before you get on, at tobacconists, news kiosks or at ticket machines. Stamp your ticket in the machine when you board.

Hotels are rated from one to five stars, and bargains are few and far between. Standards in budget *pensioni* vary widely from region to region, and it is pot luck whether you chance on a good place. Italy is best at characterful hotels in converted historic buildings – but you will pay accordingly. Renting a farmhouse or villa is another option, particularly in Tuscany and Umbria. Many agencies and tour operators offer self-catering deals, but the cheapest option is to look at private ads in Sunday papers or magazines such as *The Lady*. Remember to get written details of what exactly is included. Most owners require a hefty cash deposit to cover breakages.

RED TAPE, HEALTH AND SAFETY

BRITISH PASSPORT-HOLDERS do not need a visa to visit Italy. Petty theft (pickpocketing and bag-snatching) is common, especially in southern cities like Rome and Naples. Leave valuables in a hotel safe-deposit box and keep your money in a moneybelt worn beneath your clothes rather than in a 'bum bag'. Never leave valuables in a car; even when you are in the vehicle stow your bag under a seat out of sight, as thieves on motorbikes may smash the window and grab your bag from the seat. It is usually safer to park in car parks with attendants.

MORE INFORMATION Italian State Tourist Board, 1 Princes Street, London W1R 8AY, tel 020-7408 1254, brochure line (09001) 600280 (premium rate number), web site: *www.piuitalia2000.it*

COST OF LIVING £–££

JAPAN

HIGHLIGHTS

Culture
Kyoto, Tokyo

History
Hiroshima

Local colour
Kyoto, Tokyo

Nightlife
Tokyo

Scenic landscape
Hakone

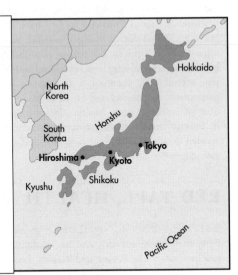

TOKYO
Good for culture, local colour and nightlife

FAST, FRANTIC and crowded, Tokyo still has a lot to offer tourists. Away from the flashing neon, pockets of traditional life thrive all over the city, despite its sprawl of ugly modern buildings, making it a bizarre mix of old meets new and East meets West.

BEST SIGHTS

Asakusa
Sensoō-ji is Asakusa's main attraction and one of Tokyo's most interesting temples – it has a narrow street of shops within the temple grounds.

Ginza
Ginza is perhaps the most expensive shopping area in the world. Look out for the Sony building on the Sukiyabashi crossing – a vast building displaying the company's newest and most high-tech products, or watch a traditional Kabuki play at Kabuki-za Theatre.

Meiji-jingu Shrine
Built in memory of the Emperor Meiji.

Shibuya
The place to go to watch Tokyo's young trendies tottering in their platform boots (or whatever the latest fashion craze is).

Shinjuku
Shinjuku train station is one of the busiest in the world. Visit the 45th floor of the Metropolitan Government Offices for one of the best views of Tokyo. The Kabuki-cho, the red light district of Tokyo, is a safe area to walk in and has some excellent restaurants.

Tokyo Disneyland
A great family day out – but if you go at a weekend or on a Japanese holiday be prepared for uncomfortably long queues for almost all rides.

BEST EXCURSIONS

Kamakura
The capital of Japan from 1192 to 1333 is within easy day-trip distance of Tokyo and has many fine temples and shrines. The huge bronze statue of Daibutsu (Great Buddha) was completed in 1252.

Nikko
Nikko also boasts some impressive shrines and temples. The extravagant Tosho-gu Shrine is not to be missed. Also visit Lake Chuzenji with its beautiful scenery and breathtaking Kegon Waterfall.

HAKONE
Good for scenic landscape

THIS MOUNTAINOUS region is especially lovely during the autumn, when the maple leaves turn spectacular colours. If the weather is clement you will also get splendid views of Mount Fuji.

BEST SIGHTS

Hakone Open–Air Art Museum
This impressive museum, set in a large area of parkland, features work by many Western artists.

Owakudani and Lake Ashi
A cable-car transports you up to steaming volcanic hot springs. Try one of the black, hard-boiled eggs that are cooked in the boiling mud. The cable-car continues up to beautiful Lake Ashi.

KYOTO
Good for culture and local colour

HOME TO the Imperial family from 794 to 1868, Kyoto has too many temples, shrines and gardens to see in just one visit.

BEST SIGHTS

Byodo-in Temple
Byodo-in is pictured on the 10-yen coin.

Gingkaku-ji Temple
Attractive, artful mounds of white sand and sloping moss gardens.

Kinkaku-ji Temple
Covered in gold-leaf, this is one of Japan's most photographed sights.

Ryoan-ji Temple
Quintessentially Japanese temple with a traditional Zen garden.

BEST EXCURSIONS

Himeji Castle
The castle was built in 1580 and is one of the finest in Japan.

Nara
Another ancient capital of Japan, Nara has its fair share of temples, shrines and national treasures. Most of the main sights are in Nara Park. The Todai-ji Temple is the largest wooden building in the world and also claims to have one of the largest bronze statues of Buddha.

HIROSHIMA
Good for history

DURING THE Second World War this city was obliterated when the first atom bomb was dropped. The shell-like remains of the Industrial Promotion Hall (now called the Gembaku Domu, or A-bomb Dome) have been left untouched since 8.15am on 6 August 1945.

BEST SIGHTS

Miya-jima
Easily reached from Hiroshima, Miya-jima island is a peaceful place with a 'floating' red torii gate, part of Itsukushima-jinja Shrine, in the bay.

Peace Memorial Park
The cenotaph holds the names of all those killed by the bomb.

The A–bomb Museum
A powerful and moving museum which conveys its message with force.

WHEN TO GO

THE BEST times to visit Japan are spring and autumn. Spring, when the cherry blossom is out, is also the most popular time for Japanese to travel within Japan, so be prepared for large crowds, especially in Tokyo and Kyoto. If possible, avoid 'Golden Week' (end of April to beginning of May), when the entire population of Japan is on holiday. Summer is very hot and humid, and September is the typhoon season.

	Average daily maximum temperature °C											
London	6	7	10	13	17	20	22	21	19	14	10	7
Tokyo	8	9	12	17	22	24	28	30	26	21	16	11
	JAN	FEB	MAR	APR	MAY	JUN	JUL	AUG	SEP	OCT	NOV	DEC
Tokyo	5	6	10	10	10	12	10	9	12	11	7	5
London	15	13	11	12	12	11	12	11	13	13	15	15
	Average number of rainy days per month											

PACKAGE TRAVEL

JAPAN IS often featured by tour operators as part of a Far Eastern tour, with combinations including Hong Kong, Thailand and Bali. If you want to spend your whole holiday in Japan a popular itinerary includes Tokyo, Kyoto and Nara. Specialist operators offer more extensive options for those who want to see more of the country.

Tour operators

General: Dream Journeys, Far East Gateways, Gold Medal, Kuoni, Nomadic Thoughts, Premier Holidays, Silverbird, Virgin Holidays
Specialists: Creative Tours, Japan Experience, Travelsphere, World Dreams **Other activities**: Ace Study Tours, British Museum Traveller, Exodus, Explore Worldwide, Prospect

---

INDEPENDENT TRAVEL

JAPANESE PEOPLE are generally very friendly, keen to practise their English and help you at the same time. The major tourist centres like Tokyo, Kyoto and Nara cater well to visitors: the only time you might encounter problems is if you venture off the beaten track.

The easiest way to get around Japan is by the very efficient and extensive rail network. If you intend to travel any distance in Japan it is worth buying a Japan Rail Pass which allows unlimited travel on the entire Japan Railway (JR) network, including the bullet train (*shinkansen*), JR ferries and JR buses. You must buy a voucher in your home country and validate it once you arrive in Japan. Passes for children aged 6–11 are half-price. In the Hakone region you can buy a Hakone Free Pass, valid for several days: it allows free travel on all forms of transport.

Accommodation is not cheap, although a few budget options are available. The Japanese Inn Group is an organisation of *ryokans* (traditional-style inns where you sleep on a futon mattress on the tatami matting floor) and *minshku* (Japanese B&Bs). For details, ask the tourist office or see its web site (*www.members.aol.com/jinngroup/*). Youth hostels are another budget option, as are some of the cheaper business hotels (which have small Western-style rooms). For an unusual experience there are also capsule hotels (which mostly only accept male guests), where you pay for a coffin-sized pod with a TV above you and access to a communal bath, plus bar and restaurant.

RED TAPE, HEALTH AND SAFETY

BRITISH PASSPORT-HOLDERS do not need a visa to visit Japan. Japanese people are famed for their honesty, and there are no particular crime or health problems – just take the usual precautions (see page 12).

MORE INFORMATION Japan National Tourist Organisation, 20 Savile Row, London W1X 1AE, tel 020-7734 9638, web site: *www.jnto.go.jp/*

COST OF LIVING £££

JORDAN

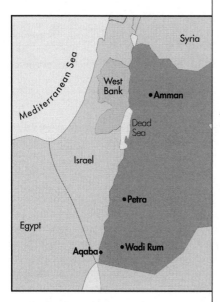

HIGHLIGHTS

Culture
Amman, Madaba

History
*Desert castles, Jerash,
Kerak, Petra, Umm Qeis*

Local colour
Wadi Rum

Outdoor activities
Aqaba, Wadi Rum

Romantic escapism
Petra, Wadi Rum

Scenic landscape
*Dead Sea, Petra,
Wadi Rum*

AMMAN
Good for culture, history and scenic landscape

BUILT ON a series of narrow ravines crammed with small white apartment blocks, Amman is a useful base for visiting northern Jordan.

BEST SIGHTS

National Archaeological Museum
Built next to the original citadel, with its ruins of Roman, Byzantine and Islamic buildings, this small but impressive museum has fragments of the Dead Sea Scrolls, plus some fine Roman sculpture.

Roman Theatre
This is the bustling, well-preserved hub of the city. A walk around its nearby streets will reveal a fascinating mix of shops selling Arab bread,

galvanised buckets, or carpets woven with an image of the late King Hussein. A folklore museum beside the theatre offers insights into the customs and costumes of the Bedouin.

BEST EXCURSIONS

Bethany Beyond The Jordan
The recently discovered site of the baptism of Jesus Christ. Archaeologists have uncovered an early Byzantine church built over the cave where John the Baptist lived and near an oasis where they believe Jesus was baptised.

Dead Sea
The lowest point on earth, the Dead Sea basin radiates furnace-like heat. The high salt content means that floating, rather than swimming, is the only option – but don't shave beforehand, as the salt can be agony if you have any cuts! The Dead Sea Spa Hotel near Suweimeh offers daily rates for bathing.

Desert castles
Out in the barren eastern desert is a scattering of palaces and forts built by the luxury-loving Omayyad caliphs, rulers of the Arab world from AD 661 to 750. They can be covered in a day-trip from Amman.

Furthest east is the squat black fort of Azraq, where Lawrence of Arabia wintered – more interesting for its history than its features. By contrast, the walls of the tiny barrel-vaulted pavilion of Qasr Al-Amra, where the caliphs rested in steam baths after hunting, are covered in lavish frescos. Finally there are the imposing walls and decorative stone windows of Qasr Al-Karaneh. The castle contains almost 100 rooms on two floors, including lofty camel stables.

Jerash
As part of the league of ten free cities known as the Decapolis, Jerash flourished under Roman rule. Well preserved, it stretches over a vast area. From the magnificent Oval Plaza, you walk along a colonnaded main street lined with temples, a market and a splendid nymphaeum, or public fountain. A ceremonial stairway leads to the Temple of Artemis, which has a pillared sanctuary on top of a stone platform (if you slide your little fingers below the base of a column, you can feel it moving in the wind!). Two restored theatres sit at either end of the site.

Madaba
The Christian roots of this town, which was prosperous in Byzantine times, are much in evidence. St George's church contains a remarkable

sixth–century mosaic map of the Near East. For more mosaics, visit the archaeological park in the centre of town, where the remains of a Byzantine church lie on top of a Roman house. The mosaic floor of the Hippolytus Hall shows mythological figures, while in the Church of the Apostles another huge mosaic is being renovated.

Ten minutes from Madaba, Mount Nebo is the point from which Moses gazed at the Promised Land; a monastery marks the spot where he is said to be buried. Mosaics in the chapel show local wildlife, while nearby is Moses' spring, where fresh water greens the hillside.

Umm Qeis

In a stirring location overlooking the Golan Heights (be prepared for military checkpoints and restrictions) is the former Decapolis city of Gadara. The remains of the Byzantine basilica include a striking mix of black basalt and white limestone columns with a row of vaulted shops beneath, and a basalt theatre. Climb up behind the nymphaeum for a view of the Sea of Galilee, or Lake Tiberias.

KING'S HIGHWAY
Good for history and scenic landscape

THE DESERT Highway is the quickest road to the south, but the scenery is mainly flat and arid. Far more interesting is Route 35, known as the King's Highway since biblical times. This road twists through small, shallow valleys filled with grazing goats and sheep and pockets of fertile farmland.

A string of fortified towns along the way became a significant part of the Crusader empire, preying on caravan trains heading northwards.

Dana Nature Reserve

People have returned to the medieval village of Dana where they are preparing crops and crafts for the tourist market. The Dana guest-house sits on a cliff offering stunning views along the Wadi Dana. Rangers provide an excellent series of guided nature walks.

Kerak

The most magnificent castle is at Kerak, where dramatic sloping stone escarpments and chunky yellow stone walls are perched on the side of a deep ravine. Many of the sprawling, labyrinthine ruins are virtually subterranean, as the knights and followers wanted to keep cool.

AQABA
Good for outdoor activities

JORDAN'S ONLY access point to the sea is not a particularly attractive resort. The town is lively in the evening, but the hotels are showing signs of wear. The beach is only a small strip of sand. The aquarium at the Marine Sciences Centre has an excellent display of local underwater life.

BEST WATER SPORTS

The most worthwhile sight is the wonderful coral reef fringing the coast. The Royal Jordanian Diving Centre offers tuition and easy access to the reef.

PETRA
Good for history, romantic escapism and scenic landscape

FEW ANCIENT wonders can match Petra's magical location: a lost kingdom hidden from sight by arid mountains and reached only through a natural gorge. Forgotten by the West until its rediscovery by the Swiss explorer Jean-Louis Burckhardt in the early nineteenth century, Petra retains its grandeur and romance despite the influx of tourists.

The Nabataeans, a nation of traders at the time of Christ, carved tombs and monuments on an extraordinary scale out of the reddish sandstone. The colours are truly staggering, reflecting every hue of a rosy rainbow.

You need at least two days to make the most of Petra. Be prepared for plenty of walking and climbing – tackle the High Place of Sacrifice and the monastery on separate days, as they are both strenuous climbs. The coolest and least crowded times are early morning and after 4pm. Note that horses are expensive and take you only 300 metres to the entrance of the gorge; elderly or disabled visitors can hire a carriage to reach the Treasury.

BEST SIGHTS

Treasury
The city's first and most unforgettable monument. The scale and colours are extraordinary – as you move forward, details of the columns, pediments and carved horsemen come into focus. Morning sunshine illuminates the Treasury, so be sure to arrive before 10am.

Viewpoints around Petra

The High Place of Sacrifice is a dramatic table mountain once used for animal sacrifices. Nearby are the reliefs of a Nabataean goddess and a lion, and the Garden, Roman Soldier and Renaissance Tombs. In the main valley are the Royal Tombs – the three-storey Palace Tomb, the biggest in Petra, is collapsing to reveal the crazy swirling patterns of the rock beneath. The façades of the Royal Tombs can be seen from the outcrop of El-Habees at the end of the main valley. The Ed-Deir monastery is an even bigger version of the Treasury, though less intricately carved. The forum museum displays Nabataean pottery and jewellery.

BEST EXCURSIONS

Little Petra

About 20 minutes' drive from Wadi Musa, Siq El-Baared, or Little Petra, is a gorge with some well-preserved tombs and a view across the mountains.

Umm El-Biyarah

This is the highest mountain in Petra, with spectacular views. The path is a little tricky to find (hire a guide).

WADI RUM

Good for local colour, outdoor activities, romantic escapism and scenic landscape

THIS COLOURFUL landscape of sandstone outcrops was the location for the film *Lawrence of Arabia*, and is home to the Bedouin people.

BEST LOCAL COLOUR

The Bedouin are happy to welcome travellers to their encampments, where they inhabit low, open-sided tents of black goat's wool. If you join a group you will probably be treated to communal singing around the fire and a meal of *mensaf* (boiled and roasted goat).

BEST EXCURSIONS

There are plenty of Bedouin in Rum village who can organise a night in the desert, a camel ride, or a four-wheel-drive tour visiting strange rock formations and enigmatic carvings and inscriptions. Some over-night trips are more touristy than others – the tourist office inside Wadi Rum Rest House can give you comprehensive information. Guides can also take you on longer treks and climbs.

WHEN TO GO

MARCH TO May and September to November are the best times to visit, with hot days and cool nights. Aqaba is not warm all year round; Amman and Petra can get very cold in winter. Summer can be uncomfortably hot.

Average daily maximum temperature °C

	JAN	FEB	MAR	APR	MAY	JUN	JUL	AUG	SEP	OCT	NOV	DEC
London	6	7	10	13	17	20	22	21	19	14	10	7
Amman	12	13	16	23	28	31	32	32	31	27	21	15
Amman	8	8	4	3	1	0	0	0	0	1	4	5
London	15	13	11	12	12	11	12	11	13	13	15	15

Average number of rainy days per month

PACKAGE TRAVEL

TOUR OPERATORS offer a large range of trips, from cheap overland jaunts to full-blown archaeological expeditions with lecturers. They all follow a similar route and take around seven to ten days – be sure to choose one that allows enough time at Petra (minimum two days) and Jerash (half a day). Some tours combine Jordan with Israel, Syria or Egypt.

Tours of Jordan follow a predictable route, starting from Amman and stopping off at Jerash, Madaba, the Dead Sea, Mount Nebo, Kerak and Petra, occasionally diverting off the beaten track before finishing in Aqaba on the Red Sea. Some packages focus on Petra, taking you from Amman to Petra and back again – you can book these in the UK and from Israel.

Tour operators

Adventure: Exodus, Explore Worldwide, Guerba, Top Deck **Birdwatching**: Naturetrek **Cultural**: Andante, British Museum Traveller, Coromandel, Prospect, Ramblers Holidays **General**: Abercrombie & Kent, Bales Tours, Cox & Kings, Hayes & Jarvis, Jasmin Tours, Kuoni, Page & Moy, Saga, Somak, Titan HiTours, Travelsphere, Voyages Jules Verne **Religious**: Inter-Church Travel, McCabe Travel **Scuba diving**: Longwood, Regal Holidays **Tours from Israel**: Goldenjoy, Pullman Holidays (UK), Superstar Holidays

---

Travel is by coach, minibus or perhaps, on a private tour, by chauffeur-driven car. The more adventurous tour itinerary will include a couple of days in the desert on a camping safari. Other possible extensions include relaxing on the beaches of Sinai and Egypt or a visit to Lebanon.

Activities available include taking part in an archaeological dig and cultural tours, birdwatching and scuba diving.

INDEPENDENT TRAVEL

A PACKAGE holiday will work out cheaper than going independently, as tour operators get better deals on the (expensive) hotel prices, but if you want more freedom, doing it on your own is easy.

The roads are good, so car hire is a feasible option – though stick to taxis in Amman, where the road system is confusing. Alternatively, you can rent a car with a driver at most large hotels in Amman to visit the desert castles, Jerash, Umm Qeis and the Dead Sea. From Amman there are JETT buses to Petra and Aqaba.

RED TAPE, HEALTH AND SAFETY

TO OBTAIN a tourist visa for Jordan, you will need a passport valid for six months, one passport photograph and a completed application form (available from the Jordanian Consulate). A three-month single-entry tourist visa costs £27, a double-entry visa is £48. Courier your application or visit the consulate in person between 9.30am and 1pm, Monday to Friday. Visas take 48 hours to process and can be collected between 1.10 and 2.30pm, Monday to Friday. Visas for UK nationals can also be obtained on arrival at the airport in Jordan.

Inoculations against hepatitis A, typhoid and polio are recommended. Immunisation against yellow fever is essential if you arrive from an 'infected' country but is not required if you travel direct from the UK.

Jordanians are very friendly, and you are unlikely to be hassled or pressured in shops or markets. When driving, always carry your passport, as there are army checkpoints near the border. Female travellers should have no problems as long as they dress conservatively. Both men and women should cover legs and shoulders.

The Foreign Office web site provides up-to-the-minute advice on visiting Jordan. *www.fco.gov.uk/travel/countryadvice.asp.*

MORE INFORMATION The Jordanian Tourist Board web site at *www.tourism.com.jo* is an excellent resource for anyone wishing to visit the country.

Jordan Tourism Board, Representation House, 11 Blades Court, Deodar Road, London SW15 2NU, tel 020-8877 4524

Jordanian Embassy and Consulate, 6 Upper Phillimore Gardens, London W8 7HB, tel 020-7937 3685, visa information (0891) 171261 (premium rate number), web site: *www.jordanembassyuk.gov.jo/*

COST OF LIVING £-££

KENYA

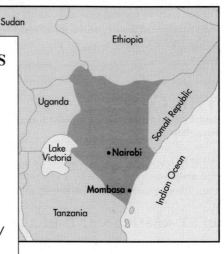

HIGHLIGHTS

**Beaches/
family holidays**
Coast

Local colour
Game parks

Nightlife
Coast, Nairobi

**Outdoor activities/
scenic landscape**
Game parks

Romantic escapism
Coast, game parks

Shopping
Nairobi

Wildlife
Game parks, Nairobi

NAIROBI
Good for nightlife, shopping and wildlife

THE NATIONAL Museum offers a good introduction to Kenya's fauna. Nairobi National Park, ten minutes from the city centre, has all the plains animals, except elephant, in a remarkably natural environment. The AFEW (African Fund for Endangered Wildlife) Giraffe Centre offers close encounters with native wildlife.

The Carnivore (a well-known tourist spot), Cantina Club and many other local clubs feature sizzling live music most nights. You should be prepared to venture into the unknown, hiring a taxi for the whole evening – much of the nightlife takes place on the outskirts of the city.

Shopping in Nairobi is lively and unusually rewarding. Let yourself in gently in the malls and curio shops. Then check out City Market's famous array of tropical fruit and veg. It also has a good range of craft stalls nearby, but beware of bag snatchers. The Tuesday 'Maasai Market' at the Globe Cinema is a great place to shop for crafts at competitive prices.

THE COAST
Good for beaches, family holidays, nightlife and romantic escapism

AS WELL as resorts and beaches, there are superb diving opportunities, and simple snorkelling can be a rewarding experience. Beware, however, the coastline can be strewn with seaweed from June to August.

BEST RESORTS AND BEACHES

Several all-inclusive beach resorts offer excellent value for money.
● Turtle Bay at Watamu and Sun 'n' Sand on the coast north of Mombasa are the best for children. Unfortunately these resorts do not give you much of a feel for Kenya.
● Diani Beach, south of Mombasa, is long and fringed with coconut palms. It has a wide variety of hotels and a number of separate restaurants, clubs and shops.
● Watamu consists of three idyllic bays. The Marine National Park, with limpid water is ideal for snorkelling and is less busy than Watamu.

BEST NIGHTLIFE

Diani Beach has some good discos away from the hotels' own (which can be bland). A few minutes north of Mombasa town is Bora Bora, the coast's best nightclub. Malindi 20 minutes' drive north of Watamu, has lively nightlife in high season.

BEST FOR ROMANTIC ESCAPISM

Lamu is the best for rustic-style exclusive hotels which are now extremely scarce, and also offers very basic guesthouses.

BEST SIGHTS AND EXCURSIONS

The ruins of the mysterious fourteenth-century town of Gedi, near Watamu, include mosques, a palace and stone houses.

BEST LOCAL COLOUR

Lamu island, at the northern end of the coast, is small. The town, Lamu, has to a large extent preserved its medieval town plan. There are no cars on the island: you get about on foot or by *dhow* (simple, wooden sailing vessel). A fine, often deserted, beach is another attraction.

GAME PARKS
Good for local colour, outdoor activities, romantic escapism, scenic landscape and wildlife

ALTHOUGH KENYA has over 40 parks and reserves only about a dozen are commonly visited. All charge daily fees.

BEST WALKING

All the following are fairly accessible by hired car or public transport and open to walkers (unlike most game parks, which are not, usually because of lions): Mount Kenya National Park (beautiful Afro-alpine vegetation); Hell's Gate (dramatic gorge with plenty of wildlife); Lake Bogoria National Reserve (impressive hot springs and greater kudu antelope); Saiwa Swamp (home of the rare sitatunga antelope).

BEST FOR ROMANTIC ESCAPISM

The most obvious romantic escapes are the 'tree hotels', modelled after Treetops, the most famous of them, where Princess Elizabeth was staying when she learned of her accession to the throne. Try The Ark, or Mountain Lodge, or, near the coast, Shimba in the Shimba Hills rainforest. All have basic rooms constructed with tree branches growing through them. Upmarket tented safari camps, such as Finch Hattons in Tsavo West, also offer memorable stays. Alternatively, private safaris, on which you camp wild and are escorted during the day on foot, horseback or by vehicle, can be booked in several parks, especially Maasai Mara.

BEST LOCAL COLOUR

In the Maasai and Samburu tribal areas traditional costume is worn, with elaborate jewellery and weaponry. Visits to local villages are often arranged while on safari – you pay a fixed fee to the headman and are then free to take photographs. The extreme poverty of the villagers can be disturbing and there is often pressure to buy souvenirs.

BEST WILDLIFE

Overall The best wildlife is to be found in the Maasai Mara, a vast plain of undulating grassland with woodland along the banks of the Mara river (crocodile and hippo). It is home to a huge variety of plains game (elephant, lion, cheetah, antelope and even rhino which are now extremely scarce). The most exciting time to visit is during the annual mass migration of wildebeest, which peaks for three unpredictable weeks some time between August and October. Despite the all-day bumpy, dusty drive or expensive flight from Nairobi, the Mara is very popular; on cheaper safaris you may feel part of a crowd, with other minibuses present every time you stop to watch a pride of lions or a herd of elephants. The park can be very muddy during rains, often immediately after Christmas. You can also go on expensive balloon safaris and microlight flights in Maasai Mara.

Samburu, a dry country reserve north of Mount Kenya, is a runner-up, with acacia woodland and superb birdlife near the Ewaso Ngiro river. It has fewer predators than the Mara, but lots of grazing animals, including rarer species of antelope and giraffe.

For birds Kakamega Forest is a patch of equatorial lowland rainforest in western Kenya. Unique bird, monkey, reptile and insect life can be seen on forest walks. This park is not included in ordinary package safaris. Access by hired car or public transport is straightforward, but the park is a full day's journey from Nairobi.

For flamingos The endless flocks are usually seen at Lake Nakuru or Lake Bogoria, but the birds are nomadic and very unpredictable. Both parks are three hours' drive on good roads from Nairobi.

For views of Kilimanjaro Amboseli is a very busy park of flat plains and swamps, easily reached from Nairobi or the southern coast. It is most famous for its herds of elephant and other plains game, including cheetah and lion, set against the backdrop of Mount Kilimanjaro, over the border in Tanzania. The park is small and there are always other vehicles but the facilities are good and the game drives shorter and therefore less exhausting.

For scenery Tsavo West has hilly, volcanic scenery and a beautiful oasis, Mzima Springs, with hippos and crocodiles. Aberdare is a cool mountain park with rainforest on the lower slopes and moorland on the tops. Observe dramatic waterfalls from many walking routes.

WHEN TO GO

KENYA HAS three seasons: low from Easter to 30 June, mid-season from 1 July to 30 November and high season from 1 December to 31 March. The 'long rains' fall during the low season, when beaches are often wet in the morning. During the 'long rains' safaris can be less rewarding as the animals are dispersed away from rivers and waterholes.

	Average daily maximum temperature °C											
London	6	7	10	13	17	20	22	21	19	14	10	7
Mombasa	32	32	33	31	29	29	28	28	29	30	31	32
	JAN	FEB	MAR	APR	MAY	JUN	JUL	AUG	SEP	OCT	NOV	DEC
Mombasa	5	4	8	16	18	13	14	15	13	13	11	10
London	15	13	11	12	12	11	12	11	13	13	15	15
	Average number of rainy days per month											

	Average daily maximum temperature °C											
London	6	7	10	13	17	20	22	21	19	14	10	7
Nairobi	27	28	28	26	25	24	23	23	26	27	25	25
	JAN	FEB	MAR	APR	MAY	JUN	JUL	AUG	SEP	OCT	NOV	DEC
Nairobi	5	4	8	16	14	5	4	5	4	7	16	11
London	15	13	11	12	12	11	12	11	13	13	15	15
	Average number of rainy days per month											

PACKAGE TRAVEL

THE BASIC choice of package holiday is between beach-only and safari-and-beach. If you opt for a beach-only option you can still quite easily book a one- to three-night safari. Cheaper packages use charter flights to Mombasa, while the more expensive safari packages tend to use scheduled flights to Nairobi (usually British Airways or Kenya Airways). If you are going on safari, it is best to schedule your trip for early in your holiday, and relax on the beach afterwards. Some tour operators combine safaris in Kenya with ones in neighbouring Tanzania. Many Kenya specialists are tailor-made safari experts. A few companies offer Kenyan safaris in combination with beach holidays in Zanzibar, Mauritius or even Dubai. If you are going on a Mombasa-based safari-and-beach holiday with the safari first, you need to bear in mind that after the overnight flight your transfer inland to the national parks will take two to three hours, in high temperatures. Similarly, if you are going directly to a coast hotel, you should find out what the transfer time is. Some journeys take as little as 20 minutes, but the one to Malindi takes about two hours.

Accommodation on the coast varies considerably in quality, from just-about-adequate beach hotels to state-of-the-art palaces. You generally get what you pay for, with food, room size and the variety of facilities on offer being the first casualties of competitive pricing. But further probing of your travel agent or a detailed guide book may reveal good-value hotels that have facilities well above average for the price. Holiday reps tend to have responsibility for several properties at one time and often visit each hotel only once or twice a week. If you have a problem it is often easier to befriend the reception staff, who may go out of their way to transfer you to a more suitable room if one is available.

Accommodation in Nairobi is usually in good-quality international-style hotels close to the city centre. Most packages that include Nairobi treat it only as a necessary one-night stay.

Accommodation in the game parks is generally in lodges – hotels in the bush designed to provide the best opportunities for relaxation and game viewing. These are built either as conventional hotels, sometimes with the rooms in chalets known as *bandas*, or as comfortable tented lodges, which have 'rooms' made of canvas, with separate, thatched, waterproof roofs, mosquito screening and built-in bathrooms.

Other than safari holidays, activities include birdwatching and adventure holidays. Scuba diving and deep-sea fishing are also available.

Tour operators

Adventure: Sherpa **Birdwatching**: Limosa, Sunbird **General**: Abercrombie & Kent, Airtours, Bales Tours, British Airways Holidays, Cosmos, CV Travel, Elite Vacations, Hayes & Jarvis, Kuoni, Thomson, Tradewinds, Worldwide Journeys **Specialists**: African Safari Club, Guerba, Kumuka Expeditions, Okavango Tours & Safaris, Safari Consultants, Somak **Tailor-made specialists**: Africa Archipelago, Africa Exclusive, Africa Travel Centre, Cazenove & Lloyd Safaris **Walking/trekking**: Exodus, High Places, KE Adventure, Sherpa **Wildlife**: Abercrombie & Kent, Naturetrek, Wildlife Worldwide

---

INDEPENDENT TRAVEL

CHARTER FLIGHTS to Mombasa are usually available for two- to three-week stays; scheduled flights go to Nairobi.

Independent beach holidays need some research, as there are only a few cheap or reasonably priced hotels on the beach itself. Staying in package-standard hotels on the beach will cost you more than if you were on a package. Inland hotels have a greater range of prices. You can usually find something modest but comfortable quite cheaply.

A British driving licence is sufficient, but car hire is expensive. Driving is on the left. The commonest hire vehicle is a Suzuki jeep. Check that your vehicle has the necessary windscreen documentation and spare tools. Police can be troublesome over this or other perceived infringements of the law, but they are only trying to extract money from you. Be polite and good-humoured and you will be allowed on your way. Roads, other road users, pedestrians and animals can all be very unpredictable: drive cautiously, and never drive at night.. Hiring a car is one way to visit the game parks independently, but buy appropriate game park maps.

The other way to visit the parks independently is on a locally organised lodge or camping safari, bookable with safari operators in Nairobi or at most coast hotels. Follow word-of-mouth recommendations to get the latest on suitable companies. Try where possible to book directly with the operator, rather than through an agent. One common source of disappointment is having to spend a long time travelling to the parks, ending up with insufficient time on game drives within them.

If you want to travel around Kenya but do not mind not getting into the parks, the country is well served by buses, which charge very reasonable fares. Book seats in advance. For off-the-cuff local travel, you can use *matatus* (shared taxi-minivans), but they are notoriously unsafe.

A single rail route runs from Mombasa to Nairobi, then forks west to Kisumu on Lake Victoria, or north-west to Uganda. If you are heading on from Nairobi to the coast, this is the best way to travel. The first-class ticket includes dinner, bed with sheets and blankets, and breakfast. Although most rolling stock is now modern, the journey is a leisurely one, and the service full of charming old-fashioned touches. It is important to book ahead.

Many independent travellers take the opportunity to climb Mount Kenya. Clothing and equipment can be hired in Nairobi or before the ascent. Although any reasonably fit person can reach Point Lenana among the glaciers, you should not rush the climb, as altitude sickness can be very dangerous. Most hikers hire porters/guides. Allow at least four days. The view from the top is only occasionally really clear.

RED TAPE, HEALTH AND SAFETY

BRITISH PASSPORT-HOLDERS do not at the time of writing require a visa, but check with your tour operator or airline.

Consult your GP about the latest recommended vaccinations; anti-malaria tablets are also advisable. To avoid getting bitten use mosquito repellent and always sleep under a mosquito net. Stick to bottled water; in hotels and restaurants the water is boiled first.

Muggings and armed attacks can occur at any time, particularly in Nairobi and Mombasa. Avoid travelling after dark. Do not accept food or drink from strangers. Car-hijackings can also occur – do not attempt to escape from hijackers or resist their demands.

The Foreign Office Travel Advice Unit advises visitors to avoid the North Eastern Province, the Tana River district of Coast Province and the Isiolo and Marsabit district of Eastern Province (apart from the Samburu Game Reserve and, when accompanied by tour operators, the Shaba Game Reserve). Visitors to Lamu Island are advised to travel by air. For further advice, see page 11.

MORE INFORMATION Kenya National Tourist Office, 25 Brooks Mews, London W1Y 1LF, tel 020-7355 3144, web site: *www.visit-kenya.com*

Kenya High Commission, 45 Portland Place, London W1M 4AS, tel 020-7636 2371

COST OF LIVING £-££

LATVIA

HIGHLIGHTS

Food/wine
Riga

Family holidays
*Gauja National Park,
Jurmala*

Nightlife
Riga

Culture
Cesis, Jelgava, Rundale

Outdoor activities
Gauja National Park

RIGA AND AROUND
Good for culture, family holidays, food/wine and nightlife

THE 800-YEAR-OLD capital has been restored to its former style with the tearing down of most buildings linked with the Soviet era. Bland concrete has given way to Gothic brick, Renaissance stone and Jugendstil (art nouveau) tiles, coffee houses have replaced canteens, Mercedes outnumber Ladas, and Riga is again a truly capital, cosmopolitan city. Thai restaurants are as common as Latvian ones, and the selection of whiskies available in most bars puts many British pubs to shame.

BEST SIGHTS

Dom Cathedral
This gothic cathedral has always reflected Riga's fortunes. It flourished in the late nineteenth century when its massive organ was built but was badly damaged in 1944; some stained glass is yet to be replaced. When the cloister and garden are fully restored in 2001, the cathedral and its square will again be the heart of Riga.

Jugendstil architecture
Riga's best 'museum' is in Alberta Street, where every building is a masterpiece from the late nineteenth century. Do not begrudge the climb up the circular staircase in the Janis Rozentals Museum – the reward is five storeys of continuous murals by the artist (1866–1916).

Motor Museum
The Russians must be sorely regretting their failure to remove this collection when they left in 1991. The vanity of each Soviet leader is fully exposed through their cars displayed here, as is the driving inability of Leonid Brezhnev with his crashed Rolls Royce.

Waxworks
An hour here brings to life the famous and infamous from Latvia's history over the last hundred years or so. Latvians are supposed to be dour; here they are definitely the reverse.

BEST EXCURSIONS

Jelgava
The eighteenth-century Italian architect Bartolomeo Francesco Rastrelli built a second palace here (see also 'Rundale Palace' opposite). Jelgava was soon surrounded by a large town. The interior of the palace is now an agricultural college but the exterior is much as when it was built. The Dukes of Courland, who ruled over Latvia for 200 years, are buried in a variety of wooden and metal coffins, incongruously displayed in a vault next to a student basement café.

Jurmala
Riga's seaside resort has always been popular with those in power in Latvia. Villas survive from the era of the Baltic Germans as well as from the Soviet period. Now the town and its long beach are open to all. Cars are largely banned, so the loudest noise is likely to come from an open-air concert or from a tourist who has found a good piece of amber on the beach. (Those not so lucky can still buy it cheaply at the local market.)

Rundale Palace

Many tourists see a visit here as a substitute for St Petersburg as Rastrelli put just as much effort into building Rundale as he did for the Winter Palace (Hermitage). Although the paintings displayed are poor quality, the furniture, woodwork and spacious reception rooms can be positively compared with the Hermitage. Allow a day to do justice to the Palace, the gardens and the exhibition about religious persecution in Soviet times.

GAUJA NATIONAL PARK
Good for culture, family holidays and outdoor activities

JOIN RIGANS at the weekends in Gauja National Park, or enjoy it in greater solitude at other times. Explore the dungeons, towers and walls of the medieval castle at Cesis, then take in the 60 miles of protected landscape which straddles the River Gauja with minimal access for cars and coaches. To follow the course of the river, hire a bicycle, horse or canoe. It is possible to stop frequently at cliffs, caves and gardens.

BEST SIGHT

Turaida Castle

Turaida is an isolated village on a hillside. The name means 'garden of God' and a climb up the castle tower offers a varied landscape of lakes, forests and flowers in complete contrast to Riga only 30 miles away. The Sculpture Park outside contains modern representations of themes from nineteenth-century Latvian songs. Visit in the autumn if possible when green gives way to red and orange.

WHEN TO GO

RIGA IS usually spared the worst of the Russian winter so even in January temperatures do not drop much below freezing. The long

	Average daily maximum temperature °C											
London	6	7	10	13	17	20	22	21	19	14	10	7
Riga	-4	-3	2	10	16	21	22	21	17	11	4	-1
	JAN	FEB	MAR	APR	MAY	JUN	JUL	AUG	SEP	OCT	NOV	DEC
Riga	19	18	16	13	13	11	12	16	17	19	19	21
London	15	13	11	12	12	11	12	11	13	13	15	15
	Average number of rainy days per month											

nights at that time of year are uninviting in the countryside but Riga keeps its vitality year-round. Latvia is crowded in July (the Scandinavian and German holiday period), but otherwise spring, summer and autumn offer equally varied weather, and attractions and music festivals take place throughout the year. Never forget an umbrella, but don't assume you will always need it.

PACKAGE TRAVEL

YEAR-ROUND CITY breaks to Riga are based on the many four- and five-star hotels now open. A big buffet breakfast and the large Riga airport tax are always included in the price. Jurmala offers a wide range of accommodation; many other towns still have only one satisfactory hotel. Baltic specialists can arrange itineraries around the country, often including Estonia and Lithuania.

Tour operators

City breaks: Regent Holidays, Scantours, Specialised Tours **Culture**: Martin Randall **Cycling**: Exodus, Regent Holidays **Specialists**: Intourist, Regent Holidays, Specialised Tours **Walking**: Explore Worldwide

---

INDEPENDENT TRAVEL

RIGA IS easily reached from all over Britain. SAS Scandinavian Airlines has several connections every day via Copenhagen and Stockholm from the London airports, Birmingham, Manchester, Glasgow and Edinburgh. British Airways has a direct flight four times a week from Gatwick and daily connections via Helsinki with Finnair. Discount air fares are available from tour operators that specialise in the Baltic States; these companies also have discounted rates at the main Riga hotels. Riga has very little two- or three-star accommodation although this category is easily available elsewhere.

Car hire is expensive in Lativa – about £40 per day – and recommended only for tourists wanting to visit many small towns in a hurry. An extensive and efficient bus and train network operates throughout the country, with very low fares. Buses also link the main towns with Estonia and Lithuania.

RED TAPE, HEALTH AND SAFETY

BRITISH PASSPORT-HOLDERS do not require a visa for Latvia. Medical care in local hospitals is of a high standard and visitors should find that travel insurance will cover the low medical charges. English is widely spoken in hotels, shops and restaurants in Riga, but much less elsewhere.

Pickpockets can be a nuisance in Riga and late-night violence outside nightclubs is common – take the usual precautions (see page 12). Theft of and from cars is a frequent occurrence and it is advisable to leave vehicles overnight in a guarded car park. Visitors should beware of poorly maintained roads and pavements. Museums are often closed two days a week (usually Monday and Tuesday) and have eccentric and short opening hours.

MORE INFORMATION Latvian Embassy, 45 Nottingham Place, London W1M 3FE, tel 020-7312 0040

COST OF LIVING *££*

LITHUANIA

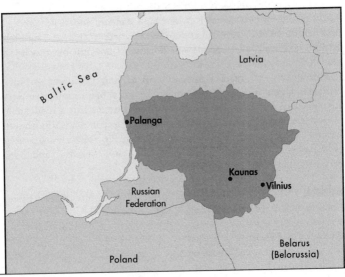

HIGHLIGHTS

Beaches
Druskininkai

Food/wine
Vilnius

Nightlife
Vilnius

Romantic escapism
Trakai

Culture
Kaunas, Vilnius

History
Kaunas

Outdoor activities
Lake Galvé

Wildlife
Curonian Lagoon

Family holidays
Palanga

Local colour
Druskininkai, Hill of the Crosses

L ITHUANIA WAS the first of the Baltic States to declare indepen-dence in March 1990. It is friendly and more cosmopolitan than its neighbours, and the people are genuinely proud to fly the Lithuanian flag. As a predominantly Catholic state for centuries, the cities have Central European influences, with some fine baroque churches. The countryside is flat but largely unspoilt and agriculture remains on a fairly traditional level.

VILNIUS
Good for culture, food/wine and nightlife

IN THE sixteenth and seventeenth centuries the capital of Lithuania was a wealthy merchant city and a centre for trade with the Baltic area. It is the most northerly stop on the Baroque Trail. In the last few years, the buildings of the Old Town have been painted mustard-yellow which the Baltic winters are just starting to weather. The secret courtyards and cobbled streets are a delight to explore, and Cathedral Square, dominated by the clock tower and classical façade of Vilnius Cathedral, acts as a focal point for tourists.

BEST SIGHTS

Church of Saint Peter and Paul
The interior of this church, which was built on the site of an ancient pagan temple to the goddess of love, is decorated in high baroque style with over 2,000 statues clinging to the roof, and pillars depicting mythical scenes. Two other churches worth visiting are St Casimir's and St Michael's.

BEST CULTURE

State Opera
The Opera House, on the banks of the Neris river, is sometimes compared to a giant skateboard ramp. The repertoire has been broadened following liberation from the strictures of Soviet-approved operas.

BEST FOOD

Lithuanian cuisine tends to be heavy and stodgy. However, it is worth a visit to the chain known as Rita's Place, where folk musicians liven up the evening with energetic displays of rustic dancing.

BEST NIGHTLIFE

In the post-Soviet era, a vibrant club scene has developed in Vilnius, most famously The Iron Wolf, a kitsch nightclub decorated with hammer-and-sickle style memorabilia. The dance floor is dominated by a giant MiG fighter embedded in the wall, and when the music gets too much, there's a Lenin chill-out room in which to recover.

KAUNAS
Good for culture and history

LITHUANIA'S SECOND city and centuries-old commercial centre has a good range of museums and galleries and some fine architecture. It also has a thriving café culture serving the large student population of the city.

BEST SIGHTS

Čiurlionis Art Museum
A mixture of folk paintings and serious works devoted to Lithuania's artistic heritage and including a large section on the soulful painter and musician Mikalojus Čiurlionis.

Devil's Museum
Formerly a private collection of over 1,700 bizarre effigies and statues of the devil. The exhibits range from the grotesque to the folksy and include depictions of devils from around the world.

Kaunas Castle
A river fortress marking the foundation of the city. Now largely ruined, but housing a small museum.

TRAKAI
Good for outdoor activities, romantic escapism and scenic landscape

THE ANCIENT Lithuanian capital west of Vilnius is situated among lakes and forests, with some spectacular romantic castles and delightful walks through the forests. The restored Gothic castle on an island in the middle of Lake Galvé dates from the early fifteenth century and is linked to the mainland by a series of footbridges.

BEST WATER SPORTS

Lake Galvé
This is a popular weekend retreat for Lithuanians. You can take a yacht trip or hire a rowing boat; jet skis and speedboats are also available here.

NORTHERN LITHUANIA
Good for local colour

BEST SIGHT

Hill of the Crosses
An extraordinary pilgrimage site near the town of Šiauliai formed from thousands of crosses built up over the years in defiance of the Soviet authorities. It is a chilling and eerie place.

SOUTHERN LITHUANIA
Good for beaches and local colour

BEST SIGHT

Druskininkai
This nineteenth-century spa town near the border with Belarus was developed during the Soviet era when there were nine sanatoria with over 5,000 beds for spa patients. A few spas still remain, offering mud baths, mineral baths and massages.

WEST COAST
Good for family holidays and wildlife

BEST RESORT

Palanga
● The only real Lithuanian seaside resort is 11 miles south of the Latvian border.
● During the summer the town becomes overcrowded with visitors enjoying the long sandy beach, sanatoria and surrounding pine woods.

BEST NATURE RESERVE

Curonian Lagoon
A unique natural feature formed by a 60-mile long spit of land. The spit villages, known collectively as Neringa, survived development in the 1960s and remain delightful hideaways where fresh fish is landed every day. The surrounding woodland is home to some rare flora and fauna, including an elusive herd of wild boar, and the sand dunes provide weird backdrops to walks along the coast.

WHEN TO GO

CITY BREAKS to Vilnius are popular at any time of the year, and especially during the International Music Festival in June and the Jazz Festival in October. Resort areas are limited to the short season over the summer months when it can be sunny but mild. During the winter temperatures can drop alarmingly, especially inland.

	JAN	FEB	MAR	APR	MAY	JUN	JUL	AUG	SEP	OCT	NOV	DEC
Average daily maximum temperature °C												
London	6	7	10	13	17	20	22	21	19	14	10	7
Vilnius	-5	-3	1	12	18	21	22	22	17	11	4	-2
	JAN	FEB	MAR	APR	MAY	JUN	JUL	AUG	SEP	OCT	NOV	DEC
Vilnius	20	17	15	13	17	12	11	13	13	15	17	21
London	15	13	11	12	12	11	12	11	13	13	15	15
Average number of rainy days per month												

PACKAGE TRAVEL

A HANDFUL of tour operators run packages to Lithuania, or touring holidays incorporating the neighbouring Baltic States of Estonia and Latvia. Tailor-made itineraries can usually be arranged. Specialist operators can arrange art and music breaks as well as wildlife breaks and shooting holidays. Vilnius is also starting to feature in some mainstream operators' city-break brochures.

Tour operators

General and specialist: Norvista, ScanMeridian, Scantours, Specialised Tours, Yes Travel **Activities**: Ace Study Tours, Midas (battlefields), Ramblers Holidays (walking)

INDEPENDENT TRAVEL

DIRECT FLIGHTS to Vilnius are available with Lithuanian Airlines from Heathrow. Otherwise the best connections are with SAS via Copenhagen or Stockholm, or Austrian Airlines via Vienna. Local tour operators such as Lithuanian Tours offer themed itineraries based around Vilnius and can arrange guides and transport.

Car hire can be expensive and difficult to arrange unless you do it through your hotel. The roads are good, and well signposted. Cheap accommodation is available, a number of agencies arrange stays in private homes and there is a thriving Youth Hostels Association. The cities have a wide range of cheaper guesthouses, most offering good basic rooms, and large Soviet-style hotels offering cheap beds, but many of the latter are a bit soulless and in need of major refurbishment. A number of new resort-style hotels have sprung up around Vilnius, often developed in partnership with western businesses.

Within the country, it is easiest to get around by bus, but there are good train connections to neighbouring countries via Vilnius. Information is usually supplied in English, and English-speaking information booths exist in most of the cities.

RED TAPE, HEALTH AND SAFETY

BRITISH PASSPORT-HOLDERS and UK citizens do not require a visa to visit Lithuania. No immunisations are necessary, although the state of health care is not entirely up to Western standards. Serious street crime is rare, but as in other developing countries in the region incidents are on the increase.

MORE INFORMATION Lithuanian Embassy, 17 Essex Villas, London W8 7BP, tel 020-7938 2481

COST OF LIVING

MALAYSIA

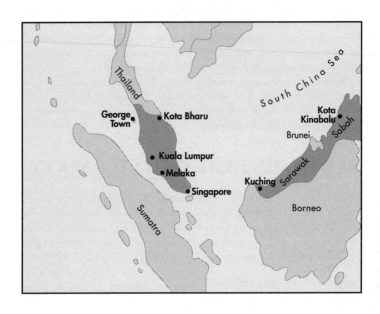

HIGHLIGHTS

Beaches
*Kelantan,
Langkawi,
Penang,
Terengganu*

Culture
*Kelantan,
Melaka,
Sarawak,
Terengganu*

**Family
holidays**
Kuala Lumpur,

*Penang, Sabah,
Terengganu*

Flora
*Pahang, Sabah,
Sarawak*

Food
*Kuala Lumpur,
Melaka, Penang*

History
*Kuala Lumpur,
Melaka,
Penang,
Sarawak*

Local colour
*Kelantan,
Melaka,
Sabah,
Sarawak,
Terengganu*

**Outdoor
activities**
*Labuan,
Langkawi,
Pahang,
Sabah,
Sarawak*

**Romantic
escapism**
*Langkawi,
Sabah*

Shopping
*Kelantan,
Kuala Lumpur,
Labuan,
Melaka,
Sarawak,
Terengganu*

Wildlife
*Pahang, Sabah,
Sarawak*

A LATE DEVELOPER, Malaysia remains unspoilt and enticingly unexplored – the wild outdoors often lies right outside your window. Within the narrow, peninsular mainland (Western Malaysia) and the states of Sabah and Sarawak on the island of Borneo (Eastern Malaysia) are found no less than 14,500 species of plants and 200 different mammals including the endangered 'old man of the forest', the shaggy-haired orang-utan. Most excursions can be made from a comfortable base, and the country has something to offer every type of holidaymaker.

KUALA LUMPUR
Good for family holidays, food, history and shopping

CHOOSE A CENTRAL hotel to avoid too much walking: traffic is fast and the streets narrow. Many locals speak English and are helpful to visitors.

BEST SIGHTS

National Museum
Exhibits on Nonya (Malaysian-born or 'Straits' Chinese) culture and a Malay *kampung* (traditional village).

Orchid Garden and Butterfly Park
Walk along paths lined with rare orchid species and other tropical plants, or enjoy the sight of 6,000 dazzling butterflies. Both spots are crowded at weekends.

Petronas Twin Towers, Sultan Abdul Samad Building and Railway Station
Petronas Twin Towers is the world's tallest building. Sultan Abdul Samad Building (opposite the Tudor-style Selangor Club on Jalan Raja) is grand and colonial, while the railway station is flamboyant Indo-Saracenic.

BEST SHOPPING

Local shopping offers variety and value in everything from street markets to multi-storey malls. Recommended are Bukit Bintang Plaza, Sungei Wang Plaza, Lot 10, Suria KLCC and the ASEANA complex of Asian crafts. For bric-a-brac, clothing and leatherware, try Petaling Street. The Central Market is fun for families and Pasar Malaam Night Market sells everything under the moon.

All shopping centres offer Malay, Chinese, Indian and American food courts; street stalls have the cheapest eats.

BEST EXCURSIONS

Port Dickson
Old-world resort with a pleasant beach and Yacht Club – but avoid weekend crowds.

Selangor
Visit the Blue Mosque, Sunway Lagoon theme park and the Royal Selangor Pewter Factory.

KELANTAN
Good for beaches, culture, local colour and shopping

KELANTAN IS an ultra-conservative Muslim state where alcohol is banned and bikinis are frowned upon. It has many colourful traditions and cottage industries. Shop for embroidered *songket* textile, bamboo ware, kites and batik.

BEST SIGHTS

Khota Bharu
A quiet town with a big central market, run by women traders who object to being photographed. See top-spinning, shadow plays and dancing at the Cultural Centre.

Pantai Cahaya Bulan
Good swimming, but rather less exotic than its name – the 'Beach of Passionate Love'– suggests, as rubbish can be a problem. The road passes picturesque handicrafts villages under the palms.

MELAKA
Good for culture, food, history, local colour and shopping

AN ENGAGING old town whose architectural gems include Portuguese, Dutch and British buildings, Chinese temples and Nonya houses. It is easily seen on foot. Snap up antique furniture and clocks on Jalan Hang Jebat.

BEST SIGHTS

Baba Nonya Heritage Museum
Museum illustrating the Nonya's opulent lifestyle in the early 1900s.

Cheng Hoon Teng
The oldest Chinese temple in Malaysia (1646).

Red Square
The town's historic centre, with Dutch colonial buildings.

PAHANG
Good for flora, outdoor activities and wildlife

THE VAST Taman Negara National Park is a priority for nature-lovers. In the west, the Cameron Highlands offer a cool retreat from the steamy coast. Shop for batik, driftwood artefacts, tea and coffee.

BEST EXCURSIONS

Cameron Highlands
Quaint Ceylon-type hill resorts are set among rolling tea estates. Some hotels have log fires.

Taman Negara
This 130 million-year-old region of virgin rainforest offers boating. Walkways in the tree canopy are filled with brilliant birds. Don't forget your binoculars.

PENANG
Good for beaches, family holidays, food/wine and history

PENANG, A small island off the west coast of western Malaysia, is fringed by some of Malaysia's best beaches. It is a favourite family destination. Popular resorts include Batu Ferringhi, with de-luxe hotels, water sports and discos. The state is renowned for cheap shopping and seafood – chilli crab is a speciality.

BEST TOWN

The capital George Town is a clutter of traditional Chinese shop-houses, modern shopping complexes and places of worship. Trishaws are a novel means of sightseeing.

Fort Cornwallis
Francis Light stepped ashore here to claim Penang for the British Crown in 1786.

Penang Hill
Travel by funicular railway for spectacular views. The summit reaches 2,693 feet.

Snake Temple
A temple with real snakes curling around the altar.

PERAK
Good for beaches, family holidays and history

THE EASY-GOING western state is known for tin mining and pomelos, a fruit beloved by the Chinese, who dominate the capital Ipoh. In the city the railway station, St. Michael's School and the snooty Royal Ipoh Club exude images of the colonial era.

BEST SIGHTS AND EXCURSIONS
Kuala Kangsar
Peaceful old royal town whose highlights are the *Istana*, or former palace, and the voluptuous Ubudiah Mosque.

Pankor Luat Island
Good beaches plus exclusive and expensive accommodation, ideal for honeymooners.

Taiping Lake Gardens
An attractive picnic stop on the West Coast Highway.

SABAH
Good for family holidays, flora, local colour, outdoor activities, romantic escapism and wildlife

MALAYSIA'S MOST exotic flora and fauna, plus adventure sports such as rafting and diving. The relaxed capital, Kinabalu, is well situated for excursions, while beach lovers will enjoy Tanjung Jara resort. Try wall-diving along the reef's edge in the Sipadan and Layang-Layang Islands. Shoppers can find tribal artefacts and Filipino curios.

BEST SIGHTS AND EXCURSIONS
Kota Kinabalu National Park
Park containing 1,200 species of orchids as well as the giant rafflesia, largest plant in the world. Mount Kota Kinabalu (13,455ft) is Asia's highest peak.

Poring Hot Springs
The sensual experience of lying in a hot tub surrounded by jungle.

Sabah Museum

Natural history, ethnography and ceramics collections plus a heritage village, close to Kinabalu.

Sepilok Orang-utan Sanctuary

Befriend orang-utans rescued from forest fires and logging-camps.

SARAWAK

Good for culture, flora, history, local colour, outdoor activities, shopping and wildlife

MALAYSIA'S LAST truly wild frontier, whose interest lies in its fascinating tribal culture and spirit of adventure. Damai Beach Resort is the best beach.

BEST TOWN

Kuching

The atmospheric capital has waterfront bazaars and buildings dating from the time of the White Rajahs (the nineteenth-century British ruling class). Take a sunset cruise on the Sarawak river or visit the Sarawak Museum, Fort Margherita or the Law Courts. Shops sell pottery, basketware and Iban curios.

BEST EXCURSIONS

Mulu and Niah National Park

Extensive cave systems of international repute – the Great Cave covers an area equal to 13 soccer fields.

Up-river safaris

Meet the Ibans, former headhunters who live in longhouses shared by as many as 100 family members.

TERENGGANU

Good for beaches, culture, family holidays, local colour and shopping

VILLAGE LIFE is centred on farming and fishing; local wares are silk and batik textiles. The capital, Kuala Terengganu, has colourful shop-houses and a boat-building yard. Tanjung Jara is the best beach.

331

BEST EXCURSIONS

Kampung Merang
Charming village with cheap accommodation among the coconut plantations.

Kenyir Lake
An angler's paradise, but swimming is prohibited because of the ferocious *toman* fish.

Pulau Perhentian
Tranquil island with powder-sand beaches and excellent snorkelling.

Rantau Abang Beach
See leatherback turtles lay their eggs at night between May and September. Good Visitor Centre.

Suterasemai Silk Centre
Everything you always wanted to know about silkworms.

WHEN TO GO

MALAYSIA HAS an equatorial climate with high humidity and heavy rainfall, but it is rare not to enjoy sunshine at some stage of the day. Because Western and Eastern Malaysia are so far apart, they have

	Average daily maximum temperature °C											
London	6	7	10	13	17	20	22	21	19	14	10	7
Kuala Lumpur	32	33	33	33	33	33	32	32	32	32	32	32
	JAN	FEB	MAR	APR	MAY	JUN	JUL	AUG	SEP	OCT	NOV	DEC
Kuala Lumpur	14	14	17	20	16	13	12	14	17	20	20	18
London	15	13	11	12	12	11	12	11	13	13	15	15
	Average number of rainy days per month											

	Average daily maximum temperature °C											
London	6	7	10	13	17	20	22	21	19	14	10	7
Kuching	29	30	31	32	32	33	32	33	32	32	31	31
	JAN	FEB	MAR	APR	MAY	JUN	JUL	AUG	SEP	OCT	NOV	DEC
Kuching	24	21	22	20	21	15	18	19	20	24	26	25
London	15	13	11	12	12	11	12	11	13	13	15	15
	Average number of rainy days per month											

different monsoon seasons. On the peninsula, April to May and October are wet, while November to February is wet season on the east coast. Avoid the monsoon season if possible. September and March are the best months to travel.

A good time to visit is during a shopping carnival, or an occasion such as the colourful Hindu Thaipusam Festival (check dates with the Tourism Promotion Board, overleaf).

PACKAGE TRAVEL

TOUR OPERATORS package every aspect of Malaysia and the islands. Holidays range from 18-day coach tours to specialised nature, golf and diving packages. Some companies offer self-drive packages including accommodation. Flights converge on Kuala Lumpur from worldwide destinations, and Malaysian Airlines operates an excellent domestic network.

Tour operators

Birdwatching and wildlife: Discover the World, Limosa, Nature-trek, Sunbird, Wildlife Worldwide **General and specialist**: Asian Journeys, Distant Dreams, Exodus, Far East Gateways, Jetset, Kuoni, Magic of the Orient, Malaysia Experience, Travel 2, Somak, World Dreams **Other activities**: Dive Worldwide, Holts' Tours (battle-fields), Regal (scuba)

INDEPENDENT TRAVEL

INDEPENDENT TRAVEL is easy and cheap in the peninsula, which has an excellent infrastructure for sightseeing by train and bus. Driving is on the left and there are frequent petrol stations with toilet facilities. Watch out for reckless drivers on the busy Kuala Lumpur to Johor Bahru highway. In quiet states such as Kelantan, you may be the only driver on the road. Travel in Eastern Malaysia is mainly by air or boat.

Hotels range from sophisticated urban establishments and dazzling island resorts to simple guesthouses. In the low season, you can bargain for a room.

RED TAPE, HEALTH AND SAFETY

COMMONWEALTH CITIZENS do not require a visa, but an onward/return ticket is required. Scruffy visitors may be refused entry. Be warned that drug smuggling carries the death penalty.

Inoculation against hepatitis and tetanus is advisable; the latter is compulsory for travellers from yellow-fever regions. Malaysia gets a good bill of health; the most common illness is a cold from air-conditioned hotels. Check current anti-malarial precautions and remember to take insect repellent. Bottled water is available everywhere.

Bag-snatching occurs in crowded areas – take the usual precautions (see page 12). At the time of going to press, some tourists had been kidnapped from several remote diving resorts off Sabah by terrorist factions. Tourists concerned about safety should consult the Foreign Office Travel Advice Unit (see page 11). Generally speaking Malaysia is safer than most Asian countries, but women risk exposure to insult if scantily dressed. Pack lightweight cotton clothes with a jacket for high altitudes.

MORE INFORMATION Malaysian Tourism Promotion Board, 57 Trafalgar Square, London WC2N 5DU, tel 020–7930 7932, web site: *www.tourism.gov.my*

COST OF LIVING £

THE MALDIVES

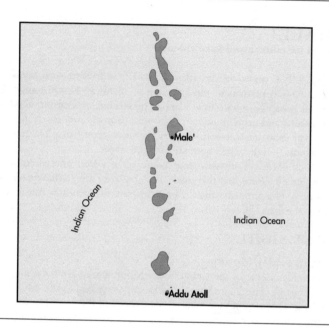

HIGHLIGHTS

Beaches/ scenic landscape
Resort islands

Culture/ local colour
Addu Atoll, Male'

Family holidays
Biyadoo, Holiday Island, Kanifinolhu, Laguna Beach

Outdoor activities
Bathala, Dhigufinolhu, Ellaidoo, Filitheyo, Helengeli, Kuredu, Maayafushi, Tari Village, Vaadhoo

Romantic escapism
Banyan Tree, Coco Palm Resort, Rihiveli, Soneva Fushi

THE MALDIVES is a chain of some 26 coral atolls extending 450 miles across the Indian Ocean south-west of Sri Lanka. Each atoll has a ring of reefs, sandbars and islands around a lagoon – officially there are 1,192 islands altogether, none larger than a mile across. About 200 islands have Maldivian communities and another 90 or so islands have been developed as tourist resorts. Most islands are so tiny you can stroll around them in ten minutes.

MALE'
Good for culture and local colour

THE TINY capital of this Islamic republic is packed with people – some 65,000 permanent residents and as many as 30,000 temporary visitors on a one-square-mile island. The bustling waterfront, winding backstreets and many mosques can be seen in an afternoon's stroll, then you can shop for souvenirs or join the local gentry in a teashop for 'short eats' – little snacks both savoury and sweet.

Much of the action takes place down on the waterfront, where small boats called *dhonis* are the trucks and buses of the Maldives. They shuttle to the airport, which is on a separate island nearly half a mile across the water.

BEST SIGHTS

Grand Friday Mosque
The golden dome of the Grand Friday Mosque shines in the sunlight – it is actually aluminium, but it looks imposing beside the tall white minaret. At around noon on Friday the faithful assemble, quietly coming from every direction, leaving shoes by the thousands around the stairs.

Market
Every evening the fishing fleet comes in and dozens of *dhonis* pull up beside Marine Drive. Elegant silver fish, many more than three feet long, are unloaded by hand and carried across to the market, where the floor is soon tiled with tuna.

THE RESORTS
Good for beaches, family holidays, outdoor activities, romantic escapism and scenic landscape

THE COUNTRY boasts some 90 resorts, each one on its own picture-perfect, palm-fringed island with a pure white beach and a turquoise-blue lagoon. On these resort islands there is no motorised transport.

BEST WATER SPORTS

Diving and snorkelling
The Maldives is famous as a diving destination. Every resort has a

diving operation offering courses and trips daily. The whole country consists of coral atolls, and the reefs are carefully preserved, although much of the shallow water coral was killed by 'coral bleaching' in 1998 by El Niño. The coral is growing back, and it's excellent for divers going below 30 feet. The fish life is still amazing – it is like swimming in an aquarium, even with a snorkel just a few metres from the beach.

Experienced divers enjoy the wrecks, the larger marine life (manta rays, turtles, whale sharks, morays and more), and the long drift dives. Some of the best resorts for serious divers are Bathala, Dhigufinolhu, Ellaidoo, Filitheyo, Helengeli, Kuredu, Maayafushi and Vaadhoo.

Surfing

From March to November there is some great surfing in the Maldives, but only a few resorts have accessible 'breaks' (all the surf spots are 'reef breaks', where the waves break over coral reefs). Tari Village is the best resort for surfers (you have to book a surfing package), but Lohifushi is also good. Boat-based surfing trips are another possibility.

BEST FOR FAMILY HOLIDAYS

As a self-contained community, with no traffic and just one resort per island, a Maldives resort can be perfect for families. Try Biyadoo, Club Med, Holiday Island, Kanifinolhu and Laguna Beach.

BEST FOR ROMANTIC ESCAPISM

The most romantic resorts are the small and luxurious getaways such as Banyan Tree, Coco Palm Resort, Rihiveli and Soneva Fushi.

BEST EXCURSIONS

Safari boats

Increasingly popular 'safari trips' offer one or two weeks' cruising through the atolls on a live-aboard boat. These safari trips are great for getting to the more remote diving sites, visiting uninhabited islands and seeing some different scenery. Make sure you have compatible companions.

ADDU ATOLL
Good for culture and local colour

IN THE far south of the country is Addu Atoll, which was a remote RAF base from 1956 to 1976. The base is now the Equator Village resort, on the island of Gan, unique because it is linked to neighbouring islands by a causeway. A few trucks and minibuses run along the ten-mile road across the islands and causeways – this is the longest road in the country and quite exceptional.

BEST LOCAL COLOUR

Rent a bicycle from the resort, and pedal across to the adjoining islands of Feydhoo, Maradhoo and Hithadhoo. The villages have straight sandy streets, shady trees, old mosques and coral-stone houses. It is a world of its own – traditional, unhurried and as well-ordered as the tenets of Islam.

WHEN TO GO

DECEMBER TO April is the dry season (it can rain a little). It is the peak tourist season too, when resorts can be fully booked and prices are higher. Christmas to New Year is the busiest and most expensive period. From May to November the skies can be cloudy, humidity is higher and rainstorms are more likely. There are fewer people and lower prices, though August is more expensive.

Average daily maximum temperature °C											
London	6	7	10	13	17	20	22	21	19	14	10	7
Minnicoy	29	29	30	31	31	30	29	29	29	29	29	29
	JAN	FEB	MAR	APR	MAY	JUN	JUL	AUG	SEP	OCT	NOV	DEC
Minnicoy	3	1	1	3	9	17	14	12	10	11	8	4
London	15	13	11	12	12	11	12	11	13	13	15	15
Average number of rainy days per month											

PACKAGE TRAVEL

NEARLY ALL the visitors to the Maldives are on package holidays. Most mainstream tour operators cover the Maldives in their long–haul brochures and there are direct charter and scheduled flights into Male'. Most of the tourist resorts featured are scattered among the three main groups of islands: North Male' Atoll, South Male' Atoll and Ari Atoll to the west. Resorts are being developed on other atolls, offering more seclusion and less visited dive sites. Transfers from the airport are by boat or seaplane.

Many of the beach resorts occupy their own tiny island and there is a variety of styles and budgets to choose from – from the exclusive and highly sophisticated to simple, laid-back resorts with few frills. Accommodation is mostly in small bungalows which run the gamut from basic (ceiling fans and unheated water) to sublime (spacious with tropical furniture and luxury open-air bathrooms). Packages are on a half-board, full-board or all-inclusive basis – food is usually good, and served buffet-style. Entertainment is low-key with maybe an occasional barbecue or Maldivian theme evening. Each resort has its own diving centre and most offer other water sports such as canoeing, sailing or windsurfing.

Scuba diving can be arranged at the resort – there is no need to book dives or courses. You can also take a cruise through the islands or combine the Maldives with destinations such as Sri Lanka (around 400 miles away), Dubai and Singapore.

Tour operators

General: Abercrombie & Kent, Airtours, Axis, Carrier, Classic Connection, Coromandel, Cosmos, Cox & Kings, CV Travel, Distant Dreams, Elegant Resorts, Elite Vacations, First Choice, Hayes & Jarvis, JMC, Kuoni, Premier Holidays, Somak, Sunset Faraway, Thomson, Tradewinds, World Dreams, Worldwide Journeys **Multi-activity**: Club Med **Scuba diving**: Dive Worldwide, Regal Holidays

---

INDEPENDENT TRAVEL

IT IS almost impossible to travel independently. If you arrive without a hotel reservation, the immigration authorities will ask you to make arrangements with a tour operator before you leave the airport. Government policy restricts visitors to Male' and resorts in the 'tourism zone'. A permit is required to go outside this zone, for which you need a sponsor from a local island.

RED TAPE, HEALTH AND SAFETY

BRITISH PASSPORT-HOLDERS are given a free 30-day visitor's permit on arrival. Visitors should have a return ticket and US$25 for every day of their intended stay.

The Maldives is remarkably free of health problems and crime, especially the resorts, but inoculations against hepatitis A, typhoid and polio are recommended. If arriving from an 'infected' country, immunisation against yellow fever is essential. Consult your GP or a travel clinic for the latest health advice before departure. Scuba diving presents some risks, and divers should have insurance which covers them for helicopter evacuation and decompression treatment.

No alcohol, pornography, pork, narcotics, spearguns or 'idols of worship' can be brought into the country. Baggage is searched, and any alcohol will be taken and held until departure. Magazines may be regarded as pornographic if they contain advertisements showing women in underwear. Export of turtle shell (sometimes called 'tortoise-shell'), or any turtle shell products, is forbidden.

MORE INFORMATION The Maldives High Commission, 22 Nottingham Place, London W1M 3FB, tel 020-7224 2135, web site: *www.visitmaldives.com*

COST OF LIVING £-££

MALTA

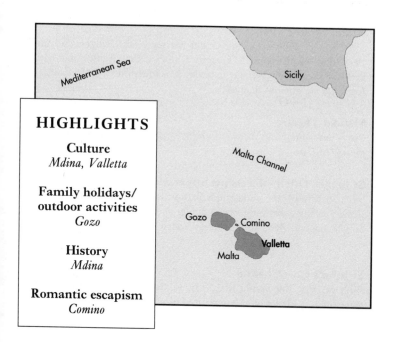

HIGHLIGHTS

Culture
Mdina, Valletta

**Family holidays/
outdoor activities**
Gozo

History
Mdina

Romantic escapism
Comino

Mediterranean Sea

Sicily

Malta Channel

Gozo · Comino

Valletta

Malta

VALLETTA
Good for culture

PLANNED IN 1565 as both a fortress and a city home for the Knights of St John, the capital still has an aristocratic air. It is comparatively small, but inside its bastion walls is a rollercoaster grid of narrow streets and endless stairs. Walk it during the daytime, when it is alive with people.

BEST SIGHTS

Admiralty House/Museum of Fine Arts
Originally a knight's private residence, Admiralty House was until 1961 the headquarters of the British Mediterranean fleet. There are 30 rooms of exhibits.

Auberge de Provence/Museum of Archaeology

This 1571 hall of residence for the Knights from Provence now contains most of the prehistoric finds from the islands.

Grand Master's Palace

The former residence of the Grand Master of the Knights and until 1928 that of the British Governor, the palace houses the Malta Parliament. The principal staterooms, courtyards and the Palace Armoury are open to the public.

Manoel Theatre

Tiny but sumptuous baroque theatre: the third-oldest functioning theatre in Europe.

St James' Ditch/Merchants Street Market

Situated beneath the eponymous bastion is a vibrant Sunday morning market selling everything from puppies and Tiger Balm to the English Sunday papers. Merchants Street is a scaled-down daily version and not as much fun.

St John's Co-cathedral

Built in 1578, this houses Malta's finest art treasures. The floor of the cathedral is made up of 400 tessellated tombs of pre-eminent Knights.

MDINA
Good for culture and history

PUT THE old capital of Malta at the top of your 'sights to see' list. Dating from the twelfth century, it has been preserved and is mostly devoid of tacky modern development. St Paul's Cathedral is a very skilful piece of Maltese baroque architecture and is built on the site where St Paul converted the Roman governor Publius to Christianity.

GOZO
Good for family holidays and outdoor activities

GOZO IS the least spoilt corner of the archipelago. Five miles from Malta, it is reached either by a heli-link or a ferry service. It is smaller, greener, more tranquil and uncomplicated. The diving, walking and rock-bathing is better than on Malta. If you want a quiet, family, villa-type holiday bypass Malta altogether and head for a farmhouse on Gozo. Do not miss a Gozitan summer *festa* (see 'When to go').

BEST SIGHTS

Mgarr harbour
Mgarr harbour has all the hubbub of a local ferry terminus and three excellent waterside restaurants. The best bar on the island, the Gleneagles, is here too.

Sannat
Sannat is good for cliff walking, and on cooler afternoons traditional lace-makers weave in the shade. The excellent Hotel Ta'Cenc is nearby.

Victoria (Rabat)
This is the hub of Gozo's cosmos. The bus terminus, morning market, powerful local wine, patriarchal 'citadel' and dinky museums make it almost a daily 'must'.

Xaghra
This is the tranquil village from which to start and finish scenic walks through what used to be the Grand Master's hunting grounds. The prehistoric 'temples' of Ggantija are easily accessed from here.

COMINO
Good for romantic escapism

FLECKED WITH sparse vegetation and overgrown dry-stone walls, Comino from afar seems barren and unappealing. But it boasts some attractive rocky bays, just one hotel and a smattering of local inhabitants. It is ideal for those who enjoy an away-from-it-all holiday after the day-tripper boats have left in the afternoon.

WHEN TO GO

DUE TO its geographical position Malta enjoys a long season: from April to October. Visit in May to see a surprisingly verdant island and its wild flowers; go in July and August if you do not mind crowds and the aroma of sun oil, and in September and October if you want to see a country gently unwind.

King Carnival, a celebration of decorated floats and open-air dancing, is held during the four days before Ash Wednesday. Holy Week celebrations include Maundy Thursday pilgrimages, Good Friday pageants and Easter Sunday processions. Village *festi*, in honour of the local patron saint, are held nearly every weekend in summer.

	Average daily maximum temperature °C											
London	6	7	10	13	17	20	22	21	19	14	10	7
Valletta	14	15	16	18	22	26	29	29	27	24	20	16
	JAN	FEB	MAR	APR	MAY	JUN	JUL	AUG	SEP	OCT	NOV	DEC
Valletta	12	8	5	2	2	0	0	1	3	6	9	13
London	15	13	11	12	12	11	12	11	13	13	15	15
	Average number of rainy days per month											

PACKAGE TRAVEL

BECAUSE OF their small size the islands can be treated as one industrial-sized resort. Just about everywhere is accessible – even on Gozo. All the hotels are three-star standard or better. It cannot be emphasised enough that long stretches of sandy beaches do not exist in Malta; but the water is more often than not substantially cleaner than on a 'costa'. Many of the principal hotels have large pools and sea access off the rocks, from which the elderly and very young should exercise caution.

Packages to Malta are cheap compared with many other Mediterranean destinations. All major tour operators go there, and most packages offer hotel and self-catering apartments in the main beach resorts. Many tour operators also offer the island of Gozo, alone or as part of a two-centre holiday. Here there are also farmhouses converted into upmarket self-catering or hotel accommodation.

Only a handful of specialist tour operators offers holidays on Comino. Package accommodation is limited to the single hotel around which most of the tourist activities on the island revolve. Specialist activities on the islands include Christian or cultural tours, golf, sailing, scuba diving and walking.

Tour operators

Archaeology: Andante **Church tours**: Inter-Church Travel **Cultural**: Martin Randall **General**: Airtours, Aquasun, Belle Air Holidays, Bonaventure, Cadogan, Chevron Air, Cosmos, Crystal, CV Travel, First Choice, Malta Sun, Panorama, Prestige, Sunspot Tours, Thomson, Unijet **Golf**: Aquasun, Belleair Holidays, Malta Direct **Scuba diving**: Belleair Holidays, Gozo Holidays, Malta Direct, Regal Holidays, Sunspot Tours **Short breaks**: Belleair, Cresta, Inghams, Malta Direct, Travelscene **Walking**: HF Holidays, Headwater, Ramblers Holidays **Other activities**: Ace Study Tours, Holts' tours (battlefields)

INDEPENDENT TRAVEL

VERY FEW British tourists visit Malta independently. The odd buccaneering soul turns up on a cargo vessel from northern Italy but most, due to the sheer economic weight of numbers, book flights and accommodation through an operator.

Air Malta, Air 2000, Britannia and British Airways operate both scheduled and charter flights. Regular ferry services leave from Naples in Southern Italy, and Catania and Syracuse on Sicily.

Malta has the cheapest car-hire rates in Europe. Driving is on the left; a British driving licence is acceptable. Some car-hire firms have a minimum age limit of 25 and a maximum age limit of 70: check when booking. Maltese driving leaves much to be desired. Most of the roads are unlit and outside the main towns there are no pavements. Extreme care should be taken when driving, and pedestrians should always walk facing oncoming traffic.

The main bus terminus is in Valletta, from where buses go to all parts of Malta, though there are also direct point-to-point services. The buses are very cheap and a great way to see Maltese life – and you avoid having to drive. Taxis are all fitted with meters.

The Gozo Channel Company operates a car-passenger ferry service between Malta and Gozo, with about 30 crossings each way daily in summer. In peak season a hydrofoil service links Malta, Gozo and Comino. Air Malta also runs a helicopter service linking Malta and Gozo (stopping at Comino on request).

RED TAPE, HEALTH AND SAFETY

BRITISH PASSPORT-HOLDERS do not require a visa. Tap water is safe to drink, and the crime rate is relatively low – just take the usual precautions (see pages 10–12). Topless bathing is illegal.

MORE INFORMATION Malta National Tourist Office, Malta House, 36–38 Piccadilly, London W1V 0PP, tel 020-7292 4900, web site: *www.visitmalta.com*

COST OF LIVING ££–£££

MAURITIUS

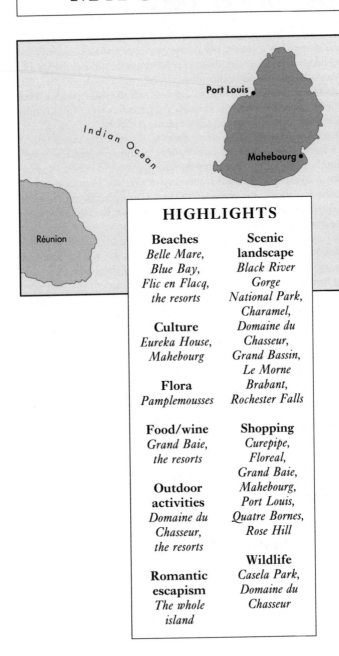

Port Louis

Indian Ocean

Mahebourg

Réunion

HIGHLIGHTS

Beaches
*Belle Mare,
Blue Bay,
Flic en Flacq,
the resorts*

Culture
*Eureka House,
Mahebourg*

Flora
Pamplemousses

Food/wine
*Grand Baie,
the resorts*

**Outdoor
activities**
*Domaine du
Chasseur,
the resorts*

**Romantic
escapism**
*The whole
island*

**Scenic
landscape**
*Black River
Gorge
National Park,
Charamel,
Domaine du
Chasseur,
Grand Bassin,
Le Morne
Brabant,
Rochester Falls*

Shopping
*Curepipe,
Floreal,
Grand Baie,
Mahebourg,
Port Louis,
Quatre Bornes,
Rose Hill*

Wildlife
*Casela Park,
Domaine du
Chasseur*

THE TRUMP card of this 93- by 76-mile island in the Indian Ocean off Madagascar is its stunning natural beauty – mystic mountains, lush countryside (much of which has been cultivated for sugar cane), dazzling beaches and endless azure sea. Tourism has boomed but this heavily populated island with 1.1 million inhabitants has created a charter-free industry while retaining its strong local culture, a heady mix of Indian, Chinese, African, Creole and European influences. There are no high-rise hotels and no blackspot areas. Mauritius is a major honeymoon destination and is also good for families and watersports enthusiasts.

PORT LOUIS
Good for shopping and entertainment

THE THRIVING capital and port has plenty to interest visitors, including a bustling central market.

Caudan waterfront
A complex with plush air-conditioned shops, multi-screen cinema and casino.

Racecourse
The world's second oldest racecourse, built in 1812. Join the locals every Saturday from May to November.

BEST EXCURSION
Eureka House
An imposing country house, built in the 1830s. Visit the restored music room, Chinese room and French East India room. Don't miss the colonial shower contraption.

GRAND BAIE AND THE NORTH
Good for beaches, family holidays, flora, food/wine, nightlife, outdoor activities, shopping and romantic escapism

GRAND BAIE is a tourist hang-out, its main drag full of shops, bars and restaurants.

BEST RESTAURANTS
Head to La Pagode or the Taj Mahal for cheap eats, or for something more upmarket, walk a little out of town to Le Capitaine Restaurant for great Creole cuisine. At Le Fins Bec restaurant you can create your

own *rhum arrangé* or flavoured rum. The Sunset Café is the perfect place to relax with a glass of Phoenix (the local brew) and watch the deep-sea marlin catches on display. Favourite Friday night spots include the Banana Café (a sand-floor bar) and Zanzibar, which packs in locals and tourists alike.

BEST SHOPPING

Sunset Pier
A development packed with upmarket shops. One of Mauritius' main industries is textiles; consequently this is the place to come for designer labels.

Factory shops
If you want cheap prices on end-of-range designer labels, head to the factory shops of Floreal, Curepipe, Quatre Bornes or Rose Hill.

BEST FLORA

The Pamplemousses district in the central north of the island is good for exotic flowers and vegetation. At the Sir Seewoosagur Ramgoolan Botanical Gardens highlights include a giant water-lily pond and a great variety of palms. Guides (who take you round for a small fee negotiated in advance) point out ginger, cinnamon, nutmeg and other herbs and spices, along with a 200-year-old Buddha tree. Look out for the giant Aldabra tortoises.

THE SOUTH
Good for beaches, culture, family holidays, flora, food/wine, history, outdoor activities, romantic escapism, scenic landscape and wildlife

THE BLACK River Gorge National Park is an area of outstanding mountainous natural beauty containing Chamarel and Grand Bassin (see opposite), along with casuarina and coniferous trees and waterfalls. A drive along the beautiful southern coast road is highly recommended.

BEST SIGHTS

Casela Park
See parrots, pheasants and the rare pink pigeons along with leopards, tigers, lemurs, monkeys and deer. Great views across the Rivière du Rempart Valley.

Chamarel

Chamarel, or 'coloured earths', is an intriguing moon-like landscape where the earth ranges in colour from purple to deep orange (believed to be the result of the uneven cooling of molten rock). A 330-ft waterfall and restaurant with views over the countryside and ocean are nearby.

Domaine du Chasseur

Large estate in the south-east, covering over 2,000 acres of forested slopes. Visitors can hike around the area or take mini safaris. Birdwatching is popular and you may also spot a Javanese deer or boar. Facilities include some rustic bungalows and a restaurant.

Grand Bassin

Spectacular crater lake, a site of pilgrimage each February and March when most of the island's Hindu population converge for Maha Shivaratri celebrations.

Mahebourg

The town's Naval Museum tells the story of the French victory in the Battle of Grand Port (1810). Other attractions include a colourful local market.

Le Morne Brabant

An imposing, partly inaccessible rock on the south-west coast, with a restaurant halfway up. In the nineteenth century slaves hid on top and, ignorant that slavery had been abolished, flung themselves off the clifftop when soldiers approached.

Rochester Falls

Unofficial guides are eager to show visitors these modest falls over stacks of rock (reached off the south-coast road via sugar-cane fields). Local divers plunge off the top and run up the bank to demand a few rupees' reward.

La Vanille Crocodile Park

A small zoo in thick forest. Nile crocodiles imported from Madagascar and farmed for their skin are on show. You will also see giant tortoises, monkeys, deer, bats, giant land crabs and lizards.

THE RESORTS

Good for beaches, family holidays, food/wine, nightlife, outdoor activities and romantic escapism

TOURISM TENDS to focus around the resorts, which are nearly all along the best beaches. **Belle Mare** is a resort area on the east coast and the site of many big hotels. The white beach here is stunning. **Grand Baie** is a lively hotel spot with plenty of entertainment close by, while right down on the south-east coast lies the Shandrani Resort on a spectacular peninsula.

Mauritius boasts world-class hotels such as the Royal Palm and the Saint Geran. New four- and five-star properties continue to be developed (including the Hilton and the Oberoi in 2000). Hotels tend to have good restaurants and offer great watersports such as water-skiing, windsurfing, sailing, kayaks, pedalos, snorkelling, scuba diving, glass-bottom boats and catamaran cruises; many have spas. The resorts offer gentle night-time entertainment such as live music – Mauritius is not a party island as the emphasis is on beach life and romance.

WHEN TO GO

MAURITIUS IS popular all year round, but especially at Christmas and New Year when prices rise. Booking well in advance is advisable. Summer runs from November to April, when average coastal temperatures are 30°C. Winter lasts from May to October and sees a warm average of 24°C. Interior temperatures in the highlands are five degrees lower. The rainy season is officially from January to May but you could encounter overcast days any time of the year. December to March is best for diving as the water is clearer. June to August is best for surfing along the south coast, and October to March is the deep-sea fishing season.

Average daily maximum temperature °C											
London 6	7	10	13	17	20	22	21	19	14	10	7
Pamplemousses 30	30	30	28	27	25	24	24	25	27	29	30
JAN	FEB	MAR	APR	MAY	JUN	JUL	AUG	SEP	OCT	NOV	DEC
Pamplemousses 21	20	23	20	19	18	19	20	17	13	13	18
London 15	13	11	12	12	11	12	11	13	13	15	15
Average number of rainy days per month											

PACKAGE TRAVEL

MOST OPERATORS offer a selection of upmarket four- and five-star beach hotels. Hotels tend to be large with good facilities including watersports (scuba) and tennis. Although popular with a large wedding and honeymoon clientele (with discounts to brides carrying a marriage certificate in some cases), the hotels are also child-friendly, with children's clubs and babysitting available. As the island is large and hotels are spread out along its coastline, many visitors are hotel-based, hiring a car for a couple of days to explore the island.

Tour operators

General: Abercrombie & Kent, Beachcomber Tours, British Airways Holidays, Cosmos, Distant Dreams, Elite Vacations, Hayes & Jarvis, Elegant Resorts, Kuoni, Seasons in Style, Silhouette Travel, Simply Golf, Somak, Sovereign Worldwide, Sunset Faraway, Tana Travel, Tradewinds, Travel 2, Tropical Places, Worldwide Journeys **Specialists**: Carrier Tours, Classic Connection, Rainbow Tours, Susie Freeman Travel, Tropical Locations **Other activities**: Dive Worldwide (diving), Simply Golf (golf)

INDEPENDENT TRAVEL

IT IS almost impossible to travel independently in Mauritius. This is not backpacker territory. If you arrive without a hotel reservation, the immigration authorities will ask you to make arrangements with a tour operator before you leave the airport. Cheap self-catering bungalows are available in Grand Baie, Flic en Flacq and on the south coast to which taxi drivers will take you, but you should at least have a contact name and telephone number before you arrive. There are also rustic chalets at Domaine du Chasseur. Car hire is easy with large rental companies on the island. One motorway runs from the airport in the south-east to Grand Baie in the north-west. The rest of the roads are slow and winding. Watch out for the locals' dare-devil overtaking and bumper-to-bumper road sense. Mauritius has a regular, cheap, local bus service and an express service from Port Louis to Grand Baie.

RED TAPE, HEALTH AND SAFETY

BRITISH PASSPORT-HOLDERS do not require a visa for Mauritius. Entry is granted for a maximum of three months.

No vaccinations are compulsory but hepatitis A and B are recommended.

The island is generally safe, although as with any tourist destination theft does occur, so visitors should use room safes, lock belongings out of sight in cars and be streetwise. Hawkers walk the beaches selling bags, sarongs, pearls and designer T-shirts, but there is no heavy hassle factor.

MORE INFORMATION Mauritius Tourist Board, 32–33 Elvaston Place, London SW7 5NW, tel 020-7584 3666

COST OF LIVING £££

MEXICO

HIGHLIGHTS

Beaches
Yucatán, west coast

Culture
*Mexico City, Yucatán,
the Colonial Heartland*

Local colour
Mexico City

Scenic landscape
Baja California

Wildlife
Baja California, Yucatán

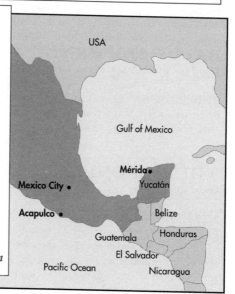

MEXICO CITY
Good for culture and local colour

THIS IS a vast, smoggy, sprawling, poverty-stricken city, but one with some exquisite historical sights and bags of character. It is a city that will grow on you; its charms are not immediately apparent.

BEST SIGHTS

Museo Nacional de Antropología
Astonishing artefacts from every mesoamerican civilisation are displayed in halls surrounding a central courtyard. The Maya collection is a must if you plan to go on to the archaeological sights in the Yucatán.

Zócalo
This vast open square in the historic centre of the city is bordered by the sinking baroque cathedral, the Palacio Nacional (coated with Diego Rivera's murals inside) and busy shopping and sightseeing streets.

BEST EXCURSION

Teotihuacán
The ancient, pre-Aztec city is an hour's drive from the city. Two great

353

pyramids dominate the site – from the summits the ceremonial design of the city unfolds along the mile-and-a-half length of the Avenue of the Dead.

BAJA CALIFORNIA
Good for wildlife and scenic landscape

THIS SLENDER finger of land has some of Mexico's most impressive desert landscapes, and a range of fascinating wildlife, including whales, seals, turtles and many seabirds.

THE COLONIAL HEARTLAND
Good for culture

NORTHWEST OF Mexico City, the five states of Aguascalientes, Guanajuato, Queretaro, San Luis Potosí, and Zacatecas contain some of the country's finest examples of colonial architecture, founded on the wealth gained from the mines in the Spanish era. In many of the splendid cities in this region, such as Guanajuato, you can stay in hotels converted from colonial mansions and haciendas (ranch estates).

WEST COAST
Good for beaches

MEXICO IS a popular sun-and-sand destination for Americans, who flock to the two biggest resorts on the west coast – Acapulco and Puerto Vallarta (also offered by British tour operators). Both have large beaches and continuous runs of fast-food outlets, malls and high-rise hotels. Other formerly sleepy resorts, such as Ixtapa and Huatulco, are being developed on a large scale in rival Cancún in the future.

YUCATÁN PENINSULA
Good for beaches, culture, scenic landscape and wildlife

BEST RESORT

Cancún
- Purpose-built resort; modern US-style hotels line a 15-mile sandbar.
- The turquoise waters of the Caribbean Sea lap one side; on the other is an inky-coloured lagoon fringed with mangroves.
- Plushest of novelty palaces are at furthest end of the sandbar,

with older hotels, malls and water-sports complexes nearer to the mainland.

● Hotel beaches and grounds are very appealing, but food and drink are ferociously expensive. Most visitors are content with the range of water sports and more leisurely beachside activities on offer, otherwise there are nature reserves to the north and south – and of course the ancient ruins.

● The Maya sites, Chichén Itzá and Tulúm, are easy day-trips.

BEST MAYA SITES

The scrub-like jungle that coats the flat Yucatán Peninsula in southern Mexico hides an untold number of mysterious ruins – the remains of the Maya civilisation that ruled before the Spanish conquest. A few lost cities have been rescued from the undergrowth.

Chichén Itzá

Probably the best-known and most visited Maya site. Complexes of temples rise from an expanse of green lawn. Kukulcan's El Castillo Pyramid is the dominating central structure, overlooking the massed ranks of sculpted columns in the Temple of the Warriors and the vast I-shaped ball court.

Cobá

An out-of-the-way site, unsung, unexploited and largely unexcavated, where one can recapture the feeling of discovery. Tramp through paths skittering with iguanas to the Nohoch Mul pyramid, for a view across the lurid green Lake Cobá and the surrounding jungle.

Palenque

The best setting of all the sites, deep in the backlands of Chiapas state, south of the peninsula, with rainforest coating the hills behind the sandy stone of what was once a powerful city. Reliefs of warriors and gods in stucco and stone guard the palaces and temples. Palenque's unique feature is a four-storey tower, a construction unknown elsewhere in pre-Columbian MesoAmerica.

Tulúm

A collection of ruins in a spectacular setting – a white sand beach overlooked by two ruined towers on the cliffs.

Uxmal

The most beautiful of the Maya cities for the elaborate decoration of the stones smothered with geometric gargoyles, zigzags and diamond lattice work. A string of smaller sites in the vicinity is worth visiting.

BEST WILDLIFE

Sian Ka'an Biosphere Reserve

Superb protected coastal region comprising diverse natural habitats, from tropical rainforest to coral reef, home to hundreds of exotic species of birds and other animals.

WHEN TO GO

THE YUCATÁN is always blisteringly hot, and breathlessly humid in the rainy season (May to September). November is a good month to travel, before prices rise for the winter season, when the weather is best.

Average daily maximum temperature °C												
London	6	7	10	13	17	20	22	21	19	14	10	7
Mérida	28	29	31	33	33	33	32	32	32	30	28	28
	JAN	FEB	MAR	APR	MAY	JUN	JUL	AUG	SEP	OCT	NOV	DEC
Mérida	4	4	3	3	6	13	15	13	17	10	6	6
London	15	13	11	12	12	11	12	11	13	13	15	15
Average number of rainy days per month												

PACKAGE TRAVEL

MAINSTREAM TOUR operators offer beach packages in Acapulco, Puerto Vallarta or Cancún, or combine a tour of the sites of the Yucatán Peninsula with a week on a beach. Prices, routes and hotels vary considerably. Some specialists will tailor-make packages for you.

Tour operators

Cultural: British Museum Traveller, Sunset Faraway, Veloso Tours, Trips Worldwide **General**: Airtours, British Airways Holidays, First Choice, Hayes & Jarvis, JMC, Kuoni, Thomson, Unijet, Virgin **Tailor-made tours**: Ace Study Tours, Bales Tours, Cox & Kings, Encounter Overland, Explore Worldwide, Journey Latin America, Latin America Travel, Nomadic Thoughts, South American Experience **Other activities**: American Adventures (camping), Exodus (cycling), Trek America (adventure camping)

INDEPENDENT TRAVEL

TRAVELLING INDEPENDENTLY in Mexico requires stamina, and it helps if you speak and understand a little Spanish. There are some excellent new highways, but away from large conurbations road conditions often leave something to be desired.

Scheduled flights go to Mexico City, charter flights to Cancún and Puerto Vallarta. Internal flights can save time and are likely to be more comfortable than a hot bus ride (the main way to get around). Long-distance buses usually have air-conditioning. These are reasonably comfortable; local rural buses considerably less so. Shared minibuses and taxis may be a better option. Trains are cheaper and even slower than buses, and are recommended only for really long journeys.

In theory, hotels and prices are regulated by the tourism authorities, but due to stupendous inflation, prices have usually increased to more than those advertised. Always ask for a reduction on the quoted price of hotels. Be sure to see the room before agreeing to take it. Air-conditioning costs more. Very few official campsites exist.

RED TAPE, HEALTH AND SAFETY

BRITISH PASSPORT-HOLDERS do not require a visa to enter Mexico. Montezuma's Revenge, or upset stomach, is the commonest health problem – see page 12 for tips on how to avoid it. Air pollution is at its highest in Mexico City between December and May. See your GP or a travel clinic for advice on recommended vaccinations.

The Foreign Office warns about the risk of armed robbery in urban areas – do not resist, and avoid travel after dark and isolated beaches at all times. For the latest advice contact the Foreign Office Travel Advice Unit (see page 11).

MORE INFORMATION Mexican Ministry of Tourism, 41 Trinity Square, London EC3N 4DJ, tel 020-7488 9392, web site: *www.mexico/travel.com/*

COST OF LIVING £–££

MOROCCO

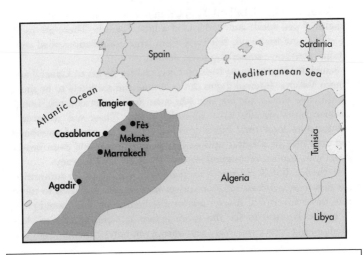

HIGHLIGHTS

Beaches
*Agadir, Asilah,
Essaouira*

Local colour
*Middle Atlas,
Northern Morocco*

Scenic landscape
*South Morocco
and Sahara*

Culture
*High Atlas,
Middle Atlas*

Outdoor activities
*Essaouira,
High Atlas,
Northern Morocco*

Shopping
*Fès, Marrakech,
Mèknes*

NORTHERN MOROCCO
Good for local colour and outdoor activities

BEST SIGHTS

Rif Mountains
The saw-toothed crags of the Rif are excellent hiking country. Visits focus on the relaxed little town of Chefchaouen, which is hardly more than a village. The cool air and friendly, pester-free ambience is a relief after Tangier.

Tétouan is worth a trip for the Medina and Andalusian heritage: Spanish is still spoken widely. Be prepared for maximum hassle.

Tangier

The word 'cosmopolitan' could have been invented to describe Tangier. It is a seedy old roué of a town that bears the marks of every race or civilisation that has passed through. Smuggling, drug-running and illegal immigrants to Spain – in fact, money made by whatever dubious means – are Tangier's real trade. The main points of interest centre on the Grand Socco at the entrance to the Medina, and the Petit Socco inside the walls. The fortified Kasbah gives great views over the sweep of the bay. Unfortunately, the touts and hustlers are so tenacious that they spoil many people's visits. Have a drink in the Tanger Inn for a taste of the Tangier that once attracted writers such as Paul Bowles and William Burroughs.

MIDDLE ATLAS
Good for culture, local colour and shopping

IF YOU do nothing else in Morocco, see the imperial cities – Fès, Meknès and Rabat. You can whizz around them quite quickly if time is limited, although two weeks is a realistic timespan. The medinas (or old towns), rather than the modern parts of the cities, are the focus of interest.

Fès

Visiting Fès's medina is perhaps the highlight of any trip to Morocco. It is a step back to another age, into a walled medieval labyrinth, whose colours, smells, noise and bustle are as much a shock to the system as, say, a first visit to India. Police have cracked down on the armies of touts and hustlers who once made this experience hellish.

The best way to take it all in is just to follow your nose through the souks (the henna souk is especially fascinating) and bazaars, ferret around, drink mint tea and not worry too much about getting lost – you will inevitably do so, but there are various walls and landmarks to help out with orientation. Try to visit the tanneries to experience local colour – an assault on the olfactory senses. The mosques and *medersas* (theological colleges) are masterpieces of architecture dating back to the twelfth century. Look for the Medersa bou Inania, Medersa el Attarine and Kairouine mosque. Sadly, the mosques are off-limits to non-Muslims, and the restored Royal Palace, Dar el-Makhzen, is not open to the public.

Meknès

Meknès owes its current position of fame to Sultan Moulay Ismail's barbarous reign in the seventeenth century; he came to power in 1672, a time when Meknès had fallen into obscurity. During his 55-year reign he endowed the town with an enormous palace and 15 miles of walls. As head of the Alawite dynasty he introduced an unprecedented period of stability to Morocco by butchering all his enemies and any dissenting elements mercilessly. The massive palace complex is the focal point of this city. Exploring Meknès involves less hassle than Fès, although it is certainly not a 'guide-free' zone. The Bab el-Mansour gateway is one of the most magnificent in the country. The usual restrictions on visiting mosques and palaces apply. The more peaceful atmosphere of the souks and bazaars is particularly enjoyable here.

Rabat

Rabat is Morocco's modern capital and seat of government. King Hassan resides here, so the city has a rather orderly feel. It is definitely the most relaxed of the imperial cities. Its main highlights are the Kasbah des Oudaias, Tour Hassan and the Necropolis of Chellah. The medina is fascinating, and the comparative lack of hassle and hustle is quite a relief but somehow less interesting than the spectacular chaos of Fès or Marrakech. Visit the neighbouring town of Salé for its unspoilt and tranquil medina.

ATLANTIC COAST
Good for beaches and outdoor activities

HUNDREDS OF miles of beaches cover the coast between Tangier and Mauritania.

BEST RESORTS AND BEACHES

Agadir
● Morocco's main package destination is clean and modern, but expensive by Moroccan standards.
● Great sheltered beaches and good restaurants but lacks Moroccan character.

Asilah
● Relaxed and low-key resort town being smartened up for wealthy Moroccan and European holidaymakers.
● Portuguese walls date from the fifteenth century.

Essaouira
● Fortified town with delightful cool blue whitewashed houses and lazy squares.
● Fantastic beaches, world-class windsurfing, no hassle or hard sell.

● Good for thuya wood carvings, thuya being the most common tree in the Essaouira hinterland.

BEST EXCURSION

Taroudannt

The walled city of Taroudannt, 53 miles inland from the coast, is unmissable if you are in the area. It is one of the highlights of Morocco. Hordes of day-trippers from Agadir invade during the day, but it retains a quintessentially south Moroccan character. Browse through the souks or explore the tanneries, kasbah and crumbly ramparts.

HIGH ATLAS
Good for culture, outdoor activities and shopping

BEST SIGHTS

High Atlas

Treks are a viable option for the fit and adventurous. Morocco's highest peak is the 13,745-ft Jebel Toubkal. The views are spectacular, but this is a fairly serious undertaking and a guide is necessary. Less hardy types could opt for a day-trip out from Marrakech to the gorgeous waterfalls of Cascades d'Ouzoud.

Marrakech

Indelibly printed on the 'sixties hippy trail, the ochre ramparts of Marrakech are now Morocco's biggest puller of tourists. The almost permanently snowcapped Atlas Mountains provide an unbeatable and incongruous backdrop to the exotic tumult of the old town. The heart of this quarter is a surprisingly open and vast square, the Djemaa el-Fna, pinpointed by the landmark Koutoubia mosque. Evening is the best time to visit, when snake charmers, jugglers, story tellers, magicians and fakirs put on a Brueghelian show for tourists and locals alike.

Islamic architecture buffs should seek out the Ali ben Youssef mosque and *medersa*, Mouassine mosque and El Badi Palace. Unlike other Moroccan museums, which can be rather disappointing, the Museum of Moroccan Arts is well worth a visit for the spectacular crafts and artefacts housed in the Dar Si Said, a lavishly decorated merchant's town house. Marrakech souks are brilliant as long as you have mastered the art of haggling. If you are unsure of your bargaining skills, beware, as the merchants are mercilessly rapacious.

THE SOUTH AND SAHARA
Good for scenic landscape

IT PAYS to hire a car and tour this region at your own pace to appreciate the awesome natural beauty of the region, with its mountains, valleys, oases and villages untouched by tourism or the twentieth century.

BEST SIGHT

Ouarzazate is worth a stop-off to see the kasbah, although there is a better one in nearby Ait Benhaddou, which has featured in many films, including *Jesus of Nazareth* and *Lawrence of Arabia*.

BEST LANDSCAPE

Dadès Valley
Stunning scenery east of Ouarzazate. Of special interest are the kasbahs around Skoura, and impressive mountains of the Dadès and Todra Gorges. From Erfoud you could extend the tour along the Ziz Valley.

Drâa Valley
This leads south-east from Ouarzazate through a spectacular variety of gorges, kasbahs, date-producing *palmeraies*, to a first glimpse of the Sahara's magnificent dunes. The towns themselves have little of interest, but offer an insight into authentic rural life.

WHEN TO GO

THE MAIN religious holiday period is Ramadan, which lasts for about a month. The faithful are expected to fast during the day, and opening times are disrupted. The end of Ramadan is marked by four or five days of family festivities (rather like Christmas) and can also be an awkward time to travel.

	Average daily maximum temperature °C											
London	6	7	10	13	17	20	22	21	19	14	10	7
Agadir	19	21	23	23	24	25	27	27	27	26	24	21
	JAN	FEB	MAR	APR	MAY	JUN	JUL	AUG	SEP	OCT	NOV	DEC
Agadir	6	4	5	3	2	1	0	<1	1	4	5	5
London	15	13	11	12	12	11	12	11	13	13	15	15
	Average number of rainy days per month											

	Average daily maximum temperature °C											
London	6	7	10	13	17	20	22	21	19	14	10	7
Fès	15	18	20	22	26	31	36	36	32	26	20	16
	JAN	FEB	MAR	APR	MAY	JUN	JUL	AUG	SEP	OCT	NOV	DEC
Fès	12	9	12	9	6	4	1	1	3	7	11	12
London	15	13	11	12	12	11	12	11	13	13	15	15
	Average number of rainy days per month											

PACKAGE TRAVEL

MOST TOUR operators offer the beach resort of Agadir or visit Tangier or Marrakech and perhaps offer a southern coach tour. Specialists offer the inland towns of Taroudannt and Fès, Zagora, Ouarzazate, southern tours, Land-Rover safaris and trekking in the High Atlas mountains. City breaks on offer are to Marrakech.

Activities include walking, horse-trekking, birdwatching, natural history tours and camping safaris.

Tour operators

Birdwatching: Limosa, Naturetrek, Ornithology, Sunbird **Camping safaris**: Acacia, Guerba, Worldwide Journeys **City breaks**: British Airways Holidays, Sovereign, Travelscene **Cultural**: Martin Randall, Prospect **General**: Abercrombie & Kent, Best of Morocco, Cadogan, CV Travel, Goldenjoy, Hayes & Jarvis, Inspirations, Moroccan Travel Bureau, Prestige, Seligo, Steppes East, Thomas Cook, Voyages Jules Verne **Walking**: Exodus, Explore Worldwide, Headwater, Ramblers Holidays, Sherpa **Other activities**: British Museum Traveller (cultural), Club Med (multi-activity), Dragoman (adventure), Solo's (singles)

INDEPENDENT TRAVEL

SCHEDULED FLIGHTS run from London to Tangier, Casablanca, Marrakech and Agadir.

High-speed trains operate between Rabat and Casablanca, and Casablanca and Marrakech; slower services link major towns and cities. There are two classes: in hot weather it is worth paying extra to go first-class for the air-conditioning.

Several companies run coach services, which cover most of the country. Although they are fast, they tend to stop at nearly every town, sometimes for as long as half an hour, which adds considerably to the length of the journey. Nevertheless, it is a good way to experience local colour, if you are not in a hurry. Coach travel is usually slightly more expensive than economy class on trains.

Morocco has a well-maintained road system as well as a network of unsurfaced mountain and desert tracks (some of which are passable only in a four-wheel-drive vehicle). Driving regulations are similar to those of France – remember the *priorité à droite*. A British driving licence is normally sufficient, but some smaller hire-car agencies may require an international driving permit. It is best not to drive at night. Look out for animals straying on to the roads, slow-moving horse-drawn carts and local children.

Hotels are classified from one to five stars, and prices are fixed by the Ministry of Tourism. Plenty of unclassified hotels vary their prices according to season and how much they think they can squeeze out of you. Rooms in cheaper hotels tend to be small, if clean and basic, and many do not have hot water – you have to use public baths or showers. More expensive hotels may be renovated older palaces or modern, 'international'-style buildings.

There are quite a few campsites, but all the extra charges for hot water, electricity, cars or motorbikes can add up, and it is often almost as cheap to plump for a hotel.

RED TAPE, HEALTH AND SAFETY

NO VISA is required by British passport-holders. For the latest advice on recommended vaccinations, see your GP or a specialist travel clinic.

Hustlers are a way of life in Morocco. On foot or motorbike, they are very persistent, trying to direct you to hotels or leatherware shops. Police have cracked down on false 'guides' in order to reduce the hassle that put tourists off visiting. It is now illegal for Moroccans (other than official guides) to escort tourists. Special tourism police enforce this.

Contact the Foreign Office Travel Advice Unit (see page 11) for the latest advice on safety and security.

MORE INFORMATION Moroccan National Tourist Office, 205 Regent Street, London W1R 7DE, tel 020-7437 0073, web site: *www.tourism-in-morocco.com*

You can also access information about Morocco at: *www.tourist-offices.org.uk/Morocco/index.html*

COST OF LIVING £

NAMIBIA

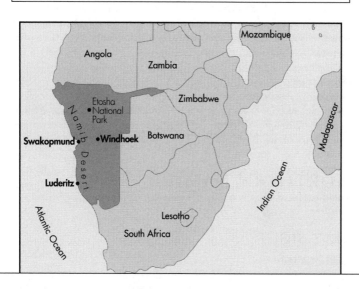

HIGHLIGHTS

Local colour	**Outdoor**	**Scenic**	**Wildlife**
Bushmanland,	**activities**	**landscape**	*Etosha*
Kaokoland and	*Etosha*	*Coast,*	*National Park,*
Damaraland,	*National Park,*	*Etosha*	*Namib–Naukluft*
Lüderitz	*Namib–Naukluft*	*National Park,*	*National Park,*
	National Park	*Namib–Naukluft*	*Skeleton Coast,*
History		*National Park*	*Waterberg*
Lüderitz			*Plateau*

SOUTHERN AND CENTRAL NAMIBIA
Good for outdoor activities, scenic landscape and wildlife

BEST SIGHTS

Fish River Canyon
The second-largest canyon in the world, yet virtually unknown so you will share the dramatic viewpoints with only a handful of other people, or maybe get the whole place to yourself. A tough five-day hiking trail is provided for those wishing for a more in-depth introduction.

Namib-Naukluft National Park

For tourists this huge national park is the most accessible area of the Namib Desert, which stretches the length of Namibia. The giant sand-dunes at Sossusvlei are an absolute must-see, particularly dramatic at sunset or sunrise. Sharply contrasting, the rocky Naukluft Plateau is an oasis for wildlife and an excellent hiking area.

Windhoek

Namibia was briefly a German colony and Windhoek, the capital, retains a Teutonic flavour, now interestingly mixed with local African styles. It is not worth setting aside more than a day to take in the atmosphere of this small, pleasant city.

NORTHERN NAMIBIA

Good for local colour, outdoor activities, scenic landscape and wildlife

BEST SIGHTS

Bushmanland

The Bushman people (more correctly called San) are Namibia's original inhabitants, a fascinating race adapted to desert life, now pushed to the country's margins and on the verge of extinction. Their current homeland, a remote, roadless area, is accessible only by organised tour or skilful self-drive.

Etosha National Park

One of the finest wildlife reserves in Africa; a semi-desert landscape with waterholes that attracts huge herds of animals. Excellent game-viewing, good accommodation options and straightforward access (by hire car or locally organised tour).

Kaokoland and Damaraland

Kaokoland is the most remote of all Namibia's wild areas – its rugged landscape may be appreciated only by true wilderness fans. The local Himba people are culturally intact, maintaining traditional dress and lifestyle. Damaraland is more accessible, and has the intriguing 'natural gallery' of ancient Bushman rock art at Twyfelfontein.

Waterberg Plateau

A smaller park, often overshadowed by Etosha National Park, but with a contrasting rocky and vegetated landscape. Game-viewing is reward-ing but more specialised. Wilderness hiking trails are also available.

THE COAST
Good for history, local colour, scenic landscape and wildlife

ICY OCEAN currents hinder plant-growth on Namibia's coast, so the waves break on the edge of the desert. Some people call it 'the biggest beach in the world' but, with cold winds and frequent mists, don't expect typical seaside resorts. Once again, Namibia's stunning natural landscapes, plus a few eclectic historical pockets, constitute the main attractions.

Lüderitz
This is a small port, out on a limb some 190 miles across the empty desert from the next big town, Keetmanshoop. The German heritage is more evident here, hence the town's nickname: 'Bavaria on the beach'. Nearby is Kolmanskop – a diamond mine ghost town gradually being reclaimed by the dunes.

The Skeleton Coast
A stark, dry region, with harsh temperatures and occasional valley oases which support a surprising range of wildlife, including Namibia's famously hardy desert elephants. The northern part of the Skeleton Coast can be reached only by exclusive fly-in safari, while the southern sections are more accessible to independent tourists.

Swakopmund
This compact holiday and sea-fishing centre for Namibians and South Africans now welcomes the recent influx of other nationalities and is a good place to arrange wildlife safaris or desert tours (by car or camel). Best sights nearby, apart from suburban sand-dunes, include the Cape Cross seal colony – also the site of a fifteenth-century Portuguese landing.

WHEN TO GO

THE BEST time to visit Namibia is between May and August when the weather is relatively cool. From August to November it is hot, and from November to April the weather is hot and humid, although in these less popular periods there is more space in the parks and less need to book ahead for accommodation.

Namibia is very popular among South Africans, and busy in school holiday periods – roughly: most of December and the first half of

January; the second half of March and the first half of April; the end of June and the first half of July; the end of September and early October.

Average daily maximum temperature °C												
London	6	7	10	13	17	20	22	21	19	14	10	7
Windhoek	30	29	27	26	23	20	21	24	27	29	30	30
	JAN	FEB	MAR	APR	MAY	JUN	JUL	AUG	SEP	OCT	NOV	DEC
Windhoek	12	11	10	5	2	0	0	0	1	3	7	7
London	15	13	11	12	12	11	12	11	13	13	15	15
Average number of rainy days per month												

PACKAGE TRAVEL

SEVERAL UK companies organise tours to Namibia, some as longer journeys around southern Africa, although Namibia's size means a minimum two weeks are required to do the country justice. Mainstream tour operators offer a selection of tours of the country by coach, minibus or four-wheel-drive vehicles. Most offer a taste of a safari with visits to national parks and game reserves, while others focus on game viewing.

A two-week highlight tour might include visits to Windhoek, the Namib Desert, the Sossusvlei sand dunes, Swakopmund and the Skeleton Coast, the seal colony at Cape Cross, the Etendeka Mountains and of course a trip into the Etosha National Park. Some include internal flights to avoid long road journeys.

Accommodation is in hotels, guest farms, private lodges, bungalows or luxury permanent tented bush camps and is generally of a good standard.

Tour operators

Adventure: Acacia, Encounter Overland, Exodus, Explore Worldwide, Guerba, Kumuka Expeditions **Birdwatching/wildlife**: Naturetrek, Sunbird, Wildlife Worldwide **General**: Abercrombie & Kent, Cox & Kings, Cricketer, Somak, South African Airways, Sunvil, Thomas Cook, Travelsphere, Worldwide Journeys **Specialists**: Abercrombie & Kent, Africa Exclusive, African Explorations, Africa Travel Centre, Art of Travel, Carrier, Cazenove & Loyd Safaris, Cedarberg, Cox & Kings, Definitive Africa, Okavango Tours & Safaris, Safari Consultants, Safari Drive, SAR Travel, Scott Dunn World, Somak, Temple World, Tim Best, Wild Africa Safaris

---

Upmarket safari specialists can take you off the beaten track in search of better game viewing and to more exclusive lodges and bushcamps. It will probably cost more to stay in tents rather than hotels.

Many of the specialist tour operators to Namibia organise individual itineraries based on your requirements and budget.

Self-drive holidays are also on offer – with or without a pre-arranged itinerary but remember, distances are vast.

Activity holidays include safaris, birdwatching and wildlife, horse-riding safaris, cultural tours and adventure trips.

INDEPENDENT TRAVEL

NAMIBIA CONSISTS mainly of desert and semi-desert and is about three times the size of Britain, with one of the lowest population densities in the world. This gives the country a distinctive sense of space.

Access by air from Britain is straightforward; Air Namibia offers direct flights, and Windhoek can be reached on several other European and southern African airlines. There are buses between the main towns but not into wilderness areas (i.e. to the best sights). Independent travellers usually find their own way between the towns and then arrange tours locally in Windhoek, Swakopmund or Etosha to see the wildlife or natural landscape areas.

Another option is to hire a car. Even main roads in Namibia provide a sense of emptiness and adventure, without the logistical worries involved with driving in some other parts of Africa. Rates for saloon cars (which can be used to reach many areas) are around £50 to £75 per day. Four-wheel-drive (for remote areas) is around double this. If your budget is limited, hiring a car for even a few days means you see much more. If you are planning to hire a car for your whole visit, a fly-drive package is worth considering.

One disadvantage of independent travel here is that much national park accommodation must be booked in advance. Namibia's efficient national park reservation system limits over-crowding, but assumes all visitors have fixed itineraries. Less rigid travel is not impossible, but may be tricky at busy periods.

RED TAPE, HEALTH AND SAFETY

NAMIBIA GAINED independence from South Africa in 1990 and only since then has it opened up to tourists from Britain and elsewhere. Visas are not required by British citizens, but do check the current regulations at the Namibia High Commission in London before departure in case procedures change. You can stay in the country for three months but must be able to produce a passport valid for six months and a return ticket.

Hepatitis A, typhoid and polio inoculations are recommended. If entering Namibia from an 'infected' country, you must show proof of immunisation against yellow fever. There is a low malaria risk but prophylaxis is usually recommended – see your GP or a travel clinic.

Health conditions are generally good; you are unlikely to come into contact with many exotic diseases, although the usual commonsense rules concerning food and water apply (see page 11). Sunburn and dehydration are a real risk, so be sure to cover up and drink plenty.

In the national parks some animals can be dangerous. Take heed of the rules about not approaching the elephants or feeding the lions.

Namibia is a safe country; the risk of robbery or theft is very low. Avoid the township areas at night. Contact the Foreign Office Travel Advice Unit (see page 11) for up-to-date advice.

MORE INFORMATION Namibia Tourism, 6 Chandos Street, London W1M 0LQ, tel 020-7636 2924,
web site: *www.iwwn.com.na/namtour*

COST OF LIVING £$£$

NEPAL

HIGHLIGHTS

Culture/history
Kathmandu and the valley

Local colour
Himalayas, Kathmandu and the valley

Outdoor activities
Himalayas, Pokhara

Romantic escapism
Pokhara

Shopping
Kathmandu and the valley

Scenic landscape
Himalayas, Pokhara, the Terai

Flora/wildlife
The Terai

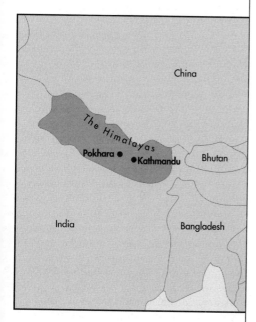

KATHMANDU AND THE VALLEY
Good for culture, history, local colour and shopping

AS RECENTLY as the 1960s, life in Kathmandu and its isolated valley was essentially medieval, revolving around agriculture and spiritual devotion. But things are changing fast and it is now one of the most polluted cities in the East. Uncontrolled development and the advent of mass tourism mean the old tranquillity is lost forever. This said, Kathmandu remains a magical place, crammed with temples, palaces, exotic markets, Tibetan refugees, and an architectural tradition which transports the visitor back to the Middle Ages. Woodcarving, sculpture and religious iconography have been the creative responses to Nepal's spiritual diversity, historical richness and cultural exchange – the legacy of its unique geographical position.

Most of your exploration can be done on foot, soaking up the atmosphere. Take time to scour the backstreets: at every turn you will stumble upon sacred shrines, enchanting courtyards and examples of the cultural melting-pot that is Kathmandu – pagoda-style palaces, Hindu temples, Tibetan *stupas* (onion-shaped domes crested with gold, with Buddha's all-seeing eyes painted on the top), souvenir shops, and people – lots of people.

BEST SIGHT

Durbar Square
Old Kathmandu's focal point, bursting with medieval temples, hawkers and holy men. Locals throng the busy vegetable market. You may get a glimpse of the Kumari, a living child-goddess at Kumari Behal. Sit on the steps of the Maju Deval Shiva temple and be entertained by touts and tourists alike. Durbar means 'palace': each town has its own palace and corresponding square.

BEST TEMPLES

Boudanath
This is a vast *stupa* in what is now a dirty but fascinating suburb of Kathmandu. Hundreds of Tibetans come here daily to walk *koras*, or circumambulations, of the immense dome, and to twirl their prayer-wheels and chant mantras. You will also see them performing prostrations on special boards – some do thousands at a time. The setting and atmosphere is other-worldly.

Dashinkali
At this isolated Hindu temple complex, visitors face one of the most confronting, yet fascinating experiences in Nepal. The goddess Kali is destroyer of demons, and to perform her work effectively she demands regular blood sacrifices. On Tuesdays and Saturdays goats, chickens, buffalo and sheep are despatched in a steady stream over her image. This is a religious ceremony, but still, it is not for the faint-hearted.

Pashupatinath
The Hindu place of pilgrimage draws devotees from all over the subcontinent. Wandering *sadhus* (holy men), Tantric iconography, ritual bathers in the holy Bagmati river and cremations on the burning *ghats* are just some of the sights you will see at this temple complex the size of a village.

Swayambunath

A white *stupa*, within walking distance of the centre of Kathmandu. Swathed in colourful prayer-flags and surrounded by clusters of small satellite temples, this is Nepal's most famous Buddhist pilgrimage site. It is also known as the Monkey Temple, thanks to the amusing, and thieving, simian population.

BEST EXCURSIONS

Bhaktapur

This town retains the strongest feel of the Middle Ages. Many old, architecturally fine buildings have been restored, and the Nyatapola Temple is the tallest in the valley, as well as one of the most elegant of the traditional Nepali temples. Its five ornately carved storeys resemble a medieval wedding cake. In Durbar Square you can spy on tiny, carved copulating elephants high up in the Shiva-Parvati temple, or on cavorting couples performing Tantric union on the Pashupatinath Temple.

Patan

Patan is adjacent to Kathmandu and can be reached by taxi in 20 minutes. It also has its own Durbar Square which is a veritable forest of wooden pagoda-style temples, all elaborately carved and guarded by stone animals on the first level – lions, snakes and peacocks. From here, avenues extend to the four Ashoka *stupas*, which, legend has it, date back to 500 BC. The Golden Temple is a unique monastery full of Buddha images and frescos, and the Kumbeshwar Temple is five storeys of ornate religious statuary.

HIMALAYAS
Good for local colour, outdoor activities and scenic landscape

'THE KINGDOM of the Gods' is blessed with the highest mountain range in the world – Mount Everest soars to 29,030ft. From the lowlands of the Gangetic Plain, the Himalayas rise in fairy-tale peaks and valleys to the barren Tibetan plateau. Annapurna and Everest dominate, but the trekking possibilities are endless. Climbing among breathtaking panoramas, through remote medieval villages, you experience the people as much as the scenery.

BEST OUTDOOR ACTIVITIES

Trekking can be as arduous as you like, but you do need a modicum of fitness. In return you will behold the most inspiring scenery in the world, and encounter people as hospitable as they are hardy. Popular treks are around the Annapurna Circuit and the Langtang and Jomsom

Treks. Several shorter treks start from Pokhara. Overnight accommodation is basic, usually in simple mountain lodges. For most treks, with the exception of Annapurna, Everest and Langtang, permits are required. This takes a day at Kathmandu's Immigration Office, or in Pokhara, but allow two days to be prudent.

White-water rafting expeditions are available for the novice and the expert. For the average newcomer, the Karnali river offers trips where you can float along admiring the scenery and running a few small rapids.

POKHARA
Good for outdoor activities, romantic escapism and scenic landscape

IF YOU can, fly to Pokhara through the Himalayas, and sit on the right-hand side of the plane for staggering snow-capped views. Pokhara has the perfect recipe for relaxing: a mild climate, a beautiful setting next to the large, limpid lake known as Phewa Tal, the awe-inspiring backdrop of the Annapurna Range, and plenty of hotels and restaurants. Row out and contemplate the reflection of Machhapuchhare, or Fish Tail Mountain, in the lake or shop at the Tibetan stalls.

THE TERAI
Good for flora, scenic landscape and wildlife

THIS NARROW strip of fertile plain at the foot of the Himalayan range is home to half the human population of Nepal, as well as to elephants, rhinos, Bengal tigers, leopards, sloth bears, crocodiles, dolphins and innumerable species of birdlife. The wildlife is best viewed at the Royal Chitwan National Park, where the animals roam freely through 500 square miles of open grassland, riverine vegetation and hardwood forests. Stay in rustic luxury inside the park for a true safari experience.

The Terai is a tropical zone, very distinct from the temperate and alpine areas of the Himalayas: plant life includes sal forests, tall elephant grasses and acacia and rosewood.

WHEN TO GO

FOR PERFECT visibility and a mild temperature, choose October to November. It is too cold in December and January, too hot in May and June, and the rainy season is between July and September.

To see the flowers, especially the rhododendrons, which bloom in the temperate mountain regions in the lower Himalayas, choose February to April, although views may be obscured by haze.

Average daily maximum temperature °C												
London	6	7	10	13	17	20	22	21	19	14	10	7
Kathmandu	18	19	25	28	30	29	29	28	28	27	23	19
	JAN	FEB	MAR	APR	MAY	JUN	JUL	AUG	SEP	OCT	NOV	DEC
Kathmandu	1	5	2	6	10	15	21	20	12	4	1	0
London	15	13	11	12	12	11	12	11	13	13	15	15
Average number of rainy days per month												

PACKAGE TRAVEL

SEVERAL TOUR operators offer Nepal as part of a tour of Northern India, combining a couple of days' sightseeing with some relatively gentle trekking. Specialists and adventure tour operators tend to focus on trekking and expeditions of varying levels of difficulty, although sightseeing and cultural tours, white-water rafting, mountain biking and mountaineering are also available.

Tour operators

Adventure and Trekking: Alternative Travel Group, Dragoman, Encounter Overland, Exodus, Explore Worldwide, Guerba, Peregrine Adventures, Walks Worldwide **Battlefields**: Holts' Tours **General**: Abercrombie & Kent, Asian Journeys, Bales Tours, Coromandel, Cox & Kings, Imaginative Traveller, Kuoni, Silverbird, Steppes East, Travelsphere, World Dreams, Worldwide Journeys **Mountain Biking**: Exodus, KE Adventure **Mountaineering**: Himalayan Kingdoms, KE Adventure, Sherpa **Specialists**: Classic Journeys, Himalayan Kingdoms **Tailor-made specialists**: Mysteries of India, Trans Indus **White-water rafting**: Adrift **Wildlife**: Birding, Naturetrek, Limosa, Sunbird, Wildlife Worldwide

---

Two-week sightseeing tours typically start from Kathmandu, exploring Patan, Bhaktapur, Boudanath and Pashupatinath before travelling on to Pokhara. They also fit in a couple of days trekking and a visit to the Royal Chitwan National Park to observe the wildlife. Accommodation is generally in hotels; trekkers mostly live under canvas or basic 'tea houses'.

INDEPENDENT TRAVEL

YOU CAN FLY direct to Nepal from the UK. Give yourself plenty of time to get around; in general, bureaucracy is nowhere near as time-consuming as in India. Travel inside the country is by bus or plane; bus journeys are long and gruelling, but cheap; plane journeys are short, exciting and also relatively cheap (get tickets locally). In the Kathmandu valley, travel by taxi is cheap and easy, but agree a price before you start. Most of your sightseeing can be done on foot. Hotels of all standards in Kathmandu can be booked from the UK. Pokhara has no shortage of accommodation, and you will be met by touts at the bus station and airport.

You can make your own arrangements for trekking, applying for the permits when you arrive, or, if you require porters (who can create elaborate camps, as well as cook for you), a local agent will help.

RED TAPE, HEALTH AND SAFETY

VISAS ARE required. To obtain a visa allowing 60 days' stay in Nepal you need an application form (from the Nepal Embassy), your passport, one passport photograph and £20 cash. Apply by mail (courier your application) or in person to the Nepal Embassy, open 10am to 12pm, Monday to Friday. Allow 24 hours for processing personal applications, two weeks for postal applications.

Inoculations against hepatitis A, polio, meningitis (depending on the area visited and the time of year) and typhoid are recommended. If arriving from an 'infected' country, immunisation against yellow fever is essential. Some areas are affected by malaria – check with your GP or a travel clinic about malaria protection. If you are trekking above 10,000ft you may experience altitude sickness – see page 10 for precautions. The biggest health problem for visitors to Nepal is diarrhoea – follow the precautions on page 12 to avoid stomach upsets.

Bad driving and poor vehicle maintenance cause many accidents; travel by long-distance bus is a particular cause for concern.

Due to political unrest it is advisable to avoid street demonstrations. For more information, contact the Foreign Office Travel Advice Unit (see page 11).

MORE INFORMATION Tourist Information, Nepal Embassy, 12A Kensington Palace Gardens, London W8 4QU, tel 020-7229 1594/6231, web site: *www.welcomenepal.com*

COST OF LIVING £

THE NETHERLANDS

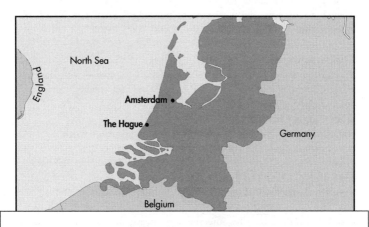

HIGHLIGHTS

Beaches	Leiden,	Flora/wildlife	Local colour
Wadden Islands,	*Zuiderzee-*	*De Hoge Veluwe,*	*Aalsmeer,*
Zuid-Holland	*museum*	*Giethoorn,*	*Alkmaar,*
		Wadden Islands	*Het Nederlands*
Culture	**Nightlife**		*Openlucht-*
Amsterdam,	*Amsterdam,*	**History**	*museum,*
Delft, Haarlem,	*Rotterdam*	*Amsterdam*	*Hoorn,*
The Hague,			*Giethoorn*
Het Loo Palace,			

AMSTERDAM
Good for culture, history and nightlife

BEST SIGHTS

Anne Frank's House
The house where Anne Frank and her family hid from the Nazis before being betrayed is well worth the long queues.

Canal trip
A trip in a perspex-roofed boat is by far the best way to see the canalside architecture and to admire the ranks of bell, neck and step gables.

Heineken Brewery
The good-value and informative tours provide everything you ever wanted to know about the city's most famous product, as well as the chance to explore the historic old building (closed temporarily for refurbishment until early 2001).

Rijksmuseum
A pilgrimage to Rembrandt's *Nightwatch* is a must – you can also admire the works of Frans Hals, Ruisdael, Bol and Steen.

Van Gogh Museum
This collection charts the evolution of the tragic artist's work.

NOORD HOLLAND
Good for culture and local colour

LONG SANDY beaches line the west coast; former seaspots on the eastern side have become lakeside towns on the now enclosed Ijssel-meer. The countryside is flat and criss-crossed with canals and polders.

BEST SIGHTS

Alkmaar
This town, enclosed by a canal, is renowned for its weekly cheese market.

Bloemenveiling (flower auction)
Daily flower auctions are held in the early morning in a 156-acre building near Aalsmeer. Visitors can watch the proceedings from footbridges.

Edam
Less touristy than its neighbours Marken and Volendam, this town is home of the famous cheese – red-waxed for export, otherwise yellow.

Haarlem
The museum named after Frans Hals contains a gallery of his portraits of the town's dignitaries and a good general collection of paintings by sixteenth- and seventeenth-century Dutch artists. The Teylers Museum offers an eclectic mixture of art and scientific exhibits.

Hoorn
Hoorn has lots of attractive façades and old Dutch barges, as well as a wide selection of restaurants and cafés.

Zuiderzeemuseum

The indoor section (*Binnenmuseum*) and outdoor section (*Buitenmuseum*) make up the outstanding museum in Enkhuizen showing what life was like on the Zuiderzee before 1932.

ZUID HOLLAND
Good for beaches, culture and nightlife

BEST SIGHTS

Arnhem

Laden with many layers of history. Site of the infamous 'Bridge too Far', which halted British paratroops and their attempts to cut the Second World War short. Good museums and lively nightlife today.

Delft

As attractive as its eponymous pottery, this well-preserved historic town is an oasis of calm after hectic Amsterdam. It has pretty, shaded canals and a historical centre.

Gouda

The attractive main square (Markt) has a fifteenth-century Gothic Stadhuis (Town hall). St Janskerk has beautiful stained-glass windows.

The Hague (Den Haag)

The Hague, the country's diplomatic centre and seat of government, is a sophisticated city with many parks and gardens, and is close to the sea. The Mauritshuis is one of the finest picture galleries in the world.

Keukenhof Park

Over 70 acres of gardens where you can wander among daffodils, narcissus and hyacinths in late March/early April, and six million tulips from mid-April until the end of May. Bulbs can be bought there.

Kinderdijk

Nineteen traditional Dutch windmills, built in the 1740s, are spread along the canals, meadows and reedbeds close to the River Leek about nine miles east of Rotterdam.

Leiden

Rembrandt's birthplace is the oldest university town in the country and has a very attractive old town centre dissected by canals, and the oldest botanical gardens in Europe.

Rotterdam

This ambitious city stole the right to stage the Euro 2000 Football final from under Amsterdam's complacent nose. It has recovered from devastating Second World War bombing by imaginatively blending old and new. Home to some of Europe's most intriguing avant garde architecture as the city rebuilds in an effort to match the Dutch capital. Also funky bars, quality shopping and eclectic restaurants.

THE NORTH
Good for beaches, flora/wildlife and local colour

OF THE three provinces that make up the north of the country, Friesland is the most popular with tourists, although Groningen town attracts quite a number of visitors.

BEST SIGHTS

Barrier Dam (Afsluitdijk)
After devastating floods in 1916 the Zuiderzee was restrained by the building of a huge dam. This left the Waddenzee beyond the barrier and created an internal freshwater lake, the Ijsselmeer.

Giethoorn
The heart of this fenland area can be reached only by bicycle, boat or on foot. Thatched houses and neat gardens are tended by locals in traditional dress. It is very touristy in summer.

Wadden Islands
The five islands (Schiermonnikoog, Texel, Vlieland, Terschelling and Ameland) off the Netherlands' north-west tip are quiet, with beautiful beaches and lots of flora and fauna; they are popular with the Dutch.

CENTRAL NETHERLANDS
Good for culture and flora/wildlife

BEST SIGHTS

De Hoge Veluwe
This 13,300-acre national park is rich in birdlife and wildlife.

Het Loo Palace
On the edge of the Hoge Veluwe is this magnificent palace built by William III and Mary in 1685. The gardens, including the Privy garden, have recently been restored.

Rijksmuseum Kroller-Muller
One of the country's most important art collections is housed in this museum in the middle of the Hoge Veluwe.

THE SOUTH
Good for food/wine and local colour

BEST BASE

Maastricht
Famous for the signing of the Maastricht Treaty in 1992, this sophisticated, cosmopolitan city offers a good range of hotels, restaurants and shopping. European rather than specifically Dutch in feel, it is an ideal place to spend a couple of days.

BEST SIGHTS

Het Nederlands Openluchtmuseum (Netherlands Open-Air Museum)
Spread over 110 acres, this museum has brought together examples of houses, windmills, barns, cottages and numerous other traditional buildings from all the provinces of the Netherlands. If you have too little time to travel around the country you can experience the variety in this microcosm.

Stormvloedkering Oosterschelde (Storm Surge Barrier) and Delta Expo
This exhibition details the extraordinary engineering achievement of the Delta Plan. Drawn up after the disastrous floods in 1953 and later revised, it took over 30 years to complete. Boat trips take you up to the barrier.

WHEN TO GO

GOOD WEATHER cannot be guaranteed, so the cities are all-year destinations. Amsterdam is statistically one of Europe's wettest capitals. The Wadden Islands are at their best between May and September, but if you want to see the bulbfields visit in April and May.

		Average daily maximum temperature °C										
London	6	7	10	13	17	20	22	21	19	14	10	7
Amsterdam	3	4	8	12	16	19	21	20	18	13	8	5
	JAN	FEB	MAR	APR	MAY	JUN	JUL	AUG	SEP	OCT	NOV	DEC
Amsterdam	22	18	17	14	14	13	17	17	17	21	22	23
London	15	13	11	12	12	11	12	11	13	13	15	15
		Average number of rainy days per month										

PACKAGE TRAVEL

MANY TOUR operators offer city breaks to Amsterdam. Outside Amsterdam, self-catering in holiday villages is popular, either in mobile homes or chalets. Coach tour operators feature short trips to the bulbfields or visits to the northern countryside in spring.

Tour operators

Camping: Eurocamp, Eurosites, Select Sites **City breaks**: Bridge Travel Service, British Airways Holidays, Cresta, Crystal, Inghams, Inntravel, Kirker, Made to Measure, Osprey, Premier, Simply Travel, Sovereign, Thomson, Time Off, Travelscene **Coach tours**: Armchair, Shearings **Cultural**: Ace Study Tours **Cycling**: Anglo Dutch, Bike Tours **General**: Amsterdam Travel Service, DFDS Seaways, Stena Line **Other activities**: Anglers World (fishing), Eurovillages (holiday villages), French Country Cruises, Ffestiniog Travel (rail tours), Holts' Tours, Midas (battlefields), Limosa (bird-watching), On the Piste (day-trips), Solo's Holidays (singles), Swan Hellenic (river cruises)

INDEPENDENT TRAVEL

FLIGHTS TO Amsterdam airport (Schipol) from London and many other UK airports are widely available. Schipol is linked to Amsterdam city centre by a frequent, fast train service. The budget airline easyJet has recently undercut many of the major airlines, forcing prices down across the board.

Car hire is extremely expensive; if you are planning to tour you should bring your own car. The fastest route to the Netherlands by car is via the Dover to Ostend jetfoil or Le Shuttle to Calais. Both routes link in with a good motorway system to the Netherlands. Stena offers excellent deals for a car and four passengers from Harwich to the Hook of Holland, but the journey takes six-and-a-half hours.

Ultra-fast Eurostar trains from London connect with similarly fast Thalys services in Brussels, which then travel on to Amsterdam. Holland's internal rail network is fast and efficient. Rover cards (*Dag Karten*) are valid for up to nine days and offer considerable savings. Unless you are planning extensive touring it is advisable to fly and use trains. Parking is expensive, and a car can be a liability in the cities.

The cheapest way to travel around is by buying a *Stippenkaart*, which is valid on all buses, trams and metros countrywide.

All types of accommodation are available, from smart hotels to self-catering apartments, and are generally of a high standard. Hotels are priced according to their facilities; two- and three-star hotels are perfectly adequate. They are all usually spotless. Tourist offices have comprehensive lists of what is available and can make bookings for you. Advance booking is essential in summer and always advisable in Amsterdam.

Holland also has a very well-developed network of cheap and clean youth hostels – a useful web site is *www.hostellinginternational.com*

RED TAPE, HEALTH AND SAFETY

BRITISH PASSPORT-HOLDERS do not require a visa. The Netherlands has no particular health or crime problems – just take the usual precautions (see pages 10–12).

MORE INFORMATION Netherlands Board of Tourism, 18 Buckingham Gate (PO Box 523), London SW1E 6NT, tel (09068) 717777 (premium rate number), web site: *www.holland.com*

COST OF LIVING *£££*

NEW ZEALAND

NORTH ISLAND
Good for beaches, culture, food/wine and outdoor activities

BEST BASES

Bay of Islands
The attractive, weatherboarded town of Russell or Paihia on the opposite shore is the best base for exploring this historically important area of wooded hills and small beaches. Settlers came here for the whaling and the kauri trees, impressive forest giants which survive now only in isolated pockets. They grow near Bay of Islands at Puketi Forest, but to see the largest specimens head for Waipoua on Highway 12, easily combined with a loop journey back to Auckland. Maori tribespeople run dolphin-watching tours into the Bay.

Coromandel peninsula

A popular spot for weekending Aucklanders, the Coromandel peninsula is a wild, wooded spit of land with golden beaches and forest walks. Once the scene of New Zealand's first gold-rush, it now attracts tourist summer onslaughts. It is a good area for walks and birdwatching.

Napier

This stylish, brightly painted town has a pleasant ocean-front atmosphere. Destroyed by an earthquake in 1931, the town was rebuilt according to the most progressive ideas of the time, entirely in art deco style. The rich wine-producing region around Napier is known as Hawkes Bay; 22 wineries are open to the public. The oldest is the Mission; you can take an organised tour or wander around and chat to the staff. At the end is the sampling table – and a chance to stock up at discount prices for New Zealand's many BYO (bring-your-own) restaurants.

Tongariro National Park

A popular ski resort area in the season, this is also excellent tramping country for experienced hill-walkers, with expansive views of the classic volcanic cone of Ngauruhoe and the active Ruapehu. Mountain Air operates tourist flights over the volcanoes.

Wellington

Windy Wellington, New Zealand's capital, is in a fine waterfront location and has a sophisticated edge over its commercial rival Auckland. Swanky modern buildings stand beside weatherboard houses, and along the quay at Queen's Wharf are some stylish converted warehouse restaurants. Here, too, is Te Papa, New Zealand's new and controversial national museum.

BEST GEOTHERMAL SIGHTS

Rotorua

The faint whiff of sulphurous gases is ever-present here – the best base for day-trips to geothermal sites and Maori cultural attractions. Most Maori 'experiences' on offer at Rotorua come as packaged and processed as cheese slices, but a few Maori-owned companies do run more authentic visits to traditional *hangi* dinners and dance displays; choose carefully.

Waimangu Valley

You can see all types of geothermal activity and experience them going on under your feet. Scorching streams, bubbling lakes and small geysers culminate in the electric-blue pool at Inferno Crater.

Waiotapu
Further down Highway 5, the landscape is a little less dramatic, but cauldrons of boiling mud and the aptly named Champagne Pool make it a worthwhile trip.

Whakarewarewa
Visit the Prince of Wales and Pohutu geysers at the best 'quickie' geothermal sight; exhibitions and shows are to be seen at the Maori Arts and Crafts Institute there.

AUCKLAND

A BUSINESS and commercial centre, New Zealand's largest city has some good sights based on its maritime traditions, but most visitors soon head off for attractions such as the Bay of Islands or Rotorua.

BEST SIGHTS

The Maritime Museum has an interesting waterfront collection of boats, from outrigger canoes to America's Cup winners. Displays include a reconstruction of an immigrant ship plus a computer database with the names of the settlers who passed through Auckland harbour. At the National Museum the fine display of Maori carvings is seen in the context of the South Seas region. The museum is surrounded by attractive parkland. The aquarium at Kelly Tarlton's Antarctic Encounter and Underwater World, reached by a snowcat journey through a penguin colony, is fun for children, but the highlight is the display of Captain Scott's Antarctic base camp. (Scott used New Zealand as his final departure point for Antarctica.) Don't miss Auckland Zoo with its exhibits of nocturnal kiwis and tuataras (a type of lizard) – the oldest living animal on earth.

A short ferry journey across from Auckland quayside, is Devonport, a bright, lively village of restaurants and cafés.

SOUTH ISLAND
Good for beaches, flora, outdoor activities and wildlife

SOUTH ISLAND, with its vast wilderness of forests, lakes and mountains, is perhaps New Zealand's greatest attraction. Visitors come for the wildlife, walks, outdoor sports and simply to enjoy the beauty of the place: towns and settlements are few and far between.

BEST BASES

Christchurch

A very 'English' city with its cathedral square and willow-lined river (complete with punts), Christchurch is a settlement that was planned from England by Anglicans who believed the world was turning evil and wanted to make a fresh start in a New World. You will find plenty of pubs and BYO restaurants (bring your own wine).

Just south of Christchurch, the Banks peninsula has some fine harbours built on the craters of extinct volcanoes. Walking is the most popular activity for visitors, and there are pretty villages such as Akaroa – an early French settlement – to visit. The superb glaciers and ice walls of Mount Cook National Park can be visited from the west by helicopter, or by driving in from the east to Mount Cook village. Walks with unforgettable views are the main attraction here.

Nelson

Reputedly the sunniest place in New Zealand, Nelson is a pleasant town at the centre of a large fruit- and vine-growing region. It is also close to some of the country's best beaches. Nelson Lakes National Park is 70 miles from the town and a popular walking area in summer, with views of Lake Rotorua. Abel Tasman National Park is a coastal park with some fine remote beaches accessible from the long-distance coastal path. Wine is produced in Marlborough.

Queenstown

During a period of only 20 years (mid-1970s to mid-1990s) bustling, bungee-jump capital Queenstown has developed from a genteel, elderly resort into the adventure-sports capital of the South Island. It is also hugely popular with backpackers. Thrill-seekers will find everything they ever wanted, from jetboat rides on the Shotover River to whitewater rafting and bungee jumps out of helicopters. Less frenetic are the four-wheel-drive safaris to explore forgotten gold-mining outposts like Skippers Canyon and Macetown. The scenery is stunning, and there is always a chance that you will find a nugget. The former goldrush settlement of Arrowtown still thrives, a pretty street of weatherboard cottages with a good local history museum.

BEST WILDLIFE

Dunedin

A university town with stylish cafés, restaurants and bars, Dunedin can be a lively place in term-time. More importantly, it is the jumping-off point to explore the least-developed corner of this wild country. The royal albatross colony at the end of the 18-mile-long Otago peninsula is the only easily accessible nesting place in the world for the world's largest seabird. The birds lay their single egg around November, and 11 months later the chick finally flies away. You will get closer by taking the tour on land – coach trips up to the observation centre – but sea tours of the harbour might include views of blue penguins, fur seals and, more rarely, a whale. Just along the coast is Penguin Place where early risers can watch a dawn parade of rare yellow-eyed penguins waddling towards the sea.

Kaikoura

Fenceposts made from the bones of humpback whales betray Kaikoura's past as a whaling station. This small peninsula is located close to a prime feeding area for the whales and now that they are no longer slaughtered the chance of spotting a sperm whale is quite good. Boat trips run by local Maoris use echo-sounders to locate the animals before moving closer: if nothing appears then you get your money back. Helicopter trips are slightly more expensive but can often succeed in marginal weather conditions. From October onwards, swimming with the dolphins is also a big attraction.

BEST SCENIC LANDSCAPE

Doubtful Sound

Less popular than Milford, perhaps because the scenery is less stunning, Doubtful Sound is in many ways a more typical fjordland sight, with its vast primeval forests and brooding unvisited side channels. Day trips start with a boat journey across Lake Manapouri and then a coach trip up a dirt track to Doubtful and a second boat ride up the fjord.

Franz Josef and Fox Glaciers

These two neighbouring ice tongues curl down from Mount Cook almost to the Tasman Sea. Franz Josef has the more spectacular valley but Fox has fewer visitors. Guided tours will take you up the blue face of the glacier if you are fit and have sufficient nerve. Less energetic are the helicopter flights through the spectacular ice valley up to Mount Cook. Choose a trip that lands on the snowfield below the summit and have a memorable snowball fight.

Milford Sound

According to Rudyard Kipling this is the eighth wonder of the world, and few would dispute his description of this magnificent fjord, its sheer sides streaked with waterfalls and scars left by forest landslips. Mitre Peak dominates the boat journey from Milford to the sea, where you might spot penguins and seals. The drive up from Te Anau is almost as spectacular in itself.

Punakaiki

On the wild west coast, this little oasis of bizarre plants and geological freaks is a great one-night stop-over. The rocks, piled up like pancakes, are blasted with fountains of spume from the sea. Check on the high tide times if you are planning a quick stop.

WHEN TO GO

TEMPERATURES IN New Zealand vary more according to altitude than latitude. You can be skiing and swimming on the same day. Take warm clothes and waterproofs (unless you are there only in the height of summer and not planning to do any serious walking). Be very cautious about exposure to the sun, as its rays can burn quickly in the relatively unpolluted atmosphere – it is advisable to carry (and apply) suncream and sunblock at all times, even on cloudy days.

Because Christmas occurs in summer in New Zealand, most New Zealanders take their annual holiday in either December or, more commonly, January. If you want to beat the crowds remember to book accommodation and activities early.

	Average daily maximum temperature °C											
London	6	7	10	13	17	20	22	21	19	14	10	7
Auckland	23	23	22	19	17	14	13	14	16	17	19	21
	JAN	FEB	MAR	APR	MAY	JUN	JUL	AUG	SEP	OCT	NOV	DEC
Auckland	10	8	9	10	12	13	13	11	10	10	10	10
London	15	13	11	12	12	11	12	11	13	13	15	15
	Average number of rainy days per month											

PACKAGE TRAVEL

MOST TOUR operators offer detailed individual itineraries. You can select from car hire, bus and rail passes, accommodation passes, guided walks, self-drive touring itineraries, motor homes, coach tours and two- or three-night tours around popular areas such as the Bay of Islands or Franz Josef and Fox glaciers. Accommodation ranges from backpackers' hostels and clean motor camps, farm- or homestays and motels to exclusive lodges in the countryside. Activities include whale-watching, trekking, wine tours and birdwatching.

Tour operators

General and specialist: AAT Kings, All-Ways Pacific, Australian Pacific Tours, Austravel, Bakers Dolphin, Bridge the World, British Airways Holidays, Cadogan, Classic Connection, Distant Dreams, Jetset, Kuoni, Noble Caledonian, Qantas Holidays, Saga, Trailfinders, Travel 2, Travelbag, Travelmood, Travelsphere **Walking**: Explore Worldwide, Ramblers Holidays **Other activities**: Ace Study Tours, Arblaster & Clarke (wine), Discover the World, Hemmingways, Limosa (birdwatching), Naturetrek (wildlife), Ornitholidays, Solo's (singles), Waymark (walking)

INDEPENDENT TRAVEL

IF YOU have time to travel for longer than three weeks, journeying to New Zealand is the perfect opportunity to stop over in some exotic destinations on the way. If you decide to go in one direction without backtracking, a round-the-world ticket can be a good option and excellent value. There are plenty of discounted fares to New Zealand, particularly outside high season (December to February) – bear in mind that the cheaper ones may include compulsory stop-overs which make your flight longer.

New Zealanders drive on the left-hand side of the road, and it is compulsory to wear seat-belts at all times. The open road speed limit is 60mph (100km/h) and in built-up areas usually 30mph (50km/h). Roads are generally uncluttered, although you can expect some congestion around busy holiday times. Almost all roads are tar-sealed, although some country back roads are not. The few motorways are usually around the major cities. Signposting is good.

You have to be over 21 and hold either a British driver's licence or international driving permit before you can hire a car or camper-van. All major international car hire firms are represented in New Zealand.

If you are a member of the AA in Britain, take your membership card with you, as it has a reciprocal agreement with the AA in New Zealand. This gives you the benefit of free detailed maps, emergency breakdown services and free technical advice about your car.

Hiring a camper-van (or motor-home) is very popular and a great way to tour some of the more remote areas. However, it is not necessarily cheaper than hiring a car and staying in budget accommodation, particularly in high season. Depending on the size of your party you can hire a two-, four- or six-berth van.

Public transport, although extensive, can be slow and expensive. At least one rail journey, however, is recommended. The best include the Geyser Express from Auckland to Rotorua, the South Island's trans-alpine or the Auckland-to-Wellington day trip.

There is no shortage of accommodation in all the tourist spots, but try to book in advance during the highest season (mid-December to end January, Labour Weekend and Easter). If you plan to travel extensively, staying in motels is your best bet as most have rooms with two double beds, are priced per room, and are therefore very good value for families. Cabins in Motor Camps are excellent value but tend to be snapped up quickly during summer holidays.

If you stay in B&Bs, homestays or farmstays you will get to meet more New Zealanders, and these places are good if you intend to spend a long time in one place – tourist information centres have comprehensive details of those in their area. B&Bs are rare and tend to be priced per person and are better value for single travellers. Homestays or farmstays are priced according to the number of people per group.

If you want to book in advance, the New Zealand Tourism Board publishes a *Where to Stay* guide which lists all kinds of accommodation (though it is not entirely comprehensive) along with their official facility and quality rating, called Qualmark, which is gradually being introduced throughout the country.

RED TAPE, HEALTH AND SAFETY

BRITISH PASSPORT-HOLDERS do not need a visa and will be issued a permit upon arrival to stay in the country for up to six months, provided that: your passport is valid for at least three months beyond the date you will be leaving New Zealand; and you hold a fully paid onward or return ticket to a country you have permission to enter.

Keep aside $20 per person for your New Zealand departure tax.

No vaccinations are required before you enter New Zealand. Tap water is safe to drink. If you are planning to take part in any outdoor activities make sure that you take out comprehensive travel insurance. Sandflies, irritating midge-like, blood-sucking insects, are small black flies that live on the ground, so the bites are usually around the ankles. Wear plenty of insect repellent and shoes with thick socks if you are spending any time near water.

MORE INFORMATION The New Zealand Tourism Board, New Zealand House, 80 Haymarket, London SW1Y 4TQ, tel (0839) 300900 (premium rate number), web site: *www.nztb.govt.nz*

COST OF LIVING £

NORWAY

HIGHLIGHTS

Beaches
Arendal, Kristiansand

Culture
Oslo, Røros, Tromsø, Trondheim

Family holidays
Oslo

Local colour
Northern Norway

Outdoor activities
Lillehammer, Stavanger, Voss

Scenic landscape
Western fjords

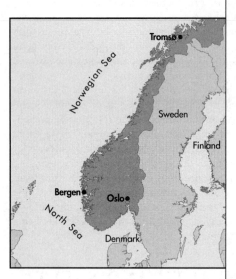

OSLO
Good for culture and family holidays

OSLO IS the oldest of the Scandinavian capitals and feels more like a wealthy provincial town than a capital city. Its charms may be low-key, but this spacious, graceful city is filled with excellent museums and enjoys a vibrant outdoor life. Beaches, islands, forests, lakes and hills are only minutes away from the centre.

BEST SIGHTS

Akerhus Castle
Built around 1300, the original castle was modernised by Christian IV in the seventeenth century. The Resistance Museum in the grounds documents Norwegian resistance in the Second World War.

Bygdøy Peninsula
The collection of five museums across the bay includes the Kon-Tiki Museum, displaying the balsa raft in which Thor Heyerdahl crossed the Pacific in 1947, the Fram museum with Amundsen's famous Polar challenging ship and the outstanding Viking Ship Museum.

Frogner Park
This houses the marvellous Gustav Vigeland Sculpture Park and Museum, with fantastical works by the renowned Norwegian sculptor.

Munch Museum
The museum contains 5,000 paintings and drawings from the great Edvard Munch, creator of *The Scream* and other psychologically challenging and sometimes disturbing pieces. The exhibitions are continually changing and help to explain different aspects of the artist's life and work.

National Gallery
The country's finest collection of art includes Greek and Roman sculpture, sixteenth- and seventeenth-century religious painting and a more-than respectable gathering of works by the likes of Monet, Picasso and Cézanne.

National Museum of Contemporary Art
Quite apart from the Scandinavian sculpture and paintings, the art nouveau building in itself is quite breathtaking.

SOUTHERN NORWAY
Good for beaches and outdoor activities

BEST SIGHTS

Frederikstad
Located between Oslo and the Swedish border, this remarkably preserved seventeenth-century fortified town is well worth a visit.

Lake Mjøsa
Norway's largest lake lies in gentle landscape. The major winter-sports centre Lillehammer hosted the 1994 Winter Olympics.

Stavanger
Stavanger is Norway's fourth largest city and was once the location of over fifty sardine canneries. It has an appealing old town and a fine

museum devoted to its fishing and canning past. It is also a good base for hiking in nearby Rogaland or for boat trips on the local fjords.

BEST RESORT

● Kristiansand, a major resort on the south coast, has great beaches.
● To the east are attractive, less crowded beaches, islands and resorts, such as Arendal.

THE WESTERN FJORDS
Good for scenic landscape

THE SPECTACULAR western fjords are most people's idea of Norway, and these dramatically beautiful inlets rarely disappoint.

BEST SIGHTS

Bergen
Norway's second-largest city, and European city of culture for 2000, offers medieval buildings, intriguing museums and lively street life. The huge fish market of Torget is unmissable and the Bryggens Museum contains everything from medieval tools to skeletons. South of Bergen is Troldhaugen, a dramatic setting on the fjord side, where the composer Edvard Grieg, famous for the Peer Gynt Symphony and Piano Concerto, lived and worked.

Alesund
A town renowned for its art nouveau and architecture, this is a good base for exploring the surrounding fjords. The town's newest attraction is the Atlantic Sea Park, Scandinavia's largest aquarium.

BEST FJORDS

Aurlandsfjord
A spectacular train journey, which is a real white-knuckle ride, leads to the town of Flåm on this narrow and most picturesque fjord.

Geirangerfjord
This tiny, snaking inlet offers some of Norway's most dramatic scenery, with precipitous cliffs, plunging waterfalls and dizzying views. Best viewed from the aptly named Eagle's Highway, which snakes around the mountains above.

Hardangerfjord
The broad 75-mile Hardangerfjord cuts inland from Bergen. Voss,

halfway up the fjord, is an excellent winter-sports centre and provides the best base for further exploration of the region.

Nordfjord

Despite high mountains falling to the waterside, this is the most accessible of the fjords by car. The mountain road that links Sognefjord and Gerangerfjord winds round the head of the fjord and is an excellent but hair-raising way to take in the scenery. It also gets you close to the mighty Jostedalsbreen Glacier where you can take guided walks on the ice field.

Romsdalfjord

One of the few fjords accessible by train (at the town of Åndalsnes). The most appealing base in the area is Molde, which hosts an international jazz festival every July.

Sognefjord

This is Norway's deepest, longest and most popular fjord. Balestrand and Sogndal are good bases for exploring. There are fine traditional stave churches in the area.

NORTHERN NORWAY
Good for culture and local colour

BEST SIGHTS

Lofoten & Vesterålen Islands

These dramatic, weather-beaten (yet surprisingly mild) islands may be on many cruise ships' itineraries, but they have preserved their own identity and distinctive culture. Vestvågøy is the most charming island.

Nordkapp

The North Cape is (arguably) Europe's most northerly point. Looking off this stark cliff with reindeer-specked tundra behind and bleak mountains to the sides, the visitor truly feels on the edge of the world.

Røros

Once a copper-mining centre, the grass-thatched cottages and restored mine-works of this carefully preserved town are now a UNESCO World Heritage Site.

Tromsø

The world's most northerly university town and undisputed capital of the north is lively and interesting, particularly if you are lucky enough to see the fabulous Northern Lights. Tromsø is nicknamed 'Gateway to the Arctic', and the Polar Museum has an interesting section devoted to Roald Amundsen, explorer of the North-West passage. The Tromsø Museum has a fascinating and varied collection of exhibits, especially the religious art section.

Trondheim

Once the site of the early Norse parliament, Norway's third city is a compact, friendly place with a fine medieval centre. The magnificent cathedral of Nidaros Domkirke, dating from the eleventh century, is the traditional burial-place of Norwegian monarchs. Visit the Museum of Applied Art to see a superb collection of clothes, furniture and other applied work from the Renaissance onwards.

BEST FOR SKIING

Norway has thousands of miles of maintained cross-country ski routes and countless downhill runs. Holmenkollen near Oslo (where you can stand at the top of the fearsome Olympic ski jump), Lillehamer (site of the 1994 Olympics) and the area surrounding Gudbandsdalen region are the most popular spots. For summer skiing head for the glaciers near the towns of Finse or Stryn, or to the Jotunheimen mountains.

WHEN TO GO

GENERALLY SPEAKING, Norway is driest in June and warmest in July. It is usually drier inland than on the coast. Until early June some mountain passes remain blocked by snow – July and August are the best months for driving.

Many museums and galleries have restricted opening hours outside the peak summer months, and some close altogether from September.

	Average daily maximum temperature °C											
London	6	7	10	13	17	20	22	21	19	14	10	7
Oslo	-2	-1	4	10	16	20	22	21	16	9	3	0
	JAN	FEB	MAR	APR	MAY	JUN	JUL	AUG	SEP	OCT	NOV	DEC
Oslo	15	12	9	11	10	13	15	14	14	14	16	17
London	15	13	11	12	12	11	12	11	13	13	15	15
	Average number of rainy days per month											

		Average daily maximum temperature °C										
London	6	7	10	13	17	20	22	21	19	14	10	7
Tromsø	-2	-2	0	3	7	12	16	14	10	5	2	0
	JAN	FEB	MAR	APR	MAY	JUN	JUL	AUG	SEP	OCT	NOV	DEC
Tromsø	18	17	19	18	18	18	15	19	21	21	18	19
London	15	13	11	12	12	11	12	11	13	13	15	15
		Average number of rainy days per month										

PACKAGE TRAVEL

OPTIONS INCLUDE scenic tours by rail, bus and boat, car tours to pre-booked hotels and coastal tours of spectacular fjord scenery. Rent a country cottage, stay in a chalet in a holiday centre, visit the Arctic Circle, go on a whale safari, or dog sledging, or take a city break. Activity tour operators offer birdwatching, walking, battlefield and study tours.

Tour operators

Birdwatching: Limosa **City breaks**: Bridge Travel, British Airways Holidays, Cresta, Crystal, Inghams, Osprey, Premier, Time Off, Travelscene, Yes Travel **Specialists**: Fjord Line, Inntravel, Norvista, DFDS Seaways, Scandinavian Travel Service, Scan-Meridian, Scantours, Sovereign, Specialised Tours, Taber Holidays **Walking**: Explore Worldwide, Headwater Holidays, Waymark **Other activities**: Ace Study Tours (study tours), British Museum Traveller (cultural), Discover the World (wildlife), Eurocamp (camping), Ffestiniog Travel, Great Rail Journeys (rail tours), Holts' Tours (battlefields), Solo's (singles), Arctic Experience (whale watching)

INDEPENDENT TRAVEL

DIRECT DAILY flights leave the UK for Oslo, Bergen and Stavanger, many with low-cost airlines. Ferries run two or three times a week from Newcastle to Stavanger and Bergen.

Despite the frequently harsh weather in Norway, the bus, rail and ferry systems are remarkably reliable. Train tickets are expensive, although several discounts are available. Buses are considerably better value and reach many destinations not accessible by train. In contrast, tickets for the coastal ferries are pricey. Sometimes internal flight prices compare favourably with train fares, and some companies offer discount air passes. Ask at the Norwegian Tourist Board office in London.

Car rental is expensive. A standard British driving licence is sufficient documentation. Cycling is popular, and bike rental places abound.

Hotel rooms are very pricey, although you may get summer or weekend discounts. Investigate hotel discount schemes for considerable savings. The Norwegian Tourist Board and Norwegian State Railways Office in London can supply details. Small pensions and inns are the next cheapest option.

Most of the 300 youth hostels in Norway have a few double or family rooms and offer the best value for money in the country. You will almost certainly have to book them in advance.

A huge network of campsites exists in Norway, and campers have the legal right to camp rough in any open area. Most campsites also have *hytter* or cabins, often well equipped and a cost-effective option for groups and families.

Tourist offices can make reservations for hotels and for rooms in private homes, although they may charge a small fee.

RED TAPE, HEALTH AND SAFETY

BRITISH PASSPORT-HOLDERS do not require a visa. Norway has no particular health or crime problems: just take the normal precautions (see pages 10–12).

MORE INFORMATION Norwegian Tourist Board, Charles House, 5 Lower Regent Street, London SW1Y 4LR, tel 020-7839 6255, web site: *www.visitnorway.com*

COST OF LIVING £££

OMAN

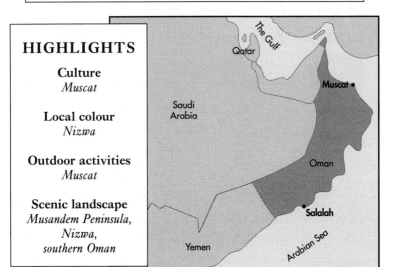

HIGHLIGHTS

Culture
Muscat

Local colour
Nizwa

Outdoor activities
Muscat

Scenic landscape
*Musandem Peninsula,
Nizwa,
southern Oman*

MUSCAT
Good for culture and outdoor activities

THE OMANI capital has a large number of museums. Two that should not be missed are the Sultan's Armed Forces Museum, which offers the best overview of the country's history, and the Natural History Museum which has excellent displays on the country's flora and fauna. The city also boasts the only decent aquarium in the Gulf region.

BEST SIGHT

Mutrah Souk
The best traditional souk in the Gulf region. Take some time to wander its alleyways looking at everything from spices to silver-clad daggers.

BEST WATER SPORTS

Al–Bustan Palace Hotel
There is a charge for admission to the beach at the Al–Bustan Palace Hotel if you are not staying in the hotel, but it is worth it. The facilities are excellent, and you can rent equipment for a wide variety of water sports.

NORTHERN OMAN
Good for local colour and scenic landscape

BEST SIGHTS

Jabrin
In a country with many old, well-restored fortresses, this is the single best one to see. A visit can easily be combined with a trip to Nizwa.

Musandem Peninsula
A remote area separated from the rest of Oman by the UAE's east coast, the Musandem offers the dedicated traveller some of Arabia's most spectacular scenery. It has a stark, rugged beauty with mountains rising steeply from the sea and little or no flat coastline. The main town is Khasab. Try to fly there from Muscat if possible. This saves time, eliminates the need for a UAE visa and is surprisingly affordable, even for those on a budget. Note that Khasab has only one hotel and it is not very big. Do not arrive without a reservation.

Sohar
The coastal town of Sohar was Oman's most important port for six centuries (up to the thirteenth century), and is the traditional home of Sinbad the Sailor. Its distinctive white fort merits a diversion.

Sur
It is a four-hour car journey from Muscat to Sur. The town's two forts and the good beaches available at its main hotel are worth it, but only if you are not pressed for time.

BEST LOCAL COLOUR

Nizwa
The cultural centre of Oman's interior, Nizwa is worth the trip for its well-restored fort and large market area. Adjacent to the market are workshops where you can see daggers and other handicrafts being made. The town also provides a good base for exploring the striking Jebel Akhdar region with its dramatic mountains rising up from the desert (mountain biking in this area is increasingly popular with the ex-pat community), a welcome relief from the flat, rather featureless terrain closer to Muscat. It is advisable to see the area on an organised tour – or hire a four-wheel-drive vehicle.

SOUTHERN OMAN
Good for scenic landscape

BEST CITY

Salalah
The capital of Oman's Dhofar province offers a completely different climate and pace of life from Muscat. The hills above the city are lush and green in the autumn, watered by the rains of the Indian monsoons. Don't miss Job's Tomb, a mosque perched on a hill overlooking the city. The small museum in the city centre has a display on the British traveller and author Wilfred Thesiger, who spent time in Salalah while making some of the journeys recounted in his classic *Arabian Sands*.

Ubar
Avoid this remote site of a 'lost city', thought to have once been a great and rich trading metropolis. It is three hours by car from Salalah and frequently disappoints all but the most dedicated students of archaeology (there is little to see).

BEST BEACHES

Mughsail
There are fine beaches at Mughsail, 17 miles west of Salalah. Salalah's Holiday Inn Hotel offers a good beach club.

BEST EXCURSION

Taqa
Taqa, 14 miles east of Salalah, has an interesting small fort and a cemetery containing the grave of the Sultan of Oman's mother. Just outside the town are several spring-fed oases.

WHEN TO GO

OMAN IS very hot for most of the year. From mid-October to mid-March is the best time to visit. From June to September the Salalah area is soaked by monsoon rains.

Avoid visiting during Ramadan, the Muslim month of fasting. In the years 2000–2003 Ramadan will fall in November and early-to-mid December. During Ramadan the faithful are expected to fast from sunrise to sunset, and opening times are disrupted. Visitors cannot eat, drink or smoke in public places and alcohol is prohibited. The end of

Ramadan is marked by four or five days of family festivities (rather like Christmas) and can also be an awkward time to travel.

	Average daily maximum temperature °C											
London	6	7	10	13	17	20	22	21	19	14	10	7
Muscat	25	25	28	32	37	38	36	33	34	34	30	20
	JAN	FEB	MAR	APR	MAY	JUN	JUL	AUG	SEP	OCT	NOV	DEC
Muscat	2	1	1	1	0	0	0	0	0	0	1	2
London	15	13	11	12	12	11	12	11	13	13	15	15
	Average number of rainy days per month											

PACKAGE TRAVEL

NOT MANY tour operators feature Oman, and those that do tend to be smaller specialist operators. Four-wheel-drive tours of the country generally start from Muscat. These may take in forts, wadis, sand dunes and markets and visit Nizwa, Jabrin, Wahiba Sands, Sur Beach and the old frankincense trading centre at Salalah. They are generally escorted, although some operators organise self-drive and chauffeur-driven tours.

Accommodation is generally in upmarket hotels with the opportunity to camp out in the wilderness on some tours. Note that most of the local agents leave brochures in the lobbies of the bigger hotels. But beware – most of their tours presume four or more people, and solo travellers or couples are likely to be charged the full price for four people if they cannot fill the vehicle.

Activity holidays include birdwatching and mountain biking, and tailor-made holidays can be arranged.

Tour operators

Adventure: Exodus, Explore Worldwide **Birdwatching**: Limosa, Naturetrek, Ornitholidays **General**: Steppes East, Somak, Elite Vacations **Specialists**: Abercrombie & Kent, Arabian Odyssey, Axis, Coromandel, Cox & Kings, Explore Worldwide, Jasmin Tours, Kuoni **Tailor-made specialists**: Eastravel, Nomadic Thoughts, Peltours

---

INDEPENDENT TRAVEL

A DIRECT service is available from the UK to Muscat. Overland, the Omani capital can be reached via a twice-daily air-conditioned coach from Dubai, in the United Arab Emirates. Internal flights link Muscat with a handful of other cities, most notably Salalah in the south, and Khasab in the Musandem Peninsula.

An extensive coach network aids internal travel, although aside from the coaches travelling between Muscat and Salalah, few are air-conditioned. Prices are very low by UK standards and reservations are rarely necessary except on the Muscat to Salalah route. Shared taxis and minivans go everywhere the coaches go and also travel to many smaller places not served by the coaches. Taxi and minivan fares are only slightly higher than coach fares and it is worth the extra outlay for the extra flexibility.

Car hire is widely available in Muscat but is often very expensive. Note that rented cars rarely come with unlimited mileage, and as the distances in Oman, and even within Muscat itself, are often great the extra charges can soon mount up.

In Muscat and Salalah hotels are available in all price ranges except the very cheapest. Outside of these two cities, however, there is little moderately priced accommodation. If you like Indian food, eating cheaply is never a problem.

Entry to most forts and archaeological sites is free, but requires a permit issued by the Ministry of Culture and National Heritage. The ministry's office is in a building attached to the Natural History Museum in Muscat. Permits are issued free of charge in a few minutes.

RED TAPE, HEALTH AND SAFETY

FOR A single-entry, three-month visa you will need a passport valid for six months, a completed application form (available from the embassy; send an sae), proof of funds or current employment, evidence of your travel itinerary and £40 (cash, postal order or, if submitted in person, cheque). Send your application by registered delivery or apply at the embassy in person between 9.30am and 12.30pm, Monday to Friday. The visa usually takes one week to process and must be used within three months of issue. Multiple-entry visas are also available.

Sanitary conditions in Oman are very high. Cities and towns are always extremely clean and orderly, and the tap water is safe to drink. Make sure your hepatitis A, typhoid and polio vaccinations are up to date – check with your GP or a travel clinic. You may wish to consider taking anti-malaria medication, particularly if you plan to travel in the south of the country.

Life in Oman is very safe. Always bear in mind, however, that it is, by Western standards, an extremely conservative country. Shorts and tight or revealing clothing are considered offensive on both men and women and may get you into trouble with the local authorities. Foreign women are not required to cover their heads while travelling in Oman, but it is prudent to dress conservatively (wear loose trousers or a long skirt).

MORE INFORMATION Embassy of Sultanate of Oman, 167 Queens Gate, London SW7 5HE, tel 020-7225 0001, visa information (09001) 600567 (premium rate number), web site: *www.mistral.co.uk/ squ/oman.htm.*

COST OF LIVING £££

PERU

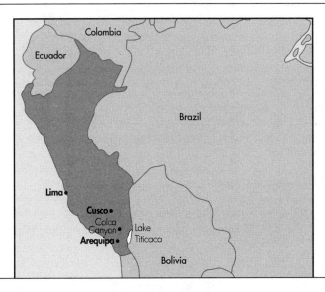

HIGHLIGHTS

Culture	Local colour	Outdoor	Shopping
Arequipa,	*Sacred Valley*	**activities**	*Cusco*
Cusco,		*Huaraz*	
Lima	**Romantic**		**History**
	escapism/	**Flora**	*Arequipa,*
Wildlife	**scenic**	*Manu*	*Cusco, Lima,*
Manu	**landscape**	*National Park*	*Matchu Pitchu,*
National Park,	*Colca Canyon,*		*Nasca,*
Paracas	*Huaraz,*	**Nightlife**	*Sacred Valley,*
National	*Lake Titicaca,*	*Cusco, Lima*	*Trujillo*
Reserve	*Matchu Pitchu*		

LIMA
Good for culture, history and nightlife

THIS VAST, sprawling city offers a challenging initiation into Peru's history and culture. At the heart of Lima, around Plaza de Armas, the fairly dilapidated colonial centre has preserved much of its charm and atmosphere. In addition to the wealth of fine architecture here, the city has a richly decorated cathedral and a good selection of museums.

BEST SIGHTS

Convento de los Descalzos

Guided tours offer an intriguing glimpse of the way Franciscan friars lived when they occupied this beautiful convent during the colonial and early Republican periods.

Miraflores

The bourgeois seaside suburb of Lima is an important social centre with shops, a handicrafts market, upgrade hotels, many restaurants, video bars and discos. Further south are a number of popular beach resorts (better for surfing than swimming, because of pollution and strong currents).

Museo de la Nación

The large anthropological and archaeological museum includes interesting displays on Peru's many ruined sites, with a superb collection of pre-Columbian ceramics and textiles, as well as an active programme of cultural activities.

Museo de Oro

Impressive displays include pre-Columbian gold, ceramics, mummies and Spanish colonial arms. Thousands of well-presented exhibits give a chronological history of Peruvian culture from the second century BC.

PARACAS NATIONAL RESERVE
Good for wildlife

BOAT TRIPS visit the Islas Ballestas, a few hours down the coast from Lima, guano islands that are teeming with noisy sea lions, pelicans, penguins and an abundance of other birdlife. This impressive reserve claims one of the highest concentrations of marine birds in the world.

NASCA
Good for history

CUT INTO the arid crust of the Atacama Desert are the mysterious Nasca Lines – some abstract, some forming the outlines of animals – which date from around the third or fourth century BC. The purpose of the lines, which because of their scale are best appreciated from the air, has been the subject of much speculation. How an ancient civilization – without the use of technology – produced these impressive designs, also remains largely a mystery. Also in the area are many cemeteries with mummified human remains strewn across the bleak desert landscape.

AREQUIPA
Good for culture and history

A PLEASANT city at the foot of a snow-capped volcano, Arequipa possesses some attractive colonial buildings made of sillar, the local white volcanic stone, and has a relaxed atmosphere aided by an all-year sunny climate. It is also home to a number of fine churches, a cathedral and a couple of museums.

BEST SIGHT

Santa Catalina Convent
Almost a miniature town in itself, the convent feels very remote from the lively city beyond the monastery walls. It comprises calm courtyards, flower-filled cloisters and the personal quarters of the 400 or so nuns, whose forebears once lived here in total isolation.

COLCA CANYON
Good for romantic escapism and scenic landscape

A BEAUTIFUL, unspoilt area, a few breathtaking hours' drive from Arequipa, where you can absorb local life in the primitive Andean villages that dot the terraced mountainsides. You can often spot condors at Cruz de Cóndor, one of the deepest points of this dramatic canyon. Most visitors opt for the cheaper day-trips, but this is worth an overnight stay, to acclimatise to the extreme altitude, and to properly appreciate the superb setting.

LAKE TITICACA
Good for romantic escapism and scenic landscape

A TRANQUIL and idyllic region where weary travellers can recuperate and take in the spectacular views across the still waters of the high-altitude lake.

BEST ISLANDS

A number of islands are worth visiting, including the floating Uros islands made of piles of reeds and the peaceful Amantani and Taquile islands.

CUSCO
Good for culture, history, nightlife and shopping

ONCE THE capital of the Inca empire, Cusco is today the heart of tourism in Peru. It is a beautiful city with plenty to offer, including markets and shops selling local crafts, many restaurants and bars catering to Western tastes and a vibrant lifestyle. The city is notable for its numerous colonial churches.

BEST EXCURSION

Many Inca ruins can be found in almost every street in the city centre and on its outskirts. An enjoyable way to visit the ruins around the city is on horseback – you can book an expedition with one of the many tour companies.

THE SACRED VALLEY
Good for history and local colour

MANY FASCINATING villages and ruins interrupt the gentle slopes of this attractive valley overlooked by dramatic, snow-capped peaks.

BEST SIGHTS

Chinchero
Bustling Sunday market and dramatic Inca terracing on the valley hillside.

Ollantaytambo
The monolithic temple fortress of this striking Inca town is a superb example of the sophistication of Inca engineering.

Pisac
There is a notable Inca fortress here strategically perched on a ridge, high above the valley. The town of the Pisac, below, has an excellent Sunday market.

MACHU PICHU
Good for history, romantic escapism and scenic landscape

THIS ANCIENT Inca city perched amid its stunning setting of lush, dramatic mountains is truly magical. Shrouded in mystery by the mist and low clouds, the ruined city is at its most enchanting at dawn. It is worth the strenuous four-day hike along the Inca trail to have the place to yourself before the tourists arrive on the train from Cusco.

MANU NATIONAL PARK
Good for flora and wildlife

THIS NATURE reserve is situated in the Amazon basin which provides a third dimension to the Peruvian landscape, otherwise characterised by desert or mountains. Extremely rich in tropical flora and wildlife, the Manu National Park is still relatively unexplored.

Organised tours of the park, mostly by river, usually include basic food and involve fishing, hunting and sleeping in hammocks.

HUARAZ
Good for outdoor activities, romantic escapism and scenic landscape

BEST WALKING

Cordillera Blanca mountains
Huaraz is the focal point of the Cordillera Blanca mountain range and is the most popular starting-point for trekking in this spectacular region. Dramatic mountain scenery provides the setting for many excursions in the area.

TRUJILLO
Good for history

INTERRUPTING THE monotonous desert scenery of northern Peru's coastline is the oasis of Trujillo, which has numerous old churches and some picturesque colonial buildings.

BEST EXCURSION

Chan Chán
Most visitors to Trujillo come to explore the nearby ruins of Chan

Chán, an extraordinary, vast adobe city which was built by the Chimú kings in the first century AD. Within the 12 square miles of the walls lies an entire city with ruined streets, houses, temples and palaces.

WHEN TO GO

EACH AREA of Peru has its own climate and so *when* you go depends very much upon *where* you go. The dry season falls between April and October and it is best to visit during these months. The most popular period for tourism (around Cusco in particular) is June to August, during which time prices tend to be higher.

Average daily maximum temperature °C											
London	6	7	10	13	17	20	22	21	19	14	10	7
Lima	28	28	28	27	23	20	19	19	20	22	23	26
	JAN	FEB	MAR	APR	MAY	JUN	JUL	AUG	SEP	OCT	NOV	DEC
Lima	1	0	0	0	1	1	1	2	1	0	0	0
London	15	13	11	12	12	11	12	11	13	13	15	15
Average number of rainy days per month											

PACKAGE TRAVEL

MOST SPECIALIST tour operators will create individual itineraries with a diverse choice of escorted tours and excursions. Machu Pichu and Cusco are the highlights of most tours, with Arequipa, the Colca Canyon and Trujillo accompanying sights of interest in the Andes.

You can take a trip into the Amazon jungle from Iquitos or Puerto Maldonado to stay in jungle lodges for a couple of days, viewing the jungle wildlife with guides.

Transport may be by coach, minibus or public transport. The rail journey from Cusco down to Lake Titicaca, which takes you through tremendous Andean scenery and fertile valleys, is often included on many tours. Trips to the Nasca Lines are also popular and some operators offer visits to the Islas Ballestas off the Pacific coast.

Activity holidays include escorted treks along the Inca trail, mountain trekking in the Cordillera Blanca or environmental expeditions. You can also try mountain biking and white-water rafting. Wildlife and ornithological holidays are also available.

Peru can be combined with Bolivia, Ecuador, Chile and other South American countries.

Tour operators

Adventure: Dragoman, Encounter Overland, Exodus, Explore Worldwide, Guerba, Travelbag **Archaeology**: Andante **Biking**: Exodus **Birdwatching**: Sunbird **Cultural**: British Museum Traveller **General**: Abercrombie & Kent, Bales Tours, Cox & Kings, Hayes & Jarvis, Kuoni, Last Frontiers, Worldwide Journeys **Specialists**: Journey Latin America, Passage to South America, Trips Worldwide, Veloso Tours **Trekking**: KE Adventure, Walks Worldwide **Wildlife**: Discover the World, Reef and Rainforest

INDEPENDENT TRAVEL

INDEPENDENT TRAVEL in Peru is mostly for the adventurous, but with tourism rapidly on the increase it is becoming easier. Standards of travel and accommodation are improving.

Simple accommodation is easy to find on arrival in most places along the traveller trail, but more expensive hotels should be booked in advance. In places such as Cusco, many tourist agencies arrange excursions offering a good compromise between independent and package travel.

It is fairly easy to find transport between the main tourist destinations in Peru, which has over 1,300 miles of railway and a few major roads including the Pan-American Highway, which runs along the whole Peruvian coast. Travelling by train is fun and scenic and preferable to the buses, which can vary greatly and can be exhausting due to poor roads. For those with little time or those wishing to forfeit the experience of overland travel, flights are cheap and easy to reserve.

RED TAPE, HEALTH AND SAFETY

NO VISA is required for Western Europeans, Canadians, Americans, Australians or New Zealanders. A Tourist Card is issued on arrival allowing a visit of up to 90 days.

Inoculations against typhoid, hepatitis and polio are recommended as are malaria tablets if you are visiting the jungle. Visit your GP or a travel clinic for further advice, and follow the precautions on page 12 to prevent stomach upsets. Altitude is often a problem in the Andes and you should allow yourself time to acclimatise – see page 10 for hints on combating altitude sickness. Take warm clothing, as temperatures in the mountains can be bitterly cold at night.

Today terrorism is no longer a threat in the main tourist areas and theft is likely to be the main hindrance. Watch your belongings at all times, especially on buses and trains and in markets. Be warned that the consequences for possession of illegal drugs can be particularly severe.

The Foreign Office advises that travellers register with the British Embassy in Lima on arrival in Peru. For more information, contact the Foreign Office Travel Advice Unit (see page 11).

MORE INFORMATION Tourist Section, Embassy of Peru, 52 Sloane Street, London SW1X 9SP, tel 020-7235 1917/2545, web site: *www.rcp.net.pe/promperu/TURISMO*

Peru Tourist Service, 47 Causton Street, London SW1P 4AT tel 020-7976 5511.

COST OF LIVING £

POLAND

HIGHLIGHTS

Culture	Nightlife	Outdoor activities
Gdansk, Krakow	*Warsaw*	*Tatra Mountains*

WARSAW
Good for nightlife

TODAY IT is hard to think of Warsaw as a city totally destroyed by the retreating Nazis in 1944 and then rebuilt under strict Soviet control. For 1,000 years Poles have had to be resilient as one power after another occupied them, but hopes of independence were never allowed to waver. More than any other Eastern European capital, Warsaw managed in the 1990s to create a capital where its past is not forgotten, but it is well hidden in the museums.

BEST SIGHTS

Royal Castle
Destroyed, like so much else in Warsaw during the Second World War, the castle was fully restored only in 1981. This was undertaken so

well that it is hard to believe that any damage was done at all. It is now an appropriate symbol of Polish statehood, with its marble ballroom, tapestry displays and even a throne room. Twenty-first-century visitors can enjoy a retreat into eighteenth-century opulence.

Town Hall Square Historical Museum
The full horror of German and Russian activity in Warsaw from 1939 can be appreciated by watching the film shown in the museum's cinema. The surrounding exhibits, however, cover several centuries of history. It is a relief to see that there were many happier times in Warsaw.

Wilanow Palace
John III, Poland's king at the end of the seventeenth century, built this as his summer palace. If you visit in good weather try to spend as much time outside in the gardens as indoors amongst the Polish paintings. John brought in the best European talent: landscape artists from England, furniture designers from France and sculptors from Italy. Return in the evening for an indoor or outdoor concert.

KRAKOW
Good for culture

KRAKOW WAS for many centuries the capital of Poland, and perhaps still is, as far as many visitors and overseas Poles are concerned. Foreign invaders intruded less here than in Warsaw and Gdansk: they respected the city and its Polish heritage and became quickly assimilated. The spirit of Casimir the Great (1333–1370) who unified Poland, established a legal system, made peace with all his neighbours and warmly welcomed Jewish traders has perhaps finally returned.

BEST SIGHTS

Auschwitz
An hour away by bus is this small town that is forever associated with Nazi terror. The excellent English tour (daily 11.30am) takes you round the heart-wrenching blocks, now filled with memories and mementoes. Nearby Birkenau, left untouched since the war, is equally chilling and memorable.

Rynek Glowny (Market Square)
Climb the (slightly leaning) fifteenth-century Town Hall tower before doing anything else. There is no better way to take in the whole square, remarkably left intact by twentieth-century developers, bombers and soldiers.

Sukiennice (Cloth Hall)

A wander through this building gives a congenial lesson in architectural history from the thirteenth to the nineteenth century. Part of the National Gallery is housed on the first floor. Finish up in the market on the ground floor, where prices are, if no longer medieval, at least still very reasonable.

Wieliczka Salt Mine

The mine is included on the UNESCO World Heritage List, and a half-day here is time well spent. The miners have long gone, leaving sculptors and nature to work together (the stalagtites and stalagmites are shaped by artists). The Warsaw Chamber, at 400 feet underground, is one of the world's deepest concert halls.

GDANSK
Good for culture

STILL OFTEN known by its former name of Danzig, the town has been an important German port since its founding in the eleventh century. Intermittently Poland did thrive here, as in the sixteenth century, but only since 1990 when Russian troops began to leave has national pride begun to reassert itself again. Recent Soviet ghosts, just as much as earlier Swedish and Teutonic ones, lurk around each corner, but Polish signs and goods are now displayed and local books, plays and music flourish.

BEST SIGHTS

St Mary's Church

Nothing symbolises Polish devotion better than a visit to this fifteenth-century church; big in every sense, it accommodates 25,000 people and the tower is nearly 400 feet high. Serious art and architecture scholars could spend an entire day inside. Climb the tower for a view of the whole church and a more extensive one over the city.

Old Town Hall

The centrepiece here is the 'Red Room' which has no link with the communist era, but was the Council meeting room from the eighteenth century. The painted ceiling, the fireplace and the portal were all hidden in 1942 and returned after the war. This is one of the very few original interiors left in Gdansk. Arrive on the hour to hear the bells pealing. The museum on the second floor gives a realistic portrayal of the fighting in the Second World War.

BEST EXCURSION

Westerplatte

There is an eerie peace on this promontory that juts into the Baltic Sea and which now houses just a ruined barracks and some smaller guardhouses. This contrasts with the seven-day bombardment of the Polish garrison which began here at dawn on1 September 1939 and which signalled the beginning of the Second World War.

Equally important to the history of Poland are the now-deserted shipyards seen en route to Westerplatte. In 1980 a general strike was called here, and Solidarity was founded by Lech Walesa. Ten years later he was elected as Poland's first post-communist president.

TATRA MOUNTAINS
Good for outdoor activities

IN THE Tatra Mountains you can ski in the winter or walk in the summer. The Poles are as versatile with wood in the countryside as they are with stone and brick in the towns; most houses are built by their owners.

BEST BASE

Zakopane

Still almost a village, this town in the centre of the Tatra Mountains manages to cater for all pockets. Five-star hotels rub shoulders with backpackers' hostels, and the nightlife and restaurants meet the needs of different ages.

WHEN TO GO

	Average daily maximum temperature °C											
London	6	7	10	13	17	20	22	21	19	14	10	7
Warsaw	0	0	6	12	20	23	24	23	19	13	6	2
	JAN	FEB	MAR	APR	MAY	JUN	JUL	AUG	SEP	OCT	NOV	DEC
Warsaw	15	14	11	13	21	13	16	13	12	12	12	16
London	15	13	11	12	12	11	12	11	13	13	15	15
	Average number of rainy days per month											

SPRING AND autumn offer a mild and relatively dry climate, lower hotel prices and the absence of large coach parties at every major site. Summer can be hot and somewhat humid. City breaks can be taken at any time but Gdansk is best avoided in the winter; being furthest north it is cold and has little daylight. Shrewd shopping at pre-Christmas markets can probably repay the air fare from Britain.

PACKAGE TRAVEL

SEVERAL CITY-BREAK specialists and operators to Eastern Europe offer year-round short-stay programmes in Gdansk, Krakow and Warsaw. Accommodation is usually in four- or five-star hotels as few satisfactory hotels exist in lower categories. Outside these three cities, the situation is reversed, with little high-quality accommodation but many three-star hotels of a good standard. A visit to Poland can easily be combined with one to the Czech Republic, Kaliningrad or Lithuania. Coach tours usually include time in Belgium and Germany en route. Activity holidays include battlefields, bird-watching, walking, Jewish history and skiing.

Tour operators

Battlefields: Holts' Tours, Midas **City breaks**: British Airways Holidays, Bridgewater Travel, Cresta, Danube Travel, Inghams, Magic Cities, Osprey, Regent Holidays, Thomson, Travelscene **Cultural**: Ace Study Tours, British Museum Traveller, Martin Randall **Specialists**: Danube Travel, Polorbis, Regent Holidays, Tazab Travel **Walking**: Exodus, Explore Worldwide, Ramblers, Naturetrek, Waymark

---

INDEPENDENT TRAVEL

GDANSK, KRAKOW and Warsaw all have direct flights from London, mostly operated jointly between British Airways and LOT Polish Airlines; Warsaw is also served by a similar 'code-share' flight from Manchester. With a change of plane in Amsterdam, Warsaw can also be reached from most UK regional airports with KLM. SAS Scandinavian Airlines has connections via Copenhagen to its Gdansk and Warsaw services. These are useful for passengers who may wish to combine a stay in Poland with a visit to Lithuania or Kaliningrad where SAS also operates. The cheapest option, although not the most comfortable, is to fly to Berlin and then to continue by bus to Poland.

Hotel prices are high in Warsaw year-round because of constant demand from business travellers as well as from tourists. In Gdansk and

Krakow prices have increased as these towns become better known. Elsewhere plenty of bargains are available.

Car hire is expensive. Choose a reputable firm offering modern vehicles. With parking difficult in the larger cities, car hire is most suitable for tourists wanting to visit small villages off the beaten track. Travelling around Poland by train or bus is cheap, convenient and relatively comfortable. This also applies to international services that link Poland to Germany, Kaliningrad and Lithuania. Advance reservations on domestic trains and buses are rarely necessary but are advisable for longer journeys out of Poland.

RED TAPE, HEALTH AND SAFETY

BRITISH PASSPORT-HOLDERS do not require a visa for Poland. Customs and immigration is easy for visitors arriving by air. Those arriving by car must expect long delays and searches. Public buses always jump the queue at international borders.

Hospitals are well maintained and hygiene standards are high; no inoculations are necessary.

There is always a charge for public toilets in Poland, even in restaurants. Keep a supply of small change for them (the amount charged does not always reflect the standard).

MORE INFORMATION Polish Tourist Board, 1st Floor, Remo House, 310–312 Regent Street, London W1R 5AJ, tel 020–7580 8811, web site: *www.poland.net/travelpage/*

COST OF LIVING *££*

PORTUGAL

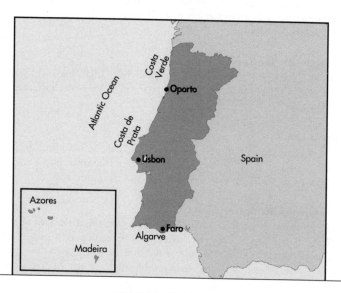

HIGHLIGHTS

Family holidays
Algarve

Local colour
Costa de Prata, Costa Verde, Oporto

Nightlife
Algarve, Lisbon

Flora
Azores, Madeira

Beaches
Algarve

Culture
Costa de Prata, Lisbon

Outdoor activities
Algarve, Azores, Madeira

Scenic landscape
Costa Verde, Madeira

Wine
Madeira, Oporto

LISBON
Good for culture and nightlife

ALTHOUGH IT is not the most exciting European capital, Lisbon has a charming laidback atmosphere and is conveniently small-scale for a city break. The city itself boasts a few great buildings but there is plenty of architectural detail and decoration to admire – an intoxicating mix of influences from Europe and North America. It enjoys a thriving bar scene.

BEST SIGHTS

Calouste Gulbenkian Museum
Part of a complex that includes shady grounds, concert halls, an outdoor amphitheatre and exhibition spaces, the museum is divided into ancient, non-European and European art.

Castelo de São Jorge
Moorish castle strengthened and embellished by later kings, laid out as park with gardens, peacocks and deer, terraces, pricey café, and rampart walkways.

Expo Urbe
The former site of Expo 98 has now been transformed into a leisure, residential and nightlife area. Also on site is Oceanarium, Europe's largest aquarium, with four habitat zones and a gigantic tank.

Jéronimos Monastery
An exuberant Manueline building in the western suburb of Belém, one of the few to have survived Lisbon's 1755 earthquake: exotic and nautical themes prevail. Downriver is Torre de Belém from the same period – a former defensive tower softened by fancy balconies and pinnacles.

National Museum of Ancient Art
An extensive collection of artistic treasures out in the leafy suburb of Lapa.

National Tile Museum
Attractive museum in a sixteenth-century convent that charts the development of *azulejos*, or painted tiles.

Tram 28
This legendary old tram rumbles right through the heart of the city, opening up an illuminating cross-section of Lisbon life, as it navigates the city's famous hills on its way up to Castelo de São Jorge.

THE ALGARVE
Good for beaches, family holidays, nightlife and outdoor activities

IF YOU are looking for a resort-based holiday, with great beaches, a comfortable and convenient hotel, and good facilities, the Algarve is an excellent choice. However, insensitive development blight continues, and large numbers of tourists crowd the most popular beaches. West of Lagos, however, you can still find empty stretches of sand.

Outside the summer season the Algarve is also anxious to attract the golfer – there is a golf course within 10 minutes of nearly every major resort, and many hotels and villa complexes will also offer you discounts on green fees.

BEST SIGHTS

The natural beauty of the Algarve's coastline is the highlight of any trip. Boat trips are offered all along the coast, but the most dramatic coastline is between Albufeira and Carvoeiro. The best views are at Benagil and particularly Algar Seco, where viewing steps and a tunnel have been built into the rock.

Faro is worth a day-trip for its eighteenth-century port buildings around the seafront and the small medieval walled town, or an evening outing to sample the healthy nightlife of the bars and clubs around Conselheiro Bivar and Do Prior.

A 45-minute drive east of Faro, the idyllic town of Tavira straddles the River Gilão, with traditional Algarvan houses covered in decorative tiles and atmospheric riverside restaurants. West of Faro, Silves was once the splendid Moorish capital of the region, and Cabo do São Vincente, the most westerly point of Europe, is the site of the renowned school of navigation set up by Prince Henry the Navigator in 1418.

BEST RESORTS

Most resorts have huge stretches of top-quality beach. The final choice comes down to whether you want a proper town with busy nightlife or a purpose-built villa/apartment complex with sports facilities.

Albufeira
● Old Moorish town slowly being overwhelmed by tourism, though the fishing tradition remains alive.
● Acres of golden beach below the town.
● Lively place at night, especially the tacky neon stretch of Largo Cais Herculano; for a quieter time, stick to the white-walled alleys and staircases of the town above, with a choice of small quiet restaurants.
● Montechoro, or 'The Strip', just under two miles from Albufeira's old town, is the liveliest nightlife zone on the Algarve, with dozens of buzzing bars and nightclubs. The old town offers a quieter alternative with good restaurants and less frenzied nightspots.

Alvor
● Agreeable old town above the harbour.

- Long, straight, golden sandy beach flanked by strange rock formations. A good family resort.
- Beachside development, though high-rise, is on a fairly human scale.

Carvoeiro

- Steep narrow sandy cove means that the old part of the fishing village has kept some measure of charm and intimate quality.
- Large number of bars and restaurants, several run by British ex-pats.
- Modern development on the two roads leading up the valley away from the sea or on the clifftops above the town.
- First sizeable beach is closer to Ferragudo, a largely unspoilt fishing village.

Lagos

- Historic and picturesque fortified port, steep cobbled streets dotted with small churches, restaurants, and intriguing shops.
- Very popular with younger independent travellers who fuel its vibrant nightlife scene.
- Few hotels; nearest beaches at Meia Praia, a 5-minute drive away. However, more impressive beaches, coves and grottoes just west of the old walls.

Quinta do Lago

- Attractive, though large, purpose-built resort with beautiful shoreline.
- Mostly low-rise villa complexes dotted between several golf courses. Golf is the year-round attraction.
- Southern half of the resort is preferable, as it is close to the natural beauty of the Ria Formosa lagoon and the dunes beyond.
- Huge beach of fine sand, stretching into the distance.

Salema

- Small, generally uncommercialised resort with an authentically scruffy old town.
- Bustling fisherman's beach.
- A good base for independent travellers.

Vale do Lobo

- Swanky, purpose-built resort with its own cricket pitch, two golf courses, a large tennis centre, a driving range and aerobics classes.
- Orderly and efficient small development, too orderly for some.
- Long, narrow beach backed by sandstone cliffs.

COSTA DE PRATA
Good for culture and local colour

THIS AREA has some important historical sights and good beaches, but much of it is flat and featureless, interrupted only by the occasional large stretch of pine woods; the coast often suffers from strong winds. The resorts, though scarred by the occasional tower block, often sustain a traditional way of life, but the beaches are not as good as those of the Algarve. Fierce Atlantic rollers also make sections of the coastline hazardous for bathers, though heaven for surfers.

BEST RESORTS

Cascais
● One-time fishing village that made it big, with a reputation for the best seafood on coast.
● Good for stay-put holiday, but the quality of bathing water is dubious. Compared to the Algarve, Cascais is blighted by poor-quality sand and dirty water.
● Nicest resort beach is Praia da Conceição; biggest and best beach in the area is Praia do Guincho, 4 miles west of town.

Ericeira
● Low-key Portuguese family resort, popular with surfers.
● Large, intermittently rocky beach shared by sun-worshippers and fishermen, who use tractors to haul the boats up the shore.
● Pleasant town built around square lined with plane trees.

BEST SIGHTS

Batalha
The Flamboyant Gothic church of this monastery is notable for its profusion of pinnacles, buttresses and open balustrades.

Coimbra
The riverside home of one of the country's leading universities has a youthful energy that sits well with its mature medieval charm. The university library is very fine, while the Machado de Castro Museum's diverse collection includes a range of sinister hand-shaped reliquaries.

Fátima
A piazza that can hold up to 300,000 pilgrims fronts a neoclassical 1930s basilica commemorating appearances of the Virgin Mary to three local children in 1917. View spectacular pilgrimages on 13 May and 13 October, when all the massive car parks around town are full.

423

Mafra

The astonishing monastery-palace of Mafra combines Italian neoclassical and German baroque architecture. The tour is recommended.

Sintra

Beloved by Lord Byron, this historic town among wooded hills was for centuries the royal family's summer residence, and has a profusion of palaces. The Royal Palace is most memorable for its domed Hall of Arms. The hill above is crowned by the Pena Palace, an orgy of mock-medieval kitsch.

OPORTO
Good for local colour and food/wine

AT LAST emerging from Lisbon's shadow, Oporto has much to offer. Three fine bridges span the River Douro, linking the port centre of Vila Nova de Gaia with the intriguing, dignified city on its right bank. The narrow alleyways of the Italianate old town lead down to the riverside. Numerous tea houses and grand coffee shops are dotted around the city. The main sights are in the old quarter, including the Church of St Francis, with a staggeringly ornate rococo interior, and the rich art collection of the Soares dos Reis Museum. Not to be missed is a tour of the port wine warehouses across the river. Free guided tours are available at most lodges – you get to sample the wine and see the oak casks with their precious maturing contents.

COSTA VERDE
Good for local colour and scenic landscape

THE COSTA Verde is one of the most rewarding areas of Portugal to tour, offering a combination of mountain scenery, sandy beaches, historic towns and unspoilt villages – all contained within a fairly compact area.

BEST RESORTS

The coast has many long sandy beaches, but the relatively cold water and frequent onshore winds limit their appeal for stay-put sunbathing and swimming holidays.

Ofir

● Some of Costa Verde's best beaches – large expanses of sand with dunes and pine woods behind.
● Several hotels, restaurants and bars, but other tourist facilities limited.

Viana do Castelo
- Attractive setting on wooded estuary of River Lima.
- Busy town with striking views from Sta Luzia hill.
- Nearest beaches two miles away on other side of river.

BEST SIGHTS

Amarante
This wine-making town lies on the edge of the Serra do Marrão and is famous for its pastries and setting. Its tiers of balconied houses rise steeply up the slopes on either side of the River Tamega, around the sixteenth-century convent of São Gonçalo.

Barcelos
Home of the painted pottery cockerels (now an emblem of Portugal), this is a picturesque riverside town with a popular Thursday market.

Guimarães
The old quarter of the original capital of Portugal contains lovely squares and narrow fifteenth-century streets, while in a park stands the Palace of the Dukes of Bragança, housing a collection of tapestries and furniture.

Peneda-Gerês National Park
Some of Portugal's most dramatic scenery is to be found among these magnificent mountains, forests and artificial lakes. The high peaks of the Serra de Gerês are harsh, with sparse vegetation, but around the lakes the slopes are gentler, and there are opportunities for fishing, swimming and boating. The spa town of Gerês, dotting the tree-covered slopes near the head of Caniçada Lake, is a peaceful place in which to stay.

Valença do Minho
The cobbled streets of this fortified hilltop settlement overlooking the river frontier with Spain are crowded with souvenir shops, but it still has considerable charm and character.

MADEIRA
Good for flora, food/wine, outdoor activities and scenic landscape

THE ISLAND lies in the Atlantic, on the same latitude as Morocco. A holiday here may involve strolling in formal gardens and mosaic-paved shopping streets, visits to a wine lodge to learn how the various

Madeira wines are made, or expeditions into the hinterland, perhaps following the *levadas* (irrigation channels) that criss-cross the island.

BEST BASE

Funchal

Most people choose to stay in Funchal, a large, bustling town with several museums, a good market, plenty of shops, a casino, and a pleasant if touristy port area and old town to explore. The São Francisco Wine Lodge offers tours on the making of Madeira wine, plus generous tastings; the Museum of Sacred Art contains fine pieces and Flemish art while the Quinta das Cruzes Museum offers glimpses of leading Madeiran families' lifestyles in the eighteenth and nineteenth centuries. The Botanic Gardens give an excellent introduction to Madeira's subtropical flora.

BEST EXCURSIONS

Curral das Freiras

A tiny mountain village, founded by nuns as a refuge against pirates.

Porto Moniz and Paúl da Serra

The thrilling corniche road along the northern coast to Porto Moniz features rock tunnels and cascades of water tumbling down cliff faces.

THE AZORES
Good for flora and outdoor activities

OTHER THAN sailors, walkers and plant-lovers are the commonest visitors, coming for the attractive and not-too-strenuous coastal and hill walks and the enormous variety of trees, flowers and grasses.

BEST ISLANDS

Faial

- The most touristy island, much frequented by yachts.
- Prettiest main town Horta has good restaurants and local shopping.
- Excellent walks around the central volcanic cauldron.
- Most deserted beach is at Faja da Praia do Norte in the north-west.

Flores

- Remote, particularly attractive to botanists and walkers.
- Seven lakes in rugged interior and waterfalls that drop into the sea.

Graciosa
- Remote, sleepy, away-from-it-all island.
- Handsome town of Santa Cruz with wide square.
- Volcanic crater with lake of sulphurous water inside huge grotto.

Pico
- Mostly visited as day-trip from Faial.
- Best volcanic landscape, with the highest peak: for good climbers.
- Whaling museum at Lajes.

Santa Maria
- Tiny, bypassed by most tourists – you can tour the whole island by car in half a day.
- Two first-class beaches of golden sand: Praia attracts more sunbathers, while São Lourenço Bay has a prettier setting.
- Most attractive part is in the east, around Pico Alto.

São Jorge
- Lovely, wild rugged landscape, with central plateau punctuated by volcanic cones, and almost vertical shore cliffs.
- Superb coastal hill walks, the best being on the north coast.
- Only beach is at Faja do João Dias, an hour's walk from the road.

São Miguel
- Largest and one of the busiest islands.
- Several black sand beaches; the best are on the enclosed bay near Porto Formoso on the north coast, and near Ribeira Quente and Vila Franca do Campo on the south.
- Natural sights include the Terra Nostra forest park in the east and the lakes in the crater of Sete Cidades in the west.

Terceira
- Busy, the most densely populated island, with villages and towns forming an almost continuous ring round its shores.
- Fine volcanic landscape in the middle, with sulphurous fumaroles and the cave of Alvar do Carvão, but otherwise the least appealing.
- The only beach is at Vila Praia da Vitoria.

WHEN TO GO

THE MOST colourful time to go to Lisbon is at Carnaval, which takes place around Shrove Tuesday, and in June, when three major saints' days (St Anthony, St John, and St Peter) are celebrated with processions, concerts, fireworks and street parties.

On the Algarve and the Atlantic coast, it is cheaper and less crowded in June and September. From October till April the weather is good for walking. For golfers, October and May are good times to choose. The Algarve features as a winter destination in brochures, and resort hotels stay open throughout the year.

Madeira's major event is an annual flower festival in late April, when colourful floats traverse Funchal. There's also a September wine festival.

The islands of the Azores are among the few places left near Europe where you can still happily go in July and August – there are no great crowds, and the weather is pleasantly warm, not sweltering. But count on a few rainy days and book your hotels in advance.

	Average daily maximum temperature °C											
London	6	7	10	13	17	20	22	21	19	14	10	7
Lisbon	14	15	17	20	21	25	27	28	26	22	17	15
	JAN	FEB	MAR	APR	MAY	JUN	JUL	AUG	SEP	OCT	NOV	DEC
Lisbon	15	12	14	10	10	5	2	2	6	9	13	15
London	15	13	11	12	12	11	12	11	13	13	15	15
	Average number of rainy days per month											

PACKAGE TRAVEL

MANY BRITISH tour operators offer city-break packages to Lisbon and an increasing amount to Oporto.

All the mass-market tour operators feature package holidays in hotels in the Algarve. Prices can be expensive compared with other Mediterranean resorts, but they drop outside July and August. Restaurant food is generally inexpensive, so you may want to book only B&B. As with hotels, villa accommodation can be pricey, particularly at the 'exclusive' purpose-built resorts, but the mid-range self-catering villas and apartments are good value.

In northern Portugal specialist operators feature holidays in *pousadas* – state-run hotels, often in converted historical buildings. You can use one as a base for day-trips, or combine several on a touring holiday.

Most package holidays to Madeira are based in Funchal – some hotels are more than half an hour's walk from the hub of things, although the bus service is good and taxis reasonably cheap. Specialist operators offer wider coverage of the islands, including the government-run *pousadas* in the interior. For beach-bums, some operators offer two-centre holidays based on a week in Funchal and a week on Porto Santo.

Specialist tour operators offer stay-put hotel packages or tailor-made island-hopping trips to the Azores. If you are staying put, choose an island in the middle group, from where you can easily visit others on boat trips. Specialist activities on offer include walking, wine-tasting, flora and birdwatching, as well as pilgrimages to Fátima.

Tour operators

City breaks: Kirker, Time Off, Travelscene **General**: Abreu, Airtours, Alternative Travel Group, Cadogan, Caravela, Cosmos, Crystal, First Choice, Inghams, JMC Travel, Manos, Mundi Color, Prestige, Sunvil, Thomson, Unicorn Holidays, Unijet **Specialists**: Bonaventure, Casas Cantabricas, Destination Portugal, Magic of Portugal **Villa specialists**: CV Travel, Individual Travellers Spain & Portugal, Meon, Something Special, Travel Club of Upminster, Villa Club, Vintage Travel **Other activities**: Arblaster & Clarke, Exodus, Explore Worldwide, Holts' Tours (battlefields), Longmere Golf, Longshot Golf, Serenity Golf, Simply Golf, Martin Randall (cultural), Winetrails (wine)

INDEPENDENT TRAVEL

YOU WILL not save money by going independently to the seaside, but it is worth considering if you are going to tour – though check the fly-drive deals first. British Airways flies direct to Lisbon and Porto from Heathrow and from Manchester to Faro in summer. TAP Air Portugal flies to Lisbon, Porto and Faro from Heathrow, and from Manchester to Lisbon. Since Go started no-frills budget flights to Lisbon in 1999, independent city breaks have become a cost-effective option. Cheaper charter flights are also available to Lisbon all year round (more so in summer) from Gatwick, Luton and Manchester, but most are based on one- or two-week holidays. Charter flights are available from most regional airports to Faro on the Algarve.

Car hire is relatively cheap, but Portugal has one of the worst accident records in Europe. By law, motorists must carry some form of identification with a photo or face an on-the-spot fine. A passport will suffice (photocopies are not valid). Make sure you also have your driving licence and the hire-car contract (or logbook for private cars). Front seat-belt use is compulsory.

A pleasantly relaxed and inexpensive rail network connects Lisbon with the main northern towns and the Algarve. The Portuguese railway company CP sells a *Bilhete Turístico* rail pass, valid for first-class travel on all trains except Lisbon-Madrid. Long-distance buses, usually quicker than trains, also link the main centres, but are more expensive. Services tend to be less frequent at weekends. Buses are the main form of local transport; rail services also run between Lisbon and Cascais, and along the Algarve coast.

There are direct scheduled and charter flights from London to Funchal. Car hire and petrol on Madeira are expensive, but if you want the freedom to explore, hiring is worthwhile. Madeira's roads are steep, twisting and bumpy: you are rarely out of second gear. Taxis are plentiful, and available for half- or whole-day charters at rates set down by the Funchal tourist office. Coach tours are another popular and good-value way of seeing the island, and often include lunch.

You can visit the Azores independently by flying to Lisbon and then on to São Miguel or Terceira. But leave your itinerary flexible – local planes and boats are simpler to book on the spot. The local airline, SATA, connects all islands except Corvo on small, reliable planes (weather permitting). It is easy to make bookings on the spot. Ferries ply between all the islands and are cheaper but take longer. They are most useful on the short distances between islands in the middle group. Taxis are commonly used for getting around all the islands.

Hotels are officially graded from one to five stars; there is a separate one- to four-star system for simpler *pensões* and *residencials*. *Pousadas* are state-owned inns, often in scenic or historic locations, offering reliable standards of comfort. *Estalagens*, classified as three or four stars, are similar to *pousadas* but privately owned, and standards are more variable.

The *Turismo de Habitação* scheme offers bed and breakfast in privately owned accommodation ranging from simple farmhouses to palatial seventeenth-century mansions.

Campsites are generally very simple and cheap, except for a few well-equipped sites on the Algarve. They are graded on a four-point scale. For budget-conscious travellers Portugal has a well-maintained and widespread youth hostel network (*www.hostellinginternational.com*).

RED TAPE, HEALTH AND SAFETY

BRITISH PASSPORT-HOLDERS do not need a visa to visit Portugal.

Tap water in most parts of the country is safe to drink, but check with the locals. The usual problems with petty theft occur – see page 12.

MORE INFORMATION Portuguese National Tourist Office, 22–25A Sackville Street, London W1X 2LY, tel 020-7494 1441, web site: *www.portugal.org*

COST OF LIVING ££

RUSSIA

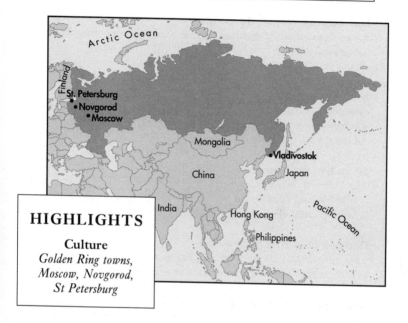

MOSCOW
Good for culture

THE CITY is very much in the vanguard of the new Russia: new energy, new business, new money, new crime. The latest grandiose gesture is the vast new cathedral, complete with gold onion domes, built by the river in record time. Moscow is not exactly beautiful, but it is a fascinating (and very expensive) place, with plenty to do in a week. It is best to combine guided tours with striking out on your own.

BEST SIGHTS

Opening times vary greatly; some sights are available only on guided tours. Long queues can build up on Sundays for the big museums – go early in the morning.

Kremlin
Inside the swallow-tailed red walls, the complex of stuccoed palaces and domed cathedrals takes at least a day to explore. By far the most

431

beautiful part of it is the Cathedral Square: there is a church here for every major event in the lifespan of a tsar.

Leo Tolstoy House Museum
An evocative literary museum, giving a rare glimpse into the great writer's daily life.

The Metro
Moscow's underground system is one of its greatest works of art – cathedral-like halls, marble columns, murals and statuary. Of the many stations worth seeing, Ploshchad Revolyutsii, Komsomolskaya and Arbatskaya are especially interesting.

Novodevichy Convent
The restored convent is a peaceful place of red and white buildings within fortified walls. In the adjoining cemetery you can pay tribute to Russian greats including Gogol, Chekhov and Prokofiev.

Pushkin Fine Arts Museum
The museum houses ancient and European art, notably a splendid collection of French Impressionist and post-Impressionist paintings.

Red Square and St Basil's Cathedral
The vast cobbled square is dominated by GUM, a palatial indoor shopping centre now housing smart Western designer chains at exorbitant prices, and by St Basil's Cathedral, Moscow's most exotic and photographed building (the interior is less remarkable). Lenin's embalmed body still lies in the Mausoleum beneath the Kremlin walls.

Tretyakov Gallery
The greatest collection of Russian art resides in a restored building with good facilities. The medieval icons are particularly fine.

GOLDEN RING
Good for culture

THE 'GOLDEN ring' of medieval Russian towns around Moscow contains a panoply of early Russian art and architecture: churches, monasteries and kremlins (fortresses). All can be visited on day-trips or overnight stays from Moscow, by public transport or guided tours.

BEST SIGHTS
Little Suzdal is the most picturesque and the most visited. Also very

worthwhile is Sergiev-Posad (formerly Zagorsk), with its fortified complex of the Trinity Monastery of St Sergei, one of Russia's most important religious landmarks, associated with the great icon painter Andrei Rublev. Other towns in the Golden Ring include Vladimir, Yaroslavl and Rostov-Veliky.

ST PETERSBURG
Good for culture

AN ASTONISHINGLY beautiful city, of almost perfect symmetry and dazzling vistas, St Petersburg was purpose-built in the eighteenth century as a 'new town', mainly by Europeans, on Peter the Great's orders. The result is a striking combination of Italianate architecture and northern light (in summer the nights are as light as day). As one of Europe's greatest treasure-troves of art, it deserves up to a week of your time.

BEST SIGHTS

Alexander Nevsky Monastery
In one of the two walled cemeteries here you can pay your respects to Tchaikovsky, Mussorgsky, Rimsky-Korsakov and Dostoyevsky.

Dvortsovaya Ploshchad and Nevsky Prospekt
The Palace Square is a vast theatrical space enclosed by the stuccoed Winter Palace and the classical curve of the Staff Headquarters. Nevsky Prospekt, the city's main avenue, leads off from here, crossed by canals, flanked by classical, baroque and art-nouveau façades and seething with people and street traders for its entire six-mile length.

The Hermitage
You could spend the whole week in this, one of the world's greatest museums, purpose-built to house the royal art collections in some 400 halls which contain two million works of art from all periods of history. The opulent interiors match the richness of the collection.

Literary museums
Lovers of Russian literature should visit the Pushkin Flat Museum and the Dostoyevsky House; in the latter you can see the study where he wrote *The Brothers Karamazov*.

Peter and Paul Fortress
This is a mini eighteenth-century town built as a bastion against the

Swedes on the right bank of the Neva. Peter the Great's grave is here, in a church with a thin gold spire.

Royal palaces
Petrodvorets (the Summer Palace), best visited by hydrofoil during the summer months, and Catherine's Palace at Pushkin are baroque echoes of the Winter Palace in St Petersburg in appearance. Pavlovsk is a classical building whose gardens were inspired by those of Versailles in France.

NOVGOROD
Good for culture

NOVGOROD IS one of Russia's oldest towns (founded by Vikings), south of, and easily visited from, St Petersburg — an overnight stop is best. It bristles with blue and gold domes of monasteries and churches.

WHEN TO GO

VISIT IN summer, when temperatures are pleasantly warm; the Moscow winter is grim and long. St Petersburg, further north but with a milder climate than Moscow, is particularly beautiful during the 'white nights' in June (there is also a festival of that name) or during the winter, covered in snow (the buildings are well-heated).

Average daily maximum temperature °C											
London	6	7	10	13	17	20	22	21	19	14	10	7
Moscow	-9	-6	0	10	19	21	23	22	16	9	2	-5
	JAN	FEB	MAR	APR	MAY	JUN	JUL	AUG	SEP	OCT	NOV	DEC
Moscow	18	15	15	13	13	12	15	14	13	15	15	23
London	15	13	11	12	12	11	12	11	13	13	15	15
Average number of rainy days per month												

PACKAGE TRAVEL

THE CHOICE of packages to Russia is still somewhat restricted. Most operators offer city breaks in either Moscow or St Petersburg, or a two-centre holiday in both cities with transfers by air or rail. Other options include the Trans-Siberian, Trans-Mongolian and Trans-Manchurian rail routes, which link Moscow and Vladivostok in the far east and China (where destinations include Beijing and Guangzhou). Alternatively, there are activity holidays based on walking, birdwatching or river cruises.

Tour operators

Cultural: Ace Study Tours, Exodus, Inscape, Martin Randall, Prospect, Travel for the Arts **River cruises**: Abercrombie & Kent, Noble Caledonian, Swan Hellenic, Voyages Jules Verne **Specialist**: Intourist, Norvista, Regent Holidays, Scantours, Steppes East **Other activities**: Cosmos (coach), Explore Worldwide (adventure), Holts' Tours (battlefields), Jagged Globe (trekking), Ornitholidays (birdwatching), Solo's (singles), Wildlife Worldwide (wildlife)

INDEPENDENT TRAVEL

YOU WILL not save money by taking a package to Russia, but you may save yourself some hassle. Once there you can strike out on your own by using the cheap and generally excellent public transport or joining the readily available organised tours. The best policy is to use a combination of both and explore on your own once you feel more confident. You can also go independently, booking your flight and accommodation from the UK. It helps to know some Russian (and the Cyrillic alphabet).

Aeroflot, an airline which has always had a poor reputation, has now been broken up into several smaller airlines, leading to further doubts about safety. As a result, domestic flights are probably best avoided. Trains are more reliable, and cheap, though they are slow. The ultimate rail journey is on the Trans-Siberian Railway from Moscow to Vladivostok, a unique six-day experience.

Although car hire is now easily available, the traffic in the cities is nightmarish, the standard of driving abysmal and the roads outside the cities mainly in very bad condition, with signposting rather poor and in Cyrillic only.

There is a dearth of moderately priced, reasonable-standard hotels. For most tourists the choice is between the featureless square blocks inherited from the Soviet era and the new generation of luxury hotels that are affordable only by business travellers. As a guide, a three-star hotel will usually be a 1960s/'70s tower block with several restaurants and a bar or a nightclub. Always check the menus and prices in hotel restaurants before you order – some have the attitude that foreigners are there to be fleeced. When booking a package, check the location

435

of your hotel – if it is way out of the centre, make sure it is near a metro station. Specialist agencies can arrange B&B accommodation in private households (mainly in blocks of flats), and both Moscow and St Petersburg now have youth hostel accommodation.

RED TAPE, HEALTH AND SAFETY

IT IS best to let your travel agent or tour operator get your visa for you; essentially, the more you pay the quicker it will arrive (it can cost anything from £30 to £150). Three passport photographs, a completed visa form, passport and voucher from a recognised tour operator are required. An ordinary tourist visa usually takes two weeks to process. Applications will be rejected if all accommodation in Russia has not been pre-booked.

Although reports of crime in Russia are exaggerated in the Western press, you should take the same precautions as you would in any big city – do not carry valuables and cameras ostentatiously and do not leave them lying around in your hotel. For the latest advice, contact the Foreign Office Travel Advice Unit (see page 11).

MORE INFORMATION Russian National Tourist Office, 167 Kensington High Street, London W8 6SH, tel 020-7937 7217.

The largest operator is Intourist, Intourist House, 219 Marsh Wall, London E14 3PD, tel 020-7538 8600, visa information (09001) 171271 (premium rate number)

COST OF LIVING *££–£££*

THE SEYCHELLES

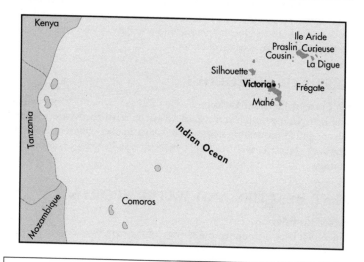

HIGHLIGHTS

Beaches *La Digue,* *Frégate,* *Mahé,* *Praslin*	**Food/wine** *Mahé,* *Praslin*	**Outdoor activities** *La Digue,* *Mahé, Praslin*	**Scenic landscape** *La Digue*
Flora *Praslin*	**Local colour** *Mahé*	**Romantic escapism** *Frégate*	**Wildlife** *Bird Island,* *La Digue,* *Praslin*

THE SEYCHELLES is a group of islands in the western Indian Ocean off the coast of east Africa, north of Madagascar. There are 115 named islands.

MAHE
Good for beaches, local colour and outdoor activities

MAHE, DOMINATED by the green hump of Morne Seychellois, is the hub of the islands, and the one with most to offer tourists. You can choose from 75 beaches, learn to dive, try parascending, visit a tea plantation, or the casinos. The Creole fish curries are excellent.

Victoria

As capitals go, Victoria is definitely in the modest league. It is about the size of an average English market town, and you can wander round it on foot. The centre of town is the silver clock-tower, erected in 1903 as a tribute to Queen Victoria and a replica of one which stands on Vauxhall Bridge Road in London.

BEST LOCAL COLOUR

Sir Selwyn Clarke Market

The best place to catch some local colour in Victoria, where massive fish are gutted for waiting housewives. Other market stalls sell colourful arrays of spices as well as tiny bottles of vanilla essence and fiery chutneys.

BEST BEACHES AND WATER SPORTS

Anse Intendance

The beach here is stunning, but beware of the currents.

Anse aux Pins

Located on the east coast, this beach offers the chance to see the local fishermen selling off their catches during the day and repairing their wicker creels.

Anse Takamaka

A lovely beach in the south-west of the island with fine snorkelling. Care is required owing to hazardous currents.

PRASLIN

Good for beaches, flora, outdoor activities and wildlife

PRASLIN SEEMS simple and undeveloped after Mahé. You can hire a car or bicycle to get around. Most hotels are close to the beaches.

BEST EXCURSION

Vallée de Mai forest

When General Gordon of Khartoum discovered this eerie forest, he believed he had found the Garden of Eden. The unique tropical habitat (a UNESCO World Heritage Site) includes coco de mer trees, whose thick stems shoot 80 feet into the air while their palms fan out like parasols, creating a canopy.

BEST BEACHES AND WATER SPORTS

Praslin offers numerous diving and water sports opportunities. There are a couple of straggling settlements at Baie Ste-Anne near Anse Volbert in the north and at Grand Anse in the south; Anse Lazio is pleasant.

LA DIGUE
Good for beaches, outdoor activities, scenic landscape and wildlife

LA DIGUE, half-an-hour from Praslin by boat, is the most photogenic island, and the best partner for Mahé if you visit only two islands.

BEST BEACH

Anse Source d'Argent
An idyllic beach lapped by turquoise waters and backed by huge rocks like giant elephants' feet. You can make your way to the beach by ox-cart.

BEST WILDLIFE

The black paradise flycatcher, one of the world's most threatened birds, can be glimpsed on La Digue at the nature reserve.

BIRD ISLAND
Good for wildlife

BIRD ISLAND – only 12 feet above sea-level – is flat with open vistas. Most of the island (you can walk around it in a couple of hours) is protected by coral reef, but there are gaps, and swimming on the west side of the island is sometimes very rough. Take plastic sandals to protect your feet from coral and sharp pebbles while swimming.

BEST WILDLIFE

Most visitors come to watch birds from May to September. Beginners are given an observation check list to help them get started. On the observation platform watching the roosting of the sooty terns – a spectacular piece of theatre, set against the backdrop of a tropical sunset – you may feel overwhelmed by the sheer volume of birds which descend.

FREGATE
Good for beaches and romantic escapism

FREGATE IS a truly special island. You can see the golden beaches as the plane approaches and then enjoy the island's distinctly exclusive feel.

BEST BEACH

Anse Victorin
The beach is about 25 minutes' walk through dense vegetation from the bungalows. Brave the final, steep descent: it is worth it. Beware of the strong current.

OTHER ISLANDS
Good for beaches, flora, outdoor activities and wildlife

Aride
The most important nature reserve of the granitic islands, lying five miles north of Praslin. It is owned by the Royal Society for Nature Conservation and is partially surrounded by coral reef, making it equally popular with birdwatchers and divers. Wright's gardenia blooms here.

Cousin
From Praslin you can take a trip to Cousin, a bird sanctuary open to the public three days a week. The warden will introduce you to fairy tern, black noddies, brush warblers and white-tailed tropic birds. Be sure to bring insect repellent.

Curieuse
This island can be twinned with Cousin on the day-trip from Praslin. On a walk through the dense vegetation you can identify vegetation including cinnamon, lime, coco de mer, takamaka, papaya and almond trees. If you are lucky you might see a hawksbill turtle as you creep across the narrow turtle causeway.

Denis
Among the islands Denis is the fisherman's friend. If big-game fishing doesn't appeal, you can spend your time on astonishingly white beaches. Day-trippers are not allowed.

Desroches
Desroches, a platform reef, is the largest of the Amirantes group of

islands, and lies 142 miles south-west of Mahé. Its remoteness gives it a special appeal, as do its excellent water-sports facilities. The island's only hotel is the comfortable Desroches Island Lodge.

Silhouette
Silhouette is a large, forested, lumpy granite island rather less developed than the others, though the single hotel is smarter than you might expect. Cinnamon and coconut plantations flourish beneath the slopes of Mount Dauban, where rainforest and pitcher plants survive..

WHEN TO GO

THE WEATHER is generally humid and warm, and the year is divided into two monsoon seasons. The heaviest rain sets in during the north-west monsoon season, between December and late March, with the number of rainy days peaking in December and January. Even during the south-east monsoon between April and October sudden torrential downpours are common. The temperature is fairly even all year.

For those interested in diving, underwater visibility is best when the sea is at its calmest in the interval between the two monsoons in April/May or October/November.

	Average daily maximum temperature °C											
London	6	7	10	13	17	20	22	21	19	14	10	7
Victoria	31	31	32	33	32	30	29	29	29	31	31	31
	JAN	FEB	MAR	APR	MAY	JUN	JUL	AUG	SEP	OCT	NOV	DEC
(Mahé)	21	17	14	18	14	15	14	14	15	13	17	21
London	15	13	11	12	12	11	12	11	13	13	15	15
	Average number of rainy days per month											

PACKAGE TRAVEL

FOURTEEN ISLANDS are widely used by UK tour operators, and about a dozen others can be visited easily on rather pricey day-trips. Mahé is the most developed and varied island if you want to stay put and has the most accommodation to choose from.

Island-hopping involving stays on a combination of islands is a reasonably flexible option – a choice of Mahé, La Digue, Frégate and Bird Island offers variety with a blend of water sports and unforgettable birdlife, while Silhouette, Desroches and La Digue are good for getting away from it all.

Package accommodation tends to be in large, modern, usually low-rise hotels of a good standard. Accommodation in smaller hotels and guesthouses is also available. Self-catering is on offer on Mahé, Praslin and la Digne although as the cost of living is high this may not be much of a saving on hotel package prices. Activity holidays on offer include birdwatching and scuba diving, or you can take a cruise around the islands.

Tour operators

Birdwatching and wildlife: Abercrombie & Kent, Naturetrek, Ornitholidays **General**: British Airways Holidays, Classic Connection, Distant Dreams, Elite Vacations, Hayes & Jarvis, Kuoni, Reef & Rainforest, Somak, Sunset Faraway, Tropical Places, Worldwide Journeys **Flora**: Cox & Kings **Tailor-made specialists**: Seychelles Travel, Silhouette Travel, Tana Travel

---

INDEPENDENT TRAVEL

THERE ARE no UK charters. Scheduled flight fares are prohibitive, but it may be worth contacting a consolidator.

Mahé is the hub of the transport network and all inter-island flights are channelled through it. Several return flights link Mahé and Praslin during the day; connections to the other islands are not as regular.

Car hire is available only on Mahé and Praslin. Driving is on the left. Bicycles are for hire on Praslin, Mahé and La Digue.

Diving schools around the islands offer lessons; enthusiasts can take the top-of-the-range Divemaster course. Snorkelling equipment is available for hire or free of charge at many hotels. Mahé and Praslin are particularly good for snorkelling and water sports.

If you are travelling via a yellow-fever region, you will need a certificate proving that you have been inoculated.

RED TAPE, HEALTH AND SAFETY

BRITISH PASSPORT-HOLDERS do not require a visa. A visitor's permit is issued on arrival provided you have a valid passport, return ticket, pre-booked accommodation and sufficient funds to cover your stay.

Vaccinations for polio, hepatitis A and typhoid are usually recommended – consult your GP or a travel clinic for the latest advice.

Consisting of around 115 islands, the Seychelles retain a French identity and except for red pillar-boxes and a requirement to drive on the left, little remains of 160 years of British rule. Everything except fish – around which Creole cooking revolves – and fruit is imported. Take precautions against stomach upsets (see page 12). Swimmers and divers should beware dangerous currents, particularly on Mahé. Wear plastic shoes at all times when swimming to avoid painful stings from sea urchins and cuts from coral, many species of which are poisonous.

Contact the Foreign Office Travel Advice Unit for up-to-date information on crime and safety matters (see page 11).

MORE INFORMATION Seychelles Tourist Office, 48 Glentham Road, London SW13 9SS, tel 020-8741 6262, web site: *www.seychelles.uk.com*

COST OF LIVING £££-£££

SINGAPORE

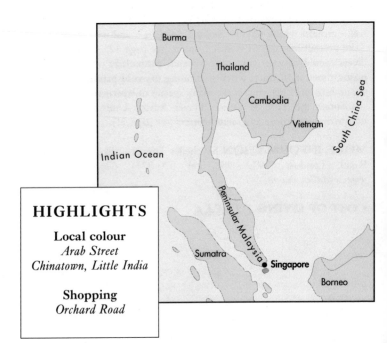

HIGHLIGHTS

Local colour
Arab Street
Chinatown, Little India

Shopping
Orchard Road

ALTHOUGH THE popular image is of a modern, soulless, business city, best known for its shopping, Singapore provides an ideal, easily digestible 'taster' of the cultures and food of South East Asia. Vast shopping malls aside, there are plenty of other reasons to visit the main island of Singapore and perhaps one or two of the 60 smaller islands within its territorial waters.

For those who do come to exercise their credit cards, shops are generally open 10–12 hours a day, seven days a week. In Singapore's air-conditioned malls (mostly located on Orchard Road) many shops have fixed prices, but haggling is sometimes accepted most readily in districts such as Chinatown.

BEST SIGHTS

Arab Street
The Muslim centre of Singapore is the place to go shopping for batik and sarongs, leatherware and rattanwork, and visit the gold-domed Sultan Mosque.

Chinatown

Over the past few years many of the old colonial shopfronts and alleyways have been restored and gentrified, and smart shops and restaurants have appeared, but you can still get a glimpse of the old ways in the temples and markets as you hunt down some traditional Chinese arts and crafts.

Gardens and zoo

Singapore's climate and fertile land provide ample opportunity for enjoying green spaces. The Mandai Orchid Gardens and the Singapore Botanic Gardens are both excellent places in which to see the orchids for which Singapore is so renowned. The zoo tries to reproduce natural conditions for as many captive species as possible, and the award-winning Night Safari provides a tour in microcosm of the world's jungles, plains and savannahs.

Little India

Singapore has a vibrant Indian community. In the area of Little India, around Serangoon Road, you can savour the heady aromas of the spice shops, hear Indian music and eat an Indian meal, served on a banana leaf, with your fingers. A 'psychic' parrot will tell your fortune.

Raffles Hotel

Although expensive to stay at, Raffles is still worth a visit, if only for a Singapore Sling in the Long Bar and to imagine life in the colonial days of old. The hotel now sets its sights firmly on the tourist market – both those who stay there and those wishful thinkers who just want to look around and perhaps buy something from the rank of souvenir shops within the hotel grounds. A small museum provides a fascinating insight into celebrity guests, including Charlie Chaplin, Elizabeth Taylor and Noel Coward.

Sentosa Island

This huge family-fun park (crowded with local people at weekends) has something for everyone: a very impressive aquarium (including a 'touch pool' for braver souls), Fantasy Island – a large water theme park – several good museums, a man-made beach, and even a musical fountain which plays music and flashes its coloured lights at night as jets of water shoot skywards. Take the cable car for a bird's-eye view of Singapore.

WHEN TO GO

LOCATED CLOSE to the equator, Singapore is hot and humid all year round and at its wettest from November to January (although the difference between this season and other months of the year is not so dramatic that you should completely rule this period out). Its mix of cultures means that Singapore has a particularly good range of colourful Chinese, Muslim and Hindu events and festivals.

Average daily maximum temperature °C												
London	6	7	10	13	17	20	22	21	19	14	10	7
Singapore	30	31	31	31	32	31	31	31	31	31	31	31
	JAN	FEB	MAR	APR	MAY	JUN	JUL	AUG	SEP	OCT	NOV	DEC
Singapore	17	11	14	15	15	13	13	14	14	16	18	19
London	15	13	11	12	12	11	12	11	13	13	15	15
Average number of rainy days per month												

PACKAGE TRAVEL

CITY BREAKS in Singapore are on offer, but the destination is used more often as a starting point for a tour of the Far East. Brochures offer a choice of hotels and pre-purchased excursions. Multi-centre holidays with any combination of other Far East destinations such as Bangkok, Bali, Indonesia and Hong Kong can be arranged.

The train journey on the Eastern and Oriental Express between Singapore and Bangkok is also offered by several tour operators; various cruises start from Singapore.

Tour operators

General: Bales Tours, British Airways Holidays, Distant Dreams, Far East Gateways, Gold Medal, Hayes & Jarvis, Jetabout, Kuoni, Magic of the Orient, Pearl of the Orient, Premier Holidays, Qantas Holidays, Sunset Faraway, Tradewinds, Travelbag, Tropical Places, World Dreams

---

INDEPENDENT TRAVEL

FREQUENT DIRECT flights go to Singapore, but it is also an ideal stop-over point on a long-haul flight to Australia or New Zealand. Changi International Airport is so well equipped that it is almost worth stopping there just to experience the fitness centre, business centre, free film shows and shops and restaurants.

Getting around in Singapore is not a problem as both the bus service and MRT (underground train) services are frequent, reliable and extensive. Taxis are metered – and clean, as drivers can be fined for driving a dirty cab. Trishaws are now used mainly as a tourist attraction; if you want to experience a ride, make sure you agree the fare beforehand.

The main tourist enclave of smart hotels is around Orchard Road. It is best to book in advance and ask for a discount, as cheaper rates are not usually available to people who walk in off the street. The main budget accommodation area is in cheap Chinese hotels around Bencoolen Street and Beach Road. Rooms may be small, and usually have a fan, with shared toilet and shower.

RED TAPE, HEALTH AND SAFETY

BRITISH PASSPORT-HOLDERS do not require a visa; a 14-day stay permit is usually issued on arrival.

No vaccinations are required, and Singapore is not a malarial area. Most visitors to the country comment on how very clean it is, which is perhaps not surprising when you consider that there are hefty fines if you get caught littering the streets (fines are also levied on those caught eating, drinking or smoking on MRT trains or even not flushing the public toilet). Tap water is safe to drink, and food from hawkers' stalls is generally fine. Dehydration is the main problem, due to the heat and humidity – make sure that you drink plenty of fluids.

The crime rate is low as a result of the harsh punishments meted out to offenders.

MORE INFORMATION Singapore Tourism Board, Carrington House, 126–130 Regent Street, London W1R 5FE, tel 020-7437 0033, web site: *www.travel.com.sg/sog*

COST OF LIVING £–££

SOUTH AFRICA

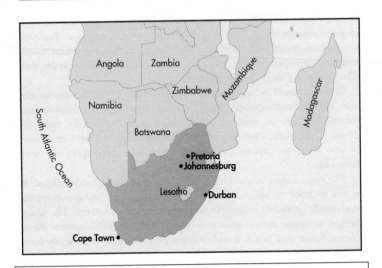

HIGHLIGHTS

Beaches
Durban,
Western Cape

Outdoor
activities
Western Cape

History
Johannesburg,
Pretoria

Family
holidays
Western Cape

Food/wine
Western Cape

Wildlife
Durban,
Kruger
National Park,
Western Cape

Culture
Cape Town,
Durban,
Johannesburg,
Western Cape

Scenic
landscape
Cape Town,
Garden Route,
Western Cape

Nightlife
Cape Town

Shopping
Cape Town,
Johannesburg,
Western Cape

CAPE TOWN
Good for culture, nightlife, shopping and scenic landscape

SOUTH AFRICA'S oldest city nestles in a bowl against the dramatic backdrop of majestic Table Mountain. One of the finest views of the city is from the sea, so be sure to take a boat trip around Table Bay. Inequality of wealth and strong racial tensions still pervade, but sightseeing is generally hassle-free provided you avoid the established no-go areas such as the Muslim Quarter, which should be visited only as part of a guided tour.

BEST SIGHTS

Castle of Good Hope
South Africa's oldest occupied building, completed in 1676, today houses a small museum of period furniture and paintings. There are also guided tours around the preserved dungeon cells.

Public Gardens
The gardens offer some respite from the throb of traffic, together with an opportunity to view some of Cape Town's finest historic buildings, including the handsome Houses of Parliament (tours available), the National Gallery, with its notable collection of modern South African works, and the South African Museum.

Robben Island
Regular day tours leave Cape Town's waterfront for this barren island and former prison, where Nelson Mandela and a host of other African political figures were incarcerated during the apartheid era.

Table Mountain
No visit to Cape Town is complete without a trip to the top of its most famous landmark. Most visitors take the five-minute cable-car ride to the top – to avoid queuing, book in advance through the information office in Adderley Street or in the Victoria & Alfred Waterfront Visitor Centre. You can also reach the summit on foot by taking one of the many way-marked paths, with differing levels of difficulty; some are suitable only for highly experienced hikers.

Victoria and Alfred Waterfront
Cape Town has an excellent collection of bars and restaurants, but many of those in the city centre can be rather gritty, if not a little sleazy. The redevelopment of the V&A Waterfront has established a lively collection of restaurants, bistros and bars alongside the busy harbour front.

WESTERN CAPE
Good for beaches, family holidays, flora, food/wine, outdoor activities, shopping, scenic landscape and wildlife

THE WESTERN Cape has a character distinct from anywhere else in Africa, determined by its Mediterranean-type climate, unique vegetation (it is regarded to be a distinct floral kingdom, one of only five in the world), magnificently rugged hills, valleys swathed in vineyards, and host of beach resorts.

BEST VINEYARDS

Stellenbosch

The heart of South Africa's wine industry is about an hour's drive from Cape Town, concentrated around the towns of Stellenbosch, Paarl and Franschhoek. Of these, the most historic is Stellenbosch, established towards the end of the seventeenth century in the Eerste River valley. The university town has a striking collection of buildings in Cape Dutch style: of particular note are those found in the village museum, a collection of restored historic houses furnished in period style, including Schreuder House, dating from 1709, and believed to be South Africa's oldest surviving town-house.

Wine enthusiasts will find no shortage of vineyards and estates radiating from the town centre, linked by well-signed touring routes. Perhaps the pick of the crop are Rust-en-Vrede, a small and rather private estate with a chocolate-box setting and superb red wines, and Delheim, an altogether more touristy experience, with informative and amusing guided tours.

BEST SCENIC LANDSCAPE

Cape Peninsula

The Cape Peninsula's dramatic coastline, long white sandy beaches and imposing mountains provide some of the region's most striking scenery. Keen walkers can attempt the ascent of Chapman's Peak (exertion moderate) for fine views of the peninsula, or the network of trails that criss-crosses the extensive Cape of Good Hope Nature Reserve.

Most visitors to the Nature Reserve make straight for Cape Point. A steep headland rears above the huge car park, with a trail leading up to the promontory. On the way, the road passes through the unique heath-like *fynbos* habitat, studded with wild proteas and home to a number of large mammals and birds endemic to the Western Cape. A greater number of plant species occur naturally in this tiny reserve than in the whole of the British Isles.

There is no commercial hullabaloo at the Cape of Good Hope proper – just a rocky coastline and white sand beach buffeted by spume-spraying breakers, plus another walk to the top of the headland.

BEST BEACHES

The Western Cape's long sandy beaches provide the perfect setting for exhilarating walks, but not all are suitable for bathers and sun-worshippers, particularly those on the exposed Atlantic coast, which are prone to strong, sand-lifting winds. The western waters are also significantly colder than those on the eastern coast.

Bloubergstrand
● Long sandy beach with terrific views across Table Bay towards Cape Town and across to Robben Island.

Boulders
● Lovely beach set in sheltered cove, good for families.
● Home to hundreds of jackass penguins.
● On the Western Cape's exposed Atlantic coast, so can be chilly and windswept.
● Popular for windsurfing and boardsailing.

Camps Bay
● Good for young trendies: distinctly Californian feel with volleyball on the beach, beauty competitions etc.
● A lovely long beach, backed by a palm-lined promenade and the coast road.
● Extremely exposed to the elements. Water is cold and invigorating.
● Excellent cafés and restaurants.

Clifton
● Popular with young trendies, hence crowded at weekends and in high season – limited parking.
● Four fantastic beaches sheltered from the winds.
● Superb views of the Twelve Apostles, an extension of the Table Mountain range.

Fish Hoek
● Good for families.
● Low-key town with wide sandy beach and a pleasant promenade right on the sea.
● East coast location brings warmer waters and less exposure to wind.
● Attracts an older crowd.

Hout Bay
● Good for families, with wide sandy beach backed by low-rise buildings and many good eateries.
● Characterful fishing town with a working harbour.
● In a stunning setting perched between the Sentinel and Chapman's Peak.

Llandudno
● Good for surfers.
● Picturesque village set into cliff, with wide sandy bay, weathered boulders to clamber over and rock pools to explore.
● Limited parking and facilities.

Noordhoek
● Beautiful long sandy beach beneath Chapman's Peak – useful for walkers.
● Cold water and very exposed.
● Popular with horse-riders and dog-walkers.

Sea Point
● Lively resort with English feel, close to Cape Town, popular with younger set and gay crowd.
● Long but rather scrappy beach backed by major road.

THE GARDEN ROUTE
Good for scenic landscape

SOUTH AFRICA'S most scenic coastal terrace stretches from Mossel Bay in the west to the Tsitsikamma area in the east. The attractive shoreline borders the Indian Ocean, and bays and high cliffs give way to a striking hinterland of imposing mountains, spectacular passes and waterfalls.

BEST BASES

Kynsna
As well as a scenic lagoon and lush, indigenous forest, there is a little museum complex and an eclectic range of arty-crafty shops.

Victoria Bay
Relaxing, laid-back resort with a lovely little cove beach flanked by rocky foreshore and rows of Edwardian houses with verandas.

BEST SIGHTS AND EXCURSIONS

Addo Elephant National Park
This recently extended national park, a short distance from the city of Port Elizabeth, is the most southerly major game reserve in Africa. Best known for its population of about 300 elephant – the rangers at the gate will tell you where the latest sightings have been – the park also harbours buffalo, black rhino, vervet monkeys and a variety of antelope.

Mossel Bay

As well as a fine, crab-strewn beach, the resort has an interesting cluster of museums, a homage to its role as a water station for the fifteenth-century Portuguese navigator Bartholomew Dias.

Nature's Valley

A gorgeous blend of ocean, lagoon and milkwood brush, with serene reflections of the wooded mountains in the Groot River, and birds of prey that swoop low over the Bloukrans Pass.

Oudtshoorn

An excellent set of amusements for children includes ostrich farms where you can ride one of the birds, the Cango Caves with their stalactites and stalagmites, and the Cango Crocodile Ranch.

JOHANNESBURG
Good for culture, history and shopping

SOUTH AFRICA'S largest city appears to have little to recommend it to holidaymakers: seldom attractive, notoriously crime-ridden, this congested urban sprawl – known to the Zulus as Egoli, or 'City of Gold' – has lost its glitter in recent years. As a result, perhaps the majority of Johannesburg's visitors prefer to head for established tourist centres such as the Sun City complex, the national parks or Cape Town.

Certainly, little remains of pioneer Johannesburg, and monuments to the heady gold-digging days have been swallowed up by tower blocks. Crime figures, too, are for once not exaggerated and it pays to be cautious when sightseeing; take guided tours where possible. However, Johannesburg is also a cultural melting-pot, where the Rainbow Nation's many influences converge (not always harmoniously) to create a vibrancy and character less evident in other South African cities. The city boasts museums, galleries, renowned theatrical performances and excellent shopping – all of which are worth a day or two of your time.

Be sure to see the city centre's impressive skyscrapers before heading to Gold Reef City for a reconstruction of Johannesburg's gold-digging days. Touristy it may be, but it is worth bumping around in a horse-drawn carriage and descending an old mineshaft for a glimpse of the workings of South Africa's most lucrative industry. For a more emotive experience, a tour of Soweto, to the south-west of the city, reveals some of the harshness and inequalities of the nation's more recent history and highlights many of the problems faced by the 'New South Africa' in the aftermath of the apartheid era.

PRETORIA
Good for history

JUST 35 miles north of Johannesburg, Pretoria has an altogether different character. Famed for its beautiful jacaranda trees (a riot of colour in spring), charming parkland areas and cluster of handsome and historic buildings, South Africa's administrative centre is instantly more appealing and visitor-friendly than its near neighbour. Be sure to take in the striking Union Buildings, built in 1913 and designed in neoclassical style by the British architect Herbert Baker. And for lovers of more recent man-made attractions, Pretoria is within striking distance of Sun City, a purpose-built holiday resort, offering a wealth of luxurious hotels, casinos and leisure activities, guaranteed to keep even the most active visitor amused.

KRUGER NATIONAL PARK
Good for wildlife

NO VISIT to South Africa would be complete without seeing some of its striking wildlife. Whatever your base, you are likely to be within driving distance of a conservation area (for example, Pilanesberg near Sun City is a small but fascinating game reserve), but for the ultimate wildlife experience, head for the Kruger National Park, as one of the neighbouring private reserves, in Mpumalanga. Named after Paul Kruger, president of the first Republic of South Africa, this vast reserve covers almost 8,000 square miles and is well-stocked with game, including the all-important 'big five' of elephant, buffalo, rhino, lion and leopard, alongside zebra, giraffe, hippo and wild dog. Accommodation in park lodges is inexpensive and comfortable, but book in advance, as Kruger is one of South Africa's premier tourist spots and always busy.

Sharing an unfenced boundary with the Kruger Park, a cluster of private reserves protects a similar selection of big game, but offers an altogether more exclusive experience. Game drives in open four-wheel-drive vehicles are led by highly knowledgeable rangers, and close encounters with big cats and nocturnal predators are virtually guaranteed. The largest of the private reserves is Sabi Sands, which consists of a number of different properties – including the legendary Mala-Mala, Sabi-Sabi and Londolozi Lodges – managed as one ecological unit.

DURBAN
Good for culture, wildlife and beaches

THE LARGEST port on the east coast of Africa, Durban is also a lively resort town, its popular sandy beach lined with hotels, restaurants, museums, aquariums and – somewhat bizarrely – rickshaws. Linguistically, Durban is the most English of South African cities, while its cultural character, determined by the predominantly Zulu populace, is spiced up by a large and influential Asian community. The bustling and aromatic Indian Market is well worth visiting, provided that you leave your valuables in your hotel. In common with other South African cities, crime is a genuine cause for concern in Durban itself, but nearby resorts such as Umhlanga Rocks and Amanzimtoti are safe enough.

BEST EXCURSIONS

The Drakensberg
Three hours inland of Durban, the Drakensberg (Dragon's Mountains) is particularly popular with hikers and ramblers. A series of reserves protects this extensive range: the Royal Natal Park is the most impressive scenically, while Giant's Castle Game Reserve has abundant game and some excellent rock art.

Zulu Cultural Lodges
Centred around Eshowe, two to three hours' drive north of Durban, these lodges offer lively and informative introductions to the vibrant complexities of Zulu culture. The most famous and busiest is Shakaland, originally the set for the television series *Shaka Zulu*. A recommended alternative, more low-key and intimate, is Simunye Cultural Lodge. Set in a beautiful wooded gorge, it is reached from the main road by ox-wagon.

Zululand Reserves
The cluster of game reserves in the north of KwaZulu-Natal province are referred to collectively as the Zululand reserves. Hluhluwe-Umfolozi offers the best all-round self-drive safaris (all the 'big five' and the world's largest concentrations of both black and white rhino), while Mkuzi is more untrammelled and scenic. Ndumo has arguably the finest birding in the country, and the private Phinda Resource Reserve ranks with Africa's classiest luxury game lodges. St Lucia Estuary, recently proclaimed a UNESCO World Heritage Site, is a must for anglers and birdwatchers, and offers some excellent walking trails

among non-dangerous game. Sordwana Bay is the best diving and snorkelling site in South Africa.

WHEN TO GO

THE WESTERN Cape has a Mediterranean-type climate with long, hot summer days and wet, cool winters. Even in summer the region is prone to strong gale-force winds that can last for several days. The best times to visit are undoubtedly in spring (September/October) and autumn (March/April), when you can count on pleasantly warm temperatures with perhaps a few rainy days.

Average daily maximum temperature °C											
London	6	7	10	13	17	20	22	21	19	14	10	7
Johannesburg	25	25	24	21	19	16	17	19	23	24	24	25
	JAN	FEB	MAR	APR	MAY	JUN	JUL	AUG	SEP	OCT	NOV	DEC
Johannesburg	15	11	10	10	5	2	1	2	3	10	15	15
London	15	13	11	12	12	11	12	11	13	13	15	15
Average number of rainy days per month											

Average daily maximum temperature °C											
London	6	7	10	13	17	20	22	21	19	14	10	7
Cape Town	26	26	25	23	20	18	17	18	19	21	24	25
	JAN	FEB	MAR	APR	MAY	JUN	JUL	AUG	SEP	OCT	NOV	DEC
Cape Town	5	5	5	9	13	12	12	13	10	9	5	5
London	15	13	11	12	12	11	12	11	13	13	15	15
Average number of rainy days per month											

PACKAGE TRAVEL

INCREASING NUMBERS of tour operators list South Africa in their brochures, offering a variety of accommodation and tours and a good deal of flexibility. Several tailor-made tour operators specialise in Africa and organise tours and safaris (see below), such as deluxe train journeys, tours of the Garden Route and the winelands, city breaks in Johannesburg and Cape Town, game reserves, safaris and escorted tours. Accommodation standards are high, ranging from upmarket excellentvalue B&Bs and luxurious country houses to plush tented camps and lodges in the private reserves adjacent to the Kruger National Park.

Activity holidays include battlefield tours, wildlife tours, wine or rail tours, birdwatching and safaris.

Tour operators

Adventure: Acacia, Kumuka Expeditions **Battlefields**: Holts' Tours, Midas **Birdwatching**: Ornitholidays, Sunbird **General and specialist**: Abercrombie & Kent, Bluebird, British Airways Holidays, Carrier, Definitive Africa, Elite Vacations, SAR Travel, Somak, South African Affair, South African Airways, Thomas Cook, Tradewinds **Tailor-made specialists**: Africa Exclusive, Cazenove & Loyd Safaris, Okavango Tours & Safaris, Safari Consultants, Tailor-Made, Wild Africa Safaris **Wildlife**: Discover the World, Naturetrek, Wildlife Worldwide **Other activities**: Ace Study Tours, Andante (archaeology), Arblaster & Clarke (wine), Cox & Kings (flora), Dive Worldwide, Regal (scuba), Exodus (walking), Explore Worldwide (walking), Solo's Holidays (singles), Winetrails (wine)

INDEPENDENT TRAVEL

SCHEDULED AND charter flights connect London to Johannesburg and Cape Town. Internal flights are the best way to cover long distances, but can be expensive – it is worth checking in advance about any special packages offered by SAA (South African Airways) to foreign visitors, regardless of whether they are flying to the country with another airline. Otherwise, the best way to get around is by car (most major international rental companies are represented). Driving is on the left.

Train and/or coach services connect all major centres, but their schedules are somewhat restrictive. A more flexible option is the Baz Bus: a hop-on, hop-off door-to-door coach service which links the better backpacker hostels in all major centres (and most minor ones). Backpacker hostels are the best places to arrange camping safaris, affordable day excursions, and cheap car rental.

Public transport within most cities cannot be recommended as safe, although the Cape Peninsula has a good network of local trains with links to Stellenbosch. The Outeniqua Choo-tjoe is a narrow-gauge steam train that links George with the popular resort of Knysna, running through woodland, along the coast, and across the Kaaimans River Bridge.

Accommodation is excellent and generally inexpensive by international standards. Bland chain hotels are supplemented by a range of cheaper and characterful B&Bs. A network of backpacker hostels, spread across South Africa's main tourist centres, offers private rooms as well as dormitories and camping space. Availability should not be a problem in spring and autumn, but as South Africa is increasing in popularity it may be advisable to book at least a few days ahead.

RED TAPE, HEALTH AND SAFETY

VISAS ARE not required for British passport-holders. No immunisations are required. Malaria is absent from most of the country – exceptions being the Kruger Park area and the coastal belt north of Durban, where precautions should be taken, particularly during the wet summer months.

Leaflets giving advice on safety and security are displayed in the airport and the Waterfront Visitor Centre in Cape Town. The level of violent crime is increasing, particularly in Johannesburg but also in other major cities. Avoid isolated areas, and do not carry expensive jewellery or lots of cash. The Foreign Office Travel Advice Unit advises avoiding townships and surrounding areas. For the latest information contact the Foreign Office Travel Advice Unit (see page 11).

MORE INFORMATION South African Tourism Board, 5 Alt Grove, London SW19 4DZ, tel 020-8944 8080, brochure line (09063) 640600 (premium rate number), web site: *www.satour.co.uk*

COST OF LIVING £

SPAIN

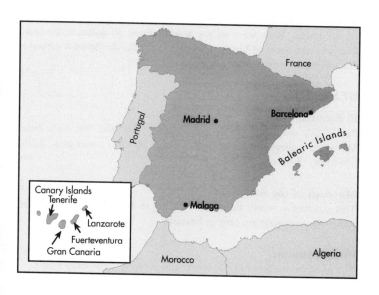

HIGHLIGHTS

Beaches
*Andalucía,
Balearics,
Canaries,
Catalonia,
northern Spain*

**Family
holidays**
*Andalucía,
Balearics,
Canaries*

**Flora/
wildlife**
Andalucía

Food/wine
*Barcelona,
Catalonia,
Levante,
northern Spain*

Local colour
*Andalucía,
Aragón,
Extremadura,
northern Spain*

Nightlife
*Andalucía,
Balearics,
Barcelona,
Canaries,*

*Catalonia,
Madrid*

**Outdoor
activities**
*Andalucía,
Catalonia*

Culture
*Andalucía,
Aragón,
Barcelona,
Bilbao,
Castile,
Catalonia,
Madrid*

**Romantic
escapism**
*Andalucía,
Extremadura*

**Scenic
landscape**
*Aragón,
Canaries,
Catalonia,
Extremadura,
northern Spain*

Shopping
Barcelona

MADRID
Good for culture and nightlife

WHAT MADRID lacks in physical beauty it more than makes up for on the inside. With three of the world's finest art galleries, first-rate shopping and some of Europe's liveliest nightlife, the Spanish capital is one of Europe's more engaging cities

BEST SIGHTS

El Escorial
Phillip II's sixteenth-century palace, about an hour by train from Madrid, is a megalomaniacal sort of place: 16 inner courtyards, 2,500 windows, 15 miles of passageways.

Museum of the Americas
This museum is worth the metro ride out to Moncloa, even if all the audio-visual displays are only in Spanish.

Prado Museum
The museum has about 9,000 works and room to show only 1,500.

Reina Sofía Museum
This superb collection of twentieth-century art includes Picasso's masterpiece *Guernica*.

Thyssen–Bornemisza Museum
One of the most famous private art collections in the world.

CASTILE
Good for culture

VISITORS KEEN on Spanish art, architecture and history will enjoy exploring the great central tableland around Madrid known as Old and New Castile (Castilla-y-León and Castilla-La Mancha). Despite the capital's radiating influence, Castile still has a rural, provincial air. The continental climate in this high plateau is extreme; choose spring or autumn for comfortable travelling.

BEST CITIES

Burgos
The spires of an outstanding Gothic cathedral dominate this provincial

capital, where El Cid's ghost hovers. Just outside its well-preserved old quarter lie three exceptional monasteries.

León
The oldest glasswork of León's splendid cathedral is 700 years old, but its famous pilgrim *parador*, the Hostal de San Marcos, and the twelfth-century frescos are equally memorable.

Salamanca
Spain's most famous university city offers a showcase of Renaissance architecture, and a magnificent Plaza Mayor.

Segovia
This delightful town's prize monument is its Roman aqueduct. Also visit the fairy-tale folly castle and a cluster of Romanesque churches.

Toledo
Toledo is one of Spain's greatest tourist attractions. The old town, dramatically poised above the Tagus gorge, is stacked with art and architecture from many periods.

Valladolid
Valladolid's main attraction for visitors is its architecture. The Collegio de San Gregorio houses a stunning collection of sculpture by many of Spain's best Renaissance artists.

ARAGON
Good for local colour and scenic landscape

THE VARIETY of scenery in this little-known and depopulated region is astonishing. Best are the high peaks of the Pyrenees, spectacularly encapsulated in the Ordesa National Park. Aragón's largest cities, though not beautiful, contain a remarkable heritage of Moorish monuments. In unspoilt rural areas it is still possible to see ancient ways of life, including some of Spain's strangest *fiestas*.

BEST SIGHTS

Ordesa and Monte Perdito National Park
This is one of Spain's oldest national parks. Snow makes the park accessible only in summer without specialist climbing gear, and most of it can be visited only on foot.

Teruel
Teruel offers a striking assembly of Mudejar towers in ornate brickwork and one of Aragón's best provincial museums. The cathedral displays dazzling craftsmanship.

Zaragoza
Zaragoza fared badly in both the Peninsular and the Civil Wars, and today forms a dusty sprawl of brick along the Ebro. The most impressive buildings are the multi-domed basilica of Nuestra Señora del Pilar, and the Catedral de la Seo.

ANDALUCIA
Good for beaches, culture, family holidays, flora, local colour, nightlife, outdoor activities, romantic escapism and wildlife

---

FLAMENCO DANCERS, acoustic guitars and matadors originate from here. Andalucía also offers excellent-value sun-and-sand packages for all ages.

BEST CITIES

Cadiz
Europe's oldest city is strangely untrammelled by the tourist hordes. With good beaches, numerous tapas bars, an intoxicating history and that famous *gaditano* – love of partying – Cadiz is one of Europe's undiscovered cities.

Córdoba
Córdoba is the smallest of Andalucía's three great cities but perhaps the most enjoyable to explore. The compact old town is packed with tiny alleyways of whitewashed houses. The Jewish quarter is home to a delicately ornamented synagogue, one of only three remaining in Spain.

Unmissable is the Mezquita, the greatest mosque in the Western world. The Alcázar de los Reyes Cristianos, once the residence of Fernando and Isabella, the city's Christian 'liberators', has Roman mosaics and beautifully kept geometrical gardens. Visit the Torre de la Calahorra for its panorama of the Roman bridge, water wheel and old town.

Granada
The 'modern' city is pleasant enough, but most visitors come to see the world-famous Alhambra palace, the most perfect example of

Moorish architecture in Europe. Highlights are the Patio of the Lions and the luxuriant gardens, which provide a grand approach to the Generalife, the rulers' summer palace. Opposite the Alhambra hill, the Moorish quarter (Albaicín), affords fine views.

The stark Renaissance cathedral is disappointingly conventional, but the adjacent Gothic Capilla Real (Royal Chapel) – mausoleum of Fernando and Isabella – is more flamboyant. On the outskirts of town, La Cartuja is an outrageously lavish Carthusian monastery.

Seville

Andalucia's capital is an exotic cocktail of Moorish and Spanish influences, with a string of historic attractions that complement the modern developments that sprouted up for World Expo 1992. The most beautiful part of the enormous Gothic cathedral is the Giralda, a gloriously golden twelfth-century minaret, with a magnificent panorama from the summit.

The Alcázar is a tranquil (though often tourist-thronged) royal palace. Visit the Museum of Fine Art in the delightfully restored Convento de la Merced. Highlights of the María Luisa Park are the Plaza de España, the Popular Arts Museum and the Archaeological Museum. The quintessential Sevillana experience is to spend a night exploring the numerous tapas bars in the city that many Spaniards rate as the 'Tapas Capital of Spain'.

One of Europe's most important wildlife habitats is Doñana National Park; it is best visited in the wet winter and spring months.

BEST RESORTS

Each of Andalucía's four *costas* has a distinctive character. If you choose your resort and accommodation carefully you will find the ambience of the Costa del Sol more cosmopolitan than you might expect, restaurants and bars for all tastes, and prices kept low by fierce competition. East of the Costa del Sol (Costa Tropical and Costa de Almeria) beaches are wider and less crowded, although the sand is coarse and grey. The best beaches of all are on Andalucía's Atlantic Coast, the Costa de la Luz, though strong winds often gust in from the ocean.

Conil de la Frontera (Costa de la Luz)

● Vast, desert-like beach, more sheltered than others, stretching for four miles to Cape Trafalgar, and backed by a few largish hotels.
● Smaller pensions, low-key bars and craft shops in village centre, and excellent fish restaurants along seafront.
● Popular with Spaniards and Germans.

Mojacar (Costa de Almeria)
● Arty Moorish village of white sugar-cube houses and steep, narrow streets, set amid rugged hills three miles above greyish beach, backed by low-rise apartment and hotel buildings.
● Plenty of trendy bars in old town; more traditional resort-style family fun down below along seafront – and several loud open-air discos.
● Feels rather isolated: a long way from Andalucía's top sights.

Nerja (Costa del Sol)
● Prettiest of Costa del Sol resorts, ringed by mountains.
● Whitewashed houses clustered round aprons of sand, with palm-fringed promenade jutting into sea.
● Generally low-rise development.
● Very good children's facilities and low-key nightlife.
● Good walks in and around the town.

Torremolinos (Costa del Sol)
● Brash and irredeemably ugly, with densely packed tower blocks, but constantly lively and certainly never dull. Adjacent Benalmadena Costa has a lively and glitzy marina.
● Wide range of restaurants to suit all tastes and budgets, golf courses nearby, good water sports, Aquapark and Tivoli World, a child-centred amusement park for family fun.

BEST SIGHTS AND EXCURSIONS

Almerian desert
Go to one of the daily shows at one of three movie sets in this rugged desert landscape; hundreds of films were shot here, including *The Good, the Bad and the Ugly*. From the appealing small town of Sorbas the local tourist office arranges caving excursions into contorted volcanic caverns. Nearby Nijar is also worth visiting for its distinctive ceramics.

Las Alpujarras
A chain of white mountain villages spread out between the sea and the Sierra Nevada. In many, donkeys file through narrow streets, and labourers tend fertile orchards of vines, oranges, bananas and olives. The most developed villages are Capileira, Bubión and Pampaneira. Trevélez, the highest village in Spain, also makes a good base. Throughout the region, there are good walks along (mostly) well-maintained paths, plus opportunities for horse-riding and cycling.

Carmona
Half an hour's drive from Seville, this walled, hilltop town is visible for miles. The historic quarter is small but well-preserved.

Jaén and Renaissance towns

The provincial capital of Jaén is dull, but the surrounding landscape is dramatic; a staggeringly beautiful sierra of jagged rocks in shades of blood-red and vermilion. Cazorla is the main town: an animated place with a superbly located *parador* set 15 miles from town within the Nature Park. Further north, Ubeda and Baeza have ornate palaces and churches sculpted in golden stone.

Jerez de la Frontera

The main reason for visiting is a trip to a sherry *bodega*, best arranged through the tourist office. You might also enjoy the Royal Andalucían School of Equestrian Art. The town has a bizarre hybrid Gothic-Renaissance cathedral and a Moorish alcázar.

Ronda and the Pueblos Blancos ('white towns')

A few miles inland, against a backdrop of pine-clad mountains, olive groves and rocky crags, the *pueblos blancos* make a pleasant break from the seaside crowds. Ronda, in a wonderful location atop a deep chasm, is the biggest and most visited, with attractive seventeenth-century mansions, a new museum and one of Spain's most famous bull rings. Vejer de la Frontera is one of the most unspoilt; Arcos de la Frontera is more developed but has a fine church and *parador*. Others worth seeking out include El Bosque, Grazalema, Zahara de la Sierra, Setenil, Ojén, Casares, Coín and Mijas; the latter two are distinctly on the tourist trail but none the less pretty.

BARCELONA
Good for culture, food/wine, nightlife and shopping

BARCELONA'S WATERFRONT was given a major facelift in honour of the 1992 Olympics. The old medieval alleyways cluster round the immense Gothic cathedral, through the regular grid pattern of wide streets, known as the Eixample, to the leafier suburbs. Elegant turn-of-the-century cafés, lively *cava* bars, and waterfront tapas bars provide endless opportunities for sampling local food and drink.

BEST SIGHTS

Aquarium
Newest of the top sights on the restored waterfront. State-of-the-art displays, and moving walkways to view the streamlined sharks.

Marès Museum
Wonderfully eclectic display of medieval sculpture.

Miró Foundation
Bright and attractive with changing exhibitions of varied media.

Modernist architecture
The rich concentration of Modernist buildings on plush Eixample boulevard includes Gaudí's La Pedrera (which can be visited) and Casa Batlló. His unfinished church, La Sagrada Familia, is well worth visiting. Take the lift up one of the spires to appreciate it better.

National Museum of Catalán Art
Collection of Romanesque art in the National Palace on Montjuïc.

Nou Camp
Home to one of the world's greatest football teams. The impressive 120,000-capacity Barcelona C stadium has a museum as well as offering guided tours. Taking in one of the home games, especially against arch-rival Real Madrid, gives a more evocative insight into Catalan nationalism than any museum.

Picasso Museum
This museum, dedicated to arguably the city's finest son, showcases much of his best work.

The Ramblas
Irresistible ribbon of flower and bird stalls, plus lively street theatre.

CATALONIA
Good for beaches, culture, food/wine, nightlife, outdoor activities and scenic landscape

THIS SMALL triangle of land bound by the Pyrenees to the north, the Mediterranean to the east, and Aragón and Valencia to the west, may be on the Iberian fringe geographically and culturally (Catalán is the strongest of Spain's regional languages), but has made a central contribution to Spain's economic miracle.

BEST CITY

Tarragona
Though the modern city is provincial and dull compared with Barcelona, Tarragona's history dates from the sixth century BC. Visit the Archaeological Museum, the cliff-top amphitheatre, stumpy remnants of the Roman forum, the paleo-Christian necropolis further west, and the Tarragona History Museum. The cathedral is the largest in Catalonia, and the old quarter is also worth exploring.

BEST RESORTS

North of Barcelona, the Costa Brava, or more specifically the unattractive and overdeveloped resort of Lloret del Mar, is considered the birthplace of package tourism, but away from the main resorts the coast remains wild and rugged, with fine golden sand and sparklingly clear water. To the south, the Costa Dorada is less scenic but is a good base for visiting Port Aventura, Spain's answer to Disneyland.

Aiguablava (Costa Brava)
● Good for secluded villas. There are just two hotels.
● Series of tiny inlets with golden sand and turquoise water, backed by thick pine groves and craggy cliffs.
● More life and facilities at nearby Tamariu (a larger but unspoilt resort).

Cadaqués (Costa Brava)
● Cluster of whitewashed, cubic houses in secluded bay.
● Stamping ground for the avant-garde, thanks to nearby former residence of Salvador Dalí; galleries and artists' workshops abound.
● Laid-back ambience, with pavement cafés and rakish jazz clubs.
● Not for beach lovers – the strip of sand is narrow and grey.

Calella de Palafrugell/Llafranc (Costa Brava)
● Twin resorts linked by a coastal path; Llafranc is smaller but more conventionally resort-like; Calella is more of a fishing village, though larger.
● Scenic location backed by hills, and wide, sandy beaches.
● Plenty of seafront cafés and fish restaurants, particularly in Calella.

Cambrils (Costa Dorada)
● Best base for visiting Port Aventura, with good family facilities.
● Developed, with large package hotels, but retains fishing village feel.
● Huge saddle of fine sand backed by pleasant promenade lined with restaurants and pavement cafés.

Sitges (Costa Dorada)
● Mobbed by Barcelonan summer refugees, popular with the gay community, and never dull, with a plethora of bars, restaurants and discos.
● Sophisticated and stylish despite the development, with many fine buildings in narrow back streets.
● Long golden beach; young and lively in the centre; quieter and more family oriented on outskirts.

● Three excellent museums; the Romantic Museum, with collection of dolls and musical instruments, should not be missed.

Tossa de Mar (Costa Brava)
● Developed but mostly low-rise resort, backed by mountains.
● Two decent beaches of slightly gritty sand, with pleasant promenades.
● Walled twelfth-century old town on crest of western headland.
● Range of bars and restaurants: both traditional Spanish and British.

BEST SIGHTS AND EXCURSIONS

Aigüestortes National Park
Visit this national park, with its forested tracks, rocky crags, valleys and streams. Follow the walk to the deep green waters of Sant Maurici lake.

Figueres
Visit the eclectic Salvador Dalí Theatre-Museum, every bit as surreal as any of his work and housing his tomb.

Girona
Girona's tall Gothic cathedral stands out atop the concentric rings of old houses and labyrinth of steep narrow streets which make up the Jewish quarter. The City Museum is worthwhile, and the Cinema Museum excellent, particularly for children. The Romanesque cloister and rich treasury are also worth a visit.

Montserrat
Riding high up rugged mountainside by cable car is part of the fun of the trip up to this atmospheric monastery. The monastery building at Montserrat is bland but its setting is spectacular. Visit the three museums or take the funicular to the mountain-top hermitages.

Port Aventura
Spain's answer to Disneyland mirrors its rival's layout of themed lands and combination of live shows and rides. Tame rides exist for small children.

Pyrenean foothills
A trail of outstanding Romanesque churches and exhibits include the Episcopal museum at Vic; the cloister and twelfth-century portal at Ripoll; a cathedral, cloister and museum at La Seu d'Urgell. Also explore the tiny Romanesque churches at Sant Joan de les Abadesses, Camprodon, Baguerge, Tredòs, Gessa and Salardù.

Santa Maria de Poblet

Santa Maria de Poblet is home to Catalonia's best-known Cistercian monastery. Highlights include the delicate cloister and the Royal Pantheon. Six miles south, at Montblanc, a museum traces the history of the monastery and local trade.

Vilafranca del Penedès and the wine region

For an introduction to Catalonia's best wines, visit the museum at Vilafranca. For wine-tasting, head out to Pacs del Penedès and the Torres *bodega*. Close by, Sant Sadurní d'Anoia is the *cava* capital.

EXTREMADURA
Good for local colour, romantic escapism and scenic landscape

EXTREMADURA IS one of Spain's poorest, least developed areas. Tourism is filtering into the area, particularly in the historic towns and cities, but elsewhere visitors will find little English spoken. The best scenery is in the north, but most of the interesting towns are in the south.

BEST SIGHTS

Cáceres

The modern development is unattractive, but the vast, arcaded plaza, palaces and churches propel you back in time. Three palaces, two churches and the remains of a Moorish bath are worth a visit.

Guadalupe

The winding mountain road makes a visit to the wonderful monastery at Guadalupe feel like a pilgrimage.

Mérida

Although the modern city is disappointing, Mérida was once the cultural centre of Roman Spain. The ruins most worth seeing are close together, near the 60-arch bridge spanning the Guadiana.

Plasencia

Plasencia has quaint alleyways and a part Gothic, part Romanesque cathedral.

Trujillo

The main square is lined with extravagant palaces, but the Méson la Troya, a wonderfully eclectic and inexpensive restaurant is just as much of a crowd-puller.

Zafra and southern towns

Southern Extremaduran towns and villages have an Andalucían flavour, with whitewashed houses lining narrow streets. Zafra has a fine sixteenth-century church. The pinnacles and spires of Jerez de los Caballeros are visible for miles around.

BEST TOURING

Hervás and the Jerte valley

The Jerte valley is full of cherry orchards and olive groves, whilst Hervás, close by, has an unusually well-preserved Jewish quarter.

La Vera

Fruit trees, vines and olive groves abound in the land around the villages of La Vera. Garganta la Olla and Jarandilla de la Vera are the most picturesque places.

NORTHERN SPAIN
Good for beaches, food/wine, local colour and scenic landscape

THE WEATHER is less predictable than in the south but the beaches are not scarred by tower blocks, and the few 'developed' resorts retain a quirky individuality. Inland, the Picos de Europa mountain range offers excellent outdoor pursuits, and there are numerous churches, museums and villages to explore.

Throughout the Basque country and Navarra, you will hear the arcane Basque language (spoken by a minority) and follow Basque road signs. In rural Galicia, Gallego, similar to Portuguese, is the main tongue, and the culture has Celtic roots; bagpipes (*gaitas*) are as much a part of local celebrations here as in Scotland.

BEST RESORTS

Baiona

● Ranged round a gently curving bay within a small fjord.
● Gleaming cafés on the waterfront, traditional tapas bars in the old town, fancy *solanas* (enclosed balconies), and wrought iron balconies.
● Best resort in Galicia, popular with Spaniards; foreigners tend to stay at the secluded castle-*parador* on a pine-clad promontory.
● Best beaches just outside town, or a ferry ride to the Islas Cíes.

Comillas

● Former summer residence of Alfonso XII: an air of regal refinement lingers in faded mansions and cobbled streets of old town.

- Flamboyant folly designed by Gaudí – now an exclusive restaurant.
- Messy modern seaside resort, packed with Spaniards in summer.
- Lively, with plenty of eating possibilities, and fine, wide strip of sand.

Fuenterrabía (Hondarrabia)
- Fishing village with a large, creamy sand beach in sheltered bay.
- Walled medieval quarter on hilltop, with narrow, cobbled streets, and sixteenth-century castle (now a *parador*) with stunning sea views.
- Lively and distinctly French ambience.
- Excellent restaurants.

Laxe
- Traditional fishing village where you can still see people mending nets and bringing in the catch.
- Slowly growing as a resort, with paved promenade planted with baby palm trees, and long sheltered beach.
- Pleasant old town of stone and whitewashed houses.
- Limited accommodation.

Luarca
- Civilised and relaxed former fishing village; the harbour is overlooked by elegant houses and fishermen's cottages.
- Two beaches of hard-packed sand, backed by slate cliffs, and lined with old-fashioned changing cabins.
- Good selection of bars and fish restaurants round harbour.

Muros
- Most developed fishing village, with bars, disco and artificial beach.
- Smartly renovated main plaza overlooks the fjord; rustic back streets.
- Plenty of unpretentious fish restaurants.
- Best beach (Playa de San Francisco) is situated about three miles out of town.

San Sebastián (Donostia)
- Slightly faded but still chic.
- Beautiful scallop-shaped bay with two sandy beaches, closed in by wooded promontories and backed by frilly pavilions.
- Easy-going ambience ideal for both families and couples.
- Picturesque harbour, with arcaded fishermen's cottages, and many restaurants serving delicious local specialities.

Santander
- Vestiges of *belle époque* panache and exuberant, but fading, grand hotels.

● Fine golden beach.
● Colourful fish market, much-restored Gothic cathedral, and Museo de Bellas Artes.

San Vicente de la Barquera
● Costa Verde's most relaxed resort, popular with Spanish families.
● Pavement cafés and seafood restaurants in arcaded main street, pizzerias and lively bars by waterfront.
● Sleepy, walled old town with thirteenth-century church.
● Exposed but large sandy beach across estuary and arched bridge.

Viveiro
● Old town of narrow streets and flaking ochre plazas rises up on one side of the *ría*, around a splendid Gothic church.
● Best nearby beach, Playa de Area, across the *ría*, backed by grassy dunes and sheltered by two promontories.
● Plenty of bars, restaurants and cafés for all tastes.

BEST INLAND BASES

Leyre
Above the Yesa reservoir in the craggy Pyrenean foothills, is an eleventh-century monastery; part of it now houses a restaurant and hotel. Stay for compline, when the brothers sing Gregorian chant in candlelit, incense-laden gloom.

Olite and the Pilgrim route
A tourist honeypot, thanks to its Disneyesque castle, Olite is a good base for exploring the Pilgrim route. Nearby is a fine Cistercian church, the Monasterio de la Oliva, and many smaller villages.

Pamplona (Iruñea)
Famed for July's frenetic San Fermin festival, when bulls are let loose in the street, Navarra's provincial capital has faded *belle époque* buildings and wonderful cafés round the main square, an atmospheric old town, with Gothic cathedral and a good museum.

Santiago de Compostela
Santiago, home to St James the Apostle's remains, is the focus of one of the most important medieval pilgrimages. Tourists flock to view the city's architecture of golden-grey, mineral-flecked granite. The cathedral is the centrepiece. The Museo do Poblo Gallego is a former convent.

Santillana del Mar
The medieval ruralism of this misleadingly named inland village is best enjoyed after the coach parties have gone. A fine Romanesque church and an outstanding museum of religious art are the main sights.

BEST SIGHTS AND EXCURSIONS

Altamira caves
If you can, visit Spain's most important prehistoric cave paintings (only 25 people a day). Bookings are made more than six months in advance; if you are lucky, and you arrive early, you may inherit a cancellation.

Betanzos
Three medieval churches add focus to a wander through the back streets of this market town; the fourteenth-century San Francisco is the best.

Bilbao
The revamped old quarter, or Casco Viejo, is full of smart shops, restaurants and tapas bars. Art lovers should visit the Museo de Bellas Artes and the stunning Guggenheim Museum near the River Nervion.

Celanova
A small and not particularly interesting modern town hides a fascinating monastery with a florid baroque façade and vaulted cloister.

Guernica
Thanks to the Luftwaffe's bombs the town is mostly drab and modern.

Haro and the Rioja vineyards
You will see plenty of *degustación* signs, and the state-owned co-operative in Haro, a cheerful small town, is a good place to see the traditional processes. The Palacio Winery outside Laguardia is also worth a visit.

Islas Cíes
Of the three islands reached by ferry from Vigo, one is an out-of-bounds bird sanctuary. The others are linked by a tremendous white sand bar. Swimming is sheltered and Praia de Figueiras is very beautiful.

La Guardia
A rather tacky fishing village worth visiting to see Monte Santa Tecla, a superbly preserved Celtic *citanía* (fortified hill settlement), with scores of circular stone huts, two rebuilt, and extensive coastal views.

Lugo

The surrounding Roman city walls, made of local slate, are 50 feet high, over 20 feet thick, and defended by 85 towers, with ten gates.

Mondoñedo

The central point is the plaza, sloping from a row of arcaded houses to the golden façade of the eighteenth-century cathedral.

Oviedo

Asturias's industrial capital is worth visiting only if you have an interest in pre-Romanesque churches. The Archaeological Museum's collection ranges from prehistoric flints to more contemporary folk art.

Pontevedra

A lively, atmospheric market city on the river estuary. Highlights are the Museo Provincial and the Santa María Mayor church.

Tui

The cathedral of Galicía's main frontier town is an austere Romanesque-Gothic structure. The interior is more elaborate.

BEST SCENIC LANDSCAPES

Picos de Europa

Some of the walking routes can be quite strenuous, though the attractive file through the Cares Gorge is suitable for all (and very popular). Potes is the main centre for arranging jeep and horseback safaris, Carmona is one of the loveliest of the villages, while the most popular excursion is the cable-car ascent at Fuente Dé. Covadonga, a kitsch Catholic shrine, is fun. Higher up the hill, two deep azure lakes are popular lunch spots.

Sils Gorge

Inland, Galicía's most memorable drive follows a gorge of cascading rock, with lush woods and tiny terraced plots of maize and vines. Sited on a spur above the gorge, the former monastery at San Esteban de Ribas de Sil has a rather dull church, but three lovely cloisters.

THE LEVANTE
Good for food/wine

THE COASTAL regions of Valencia and Murcia, known collectively as the Levante (the East) are justifiably less visited than their neighbours. But to dismiss the area altogether is unfair; the climate is warm and sunny year-round, the three main cities are appealing, and even the most developed resorts are fun, with plenty of British camaraderie.

BEST RESORTS

The best resorts are clustered around the peninsula separating the Costa del Azahar in the north from the Costa Blanca in the south.

Benidorm (Costa Blanca)
● Much maligned, indisputably kitschy, with high-rise architecture that is more city- than resort-like, but effervescent, fun and friendly.
● Broad, palm-lined boulevards and a tiny, pretty old quarter, though overrun with 'British' bars.
● International crowd from across northern Europe and plenty of Spanish visitors ensure wide choice of bars and cuisines.
● Two decent sandy beaches: Playa de Poniente, backed by hills and promenade, is more attractive than Levante.
● Good for long stays out of season, but best avoided in high summer.

Jávea (Costa Blanca)
● Best of the low-key resorts for a stay-put holiday, nestling in a dip below the pine-clad San Antonio headland.
● Mostly apartment and villa accommodation, the most appealing of which is scattered on the hillsides outside town.
● Year-round resort, popular with retired British, with sandy beach.

Peñiscola (Costa del Azahar)
● Best resort on the flat, featureless coastal plain south of Valencia, with lovely old town built on a rugged crag and capped by a castle.
● Atmospheric narrow streets, particularly at night, when castle is floodlit, but tortuous in high season when packed.
● Excellent fresh fish, lively fishing port and a daily fish auction.
● Not recommended for long stays; though long and sandy, the beach lacks shade and is backed by main road.

BEST CITIES

Alicante
Many unjustifiably dismiss Alicante as a cheap charter-flight destination for Costa holidays, but those who stay a night or two will discover the perfect place for aimless strolling and lingering at pavement cafés. In the old Santa Cruz quarter, the patchwork of tiny houses may be sprucely decked with geraniums, or decaying, with peeling façades and graffiti.

Castillo de Santa Bárbara affords extensive views over town and sea, while the Museo de Arte Siglo 20 (Museum of Twentieth-Century Art) has an unexpectedly impressive and comprehensive collection.

Four miles north is San Juan, with a long sandy beach and palm-planted promenade; it surpasses the main town beach for sun-bathing and swimming. Frequent ferries ply visitors to the little off-shore island of Tabarca, a small fishing settlement with a few bars/restaurants, and good beaches.

Murcia

Murcia is not the most enticing of capitals but retains an elegant, if small, old town, and makes a pleasant overnight stop. The pedestriani-sed centre, with pavement cafés, is particularly lively in the evenings.

The Casino, a florid late nineteenth-century structure now used for exhibitions and concerts, and the cathedral, whose magnificently the-atrical baroque façade hides a plainer Gothic interior and two elaborate chapels, are worth a visit. The small museum displays melodramatic works by the eighteenth-century Murcian sculptor Francisco Salzillo.

Valencia

Spain's third-largest city is a curious hotch-potch, but has some atmospheric corners and impressive buildings, sunny plazas with trendy cafés. Evening entertainment is lively – as is shopping. The cathedral, which fronts on to Valencia's prettiest square, Plaza de la Virgen, is best known for housing the so-called Holy Grail, brought to Spain in the fourth century. The Miguelete tower is fun to climb.

Visit the Colegio de Patriarca (Patriarch Collegiate Church) on a Friday morning, when there is a dramatic service, complete with incense; it has a small museum. The 5,000 ceramics in the Museo Nacional de Cerámica date from Iberian times to the twentieth century – a must for lovers of Spanish *azulejos* (ceramic tiles).

BEST INLAND SIGHTS

With flat, featureless plains, this is not an ideal area for scenic touring, but pleasant excursions can be made from the main resorts and cities.

Guadalest

Explore the mountains inland from Benidorm, part wild, part terraced with olive, almond and citrus groves; visit the pretty waterfalls at Algar and a couple of caves, the best is at Canolobre. The medieval village of Guadalest, ingeniously clamped to a rock, is topped by a ruined castle.

Morella

Fortified Morella has the appearance of a stylised medieval painting and is unmissable. Main sights are the fourteenth-century Gothic Basilica of Santa María la Mayor, thirteenth-century Monastery of San Francisco and the castle ramparts, from which the views are phenomenal.

BALEARIC ISLANDS
Good for beaches, family holidays and nightlife

THE BALEARICS offer a variety of options, from family beach holidays to luxurious isolation, quiet villas and non-stop nightlife.

IBIZA

IBIZA TOWN itself is the main focus of the island's nightlife; it also has an appealing old town to explore by day or night.

BEST RESORTS

● Portinatx has three beaches linked by a path across low headlands. Good mix of ages, bars for old and young, enjoyable atmosphere. The drawback is that the beaches are crowded.
● Santa Eulalia del Río is centred on a small crescent of beach, backed by a neat promenade. If the beach gets too crowded, you can take ferries to nearby coves.
● Cala Sant Vincent has only a handful of hotels in a quiet cove with a magnificent sandy beach.

MAJORCA

THE LARGEST and most scenically varied of the islands, Majorca probably has a sun-and-sand resort to suit every taste as well as more than enough sights to satisfy seasoned travellers.

BEST RESORTS

● Magaluf is the place to stay for raucous nightlife and excellent beaches; Torrenova and Cala Viñas are quieter areas of the resort.
● Palma Nova is similar to Magaluf but slightly less frenetic at night.
● Plenty of space on the huge beach at Sant Ponsa but central area is built-up with hotels and anonymous eateries.
● San Vicente is on a more exposed part of the north coast; many of the villas and hotels are set right back and fringed with pines.
● Nearby Puerto Pollensa is low-key, with a long narrow beach of fine

sand and some good hotels and restaurants, far removed from the noisy excess found elsewhere on the island.

● Cala Ratjada, on the east coast, is very popular with German tourists. It comes the closest to being an authentic resort town. Lively at night, with a variety of clubs and bars.

● Canyamel and Cala Santanyi are small, attractive resorts with excellent beaches and a relaxed atmosphere.

● Purpose-built Cala d'Or spreads itself around a series of coves and tiny beaches. The pedestrianised centre, close to the smart marina, contains a good mix of bars and restaurants – stay in the central area, around Cala d'Or or Cala Gran, if you want to explore this part of the island.

BEST INLAND BASES

The Tramuntana Mountains rear out of the sea on Majorca's western coast, a jumble of gnarled peaks and sheer cliffs. For touring or escaping the coastal crowds make your base here. Banyalbufar, a simple village of tidy cobbled streets, is surprisingly lively in the evening. Deià is a popular refuge for artists and writers, including the late Robert Graves, and has a couple of very smart hotels.

BEST SIGHTS AND EXCURSIONS

Visit sophisticated, self-assured Palma for the cathedral, Almudaina Palace and Museum of Majorca. Art galleries and exhibitions are plentiful.

Valldemossa owes its fame to the long stay of the composer Frederick Chopin and his lover George Sand, who lodged in the Carthusian monastery. The cells they lived in have become a museum dedicated to Chopin's life and work; views from the terrace are fabulous.

Cuevas de Artá and Cuevas de Campanet are the best of Majorca's four sets of heavily promoted limestone caves (all are similar).

The rattling old train to Soller rumbles out of Palma, traversing stunning mountain scenery and orange and lemon groves, as it ambles towards the north-west coast of the island. Here you can connect with a wonderful old tram to Puerto Soller.

MINORCA

MINORCA'S PURPOSE-built resorts are designed for sedate convenience, ideal for holidaymakers who want sun and sand on their doorstep, a safe and friendly atmosphere and organised events.

BEST RESORTS

● Son Bou's mix of well-finished apartments and hotels is partly spoiled by two outdated high-rise buildings on the fringes. The beach, separated from the resort by dunes and reed beds, is huge, with fine white sand.

● Santa Galdana has bars and restaurants on the edge of a bay enclosed within steep cliffs and an attractive river inlet where boats congregate.

● Remote beaches include Cala Turqueta which, despite being reached by a dirt track, attracts lots of visitors in season. Cala Mitjana at Santa Galdana is another pretty but busy beach.

● Fornells is a lively resort packed with fish restaurants along a harbour; the nearest beach is a few miles away.

BEST SIGHTS AND EXCURSIONS

Minorca's capital Mahón has charming architecture. The town museum, in an old Carmelite cloister, gives a flavour of the British occupation. Ciudadela is older and smaller and reflects much better its Moorish and Spanish heritage, with honey-hued medieval buildings and shady alleys.

In megalithic times hundreds of huge circular buildings, *talayots*, were erected on the island. The most atmospheric remains include Torralba d'en Salort, an extensive settlement with a huge T-shaped stone, and Navetas d'es Tudons, shaped like a small sawn-off pyramid.

CANARY ISLANDS
Good for beaches, family holidays, nightlife and scenic landscape

SEVEN VOLCANIC islands make up the Canary archipelago. Tourism offers a more stable income than the traditional cash-crops of bananas and tomatoes, and the Spanish life-style is submerged beneath millions of foreign visitors. Sun-lovers should head for the eastern islands of Lanzarote or Fuerteventura, or the southern resorts of Tenerife and Gran Canaria. Collectively, the islands offer an astonishing range of natural scenery: lava deserts, cactus canyons and fever-chart mountains. In parts of the larger islands, unchecked development has drowned the coast in concrete. Most accommodation is purpose-built.

TENERIFE

THE LARGEST and most varied of the Canaries is good for island-hopping: Tenerife acts as the main route hub for the other islands. The beaches consist mainly of black volcanic sand or are man made.

BEST RESORT

● Puerto de la Cruz, though not a beach resort (there are only black sand strands pounded by choppy seas on its fringes), is by far the best of the island's main resorts. It has retained an old town of style and character among the ghastly high-rises that provide you with your first impression.

BEST SIGHTS AND EXCURSIONS

Santa Cruz de Tenerife, the island's capital, is relaxing, with a shady boulevard, archaeological museum and fortress. Beyond the town lies Las Teresitas, a man-made beach of golden sand – best on the island. The old university town of La Laguna has more colour, with cobbled streets and pretty squares dominated by old churches, not least the peach-coloured cathedral. The summit of Mount Teide in Las Cañadas National Park is a spectacular region of rough-edged craters, lava flows and weird rocks, and is the island's most popular excursion.

LANZAROTE

A FAVOURITE among the Canary Islands, Lanzarote is more sensi-tively developed than the other large islands; its reputation as an upmarket destination is due to the mainly low-rise self-catering accommodation.

BEST RESORTS

● Playa Blanca is an isolated resort with a low-key, family atmosphere and plenty of self-catering accommodation. It is close to the very good cliff-backed cove beaches of Papagayo, popular with naturists, though you need transport (a bike would do).
● Puerto del Carmen, by far the biggest resort, is a low-rise develop-ment based on a long, often wide, decent beach behind which a strip of bars and restaurants runs; more interesting fish restaurants are to be found by the harbour.

BEST SIGHTS AND EXCURSIONS

Lanzarote's volcanic landscapes are amazing. The Timanfaya National Park is a lunar landscape of twisted rocks and lava. A circular tour by bus starts at the visitor centre. Also visit Cueva de los Verdes, a lava cave formed by a great tube of molten material solidifying into an underground tunnel; Jameos del Agua, a restaurant and nightclub in several landscaped caves; and Los Hervideros – the sea rushes in and out of underground lava caves, spouting out of blowholes.

GRAN CANARIA

THIS THIRD-LARGEST island has the highest population, and its bustling capital, Las Palmas, has a sense of history and shabby, sometimes seedy, cosmopolitanism that is lacking anywhere else in the islands.

BEST RESORTS

● Puerto Rico consists of a pleasant beach and marina surrounded by steep hillsides terraced with white shoe boxes. A pedestrian walkway leads to a newly built beach at Playa de los Amadores, which relieves congestion on the undersized original.

● Puerto de Mogán, Gran Canaria's most attractive resort, is a smart little low-rise development, based around a marina crammed with cabin cruisers. A wide choice of bars and restaurants compensates somewhat for a small, scruffy beach.

BEST SIGHTS AND EXCURSIONS

Coach parties descend on the pretty village of Cruz de Tejeda. Other options include the shrine of Teror, where votive offerings are left for the Virgin of the Pine Trees, and the spectacular road west to the market town of San Nicolás de Tolentino.

Regular buses take you to the island's two main family-oriented attractions: the landscaped grounds and performing parrots of Palmitos Park and the Wild West show of Sioux City.

FUERTEVENTURA

THIS IS a bleak, sparsely populated island. Its biggest assets are its enormous beaches, lonely and desolate in places but good for windsurfers and anyone who yearns to live like Robinson Crusoe.

BEST RESORTS

● Caleta de Fustes is a tasteful, low-key development of apartments built around a pleasant, sheltered bay of white sand.

● The beaches shelve gently, making it ideal for children, and there is a smart marina.

● Costa Calma is the island's smartest development, catering almost exclusively for the large German market.

● Its accommodation is mostly low-rise, and it has a laid-back feel at night.

BEST SIGHTS AND EXCURSIONS

The best of the island lies within a triangle bounded by Pajara and Tuineje, with the windmill at Llanos at its peak. Between the old capital of Betancuria and Antigua you travel over steep roads, with a volcanic valley unfolding below.

LA GOMERA

EASILY ACCESSIBLE by ferry from Tenerife, La Gomera makes a popular day-trip. With an attractive *parador* and a well-equipped resort hotel, it has the best-quality accommodation of the smaller islands, but comparatively little choice.

The buckled terrain of the interior (partly a national park) is beautiful and full of botanical interest – marvellous for walkers, but slow for drivers. A lack of sand and cooler, damper weather than the main islands make it unsuitable for beach-lovers.

LA PALMA

THE WORLD'S steepest island rises dramatically around a vast volcano crater. Lush vegetation cloaks the island with forests, flowers, vines and subtropical crops. The capital of Santa Cruz de la Palma is one of the Canaries' most elegant and pleasing towns. Less tourist-oriented than most of the other islands, it offers a genuinely peaceful hideaway and spectacular touring, but few good beaches.

EL HIERRO

LITTLE TOURIST development has taken place on this, the smallest of the Canary Islands. A pine-covered ridge follows the curve of its boomerang shape, half of the rim of a volcanic crater, whose mirror image is submerged beneath the sea.

WHEN TO GO

THE CANARY Islands are the best choice for a winter break: even in the depths of winter you can expect better weather than during an English summer. The islands' south coasts are drier than the northern ones. Southern Spain and the Balearics are much cooler than the Canaries in winter, but they still get a fair amount of sunshine and many hotels stay open. Some tour operators offer special long-stay holidays of several months for pensioners.

Summer weather is warm and dry almost everywhere, but if you are going slightly out of season (e.g. April or October) you will be better off further south rather than on the Costa Brava or Dorada. The Andalusian cities, especially Seville, can be overbearingly hot at the height of summer.

	Average daily maximum temperature °C											
London	6	7	10	13	17	20	22	21	19	14	10	7
Madrid	9	11	15	18	21	27	31	30	25	19	13	9
	JAN	FEB	MAR	APR	MAY	JUN	JUL	AUG	SEP	OCT	NOV	DEC
Madrid	8	7	10	9	10	5	2	3	6	8	9	10
London	15	13	11	12	12	11	12	11	13	13	15	15
	Average number of rainy days per month											

	Average daily maximum temperature °C											
London	6	7	10	13	17	20	22	21	19	14	10	7
Malaga	17	17	18	21	23	27	29	30	27	23	20	17
	JAN	FEB	MAR	APR	MAY	JUN	JUL	AUG	SEP	OCT	NOV	DEC
Malaga	7	6	8	6	4	1	<1	1	2	6	7	8
London	15	13	11	12	12	11	12	11	13	13	15	15
	Average number of rainy days per month											

PACKAGE TRAVEL

MOST TOUR operators offer classic stay-put sun-and-sea holidays to one of the *costas* or Spanish islands, but the choice of holidays is vast and covers all tastes and pockets, from independent car touring and staying in *paradores* to golfing, wildlife and rambling.

If you are looking for a good-value, stay-put package, shop around. Several tour operators may offer packages to the same resort and the same hotels, with big price differences.

Tour operators

Battlefield: Holts' Tours, Midas **City breaks**: British Airways Holidays, Cresta, Inghams, Kirker, Made to Measure, Osprey, Sovereign, Time Off, Travelscene **Cultural**: Ace Study Tours, Andante, British Museum Traveller, Inscape, Martin Randall, Prospect, Walking Safaris **General and specialist**: Airtours, Bonaventure, Cadogan Travel, Club Cantabrica, Cosmos, Cresta, Crystal, EHS Travel, First Choice, Globespan, Inghams, Inntravel, JMC Travel, Longmere International, Magic of Spain, Mundi Color, Page & Moy, Panorama, Shearings, Siesta International, Sovereign, Spanish Harbour Holidays, Sunset Holidays, Sunvil, Thomson, Travel Club of Upminster, Unijet **Horseriding/walking**: Alternative Travel Group, Andrew Brock Travel, Exodus, Explore Worldwide, Headwater, HF Holidays, Inntravel, Ramblers Holidays, Waymark **Villa specialists**: Carefree Spain, Casas Cantabricas, Continental Villas, CV Travel, Individual Travellers Spain & Portugal, Lanzarote Leisure, Meon, Palmer & Parker, Spanish Affair **Wildlife/birdwatching**: Discover the World, Limosa, Ornitholidays, Sunbird, Wildlife Worldwide **Wine tours**: Arblaster & Clarke, Winetrails **Other activities**: Club Med (all-inclusive), Cox & Kings (flora), Eurocamp, Golf Holidays International, Insight Holidays (coach tours), Longshot Golf, Minorca Sailing Holidays, Sherpa, Simply Golf, Solo's Holidays (singles), Waymark

---

INDEPENDENT TRAVEL

YOU ARE unlikely to be able to match the deals on offer to the coastal resorts, and most accommodation is block-booked in any case. For inland Spain, however, you may save money, particularly if you take your own car and stay in *hostales* (guesthouses). These offer fewer facilities but may have more character than hotels – there are plenty of them inland. The state-run *paradores* are a good option for those with more money – they offer comfortable rooms in an assortment of often unforgettable buildings, including converted castles, palaces and convents (other guests are more likely to be American than Spanish).

Cheap seat-only charters are plentiful, and cities that are served only by expensive scheduled flights from London can often be accessed from a nearby charter airport – fly to Girona for Barcelona, for example, or to Malaga for Seville. Iberia's Moneysaver fares allow you to fly into one airport and depart from another.

Ferries cross from Plymouth to Santander and Portsmouth to Bilbao – special deals are often available. If you are taking your car over, a 'bail bond' from your insurer is recommended to prevent your car being impounded in the event of an accident.

British licences are accepted for car hire (minimum age 18); those with old green licences may need an international driving permit. Rates are lower in resorts, and it is cheaper to pre-book. Alternatively, the rail network covers the mainland comprehensively. Tourist passes allowing unlimited travel for fixed periods are available in the UK.

RED TAPE, HEALTH AND SAFETY

BRITISH PASSPORT-HOLDERS do not need a visa to visit Spain. Since 1994 ETA (the Basque separatist movement) has been setting off small bombs in tourist resorts, with the aim of disrupting the tourist industry. Travellers should remain alert and report any suspicious bags or objects to the police. For the latest advice contact the Foreign Office Travel Advice Unit (see page 11). Pickpocketing and bag-snatching are common in cities – see page 12 for advice on taking care of your possessions.

MORE INFORMATION Spanish Tourist Office, 23 Manchester Square, London W1M 5AP, tel 020-7486 8077, web site: *www.tourspain.es*

COST OF LIVING £–££

SRI LANKA

HIGHLIGHTS

Beaches
Tangalla, Unawatuna

Culture
Anuradhapura, Sigiriya

Local colour
Ambalangoda, Kandy

Outdoor activities
*Benota, Beruwela,
Hikkaduwa*

Scenic landscape
Kandy

Shopping
*Ambalangoda, Colombo,
Ratnapura*

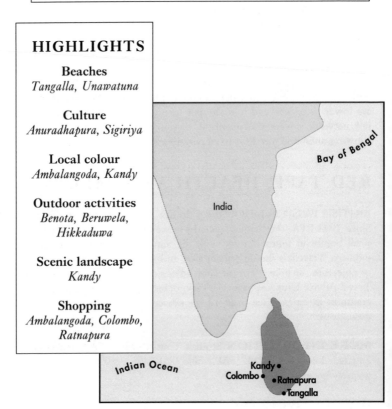

S RI LANKA, so legend has it, is the country where serendipity was invented. Although the island has been established as a tourist destination for some time, it is still charmingly unspoilt, and off-the-beaten-track exploration is so easy that it really is possible to make wonderful discoveries (deserted beaches, intriguing temples) completely by accident. The local cooking is superb – particularly on the coast where fish-based curries are, naturally enough, a speciality – and the Sri Lankan people are warm, friendly and generous.

The Sinhalese, who make up around 70 per cent of the population, are mainly Buddhist, and Buddhism has a distinctive influence, architecturally and culturally, over the whole island. Other influences stem from Sri Lanka's minority communities, including the Tamils, who represent around 15 per cent of the population and live mainly in the north; and from the island's colonial past.

The capital, Colombo, has little to interest most visitors, who are better advised to divide their time between the tropical beaches of the south and west, and the fascinating cultural sites of the interior.

THE COAST
Good for beaches, outdoor activities and shopping

THE COASTLINE that stretches southwards from Colombo boasts mile after mile of unspoilt, uncrowded, palm-fringed sand. All the best beach resorts are here. As a rule of thumb, the further you go from Colombo, the more basic the facilities.

BEST RESORTS

Bentota and Beruwela
● These twin centres are Sri Lanka's main package resorts.
● Facilities include well-equipped hotels and fine beaches which are good for water sports.

Hikkaduwa
● The small town of Hikkaduwa, further down the coast, has a relaxed atmosphere. It is tourist-oriented and attracts a balanced mix of independent travellers and those on package holidays.
● Scuba divers can travel out from the bay by dive boat to explore nearby shipwrecks. The coral in the bay itself, once spectacular, is now badly damaged but is still visited by turtles.
● The southern beaches are popular with surfers from November to April.

Unawatuna and Tangalla
● Further south are Unawatuna and Tangalla, both low-key, relatively remote resorts, with superb, curving beaches.

BEST LOCAL COLOUR
Ambalangoda
Ambalangoda, a small coastal town famous for its traditional, lurid wooden masks worn in dance-dramas, devil-dances and processions, has a small, informative museum and workshops with masks for sale.

THE INTERIOR
Good for culture, local colour, scenic landscape and shopping

BEST SIGHTS AND EXCURSIONS

Adam's Peak

Adam's Peak is a short journey from Nuwara Eliya. At its summit is a huge 'footprint' which Buddhists claim to be that of the Buddha; Hindus ascribe it to Lord Shiva; Christians say it is the mark of St Thomas of India; and Muslims believe it to be the first terrestrial footprint of Adam after he was cast out of heaven.

During the pilgrimage season (December to April) a great number of visitors make the climb to the hilltop temple. The mountain is beautiful at dawn.

Anuradhapura

Sri Lanka's most sacred early capital is still an important pilgrimage site. The town was the seat of the Sinhalese kings from the fourth century BC to the tenth century AD, and a number of important *dagobas* (Buddhist shrines) and royal palaces were founded here.

The town's spiritual focus is the Sri Maha Bodhi, or sacred bo tree. This, the oldest historically documented tree in the world, grew from a cutting taken from the tree under which the Buddha is said to have attained enlightenment. It has been a site of worship for 23 centuries.

Kandy

Kandy is famous for the Temple of the Tooth, an important pilgrimage site housing a sacred relic of the Buddha, and for the Perahera, Sri Lanka's most lavish festival, with spectacular processions of elephants, musicians and dancers (held over two weeks in early July).

It is also an excellent base for further exploration of the central highlands and tea estates.

Nuwara Eliya

This hill station is surrounded by scenic countryside.

Pinawela elephant orphanage

A must for elephant enthusiasts: the animals are well-kept and visitors can accompany the herd to a nearby river at bathing time when the water levels are low enough.

Ratnapura

The capital of Sri Lanka's thriving gem trade offers excellent shopping opportunities. Gems mined in the region include sapphires, rubies, aquamarines, zircons, cat's eyes, quartz and amethysts plus Sri Lanka's 'signature' gemstone, the feldspar or moonstone. Gems, uncut, cut, and made into jewellery, are sold all over Sri Lanka but Ratnapura has a particularly high concentration of dealers. You can also visit the mines.

Sigiriya

Part military stronghold and part elaborate status symbol, Sigiriya was built in the fifth century by Kasyapa, illegitimate son of King Dhatusena of Anuradhapura, on top of the 656-feet-high Lion Rock. Kasyapa murdered his father and, fearing reprisals, created the lavishly decorated citadel: fragments of magnificent frescos depicting nymphs remain. Kasyapa also installed superb water gardens.

WHEN TO GO

THE MAIN tourist season runs from December to March, when it is mainly dry in the most-visited areas of the island (the west and south coasts). The dry season on the east coast (much of which is currently inaccessible) is from May to September.

During the monsoon (May to September in the centre, south and west; October to December in the centre, north and east) conditions can be severe – the rain varies from light and refreshing to prolonged and drenching – but it doesn't rain all the time, and you can still swim from the reef-protected beaches.

	Average daily maximum temperature °C											
London	6	7	10	13	17	20	22	21	19	14	10	7
Colombo	30	31	31	31	31	29	29	29	29	29	29	29
	JAN	FEB	MAR	APR	MAY	JUN	JUL	AUG	SEP	OCT	NOV	DEC
Colombo	7	6	8	14	19	18	12	11	13	19	16	10
London	15	13	11	12	12	11	12	11	13	13	15	15
	Average number of rainy days per month											

PACKAGE TRAVEL

THE MAIN package holiday choices to Sri Lanka are classical tours visiting historical and colonial sights throughout the centre and south, and a selection of beach hotels along the south-west coast.

Tours that take in the highlights of the country generally run for seven to nine days; transport is by coach or private chauffeur-driven car. A typical itinerary will start at Colombo and take in Anuradhapura,

Sigiriya, Polonnaruna, Kandy, Nuwara Eliya, Ratnapura and the Yala National Park. Beach hotels are offered on a half-board, full-board or all-inclusive basis and can be added on to the end of a tour. Alternatively, you can combine Sri Lanka with the Maldives, India, Bangkok or Singapore.

Activity holidays on offer include cultural tours, adventure tours, birdwatching or cycling.

Tour operators

Adventure: Explore Worldwide, Guerba, Travelbag **Archaeology**: Andante **Birdwatching**: Limosa, Naturetrek, Sunbird **Cultural**: Coromandel, Cox & Kings, Prospect **Cycling**: Exodus **General**: Abercrombie & Kent, Airtours, Asian Journeys, Bales Tours, British Airways Holidays, Classic Connection, Cosmos, Cricketer, Elite Vacations, First Choice, Hayes & Jarvis, Kuoni, Magic of the Orient, Manos, Premier Holidays, Saga, Sri Lanka Holidays, Somak, Steppes East, Sunset Faraway, Thomson, Titan HiTours, Tradewinds, Trailfinders, Travelsphere, Unijet, World Dreams, Worldwide Journeys

---

INDEPENDENT TRAVEL

THANKS TO its extensive network of public transport, much of Sri Lanka is easily accessible to the independent traveller.

From Colombo, the old-fashioned but reasonably efficient railway runs south to Matara, stopping at the major coastal resorts of Mount Lavinia, Beruwela, Bentota, Hikkaduwa, Galle and Unawatuna on the way. It is a slow but interesting journey, with the track running right along the beach at times. Heading into the central highlands, regular trains serve Kandy and Anuradhapura (the journey to Kandy is particularly scenic), and it is possible to reach Adam's Peak, the Pinawela elephant orphanage and Sigiriya by using a combination of trains and buses.

Travelling by bus is a cheap way to get from town to town, although the buses can be crowded. Every town has a bus station but buses will stop *en route* if you indicate. Privately owned minibuses run along commuter routes: these are air-conditioned, fast, and have higher fares. The best choice for a short journey is to take one of the ubiquitous *tuk-tuks* (motorised rickshaws); make sure you agree the fare in advance.

Bicycle hire is cheap in busy centres such as Hikkaduwa and Polonnaruwa, where you can hire a gearless bone-shaker by the hour or by the day.

Well-visited centres such as Kandy, Anuradhapura and Hikkaduwa have an abundance of simple, inexpensive guesthouses. Some operate like small hotels, whereas others are family-run and will provide a room plus as many (generally excellent) meals a day as you wish in a homely atmosphere. In less-visited towns you may find it necessary to ask someone to direct you to a guesthouse since they are not always clearly marked.

RED TAPE, HEALTH AND SAFETY

BRITISH PASSPORT-HOLDERS do not require a visa to enter Sri Lanka for a stay of 30 days or less. If you wish to stay longer than 30 days a three-month visa is available from the Sri Lanka High Commission for £32.

Since malaria and dengue fever are a danger in some parts of the island (particularly the hill country) it is advisable to take a course of anti-malaria drugs and take all possible measures to avoid being bitten. Not all hotels and guesthouses automatically provide mosquito nets, so it is a good idea to take your own. Immunisation against polio, tetanus and typhoid is also recommended.

In general, standards of hygiene in Sri Lanka are high and visitors who follow a few basic rules should enjoy a completely healthy stay (see the precautions on pages 10–12).

Although the vast majority of Sri Lankans are genuinely friendly and welcoming towards tourists, it is best to be wise to the fact that touting and hustling do occur: representatives on organised tours get commission on goods purchased by tourist groups, and the more devious touts will go to great lengths to disguise their interest in you as friendship, when their sole purpose is to lead you to a guesthouse, taxi stand or gem shop for a commission. These activities are widespread and can be a considerable nuisance. Although crime is not a cause for great concern, it is a good idea to take the usual precautions against petty theft, particularly in the capital (see page 12). Until a lasting peace settlement brings an end to the long-running Sinhalese-Tamil troubles, the north of the island (the area east of Polonnaruwa and north of Anuradhapura, including Wilpattu National Park and Trincomalee) is out of bounds to travellers. The Foreign Office advises minimising time spent in Colombo as bomb attacks are possible – for more information, contact the Foreign Office Travel Advice Unit (see page 11).

However, the rest of the country is, at the time of writing, safe to visit, and by sticking to the south, west and centre (an area which, in any case, includes some excellent coastal resorts and most of the best cultural sites) tourists are unlikely to be affected by the unrest.

MORE INFORMATION Sri Lanka Tourist Board, 22 Regent Street, London SW1Y 4QD, tel 020-7930 2627, web site: *www.lanka.net/ctb*

Sri Lanka High Commission, Consular Section, 13 Hyde Park Gardens, London W2 2LX, tel 020-7262 1841 (*send an sae for visa application*)

COST OF LIVING £-££

SWEDEN

HIGHLIGHTS

Beaches
*Islands, northern and
southern Sweden*

Culture
*Gothenburg, southern
Sweden, Stockholm*

Family holidays
Gothenburg, Stockholm

Nightlife
Islands, Gothenburg

Outdoor activities
*Båstad, Härjedalan,
Lake Vättern, Ystad*

Scenic landscape
Arctic Circle, lakes

STOCKHOLM
Good for culture and family holidays

STOCKHOLM IS a former cultural capital of Europe and is Scandinavia's most beautiful city. The compact Swedish capital is spread across a series of islands and offers wonderful waterfront views, superb pastel-shaded buildings and a bewildering collection of museums.

BEST SIGHTS

Gamla Stan
Elegant seventeenth- and eighteenth-century houses crowd the islands that make up the old town. Stortoget, Gamla Stan's main square,was the original heart of the city, and was used by Christian II in 1520 as an execution site during the 'Stockholm bloodbath'. This and Gamla Stan's narrow alleys and maze-like streets are now the centre of the modern city's tourist industry.

Kungliga Slottet

With 608 rooms, the Royal Palace is Europe's largest residence. Its triumphant mid-eighteenth-century construction is lavishly decorated in the rococo style with a baroque interior. The treasury and armoury are particularly worth visiting.

Medeltidsmuseum

The history of Stockholm is brought to life with reconstructed houses and exhibitions of archaeological finds.

Moderna Museet

A fine modern art museum which displays work by most major twentieth-century artists, including Dalí, Picasso, Warhol and Bacon.

National Art Museum

A huge, eclectic and fascinating collection of pure and applied art, ranging from ancient tapestries and art-nouveau coffee pots to Russian icons and some important works by Rembrandt.

Skansen

Also to be found in the Djurgarden, the world's first open-air museum contains around 150 reconstructed buildings, from windmills to tiny Lapp Saame houses. Also nearby are the Tobacco museum and aquarium.

Storkyrkan

For centuries the kings and queens of Sweden have been married and crowned in the 'Great Church', notable for its splendid interior, flamboyant royal pews and immense altarpiece.

Vasa Museum

Situated on the western shore of the Djurgarden, Stockholm's Royal park, this museum is devoted to the mighty 204-ft-long warship *Vasa*, which sank in 1628 on its maiden voyage and was preserved in mud for 300 years. The ship is almost complete and is now the centre of an excellent exhibition.

BEST EXCURSIONS

Drottningholm

This marvellous royal palace, built by the father and son Tessin architects, in a beautiful leafy setting is commonly known as the Swedish Versailles. Rococo decoration fills the interior, and the famous theatre, built in 1766, is still in use. The Royal apartments are a highlight, and the Royal Armoury, the Royal Treasury and the Gustave III museum of antiquities are also excellent.

Gripsholm

Dating originally from the fourteenth century, Gripsholm is everyone's idea of what a castle should be – turrets and battlements, great halls and dungeons.

Millesgården

The outdoor museum of the work of the great Swedish sculptor Carl Milles is a spectacular collection of monumental classical figures.

Uppsala

This ancient university city, situated on the River Fyrisan, contains a castle, sixth-century burial mounds and the largest cathedral in Scandinavia.

GOTHENBURG
Good for culture, family holidays and nightlife

SCANDINAVIA'S LARGEST port is also one of Sweden's liveliest and most enchanting cities, with broad avenues, extensive parks and plenty of bars and restaurants. Gothenburg lies in the heart of Scandinavia and is a good base from which to visit Stockholm, Oslo and Copenhagen.

BEST SIGHTS

Art Museum

The museum has a vast and varied collection; it is strongest on the Impressionists but also includes work by modern Scandinavian artists.

Liseberg

This is the city's major amusement park – and answer to Copenhagen's Tivoli. It has over 30 rides, and a host of restaurants, cafés, bars and places for pleasant strolling around the huge gardens with their hanging illuminations.

Maritima Centrum

There are boats of all sizes and shapes to scramble over at this outdoor maritime museum, which claims to be the world's largest.

SOUTHERN SWEDEN
Good for beaches, culture and outdoor activities

BEST SIGHTS

Båstad
The Swedish answer to Wimbledon, this delightful town hosts the Swedish Open but is also notable for its beaches and the rugged Bjäre peninsula nearby, which offers fine walking and swimming.

Bohuslän
This coastline north of Gothenburg up to the Norwegian border is a popular holiday destination, with picturesque fishing villages, fjords and islands. Strömstad is the main resort.

Halland
South of Gothenburg, the Halland coastline is almost one long beach. Varberg has a thirteenth-century castle and 'Bocksten Man' – a grisly fourteenth-century murder victim preserved in a bog. Other towns worth visiting in the region are Falkenberg and Halmstad.

Kalmar
This historic east-coast town has a spectacular castle on an island and a superb exhibition dedicated to the seventeenth-century warship *Kronan*.

Kristianstad
This entrancing town was created by the Danish king Christian IV in the early seventeenth century, when southern Sweden was part of Denmark. Elegant buildings, swish shops and agreeable cafés abound. The town is also home to Sweden's oldest film studio and an intriguing film museum.

Lund
The historic university town flaunts its exquisite medieval centre and stunning twelfth-century Romanesque cathedral, considered by many to be the finest medieval building in Scandinavia. The church has scarcely changed since it was consecrated in 1145 and contains a fascinating astronomical clock and atmospheric crypt.

Malmö
A short journey across the water from Copenhagen, and now linked by the Kulturbo tunnel and bridge, Malmö is a neat and handsome city, with canals, parks and a historic centre. Lilla Torget, the most

picturesque square in the city, is surrounded by half-timbered buildings. In the Malmöhus, an impressive red castle, is a series of excellent museums of art, city history and militaria.

Skåne and Blekinge coasts
The coasts of these two southern Swedish provinces are speckled with fishing villages and good beaches. There is a notable Viking site at Ales Stennar, and the country's finest Bronze Age burial ground, Kunga-graven, is near Simrishamn.

Ystad
An attractive town at the southern tip of Sweden, Ystad has neat medieval buildings and good hiking possibilities nearby.

SWEDISH ISLANDS
Good for beaches and nightlife

Gotland
Gotland has acquired a reputation for frenetic, youthful fun in summer, when beaches and bars are packed. It also enjoys a remarkably mild climate and a huge concentration of medieval country churches. Visby, Gotland's capital, was one of the major cities of medieval Europe, its wealth demonstrated by the magnificent thirteenth-century wall enclosing the town, many churches and splendid buildings.

Öland
A popular Baltic holiday island, Öland has gentle green countryside, promising beaches, windmills, castles and burial mounds. The main town is Borgholm.

CENTRAL LAKE REGION
Good for outdoor activities and scenic landscape

BEST SIGHTS

Dalarna
North of the 'great lakes' of Vänern and Vättern, this beautiful region around Lake Siljan is renowned for its gentle, lush countryside, folk traditions and handicrafts. The town of Mora was home to the painter Anders Zorn, whose works, home and studio can be visited. The Grönlitt bear park provides a rare opportunity to watch brown bears in their natural environment.

'The Glass Kingdom'
Between Kalmar and Växjö lie many of Sweden's best-known glass-works. The Kosta Boda factory and shop in Kosta are worth a visit.

Karlsborg
Work on this monumental fortress started in 1818 but stopped in 1909 when it was realised that the castle would be obsolete before it was ever finished, due to altered defence theories and weapons technology.

Lake Vättern
The best bases from which to enjoy the natural attractions of long Lake Vättern are the towns of Gränna, Vadstena and Motala. Ferries run from Gränna to the fascinating island of Visingö.

Linköping
This living and working nineteenth-century town is home to one of Sweden's most notable cathedrals and an entrancing open-air museum.

Mariestad
This compact lakeside town has a fine medieval quarter; the Gothic cathedral dates from 1232 and is carved completely from limestone. Cruises on huge Lake Vänern and the Göta Canal are available from here.

Norrköping
Norrköping is a good base from which to see the ancient rock carvings of Himmelstalund, the magnificent eighteenth-century Löfstad Manor, and the popular Kolmården Djurpark – a huge complex of safari park, zoo and dolphinarium which is a great favourite with children.

NORTH SWEDEN
Good for beaches, outdoor activities and scenic landscape

BEST SIGHTS

Bothnian coast
North of Stockholm the coast stretches up towards Finland, offering low-key attractions: empty beaches, fine walking and pleasant towns. Among the most interesting stop-overs are Skellefteå, Hudiksvall, Umeå, Gävle, Luleå and Skuleskogen National Park.

Härjedalan country
There is excellent hiking country north of Dalarna: the town of Sveg

makes a good base. Åsarna, near the pretty village of Klövsjö, offers fine skiing.

Östersund

Located by the Storsjön lake, this sizeable town has huge open-air museums, at which the Swedes excel. West from here, jagged mountains and fast-flowing rivers lead towards the Norwegian border and Sweden's highest-profile ski resort, Åre.

The far north

The chief attractions of northern Sweden are natural. A series of national parks within the Arctic Circle provide spectacular hiking in settings of soaring mountains, endless forests, icy rivers and herds of reindeer. Muddus is the most accessible and beginner-friendly park, while the most popular trail is the 310-mile-long Kungsleden (Royal Route) from Abisko. Be warned that exploration is feasible only in July and August – when the mosquitoes are at their worst. The major towns of Jokkmokk, Gällivare and Kiruna offer insights into the importance of mining in the region and also the native Same culture. The far north is the best place to see the spectacular Northern Lights. While special viewing cabins can be found, the best views lie off the beaten track – though this is a treacherous pursuit especially in winter months.

WHEN TO GO

TEMPERATURES IN high summer are about the same in southern Sweden as in southern England, but Sweden gets more sunshine. Summer days are noticeably longer than in southern England (and winter days shorter). Midsummer is celebrated in many parts of the country, while Stockholm becomes deserted.

	Average daily maximum temperature °C											
London	6	7	10	13	17	20	22	21	19	14	10	7
Stockholm	-1	-1	3	8	14	19	22	20	15	9	5	2
	JAN	FEB	MAR	APR	MAY	JUN	JUL	AUG	SEP	OCT	NOV	DEC
Stockholm	16	14	10	11	11	13	13	14	14	15	16	17
London	15	13	11	12	12	11	12	11	13	13	15	15
	Average number of rainy days per month											

PACKAGE TRAVEL

PACKAGE TRAVEL can include scenic tours by rail, bus and boat, touring by car to pre-selected hotels, renting a country cottage, staying in a chalet in a holiday centre, canal cruises, cruises to islands in the Baltic Sea, staying on a working farm or simply taking a city break. On offer from activity tour operators are walking, battlefield and study tours and birdwatching.

Tour operators

City breaks: Bridge Travel, British Airways Holidays, Cresta, Crystal, Inghams, Osprey, Thomson, Time Off, Travelscene, Yes Travel **Walking:** Explore Worldwide, Waymark **Specialists**: Norvista, DFDS Seaways, Scandinavian Travel Service, Scan-Meridian, Scantours, Sovereign, Specialised Tours, Taber **Other activities**: Ace Study Tours, Anglers World, Discover the World (wildlife), Go Fishing (fishing), Martin Randall (cultural), Solo's Holidays (singles)

INDEPENDENT TRAVEL

BY FAR the easiest way to reach Sweden is to fly – there are several flights a day from the UK to Stockholm, Gothenburg and Malmö. Ferries from Newcastle and Harwich to Gothenburg are usually cheaper but take at least 24 hours.

The public transport system in Sweden is as efficient as it is everywhere else in Scandinavia. Almost all cities operate excellent discount card schemes which usually cover free local transport and entry to sights plus a range of other bargains. Train travel is often scenic but generally expensive – it can actually be cheaper to use SAS's internal flights, for which several discounts are available. The cheapest travel option is long-distance bus. Car hire is expensive. A full British driving licence is sufficient documentation.

Given that Sweden is generally a costly country to visit, it is a surprise to find so much good-value accommodation available. Hotels offer a wide range of discounts – particularly in the summer – including a variety of hotel passes, which must be bought in advance. In Stockholm, Gothenburg and Malmö discount cards are available which include a room, local transport and admission to sights for one price.

A cheaper option is a private room or bed and breakfast, often on a farm. Local tourist boards can supply details.

The best-value accommodation is undoubtedly in youth hostels. These are almost always of a very high standard, family-oriented with private rooms, and to be found all over the country. Because of their popularity, advance booking is advisable.

The quality of campsites is also very high, and many have cabins with their own cooking facilities – ideal for groups. As in Norway, the right to camp rough is enshrined in law.

RED TAPE, HEALTH AND SAFETY

BRITISH PASSPORT-HOLDERS do not require a visa. There are no particular health or crime problems in Sweden; just take the usual precautions (see pages 10–12).

MORE INFORMATION Swedish Travel and Tourism Council, 11 Montagu Place, London W1H 2AL, tel 020-7870 5600, web site: *www.visit-sweden.com*

COST OF LIVING *£££*

SWITZERLAND

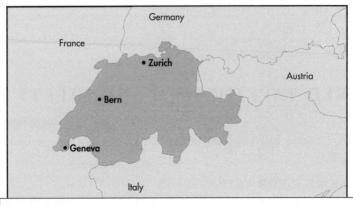

HIGHLIGHTS

Family holidays *Lake Lucerne*	**Culture** *Basle, Geneva*	**Flora** *Bernese Oberland*	*Oberland, Graubünden*
Food/wine *Rhône Valley*	**Local colour** *Bern, Rhône Valley, Ticino, Zurich*	**Scenic landscape** *Bernese*	**Outdoor activities** *Bernese Oberland*

BERN
Good for local colour

SWITZERLAND'S CAPITAL maintains a small-town atmosphere, particularly in the old town, which nestles in a curl of the Aare river. The covered arcades and historic fountain squares are best explored on foot.

BEST SIGHTS

Cathedral
The Münster has the tallest spire in the country. Treasures include sculpted figures, stained-glass and Renaissance carved choir stalls.

Zytgloggeturm
During the four minutes before each hour, this marvellous clock tower offers a mechanised display of jesters, bears and Father Time himself.

Although the clock is over 450 years old, it keeps perfect time. Guided tours are available through the tourist office.

BERNESE OBERLAND
Good for flora, outdoor activities and scenic landscape

THE GREAT peaks of the Eiger, Jungfrau and Schilthorn have made this area famous. Access to these forbidding crags is astonishingly good: railways and cable-cars reach remote points. The cost, however, can be prohibitive on prestige lines like the Jungfraujoch. Enjoy the scenery for free by using the many footpaths on the lower hillsides and meadows.

BEST BASES

Grindelwald
Even the large numbers of tourist chalet-style hotels cannot detract from the beauty of this broad U-shaped valley in the shadow of some huge peaks. The further you go up the road, the quieter it becomes.

Mürren
Built on a ledge opposite the Jungfrau range, Mürren has stunning views. In summer the walks are excellent – even the Schilthorn if you are strong enough and the weather good. Go early while any snow patches are firm.

Wengen
Slightly more developed than Mürren across the valley, Wengen is handy for its rail link over the hill to Grindelwald, and is car-free.

BEST SIGHTS AND EXCURSIONS

Alpine meadows
The Grindelwald is noted for its marked footpaths through flower-decked meadows; the species vary with altitude. The first cable-car from Grindelwald village up to Bort station or higher is an ideal starting point. June to July is probably the best time for flowers.

Jungfrau Railway
Expensive but exceptional: the route up through the rock of the Eiger to the highest railway station in the world is an engineering marvel. The views across the snowfields and peaks are magnificent on a clear day.

Oberer Glacier

At the head of Grindelwald valley, a short walk from the road brings you to the steps leading up to the glacier face, from which you can walk on to the ice. The tunnel is about 660ft long with a small grotto at the end, eerily lit by filtered light.

LAKE LUCERNE
Good for family holidays

LUCERNE HAS everything visitors crave from Switzerland: a medieval town to explore, a beautiful lake to cruise, a dizzying rack railway to an impressive peak and, of course, the associations with the William Tell legend. Lucerne and its lake (actually four lakes all linked together) is a good base and well placed for trips up to the Oberland, Engadine or Zurich.

BEST SIGHTS

Kapellbrücke Bridge

Destroyed by fire in 1993, but since restored, the thirteenth-century bridge is the focal point of the town, with many waterside restaurants and cafés looking across to its famous octagonal water tower. Stroll downriver to the Spreuer Bridge to see an original, undamaged crossing. Built in 1408, its roof is covered in 67 macabre paintings on the theme of death.

Lake cruises

One of the prettiest Swiss lakes, Lucerne has some quiet lakeside villages where you can stay. From Vitznau the oldest mountain railway in Europe sets off for Mount Rigi (5,940ft).

Mount Pilatus

Views of the lake are magnificent, and the rack-railway ascent can be built into a day-long round-trip, with a steamer to Alpnachstad and the cable-car down.

Transport Museum

The museum is well worth a visit. It is a pleasant half-hour walk along the lake from the Kapellbrücke, or take the steamer or tram to Verkehrhaus pier.

ZURICH
Good for local colour

FAMOUS AS a great financial hub, Switzerland's largest city is also a graceful, ancient place, sufficiently interesting for a short stay. The old town, on the banks of the Limmat river, can be seen on riverside walks or cruises. Zürich is well-placed for trips out to sights such as St Gallen, with its superb eighteenth-century cathedral and rococo library.

BEST SIGHTS

Grossmünster
Dating from the eleventh century, the fine minster is emblem of the city. Across the Limmat is Zürich's other cathedral, the Fraumünster.

Landesmuseum
The Swiss National Museum contains displays on Swiss life, culture, art and history.

Weinplatz
This charming sixteenth-century square of Gothic buildings is the site of the city's oldest market. Catch a river excursion here or stroll down the river along the Wühre passageway.

GRAUBUNDEN
Good for scenic landscape

A REGION that prides itself on being quite distinct from the rest of Switzerland with its own language, Romansch, Graubünden also boasts some of Europe's finest ski resorts, at St Moritz, Davos and Klosters.

BEST SIGHTS

Engadine
The Upper Engadine is well known to skiers but also has some good walks linked by cable-cars and postbuses. The best villages are down the valley from Zernez, also the gateway to the National Park. Charming Guarda is the most famous and has plenty of accommodation. Ftan and Ardez are less geared to tourism and have a more authentic bucolic atmosphere. At Tarasp a castle stands on a rock above a charming village.

Rail journeys
From Italy the finest route is via the Bernina Pass. If the weather is good, choose an open-top carriage for unrestricted views. From St Moritz the Glacier Express heads down to Chur, then up the Rhine valley to Andermatt through some of Switzerland's best scenery. Book your seat, as this is a very popular journey.

TICINO
Good for local colour

THE ITALIAN-speaking area of Switzerland is often passed over by tourists heading for the cheaper lake regions of northern Italy – a shame, because there are some lovely lakeside villages.

BEST BASE

Lugano
A handsome town of piazzas and promenades, Lugano is preferable to its neighbour Locarno. It is also close to some pretty waterfront villages like Gandria and Morcote and hill villages like Ciona and Carona.

RHONE VALLEY
Good for food/wine and local colour

FROM ITS upper reaches around Gletsch all the way to Geneva, the burgeoning Rhône river is an important communications thoroughfare. The valley itself contains many interesting towns, castles and vineyards, while the side valleys can be very beautiful – though some are marred by hydro-electric projects.

BEST SIGHTS

Château Chillon
This partly thirteenth-century castle is a 20-minute lakeside walk from Montreux. The building itself is the main attraction, and the suggested walking tour is highly recommended.

Montreux
During the TV and jazz festivals the lakeside town is packed with visitors, but usually it is just a quiet, middle-class town of elegant residences with pleasant walks and vineyards along Lake Geneva.

Val d'Hérens
Val d'Hérens is not as pretty as some villages but its traditional way of life is still fairly intact.

Zermatt
Dominated by the Matterhorn, the large resort town retains some charm. Walks and rides are all top rate, but villages like Zmutt are accessible only by bicycle or on foot.

GENEVA
Good for culture

COSMOPOLITAN AND modern, Geneva is home to dozens of wealthy residents and international organisations – as reflected in its range of restaurants, galleries and museums. Some complain that its atmosphere is sterile, but the city certainly warrants a short stay.

BEST SIGHTS

Botanic Gardens
Exotic plants and animals are found in these splendid gardens. The greenhouses are closed on Fridays.

Museum of Art and History
In the old town, this collection is strong on archaeology and painting.

Museum of the International Red Cross and Red Crescent
Compelling displays document the many atrocities perpetrated since the organisation was founded in 1863, and trace its emergent role.

BASLE
Good for culture

A PROSPEROUS centre of the pharmaceutical industry, Basle has retained its attractive old town and boasts some excellent museums.

BEST SIGHTS

Barfüsserplatz
The square is the centre of old town life and contains a fourteenth-century Franciscan church house, now a museum of the medieval city.

Münster
The façade of this twin-towered cathedral features many sculptural treasures. Inside is the tomb of Erasmus, the Renaissance scholar.

Museum of Fine Arts

One of the most important art collections in Europe includes works by Picasso, Hans Holbein the Younger, Rodin and Konrad Witz.

WHEN TO GO

THE MAIN Alpine passes are open only from May to September. But around the lakes, the season is longer – especially in the south, where Lugano enjoys relatively warm weather from April to October, though it can be wet. Most Alpine flowers are at their best in June or early July.

Average daily maximum temperature °C											
London	6	7	10	13	17	20	22	21	19	14	10	7
Geneva	3	6	10	15	19	23	25	24	20	14	8	4
	JAN	FEB	MAR	APR	MAY	JUN	JUL	AUG	SEP	OCT	NOV	DEC
Geneva	11	9	9	9	11	11	9	11	10	10	11	10
London	15	13	11	12	12	11	12	11	13	13	15	15
Average number of rainy days per month											

PACKAGE TRAVEL

BROCHURES FEATURE hotel and self-catering apartments in a wide choice of resorts in the Bernese Oberland, the Valais and the Lake Geneva region. Multi-centre holidays are also available and include travel by rail between bases. Rail tours, either independent or escorted, are also featured, often with guided walks from selected

---

Tour operators

Camping: Canvas Holidays, Eurocamp, Select Sites **City breaks**: British Airways Holidays, Cresta, Inghams, Time Off, Travelscene, Yes Travel **Cultural**: Martin Randall, Prospect **General and specialist**: Crystal, Inghams, Kuoni, Lakes & Mountains, Leger, Osprey, Sovereign, Swiss Travel Service, Thomson **Rail tours**: Ffestiniog Travel, Page & Moy **Walking**: Exodus, Explore Worldwide, HF Holidays, Inntravel, Ramblers Holidays, Sherpa, Waymark **Other activities**: Classic Tours, DER, Moswin, Premier Holidays, Solo's Holidays (singles), Ultima, Waymark (walking), Winetrails (wine)

resorts as part of the package. Rhine cruises beginning or ending in Basle are also on offer. Excursions can be pre-booked. City breaks are available to Bern, Lausanne, Geneva, Lucerne, Zürich and Interlaken, Basle and Lugano. Activity holidays include camping, Rhine cruises, walking, rail tours and wine tours.

INDEPENDENT TRAVEL

ARRANGING YOUR own holiday probably will not save you money unless you take your own car and stay in campsites. You can fly direct to Geneva from London Heathrow, Stansted, Gatwick, Luton and Liverpool; and to Zürich from Heathrow, Luton and Manchester.

The Swiss public transport system is renowned for its punctuality; it is also very well co-ordinated, with trains timed to connect with one another at major junctions, with steamers on lakes, and with buses departing from station forecourts. All sizeable places are served by rail, as branch lines have been kept open, and yellow postbuses run along virtually every public road in the Alps. Bicycles can be hired at most railway stations, though you need to be fit to get the most from them!

If you plan to use public transport, get the Swiss Card, the best of several transport discount cards. It gives unlimited travel on all trains, alpine buses and boats, and on the transport systems in 36 cities too.

Car hire is expensive, but is cheaper if you book in advance. Fly-drive deals are better value. Roads are generally well maintained and signposted. The largest towns are linked by a fast motorway network, which makes getting round the non-Alpine part of Switzerland very easy indeed. To use the motorways you have to buy a pass, which is valid for one year. There are road tunnels beneath three of the main Alpine passes (Great St Bernard, St Gotthard and San Bernardino), but elsewhere in the Alps driving can be slow and hard work. Few of the higher passes are open before May/June.

Standards of accommodation are high, so you can safely opt for the cheaper and simpler B&Bs and guesthouses. Local tourist offices hold comprehensive lists and can book for you. Many railway stations have maps with pictures of hotels you can book on the spot on a freephone.

Switzerland has a huge amount of self-catering accommodation, especially in popular ski resorts; it is generally cheaper to rent in summer than in winter. Much of this accommodation consists of apartments in large modern chalets, though traditional one- and two-family chalets still exist.

The campsite network is highly developed: most sites are inspected and approved by the Swiss Camping and Caravanning Federation. Sites in the more popular areas can be a bit cramped and regimented, though facilities are generally excellent. It is advisable to book well ahead if you plan to camp in a popular area in summer.

RED TAPE, HEALTH AND SAFETY

BRITISH PASSPORT-HOLDERS do not require a visa. There are no particular health or crime problems in Switzerland – just take the usual precautions (see pages 10–12).

MORE INFORMATION Switzerland Tourism, Swiss Centre, 10 Wardour Street, London W1D 6QF, tel 020-7851 1700, web site: *www.myswitzerland.com*

COST OF LIVING £££

TANZANIA

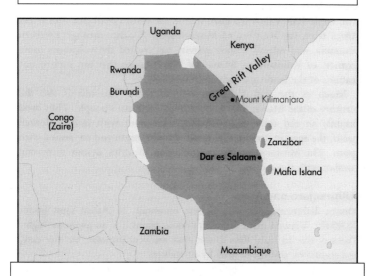

HIGHLIGHTS

Beaches
*Bagamoyo,
Dar es Salaam
North Coast,
Mafia Island*

Culture
*Northern
Tanzania,
Rift Valley*

History
*Bagamoyo,
Olduvai Gorge*

Outdoor activities
*Dar es Salaam
North Coast,
Kilimanjaro,
Mafia Island,
Mt Meru*

Scenic landscape
*Dar es Salaam
North Coast,
Kilimanjaro,
Mafia Island,
Mt Meru,
Rift Valley*

Wildlife
*Ngorongoro Crater,
Ruaha
National Park,
Sadaani
Game Reserve,
Selous
National Park,
Serengeti
National Park,
Tarangire
National Park*

NORTHERN TANZANIA
Good for culture, outdoor activities, scenic landscape and wildlife

MANY OF Tanzania's best sights are situated in Northern Tanzania, and for tourists this is by far the busiest part of the country, although it only gets really crowded around a few major attractions.

BEST SIGHTS

Great Rift Valley

The Great Rift Valley is a giant split in the earth's crust that runs across Africa from the Red Sea to Mozambique. It passes through northern Tanzania, and related seismic activity has created the volcanoes (now extinct) of Kilimanjaro, Meru and Ngorongoro that are such major features of the landscape today.

Much of the Rift Valley area in northern Tanzania is also the territory of the Maasai, best known of all Tanzania's people. They dress brightly in red robes and decorate themselves with multi-coloured beads; the men epitomise the 'noble warrior' myth and are armed with spears. The Maasai still maintain traditional lifestyles, despite increasing conflict with the modern world.

Kilimanjaro and Meru

Mount Kilimanjaro is the highest mountain in Africa (just under 20,000ft). Viewed from the surrounding plains it is an awesome sight. Treks of five to eight days to the peak are very popular, but not easy, and should be attempted only by fit walkers.

Mount Meru is 50 miles from Kilimanjaro, but overshadowed by its giant neighbour and frequently overlooked by visitors. A trek to the summit provides the best views of 'Kili', and the Arusha National Park in the foothills is a delightful mix of grassland and forest, famous for troops of black and white colobus monkey.

Olduvai Gorge

Volcanic lava laid down in the Great Rift Valley acted as a preservative, and later cut through by this gorge to reveal a cross-section of past millennia where the famous Leakey family of anthropologists and archaeologists made discoveries that changed existing theories of human evolution. The gorge is in the Serengeti National Park, and usually combined with a visit here.

BEST WILDLIFE

Ngorongoro Crater

This is a wildlife-watcher's heaven; a perfect bowl just a few miles wide, brimming with animals – lion, rhino, elephant, giraffe, zebra, hyena, wildebeest, buffalo, leopard, cheetah, jackal and numerous antelope species. Good sightings of all the African favourites are almost guaranteed, but the popularity of this relatively small area means it can have a safari-park feel at times.

Serengeti National Park

Probably the best-known of all wildlife reserves in Africa, this vast rolling grassland savanna is dotted with animals. Most famous are the herds of herbivores – notably millions of wildebeest which migrate spectacularly every year between May and July in search of fresh grazing.

Tarangire National Park

The Cinderella park of northern Tanzania, often scrubbed from busy itineraries. The wooded vegetation means wildlife watching is a touch harder than in other northern parks, but especially rewarding in the dry season when animals come from miles around to drink at the Tarangire River.

THE COAST AND ISLANDS
Good for beaches, outdoor activities and scenic landscape

Bagamoyo

The sleepy town of Bagamoyo was once a busy slave port, and later a centre for Germany's short-lived colonial rule. Some ancient buildings, and an evocative atmosphere, remain from these times, but today the idyllic beach attracts most visitors, catered for by an exclusive hotel and a handful of cheaper guesthouses.

Dar es Salaam

This is Tanzania's political and commercial centre (the official capital is Dodoma in the centre of the country). It is a big, noisy, humid, dusty and frenetic city with few real 'sights' but a very lively atmosphere and an engaging mix of African, Indian and European cultures and architecture. Nearby, the palm-fringed beaches of Dar es Salaam's North Coast are lined with luxury hotels and resorts. Offshore are small islands, popular for diving and snorkelling, although uncontrolled commercial fishing and coral collection has damaged much of the reef.

Sadaani Game Reserve

Sadaani is the only wildlife reserve on the coast ('where the bush meets the beach'), and due for upgrading to full national park status. With luck you might see a few elephants bathing in the surf.

Zanzibar and Mafia Islands

Zanzibar, in the Indian Ocean north of Dar es Salaam, is a separate state (see pages 594–8). Mafia Island, to the south of Dar, incongruously counts as part of the mainland, and is beautiful, remote and rarely visited. The island is noted for its big-game fishing and boasts a couple of exclusive luxury lodges.

SOUTHERN TANZANIA
Good for wildlife and scenic landscapes

THE SOUTHERN part of Tanzania is frequently overlooked by visitors, as its attractions are harder (and more expensive) to reach. The national parks are more specialised, and wildlife-viewing, although immensely rewarding, takes a bit more skill and patience.

Ruaha National Park
Remote Ruaha is famous for its massive herds of elephant and buffalo, as well as all the other African favourites. The rough and rocky hill country makes an interesting change to the savanna landscapes more usually encountered in wildlife areas.

Selous National Park
This is the largest wildlife reserve in Africa, situated in the low flatlands of south-eastern Tanzania, and boasts huge and varied wildlife populations. Only a small section of the park is open to visitors, but this is still big enough to get lost in for days. Most viewing is along the lush and beautiful Rufuji River. Selous is noted for containing packs of rare African hunting dog, and small groups of black rhino.

WHEN TO GO

THE NORTH of Tanzania has two dry seasons (December to February and June to October) – the best times to visit – with the former months being particularly busy. Outside these periods it rains for a few hours each day, but the wet humid weather means fewer visitors, more space and better prices. On the coast, even in the dry season, the Indian Ocean makes rain possible at any time. In the far south of Tanzania, the single dry season is from March to October.

Average daily maximum temperature °C											
London	6	7	10	13	17	20	22	21	19	14	10	7
Dar es Salaam	26	27	26	26	26	26	25	25	26	26	26	26
	JAN	FEB	MAR	APR	MAY	JUN	JUL	AUG	SEP	OCT	NOV	DEC
Dar es Salaam	13	13	19	22	17	7	5	8	12	15	17	16
London	15	13	11	12	12	11	12	11	13	13	15	15
Average number of rainy days per month											

PACKAGE TRAVEL

MANY HOLIDAY companies run tours to Tanzania, mostly a week or two 'on safari', with the option of extra days on the coast or islands, or trekking on Kilimanjaro. Costs vary, according to the standard of accommodation (everything from basic bush camps to luxury five-star hotels) and method of transport (minibus, four-wheel-drive vehicle or charter plane), as well as the actual destinations visited.

Several specialist tour operators also offer tailor-made tours around Tanzania, for individuals, couples or small groups, and base the itinerary around your particular needs and interests.

Tour operators

General and specialist: Abercrombie & Kent, Bales Tours, Cox & Kings, Distant Dreams, Hayes & Jarvis, Kuoni, Okavango Tours & Safaris, Somak, Tanzania Experience, Travelbag, Tropical Places, Worldwide Journeys **Tailor made specialists**: Africa Archipelago, Africa Exclusive, Africa Travel Centre, Carrier Tours, Cazenove & Loyd, Nomadic Thoughts, Safari Drive, Southern Africa Travel **Walking/adventure**: Dragoman, Explore, Exodus, Guerba, High Places, KE Adventure, Peregrine, Walks Worldwide **Other activities**: Dive Worldwide (scuba), Naturetrek, Wildlife Worldwide (wildlife), Solo's (singles)

INDEPENDENT TRAVEL

AIRLINES WITH flights to Tanzania from the UK include British Airways, Gulf Air, Ethiopian Airlines, KLM and Kenya Airways. For destinations in northern Tanzania, flights land at Kilimanjaro International Airport. The country's main airport at Dar es Salaam is more useful for the coast, and for the islands and southern Tanzania. From Dar, local air companies provide internal connecting flights.

Getting around the country independently is fairly straightforward on the main routes. Car hire is available, but unusual and very expensive, and not recommended for visitors without African driving experience. Trains are slow but enjoyable; buses can go terrifyingly fast. Getting into national parks or other wildlife areas is very difficult on public transport, but in Dar es Salaam and the northern towns of Moshi and Arusha it's easy to join a safari group (or have your own safari organised).

RED TAPE, HEALTH AND SAFETY

VISAS FOR Tanzania are required and available from the Tanzanian High Commission in London for £38. Your passport should still be valid for at least six months. You also need two passport-sized photographs. You can apply in person, between 10am and 12.30pm, Monday to Friday, and pay in cash. Allow 24 hours for processing. Alternatively, get the High Commission to send you a visa application form, and apply by post with an sae and £38 in postal orders. You can get more visa information from the official web site, and also download an application form.

On arrival in Tanzania you will need to show a certificate to prove that you have been inoculated for yellow fever. Your doctor or travel clinic will advise on yellow fever and other jabs required.

Precautions against malaria are important. Take anti-malaria pills, use mosquito repellent and wear sufficient clothes in the evening. Most hotels provide mosquito nets, although in cheaper places these may be missing or have big holes. If you are travelling at budget level take your own portable net.

Many people in Tanzania, especially in coastal areas and on the islands, are Muslim and traditionally conservative. Nudity is forbidden, as is topless bathing (although within the grounds of tourist hotels and resorts it is usually OK). Scanty clothing anywhere away from the beach is frowned upon.

Robberies (occasionally with violence) are not unknown in Dar es Salaam, Moshi and Arusha and also on some beach areas. Use common-sense to keep safe: avoid quiet areas at night, especially if walking alone, and keep valuables (including cameras) out of sight wherever possible.

MORE INFORMATION Tanzania Tourist Office, Tanzania Trade Centre, 78–80 Borough High Street, London SE1 1LL, tel 020–7407 0566

Tanzanian High Commission, 43 Hertford Street, London W1Y 8DB, tel 020–7499 8951, web site: *www.tanzania-online.gov.uk*

COST OF LIVING £

THAILAND

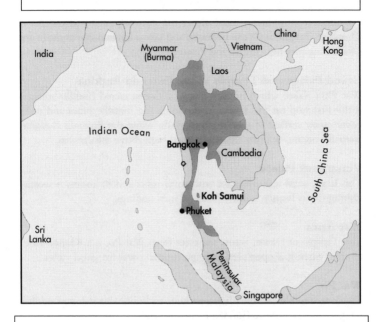

HIGHLIGHTS

Beaches/ romantic escapism
Coast

Food/wine
Bangkok, coast, northern Thailand

History
Bangkok, central and northern Thailand

Scenic landscape
Krabi, northern Thailand

Culture
Bangkok, central and northern Thailand

Outdoor activities
Coast, northern Thailand

Local colour
Bangkok, northern Thailand

Shopping
Bangkok, Chiang Mai

BANGKOK
Good for culture, food/wine, history, local colour and shopping

SPRAWLING AND steamy, full of gridlocked traffic, Bangkok is not a beautiful city, but its street life, markets and temples (*wats*) provide a sensory experience that you should not miss.

517

BEST SIGHTS

Canal tour
To discover how life is lived along the network of urban canals in Thonburi, bargain with the boatmen and take a longtail speedboat from Tha Chang pier near the Grand Palace.

Grand Palace and Temple of the Emerald Buddha
Wat Phra Kaeo, which houses Thailand's most sacred Buddha image, is the first stop on the tourist trail. Golds and metallic blues and reds cover every surface of the roof and walls, while the Emerald Buddha (actually jadeite) is a tiny figurine placed high above the crowds.

Vimanmek Palace
This large, solid teak mansion with royal relics and 81 rooms is worth visiting for its beauty and the peaceful surroundings.

Wat Arun
The Temple of Dawn, across the river from Wat Po, is a Khmer-style temple; when it is open climb up the central tower for good views.

Wat Po
This large temple complex houses a huge reclining 150-ft-long Buddha image. Hundreds more Buddha images inhabit the courtyards.

Wat Traimit
The Golden Buddha, a five-and-a-half-ton, solid gold, thirteenth-century statue, sits in this small temple in a ramshackle compound.

BEST EXCURSIONS

Ayutthaya
This was Thailand's capital until 1767, when the Burmese invaded and destroyed it. The temple remains scattered among waterways and parks are very atmospheric.

Bridge over the River Kwai, Kanchanaburi
The infamous Death Railway, where many British, Australian and Asian prisoners of war died during the Second World War, is about 80 miles west of Bangkok. The day-trip includes visits to the cemeteries and war museum and a journey along a stretch of the railway.

Damnoen Saduak Floating Market
This colourful early-morning floating market 68 miles from Bangkok is less touristy than the one in the city centre.

COAST AND ISLANDS
Good for beaches, food/wine, romantic escapism and outdoor activities

SINCE THAILAND'S growth in popularity as a package destination, resort development has been inevitable. Some resorts have been spoilt; others are a step behind, with good facilities but still enough room to breathe. For those who like the simple life, there are beaches and islands more or less untouched by tourism.

KRABI

THE BEADED limestone cliffs and sea stacks above white-sand beaches make this the most exotic and scenically spectacular coastal region of Thailand.

Krabi Town itself is unremarkable, but the coastline for several miles to the west hides dozens of idyllic beaches – the best of these is Phra Nang. Ao Nang is the most developed resort, with several hotels and bars, and enough seafood restaurants along the beachfront to provide variety for a week's stay.

PHUKET

EASE OF access combined with wonderful beaches have made Thailand's largest island a prime spot for rapid development, but it has not been spoilt entirely. Patong is the liveliest resort at night, hotels in other parts of the island run shuttle services into this resort and Phuket Town.

BEST BEACHES

South of Patong, Kata Yai and Kata Noi beaches are beautiful, with palms and an offshore island. At Nai Han the beach shelves steeply but is extremely attractive, although it is quite isolated. North of Patong, Bang Tao is a long, straight beach with shade and upmarket development. Pansea and Laem Sing are two small coves tucked under steep hillsides.

BEST EXCURSIONS

Two small islands, Phi Phi Don and Phi Phi Le, come very close to picture-book tropical paradises: they offer fine white sand and excellent snorkelling (they are very crowded in high season). Day-trips by boat from Phuket include lunch, snorkelling and a trip in a glass-bottomed boat – or you can stay overnight in bungalow complexes.

At Phang-Nga Bay, sheer-sided limestone peaks jutting from the water have been eroded into fantastic shapes. You can reach some of the islands in the bay, such as James Bond Island, where tourists mingle with souvenir sellers, on trips from Phuket by bus and ferry or longtail boat.

KOH SAMUI

KOH SAMUI has a laid-back feel. The beaches are perfect, and no building is allowed to rise higher than the coconut palms. An unconventional air prevails, despite swanky international hotels outnumbering the shanty-like beach bungalows along the island's two most magnificent beaches of Chaweng and Lamai.

BEST BEACHES

The north-east peninsula of the island shelters some very pretty sand coves, like Choeng Mon beach, which are good for peace and quiet. Chaweng beach, a wonderful four-mile stretch of sand, is the best (and most popular) beach on the island. Lamai is similar to Chaweng, although smaller and marginally less beautiful.

BEST EXCURSIONS

Over 40 small islands scattered in the sea west of Koh Samui make up Ang Thong National Marine Park and hide caves eroded out of the soft limestone rock and perfect little beaches. Day-trips run from Na Thon, and you can arrange to go snorkelling or diving.

CENTRAL THAILAND
Good for culture and history

IN THE fertile basin of the Chao Phraya river are ruins of Thai civilisations which are much older than those in Bangkok.

BEST SIGHTS

Lopburi
Easily reached on the railway line running from Bangkok to northern Thailand, this historical town is known as much for its hundreds of monkeys scampering around and stealing food as for its thousand-year-old Khmer ruins.

Sukhothai
Unification of Thailand took place here in the thirteenth century after the Khmer empire waned. Now most of the royal city is preserved as a historical park – a captivating complex of temple ruins among shady trees and lakes. Wat Mahathat, the king's temple, is the most impressive of the ruins, while Wat Si Chum has a huge seated Buddha. The best way to explore is to hire a bike.

NORTHERN THAILAND
Good for culture, food/wine, history, local colour, outdoor activities, scenic landscape and shopping

AROUND THE cities of the mountainous north a palpable air of the exotic creeps in, with the misty hills of Laos rising above the Mekong river, and hill-tribe women selling handicrafts.

BEST BASES

Chiang Mai
With scores of beautiful old temples inside the ancient walled city, Chiang Mai is the most popular destination in Thailand for visitors interested in culture and history, and is consequently touristy and commercialised.

The main centre from which to explore the north has developed rapidly over recent years. Its night market is one of the best places to buy local embroidered bags and belts as well as fake designer goods, but be prepared to bargain hard. In the factories and workshops east of town you can see painted umbrellas, teak furniture, silverware, silk and pottery being made.

Chiang Rai
If Chiang Mai is too city-like for you, Chiang Rai, about 60 miles further north, is well positioned by the River Kok and within close range of the Golden Triangle, the Burmese border and hill-tribe villages.

BEST SIGHTS AND EXCURSIONS

Doi Tung
This mountain rises abruptly from the plains close to the border town of Mae Sai. Taxis run up to the peak, where there is a small temple surrounded by bells. The views are tremendous.

Golden Triangle
Close to Chiang Saen in the tourist village of Sop Ruak stands an archway emblazoned with 'Golden Triangle'. This is the spot where Thailand, Laos and Burma meet, and the village caters for people who

just want to stand and be photographed there. There is also a small but interesting opium museum.

Hill tribes and trekking

Northern Thailand's mountains are inhabited by various tribes, each with its own distinctive language, customs, costume and jewellery. Trekking into the mountains to visit the tribes is big tourist business, and however far you walk you are unlikely to find a village that does not have regular visits from tourists. Those close to roads or rivers have become unintentional folk museums, and arguments rage about whether tourism benefits or damages the hill people.

The treks on offer vary in length and may include elephant rides or raft journeys as well as overnight stops in tribal guesthouses. Ask other travellers for recommendations before choosing a trekking company. Lists of registered guides should be available at the tourist offices.

WHEN TO GO

THAILAND IS hot and humid all year round, and wet when the monsoons arrive. The north-east monsoon drenches east-coast beaches between November and January, while the west is affected from May to November. Central and northern Thailand are at their driest and coolest from November to February (April and May are sweltering). Thailand's high season is at the same time as the British winter; the cheapest holiday deals are at other times of the year.

	Average daily maximum temperature °C											
London	6	7	10	13	17	20	22	21	19	14	10	7
Bangkok	32	33	34	35	34	33	32	32	32	31	31	31
	JAN	FEB	MAR	APR	MAY	JUN	JUL	AUG	SEP	OCT	NOV	DEC
Bangkok	1	1	3	3	9	10	13	13	15	14	5	1
London	15	13	11	12	12	11	12	11	13	13	15	15
	Average number of rainy days per month											

PACKAGE TRAVEL

ALL THE major tour operators feature Thailand for long-haul sun-and-sand holidays with a touch of the exotic. The islands of Phuket, Koh Phi Phi and Koh Samui, the mainland resort of Pattaya, the smaller resorts of Hua Hin and Cha Am and the coast around Krabi are all included in brochures. Pattaya is the most spoilt resort – and also has the down side of being a magnet for sex tourists. Accommodation is mostly in international-style hotels for one or two weeks. While many tourists visit only Bangkok and the beach resorts, plenty take tours to the north, visiting palaces and temples on the way to Chiang Mai and Chiang Rai – bases from which to take trips to the hill-tribe villages or to the Golden Triangle.

Other packaged excursions are three- or four-day tours to the River Kwai, cruises on the Chao Phraya river from Bangkok and day excursions from Bangkok to the floating market and Ayutthaya.

Tour operators

Birdwatching: Naturetrek **General**: Abercrombie & Kent, Airtours, Bales Tours, Bridge the World, British Airways Holidays, Cosmos, Distant Dreams, Elegant Resorts, Far East Gateways, First Choice, Gold Medal, Hayes & Jarvis, Jetset, Kuoni, Magic of the Orient, Oriental Magic, Premier Holidays, Saga, Silk Steps, Thomas Cook, Thomson, Tradewinds, Trailfinders, Travelbag, Travelsphere, Tropical Places, Voyages Jules Verne **Walking**: Exodus, Explore Worldwide **Other activities**: Club Med (all-inclusive), Solo's Holidays (singles), Somak (diving)

INDEPENDENT TRAVEL

DIRECT SCHEDULED flights, as well as charter flights, run daily to Bangkok from London.

Using local transport is not difficult, but the heat, the language difficulties and the pace of cross-country travel will slow you down. If your time is limited, fly – internal flights are reasonable, especially out of season. Long-distance buses come both with and without air-conditioning. Leg room is not generous, but the system is efficient. Trains are comfortable if you avoid third class, and usually have air-conditioned carriages. If you want to avoid the crush at the ticket kiosks, book in advance through a Bangkok travel agent, particularly for a sleeper or air-conditioned seat. Bangkok's new monorail should provide some relief to the traffic-bound city streets – and help out journey times.

There is no shortage of transport for short journeys; the only problem is knowing what to pay. Outside Bangkok, conventional taxis are replaced by *songthaews* – communal pick-ups with bench seats. These usually ply regular routes but will act (and charge) as taxis if empty. *Tuk-tuks* – motorised three-wheelers – seat two in discomfort, as do trishaws, which use pedal power alone. On water, longtail speedboats are powered by car engines, a propeller on a shaft acting as rudder and driving force – these are fast and very noisy. Chartering a whole boat is expensive, but you can share or join a river tour. Car hire is not recommended since alternative forms of transport are generally cheaper, quicker and more efficient. Hiring a car with a chauffeur can be a good deal and some drivers are excellent guides.

Thailand's package and business hotels are several steps ahead of their European counterparts. Low labour costs ensure plentiful staff, and service is immaculate. Facilities are generally good, too. The beach resorts and northern towns have a wide choice of accommodation, while Bangkok seems to spawn a new hotel every week. Always ask for discounts, or book from the UK via a tour operator for the best deals. Small hotels and guesthouses are found in all the popular towns and resorts, ranging from dingy doss-houses to cosy rooms in old teak houses. Budget rooms are separated by flimsy plywood partitions, with space simply for a bed and a bag – and maybe a fan if you are lucky.

RED TAPE, HEALTH AND SAFETY

TOURIST VISAS are required for stays of longer than 30 days. If you need to stay longer you will require either a 60-day tourist visa or a 90-day non-immigrant visa. For more information contact the Thai Embassy.

Protection against hepatitis A, polio, typhoid and mosquito bites is recommended (though in most areas anti-malaria protection is not considered necessary). Check with your doctor or a travel clinic.

Thailand's crackdown on opium has sanitised much of what used to be quite dangerous country in the north and west. But insurgent groups in Burma and the presence of bandits make it unwise to stray too far on your own in remote areas. Check with police.

Thai touts work by friendliness, not aggression. Be firm when saying no to being taken to the local handicraft shop, and beware of anyone who tries to interest you in buying gemstones. For the latest safety advice, contact the Foreign Office Travel Advice Unit (see page 11).

MORE INFORMATION Tourism Authority of Thailand,
49 Albemarle Street, London W1X 3FE, tel 020-7499 7679,
brochure line (0839) 300800 (premium rate number)
web site: *www.tourismthailand.org/*

The Royal Thai Embassy, 29 Queens Gate, London SW7 5JB,
tel 020-7589 2944, information line (0891) 600150 (premium rate number)

COST OF LIVING £

TUNISIA

HIGHLIGHTS

Beaches
Central and southern Tunisia, Tunis and the north

Culture/ family holidays
Central Tunisia, Tunis and the north

Outdoor activities
Tunis and the north

Local colour
Central and southern Tunisia

Scenic landscape
Southern Tunisia

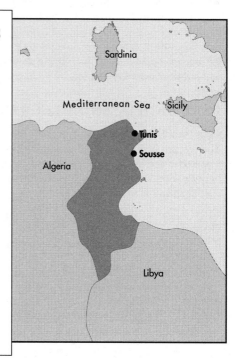

Sardinia

Mediterranean Sea · Sicily

Algeria

● Tunis

● Sousse

Libya

TUNIS AND THE NORTH
Good for beaches, culture, family holidays and outdoor activities

BEST RESORTS

Hammamet
● The broad sweep of Hammamet's bay is the premier package holiday destination in Tunisia.

● Good-value, low-rise hotels here come as a surprise to many people who might expect a North African destination to be less sophisticated.

● The development stretches for miles on either side of the town centre, and provides accommodation for those who want a beach holiday and minimal interaction with local people and culture.

Tabarka
● Close to the border with Algeria in the north-western corner of Tunisia, Tabarka is a fast-growing resort with a relaxed feel, offering

525

sandy beaches and rocky coves as well as sailing, diving and windsurfing.

● Despite the expansion during the 1990s of the old port into the luxury marina of Porto Corallo, the forests of cork oaks give the area an almost Provençal feel, while the town itself focuses around a lovely little bay with a Genoese fort.

● Golf facilities are nearby, and diving sites around areas of increasingly rare Mediterranean coral.

BEST SIGHTS AND EXCURSIONS

Cap Bon Peninsula

The 'garden of Tunisia' produces a cornucopia of fresh produce and is a welcome break from Hammamet. It is worth a trip for the undeveloped beaches around the charismatic fishing town of Kelibia, and the Carthaginian ruins of Kerkouane.

Dougga

If you want to visit one of Tunisia's excellent Roman sites, Dougga is perhaps the most interesting. The Tebersouk Mountains provide an impressive backdrop as you explore the extensive ruins. The highlight is the remarkably well-preserved Capitol built in AD166 and dedicated to Jupiter, Juno and Minerva. Other Roman sites in the north worth a visit are Bulla Regia and Thuburbo Majus.

TUNIS

FOR A capital city, Tunis is very relaxed and feels as if it belongs on the other side of the Mediterranean, especially with its French-style pavement cafés. It is cosmopolitan and liberal by Islamic standards, and presents no real culture shock for first-timers. However, it is not all that exciting either.

BEST SIGHTS

The *medina* is as hassle-free as you are likely to find, providing a laid-back introduction to haggling in the *souks* around the Great Mosque, which dates from the ninth century. The Bardo Museum, a short bus ride from the city centre, is the best in the country and an essential port of call for the superb collection of Roman mosaics taken from sites like Dougga and Thuburbo Majus. By far the most impressive is the third-century mosaic of the poet Virgil pictured being attended by two muses as he writes the famed *Aeneid*.

BEST EXCURSIONS

Carthage is a suburb of Tunis's urban sprawl and one of Tunisia's most famous archaeological sites. However, you should not expect too much, as the Romans totally levelled the original Phoenician city, and the various sites are very spread out and not particularly well kept. It is worth a wander for a few hours. Sidi bou Said is an engaging little village of whitewashed houses and avoids being a complete tourist trap. Perched on cliffs north of Tunis, the romantic atmosphere is refreshing but it can get busy when the tourist buses descend.

CENTRAL TUNISIA
Good for beaches, culture, family holidays and local colour

BEST RESORTS

Monastir

● Nine miles south of Sousse, Monastir is a centre for package tourism. The once fairly typical Tunisian town has been transformed into a showpiece tourist resort, complete with pristine streets and lampposts from the turn of the century.

● The heavily restored eighth-century Ribat has been the setting for several films, including *Life of Christ* and *Life of Brian*.

● It also has a Great Mosque and a chic 400-berth marina area where you can enjoy a drink or a meal.

Sousse

● Most visitors to Sousse go for the package hotels lining the strip of beach between the centre and the characterless development of Port el Kantaoui to the north, which is totally un-Tunisian.

● Sousse proper has a couple of interesting items in the *medina*, such as the ninth-century Ribat and Great Mosque.

● The *medina* is good for browsing in the bazaars, although it is geared very much towards the tourist trade and prices are accordingly high. Stuffed toy camels are a speciality.

BEST SIGHTS AND EXCURSIONS

El Djem

The impressive Roman amphitheatre that rises out of the dry and dusty olive-growing plains at El Djem is a sight to behold. It is slightly smaller than the Colosseum in Rome, but better preserved. Nothing detracts from this awesome monument to the civilisation that once flourished here. The museum has stunning mosaics, and classical concerts are held during the July and August music festival.

Kairouan

Kairouan is the fourth holiest city in Islam after Mecca, Medina and Jerusalem, and is culturally significant as it is the most ancient seat of Islam in the Maghreb. The Great Mosque dates from the seventh century with marble pillars, ancient pulpits and a staircase constructed from Christian tombstones. Other important monuments are the Agh-labid Basins, and the Zawiyyas of Sidi Sahab and Sidi Abid el–Ghariani. Kairouan is also an important centre of carpet production.

Sfax

The main reason for visiting Sfax, a largely industrial city, is to see an authentic working *medina*. It is a hive of activity with scores of tailors, engravers and furniture makers, yet the *souks* provide the opportunity to enjoy a relaxed browse without being made to feel like a tourist. The Dar Jellouli Museum boasts a fine collection of arts and crafts from the era of the *beys* (a *bey* was governor of a province in the Ottoman Empire). The Kerkennah Islands off the coast offer the chance to wind down completely. The fishing villages of Cherque and Gharbi are the main inhabited islands and can easily be reached by ferry.

SOUTHERN TUNISIA
Good for beaches, local colour and scenic landscape

THE SOUTH of Tunisia is in many ways the most fascinating area, and for the adventurous it offers the most rewarding sights and experiences. However, it can get extremely hot in summer.

BEST BASES

Matmata

The Berber people live underground here because of the searing heat. It is a lunar, almost surreal, landscape of craters and TV aerials seemingly sticking out of the ground. The craters are in fact circular wells from which the dug-out rooms radiate in these underground dwellings. You can stay in an underground hotel – an unusual experience. A number of scenes from the *Star Wars* films were shot at Matmata, including *The Phantom Menace*. The nearby village of Haddej has similar attractions but without the crowds. You can also make a side trip to Toujane along a very rough road with stunning views.

Tozeur

In Tozeur, you really feel that you are in the desert. Four-wheel-drive tours can be taken from here, and there are plenty of palmy oases and dunes to be seen, as well as the magnificent mountain oases of Chebika,

Mides and Tamerza. The town is on the northern shore of the great salt lake of Chott el jerid, which you can visit on foot or by rather rickety horse-drawn carriage (*calèche*). The excellent Dar Cherait museum depicts scenes of Tunisian life, past and present. Detour to Nefta to wander round its old town and oasis (*palmeraie*).

BEST RESORT

Djerba
● Just offshore, in the Gulf of Gabès, the island of Djerba is a well-developed package destination with good beaches.
● It claims to be the 'Land of the Lotus Eaters' in Homer's *Odyssey*.
● The people of Djerba have a reputation for friendliness and it is a relaxed place for a family holiday.
● The village of Guellala is known for its pottery.

BEST SCENIC LANDSCAPE

Berber settlements
South of Matmata are the *ksour*, fortified Berber settlements built from multi-storey arched granaries called *ghorfa*. Ksar Ouled Soultane has the best-preserved structures, which are more than 400 years old, but Chenini is perhaps the highlight of the *ksour* area. The whole setting is superb, with houses carved out of the cliffside and a ruined *ksar* perched above on the ridge.

Chott el jerid
The *chott* is a massive salt lake covering 2,000 square miles. The principal interest is the range of colours that form on its normally dry surface because of the chemicals in the muddy soup beneath the hard crust. Mirages and surreal optical effects are frequently seen on sunny days. A raised causeway allows visitors to cross the *chott*.

Douz
The Great Dune of Douz is the ideal location for posing as Lawrence of Arabia and looking out over the mighty *erg* (the shifting sand dunes) that stretch to the horizon and beyond. The Douz Museum explores the culture of the southern Jerid and is well worth a visit.

Seldja Gorge
You can take a scenic train ride along this spectacular gorge from Metlaoui to Redeyef. The nineteenth-century 'Red Lizard' train was once the Bey of Tunis's private train and has been refurbished for tourists.

WHEN TO GO

BASICALLY, THE further south you go, the hotter it gets. Northern Tunisia has a typical Mediterranean climate, with hot summers and mild, wet winters. By contrast, parts of the Sahara in the south may not have rain for years. The major religious holiday period is Ramadan, which lasts for about a month. The faithful are expected to fast during the day, and opening times tend to be disrupted. The end of Ramadan is marked by two days' holiday for the whole country (rather like Christmas) and can also be an awkward time to travel.

	Average daily maximum temperature °C											
London	6	7	10	13	17	20	22	21	19	14	10	7
Tunis	15	16	18	21	25	29	32	32	30	25	21	16
	JAN	FEB	MAR	APR	MAY	JUN	JUL	AUG	SEP	OCT	NOV	DEC
Tunis	13	11	11	8	5	2	1	3	5	9	9	11
London	15	13	11	12	12	11	12	11	13	13	15	15
	Average number of rainy days per month											

PACKAGE TRAVEL

MASS-MARKET TOUR operators feature the coastal resorts of Hammamet, Port El Kantaoui, Sousse and Monastir. Specialists also feature Djerba in the south and have escorted tours inland into the Sahara. Fly-drive and two-centre holidays are also available, with a week on the coast combined with a week in Djerba or touring. Activity holidays include golf, archaeology and cultural tours.

> **Tour operators**
>
> **Cultural**: Andante, British Museum Traveller, Martin Randall
> **General and specialist**: Airtours, Cadogan, Cosmos, First Choice, Panorama, Prestige, JMC Travel, Thomson, Wigmore Holidays
> **Other activities**: Andante (archaeology), Club Med (multi-activity), Explore Worldwide (walking), Holts' Tours (battlefields), Longshot Golf (golf)

INDEPENDENT TRAVEL

THE CHEAPEST fares are for charter flights, which go to Monastir and Tunis. Scheduled flights go to Tozeur, and internal flights from Tunis to Djerba, Tozeur and Sfax.

For long-distance travel the best way of getting around is by bus. The national bus company, SNTRI, provides good coverage of the main towns and cities, but book in advance. Regional bus companies serve smaller areas; these tend to be slower and are not air-conditioned. Trains are modern and efficient, but the rail network is limited. It is worth paying a bit extra for more comfort in first-class.

Shared long-distance taxis (*louages*) take five passengers and leave when full. Determine the fare before you get in; all drivers are required to carry a list of tariffs set by the government.

Car hire is expensive; it is probably best if you book through your travel agent or tour operator before you arrive. Most rental companies set a minimum age of 21. A British driving licence is sufficient; usually it must have been valid for at least a year. Roads are excellent; some in the south are unsurfaced but can be negotiated with care.

Most hotels are inspected and classified under the government rating system, and are required to display the tariff in reception. In popular package destinations you will come across five-star luxury resorts with all facilities – such places are usually cheaper if they are booked through a tour operator – but in other towns and *medinas* there are plenty of cheap one-star and unclassified hotels (you will often be expected to use public bath-houses). The few campsites are very basic. You can camp on beaches or in parks – check with the owner first.

RED TAPE, HEALTH AND SAFETY

BRITISH PASSPORT-HOLDERS do not require a visa for a stay of up to three months.

Polio, typhoid and tetanus vaccinations are usually recommended – consult your GP or a travel clinic for the latest advice, and see tips on page 12 about avoiding stomach upsets. For the latest advice on safety and security, contact the Foreign Office Travel Advice Unit (see page 11).

MORE INFORMATION Tunisian National Tourist Office, 77A Wigmore Street, London W1H 9LJ, tel 020-7224 5561, web site: *www.tourismtunisia.com*

COST OF LIVING £

TURKEY

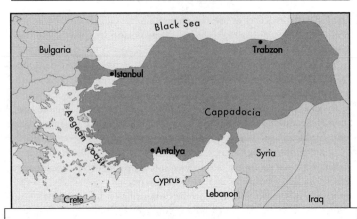

HIGHLIGHTS

Culture	Family	Mediterranean	Outdoor
Aegean coast,	**holidays**	*coast*	**activities**
Black Sea coast,	*Mediterranean*		*Cappadocia*
Istanbul,	*coast*	**Nightlife**	
Konya,		*Aegean coast,*	**Scenic**
Mediterranean	**Local colour**	*Mediterranean*	**landscape**
coast,	*Black Sea coast,*	*coast*	*Black Sea coast,*
Nemrut Dagi	*Istanbul,*		*Cappadocia*

ISTANBUL
Good for culture and local colour

ONE OF the world's great romantic cities, Istanbul straddles the European and Asian shores of the Bosphorus. Most of the best-known sights are grouped together in the Sultanahmet district in the European side, while major hotels, shopping and nightlife are concentrated in the more modern Taksim area, across the Golden Horn. The main financial and business area has migrated several miles north, where ultra-modern high-rise building is concentrated.

BEST SIGHTS

Aya Sofya
Emperor Justinian's great sixth-century church, seized and turned into a mosque by the Ottoman conquerors in 1453, is now a museum. The

impressive Byzantine mosaics and vast interior space are likely to be shrouded in scaffolding for some years.

Blue Mosque
Named for its exuberant blue tiles, the seventeenth-century Blue Mosque stands opposite Aya Sofya, its dome and minarets mirroring those of the older church. Sound and light performances take place in summer.

Chora Church (Kariye Camii)
The gorgeous fourteenth-century Byzantine mosaic- and fresco-filled church has been restored and turned into a museum.

Covered Bazaar/Egyptian Bazaar
The sprawling, always busy Covered Bazaar is the place to buy leather jackets, T-shirts, etc., while the aromatic Egyptian Bazaar serves up spices and herbs, dates and Turkish delight.

Dolmabahce Palace
Mustafa Kemal Atatürk died in this vast Victorian palace in 1938 – the clocks are still set at the time of his death. Visits are by guided tour only, and the palace is often very crowded in summer.

Topkapi Palace
This sprawling complex of kiosks and courtyards overlooks the Bos-phorus, and is where the Ottoman Sultans and their myriad concubines lived from 1453 to 1839. Highlights include the Harem, Imperial Treasury and Suite of the Felicitous Cloak displaying relics of the Prophet Mohammed. Topkapi crawls with coach parties and is best visited out of season.

Turkish and Islamic Arts Museum
A stunning collection of ceramics, carpets, calligraphy and other arte-facts is displayed in a sixteenth-century palace off historic Hippodrome. The ethnography section has showcases of nomadic *kilims* and tents.

Yerebatan Sarayi (Underground Palace)
This is an atmospheric underground cistern, with the roof supported by 300 Byzantine columns rising from the water. You can tread the boardwalk while music plays.

AEGEAN COAST
Good for culture and nightlife

THE AEGEAN coast boasts several large, brash resorts suitable for young people in search of lively nightlife. Within easy reach of several spectacular archaeological sites, these resorts make attractive bases for sightseers provided the hotels are chosen with care. The coves and inlets of this coast are extremely beautiful, and boat trips are a highlight of any visit. Turkey's second-largest port, Izmir, is the export centre for the rich agricultural hinterland – figs, sultanas, tobacco, cotton, olive oil. It has top-grade hotels and is a good tourist base for reaching the archaeological treasures north and south, with frequent long-distance bus links. You can also take day-trips to several Greek islands.

BEST RESORTS

Not all of the big resorts have decent beaches, so it is wise to select a hotel with its own pool. The closer you are to a town centre, the more chance there is of being disturbed by the nightlife. However, the quieter hotels on the outlying beaches can seem very characterless.

Altinkum
● The name means 'Golden Sand' – a newly built family resort with broad beach and paddling depth for children for at least a hundred yards to the safety line.
● The resort developers also remembered to build a good choice of waterfront restaurants and bars, and some discos; otherwise sleepy outside the main season.

Assos
● Tiny gem of a fishing harbour with half a dozen simple hotels and restaurants.
● Ruins of Behramkale on hill above; good beach 2½ miles to east.
● Perfect for getting away from it all; tricky to get to and therefore quiet.

Ayvalik
● Medium-sized resort set around pretty harbour ringed with fish restaurants.
● Best beaches 5 miles to the south.
● Boat trips to Lesbos (pricey) and Alibey Island for fish dinners.
● Good base for excursions to Bergama (Pergamon), Troy and the Dardanelles (a long haul).

Bodrum

● Large, attractive resort encircling yachting harbour, with excellent Castle of St Peter/Museum of Underwater Archaeology to the south.

● Few disappointing remains of Mausoleum of Halicarnassus, one of the Seven Wonders of the Ancient World.

● Well-known for Halikarnas outdoor disco and similar venues churning out deafening sounds until the early hours. Nearby Gumbet has similarly loud and popular disco scene and is utterly lacking in charm or style.

● Boat trips to Kos and Rhodes and to ruins at Knidos.

● Relatively secluded beaches on adjoining Bodrum peninsula.

Çeşme

● Fifty miles from Izmir, past a string of beaches, fishing villages and the ninth-century BC sites of Erythrai and Teos.

● A spa resort where hot springs bubble into the sea, just offshore, overlooked by a fourteenth-century Genoese castle.

BEST SIGHTS AND EXCURSIONS

Bergama (Pergamon)

Less visited than Ephesus, ancient Pergamon offers several disparate attractions – an acropolis with ruined theatre and assorted temples, an *asclepion* (or medical centre), and a fine archaeological museum – scattered around a sleepy, traditionally Turkish town.

Ephesus

Too popular for its own good, this spectacular archaeological site is complete with Roman theatre, library, houses, brothel and public toilets. It is a popular stopping spot for Mediterranean cruises and day-trips out of Aegean resorts. Visit out of season if possible.

Pamukkale

White-calcium travertine pools of warm, mineral-rich water fall down the hillside, well inland from the coastal resorts. Hotels above the travertines currently boast mineral-water pools but are scheduled for closure. Meanwhile, you can swim amid Roman columns at Pamukkale Motel. Nearby are the extensive ruins of Roman Hierapolis.

En route to Pamukkale, many tour companies include the Greco-Roman site of Aphrodisias – dedicated to Aphrodite, the goddess of love, nature and fertility. Dating from 4000 BC, the site flourished from the first century BC to the fifth century AD. Excavated over the past 40 years, it includes a magnificent theatre, Roman baths, and a stadium for 30,000.

Priene, Miletus and Didyma

An excursion combines three classical sites in one day, south from Kusadasi or north from Bodrum, past scenery of outstanding beauty – olives on terraced hillsides, with cypress trees.

Priene and Miletus were settled in the tenth century BC by the Ionians, but their ports were silted up by the meandering Meander river and as a result they lost their function and died.

Priene was planned on a grid pattern, with a cosy little theatre. Miletus was developed by the Romans, to include the largest theatre in Asia Minor.

Didyma was funded by the citizens of Miletus to feature a monumental Temple of Apollo, planned around 330 BC to be double the size of the Parthenon. Didyma became a centre of prophesy, ranking second in importance to the Delphic oracle.

MEDITERRANEAN TURKEY
Good for culture, family holidays, local colour and nightlife

BACKED BY the Taurus Mountains, Turkey's Mediterranean coast is squeezed into a narrow strip of shoreline, making it hard for resorts to spread far; consequently, several small, picturesque resorts just about cling on to 'fishing-village' status. The coastline is perfect for exploring in *gulets* – wooden yachts that put in at the many secluded bays.

BEST RESORTS

To the west, the best beaches are not actually in the resorts, although they are easily accessible by public transport. Further east, however, resort beaches improve considerably, and are therefore some of the best places for families with children.

Alanya

● Two hours from Antalya, past long sandy beaches, pines and banana plantations, Alanya stands like Gibraltar, jutting two miles out to sea and ending with an 800-ft cliff. However, it is a noisy, tacky resort with a busy road cutting through it.

● Alanya was a pirate lair until 65 BC, when the Romans sank their fleet.

● Later, Mark Antony gave the town and surrounding region to Cleopatra, who needed the mountain timber for her Egyptian navy. Today, beach tourism is king.

Antalya

● Sizeable town with resort areas strung out along indifferent pebble beaches to east and west.

● Thoroughly inviting centre with restored wooden houses above attractive harbour.
● Fine archaeological museum, interesting mosques and Roman ruins.
● Good base for trips to ruins at Perge, Aspendos, Side, Termessos, Olimpos and Phaselis.

Dalyan

● Small village resort, overlooked by Lycian rock tombs, site of a struggle to protect the loggerhead turtles nesting on nearby Istuzu beach.
● Low-key development with many small, attractive restaurants.
● Regular boat trips through reedbeds to sandy Istuzu beach, mud baths and ruins of Kaunos – but beware of the mosquitoes.

Datça

● Small resort on edge of remote fishing village.
● Nightlife centre and marina, plus single street of restaurants.
● Beautiful location, with views across to Greek island of Symi.
● Attractive sandy beach to west of resort.

İçmeler

● Big, modern, purpose-built resort with good standard of hotels, but lacks Turkish character of other resorts.
● Set in attractive sheltered bay within easy reach of Marmaris by boat or road.
● Wide but pebbly beach.

Kalkan

● Smallish resort with pleasant, traditional-style pensions around the harbour. Stylish, upmarket hotels on hills overlooking harbour.
● Nightlife and relatively expensive restaurants catering for yachting clientele.
● Ruins at Xanthos, Letoon and at excellent Patara beach nearby.
● Lengthy airport transfers.

Kas

● Small but growing resort with livelier nightlife than neighbouring Kalkan and wide choice of restaurants. Pick hotel on west side for quieter nights.
● Boat trips to Greek island of Kastellorizo and to idyllic Kekova and Kale. Excursions to Saklikent Gorge, Xanthos, Pinara, Patara and Myra.
● Lengthy airport transfers.
● No sizeable beach nearby.

Marmaris
● A mid-market, busy package resort jutting into a magnificent bay in a fjord-like setting. In 1798, Nelson's entire Mediterranean fleet anchored in this superb natural harbour.
● The marina is packed with yachts from mega-luxury to racy flotilla boats.
● A former Ottoman caravanserai serves as a tourist shopping centre. Above is a fortress built by Suleyman the Magnificent in 1522.

Ölüdeniz
● Wide strip of sand and shingle beach and picture-postcard lagoon make Ölüdeniz thoroughly attractive.
● Hastily built resort and village, lacking traditional Turkish culture.
● Hotels extend back from beach on a grid of orderly streets. To protect Ölüdeniz from further development, many hotels are actually in Hisarönü, an uninviting inland overspill area for holidaymakers.

Side
● One hour's drive east of Antalya, the city was developed by Greeks in the seventh century BC, and flourished in Roman times, but was abandoned after a tenth-century fire.
● A hundred years ago, Greek-speaking Muslims moved across from Crete and built a village on the site, using the ancient remains as a stone quarry.
● Owing to superb sands, Side has now become a sprawling resort combining beaches, nightlife and shopping among Roman ruins.

BEST SIGHTS

Aspendos
The finest of Turkey's many ruined Roman theatres has been restored extensively to make it easier for visitors to imagine it as it was in its glory days.

Olimpos
In the spectacular Bey Mountains National Park, Olimpos was the home of the fiery Chimaera of classical mythology. The Chimaera still manifests itself in a series of mysterious and evocative tongues of fire jumping from the rock. You can also visit the ruins of ancient Olimpos, which line a shady valley.

Termessos
Spectacular and unusual sight reached by 30-minute drive into mountains from Antalya. Sit in the silent theatre and look straight down into plunging valleys on either side.

Xanthos

A UNESCO World Heritage Site, Xanthos is dominated by a Roman theatre and Lycian pillar tombs whose sculptures now reside in the British Museum. Walk round the hill behind the car park to find less-visited rock-cut Lycian tombs.

CAPPADOCIA
Good for outdoor activities and scenic landscape

FOR SCENERY-LOVERS, Cappadocia makes a great touring base. The landscape is a panorama of cones and caves created by volcanic eruptions and the corrosive action of wind and rain on soft tufa. Humans have made an impact on it by scooping out the soil to create houses, churches, monasteries, and complete underground cities.

BEST SIGHTS

Göreme

Göreme is in a National Park, with some of the best cone-churches preserved in an open-air museum. Unfortunately the small churches are ill-suited to the coach parties that mob them; visit out of season or try to get there early.

Zelve valley

Villagers lived in the caves and cones of Zelve valley until the 1950s. Their homes now form another marginally less-visited open-air museum. Uchisar and Ortahisar boast fortresses carved out of the *tufa*, ideal perches for watching the sunrises and sunsets over the valleys.

The largest and most popular underground cities at Kaymakli and Derinkuyu can be visited on a multitude of excursions. However, both get very crowded and are certainly not suitable for anyone who is claustrophobic.

NEMRUT DAGI
Good for culture

NEAR ADIYAMAN in Central Anatolia, Nemrut Mountain is surmounted by colossal heads and other statuary fallen from the stupendous tomb of the Commagene king Antiocus I Epiphanes (64–38 BC). Popular at sunrise and sunset (but less crowded at other times), Nemrut Dagi is very remote but can be done as an excursion from Cappadocia. Even in July and August it is cold in the mornings; in winter, snow renders it off-limits.

KONYA
Good for culture

FOR THOSE interested in Turkish culture, the turquoise-domed shrine of the Mevlana (founder of the Whirling Dervishes) is one of Turkey's finest sights. However, other than the Mevlana shrine, Konya is hot, dirty and unintersting (and a long way from the coast).

BLACK SEA COAST
Good for culture, local colour, romantic escapism and scenic landscape

TURKEY'S BLACK Sea Coast offers a dramatic mountain backdrop of the Pontic Alps, which reach over 12,000 feet in the east. Coastal towns were settled by Greek traders from the seventh century BC, followed by Roman, Byzantine and Ottoman rule. Beaches and fishing villages are untouched by international tourism, and determined travellers may have to endure gruesome overnight accommodation. A road now runs along or parallel to the coast, mostly in reasonable condition. Spasmodic bus and *dolmus* services link the settlements, and even venture up the side valleys. A self-drive car makes travel much easier. The rewards in scenery, colourful lifestyle and local markets make any discomforts worthwhile. It's hard to spend much money here.

BEST RESORTS

Amasra
● The most beautiful resort of the entire coast, Amasra has two natural harbours, protected by a natural rock acropolis. A narrow neck of land connects the town centre to the mainland.
● The site has been settled for 3,000 years. Phoenician traders were followed by Greeks and then Persians, who named the city after their princess Amastris.
● The present-day terraced island hillside – called Boz Tepe – follows the town plan initiated by Queen Amastris. She beautified the town with vineyards and gardens. Most of today's houses are in traditional Turkish style.

Sinop
● Greeks colonised the perfect natural harbour in the eighth century BC, but settlements had existed from the Early Bronze Age (3000–2700 BC). The town museum tells the story.

● The first city walls from about 2000 BC now stretch for just over a mile up to 98 feet high, almost entirely in good condition.

● As a beach resort, Sinop has an active evening social life. Pontoons extend from the quayside, so that seafood restaurants are gently floating. Tea gardens play live music, with youngsters dancing between the tables.

Trabzon

● Formerly called Trebizond, this was the last stronghold of the Byzantines until they fell to the Ottomans in 1461. Many Byzantine monuments survive.

● The fabled Walls of Trebizond rise 160 feet high above ravines that themselves form a natural defence.

● Mosques, tea gardens, Turkish baths, a huge bazaar quarter, caravanserais and *hans* give a unique flavour of the Orient.

● Thirty miles inland is Sumela Monastery, founded in AD 385, which became the most important monastic settlement of Anatolia. The monastery is ruined, but the cliff setting is magnificent.

WHEN TO GO

SEVERAL RELIGIOUS festivals take place throughout the year. The most important is Ramadan, which ends with three-day family festivities and parties. It is extremely difficult to travel during this period.

	Average daily maximum temperature °C											
London	6	7	10	13	17	20	22	21	19	14	10	7
Istanbul	8	9	11	16	21	25	28	28	24	20	15	11
	JAN	FEB	MAR	APR	MAY	JUN	JUL	AUG	SEP	OCT	NOV	DEC
Istanbul	18	14	14	9	8	6	4	4	7	11	14	18
London	15	13	11	12	12	11	12	11	13	13	15	15
	Average number of rainy days per month											

PACKAGE TRAVEL

TURKEY HAS become an enormously popular package destination for those seeking a sun-and-sand holiday. Prices are relatively low, partly because the standard of accommodation in three-star hotels and below can be poorer than in other Mediterranean resorts. Cheap restaurants abound, so B&B is a good option. Two-centre holidays are also available, usually combining Istanbul with a resort on the Aegean or Mediterranean coast. City-break specialists offer Istanbul.

One of the easiest and best ways to explore the attractive coastline and visit more than one resort is to hire a berth on a *gulet*, or wooden sailing boat. Many tour operators offer two-week cruises round different parts of the coast, or one week on a *gulet* and one week in a hotel.

Self-catering complexes of villas and apartments are found mainly around the Bodrum and Marmaris peninsulas, but standards of maintenance are not as high as, for example, in the Algarve.

Tour operators

Archaeology: Andante, British Museum Traveller, Martin Randall **Birdwatching**: Limosa, Sunbird **City breaks**: British Airways Holidays, Cresta, Inghams, Kirker, Made to Measure, Osprey, Sovereign, Time Off, Travelscene **General and specialist**: Airtours, Alternative Travel Group, Anatolian Sky Holidays, Celebrity Holidays, Concept Express Ltd, Cosmos, Discovery Initiatives, First Choice, Ilios Travel, Inghams, Inspirations, JMC Holidays, Manos, Metak, President Holidays, Regent Holidays, Savile Row Tours, Simply Turkey, Sovereign, Sunquest, Tapestry, Thomas Cook, Thomson, Unijet **Walking**: Exodus, Explore Worldwide, Waymark **Other activities**: Ace Study Tours, Adrift (white-water rafting), Club Med (multi-activity), Holts' Tours (battlefields), McCabe Travel (religious tours), Swan Hellenic (Mediterranean cruises)

INDEPENDENT TRAVEL

SCHEDULED FLIGHTS go from London to Istanbul, Izmir and Antalya. Charter flights operate in summer to Antalya, Bodrum, Dalaman and Izmir.

The rail network is rather limited and slow, though trains are often cheaper than buses for getting around. First-class carriages have air-conditioning in summer; second-class do not. Long-distance buses are more popular than trains, and often several companies cover the same routes, so you have a wider, if confusing, choice.

There are lots of taxis and *dolmuses* – cars or minibuses that run along set routes, picking up and dropping off passengers along the way (you stick your hand out, and if there is room, they will stop; passengers usually make room). They cover routes both within towns and between towns and villages. Fares are cheap. Taxis in cities all have meters; in the country, agree a fare before you set off.

Car hire is expensive: it is cheaper to book from the UK or take a fly-drive package. It is wise to take an international driving permit with you. Driving is on the right, but on dual carriageways or multi-lane highways Turkish drivers will overtake in any lane. Roads are usually well surfaced and maintained, but can be narrow. Watch out for pedestrians, livestock and trucks travelling at frightening speeds.

The best-value accommodation is in *pansiyons*, which usually have friendly proprietors and simple but clean rooms. Prices are often set by the tourist authorities, which rate hotels on a scale of one to five stars.

RED TAPE, HEALTH AND SAFETY

VISITORS TO Turkey must obtain a visa/entrace stamp (£10) on arrival, at Turkish passport control. (Scottish currency in not accepted.)

Upset stomachs are the most common health problem in Turkey (see page 11 for tips on how best to avoid this). Bottled water is widely available, and it is best to drink this rather than tap water. Immunisations against typhoid and tetanus are usually recommended, but check with your GP or a travel clinic.

Street robbery is common in the major Istanbul tourist areas. Beware of approaches from strangers offering food and drink which may be drugged. Incidents of rape and sexual assault have been reported in coastal tourist resorts.

There have been no recent terrorist incidents in resort areas, and the security situation in Eastern Turkey has improved considerably. But there have been sporadic incidents involving the PKK and Turkish security forces, particularly in the provinces of Van, Hakkari, Simak, Diyarbakir and Tunceli, and neighbouring provinces in the south-east. Travellers to this region are advised to keep to the main roads and towns and to avoid travel after dark. For the latest advice contact the Foreign Office Travel Advice Unit (see page 11).

MORE INFORMATION Turkish Tourist and Information Office, First Floor, 170–173 Piccadilly, London W1V 9DD, tel 020-7629 7771, visa information 020-7589 0360, brochure line (09001) 887755 (premium rate number)

COST OF LIVING £

UNITED ARAB EMIRATES

HIGHLIGHTS

Culture
*Dubai,
northern and
eastern UAE,
Sharjah*

Nightlife
Dubai

Local colour
*Al-Ain,
northern and
eastern UAE,
Ras Al-Khaimah,*

Scenic landscape
*Liwa Oasis,
northern and
eastern UAE*

Shopping
Dubai

THE UAE is a federation of seven sovereign Emirates of which the best known are Abu Dhabi (the largest of the seven, and the capital of the federation) and Dubai. The others are Sharjah, Ras Al-Khaimah, Ajman, Umm Al-Qaiwain and Fujairah. Each Emirate takes the name of its main city.

DUBAI
Good for culture, nightlife and shopping

THERE IS more to the UAE's best-known city than its famous airport duty-free shop. Dubai is the most vibrant place in the Gulf – well worth the effort either as a stop-over or as a base for exploring the

Emirates in greater depth. Though still a very conservative place by Western standards, it is also the most relaxed city in Arabia, and an excellent introduction to the region for first-time visitors.

BEST SIGHTS

The Creek
The waterway at Dubai's heart offers some of the best views of the city. Water taxis, known locally as *abras*, criss-cross it night and day and are the best way to get from one side to the other (the main bridge spanning the Creek is the city's most notorious traffic choke-point). Rides cost only a few pence – someone will collect the money once you're underway. You can hire an *abra* for a 45-minute tour of the Creek. If you do only one thing during a Dubai stop-over, do this.

Dubai Museum
Located in a converted fort near the Bur Dubai souk (market) and the Ruler's Office (palace), the museum offers a good introduction to both the city's history and the region's way of life. The museum is much bigger than it looks, as most of the exhibit halls are underground.

Gold Souk
Even if you are only looking, the largest gold market in the Middle East has to be seen to be believed. Prices are keen – always bargain.

Sheikh Saeed's House
This large mud-brick house near the mouth of the Creek was the palace and seat of government for Sheikh Saeed Al-Maktoum, the grandfather of Dubai's present ruler. It has been restored to its original state and now houses artistic exhibits as well as providing a view of life in the pre-oil Emirates.

BEST EXCURSIONS

Al-Ain
The Buraimi oasis, about 1½ hours from Dubai by road, is shared by the UAE and Oman. Visitors can cross freely between the two countries without passports or visas. Al-Ain (the UAE side) has a small camel market (try to visit early in the morning) and extraordinary greenery. Buraimi (the Omani side) boasts a small, very traditional souk and the restored Al-Khandaq fort.

Sharjah
About 20 minutes by car from downtown Dubai, Sharjah offers a slower, more traditional way of life. Prices are far keener for oriental rugs in its modern central souk than in Dubai's high-priced boutiques.

The archaeological museum on Cultural Square is worth a visit, as is the restored traditional souk area, which is a good contrast to Dubai's more moderen, fast-paced souk.

NORTHERN AND EASTERN UAE
Good for culture, local colour and scenic landscape

BEST TOWNS

Badiyah
This east coast village is the site of the oldest mosque in the country – a small whitewashed structure along the road from Fujairah to Dibba.

Fujairah
The largest city on the east coast of the UAE, Fujairah has a small museum and is an ideal base for exploring the scenic landscapes of the east coast. Nearby Bithna has several interesting archaeological sites. The Fujairah Hilton has good beach club facilities and is a popular base for scuba-diving trips.

Ras Al-Khaimah
The northernmost of the seven Emirates that make up the UAE offers camel racing, a hot spring and a more traditional side of life that is hard to find in Dubai. This is a city of small shops and coffee houses. The fort/palace where Ras Al-Khaimah's rulers lived until the early 1960s is now a museum.

LIWA OASIS
Good for scenic landscape

THIS OASIS deep in the country's interior offers the best desert landscape. A four-wheel-drive vehicle is necessary for the best views, though some spectacular scenery can also be seen from the few paved roads running through the area, particularly the stretch between the villages of Mizaira'a and Hamim.

WHEN TO GO

GO BETWEEN November and February. The temperature during the summer months (roughly mid-April to early October) is oppressively hot with very high humidity. December can sometimes be cold and rainy, but is usually pleasantly warm. Avoid travel during the

Muslim holy month of Ramadan, which will fall in November and early-to-mid December in the years 2000–2003. The end of Ramadan can be an awkward time to travel.

	Average daily maximum temperature °C											
London	6	7	10	13	17	20	22	21	19	14	10	7
Sharjah	23	24	27	30	34	36	38	39	37	33	31	26
	JAN	FEB	MAR	APR	MAY	JUN	JUL	AUG	SEP	OCT	NOV	DEC
Sharjah	2	2	1	0	0	0	0	0	0	0	0	2
London	15	13	11	12	12	11	12	11	13	13	15	15
	Average number of rainy days per month											

PACKAGE TRAVEL

A NUMBER of package holidays to the UAE can be booked from the UK. These are usually based at beach resort hotels in and around Dubai (note – these are often far from the city centre) and may include several excursions. Stays at city hotels in Abu Dhabi also feature in the brochures of some tour operators. Only a few specialist tour operators offer tours of the UAE; packages are generally tailor-made. Tours can easily combine the UAE with Oman and various other destinations.

Excursions to places like Sharjah, Al-Ain and the east coast can be booked through a number of local agents, as can desert safaris using four-wheel-drive vehicles, camels or some combination of the two. Birdwatching is the main activity holiday on offer.

Tour operators

Birdwatching: Birding, Limosa, Naturetrek, Ornitholidays **General**: Abercrombie & Kent, Arabian Odyssey, Axis, Bridge Travel Service, British Airways Holidays, Carrier, Crystal, Eastravel, Elite Vacations, Jasmin Tours, Kuoni, Goldenjoy, Hayes & Javis, Premier, Seasons in Style, Somak, Sovereign, Sunset Faraway, Tradewinds, Travelscene, Unijet **Golf**: Longmere Golf, Longshot Golf, Simply Golf

---

INDEPENDENT TRAVEL

THERE IS a daily service to both Dubai and Abu Dhabi from the UK. There are also international flights into Sharjah but none from the

UK. You will probably land in Sharjah if you travel on a charter flight. A small number of flights are also available to Ras Al-Khaimah, Al-Ain and Fujairah, mainly from India, Pakistan, Egypt and Jordan. There are no internal flights.

No trains run in the UAE and there is no coach service between the Emirates, though coaches do run within both the Abu Dhabi and Dubai Emirates. For most travel between cities you will either need to hire a car or take a service taxi. These travel between cities for very low per-person fares. They leave when the car is full (usually seven passengers). Car hire rates are cheapest in Dubai, where it pays to shop around. The standard of the roads is excellent everywhere.

Expensive hotels and hotel/resorts are easy to find throughout the Emirates. Budget accommodation is plentiful in Dubai (which also has an excellent youth hostel) but harder to find elsewhere. Abu Dhabi and Al-Ain in particular are both quite expensive.

RED TAPE, HEALTH AND SAFETY

BRITISH PASSPORT-HOLDERS do not require a visa to enter the UAE. Sixty days' stay will be granted on entry. No specific vaccinations are necessary to enter the UAE. Except at the very bottom end of the hotel/restaurant scale, sanitary standards are very high, particularly in the main cities. You may want to stick to bottled water, less for health reasons than because the tap water is often heavily chlorinated and tastes awful.

The crime rate is very low, and safety, even at night, is not a major concern – though wild driving habits often can be.

Though liberal and open compared to other Gulf countries, the UAE is very conservative by Western standards. Despite the heat, shorts and short dresses are frowned upon anywhere except at the beach. In rural areas they may get you into trouble with the local authorities. Women should not wear tight or revealing clothing (including sleeveless tops). It is not necessary for foreign women to cover their heads or to wear the all-covering cloaks worn by local women, but it is prudent to dress conservatively in baggy trousers or long skirts.

MORE INFORMATION Dubai Department of Tourism, 1st Floor, 125 Pall Mall, London SW1Y 5EA, tel 020-7839 0580/0581, web site: *www.dubaitourism.co.ae*

COST OF LIVING £££–£££

UNITED KINGDOM

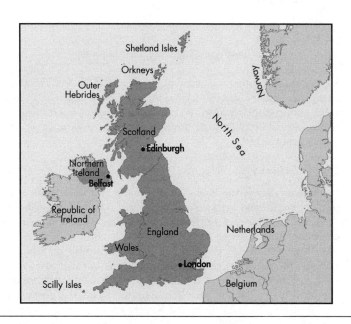

HIGHLIGHTS

Beaches
*Bournemouth,
Brighton,
Scarborough,
Torquay,
Wales*

Nightlife
London

**Romantic
escapism**
Scotland

Wildlife
*Eastern England,
Scotland*

Culture
*Central and
northern
England,
London,
Scotland,
southern
England,
Wales*

**Family
holidays**
*Southern
England*

Flora
Eastern England

Food/Wine
London

Shopping
London

**Scenic
landscape**
*Central England,
Cotswolds,
Lake District,
Northern Ireland,
Scilly Isles,
Wales,
west coast
of Scotland,
Yorkshire Dales*

History
*Central
England,
Hadrian's Wall,
Scotland,
Stonehenge*

**Outdoor
activities**
*Eastern,
northern and
southern
England,
Northern
Ireland,
Scotland,
Wales*

SOMETIMES IT is all too easy to overlook the possibilities on our own doorstep when we are trying to decide on a holiday destination. The pages that follow are a brief reminder of some of them.

LONDON
Good for culture, food/wine, nightlife and shopping

FOR ANYONE who is not afraid to be a tourist in London, Piccadilly Circus is the hub of activity – right in the middle of theatreland, close to the major shopping areas, Regent Street, Oxford Street, Covent Garden, Piccadilly and Bond Street, and within easy reach of the capital's major sights.

BEST SIGHTS

Westminster Abbey, the Houses of Parliament, Nelson's Column in Trafalgar Square and Buckingham Palace (for the daily Changing of the Guard) are all within a mile or so of Piccadilly Circus. The Tower of London, Tower Bridge and Docklands are a short bus or tube ride away. Art lovers should find time for the National Gallery. South of the river, the London Eye ferris wheel provides splendid, constantly changing views of London's skyline and it's a pleasant walk from the established South Bank Centre (including the National Theatre and the Royal Festival Hall) up to the buzzing Bankside area, home to Tate Modern, the Millennium Bridge and Shakespeare's Globe. Knightsbridge has three excellent museums – Natural History Museum, Science Museum and V&A. Kew Gardens, a few miles south-west of the city centre, offers green acres and a superb plant collection.

BEST SHOPPING

You can walk from Piccadilly to Knightsbridge, the location of Harrods department store, through two of London's prettiest parks: Green Park and Hyde Park. For trendy, slightly alternative shopping head south from Knightsbridge to the Kings Road, or west to Kensington High Street. At the weekends, markets at Camden, Portobello Road and Greenwich are tourist attractions in their own right.

SOUTHERN ENGLAND
Good for beaches, culture, family holidays and outdoor activities

THE SOUTH of England has a fair number of elegant cities, rolling countryside and resorts.

BEST RESORTS

Summer visitors might choose to visit Bournemouth, Brighton or Torquay, or seek out the beaches of Cornwall or the Scilly Isles for a longer stay at the seaside.

BEST SIGHTS

Bath

The Romans developed baths from springs discovered here by the Celts. Georgian architects later embellished this spa town with sandstone terraces and Palladian façades. Its elegant shops are another attraction.

Cathedrals

Superb cathedrals worth seeing include Canterbury in Kent, Wells in Somerset, Exeter in Devon and Salisbury in Wiltshire.

Gardens

Wakehurst Place Gardens in Sussex and the RHS gardens in Wisley, Surrey, are well-known to horticultural enthusiasts. Other areas good for garden-lovers include southern Cornwall (especially the Lost Gardens of Heligan) and southern Somerset.

Stonehenge

Europe's most famous prehistoric site is in Wiltshire, and is thought to date from about 3000 BC. Its origins and its enormous scale have amazed and baffled historians and visitors for centuries. If you are fascinated by prehistoric man, Avebury Stone Circle, Old Sarum and Silbury Hill are other ancient sites worth visiting in the region.

Windsor

For royal enthusiasts, Windsor, with its castle and extensive park, merits a visit. Just a short walk across the River Thames lies Eton College, one of the oldest schools in Britain.

CENTRAL ENGLAND
Good for culture, history and scenic landscape

THE MIDLANDS area saw the birth of the Industrial Revolution, but its many historic towns are never far from superb countryside. This area of great variety is ideally suited to touring.

BEST SIGHTS

Blenheim Palace
Not far from Oxford on the edge of the small town of Woodstock stands Blenheim Palace, home of the Duke of Marlborough and birthplace of Sir Winston Churchill. This superb baroque palace, designed by Vanbrugh, is surrounded by a vast park and gardens.

Ironbridge Gorge
Ironbridge Gorge played an important role in the Industrial Revolution. The Ironbridge Museum (a total of seven sites spread over seven miles) is outstanding and should not be missed.

Oxford
Oxford makes an excellent base for the area and is worth a couple of days sightseeing itself. The university colleges are magnificent buildings dotted around the city dating from the fifteenth century. The town also boasts excellent shops and museums.

Stratford-upon-Avon
This town of half-timbered buildings, giftshops and tea-rooms enthusiastically exploits its connection with William Shakespeare. Visit the playwright's birthplace and Anne Hathaway's cottage, or see a play at the Royal Shakespeare Theatre, if tickets are available. Nearby, Warwick Castle is an excellent family attraction.

BEST SCENIC LANDSCAPE

Cotswolds
The Cotswolds, a band of gently rolling limestone hills that cut across Gloucestershire and Oxfordshire, offer a very English experience of picturesque, manicured villages, teashops and beautiful countryside. Many houses are built of the attractive local honey-coloured stone. Hotels and restaurants abound throughout this area.

The Peak District National Park
The Park, spanning Staffordshire and Derbyshire, offers a wonderful variety of landscapes: the Dark Peak on the eastern side occupies three-

quarters of the Park with its tracts of lonely moorland and craggy heights, while the softer White Peak in the south is limestone country. Dales and river valleys cut into the rolling hills and small grey-stone villages dot the landscape.

Just outside Bakewell, magnificent Chatsworth House, home of the Duke of Devonshire, can be visited in summer.

EASTERN ENGLAND
Good for flora/wildlife, outdoor activities and scenic landscape

EAST ANGLIA is a region often bypassed by tourists but has much to offer. The north coast of Norfolk is popular with birdwatchers, while the Norfolk Broads offer one of the largest inland boating areas in Britain.

BEST RESORT

Skegness
● Traditional seaside fun, with six miles of sand providing plenty of elbow room.

BEST TOWNS

Cambridge
Take a punt out on the River Cam to enjoy views of the city's 31 university colleges. Peterhouse is the oldest, dating from the thirteenth century, and the most recent, Robinson, was built in 1979. A tour of the colleges is an instructive architectural experience.

Lincoln
A first-rate cathedral (look out for the infamous imp) stands opposite the castle at the top of Steep Hill, whose domestic architecture dates from the twelfth century.

Norwich
From the soaring grandeur of the cathedral to the microcosm of world art at the Sainsbury Centre, this fine ancient city is well worth a visit.

BEST SCENIC LANDSCAPE

John Constable, one of England's most famous landscape artists, lived and took inspiration from the countryside around Dedham and Colchester in Essex. Further north, in Suffolk, villages such as Lavenham and Southwold, once at the heart of the country's old wool trade, are some of the prettiest in Britain.

NORTHERN ENGLAND
Good for culture, outdoor activities and scenic landscape

THE NORTH of England contains the country's wildest scenery, interspersed with the major industrial cities.

BEST RESORT

Scarborough
This handsome Regency/Victorian town is 25 miles north-east of York. A popular seaside resort, it offers:
- a sandy beach with full resort amenities at the South Bay
- the quieter, more genteel North Bay.

BEST CITIES

Durham
Tiny city that magnificently crowns a rocky peninsula in a horseshoe bend of the River Wear. The cathedral is one of the finest examples of Norman architecture in Britain.

Leeds
England's third-largest city has a proud industrial past, reflected in its handsome civic buildings. It boasts impressive art galleries and museums and houses the Royal Armouries collection.

York
If time is short, head straight for York. The glorious York Minster dominates this ancient and beautiful city. A tour of the city walls shows you the Roman, Anglo-Saxon and Viking elements of the city. Two of the best of many excellent sights are the National Railway Museum and the Jorvik Viking Centre.

BEST SIGHTS

Beamish North of England Open Air Museum
Splendid recreations of past times in the North-East featuring living history, a real drift mine, and reconstructed buildings from the region.

Hadrian's Wall
The Roman emperor Hadrian constructed the wall in AD 120 to keep out the wild Northern tribes. It stretches a remarkable 73½ miles from the River Tyne in Newcastle to the Solway Firth in Cumbria, effectively dividing Scotland from England.

National Museum of Photography, Film and Television
Excellent museum in Bradford providing a concise and entertaining history of the cinema, including an IMAX screen.

BEST SCENIC LANDSCAPE

Castles of Northumberland
One of the least spoilt stretches of English coastline features a line of castle strongholds built to withstand raiders from the sea. Highlights include romantic Lindisfarne and the magnificent towers of Warkworth; bird- and seal-watchers are also well served.

Lake District
In the north-west is the Lake District, a 30-mile-long tract of lake and fell-land offering some of the most rewarding and beautiful walking, boating and touring in England. The area was a source of inspiration for William Wordsworth and other Romantic poets.

North York Moors
Head north to the wild expanses of the North York Moors and relish the views from the Cleveland Way path. Further west, the Yorkshire Dales offer gentler landscape. Throughout North Yorkshire, charming market towns and villages, splendid houses, castles and gardens blend with the magnificent scenery, making this a great touring destination. Castle Howard and Eden Camp near Malton are particularly worth visiting.

WALES
Good for beaches, culture, outdoor activities and scenic landscape

WALES HAS a distinct heritage and language, rooted in the country's Celtic past. English occupation in the Middle Ages bequeathed a string of castles, and the superb scenery extends from the industrialised valleys of the south to the mountains of Snowdonia.

BEST SCENIC LANDSCAPE

Welsh Marches
The border country between England and Wales is known as the Welsh Marches. It is marked for some of its length by Offa's Dyke, built between AD 757 and 796 by the King of Mercia. Langollen, at the northern end of the marches, is an attractive town bisected by the River Dee and the venue for the annual International Eisteddfod in August – a music competition of global renown. Look out for the remarkable Pontcysyllte Aqueduct a few miles south-east.

Further south, Hay-on-Wye is a mecca for book-lovers with 25 bookshops and allegedly over 21 miles of shelving. Tintern Abbey, immortalised by William Wordsworth, is one of the furthermost landmarks of the southern marches just north of Chepstow.

Pembrokeshire

The rugged coastline of dramatically varied scenery is best explored on foot. Inland, the misty moorlands and primeval woods of the Preseli Hills form evocative backdrops to prehistoric relics.

Snowdonia

The mountains of Snowdonia are some of the highest and most dramatic in the country, but surprisingly accessible. You could stay in the refined resort of Llandudno yet be in the heart of Snowdonia within the hour. For history, head for the Menai Straits and Caernarfon. The castle built by Edward I is the traditional site of investiture of the Princes of Wales; Prince Charles was enthroned here in 1969.

BEST RESORT

Tenby

● Georgian backdrop to several excellent beaches, the best of which is North Beach below dark cliffs.
● Take a boat-trip to Caldey Island.
● To the west, Barafundle Bay is a stunning beach of glamorous tide-washed sand (steep access).

SCOTLAND

Good for scenic landscape, culture, history, outdoor activities, romantic escapism and wildlife

THE TWO obvious destinations in Scotland – and you can fly to both – are the nation's major cities: Edinburgh and Glasgow.

Exploring central Scotland will reveal the story of Scotland's turbulent past. However, if you seek the wild, sometimes desolate beauty of Scotland, you should head for the west coast and follow it all the way up to Cape Wrath. If you take the train to Fort William and set off towards the Kyle of Lochalsh you can now drive straight on to the Isle of Skye.

BEST CITIES

Edinburgh

Central Edinburgh, predominantly medieval and Georgian in architecture, is traditionally the more attractive and refined city, but its supremacy in the arts has been increasingly challenged by Glasgow. Edinburgh's annual international arts festival, both mainstream and fringe, attracts thousands of visitors every August. The excellent National Gallery of Scotland and the National Gallery of Modern Art are both here. The glowering Castle is also well worth a visit.

Glasgow

Glasgow, a Victorian industrial town voted European City of Culture in 1990, has a number of exceptional museums; the Burrell Collection a few miles from the centre and the Kelvingrove Gallery housed near Glasgow University are two of the best.

Stirling

Stirling has an imposing castle and a memorial to Robert Bruce, who vanquished the forces of Edward I at nearby Bannockburn in 1314. More impressive is the gothic-style memorial to his co-defender of national freedom, William Wallace. Ascend the monument for great views of the Forth Valley.

BEST SCENIC LANDSCAPE

Borders

Bleak moorland switches to dense beechwoods or lush pastureland within a few minutes' journey. Unmissable sights include the serene but ruined abbeys of Jedbergh, Kelso, Melrose and Dryburgh, plus stately homes such as Mellerstain and Traquair House. On the coast are some splendid walks around St Abbs Head.

Handa Island

Handa Island, a must for ornithologists, is reached by tiny ferry from Tarbet a few miles north of Scourie. Walks from Kinlochbervie, the most northern fishing port on this coast, bring you to some stunning beaches, the somewhat inaccessible Sandwood Bay being the best.

Perthshire

Perth, a Roman city, is 36 miles north-west of Stirling. It is built around the River Tay with pedestrianised areas and renovated Georgian terraces. Its historical significance is reinforced by the proximity of Scone Abbey, where generations of Scottish kings were crowned. The rolling Perthshire hills, and the areas around Lochearn and Loch Tummel, and the festive theatre town of Pitlochry are particularly lovely.

Outer Hebrides, Orkney and Shetlands

A trip from the mainland to the Outer Hebrides, Orkney or the

Shetland Islands requires a little extra planning, but their windswept appeal is irresistible. Orkney is rich in prehistoric sites; Shetland in Viking history and seabird colonies. Some crofters still follow a traditional farming lifestyle, and local crafts include silverwork and knitwear.

Skye
A beautiful island but best seen in clear weather, so if the elements are against you head on to the Applecross Peninsula for some memorable views.

Ullapool
Ullapool is an attractive centre on the way north and the last reasonable-sized town on the west coast. From here on the roads become narrower and the scenery increasingly dramatic. A detour not to missed is the road out to Achiltibuie and the Summer Isles; then snake on round the coast joining the main road at Lochinver.

NORTHERN IRELAND
Good for nightlife, outdoor activities and scenic landscape

DESPITE ITS troubled past, Ulster retains much of its scenic allure. Though normality is still a long way off, recent years have seen a shift towards a more stable and peaceful country.

The best way to see the region is by car as outside the cities many places of interest are less easily accessed by public transport. A regular intercity train service links Belfast and Dublin – a comfortable day-trip if you start early.

The weather in Northern Ireland is notoriously fickle and the landscape is lush and green for a reason. Late spring is a good bet for sunshine but in some years rain is all too frequent.

BEST CITIES

Bangor
Bangor is a few miles east of Belfast. With a marina, a good beach, lively pubs and clubs and some fine walking just out of town, it makes for a rewarding detour. Trains leave regularly from Belfast. The short journey skirts the coast, giving great views over Belfast Lough towards the headlands of South Antrim.

Belfast
During the 1990s there was an enormous amount of redevelopment in Ulster's principal city. The Waterfront Hall in Laganside hosts

conferences and concerts. Around Queen's University is a swathe of bars and eateries fuelled by the city's insatiable appetite for socialising. There are myriad spots in which to try your first Guinness; the Crown and Robinsons are two popular bars. The area around the City Hall is excellent for shopping.

BEST BEACH

Portstewart Strand

A spectacular beach backed by towering dunes, accessed either by a cliff walk that starts at Portstewart or by road further west. The strand stretches all the way to the mouth of the Upper Bann. Take care when swimming off the beach as the currents can be strong at times.

BEST SIGHTS AND EXCURSIONS

Bushmills Distillery

One of the most popular whiskeys in Ulster, there are several variations on a theme to sample here, whether it's one of the single malts or blends. Tours and tastings are offered but phone first (tel 028–2073 1521). The distillery is about a ten-minute drive from Portballintrae.

Giant's Causeway and Carrick-a-Rede Rope Bridge

Two of the most dramatic sights in Northern Ireland. The former, a volcanic intrusion of honeycombed basalt columns that cover a section of the North Antrim coast, has World Heritage status. The renovated bridge at Carrick-a-Rede links the mainland to a small island previously used by salmon netters. Visitors can cross it during the day.

The Mournes

The paths running through this compact range of mountains offer some of the best walking in Ulster. The Brandy Path just beyond the Hare's Gap is especially dramatic, with views of the Silent Valley Reservoir away to the west sitting beneath the slopes of Slieve Binnian, Slieve Lamagan and Slieve Bearnagh. There is a wide stretch of beach at the nearby town of Newcastle and freshwater swimming in the plunge pool at Bloody Bridge just out of town to the south. Take a good map and know where you're going before setting out.

BEST SPORT

Northern Ireland has some of the best golf courses in the UK, including Portrush, Portstewart, Ballycastle, Bangor, Clandeboye and Newcastle. The lakes of Fermanagh to the west host an array of water sports and leisure activities.

THEME PARKS IN THE UK

THE UK now has over 30 theme parks, and those listed below are particularly worth a visit.

Alton Towers, Staffordshire

Alton Towers is one of the UK's largest theme parks, with over 125 rides and attractions in beautiful grounds, including Nemesis, Oblivion, the Corkscrew and the Log Flume. The park has tamer rides for children and those with weaker stomachs, also a show on ice and a 3D cinema.

Blackpool Pleasure Beach, Lancashire

One of Europe's biggest theme parks, Blackpool Pleasure Beach has over 150 rides, including the terrifying Big One, The Ride and the Grand National.

Legoland

Twelve different scenes from around Europe created from 20 million plastic bricks, plus gentle rides and play areas, all aimed at younger kids.

Oakwood Coaster Country, Pembrokeshire

As well as Vertigo and Megafobia, Oakwood also has a play area with bouncers, slides and a spider's web, plus Jake's Town with goldmine, trading post and music hall.

Thorpe Park, Surrey

Thorpe Park is the home of Depth Charge, the UK's first four-lane waterslide, as well as x: /No Way Out — a rollercoaster backwards in the dark — and Logger's Leap, a steep drop into water.

Average daily maximum temperature °C

	JAN	FEB	MAR	APR	MAY	JUN	JUL	AUG	SEP	OCT	NOV	DEC
London	6	7	10	13	17	20	22	21	19	14	10	7
Edinburgh	6	6	8	11	14	17	18	18	16	12	9	7
Edinburgh	17	15	15	14	14	15	17	16	16	17	17	18
London	15	13	11	12	12	11	12	11	13	13	15	15

Average number of rainy days per month

Average daily maximum temperature °C

	JAN	FEB	MAR	APR	MAY	JUN	JUL	AUG	SEP	OCT	NOV	DEC
London	6	7	10	13	17	20	22	21	19	14	10	7
Cardiff	7	7	10	13	16	19	20	21	18	14	10	8
Cardiff	18	14	13	13	13	13	14	15	16	16	17	18
London	15	13	11	12	12	11	12	11	13	13	15	15

Average number of rainy days per month

Average daily maximum temperature °C

	JAN	FEB	MAR	APR	MAY	JUN	JUL	AUG	SEP	OCT	NOV	DEC
London	6	7	10	13	17	20	22	21	19	14	10	7
Belfast	6	7	9	12	15	17	18	18	16	12	9	7
Belfast	20	17	16	16	16	16	19	17	18	19	19	21
London	15	13	11	12	12	11	12	11	13	13	15	15

Average number of rainy days per month

USA

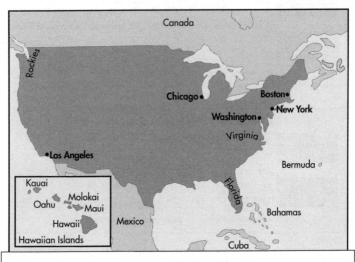

HIGHLIGHTS

Beaches
*Carolinas,
California,
Florida,
Hawaii,
Virginia*

Food/wine
*California,
Chicago,
Deep South,
New England,
New York*

History
*New York,
Virginia,
Washington DC*

Culture
*Chicago,
Deep South,
Virginia,
Washington DC*

Shopping
*New York,
Chicago*

Nightlife
*Chicago,
California,
Deep South,
Florida,
New York*

**Outdoor
activities**
*California,
Carolinas,
Florida,
Rockies*

**Family
holidays**
*California,
Florida*

**Scenic
landscape**
*Carolinas,
Deep South,
Desert States,
Hawaii,
New England,
Rockies*

WASHINGTON DC
Good for culture and history

VIRGINIA AND Washington DC have always been at the heart of American history – home to the first European settlers and to American presidents. The heart of the city is the Mall – a mile-long boulevard that leads from the Potomac River past monuments to the nation's founders and on to the Capitol where the Senate and House of Representatives are housed in a white colonnaded wedding cake of a building. The neo-classical buildings that line the Mall are the nation's cultural repository as well as the nerve centre of government.

At night head to Georgetown for a wide choice of restaurants and nightlife. There is a canal path and quiet streets to explore, with restored historic houses, including John F. Kennedy's former home.

BEST SIGHTS

Arlington National Cemetery
The final resting place of President John F. Kennedy, his wife Jackie and his brother Bobby. This vast military cemetery was started on land confiscated from Robert E. Lee, the leader of the Confederate army, whose house you can tour.

Bureau of Engraving and Printing
Guided tours of the factory where the mighty dollar is printed.

Ford's Theatre
The theatre where President Lincoln was shot looks as it did on that fateful night in 1865. Across the road is Petersen House where he died.

Library of Congress
This sumptuous nineteenth-century building has some of the choicest documents from US history.

National Air and Space Museum
The world's most famous flying machines, from the Wright Brothers' plane through Lindbergh's *Spirit of St Louis* to *Apollo 11*, are unmissable.

National Archives
A patient queue of visitors waits to catch a glimpse of the Declaration of Independence, the Constitution and the Bill of Rights.

National Gallery of Art
Includes contemporary art and several rooms on European culture.

National Museum of American History
Visiting here is like rummaging through America's attic. A bewildering collection of exhibits includes the original star-spangled banner.

National Postal Museum

The former main post office has now been converted into an entertaining museum following the story of the mail from the Pony Express onwards.

The US Capitol

Both the Senatorial and Congressional debating chambers are open when the house is not sitting.

The US Holocaust Memorial Museum

New and so popular that tickets are timed (and distributed at 10am daily). This is the story of the millions of Jews systematically killed by the Nazis in the Second World War. Moving survivors' stories are told.

Washington Monument

A conspicuous slender marble obelisk over 550 feet high. Queues for the lift up to the viewing chamber tend to be shorter at night.

White House

The home of the most powerful man in the world receives a constant stream of visitors. Exhibits show the changes made by successive occupants. Arrive at 7.30am for a chance of tickets that day.

Mall Memorials

The following memorials are all situated off the Mall.

● FDR Roosevelt Memorial depicts the four terms of FDR's presidency in sculptures and reliefs.

● Jefferson Memorial is a circular marble edifice housing a bronze of Jefferson, third president and author of the Declaration of Independence.

● Lincoln Memorial is a brooding statue of Abraham Lincoln which resides in a colonnaded memorial with the words of the Gettysburg address carved on the walls.

● Vietnam Veterans' Memorial has the names of over 58,000 men and women killed or missing in America's longest conflict chiselled into a wall of black granite. Nearby is the Korean War Veterans' Memorial with sculpted figures of 19 GIs in patrol formation.

VIRGINIA
Good for beaches, culture and history

VIRGINIA WAS one of the first parts of America to be settled by European colonists, and after Independence became one of the founding states of the USA. During the bloody Civil War, Virginia was on the losing Confederate side.

BEST SIGHTS

Historic Triangle
Three unmissable sites. Jamestown was the first English settlement in America. An excellent museum describes colonial life. At Yorktown's Victory Center there is a re-created army encampment, and an excellent film about the War of Independence. A battlefield driving tour takes you past areas where some of the worst fighting took place. Williamsburg, the former capital, has been lovingly restored to its eighteenth-century glory.

Monticello
The design of Thomas Jefferson's home exhibits his quirky genius.

Mount Vernon
George Washington's modest hilltop house has splendid views across the Potomac and 8,000 acres of grounds.

BEST CIVIL WAR SIGHTS

Appomattox Court House
See reconstructions at the scene of the Confederates' surrender under General Lee.

Fredericksberg
A pleasant town to stroll round as it escaped development. Grand Kenmore is linked to George Washington's family. Driving and walking tours of the battlefields start from the visitors' centre.

Manassas (Battle of Bull Run)
Before Manassas, both sides thought the war would be over quickly. Washington society watched the battle in which 3,500 men died.

Petersburg
A park marks siegelines at this site of strategic Federal/Confederate battles.

Richmond
Richmond has plenty of Civil War sights and a restored tobacco warehouse area near the river. The Museum of the Confederacy gives unbeatable Civil War coverage. The restored White House of the Confederacy was home to Jefferson Davis, the Confederate president who designed the Virginia State Capitol. You can also visit the Old

House of Delegates. The Richmond battlefield tour is over 100 miles long. Two sites worth visiting are Chimborazo Hospital, which describes the capital's fall, and Cold Harbour, where a route follows trenches.

BEST PLANTATIONS

Carter's Grove
Red-brick Georgian mansion provides insights into the slave system and the 1930s colonial revival.

Shirley Plantation
Beautiful Queen Anne plantation house that escaped Civil War looting.

Stratford Hall
The imposing family home of the Lees.

BEST BEACHES

Chesapeake
On the Chesapeake peninsula, try Chincoteague Island, whose main town is a prime example of smalltown America. Drive through Chincoteague Wildlife Refuge, home to wild ponies, and on to Assateague Island for a spectacular undeveloped beach.

NEW YORK
Good for culture, food/wine, nightlife and shopping

THE BIG Apple's reputation for energy and excitement is justified: you will feel something of it, even if you are there for only a few days. The city has been transformed in recent years with crime down and the feel-good factor up but there are still some no-go areas and extremes of wealth and poverty side-by-side.

BEST SIGHTS

Ellis Island
Between 1892 and 1954 all immigrants to the USA landed here, where they were processed. A short ferry ride from Battery Park, it is now a fascinating, poignant museum.

Frick Collection
Frick, a wealthy iron and steel magnate, built this palatial residence on Fifth Avenue to house his collection of European art.

Metropolitan Museum of Art
The layout of this huge collection is confusing – take a free tour round the highlights for an introduction. Note the excellent collection of Impressionists and post-Impressionists, and fascinating American wing.

Museum of Modern Art
Everyone from Rousseau to Kandinsky and Klee is represented here. There is a particularly fine gathering of Ernst and Magritte, and some wonderful work by Matisse as well as a couple of Monet's huge waterlily canvases.

Neighbourhoods
New York is a collection of district neighbourhoods, each of which is worth a stroll around: SoHo for its cast-iron buildings and boutiques; Chinatown for an authentic taste of the Orient; East Village for a more funky, Bohemian atmosphere; and Greenwich Village where the city's gay community hangs out.

Skyscrapers
The twin skyscrapers of the World Trade Center dominate Manhattan's skyline. Take an elevator to the viewing platform at the top of one of the towers to get a great view (if the weather is clear). The Empire State Building also offers stupendous views, and, unlike the World Trade Center, you can look down on the street almost 1,000 feet below.

Statue of Liberty
To land on the island you need to catch the ferry from Battery Park. You can climb up to the crown of the huge bronze lady, or just go to the top of the pedestal. Queues are likely to be long.

CHICAGO
Good for culture, food/wine, nightlife and shopping

THE WINDY City makes for a perfect all-American city break. Along with the canyon-like streets and towering skyscrapers, it's got top-notch museums, endless restaurants and shops to die for. Plus a great lakeside location – the beaches are a few blocks from downtown – and all the friendly charm of the midwest.

BEST SIGHTS

Art Institute of Chicago
An excellent collection of art and sculpture. The Impressionist collec-

tion is justly popular, but see also the unbelievably detailed Miniature Rooms and famous domestic works such as Grant Wood's *American Gothic*.

City architecture
Home of the first skyscrapers, the city is a showcase of twentieth-century architecture with some of the world's tallest buildings. A great way to see the best edifices, such as the Wrigley Building, is to take a Chicago Architecture Foundation tour, especially the river cruise. Visit Oak Park suburb to see Frank Lloyd Wright's house and studio.

Field Museum
World-class natural history museum that covers everything from cultures to vultures. Expect as much on human societies as on lions and tigers and bears.

Magnificent Mile
This stretch of Michigan Avenue is a shopaholic's paradise, with its large, vertical shopping malls, designer boutiques and department stores. Many things – such as clothes and cosmetics – are cheaper than in the UK so bring an empty case.

Museum of Science and Industry
This outstanding museum of '-ologies' is a short train ride away. Very hands-on exhibits about biology, science and technology – walk through a human heart, go down a coal mine or visit a submarine.

FLORIDA
Good for beaches, family holidays, nightlife, outdoor activities and wildlife

BEST CITIES

Miami
This sprawling, effervescent metropolis with a Hispanic flavour has a dazzling skyline, miles of sandy beaches and superb nightlife.

South Beach has one of the world's greatest concentration of art deco architecture, and Florida's trendiest, wildest nightlife. Coral Gables is a leafy Spanish–cum–Italian-style suburb built in the 1920s. Vizcaya is a twentieth-century replica of a sixteenth-century Italian estate.

Orlando
The theme-park capital of the world is far more enjoyable outside

public and school holidays. It is unbearably hot in summer but prices are cheaper.

If money is no object, stay within Walt Disney World, otherwise around International Drive or Kissimmee, a budget area close to the parks (accommodation standards vary widely).

BEST THEME PARKS

Walt Disney World, the world's largest entertainment complex, covers four theme parks. The Magic Kingdom is the essential Disney experience divided into seven themed 'lands'. Epcot is the most adult-oriented park, split into a worthy showcase of countries' architecture, culture and food, and science and technology exhibits. Disney-MGM Studios has rides and shows based on film classics, while the Animal Kingdom is a safari experience.

Universal Studios offers a theme park to rival Disney, with replicas of Hollywood film sets and its new Islands of Adventure park.

Sea World puts on exhilarating shows featuring performing killer whales and dolphins, plus polar bears and penguins displayed in imaginatively re-created habitats. Swim with dophins across the road at Sea World's new Discovery Cove park.

BEST NIGHTLIFE

Disney's relentlessly upbeat Pleasure Island is the best place for dancing. In downtown Orlando, Church Street Station, on a western theme, is more adult.

EAST COAST OF FLORIDA

VIRTUALLY ONE long, magnificent beach strung out on barrier islands, the coast is most interesting amid the yachts, mansions and country clubs of the posh Gold Coast, and least developed along the Treasure Coast.

BEST RESORTS

● Fort Lauderdale is a large family resort linked to a booming city by 300 miles of artificial waterways.
● Vero Beach is a small, peaceful enclave.
● Amelia Island has exclusive hotels, beautiful beaches and a pretty little Victorian town.

BEST SIGHTS

The Kennedy Space Center offers films and tours to Shuttle launch pads, and displays old rockets. Alongside lies the Canaveral National Seashore, Florida's largest undeveloped barrier beach, and the marshy, bird-rich vastness of Merritt Island National Wildlife Refuge.

GULF COAST

A SUCCESSION of glittering white sand beaches, cultural towns and slow-paced resorts, plus sensational sunsets.

BEST RESORTS

- Naples is an ostentatious town with dozens of golf courses, good beaches and trendy shopping.
- St Petersburg's excellent beaches line an over-developed 25-mile stretch of barrier islands.
- Sanibel and Captiva are exclusive verdant offshore islands with stunning beaches.
- Sarasota is a chic, arty town with fabulous barrier-island beaches.

BEST SIGHTS

The Salvador Dali Museum in St Petersburg contains the world's largest collection of the Spanish surrealist's works. The Ringling House and Museums in Sarasota house dazzling collections.

Tampa is a big, modern metropolis, most atmospheric in the Cuban district of Ybor City. Busch Gardens is the top attraction, a theme and safari park.

Head along the coast for greener attractions such as Rainbow River and Homosassa Springs.

THE KEYS AND EVERGLADES

THE KEYS are a 100-mile-long chain of islands; there is a dearth of good beaches but a coral reef offshore. The Everglades is an enormous swamp full of wildlife such as alligators and wading birds.

BEST SIGHTS AND EXCURSIONS

Key West is a bohemian, gay-oriented resort with laid-back nightlife, pretty 'conch houses' and literary connections: Hemingway lived here. John Pennekamp Coral Reef State Park is the best place from which to see the Southern Keys' coral, with water sports and boat trips available.

Explore the Everglades National Park on walking trails or canoe and boat trips from Flamingo. Mosquitoes are fewer and wildlife more plentiful in winter.

NEW ENGLAND
Good for food/wine and scenic landscape

IT IS almost axiomatic to say visit in the fall, when the autumn foliage turns on its pyrotechnical displays. But the six states have plenty to offer earlier in the year too. This is ideal touring territory, allowing you to combine coastal scenery such as the windswept dunes of Cape Cod or the rocky Maine coastline, with tree-shrouded mountains and immaculate villages of white weatherboarded houses.

BEST SIGHTS

Boston
Sophisticated, unintimidating city, focus of the first revolt against eighteenth-century British rule. Walk the self-guided Freedom Trail for the historic background and lunch at Quincy Market. The New England Aquarium (whale-watching trips run from outside the aquarium), the Museum of Fine Arts and the unusual Isabella Stewart Gardner Museum are excellent.

Hancock Shaker Village
This former Shaker community is now a living museum.

Mystic Seaport
A nineteenth-century whaling ship and a whaling museum can be seen at this recreated waterfront community.

Nantucket
A flat, scrub and cranberry bog-covered island, appealing for its seclusion and the attractive main harbour town rather than for its landscape.

Newport
This was the playground of the rich and famous during America's 'gilded age'. The Breakers and Marble House are the finest of nine lavish mansions open to the public. The Astors' palace, Beechwood, is also fun.

Old Sturbridge
An idealised 1830s village brought to life as a living museum.

Provincetown
This is an easy-going, culturally lively town at the tip of Cape Cod and a good place from which to take a whale-watching trip.

BEST SCENIC LANDSCAPES

Boothbay Harbour and Acadia National Park
Popular areas of Maine's spectacular, rugged coastline.

Kancamagus Highway
The road from Conway to Lincoln through the White Mountains in New Hampshire provides spectacular viewing of the foliage in the fall. Plenty of easy walking trails are located off the road, including one to the Sabbaday Falls.

THE CAROLINAS
Good for beaches, outdoor activities and scenic landscape

THE APPALACHIAN Mountains and the 500 miles of Atlantic coastline are worth exploring. Unfortunately they are at opposite sides of the Carolinas, with hundreds of miles of less fascinating country in between, so you should concentrate on one or the other, unless you have at least three weeks and do not mind long drives.

BEST INLAND SIGHTS

The Blue Ridge Parkway (BRP) is a leisurely 469-mile drive, starting in the Shenandoah National Park in Virginia and crossing the Blue Ridge Mountains, the Craggies, Pisgahs and Balsams in North Carolina. Local sights include the Linville Falls, Chimney Rock and Biltmore. Hiking is popular. The spectacular Great Smoky Mountains National Park, traversed by the BRP, is the most visited in America and particularly busy in high summer and at weekends.

Asheville
An unexpectedly cosmopolitan mountain town with an eclectic mix of buildings downtown.

Biltmore
Elaborate reconstruction of a French renaissance château built by George Vanderbilt. Napoleon's chess set and Richelieu's tapestries are on view. Slickly presented but expensive.

Chimney Rock

A monumental 258-ft column of rock with a lift inside. Lots of boardwalks and trails to follow.

Linville Falls

Well-signed and maintained woodland trails around a sheer-sided gorge where white water gushes from a chimney of quartzite.

Old Salem

The village was originally established by Moravian Protestants in the mid-eighteenth century. Wander for free or pay to hear costumed staff explain the humble life-style inside the shops and school houses.

BEST COASTAL RESORTS AND SIGHTS

An exotic brew of salt marshes, endless dunes topped with wild sea oats, inlets and islands blanketed with green rushes. Most beaches are terrific, but the resorts tend to be uninspiring. Book accommodation in any resorts and major towns along the coast well in advance.

Charleston

Charleston's gaslit cobbled streets are a feast of history and architecture. Grand *antebellum* mansions line the Battery, and rejuvenated ware-houses buzz with activity. The Calhoun Mansion is a quirky merchant's house. Middleton Place, Magnolia Plantation and Swamp Garden are the best former cotton plantations, and Patriots Point naval museum is superb.

Myrtle Beach

American Blackpool without the tower, built along a 60-mile stretch of glorious beach. North Myrtle Beach, with its fishing piers, is quieter.

Outer Banks

A long reef of narrow sandbanks off the coast which stretch down from Virginia. Ocracoke is the best place to stay.

USS North Carolina

Battleship that saw service in all the major naval battles in the Pacific. Virtually the whole ship is accessible on a self-guided tour.

DEEP SOUTH
Good for culture, food/wine, nightlife and scenic landscape

THE GRACIOUS plantation lands of Scarlett O'Hara were also musically fertile – blues, jazz and rock 'n' roll were born in the American South. Much of the wealth, supported by slavery, was curtailed by the Civil War, known locally as the War Between the States.

BEST SIGHTS

Atlanta
This modern city that played host to the 1996 Olympics has come a long way since *Gone with the Wind* – though fans of this epic tale should head for the Margaret Mitchell House, where the book was written. Best sight is the Atlanta History Center, where costumed guides escort you round a nineteenth-century plantation house; you can also visit the tomb of Martin Luther King and see his birth house or tour the CNN studios.

Cajun country
The original Acadians ('Cajun' is a corruption of Acadian) were driven out of Acadia, or Nova Scotia, by the British in the eighteenth century and settled among the bayous and swamps of southern Louisiana, bringing with them French language and customs. Lafayette is the centre of Acadiana, and you can visit a couple of recreated Acadian villages: Vermilionville and the Acadian Village.

A swamp tour is highly recommended. Small boats zigzag along bayous, home to alligators and coypus.

Memphis
Memphis's most famous sight is the much-visited Graceland, Elvis Presley's home, 12 miles south-east. You can also tour Sun Studio, scene of Elvis's first break. The Rock 'n' Soul Museum has excellent displays on the development and history of music, and jazz and blues thrive on Beale Street. The Civil Rights Museum commemorates the shooting of Martin Luther King here in 1968; the Mississippi River Museum traces the waterway's history.

Nashville
If you are not a fan of country music check out the full-scale reconstruction of the Parthenon in Centennial Park. Downtown, the Tennessee State Museum has a comprehensive civil war collection.

The main country music sights are centred around Opryland, a theme park/hotel/cable TV network spawned from the original 'Grand Ole Opry' radio programme in 1925, and Music Row, a terrace of gift shops and 'museums' of stars such as Hank Williams Jr and Barbara Mandrell.

Natchez
Virtually unscathed by the war, downtown Natchez is a grid of gracious buildings, many of which were built by cotton millionaires. Houses open all year include Stanton Hall and Longwood.

New Orleans
The lively French Quarter owes more to the Spanish in architectural terms. Here you can browse in shops selling jewellery or Mardi Gras costumes, sup on Cajun cuisine and party round the clock (for traditional New Orleans jazz try to squeeze into Preservation Hall). The Historic New Orleans Collection is a museum of local and regional history, while the Aquarium of the Americas has superb displays. Alternatively, try a Cajun cookery class or a guided cemetery walk.

Vicksburg
Vicksburg, on a bluff above the Mississippi, was the site of a decisive Civil War battle; its story is told in the National Military Park, where you can drive round a battle trail. McRaven House is a good *antebellum* house.

THE ROCKIES
Good for outdoor activities and scenic landscape

THE ROCKIES run through five states: Montana, Idaho, Wyoming, Utah and Colorado. This backbone of North America is littered with old mining towns deserted during the boom and slump of the goldrush years, but it is the awe-inspiring landscape that draws the tourists.

BEST NATIONAL PARKS AND MONUMENTS

Canyonlands
The Green and Colorado rivers have each carved a two-tier canyon on an extraordinary scale. If you are short of time, drive down the Island in the Sky section to Grand View Point for breathtaking views. If you have more time, visit the rock spires of the Needles area. The Maze remains one of the most remote parts of the USA, accessible only by jeep, involving a 150-mile detour from Moab.

Dinosaur National Monument
This vast dinosaurs' graveyard is an intriguing and humbling place – bringing home just how recent *Homo sapiens*' rule of the planet has been.

Glacier
The most northerly and remote of the parks attracts more walkers and fewer cars. The Going to the Sun Road passes beneath the Garden Wall, a glacial ridge ground away by ice to a blunt edge – see the highlights on a 'jammer' excursion.

Grand Teton
The most beautiful mountain range in the Rockies, the Tetons rise to just under 14,000 feet, mirrored in a string of forest-fringed lakes. Boats shuttle visitors across Jenny Lake to Hidden Falls. Colter Bay Visitor Center has a fine exhibition of Indian art and artefacts.

Mesa Verde
The park contains the most interesting of the ruins of the Anasazi civilisation (AD 500–1300). Three stone *pueblo* dwellings can be visited: Spruce Tree House, near the museum, Cliff Palace and Balcony House.

Yellowstone
Yellowstone is an extraordinary geological stew of over 10,000 thermal features. Old Faithful, the most reliable if not the most spectacular geyser in the park, reaches 100 feet. For a good variety of geysers, hot springs and pools take the Upper Geyser Basin Trail. The Fountain Paint Pot spouts globules of hot mud. Swim in lukewarm rapids at Firehole River.

BEST SIGHTS

Aspen
A town of clapboard houses and a winter ski resort, which is deserted in summer. A fantastic drive over Independence Pass then turns into the broad Arkansas river valley. West and east, Leadville and Redstone are two mining villages cheap to stay in and worth exploring.

Denver
Gateway to the Rockies, Denver has a mile-long pedestrianised mall which plays host to café society in summer. Excellent museums include the Natural History Museum, Denver Art Museum (one of the most important collections of American Indian art in the USA). Be sure to take the free tours of the state capitol and the Mint.

Jackson Hole

Jet-set ski resort in winter, in summer the town is a good base for exploring Grand Teton National Park. The centre is full of designer factory outlets, classy restaurants and lots of bars, and there's more than a hint of pastiche, with stagecoach rides, elk-antler arches and a nightly Old West shoot-out.

San Juan Mountains

Walkers, trout anglers and ghost-town explorers visit this alpine south-western corner of the Rockies in summer. Stay at the restored nineteenth-century mining towns of Ouray, Telluride or Durango and enjoy the glorious scenery.

DESERT STATES
Good for scenic landscape

THIS IS cowboys and Indians country, but it is the landscape of Arizona, New Mexico and Utah – vast canyons and fiery pinnacles – that stays in the memory.

BEST NATIONAL PARKS AND MONUMENTS

Arches

This is a barren red sandstone desert landscape punctuated by rock arches, cliffs and precariously perched boulders. Sunset or sunrise, when the sandstone seems to ignite, are the best times to visit.

Bryce Canyon

Not really a canyon at all, rather a steep series of 14 natural amphitheatres notable for the hoodoos – thin pinnacles of rock formed by a constant cycle of freezing and thawing.

Chaco Culture National Historic Park

A display describes building techniques of *pueblo* dwellers at this huge site between the tenth and twelfth centuries. The outstanding ruin is Pueblo Bonito, where up to 1,200 Anasazi people lived in 800 rooms.

Edge of the Cedars State Park

Informative displays of Indian artefacts with the chance to descend into the underground ceremonial hall, or *kiva*.

El Morro

The visitor centre explains how the cultures of the American Indians, the sixteenth-century Spanish conquerors and their English successors have interacted.

Grand Canyon
A 277-mile-long fissure (four to 18 miles wide at varying points) carved by the Colorado river through the rising Colorado plateau. Visit the South Rim with the hordes, or the North Rim for a more peaceful experience, and journey to the canyon floor, and wonder at the scale and the constantly changing hues of light on rock.

Montezuma Castle
Astonishing twelfth-century palace constructed high above a creek by the Sinagua people.

Monument Valley Navajo Tribal Park
Tribal members compete to take visitors by jeep, coach or horseback around the astonishing table of weird rock formations. An enjoyable trail takes you past fabulous monoliths such as the Mittens.

Walnut Canyon
Sinagua Indians settled here in 1056, using the overhangs and rock walls bound with mud to create rooms. Follow the interpretive trail.

Wupatki
An excellent interpretive trail crosses this red sandstone monument.

Zion
Sheer walls of sandstone flank the Virgin river. The visitor centre has information on short but spectacular trails like Weeping Rock or Emerald Pool that take you to hanging gardens and cascading waterfalls.

BEST SIGHTS

Hoover Dam
More than 720 feet high, this is one of America's modern engineering wonders, begun in 1931. Its reservoir, Lake Mead, can hold nearly 9.2 trillion gallons. Take a guided tour, or stand at the top and look down. Visit the museum in nearby Boulder City.

Las Vegas
Bizarrely located in the middle of the Mohave desert, Las Vegas is famous for its casinos. The hotels lining 'the Strip' are like miniature theme parks in themselves. The gambling paraphernalia remains the same, but background themes vary: ancient Rome, the gondola of

Venice, Paris, New York and even Arthurian England. Don't miss the fake volcano on the Strip, which 'erupts' every 15 minutes from dusk to midnight.

Santa Fe
Vibrant cultural centre offering a winning blend of colonial and Indian history. An excellent set of museums includes the Museum of Fine Arts, the Institute of American Indian Arts; the Museum of Indian Arts, the Georgia O'Keeffe Museum and Culture.

St George
Southern Utah's largest town, settled in the 1860s by Mormons. A hi-tech visitor centre beside the temple explains the basis of the religion.

Taos
A glorious combination of ski resort, artists' colony and historical centre, Taos in New Mexico has a stunning setting at the foot of the Sangre de Cristo mountain. You can also visit Indians who remain in their ancestral adobe houses on the Taos *pueblo* (founded nearly 1,000 years ago).

Tombstone
Famous for the 30 seconds of gunfire at the OK Corral in 1881. The 'Historama' features historical tableaux, while the courthouse has a thought-provoking display on the gunfight and a reconstructed gallows.

CALIFORNIA
Good for beaches, family holidays, food/wine, nightlife and outdoor activities

CALIFORNIA IS almost twice the size of mainland Britain. City sightseeing, combined with sampling the wild national parks and a few days lazing on the beach, would make for a varied and enjoyable holiday.

BEST CITIES
Long Beach
This rejuvenated city is the best base for touring Southern California. Restored art-deco buildings along the main shopping area, a world-class aquarium and a Russian submarine are among the attractions. Long Beach is also home to the *Queen Mary*, the classiest ocean liner ever built, now a hotel and leisure facility.

Los Angeles

LA is a great destination, but you'll need a car to get around. Top attractions include Hollywood with its Museum of Entertainment and Mann's Chinese Theatre. Universal Studios is a theme park with a tour of the backlot including the *Psycho* House, and Disneyland is just an hour away in Anaheim.

San Francisco

The state's prettiest city is a series of connecting suburbs, each with its own cultural identity, like Chinatown, Japantown and North Beach Italians. Take the cable-car from Union Square to Fisherman's Wharf for views of pastel Victorian houses or walk across the Golden Gate Bridge, symbol of the city since 1937. Nightlife can be camp and outrageous, with lots of Las Vegas-style revues catering for every possible taste.

BEST BEACHES

California's vast stretches of golden sand are surfing, not swimming, beaches, and you will need to keep a constant eye on children. Many city beaches have a distinct culture, as cyclists compete with rollerbladers.

Carmel Beach

This large cove of white sand backed by cypress-covered cliffs is ideal for sunbathing and beachcombing, but strong currents make it dangerous for swimmers.

Mission Beach, San Diego

Ideal for surfing, snorkelling, scuba-diving and fishing.

Muscle Beach, Los Angeles (Venice)

Bodybuilders congregate here to pump iron and strut around.

Pacific Coast Highway

This 400-mile road takes you through some of California's most spectacular coastal scenery, including Big Sur, a dramatic 75-mile stretch of cliffs. Good overnight stops: Santa Barbara, a Spanish-influenced town with several museums, galleries and antique shops; Morro Bay, a small fishing port and boating harbour with fish restaurants; and the Monterey peninsula resorts of Carmel, Monterey and Pacific Grove.

Santa Cruz Beach

Backed by the famous Boardwalk, whose jolly, funfair atmosphere spills over on to the sands. Great for surfing.

Santa Monica Beach

Just beyond LA's metropolitan sprawl is a long expanse of fine, golden sand patrolled by jeep-propelled lifeguards *à la Baywatch*. Santa Monica is a good base for visiting LA, with hotels for all budgets. The pier appeals to kids of all ages

Venice Beach, Los Angeles

This is where hip LA goes to hang out – cool dudes, long-limbed bronzed babes, basketball enthusiasts, and many others.

BEST SIGHTS

Malibu, a seashore sanctuary for the seriously rich, houses the John Paul Getty Museum with its controversial collection of Greek and Roman art and famous paintings, including Van Gogh's *Irises*.

Hearst Castle at San Simeon was the extravagant personal fiefdom of newspaper magnate William Randolph Hearst. Thousands of European art treasures were incorporated into the design to produce a place of regal sumptuousness and spellbinding vulgarity. Book a tour in advance.

BEST NATIONAL PARKS

Death Valley

The landscape is unforgettable: white salt pinnacles at the Devil's Golf Course; giant ripples of mud at Zabriskie Point; the amazing colours of Artist's Drive. Visit between November and April: in summer, Death Valley has the highest average temperatures on earth.

Joshua Tree

Gnarled trees where Mojave and Colorado deserts meet, thought by Mormons to resemble Joshua's arms leading them to the Promised Land.

Yosemite

The glacier-carved canyon of Yosemite Valley is readily accessible by road. Explore its stunning scenery of meadows, sheer granite walls and pine and cedar forests along marked trails. More adventurous hikers aim for Hetch Hetchy or Tioga Pass. The best views are from Glacier Point, an hour's drive away. Do not miss the giant redwoods at Mariposa Grove.

BEST VINEYARDS

The Napa Valley produces California's best-known wines, the cooler southern area being particularly suitable for chardonnay and pinot noir varieties, while the north produces excellent cabernet sauvignon. The less well-known Sonoma is the best place to get to know California's native grape variety – Zinfandel.

HAWAII
Good for beaches and scenic landscape

THE WORLD'S most isolated islands are a long flight from the UK but reward you with dramatic landscapes, idyllic beaches, year-round warmth and erupting volcanoes. Hawaii is more expensive than mainland USA. There are four main islands – Big Island, Kauai, Maui and Oahu – with Honolulu-Waikiki on Oahu the only built-up area. It's fine for a couple of days, especially if you want some nightlife, but head to the outer islands for a more relaxed life by the beach. Car hire is essential if you want to explore.

BEST SIGHT

Pearl Harbor, Oahu
The scene of Japan's surprise attack in December 1941 is now an excellent memorial-museum spanning the whole war. The destroyed *USS Arizona*, which symbolises the initial death and destruction, lies sunken beside the mighty *USS Missouri*, the world's last battleship and site of Japan's final surrender.

BEST BEACHES

Overall, Maui has the best beaches but each island has some gems with palm-fringed golden sand and crystal-clear water. The best black-sand beach (spectacular to see but not great for a day-long affair) is Punaluu on Big Island.

Stunners on Maui include Big Beach, Charley Young, Kaanapali and Kamaole III, while Oahu's top spots are Ala Moana and Malaekahana Bay. On Big Island head for Hapuna and Mauna Kea. Kauai's best beaches are Anini, Hanalei and Tunnels Beach.

BEST SCENIC LANDSCAPES

Road to Hana, Maui
An amazing three-hour drive that snakes 50 miles along the cliffs to Hana past crashing waterfalls, sheer ravines and dense vegetation. It's a narrow road with over 600 bends and 56 bridges (many one lane) but worth the effort.

Volcanoes National Park, Big Island
Where else but America would you get a drive-in volcano? The Park takes in the whole of Kilauea, which has been erupting since 1983, though the lava flows are often underground or inaccessible. You can drive around the crater, see (and smell) sulphur vents, walk over lava

fields, explore lava tubes or just go up to the newest lava where it crosses the road.

Waimea Canyon, Kauai
This mini-Grand Canyon cuts a 12-mile-long red swathe through an otherwise lush, green island. A scenic drive with spectacular look-outs runs along one side.

WHEN TO GO

HUGE VARIATIONS in weather occur from season to season and from one part of the USA to another. In general, summer is not a good time to visit Florida: the air is hot and sticky, and rainfall is heavy. But winter and spring are pleasantly mild. In New York, spring

	JAN	FEB	MAR	APR	MAY	JUN	JUL	AUG	SEP	OCT	NOV	DEC
Average daily maximum temperature °C												
London	6	7	10	13	17	20	22	21	19	14	10	7
New York	4	4	9	15	21	26	28	27	24	18	12	6
New York	11	10	12	11	12	10	10	10	8	8	9	10
London	15	13	11	12	12	11	12	11	13	13	15	15
Average number of rainy days per month												

	JAN	FEB	MAR	APR	MAY	JUN	JUL	AUG	SEP	OCT	NOV	DEC
Average daily maximum temperature °C												
London	6	7	10	13	17	20	22	21	19	14	10	7
San Francisco	13	15	16	18	19	21	22	22	23	21	18	14
San Francisco	11	10	9	6	3	1	<1	<1	1	4	7	10
London	15	13	11	12	12	11	12	11	13	13	15	15
Average number of rainy days per month												

	JAN	FEB	MAR	APR	MAY	JUN	JUL	AUG	SEP	OCT	NOV	DEC
Average daily maximum temperature °C												
London	6	7	10	13	17	20	22	21	19	14	10	7
Miami	24	25	27	28	30	31	32	32	31	29	27	25
Miami	6	6	6	8	10	13	17	16	19	15	9	7
London	15	13	11	12	12	11	12	11	13	13	15	15
Average number of rainy days per month												

and autumn are generally agreeable, though the weather can change dramatically from day to day.

For touring in the west, the summer months are best: many national parks in the northern Rockies are not open properly until June. On the coast, July and August are the worst months for fog (around San Francisco) and smog (around LA). Southern California has pleasantly mild winters.

PACKAGE TRAVEL

OTHER THAN in Orlando or in the case of city breaks to destinations such as New York, single-centre holidays are rare and limiting. A fly-drive package gives you more flexibility, or you can book twin- or multi-centre packages, or ready-made self-drive tours with pre-booked accommodation. Most tour operators specialising in the US offer a wide range of options, from tailor-made tours to airpasses, so it is easy to get the kind of deal you want.

Treat packages that offer 'free' car-hire with a pinch of salt – you will inevitably have to pay a whole range of extras when you arrive, including collision damage waiver (known as loss damage waiver in the

---

Tour operators

Battlefields: Holts' Tours, Midas **Birdwatching**: Limosa, Ornitholidays, Sunbird **City breaks**: British Airways Holidays, Cresta, Crystal, Inghams, Osprey, Premier, Sovereign, Thomson, Time Off, Travelscene **Cultural**: Explorers, Ffestiniog Travel, Martin Randall, Travel for the Arts **General and specialist**: Airtours, AmeriCan Adventures, American Connections, APT International, Archers, Bridgewater Travel, British Airways Holidays, Cosmos, Cricketer, Crystal, Delta Airlines, Florida Vacations, Funway, Getaway Vacations, Hamilton Travel, Hawaiian Dream, Inghams, Jetlife, Jetsave, Jetset, Just America, Key to America, Kuoni, North America Travel Service, Premier Holidays, Saga, Sunvil, Thomas Cook, Titan HiTours, Tradewinds, Trailfinders, Travelbag, Travelpack, Travelsphere, Unijet, US Airtours, Virgin Holidays **Rail tours**: Explorers Tours, Ffestiniog Travel **Walking**: Explore Worldwide, Ramblers Holidays, Waymark **Wine**: Arblaster & Clarke **Other activities**: Ace Study Tours (study tours), American Round-Up (ranch), Clipper Voyages (river cruising), Discover the World (wildlife), Hemmingway Travel (motor homes), Inter-Church Travel (religious tours), Naturetrek (wildlife), Ranch America (ranch), Solo's Holidays (singles)

US), top-up liability insurance (see below), airport fee, handling charge, state and local taxes, which could come to as much as £250 a week. It may be cheaper for you to book from a company that includes all these charges up front.

If you are planning to tour over quite a distance, check that the hire company will let you take the car out of the state, and which other states you can visit: some companies have limited coverage. If you want to drop the car off in a different location, you will usually have to pay a surcharge.

Most major tour operators offer holiday programmes to the USA, many in dedicated brochures. Florida, California and New England are all popular package destinations. Holidays include fly-drive, coach tours, rail tours and cruising, and accommodation is self-catering and in hotels and motorhomes. City breaks are on offer to East Coast destinations including New York, Boston, Washington DC and Chicago, and also to Las Vegas. Activity holidays include ranch holidays, covered wagon trails, walking, birdwatching, wine tours, river cruising and rail tours.

INDEPENDENT TRAVEL

FIERCE COMPETITION among airlines on the transatlantic routes means there is plenty of scope for finding special deals and cheap fares. If you are planning to travel extensively within the US, it may be worth buying an airpass. Airpasses are offered by several airlines, and their conditions vary, but most have to be bought in the UK before you go. Check the flight network of each airline: some airlines have a good range of long-distance flights, including coast to coast, while others concentrate mainly on short hops, which may require you to change.

Distances are huge, and the locals rarely walk anywhere, so unless you are just staying in a particular city, hiring a car is by far the best way of getting around. Both cars and petrol are comparatively cheap. Another possibility is the 'drive-away': if you are heading in the same direction as a car that needs to be delivered, you are given insurance, a delivery date and address and the keys, and off you go. This is not always as liberating as it sounds, as delivery dates can be quite tight – so no heading off to the east coast via Alaska – but it can be an adventure.

Rail travel is a comfortable but much less flexible option; if you are not driving it is better to use the Greyhound bus network. In cities, public transport is better and often, like San Francisco trams, part of the travel experience.

On the outskirts of most towns is a 'strip' of hotels and motels. The motel is part of the experience of touring America, and rooms are more or less standard. Bed and breakfast does exist in America, but it is more upmarket and expensive than in the UK. In cities like Washington booking through agencies may save you money on the rack rate. Alternatively the Internet is a good way to book.

RED TAPE, HEALTH AND SAFETY

THE VISA waiver programme allows British passport-holders to stay for up to 90 days without a visa if they have an onward ticket.

There are no major health risks, but it is vital that you have adequate travel insurance to cover medical emergencies and public liability. Ironically, virtually all insurance policies exclude third-party liability during the 'use or possession of any mechanically propelled vehicle' – e.g., a hire car, so it would be wise to take out optional supplementary liability cover.

Periodically reports emerge of tourists being shot/mugged/attacked, notably in Florida in recent years. The usual rules about streetwise behaviour apply (see page 12). If you are unsure about how to get to your hotel from the airport, take a taxi or courtesy bus and ask the car hire company to drop off your car at the hotel the next day, when you have had a chance to recover from the flight and are feeling more alert. The latest advice is available from the Foreign Office Travel Advice Unit (see page 11).

Many individual states have offices in the UK from which you can order tourist information. Contact numbers for some of the main destinations are listed below.

MORE INFORMATION Visit USA Association MK, US Embassy, 24 Grosvenor Square, London W1A 1AE. Travel information and brochure request line tel (09069) 101020 (premium rate number), web site: *www.seeamerica.org*

Individual states and cities Arizona (01426) 946334; California (0891) 200278; Florida (0891) 600555; Georgia 0121–445 4554; Louisiana 020-8760 0377; Memphis (01462) 440787; Mississippi (01462) 440787; Nevada (0990) 238832; New Mexico (0839) 300700; New York City 020-7437 8300; North Carolina (0990) 333123; Pennsylvania (0839) 300701; Tennessee (01462) 440784; Virginia 020-8651 4743; Washington DC 020-8877 4521; Washington State 020-7978 5233

COST OF LIVING ££

VIETNAM

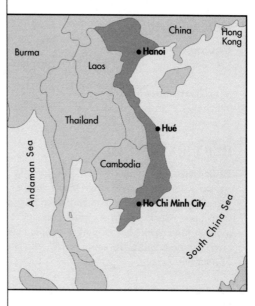

HO CHI MINH CITY AND THE MEKONG DELTA
Good for culture, local colour, nightlife and scenic landscape

HO CHI Minh City, still widely known as Saigon, is the usual jumping-off point for travel in Vietnam and provides a head-spinning introduction to a country in the throes of furious economic change. It makes a good base for exploring the Mekong Delta's quilted rice-lands, nearby war relics and the fanciful Cao Dai religious centre.

Vietnam's largest city and commercial capital retains a surprising flavour of its French colonial past, from elegant villas to coffee and croissants. After hours, choose from some of Vietnam's finest restaurants, hottest clubs and hippest bars.

BEST SIGHTS

Cholon
Visit compelling, incense-filled Chinese temples and teeming streets.

War Remnants Museum
This gives a grisly and somewhat one-sided view of what locals call 'The American War'.

BEST EXCURSIONS

Boat trips
An excursion on the Mekong Delta's skein of waterways is well worth the effort – especially if it includes the floating markets in the city of Can Tho, which sell fruit, vegetables and local commodities. Boats indicate their wares by hanging a sample from a bamboo mast in the bow. If time is short, the town of My Tho provides an excellent taster of river life.

Cu Chi
Here you can squeeze through 75 miles of tunnels dug by Viet Cong soldiers which passed under an American army base.

Tay Ninh
The flamboyant Cao Dai cathedral, dominated by the Divine Eye, takes everyone by surprise – time your visit to coincide with one of the four daily services. The cathedral is headquarters of the Cao Dai religion.

BEST NIGHTLIFE

Venues in Ho Chi Minh City range from spit-and-sawdust *bia hoi* (draft beer) bars to increasingly sophisticated clubs and discos. The most famous is Apocalypse Now, which harks back to the GI bars of the 1960s, though upfront prostitution now mars the atmosphere.

Great music and theme nights make Gecko Bar a popular hangout, while the coolest place to be seen is state-of-the-art Club Monaco. Or kick back among the fairy lights of the Rex Hotel's Rooftop Bar.

CENTRAL PROVINCES
Good for culture, history, local colour and scenic landscape

HUE'S TEMPLES and royal palaces are the highlights of central Vietnam, closely followed by Hoi An's traditional merchants' houses. South of Hoi An, the central highlands' cool, misty plateaux provide welcome respite from the plains, while further north war sights litter the Demilitarised Zone where Vietnam divided for two decades after 1954.

The main road north, Highway 1, offers dramatic views of forested mountains fringed with sugar-white sands – but beware, not all beaches are safe for swimming.

BEST SIGHTS

Central Highlands
Founded by the French, Da Lat is a quaint – though not totally unspoilt – hill station surrounded by pines and thundering waterfalls. Exploring the rest of the highlands is more problematic, but the rewards are an array of ethnic minority villages, mountainscapes and Vietnam's largest wildlife reserve, Yok Don National Park.

Demilitarised Zone
The bleak battlefields of the DMZ are a poignant memorial to the thousands who died here in the 1960s and 1970s. There is nothing particular to see, but it is hard not to respond to the sense of enormous desolation.

Names such as The Rockpile and Hamburger Hill resound from countless Vietnam War movies.

Hoi An
This pint-size town remains a captivating place despite being firmly on the tourist trail. Once a thriving port, its narrow streets are lined with ancient wooden buildings (some dating from the late sixteenth century) interspersed with eye-catching Chinese Assembly Halls, built by refugee merchants.

Nearby, seventh-century Cham temples moulder under luxuriant vegetation at My Son.

Hué
A slow-moving, cultured city on the Perfume River, Hué should not be missed. Ravaged by war and a notoriously wet climate, it is being painstakingly restored to its former glory. Known as the Imperial City

after being chosen as the new capital by Emperor Gia Long, who unified Vietnam in 1802, Hué was the country's cultural centre in the nineteenth century and remained the official capital until 1945. The emperors' lavish mausoleums rest in landscaped gardens on the outskirts; they can be reached by river boat.

HANOI AND THE NORTH
Good for culture, local colour, outdoor activities and scenic landscape

HANOI, VIETNAM'S capital, is layered in history. It is a small, rather reserved city where life proceeds at a gentler pace than in the south – though it is catching up fast.

From here most visitors take a trip to Ha Long Bay, Vietnam's premier natural attraction. The northern mountains are home to a patchwork of ethnic minorities and provide excellent opportunities for trekking.

BEST SIGHTS

Ha Long Bay
Thousands of limestone islands, some pitted with caves, speckle Ha Long Bay's expansive emerald waters, four hours by road from Hanoi. A full day's boat tour is recommended to see the best of the bay, while the more adventurous can join a sea-kayaking trip, but note that during winter months (November to March) spells of cold, drizzly weather can dampen Ha Long's beauty.

Hanoi
Despite the intrusion of flashy new high-rises, central Hanoi remains an attractive scene of lakes, shaded boulevards and stylish, French-built mansions, contrasting sharply with the neighbouring Old Quarter's intoxicating tangle of market streets. In Ho Chi Minh's Mausoleum the man himself, lying embalmed in a cold, dark hall, still draws pilgrims from around the world. The eleventh-century Temple of Literature dates back to Hanoi's earliest days and represents Vietnam's foremost Confucian sanctuary.

Northern mountains
A wild, fairly inaccessible region containing Vietnam's highest peaks. Apart from the scenery, the prime attraction is the variety of minority peoples, many still following a traditional way of life. A burgeoning trekking industry focuses around Sa Pa town, which also hosts a colourful weekend market.

WHEN TO GO

THE SOUTHERN region has a tropical climate, while the north is sub-tropical. The rainy season lasts from May to September in the north, August to January in the centre, and May to November in the south of the country. The temperature averages 25°C all year round in the south, while the north has two distinct seasons. The best time to travel in Vietnam is between January and April.

	Average daily maximum temperature °C											
London	6	7	10	13	17	20	22	21	19	14	10	7
Hanoi	20	21	23	28	32	33	33	32	31	29	26	22
	JAN	FEB	MAR	APR	MAY	JUN	JUL	AUG	SEP	OCT	NOV	DEC
Hanoi	7	13	15	14	15	14	15	16	14	9	7	7
London	15	13	11	12	12	11	12	11	13	13	15	15
	Average number of rainy days per month											

PACKAGE TRAVEL

HOLIDAY OPTIONS in Vietnam are somewhat limited. In addition to the Vietnam-based tours available, some long-haul operators offer hotels in Hanoi or Ho Chi Minh City as a stopover.

Seven-day tours visiting North and South Vietnam are typical of what is on offer. These use internal flights visiting Hanoi, Da Nang, Hué, Hoi An and Ho Chi Minh City. City tours and excursions to nearby sights are included and a cruise on the Perfume river may be part of the tour. Longer tours may include a trip to the central highlands and the town of Da Lat, or a visit to Na Trang for a boat trip round the islands and time spent relaxing on the beach. Travel is usually by minibus or coach and some operators include the Reunification Express

---

Tour operators

Adventure: Discovery Initiatives, Exodus, Explore Worldwide, Guerba, Peregrine Adventure, Symbiosis Expedition Planning **Cycling**: Exodus **General**: Asian Journeys, Coromandel, Distant Dreams, Jetset, Magic of the Orient, Silverbird, Travelsphere **Tailor made**: Regent Holidays, Silk Steps, Tennyson Travel **Other activities**: British Museum Traveller (cultural), Holts' Tours (battle-fields), Naturetrek (wildlife), Solo's (singles)

---

train journey from Hué to Hanoi in their packages. Cycle tours, trekking and sea-kayaking options are also now available.

Although changing fast, the tourism infrastructure is still relatively undeveloped so accommodation standards are variable.

INDEPENDENT TRAVEL

AS YET there are no direct flights from Britain to Vietnam, so you will probably be routed through a regional centre such as Singapore or Bangkok. Most airlines offer tickets flying into Ho Chi Minh City and out of Hanoi, or vice versa.

Local buses and trains can be fun but are slow and uncomfortable: it is worth paying extra for 'soft-class' train tickets (you get a padded seat). For night journeys there are also hard and soft berths. Increasingly visitors opt for internal flights or tourist buses plying the main routes. You can also sign up for day-trips or longer excursions with one of the many private tour operators in Hanoi, Ho Chi Minh City and other tourist centres. Make sure you know exactly what is included in the price.

Though self-drive is not available, hiring a vehicle plus driver is not exorbitant and allows greater freedom. This can be organised through a UK travel agent, or, again, a private tour operator – allow time to find a reputable agent and ensure the itinerary and costs are agreed in writing. Rental cycles, scooters and motorbikes are readily available. Only experienced bikers should attempt the rough mountain roads.

There is now a glut of hotels in Vietnam, particularly in the main cities and tourist centres. This means prices have dropped across the board and even top-class hotels offer fantastic bargains. Elsewhere the local infrastructure is rudimentary and hotels fairly basic, although standards are gradually improving. As a rule, the newest hotels offer superior standards of comfort and cleanliness. Using government-run tourist offices to book accommodation can be expensive, so it is best to book direct (using a reliable, up-to-date guidebook) or with the help of a UK agent.

RED TAPE, HEALTH AND SAFETY

ALL FOREIGN nationals need a visa to enter Vietnam, available from the Vietnamese Embassy or a specialist visa agent (see page 17).

The tourist visa costs £38 and the maximum time you can apply for is 30 days. Two passport photographs are required. Processing normally takes a week to ten days, but it is wise to allow longer in case of delays.

If you take simple, commonsense precautions you should not fall ill in Vietnam. Follow the precautions on pages 10–12 and consult your GP or a travel clinic in plenty of time about vaccinations: typhoid and hepatitis A are usually recommended. Make sure your tetanus and polio boosters are up to date. Avoid mosquito bites by regular use of repellents: dengue fever is present in the south and Japanese encephalitis in rural districts, while malaria occurs throughout the country, though there are few instances in Hanoi and Ho Chi Minh City. Anti-malaria medication varies according to your length of stay and whether you travel in the cities or off the beaten track.

Take care on the roads, as poor driving and vehicle maintenance are the cause of many accidents. While violent crime is extremely rare in Vietnam, petty crime is on the rise in Ho Chi Minh City and Nha Trang, where it's best to avoid taking cyclos (tricycle rickshaws) late at night. Women on their own should also be wary walking quiet streets after dark. Carry money, passport and other documents in a concealed money belt, don't wear flash jewellery, and keep a tight grip on your bags.

MORE INFORMATION Tourist Information Department, Embassy of Vietnam, 12–14 Victoria Road, London W8 5RD, tel 020-7937 1912 (*Press 1 when you hear the message, then ext. 203*), visa information (0891) 171228 (premium rate number)

COST OF LIVING £

ZANZIBAR

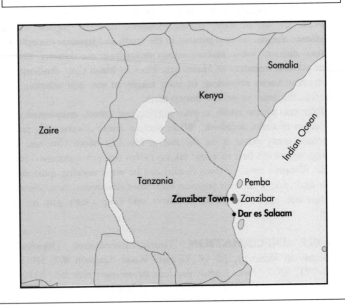

HIGHLIGHTS

Beaches
Zanzibar Island

Culture/ history
Zanzibar Town

Local colour
Pemba Island, Zanzibar Island, Zanzibar Town

Outdoor activities
Pemba Island, Zanzibar Island

Shopping
Zanzibar Town

Wildlife
Zanzibar Island

ZANZIBAR TOWN
Good for culture, history, local colour and shopping

ZANZIBAR TOWN is the capital of the state of Zanzibar. For hundreds of years it was one of the most important commercial centres in Africa and the Indian Ocean, with a thriving trade in slaves, ivory and spices – most notably cloves. Today the town still flourishes with a large and vibrant community but some of the former splendour is gone, and some areas are a touch down–at–heel.

BEST SIGHTS

Stone Town

The part of Zanzibar Town of most interest to tourists is the Stone Town, 'the old quarter': a maze of narrow streets and alleys, edged on two sides by the Indian Ocean. Until the mid-nineteenth century Zanzibar was a sultanate ruled from Oman, before coming under British colonial influence from the 1880s until 1963. Many grand buildings from these times remain – an intriguing mix of Arab, Indian, African and European styles – although the dirt and decay surrounding the fine examples can spoil a few exotic illusions. The best way (often the only way) to explore the Stone Town is on foot – the streets are too narrow for cars.

BEST SHOPPING

Browsers can spend many happy hours at the main market on the edge of the Stone Town, where fruit, spices, fish and meat are stacked in large heaps and sold by the handful, tin-full or truck-full.

Souvenir-hunters will enjoy the many shops dotted around the Stone Town. They sell jewellery and carvings from all over Africa, local cloth, spices, colonial antiques and contemporary art. Look out for the indigenous *tinga-tinga* paintings (a brightly coloured, highly stylised, almost pointillist style). There is even a more recent Zanzibari speciality – bubble bath flavoured with locally grown bananas.

ZANZIBAR ISLAND
Good for beaches, local colour, outdoor activities and wildlife

ZANZIBAR ISLAND (its proper name is Unguja, but this is rarely used by visitors) is about the size of the Isle of Wight. Together with Pemba Island it makes up the state of Zanzibar.

The accommodation on the island ranges from simple guesthouses for budget travellers, small and personal lodges for mid-range visitors to large, lively, well-equipped resort-hotels or small, quiet, exclusive hideaways.

BEST BEACHES

As befits an Indian Ocean island, Zanzibar's beaches come close to idyllic, although washed-up seaweed covers the sand at some times of year.

The best beaches are on the north and east coasts. Snorkelling or diving on the coral reefs are popular. Fishing, sailing and other water sports are available.

BEST WILDLIFE

Jozani Forest
The forest in the centre of Zanzibar Island is home to a rare species of colobus monkey, plus several other types of primate. You can observe the monkeys from nature trails through the dense vegetation.

Kizimkazi
At Kizimkazi on the southern tip of Zanzibar Island, pods (groups) of bottlenose and humpback dolphin are common. Turtles and other marine animals can also frequently be seen. Boat trips are available; with care and patience it is possible to swim near the dolphins.

PEMBA ISLAND
Good for local colour and outdoor activities

PEMBA IS undeveloped for tourism, but this is its charm. There are few 'sights' and just a handful of hotels, but some spectacular beaches. Offshore, the game fishing and diving is world-class. The marine reserve of Misali Island has a beach and excellent reefs, and is reputed to be where Captain Kidd buried treasure.

WHEN TO GO

ZANZIBAR HAS two main dry seasons: December to February and June to October, and these are the best times to visit. Outside these periods it rains for a few hours each day, but the wet weather means fewer visitors, more space and better prices. Even in the dry season, the Indian Ocean makes rain possible at any time. Some diving centres only open from August to December when water conditions are best.

Average daily maximum temperature °C											
London	6	7	10	13	17	20	22	21	19	14	10	7
Kisauni	34	34	34	33	31	30	30	30	31	32	32	33
	JAN	FEB	MAR	APR	MAY	JUN	JUL	AUG	SEP	OCT	NOV	DEC
Kisauni	8	6	12	19	15	6	5	5	6	7	10	11
London	15	13	11	12	12	11	12	11	13	13	15	15
Average number of rainy days per month											

PACKAGE TRAVEL

MANY HOLIDAY companies include Zanzibar in their brochures, but most simply offer short 'add-ons' to wider tours of Tanzania or Kenya. If you want more than a few days, only a few specialists have the first-hand knowledge and experience to provide a full, good-quality Zanzibar package.

A few fully-equipped four-star hotels are available, but Zanzibar is relatively new to tourism, so don't automatically expect the 'usual' hotel facilities. Most mid-range places are comfortable and attractive (many are in restored historic buildings) but do not provide televisions, phones and fridges in each room. This is all part of the charm. Some very exclusive places shun electricity and offer 'barefoot luxury'. To avoid surprises, when booking your holiday, check what sort of hotel you're getting.

Tour operators

Adventure: Encounter Overland, Exodus, Explore Worldwide, Guerba, Travelbag **General**: Abercrombie & Kent, British Airways Holidays, Hayes & Jarvis, Kuoni, Somak, Sovereign **Tailor-made specialists**: Africa Archipelago, Africa Exclusive, Africa Explorations, Art of Travel, Cazenove & Loyd Safaris, Definitive Africa, Safari Consultants, Safari Drive, SAR Travel, Tim Best, Wild Africa Safaris

---

INDEPENDENT TRAVEL

FLIGHTS TO Zanzibar from the UK are available on KLM and Kenya Airways. Several international airlines fly to nearby Dar es Salaam, from where local air companies provide the short hop to Zanzibar. If you want to visit Zanzibar as part of wider travels in East Africa, access is still easy. Zanzibar is linked to the mainland by regular flights and fast boat services. Zanzibar Island is fairly small, mostly rural (and mostly flat) so getting around by bus, hire car, moped or bike is easy. Tours, especially to the spice plantations, can also be arranged with companies in Zanzibar Town.

RED TAPE, HEALTH AND SAFETY

ZANZIBAR IS an independent state within the United Republic of Tanzania. Passports are needed, even if you come from another part of Tanzania. Visas for Tanzania (including Zanzibar) are required by most nationalities; application forms are available from the Tanzanian High Commission in London. When you apply, your passport should be valid for six months. You need two passport-sized photographs and £38 in cash. You can visit the High Commission in person between 10am and 12.30pm, Monday to Friday – allow 24 hours for processing. If applying by post, send your application by registered delivery and enclose an sae. You can get more visa information from the official web site (see below), and also download an application form.

A certificate to prove that you have been inoculated for yellow fever also needs to be shown on arrival in Zanzibar, even if you come from another part of Tanzania. Your doctor or travel clinic will advise on yellow fever and other jabs required. The Foreign Office strongly recommends inoculation against rabies. A meningitis risk exists in Zanzibar, if you experience symptoms that include severe headache, high temperature, dislike of bright light and a rash that does not fade when pressure is applied, consult a doctor immediately.

Precautions against malaria are important. Take anti-malaria pills, use repellent and wear sufficient clothes in the evening. Most hotels provide mosquito nets, although in cheaper places these may be missing or have big holes. If this is your budget level take a needle and thread or, better still, your own portable net.

Zanzibar is a Muslim country and the people are traditionally conservative. Nudity and topless bathing are forbidden, and scanty clothing anywhere away from the beach is frowned upon.

Buying turtle-shell (sometimes called 'tortoiseshell') products is illegal, as turtles are a protected species.

Robberies (occasionally with violence) are not unknown in the Stone Town and on some beach areas. Use commonsense to keep safe: avoid quiet areas at night, especially if walking alone, and keep valuables (including cameras) out of sight wherever possible.

MORE INFORMATION Tanzania Tourist Office, 78–80 Borough High Street, London SE1 1LL, tel 020-7407 0566, Zanzibar Travel Network web site: *www.zanzibar.net*

Tanzanian High Commission, 43 Hertford Street, London W1Y 8DB, tel 020-7499 8951/7491 3600, web site: *www.tanzanian-online.gov.uk*

COST OF LIVING £

ZIMBABWE

HARARE
Good for culture, local colour and outdoor activities

SURPRISINGLY SEDATE for an African city, Harare melds a post-Second World War provincial British feel with African flamboyance. There is nothing here you'll kick yourself for missing, but a few features are worth a look.

BEST SIGHTS

Botanical Gardens
These are full of gloriously oversized tropical vegetation.

Mbare Market
Mbare Market is worth experiencing as Zimbabwe's largest and most vibrant open-air shopping precinct.

National Gallery
The National Gallery offers a pleasant diversion, especially if you are interested in the local stone-sculpture movement.

BEST EXCURSIONS

Canoeing on the Lower Zambezi
Most canoe safaris – a Zimbabwean highlight – set out from Harare, transferring participants to the remote north of the country by air. Guided trips follow the course of the Lower Zambezi, the best of them passing through game-rich country.

Eastern Highlands
The far east of Zimbabwe is geographically distinct from the rest of the country, consisting of cool elevated grassland and forest, and highly attractive to hikers, birders, anglers, and anybody else with a yen to escape the crowds. The main city in the region is Mutare, an ideal base from which to explore the lovely forests of Bvumba National Park and majestic rockscapes of Nyanga National Park.

Epworth Balancing Rocks
A field of fantastic natural rock sculptures, including the famous 'banknote formation' depicted on Zimbabwean currency, only a 20-minute drive from the city centre.

Lion and cheetah park
A popular day-trip from the capital, this small park hosts lions, cheetahs and other wildlife in authentically African drive-in enclosures. Easily combined with a visit to the Larvon Bird Gardens, an excellent introduction to Zimbabwe's varied birdlife.

Tengenenge
A two-hour drive north of Harare, Tengenenge is the largest sculptors' community in Africa, numbering among its residents several internationally recognised artists who carve in serpentine.

VICTORIA FALLS
Good for family holidays, outdoor activities, scenic landscape and wildlife

APART FROM the obvious attraction of the mile-wide Falls themselves – one of the world's most epic geological formations – the town is the adventure capital of Africa, offering a huge range of adrenaline-pumping activities. For families, diversions include a crocodile farm, snake park and 'traditional village'.

BEST SIGHTS

Cruises
Scheduled cruises ply the Zambezi above the Falls, offering 'sundowners' and sightings of hippos and crocodiles accompanied by the truly unforgettable sounds of the impending African night.

Victoria Falls National Park
A paved walkway passes along the mile-long edge of the chasm opposite the crashing drop of the world's most voluminous waterfall. The path meanders through the tropical rainforest that thrives on the spray thrown up by the Falls plunging on to the rocks 300 feet below.

BEST OUTDOOR ACTIVITIES

An exciting one-day white-water rafting trip that runs 18 rapids below the Victoria Falls now almost overshadows the Falls themselves as the town's principal attraction.

Less macho and less adrenaline-steeped than rafting, kayaking isn't without its thrills as you negotiate small rapids, hippos and crocodiles.

Meanwhile a bungee jump plunges you 360 feet from the Victoria Falls railway bridge.

Other popular activities based out of Victoria Falls township include elephant-back safaris and microlight and helicopter trips offering aerial views of the mighty waterfall.

BEST WILDLIFE

Hwange National Park
Zimbabwe's flagship game reserve, a two- to three-hour drive south from Victoria Falls, is renowned for its dense elephant population, particularly during the dry season, and also harbours substantial populations of lions, buffalo and scores of other species. It is the most accessible of all the country's game reserves for self-drive safaris, and day trips on open landrovers can be arranged at Main Camp.

Private safari lodges
Although Zimbabwe's game density cannot match east Africa's, the standard of its game guides is excellent. The easiest way to benefit from these highly trained professionals is at one of the dozens of private safari lodges concentrated in and around Hwange National Park.

Zambezi National Park

Just four miles from the centre of town, this game reserve on the banks of the Zambezi river has a satisfyingly broad cross-section of African mammals.

GREAT ZIMBABWE
Good for culture, history and scenic landscape

GREAT ZIMBABWE is a rare phenomenon for southern Africa – a permanent structure that was built in the medieval era. It consists of several square miles of walling that was once the heart of a town of 10,000 people. The site's beauty lies in the grandeur of the walls with their stonework patterns, and its integration into the hilly landscape. Though they resemble fortifications, the walls were just a display of royal power, creating passages and enclosures that preserved privacy in a grandiose adaptation of the traditional African homestead.

BULAWAYO
Good for culture, history, local colour and scenic landscape

MANY PEOPLE find Zimbabwe's second city, Bulawayo, more appealing than the capital because so many of its colonial-era buildings have been left intact, giving it a charmingly sepia-toned ambience.

Unless you are flying around the country, it also makes a better base than Harare for exploring, because the main roads to Victoria Falls, Hwange National Park and Great Zimbabwe radiate from here.

BEST EXCURSIONS

Khami ruins

Hundreds of stone structures pepper the Zimbabwean landscape and of these, Khami, 14 miles west of Bulawayo, is second in size and significance only to Great Zimbabwe.

Khami belongs to a separate polity that arose after the collapse of the Great Zimbabwe culture, around the fifteenth century. Although less impressive than Great Zimbabwe, Khami represents a more highly developed system of architecture and urban layout which drew its inspiration from Great Zimbabwe.

Matobo National Park

Thirty miles south of Bulawayo, the Matobo National Park is packed with Dali-esque landscapes of solid granite whaleback hills. The park protects the world's most dense concentration of ancient rock paintings, some estimated to be 20,000 years old. The small game reserve in the west of the park is one of the best places in southern Africa to see endangered rhinos.

Matobo is also the last resting place of Cecil John Rhodes, the British empire-builder who died in 1902.

WHEN TO GO

ZIMBABWE IS blessed with a near-perfect sunny climate and can be visited at any time. Seasons are the reverse of Britain's, with the hottest period occurring during October and November, before the onset of the rains which bring short dramatic afternoon thunderstorms. The winter months from May to September, when barely a cloud passes overhead, are best for game viewing, as animals congregate around a few scarce water sources and are easier to spot through the sparse vegetation. After the January to April rains, the landscape is lush and the animals are at their prime, although more difficult to see.

Average daily maximum temperature °C											
London 6	7	10	13	17	20	22	21	19	14	10	7
Harare 26	26	26	26	23	21	21	23	26	28	27	26
JAN	FEB	MAR	APR	MAY	JUN	JUL	AUG	SEP	OCT	NOV	DEC
Harare 18	15	13	5	2	1	1	1	1	4	11	16
London 15	13	11	12	12	11	12	11	13	13	15	15
Average number of rainy days per month											

PACKAGE TRAVEL

PACKAGES OFFER a wide range of options and are generally very flexible. General tour operators provide a good selection of holidays and will put together various tours, activities and excursions to make up a package that suits your requirements. Many tailor-made specialists at the upper end of the market will create an individual tour. Short tours of around a week invariably include internal flights and a stay in Victoria Falls, also taking in the Hwange National Park or Lake Kariba. Longer trips might include the Matobo Hills and the deluxe train service between Bulawayo and Victoria Falls, as well as canoe trips or white-water rafting on the Zambezi and all manner of safaris.

Accommodation ranges from hotels to safari lodges, bungalows to tented bushcamps. Generally, the smaller the outfit the more exclusive your accommodation will be, but read accommodation descriptions carefully to ensure the safari lodge you are expecting is not just a hotel.

Most tour operators offer activities such as canoeing, white-water rafting and wildlife tours. Two-centre holidays with neighbouring South Africa and Mauritius are widely available.

Tour operators

Adventure: Acacia, Dragoman, Encounter Overland, Exodus, Explore Worldwide, Guerba, Kumuka Expeditions **General**: Abercrombie & Kent, Bales Tours, British Airways Holidays, Cox & Kings, Cricketer, Hayes & Jarvis, Kuoni, Okavango Tours & Safaris, Somak, Sunset Faraway, Temple World, Thomas Cook, Worldwide Journeys **Horse-riding safaris**: Campfire Adventure **Tailor-made specialists**: Africa Archipelago, Africa Exclusive, Africa Travel Centre, Art of Travel, Carrier International, Cazenove & Loyd Safaris, Cedarberg Southern Africa Travel, Definitive Africa, High Class Travel, Safari Consultants, Safari Drive, SAR Travel, Tana Travel, Tim Best, Wild Africa Safaris **White-water rafting**: Adrift **Wildlife/birdwatching**: Naturetrek, Wildlife Worldwide

---

INDEPENDENT TRAVEL

SEVERAL DIRECT flights on British Airways and Air Zimbabwe leave London for Harare each week. Flights on other carriers from London via European cities take longer, but are usually cheaper. Scores of economy buses go from the big cities to virtually every location but are crowded, erratic, none too safe and recommended only for the adventurous. A skeletal but preferable network of luxury coaches links the main centres only. To reach places outside, you must hire a car – arrange rental before you leave to save on the local tax. Main roads are very well-kept and uncongested; driving is on the left.

For covering large distances quickly, Air Zimbabwe's regular and cheap domestic flights serve Bulawayo, Harare and the main tourist areas: Victoria Falls, Hwange National Park and Great Zimbabwe. Much slower, but more romantic, is the overnight train journey from Bulawayo to Victoria Falls, which runs for part of the way along the edge of Hwange National Park.

Among the cheapest and most pleasant places to stay in Zimbabwe are government cottages in national parks. At the other extreme, the most desirable and evocative accommodation is at intimate private safari lodges which come with personalised service, guided game activities, magnificent settings and hefty price tags. In cities, hotels can be pricey, but the number of B&Bs with competitive rates is growing, and a good network of backpacker hostels offer affordable camping space, dormitory accommodation and (in most cases) private rooms.

RED TAPE, HEALTH AND SAFETY

EUROPEAN PASSPORT-HOLDERS do not need visas.

Zimbabwe is a healthy country, and apart from the real hazard of malaria, there is scant danger of contracting 'tropical illnesses' or catching a bug from the local food or water. Anti-malaria pills offering some protection against the disease are advisable. Cover up at night, use insect repellent, and sleep under a net or burn a mosquito coil at night. Health professionals also recommend ensuring that your tetanus and polio jabs are up to date; some suggest other inoculations. Get advice from your GP or a travel clinic.

For visitors Zimbabwe has two economies: a moderately expensive tourist one, charged in US dollars, and a cheap local Zimbabwe dollar one. Costs depend largely on which economy you spend most of your time in. Car hire, large hotels and safari lodges tend to be expensive, while B&Bs, backpacker lodges, eating out and transport are cheap.

Generally Zimbabwe is a safe and friendly country, although theft is a potential hazard, particularly in Harare. The incidence of passport theft is high − carry a photocopy. Driving out of town at night should be avoided because of poorly lit vehicles and badly marked roads.

Violent crime is a rarity and lawlessness bears no comparison to the sky-high levels found in parts of neighbouring South Africa. For the latest advice, contact the Foreign Office Travel Advice Unit (see page 11).

Recent disturbances in Zimbabwe have garnered plenty of international media coverage and greatly affected tourist numbers. In reality, however, the unrest has largely been confined to remote farming areas and, to a lesser extent, the capital. With the exception of a few private game ranches in farming areas, Zimbabwe's tourist attractions currently remain as safe as they have ever been. In mid-2000, the exchange rate was highly favourable to tourists, and more popular resorts such as Victoria Falls were refreshingly uncrowded.

MORE INFORMATION Zimbabwe Tourist Information, Zimbabwe House, 429 Strand, London WC2R 0QE, tel 020-7240 6169

No tourist office web site exists, but you can access information about Zimbabwe at: *www.tourist-offices.org.uk/Zimbabwe/index.html*

COST OF LIVING £

TOUR OPERATORS

AAT Kings	020-8784 2801	Asean Explorer	(01481) 823417
Abercombie & Kent	020-7730 9600	Asian Journeys	(01869) 276200
Abreu	020-7229 9905	Aspro Holidays	(01706) 260000
Acacia	020-7706 4700	Austral Tours	020-7233 5384
Ace Study Tours	(01223) 835055	Australian Pacific Tours	020-8879 7444
ACT	(01531) 660210	Austravel	020-7734 7755
Action Vacances	0161-442 6130	Austria Travel	020-7222 2430
Adrift	(01488) 684509	Austrian Airlines	020-7434 7310
Aer Lingus Holidays	020-8899 4747	Axis	020-7932 9900
Africa Archipelago	020-8780 5838	Aztec Holidays	020-8882 2999
Africa Exclusive	(01604) 628979		
Africa Travel Centre	020-7387 1211	Bakers Dolphin	0117-984 8089
African Explorations	(01993) 822443	Bales Tours	(01306) 885991
African Safari Club	020-8466 0014	Balkan Holidays	020-7543 5555
African Safari Trails	020-8941 7400	Beachcomber Tours	(01483) 533008
Air France	(0845) 0845111	Belgian Travel Service	(01992) 456146/56
Airglobe Holidays	020-7813 1122	Belleair Holidays	020-8785 3266
Airtours	(01706) 260000	Belle France	(01892) 890885
All Abroad	020-8458 2666	Bents	(01568) 780800
All Canada Travel	(01502) 585825	Best of Greece Travel	(01784) 492492
Allez France	(01903) 742345	Best of Morocco	(01380) 828533
All-Ways Pacific	(01494) 432747	Bike Tours	(01225) 310859
Alternative Travel Group	(01865) 315665	Birding	(01797) 223223
Amathus	020-7671 0900	Bladon Lines	020-8780 8800
AmeriCan Adventures	(01892) 512700	Blakes Holidays	(01603) 739400
American Connections	(01494) 473173	Bluebird Express	(01604) 858066
American Round-Up	(01404) 881777	Blue Moon Travel	020-8202 2028
AMG Travel	0161-766 5280	Bonaventure	020-8780 1311
Amsterdam Travel Service	(01992) 456056	Bowens	0121-327 3543
Anatolian Sky Holidays	0121-325 5500	Bowhills	(01489) 877627
Andante	(01980) 610 555	Bridge the World	020-7734 7447
Anderson's Pacific Way	(01932) 222079	Bridge Travel Service	(01992) 456200
Andrew Brock Travel	(01572) 821330	Bridgewater Travel	0161-707 8547
Anemone	020-8889 9207	British Airways Holidays	(01293) 722727
Anglers World	(01246) 221717	British Museum Traveller	020-7436 7575
Anglo Dutch	020-8289 2808	Brittany Direct	020-8641 6060
APT International	020-8879 7444	Butterfields	(01262) 420569
Aquasun	0161-655 4111		
Arabian Odyssey	(01242) 224482	Cadogan	023-8082 8313
Arblaster & Clarke	(01730) 893344	Campfire Adventures	(01747) 855558
Archers Direct	020-8315 5800	Canadian Affair	(0870) 753000
Arctic Experience	(01737) 218800	Canadian Connections	(01494) 473173
Argo	020-7331 7070	Canterbury Travel	(01923) 822388
Armchair	020-8560 8008	Canvas	(01383) 644000
Art of Travel	020-7738 2038	Captivating Cuba	(0870) 8870123

Caravela Tours	020-7630 9223	DA Tours	(01383) 881700
Carefree Italy	(01293) 552277	Danube Travel	020-7724 7577
Carefree Spain	(01293) 527700	David Sayers Travel	(01572) 821330
Carefree World	(01293) 527700	Definitive Africa	0161-929 5151
Caribbean Connection	0131-228 1345	Delta Airlines	(0800) 414767
Caribtours	020-7581 3517	Delta Travel	0161-274 4444
Carisma	(01923) 284235	DER	020-7290 1111
Carrier	(01625) 582006	Destination Pacific	020-7336 7788
Casas Cantabricas	(01223) 328721	Destination Portugal	(01993) 773269
Catherine Secker (Crete)	020-8460 8022	Destination Provence	(01904) 622220
Cathy Matos	020-7267 3787	DFDS Seaways	(01255) 241234
Cazenove & Loyd Safaris	020-8875 9666	Discover the World	(01737) 218800
Cedarberg Southern Africa		Discovery	020-7602 4826
Travel	020-8941 1717	Discovery Initiatives	(01285) 643333
Cedok	020-7839 4414	Distant Dreams	(0870) 0102179
Celebrity Holidays	020-7703 4249	Dive Worldwide	(01243) 870618
Chevron Air	(01723) 365368	Dominiques Villas	020-7738 8772
China Travel Service	020-7836 9911	Donald MacKenzie Travel	0141-221 4333
CIE Tours	(0870) 5143910	Dragoman	(01728) 861133
Citalia	020-8686 5533	Dream Journeys	(01784) 449832
City Holidays	(01243) 775770	Drive Ireland	0151-231 1480
Classic Collection Holidays	(01903) 823088	Driveline Europe	(01707) 660011
Classic Connection	(01244) 355320		
Classic Journeys	(01773) 873497	EasTravel	(01473) 214305
Classic Tours	020-7613 4441	EHS Travel	(01993) 700600
Clipper Voyages	020-7436 2931	Elegant Resorts	(01244) 897888
Club Cantabrica	(01727) 866177	Elite Vacations	020-8864 9818
Club Med	020-7348 3333	Encounter Overland	020-7370 6951
Collineige	(01276) 24262	Erna Low	020-7584 2841
Concept Express Ltd	020-7493 4243	Eurocamp	(01606) 787878
Conservation Corporation		European Waterways	(01784) 482439
Africa	020-7493 1312	Eurosites	(0870) 7510000
Contiki	020-7637 0802	Eurostar Holidays Direct	(0870) 1676767
Continental Villas	(01730) 233988	Eurovillages	(01606) 787776
Coromandel	(01572) 821330	Excelsior	(01202) 309555
Corsican Affair	020-7385 8438	Exodus	020-8675 5550
Corsican Places	(01424) 460046	Explore Worldwide	(01252) 319448
Cosmos	020-8464 3444	Explorers Tours	(01753) 681999
Costa Smeralda	020-7493 8303		
Countrywide	0161-224 2855	Far East Gateways	0161-437 4371
Cox & Kings	(01285) 740639	Ffestiniog Travel	(01766) 512340
Creative Tours	020-7495 1775	Filoxenia	(01422) 371796
Cresta	0161-927 7177	Finman Travel	(01942) 262662
Cricketer	(01892) 664242	First Choice	(01293) 588372
Crusader	(01255) 425453	Fjord Line	0191-296 1313
Crystal	020-7830 0600	Flightbookers	020-7757 2444
CV Travel	020-7591 2800	Florida Vacations	(01727) 841330
Cyplon Holidays	020-8348 8866	Four Seasons Leisure	0113-256 4373
Cyprair Tours	020-8359 1234	French Affair	020-7381 8519

French Country Cruises	020-8995 3642
French Golf Holidays	(01277) 824100
French Impressions	020-8324 4042
French Life	0113-239 0077
Funway	020-8466 0222
Gambia Experience	(02380) 730888
Garuda Indonesia	(01753) 687676
Getaway Vacations	020-8313 0550
Globespan	0131-441 1388
Go Fishing	020-8742 1536
Gold Medal	(0645) 213141
Goldenjoy	020-7794 9767
Golden Sun	020-7485 9555
Golf Holidays International	(01277) 228980
A Golfing Experience	020-8205 7138
Goodwood Travel	(01227) 763336
Gozo Holidays	(01923) 262059
Great Rail Journeys	(01904) 679969
Greece & Cyprus Travel	
Centre	0121-355 6955
Greek Islands Club	020-8232 9780
Greek Sun	(01732) 740317
Guerba	(01373) 826611
Hamilton Travel	020-7344 3355
Harlequin	(01708) 850300
Hartley's Safaris	(01673) 861600
Havanatour	(01707) 646463
Hawaiian Dream	020-8470 1181
Hayes & Jarvis	(0870) 8928280
Headwater	(01606) 813333
Hello Italy	(01483) 285002
Hemmingway Travel	(01737) 842735
Hermis	020-7731 3865
HF Holidays	020-8905 9558
High Class Travel	020-8933 1000
Highlife Holidays	020-8452 3388
High Places	0114-275 7500
Highway Journeys	(01256) 895966
Himalayan Kingdoms	0117-923 7163
Holiday Malta	020-8785 3222
Holiday Place	020-7431 0670
Holts' Tours	(01304) 612248
Hoseasons	(01502) 500555
Hungarian Air Tours	020-7813 4973
Ilios Travel	(01403) 259788
Imaginative Traveller	020-8742 8612

Individual Travellers	
Spain & Portugal	(01798) 869461
Infinity Tours	020-7400 7077
Inghams	020-8780 4400
Inntravel	(01653) 628811
Inscape	(01993) 891726
Insight Holidays	(01475) 742366
Inspirations	(01293) 822244
Interchange	020-8681 3612
Inter-Church Travel	(0800) 300444
Interhome	020-8891 1294
Intersky Holidays	020-8341 9999
Intourist	020-7538 8600
Irish Ferries	(0870) 5171717
Island Holidays	(01764) 670107
Israel Travel Service	(0800) 0181839
Italian Escapades	020-8748 2661
Italian Expressions	020-7435 2525
Italiatour	(01883) 621900
ITC	
(Caribbean)	(01244) 355300
(Indian Ocean)	(01244) 355320
(South Africa)	(01244) 355330
(Sports Holidays)	(01244) 355390
Jagged Globe	0114-276 3322
Japan Experience	(01703) 730830
Jasmin Tours	(01628) 483550
Jetabout	020-8741 3111
Jetlife	(01322) 614721
Jetsave Ltd	(01342) 312033
Jetset	020-7730 0852
JMC Holidays	020-8218 3300
Journey Latin America	020-8747 8315
Just America	(01730) 266 588
Just France	020-8780 4488
KE Adventure	(01768) 773966
Kerry Holidays	(0800) 393443
Key to America	020-8890 8459
Keycamp	020-8395 4000
Kings Angling	(01708) 453043
Kirker	020-7231 3333
Kosmar	020-8882 6999
Kumuka Expeditions	020-7937 8855
Kuoni	(01306) 740888
Lagrange	020-7371 6111
Lakes & Mountains	(01329) 844405

Lanzarote Leisure	020-8449 7441
Lanzotic Travel (Prague only)	(01342) 834120
Laskarina	(01629) 824884
Last Frontiers	(01296) 658650
Latin America Travel	020-7622 3300
Leger	(01709) 839839
Libra Holidays	(01253) 594111
Limosa	(01263) 578143
Longmere International	020-8655 2112
Longmere Golf	020-8655 2075
Longshot Golf	(01730) 268621
Longwood Holidays	020-8551 4494
Lotus Supertravel	020-7962 9494
LSG Theme Holidays	(01509) 231713
Made to Measure	(01243) 533333
Magic Cities	020-8563 8959
Magic of Bolivia	020-7221 7310
Magic of Portugal	020-8939 5451
Magic of Italy	020-8748 7575
Magic of the Orient	(01293) 537700
Magic of Spain	020-8748 4220
Magnum Travel	020-8360 5353
Malaysia Experience	020-8424 9548
Malta Direct	020-8785 3233
Malta Sun	020-8983 4040
Manos	020-7216 8070
Martin Randall	020-8742 3355
McCabe Travel	020-8675 6828
Meon	(01730) 268411
Metak Holidays	020-7935 6961
Midas	(01932) 407000
Minorca Sailing Holidays	020-8948 2106
Moroccan Travel Bureau	020-7373 4411
Moswin	0116-271 9922
Motours	(01892) 518555
Mundi Color Holidays	0161-848 8680
Mysteries of India	020-8574 2727
NAR	(01344) 890525
Naturetrek	(01962) 733051
Nippon Travel Agency	020-7902 2700
Noble Caledonian	020-7409 0376
Nomadic Thoughts	020-7604 4408
Normandie Vacances	(01922) 721901
North America Travel Service	0113-243 1606

North Portugal Travel	(01242) 679867
Norvista	020-7409 7334
Okavango Tours & Safaris	020-8343 3283
Oonas Divers	(01323) 648924
On the Piste	(01625) 5031111
Oriental Magic	(0990) 421888
Orientours	020-8346 1515
Ornitholidays	(01243) 821230
Osprey	020-8462 9823
PAB Travel	0121-377 7080
Page & Moy	(0870) 0106400
Palmer & Parker	(01494) 815411
Panorama	(01273) 423037
Pan Tours	020-7581 8449
Paradise Found	020-8343 8888
Passage to South America	020-8767 8989
Pax Travel	020-7485 3003
Pearl of the Orient	020-7932 0998
Peltours	020-8346 9144
Peregrine Adventures	020-8772 3700
Peter Delmann Cruises	020-7436 2931
Pettitts India	(01892) 515966
Planos	(01373) 836000
P & O European Ferries	(01992) 456654
Polorbis	020-7636 2217
Portugala Holidays	020-8444 1857
Portuguese Travel Centre	020-7581 3105
Premier Holidays	(01223) 516677
President Holidays	020-8886 7655
Prestige	(01425) 480400
Prospect	020-7486 5705
Pullman Holidays (UK)	020-7630 5111
Pure Crete	020-8760 0879
Qantas Airlines	020-7497 2571
Quest Travel	020-8547 3322
Railtours	(01902) 324343
Rainbow Tours	020-7226 1004
Ramblers Holidays	(01707) 331133
Ranch America	(01923) 671831
Reef and Rainforest	(01803) 866965
Regal Holidays	020-8304 6770
Regent Holidays	0117-921 1711
Reliancetours	020-7437 0503
Ryan Holidays	(0800) 777377

Safari Consultants	(01787) 228494	Sun Modilex	(0870) 2424211
Safari Drive	(01488) 681611	Sunbird	(01767) 682969
Saga	(01303) 771111	Sunquest	020-7499 9991
Sally Holidays	020-8395 3030	Sunselect	(01299) 271717
Sandpiper Holidays	(01746) 785100	Sunset Faraway	020-7498 9922
SAR Travel	020-7627 3560	Sunsites	(01606) 787555
Savile Row Tours	020-7625 3001	Sunspot Tours	(01580) 720295
Scandinavian Travel Service	020-7603 0768	Sunvil	020-8568 4499
ScanMeridian	020-7431 5393	Sunworld	0113-255 5222
Scantours	020-7839 2927	Superstar Holidays	020-7957 4300
Scott Dunn World	020-8672 1234	Susie Freeman Travel	(01488) 668821
Seafarer	(01202) 685500	Susi Madron's	0161-248 8282
Seasons in Style	0151-342 0505	Swan Hellenic	020-7800 2200
Select France	(01865) 331350	Swiss Travel Service	(01992) 456143
Select Sites	(01873) 859876	Symbiosis Expedition	
Serenity Golf	(01794) 521177	Planning	020-7924 5906
Seychelles Travel	(01258) 450983		
Shearings	(01942) 244246	Taber	(01274) 594642
Sherpa	020-8577 2717	Tailor-Made	020-8291 9736
Siesta International	0113-245 5580	Tana Travel	(01789) 414200
Silhouette Travel	020-8255 1738	Tanzania Experience	020-7624 5128
Silk Steps	0117-940 2800	Tapestry Holidays	020-8235 7500
Silverbird	020-8875 9090	Tasting Places	020-7460 0077
Simply Corsica	020-8541 2205	Tazab Travel	020-7373 1186
Simply Golf	0161-926 9267	TCA Holidays	(01242) 224482
Simply Simon	020-8373 1933	Temple World	020-8940 4114
Simply Travel	020-8541 2200	Tennyson Travel	020-7736 4347
Simply Turkey	020-8747 1204	Thermalia	020-7483 1898
Simply Tuscany & Umbria	020-8541 2206	Thomas Cook	(0870) 5666222
Skiathos Travel	020-8940 5157	Thomson	(0990) 502555
Skopelos Villas	(01689) 877938	Tim Best	020-7591 0300
SMS	020-7244 8422	Time for Africa	(01489) 878593
Solaire	0121-778 5061	Time Off	(0870) 5846363
Soliman Travel	020-7244 6855	Titan HiTours	(01737) 760033
Solo's Holidays	020-8951 2800	Top Deck	020-7244 8641
Somak	020-8423 3000	Tradewinds	(0870) 7510003
Something Special	(01992) 505500	Trailfinders	020-7938 3366
South African Affair	020-7381 5222	Trans Indus	020-8566 2729
South African Airways	020-7312 5000	Transun	(0870) 4444747
South American Experience	020-7976 5511	Travel 2	020-7561 2220
Southern Africa Travel	(01904) 692469	Travel Africa	(01904) 608878
Sovereign	(0870) 5768373	Travel Bug	(01273) 777167
Sovereign Scanscape	(0870) 5768373	Travelbag	020-7497 0515
Spanish Affair	020-7385 8127	Travelcoast	020-8891 2222
Spanish Harbour Holidays	0117-986 9777	Travel A La Carte	(01635) 863030
Specialised Tours	(01342) 712785	Travel Club of Upminster	(01708) 225000
Sri Lanka Holidays	020-7439 0944	Travel for the Arts	020-7483 4466
Stena Line Holidays	(0990) 747474	Travel Kumuka	020-7937 8855
Steppes East	(01285) 810267	Travel Renaissance	(01372) 744455

Travellers Czech	(01959) 540700	VFB	(01242) 240340
Travelmood	020-7258 0280	Vintage Travel	(01954) 261431
Travelpack	(0990) 747101	Virgin Holidays	(01293) 617181
Travelscene	020-8427 4445	Voyages Ilena	020-7924 4440
Travelsphere	(01858) 410456	Voyages Jules Verne	020-7616 1000
Travelux	(01580) 766000		
Trek America	(01295) 256777	Walking Safaris	(01572) 821330
Trips Worldwide	0117-987 2626	Walks Worldwide	(01524) 262255
Tropical Locations	020-7724 6644	Wallace Arnold	(01246) 555775
Tropical Places	(01342) 330713	Waymark	(01753) 516477
		Welcome Holidays	(01695) 574578
Ultima Tours	0151-347 1818	West End Travel	020-7629 6299
Unicorn Holidays	(01582) 834400	Wigmore Holidays	020-7836 4999
Unijet	(0990) 336336	Wild Africa Safaris	(01483) 579991
Up and Away	020-8289 5050	Wildlife Worldwide	020-8667 9158
US Airtours	0141-248 4844	Winetrails	(01303) 712111
		World Dreams	(01483) 751881
Vacances en Campagne	(01798) 869461	World Expeditions	020-8870 2600
Vacanze in Italia	(01798) 869461	Worldwide Journeys	020-7849 4000
Vacation Canada	(0870) 7070444		
Veloso Tours	020-8762 0616	Yes Travel	(01733) 340345

INDEX